HANDBOOK OF NORTH AMERICAN BIRDS

Sponsored by the Smithsonian Institution

California Condor (*Gymnogyps californianus*)

HANDBOOK OF

NORTH AMERICAN BIRDS

WITHDRAWN

VOLUME 4

Family CATHARTIDAE
New World Condors and Vultures

Family ACCIPITRIDAE (first part)
Osprey
Kites
Bald Eagle and allies
Accipiters
Harrier
Buteo allies

EDITED BY RALPH S. PALMER

Yale University Press   New Haven and London

Published with assistance from the foundation
established in memory of Philip Hamilton McMillan
of the Class of 1894, Yale College.

Set in Caledonia types by The Composing Room of Michigan, Inc. and
printed in the United States of America by
Vail-Ballou Press, Binghamton, New York.

Library of Congress Cataloging-in-Publication Data
    (Revised for vols. 4 & 5)

Palmer, Ralph S. (Ralph Simon), 1914–   ed.
    Handbook of North American birds.

    Vols. 1–3 "Sponsored by the American Ornithologists' Union
and New York State Museum and Science Service."
    Vols. 4–5 sponsored by the Smithsonian
Institution.
    Includes bibliographies and indexes.
    Contents: v. 1. Loons through flamingos.—
v. 2–3. Waterfowl.—v. 4–5. Diurnal raptors.
    1. Birds—North America—Collected works.
I. Title.
QL681.P35   598.297   62–8259
ISBN 0–300–04059–8 (v. 4)
ISBN 0–300–04062–8 (v. 4 & 5 set)

*The paper in this book meets the guidelines for
permanence and durability of the Committee on
Production Guidelines for Book Longevity of the
Council on Library Resources.*

10   9   8   7   6   5   4   3   2   1

CONTENTS

List of literature cited in this volume is combined with that of volume 5 and precedes the index in volume 5.

ACKNOWLEDGMENTS

As in preceding volumes, species accounts vary from single to multi-authorship (usually the latter), and credit belongs to each contributing volunteer. Almost all accounts have evolved through a process of drafting, modifying, revising, and updating; all have been read at some stage by at least one person other than the author(s). Authors vary in expertise and in their attempts to keep pace with information that is increasing exponentially. It is axiomatic that the more persons consulted, the more numerous the suggestions that data be altered or presented in some other sequence or manner. The editor of a multi-authored work must cope with this, even though the end result, after statements are modified repeatedly, may make it unclear at times to whom credit is due. There are advantages. One is an opportunity to incorporate a considerable increment of original information. I am grateful to those who have assisted in any way at any stage.

At the Smithsonian Institution, S. Dillon Ripley provided certain concrete and necessary arrangements under the stewardship of George E. Watson and later continued by Edward F. Rivinus. At the Smithsonian's National Museum of Natural History, the Bird Division staff has been supportive consistently, and the library has been indispensable.

The editor has sought widely for assistance, with reasonable success. Persons who have given time and energy freely and deserve special thanks include: Clayton M. White for essential help on many drafts, Walter R. Spofford as reader and supplier of data, Joseph R. Murphy as reader and lender of publications, Frances Hamerstrom for help in recruiting authors, Canadian Wildlife Service personnel for various kinds of assistance, Bird Banding Office of U.S. Fish and Wildlife Service for printout of earlier banding data, M. Ralph Browning for facsimile copies of source material, Allan R. Phillips for Mexican distributional and other information, Frank W. Preston for egg measurements, and the late A. W. Schorger for earlier summaries of data on foods. The names of many others appear in the text.

Out of the past, for assistance and support of the *Handbook* project in very diverse ways, these names are especially memorable: Edward A. Armstrong, Raymond G. Guernsey, Hans Johansen, Leon H. Kelso, Amelia R. Laskey, James Lee Peters, Leonid A. Portenko, Finn Salomonsen, and Marcia B. Tucker.

The personnel at Yale University Press, Edward Tripp and others, have been helpful and patient beyond reasonable measure—an understatement. Material of any consequence deserves good book design. At Yale Press they care.

RALPH S. PALMER

43° 50′ 01″ N
69° 12′ 05″ W
July 1986

INTRODUCTION

GENERAL REMARKS

The **purpose** of the *Handbook* continues to be an attempt to improve the quality of generally available information in this area of science. It is intended to be comprehensible by the interested layperson; hence, unfamiliar terminology and concepts are avoided or usually stated in generally understandable terms. The **goal** is to describe the physical appearance of both sexes at any age of each regularly occurring species and to indicate what the birds are doing in any season. This can only be approximated for a few species. **Procedure** was for the editor to draft the manuscript, this largely done before 1981, in hope of getting reasonably consistent treatment. Then, since this was an all-volunteer project, the assumption was that collaborating authors would use their expertise to correct, refine, and update the drafts (adding their signatures) within reasonable time. This has presented difficulties, better not dwelt on here.

Species are listed in the **sequence** of the sixth (1983) edition of the American Ornithologists' Union *Check-list,* and most English names are the same. New World condors and vultures evidently belong not in the Order Falconiformes but near the storks in Ciconiiformes (J. D. Ligon 1967). Yet in a linear arrangement of species they precede the others in these two volumes. The Osprey, of ancient lineage, has also been shifted in various linear arrangements.

In our area refers approximately to North America and adjacent islands north of Mexico plus Greenland, Bermuda, Baja California, and Hawaii. This is somewhat arbitrary. In the Bering Sea region, U.S. territory extends westward to include Attu (outermost of the Aleutian chain), yet its avifauna has a large Asiatic component. The Commanders, in the USSR beyond, customarily (since Stejneger's day) have been covered in some American lists. They add no species but would be covered here. Baja California (inclusion dating from Brewster and Coues) was excluded from the definition of coverage in earlier volumes but is included here. Avifaunally, it makes little sense to include Hawaii (it is distant and mainly oceanic), but it became the fiftieth U.S. state in 1959 and adds 1 living raptor species (Hawaiian Hawk *Buteo solitarius,* not covered here; see W. B. King 1981). Stragglers there from elsewhere are listed.

The species in these two volumes, predators and/or scavengers, have had a **recent history** parallel to that of such four-legged creatures as the wolf: long the enemy, to be destroyed if possible, now regarded with special favor by environmentalists and much of the public. This near-complete turnaround (raptors are still targets in some areas) has occurred mainly since the 1940s and has been accompanied by a media blitz. Raptors now have legal protection. Heavy, formerly undreamed of, monetary investment from governments and private sources has been allocated for study and to support and enhance their welfare. To a degree, this appears to be an overreaction that may quiet down or be supplanted by some other environmental "cause." Meanwhile,

1

much is being published in established technical and popular media, in addition to a great deal that tapers off into a "gray" area and to ephemeral items of even more dubious value and shorter-lived availability. No major library has all that deserves at least a glance, but a few individuals try to possess much of it. Although interest in raptors is prevalent in other parts of the world, only in North America has the proliferation of printed material about them reached such proportions. Attendance at some meetings of raptorphiles currently equals or exceeds that of any of the three major North American ornithological societies.

It might be simpler if the editor were satisfied with standardized or stereotypical species accounts, but that is not enough. For example, getting a meaningful grip on relations of raptorial birds to peoples here since long before Caucasians arrived is not easy, but a gesture is made here. On the other hand, raptor management concepts continue to evolve and to be reported in scattered sources; they may need more extensive coverage in some other work. Peculiar to raptors in some ways, but not delved into here, are the psychological aspects of avian symbols (California Condor, eagles), omens (Turkey Vulture, Caracara), and glamor (Peregrine).

English/metric Although part of the language of science, the metric system of measurement has not been adopted as generally as one would wish. For example, it is not used in our current bird guides. Some authors contributing to the present work have used it, but not all, and data cited from almost all earlier sources use English ("customary American") measure. The opening diagnosis of each raptor species uses English with metric equivalent added; then follow "technical" descriptions mainly using metric. Rather than convert everything throughout these volumes to metric or repeatedly add metric equivalents in parentheses, to the annoyance of some readers, a table of equivalents is provided.

Statistics In vogue, but avoided herein for small samples. If 61.54 percent of thirteen birds laid an egg, it is preferable to state that eight (of thirteen) did it. Except for the inclusion of SD (standard deviation), statistical applications are minimal.

Names Time brings change. For example, *Eskimo*, well entrenched in language and literature, seems unlikely to become obsolete soon. Even so, *Inuit* has supplanted it rather widely (although the last person of such persuasion with whom the editor conversed insisted he was Eskimo). Except in quotations (and except *Aleut*), Inuit is used herein. Some maps now give both English (or French) and alternative native place-names; presumably, some of the former may drop out in time. The only current barrier to wider adoption of the latter is unfamiliarity; the former are retained herein because of past and current usage. *Greenland* became *Kalâllit Nunât* in 1979; this and other native names may not come into general usage, as established Danish place-names are officially retained as alternatives.

Higher categories Previous experience indicates that technical descriptions of avian orders, families, and so on, are essentially unused in the *Handbook*. The space is better allocated to species accounts, for which the volumes are consulted—equivalent to what are commonly referred to as Bent's life histories.

Species concept Sometimes a decision must be made whether certain birds comprise two species or one (with subspecies). The editor tends to merge or combine on a selective basis where some authors would maintain separation. Examples: *Ictinia*

2

mississippiensis is treated as specifically distinct (by its author) from *I. plumbea*; *Circus cyaneus* includes *cinereus* as a subspecies (by the editor, as author).

Molting   Most of our raptors have prolonged molting once annually, as diagramed herein. After working with waterfowl, which have up to three molts per cycle, the editor found it difficult to accept the raptor pattern. It would seem that feather wear would require frequent feather renewal, but this is not the case. Also, many raptors (eagles are notable exceptions) molt from Juv. into Def. Basic (latter then repeated throughout their lives) without interposition of a "first winter" or an "immature" feather generation succeeding the Juv. That a great many species have such a recognizable intermediate stage has been repeatedly claimed and endlessly copied and/or cited, but it definitely occurs in very few species (as in the Goshawk). In retrospect, it is suspected that earlier authors, from familiarity with other birds, had problems in accepting early acquisition of "final" (definitive) feathering. Thus, there being individual variation in specimen material, young-looking variants were presumed to be "immature" or "intermediate."

Illustrations   Almost all by R. M. Mengel; in considerable measure based on layouts and reference material supplied by the editor.

Color   Less important in raptors than are shape, pattern, lightness, and darkness. The color chart in the front matter of *Handbook* 1 (correct, except that "rufous" is too pale) is followed with rare exceptions. Names like "Isabelline buff" and "russet" are avoided. The latter, for example, is a variant of "reddish brown," which is comprehensible without consulting any color chart, is inclusive enough to allow for some individual variation, and translates directly into various languages (in which its meaning is understood).

How to cite   The full names of authors (alongside their initials) were listed in the front matter in earlier volumes, and their contributions were signed with initials. Some persons have ignored these, citing the editor as though he were author of material he did not write. In the raptor volumes, authors' names are given in full at ends of the sections they contributed. They are listed neither collectively in the front matter nor in the contents adjacent to the species they wrote about, in the latter instance because it would embarrass the editor to see his own name (as author) so frequently. Except where the editor is author, the specific author should be cited.

SPECIES TREATMENT

Part of the following is adapted from front matter of *Handbook* 2.

DESCRIPTION   This follows an introductory diagnosis. Here is an example of the we-always-did-it-this-way syndrome, which continues into some currently published "standard" works. In the shotgun era, birds were routinely described from rows of skins in museum trays: first the feathering, then, from notations on the specimen labels, the colors of "bare parts" (bill or beak, eye, feet, etc.). This may have sufficed when skin ornithologists (now not numerous) communicated with one another. The procedure might be likened to looking at brands of tea along a store shelf, then having to go to the far end to find the prices. In the live bird and binocular era, millions of

CONVERSION TABLES

U.S. Customary to Metric		Metric to U.S. Customary	
to convert	*multiply by*	*to convert*	*multiply by*
Length			
in. to mm.	25.4	mm. to in.	0.039
in. to cm.	2.54	cm. to in.	0.394
ft. to m.	0.305	m. to ft.	3.281
yd. to m.	0.914	m. to yd.	1.094
mi. to km.	1.609	km. to mi.	0.621
Area			
sq. in. to sq. cm.	6.452	sq. cm. to sq. in.	0.155
sq. ft. to sq. mi.	0.093	sq. m. to sq. ft.	10.764
sq. yd. to sq. m.	0.836	sq. m. to sq. yd.	1.196
sq. mi. to ha.	258.999	ha. to sq. mi.	0.004
Weight			
oz. avdp. to gm.	28.35	gm. to oz. avdp.	0.035
lb. avdp. to kg.	0.454	kg. to lb. avdp.	2.205

ABBREVIATIONS

U.S. Customary	Metric
avdp.—avoirdupois	cm.—centimeter(s)
ft.—foot, feet	gm.—gram(s)
in.—inch(es)	ha.—hectare(s)
lb.—pound(s)	kg.—kilogram(s)
mi.—mile(s)	km.—kilometer(s)
oz.—ounce(s)	m.—meter(s)
sq.—square	mm.—millimeter(s)
yd.—yard(s)	

people cannot be bothered with that sort of separation. When they see the head, they also see the bill (or beak) and eye, which should be described together; the hind limbs belong with the underparts. So it is in field guides, and so it is here.

Descriptions follow this sequence: definitive ("final" or "adult") feathering, then condition at hatching, then feather generations in same sequence as in life up to definitive.

Plumage (capitalized) The equivalent of "feather generation." If a bird is molting, hence wearing parts of two Plumages, total vestiture is termed "feathering" or "total feathering." Under Plumage, the wing is described last. Although unimportant in raptors, so doing is consistent with previous volumes in which, for example, the body feathering may be renewed more than once without renewing the wing. It eliminates any tendency to redescribe the same wing with each change in body feathering.

Color phases So designated for raptors when differences are not bridged by a spectrum of intermediates. If they are bridged, the entire range of variation is described with the "ends" not designated as phases. This is useful, although eventually it might become a semantic exercise. For example, where extremes are bridged by variants, if dark × dark produces only dark offspring and light × light only light ones, geneticists might categorize (as phases?) these portions of the spectrum—only part of the problem of defining the physical appearance of the species. Some situations appear to be even more complex.

Counting primaries In field guides and other popular treatises that include raptors, the long outer primaries are often described, sometimes numbering them from the outermost (falconers' mode). In "technical" treatises it is standard procedure to number them from inner to outer (roughly, the sequence in which they are molted) and secondaries from outer to inner (arbitrarily, not exactly the usual sequence of molting). In the opening diagnoses (and sometimes in Field Identification) of raptors, counting primaries is from *outer inward*—as one might describe a flying bird or examine a fresh dead one or the stiff folded wing of a prepared specimen; the succeeding "technical" descriptions conform to accepted procedure (e.g., primaries numbered from *inner to outer*). Switching methods is a practical convenience for the reader and has been done consistently; *the method used is always stated.*

Wing is measured in various ways. With exceptions, Europeans have measured it flattened; Americans formerly measured across the chord of the arc (i.e., not flattened), but flattening now is widely practiced except for very large birds. Problems arise when citing from sources that measure differently. Although it is repetitious, whatever method was used is stated (if determinable).

VOICE   It is known that a few raptors have a considerable vocal repertoire with calls having particular functions; this may be true of others, but information is lacking.

DISTRIBUTION   The maps are intended to give approximate inclusive current known range, at least in our area, and it is essential that any relevant text (including Subspecies) be read. As in previous volumes, so many sources were consulted for distributional information that citing them would overburden the already extensive terminal list of references; therefore, with exceptions, sources are omitted.

MIGRATION   An element of controversy exists about some facets of this topic, partly from lack of information, but mostly from dubious conclusions drawn from extant data. North American migrants to South America are not referred to as wintering there but as being present in the austral summer.

BANDING STATUS   For most species, data for the several most recent years were not at hand. Since numbers change from year to year, the earlier data are of interest. Main places of banding are listed in diminishing order of numbers banded as derived from data at hand.

REPRODUCTION   The practice continues of naming displays in small caps where defined, the words hyphenated (SKY-DANCE); elsewhere, the 1st letter is capitalized and hyphen(s) retained.

5

Plumages/Molting: Schematic Diagram

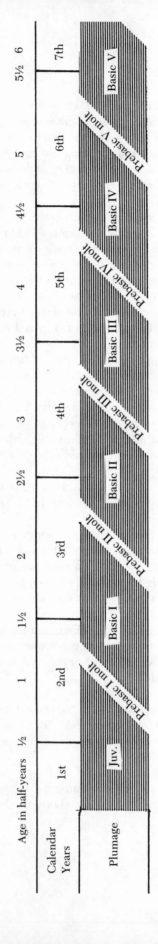

PLUMAGE (capitalized) is used in a special sense—exact equivalent of a generation of feathers—all feathering acquired by a stated molting. A portion of 1 or more Plumages (some flight feathers commonly) may be retained beyond a period of molting.

BASIC Plumage is composed of all feathers of a cycle acquired by a single molting (may include a pause) and repeated in succeeding cycles. May be stated as 1 Plumage/cycle or year, straddling 2 calendar years. If 2/cycle, they would be Basic and Alternate, and so on (see Farner and King 1972 *Avian Biology* **2** 65–102).

FEATHERING or total feathering—all vestiture worn at any point in time; may include parts of more than 1 Plumage, especially when molting. *Feathering* is preferable to *plumage* (not capitalized), the latter commonly used for whatever a bird is wearing.

NATAL DOWNS precede the first Plumage of "true" or pennaceous feathers. Diurnal raptors are generally believed to have 2 of these or, with 1 subdivided, a total of 3 (see text for Peregrine).

JUVENAL PLUMAGE succeeds the natal downs. Vestiture then consists of only this feather generation. Later, some feathering may be retained and worn with a stated Plumage. The word *juvenile*, whether loosely equated with "young" or not, is unacceptable (see Eisenmann 1965 *Auk* **82** 105).

In a few raptors, part of the Juv. is soon succeeded by Basic I. In the Am. Kestrel, for example, 1st-winter vestiture in N. Am. consists of Basic I head–body plus retained Juv. wing and tail.

PREDEFINITIVE: One or more Plumages (including Juv.) acquired before the "final" one. Beginning with loss of Juv., corresponding molts are also termed predefinitive. "Immature," "subadult," "preadult," "first winter," and so on should be avoided, being inexact and tied to assumed sexual maturity.

Many raptors have only 1 predefinitive (Juv.), contrary to much literature. Goshawk and Caracara have 2 readily recognizable ones (Juv. and Basic I); the Bald Eagle has several. In our native eagles and perhaps the California Condor, occasional individuals in an early Basic appear "retarded" or "advanced" when compared with the presumed norm. For the same reason, data from captive-reared birds must be treated with caution. Molting also can cause confusion. Sometimes it may be difficult to identify a particular predefinitive vestiture unless the bird had been banded previously at known age.

DEFINITIVE: The "final" (often incorrectly termed "adult") Plumage that recurs without significant change at each subsequent molting. See above.

California Condors have at least several "adult" predefinitive Plumages before they are known to breed. Bald Eagles, on the contrary, may begin breeding before they are "adult," that is, at a predefinitive stage. Obviously it is inaccurate to equate "adult" (a word usually to be avoided) with "definitive."

Independent of the above Individuals may be designated as *prebreeders*—have not attained breeding age, *breeders*—are breeding or have bred, *failed-breeders*—breeding cycle incomplete, and *nonbreeders*—presumably are physiologically capable of breeding but have not done so.

The above (based primarily on Humphrey and Parkes 1959 *Auk* **76** 1–31) applies to birds generally, regardless of geographical or seasonal occurrence and irrespective of number of feather generations/cycle. There is little concordance with the aging code used by N. Am. bird banders, which is tied to the calendar year.

7

FOOD   Long lists of prey consumed are not of interest in proportion to the space they fill. Data are summarized and references are given. Some of the older data take on added interest because they are not restricted to the breeding season, as are many recent studies.

Some Numbers

These volumes contain material gathered by persons ranging in age from the mid-20s to 94.

The number of references cited per species, in diminishing order, is over 200 each for the Golden Eagle, Bald Eagle. American Kestrel, Peregrine, and Northern Harrier; over 100 each for the Swallow-tailed Kite, Red-tailed Hawk, Cooper's Hawk. Merlin, Rough-legged Hawk, and Goshawk; and fewer for the remainder.

The total number of references is about 2,580 (some used frequently, i.e., a vastly greater number of citations). Very few sources predate 1800 and few predate 1850. The yearly average thereafter is approximately 3 (1850–1899), 8 (1900–1919), and 16 (1920–1939). Thereafter, approximately yearly averages, by half-decades, are 21 (1941–1945), 17 (1946–1950), 25 (1951–1955), 24 (1956–1960), 29 (1961–1965), 40 (1966–1970), 62 (1971–1975), and 85 (1976–1980 and 1981–1985). If graphed, a steep rise begins in the early 1960s and peaks in 1982. At least 550 titles appeared after large sections of these volumes had been drafted, resulting in considerable frustration in trying to update the material.

The number of wild species, meanwhile, has decreased. At this writing no California Condors are at large; the last California Condor remaining in the wild was captured and placed into captivity on April 19, 1987. Hence, the species is biologically extinct in the wild.

Family CATHARTIDAE

New World Condors and Vultures

At least all of the dark species of Vultures might better be called Condors.

AMERICAN BLACK VULTURE

Coragyps atratus

Medium-sized Am. vulture or condor. Definitive stages: length 24–27 in. (60–68 cm.), wingspread 54–69 (137–150); sexes similar in appearance and nearly so in size; beak black with light tip, and relatively long; nostrils small and narrow; head and upper neck (except nape) bare with short, scattered, black hairlike bristles, the skin nearly black; longest primaries of folded wing extend little or not at all beyond longest secondaries; tail less than ½ length of chord of folded wing and nearly square ended.

Three subspecies, 1 in our area.

NOTE **Name priority** Arbitrarily retaining current practice herein conflicts with valid earlier description plus use of *Vultur atratus* in Bartram (1791: 152, 289); type locality St. Johns R. just above L. Dexter, Fla. (see Harper 1942: 212).

DESCRIPTION *C. a. atratus.* One Plumage/cycle with Basic I earliest definitive so far as known. Inadequate data on molting.

▶ ♂ ♀ Def. Basic Plumage (entire feathering) ALL YEAR, acquired by protracted molting through the warmer months. Skin of part of **head** and upper neck with transverse ridges or folds; **iris** dark brownish, cere black; feathering of **upperparts** nearly black with brownish tinge and some gloss when new; **underparts** as upper, but neck darker; legs, **feet,** and claws blackish brown; **tail** as body, squarish ended, individual feather tips pointed (outer) or rounded (inner); **wing** upper surface as body, undersurface of primaries white or grayish over most of web, bordered and tipped blackish brown, shafts white, remainder of underwing much as body. Pterylosis was described by H. Fisher (1939).

AT HATCHING Eyes dark; down, described from various parts of the Americas, is some shade of gray, dirty white, dirty cream, buffy, light fawn, cinnamon, and so on. Nineteen specimens examined from throughout N. Am. range (J. Jackson) and 22 live chicks in Miss. varied little: all were pale pinkish buff, in contrast to the nearly white

11

down of nestling Turkey Vultures. Also contrasting with the latter, the midventral apterium of Black Vulture chicks is more restricted with no or only a narrow bare area extending down from the neck. The skin of the bare face is black, bordered above and behind the eye by short down that is similar in color to the down elsewhere, but shading to black toward the face. The down of the body extends in "Mohawk" fashion over the top of the head. Jackson followed development of 6 sets of chicks from hatching to flight and could discern no age-related change in color or texture of the down, although later it appeared slightly longer. He found that the down of newly hatched chicks seemed oily and had a characteristically repulsive odor that was transferred to his hands when he held the chicks. Although older chicks vomited, producing repulsive odors, their down seemed less oily and did not impart this odor. Every chick examined had a well-developed claw on the outer digit.

▶ ♂ ♀ Juv. Plumage (entire feathering) acquired in the span of 2–10 weeks posthatching and succeeded by Basic I during SUMMER–FALL of 2d calendar year. Beak nearly black; **head** and bare upper **neck** with scant short bristlelike down. Juv. feathering extends farther up the neck in front and back (although more in back) than in succeeding Plumages.

Juv. feathering is acquired as follows (E. Thomas 1928, J. Jackson): at 14–17 days the wing quills begin to show; at 39 days the young are almost full-sized but wing quills only 4–5 in. long and tail 2–3 in. long with no other vaned feathers evident; at about 52 days the scapulars, tertials, and most wing coverts are developed, and quills appear on breast; a week later, the dorsum is feathered, but feathers of underparts are still concealed in down; at 66 days a chick was able to fly (Thomas). (See also Reproduction, below.)

Measurements (A. Wetmore 1962); 32 ♂ WING across chord 414–445 mm., av. 426, and 28 ♀ 414–438, av. 426. Birds from the U.S. (Brodkorb 1944); WING across chord 6 ♂ 418–448 mm., and 5 ♀ 417–443.

Weight About 4¼–6 lb. (1.9–2.7 kg.). Mean and standard error for Fla. birds: 6 ♂ 1, 989 ± 32.4 gm., and 6 ♀ 2,172 ± 48 (Hartman 1955).

Albino One was reported by F. Packard (1949); a fawn-colored individual by Hailman and Emlen (1985).

Purported hybrid (McIlhenny 1937) A practical joke; see under **Turkey Vulture**.

Geographical variation Clinal: the birds (and their eggs) are smaller in the tropical portion of the range than at n. and s. ends (Brodkorb 1944, A. Wetmore 1962).

JEROME A. JACKSON

SUBSPECIES From A. Wetmore (1962). **In our area** *atratus* (Bechstein)—descr. and meas. given above; large birds; breeding range in N. Am. extends s. to include the plateau region and adjacent mts. of Mexico.

Extralimital (See E. R. Blake 1977.) *brasiliensis* (Bonaparte)—small birds; tropical Mexico s. throughout Cent. Am. and into S. Am. down to Lima, Peru, on the w. side and s. Brazil on the e. side.

foetens (Lichtenstein)—large birds; the Andes from n. Ecuador to n. Bolivia; in part of Chile; in Paraguay from n.-cent. region southward; in Argentina s. of the Rio Negro; and probably throughout Uruguay.

JEROME A. JACKSON

FIELD IDENTIFICATION   **In the air,** squat shape—wings broad and truncated, tail short and square-ended, and toes may project beyond tail. There appears to be a definite neck, while the Turkey Vulture seems to lack one. The outer primaries are light underneath and form a whitish area, unlike the gray extending along the wing in Turkey Vulture. Alternately glides or soars, then flaps rapidly; in soaring the bird does not teeter as does the Turkey Vulture. **Perched,** the Black Vulture appears darker, longer legged, longer necked, and with straighter beak than the Turkey Vulture.

JEROME A. JACKSON

VOICE   The Black Vulture is usually silent.

Hissing and grunting have been described by numerous authors. The hissing is a deep, extended sound (Jackson) that can be heard for several hundred m. (Wayne 1910). Grunting is said to sound like dogs barking in the distance (A. Saunders 1906) or the noise hogs make at feeding time (Baynard 1909). Pennock (in Bent 1937) noted a cry like *watt* or *waugh*. Young give a long, slow, deep-throated hiss that ends with emphasis when a human intrudes at the breeding site (Nicholson 1982b, J. Jackson).

When cornered or annoyed, adults may give a similar rasping hiss that has been described as a snore or halfway between a sneeze and a squeal. In Ecuador, "creaking noises" when frightened from its laying site (Marchant 1960). Very young chicks utter a sound like *phuh* or *whuh;* this evolves into *woof* or *wooft* in older ones, and finally into a long slow hiss—perhaps all are the same exhortation, varying only with lung capacity. An adult attending chicks gave a low creaking *coo* like a domestic pigeon.

JEROME A. JACKSON

HABITAT   The Black Vulture is ubiquitous in much of its range. Although it flies over and usually nests in dense woodlands, it feeds primarily in more open areas. In e. N. Am. it is relatively more abundant toward coasts. In much of its Cent. and S. Am. range it is most abundant around human habitations, perching on roofs in cities and towns or anywhere that it can at marketplaces and along streets, becoming "more or less domestic" (A. Wetmore 1965). Such also was the case in the s. U.S. before strict environmental/sanitation laws. In some areas Black Vultures are troublesome or create health problems, since their excrement washes off house roofs into cisterns. On the other hand, they dispose of garbage and thereby earn their keep.

The Black spends much time flying higher than the Turkey Vulture, watching as the latter hunts by scent and so leads the former to carrion.

JEROME A. JACKSON

DISTRIBUTION   (See map.) As far as is known, the Black Vulture is absent from Baja Calif., although there is a dubious record from Cerralvo I. in the Gulf of Calif. and an old record well s. in the Tres Marias Is. In Sonora, Mexico, van Rossem (1945) suspected that the Black had extended its range recently, because early explorers did not report that they had seen it until they arrived at tropical localities. There were no records from deserts w. of long. 130°. By the early 1960s it had spread upward and beyond into Ariz. (J. T. Marshall, A. R. Phillips). It is generally a lowland bird and only a straggler at any appreciable montane elevation. How much its close association with

13

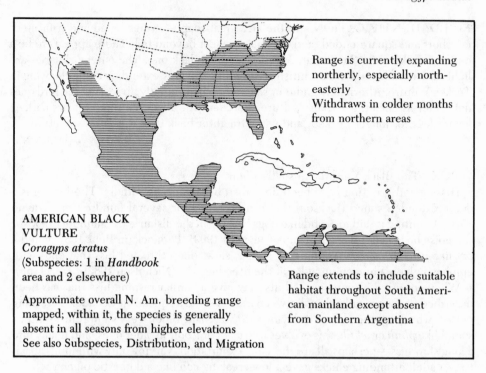

Range is currently expanding northerly, especially north-easterly

Withdraws in colder months from northern areas

AMERICAN BLACK
VULTURE
Coragyps atratus
(Subspecies: 1 in *Handbook*
area and 2 elsewhere)

Approximate overall N. Am. breeding range
mapped; within it, the species is generally
absent in all seasons from higher elevations
See also Subspecies, Distribution, and Migration

Range extends to include suitable
habitat throughout South American mainland except absent
from Southern Argentina

man may have affected its distribution needs study. (Note below that the extinct *C. occidentalis* also was contemporary with early man in our area.)

Across N. Am. the Black Vulture's upper limits of breeding have altered, one way or another, in the past 100 years; the biggest change may have been a spread northward e. of the Mississippi.

Straggler Or visitor (some records not recent) n. to Colo., N.D., s. Ont., (now a winter record), s. Que., and the Maritimes—New Bruns., Prince Edward I., and N.S. Purportedly sighted in s. Calif.

Bahamas (Bimini)—carcass found on a beach does not constitute a valid record.

The Black Vulture is generally absent from the Caribbean; reports from Cuba and Jamaica may pertain to young Turkey Vultures (J. Bond 1961), although they were accepted in J. Bond (1971). Reports from Barbados and Grenada are discounted (J. Bond 1971). Toward S. Am. it is absent from Tobago, although a few were released from captivity in 1959 and this species was seen near Little Tobago up to 1967 (ffrench 1973). Common resident in Trinidad, where it can be hunted legally (ffrench). Present on Margarita I., Venezuela.

This species is reported as **fossil** from the Pleistocene of N. Mex. (2 sites), Fla. (4), Brazil (2 or 3), Ecuador, and Peru; and from **prehistoric sites** in N. Mex., Fla. (3), and Brit. Honduras (Brodkorb 1964, with additions). (For the extinct *C. occidentalis*, Brodkorb listed many Pleistocene localities in our area, also from Nuevo León, Mexico, and from an archaeological site in Oreg.)

JEROME A. JACKSON

MIGRATION   This vulture is generally considered a resident, but individuals wander or withdraw seasonally from at least some parts of the breeding range. It tends to stay near breeding sites later in the year than the Turkey Vulture. Occasionally there appear to be local, concerted, movements or flights other than daily feeding flights. Eisenmann's (1963b) discussion of possible fall migration in Panama raised more questions than it answered. Skutch (1969) reported migration near San José, Costa Rica; the birds were in loose flocks of 25–50 and hundreds "if not thousands" passed in a morning. He saw them Sept. 8–early Dec. For spring he had fewer data, on presumably northbound birds, the 2d quarter of Apr. Both Eisenmann and Skutch are believed to be wrong in interpreting Black Vulture movements as true migrations (A. Wetmore 1965, A. R. Phillips).

JEROME A. JACKSON

BANDING STATUS   P. and B. Parmalee (1967) stated that approximately 23,700 Black Vultures had been banded in e. N. Am., some 95% of these at Avery I., La., by E. A. McIlhenny, 1934–1946. Of these, 2,832 were retrapped there at least once; very few were taken 2 or more times. (Evidently the birds are slow to forget the experience of having been trapped and handled.) Trapping was done mostly in early spring and late fall. The results indicate 1 that a certain number of birds remain locally for indefinite periods; 2 of those recaptured elsewhere, 97% were taken within 200 mi. of Avery I. and half within 2 years after banding; 3 the 2 most distant recoveries were in S.C. and Fla., 720 and 600 mi. away; and 4 many birds wander over a considerable area and local fluctuations in numbers are influenced by food supply. One bird traveled about 125 mi. in a day. Numbers of vultures banded elsehwere were, in descending order: Tex. 629, Va. 221, Tenn. 117, Ohio 12, N.C. 9, and Ind. 4.

Through Dec. 1981, 24,303 Black Vultures had been banded and there were 4,011 recoveries (Clapp et al. 1982). Until recently, main places of banding were: Tex., La., Miss., N.C., and Panama. As with the Turkey Vulture, this species is no longer being banded because of injuries resulting from excrement accumulating under the bands. Patagial and humeral markers are now used for individual identification.

JEROME A. JACKSON

REPRODUCTION   The age at which Black Vultures **first breed** is unknown, but it may be 3 or more years. There is no evidence of strong territorial behavior by breeders, although pairs typically are seen alone near their laying sites from 3 or more weeks before laying begins. Eggs typically are laid on the ground, but some also in high buildings, as in Lima, Peru. When a Turkey Vulture entered a building where a Black was incubating, the latter chased it out (P. Stewart 1974). Laying sites normally are solitary, but Black Vultures seem more likely to establish sites close to one another than Turkey Vultures. As with the latter, close sites seem to be associated with presence of an abundant food supply. Hoxie (1886) found "a dozen or more pairs" of Blacks "nesting" among dense yuccas on a 1.5-acre island in S.C., and Baynard (1909) found a large number near a heronry in a dry Fla. swamp. The only report of close laying sites in which the distance was given is that of 2 in Miss. that were within 100 m. of one another (Turcotte 1933a).

Pair formation   Pair-bond formation and renewal or maintenance activities normally occur at large winter roosting congregations, Jan.–Mar., and are characterized by aerial chases and a dance on the ground. G. Simmons's (1925) description of antics in Tex. involving presumed ♂ ♂ chasing presumed ♀ ♀ through the air and ♂ ♂ diving and displaying before ♀ ♀ may accurately portray "courtship" behavior, but the sexual identity of the participants was a supposition. Juv. Black Vultures may be fed by their parents into at least late Dec. or Jan. of their 1st year (J. Jackson 1975), and some behavior described as courtship might be parents ridding themselves of young before initiating a new breeding effort. There is great need for a detailed study of interactions of marked birds of known sex.

Audubon (1840) gave a vivid account of a "♂" strutting like a Turkey cock before a "♀" with his wings spread and head lowered. Audubon described wrinkled folds of skin about the ♂'s head as "becoming loosened" and "cover[ing] the bill." This spectacle was accompanied by the ♂ emitting a "puffing sound." Wayne (1910) described a hissing sound, heard for several hundred yds., as being associated with mating. No writers since Audubon have mentioned loose folds of skin, but Rea (in Wilbur and Jackson 1983) mentioned a throat sac in cathartids that is most conspicuous in the Black Vulture; its function apparently has not been described. It may be associated with production of sound during displays. A presumed ♂ observed "courting" in Mar. by J. Jackson had an enlarged neck, and the loose skin appeared similar to the engorged gular area of some breeding pelicans.

In a zoo, pair displays began CIRCLE-DISPLAY at the end of Mar. and were fully developed by Apr. 6 (Zukowsky 1956). Typically, the ♂ circled the ♀ on the ground, his neck stretched forward and wings uplifted, and made loud exhalings. The ♀ did a solo dance with trembling wings and rapid footsteps, moving in her own circular course. Such activity commonly occurred in the morning, and each bout lasted only 2–3 min. A. Saunders (1906) saw 3 "♂ ♂" face a "♀," spread their wings partly, and repeatedly duck their heads toward her like well-trained servants. Finally "she" flew off, the "♂ ♂" in pursuit. Other good descriptions of dances were given by Slud (1980) and Rea (in Wilbur and Jackson 1983).

Pair bond   Probably long maintained, if not for life. The same breeding sites seem to be used year after year as long as the previous year's effort was successful. Even outside the breeding season, Black Vultures commonly are seen in twos (Marchant 1960, J. Jackson). A Black Vulture may nibble the feathers of the lower neck of another, which is reciprocated (allopreening), before leaving a roost in the morning; this likely reinforces the pair bond (Haverschmidt 1977b, J. Jackson).

Jackson (in Wilbur and Jackson 1983) studied breeding phenology, laying site selection, and reproductive success, supplementing data from Miss. sites with published data, "nest" records, and data from egg collections. Earliest and mean egg dates at most latitudes suggest that the Black begins laying about 2 weeks before the Turkey Vulture, possibly since the latter is migratory. At the n. limit of the Black's range, 1st laying efforts are in late Apr., along the n. Gulf of Mexico coast in early Feb., and in s. Fla. in mid-Jan. If the clutch is lost, a replacement clutch may be laid in the same site (E. Thomas 1928, Marchant 1960). Latest dates for presumably viable eggs are in mid- to late July and likely represent 2d attempts.

Laying site   Although Black Vultures construct no nest, the site where they lay

16

typically is sheltered and dark. The pair often perches nearby for long periods, beginning 4–6 weeks before laying. This behavior is so predictable that Jackson used it to locate breeding sites in Miss.

Copulation No observations, but Grimes (in Bent 1937) may be relevant. One hopped to a branch on which the other (presumed ♀) was perched. The "♂" alighted and, with wings stretched upward, sidled close, and the other bird was forced off balance and moved to another limb. The 1st bird followed, wings still upstretched until their tips almost touched. The 2 birds "caressed" and the "♀" pecked her mate's head and breast when "he" pressed "her" too hard. This was repeated 4 times, but the "♀" appeared not to be receptive. Then the other bird folded its wings and perched quietly beside its mate. Each occasionally pecked gently at the other and once grasped each other's beak. They parted their mandibles repeatedly, but the observer, about 100 yds. distant, heard no sound. Eventually they departed.

Of 525 laying sites summarized by Jackson, 47.4% were in some type of thicket, 15.4% in a hollow tree or log, 14.9% in a cave, and 1.7% in buildings.

As with the Turkey Vulture, Jackson was able to demonstrate changes in laying sites since 1920. Until then, 26.7% of 150 sites were in tree cavities; since 1920, only 10% of 380 were in such locations. The proportion of thicket sites has increased from 32.7% to 54.5%. This change is attributable to modern forestry practices and loss of old-growth timber. Since tree cavities are more protected than thicket sites, Jackson suggested that increased vulnerability to predators may have resulted in decreased breeding success and, therefore, in population declines reported by W. Brown (1976).

In Va., the nonincubating member of a pair breeding in a building with some sawdust on the floor sometimes picked up loose material and deposited it near the laying site; but the birds frequently moved their eggs about and no material accumulated (P. Stewart 1974).

Eggs may be laid on consecutive days (P. Stewart 1974; Jackson, in Wilbur and Jackson 1983) or 2–3 days apart (Baynard 1909, Crook 1935).

Clutch size Two eggs; 1 is perhaps usually an incomplete clutch; 3 rarely found. Usually eggs can be distinguished from Turkey Vulture eggs by somewhat larger size, somewhat less pale ground color, and smaller markings. Often the 2 eggs in a clutch differ markedly in shape, size, wt., and color.

One **egg** each from 20 clutches (Tex. 18, Fla. 1, Ga. 1) **size** length 76.22 ± 4.06 mm., breadth 51.01 ± 1.56, radii of curvature of ends 18.19 ± 1.44 and 12.50 ± 1.45; **shape** oval to long oval, rarely tapering at both ends, elongation 1.48 ± 0.065, bicone −0.100, and asymmetry +0.157 (F. W. Preston). Fifty-one eggs av. 75.6 × 50.9 mm. (Bent 1937). Shell smooth, without sheen. **Color** includes a pale ground color (usually grayish green, sometimes very pale bluish, even nearly white), typically with a few large, warm, dark brownish blotches, or sometimes lighter warm browns, at or near the large end. Rarely colored quite differently—one blotched "pale purple drab," and so on (Bent 1937). Generally, 1 egg is much more heavily marked than the other.

Replacement clutches If the 1st is lost, a 2d clutch may be laid 21 days to a month later (Baynard 1909, 1910, Beal 1932, Lyle and Tyler 1934, J. Jackson). The 2d may be in the same site as the first. In Miss., Jackson found a 2d set in the same site, with fragments of shells of the predator-eaten earlier clutch still present. Turcotte (1933b) took 3 clutches at about 1-month intervals from 2 sites within 50 m. in Miss.; he

17

believed they were the product of the same ♀. H. Todd (1938) found 3 clutches laid about a month apart in the same site in Tenn.

Both sexes incubate In Va., changeovers took place at about 24-hr. intervals and were often before 0930 hrs. (P. Stewart 1974). The long axis of the eggs is parallel to the long axis of the incubating bird and apparently generally lie on the toes (P. Stewart, J. Jackson). Consequently, if the incubating bird is disturbed, the eggs are often moved—sometimes several ft.—in the bird's rush to escape (Stewart, Jackson, Marchant 1960, Housse 1940). In such open sites as buildings and thickets, an egg can get lost in the dark and not be recovered until dawn. Such long cooling of an egg might account for the variation in incubation period and the asynchrony of egg hatching in some clutches.

Incubation period Data were summarized by J. Jackson (in Wilbur and Jackson 1983). Published extremes are 21 and 41 days. Most accounts lack details sufficient to judge the adequacy of the data presented, but supporting data are more convincing for periods of 37–41 days. Variability may result from delayed start of incubation (Baynard 1909) and/or cooling of eggs during temporary loss as mentioned above. Hatching can occur on the same day or up to 3 days apart (Jackson).

Behavior, development, and care of the young Summarized here from P. Stewart (1974), J. Jackson (in Wilbur and Jackson 1983), E. Thomas (1928), and Jackson's field notes. For about the 1st 2 weeks, the young are brooded constantly, the parents alternating and maintaining a schedule similar to that during incubation. The chicks are first kept under the breast and later under a wing (Stewart). After the 1st 2 weeks, the young are brooded with decreasing frequency. Thomas noted no diurnal brooding after about 24 days, at which time the young were fed only about twice a day. For the 1st 3–4 weeks, an adult is often perched nearby and may give a spread-wing display and regurgitate in efforts to distract humans from the young (Jackson). At about 43 days, the parents cease remaining with the young at night (Stewart). Until then, Stewart observed 15–20 feeding sessions per day (contra Thomas) and heard feeding calls at night. As the chicks grew, Stewart sometimes saw the parents interrupt feeding, walk away and stand motionless, then return to feed again. Several times he saw a parent sit and stretch its neck out against the floor, possibly as an aid in regurgitating more food. After brooding ceased, the parents fed the young 3–4 times daily. Brooding was skipped on a rainy day. Usually parents alternated feedings, but several times the same parent made successive visits.

Thomas observed 3-day-old young to feed by thrusting the head into the lowered open beak of the adult to obtain a liquid, milky-appearing regurgitate. A chick's tongue is a thin troughlike structure (D. and N. Wetherbee 1961)—almost like an open pea pod (Jackson)—quite functional in obtaining liquid food from its parents. The chicks observed by Thomas preferred to feed from the corner of the parent's mouth and were fed with the adult in either a standing or brooding position. On a cold day he saw the young fed 17 times in 11¾ hrs.

On several occasions, Thomas observed an adult regurgitate solid food, which the young attempted to seize, but each time the parent reswallowed the material. Both parents fed the young, but one was more shy and contributed little food. Once the shy bird (♂?) walked to the other parent, who was brooding the young, and fed "her" in the same manner as the young were fed.

18

The young show anger or fear within a week posthatching and, as they become older, they (like adults) regurgitate when annoyed. Afterwards they eat the disgorged matter. With outstretched wings and lowered head, they give a guttural, prolonged hiss and viciously and unexpectedly lunge at intruders. Such demeanor is in striking contrast to the passivity of Turkey Vultures. Lacey (1911), however, observed young Black Vultures to feign death, as did an older bird elsewhere that had an injured wing.

Age at first flight   About 75–80 days. It has been reported as short as 66 days (Thomas) and as long as 14 weeks (Baynard 1913), but both are out of line with other reports. Young remain at the breeding site about 60 days (in Bent 1937), which is not the same as being able to fly. Jackson associated lengthened breeding site life with sites from which the young could not escape easily, such as from a deep hole or within a building where escape required leaving through a high window. In a zoo, young were fully capable of flight at 11 weeks (Zukowsky 1956). In Va., Stewart saw young aged 80 days fly 2 m. up to a loft and another 2 m. to a window, where they perched. They made gradual moves farther away until, on the 7th day away from their hatching site, they flew about 50 m. to a tree. Then they did much flying close by for 4 days and departed at age 91 days. Similar gradual site-departure was seen several times in Miss. (Jackson).

Breeding success   J. Jackson (in Wilbur and Jackson 1983) found that 61% of 49 breeding sites in Miss. lost at least 1 egg before hatching. Of 23 broods surviving to the downy stage, 17% lost 1 young and none lost both. Of 19 sites with young surviving to the feathered stage, 21% lost 1 or both young. Identifiable causes of losses include infertility, humans, other predators, and flooding. Mammalian predators on eggs and young are thought to include foxes, opossums, and dogs. Jackson saw a Com. Crow attacking a 2-day-old bird.

Duration of family bond   In Panama, for at least 5 weeks after they could fly, 2 young begged adults for food. They flapped their wings, bobbed their heads, and gave low-pitched hissing sounds. More than 15 weeks after first flying, the young begged but were not seen to be fed (McHargue 1977a).

In Miss. in Dec., J. Jackson (1975) saw 2 young with 4 adults; the young were fed by regurgitation; there was no begging; each young in turn struck its head nearly completely into the throat of an adult. This suggests parental care 6 months or more after the young can fly. For family and interfamily relations in N.C., see Rabenold (1986).

JEROME A. JACKSON

SURVIVAL   No useful data. From his Ecuadoran experience, Marchant (1960) presumed that the Black Vulture had low nesting success and that some irregularity in breeding may be characteristic of the species, which is long-lived and without enemies when adult.

The longevity record for the species is at least 25½ years (Clapp et al. 1982).

JEROME A. JACKSON

HABITS   **In our area** unless otherwise stated. The Black is more gregarious than the Turkey Vulture, that is, more typically in groups or large assemblies, whether soaring, roosting, or feeding.

A **roost** at an ammunition plant near Blacksburg, Va., where there was little human disturbance, was very large; at counts in Dec. 1973–1975 it contained 401, 1,047, and 1,133 birds, the last being 813 Black and 320 Turkey Vultures. They roosted in mature sycamore trees at the base of a river bank (Prather et al. 1976). Jackson observed a similarly large congregation where both vultures roosted on an abandoned nuclear reactor near Aiken, S.C. McIlhenny (1940) reported a large roost in LA.

In Venezuela, W. Beebe (1947) noted regular daily flights, singly and en masse, to and from feeding areas; flight was always direct both ways, with no turning aside, circling, or soaring, suggesting that the birds using a roost may have come from a distance. Rabenold (in Wilbur and Jackson 1983) presented evidence that communal roosting of Black and Turkey Vultures is an adaptation that increases foraging efficiency on a dispersed and unpredictable food supply. Based on group departures and headings from the roost, she concluded that roosts serve as centers for the transfer of information among roost members.

Flight The Black typically runs to take off from the ground, hopping 2–3 times before springing into the air, but it can spring directly upward, either in haste or when facing a breeze. The wing is adapted for soaring, but its shortness decreases lift, and more flapping is needed to maintain flight (H. Fisher 1946). Flapping rate in Fla. in summer was noted at 4.3 wingbeats/sec. (C. H. Blake). The Black neither wobbles in flight nor deviates from its course, as does the Turkey Vulture, and it can appear to be a mere speck in the sky, then drop to earth with remarkable swiftness. See Newman (1958) and Parrott (1970) for analyses of its flight.

Black Vultures tend to **hunt** visually from greater heights than Turkey Vultures, the latter using a sense of smell. The Black is said to take advantage of the Turkey Vulture's olfactory sense, following that species to food sources (M. Mitchell 1957, Stager 1964, A. R. Phillips). Blacks also tend to circle while hunting, whereas Turkey Vultures course back and forth close to the ground.

When a Black Vulture locates a carcass, sees a vulture feeding, or notes some other indication of the presence of food, it drops with great speed; the legs hang down and the wings flap furiously. While hunting, the Black keeps turning its head, apparently to watch other vultures' actions for any sign of food. Rapid descent of one is a signal to

(after Bang 1968)

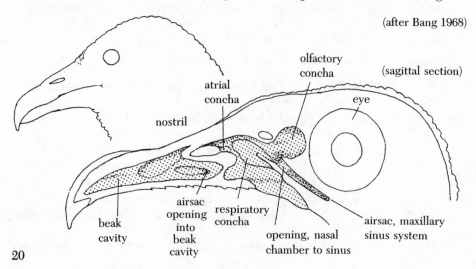

(sagittal section)

20

others, and they congregate at food at once. Such flight behavior, even if it is a mistake (no food located), can cause them to assemble quickly (Townsend, in Bent 1937). In feeding groups the Black is very aggressive, and the Turkey Vulture often has to wait (Stoddard 1978, J. Jackson).

The Black is yet another of our vultures that prefers fresh meat, but, unlike the Turkey Vulture, it favors large carcasses (P. Stewart 1978). It is far more predatory than the Turkey Vulture and hence is persecuted with more justification in some portions of its range. There are numerous records of **attacks on livestock,** especially newborn young and females in labor or shortly after giving birth. Even so, indiscriminate persecution is far from warranted.

P. W. Parmalee (1954) felt that vulture predation on livestock had dramatically increased in the preceding 10–15 years in e. Tex. (The Black is far more numerous than the Turkey Vulture there.) He queried landowners who trapped vultures and received 66 replies. Of these, 83% of the traps for which data were available were built after 1940. Vultures also were shot and poisoned, and 1 man may have been trapping them there before 1900. A conservative estimate was 100,000 vultures (mostly Black) trapped in an unspecified period. Large funnel traps, baited with dead animals, were used to capture them. Such efforts were to alleviate the problems of vultures killing newborn or incapacitated livestock and the pollution of water sources by vulture excrement. The largest number was captured in spring.

An effective method of killing the birds was to scatter dead rabbits, injected with a poison, in about a ¼-mi. radius of water holes.

Concurrent with this activity in Tex., the "vulture problem" reached such proportions in Fla. that trapping was the standard method of control in some localities.

On the Edwards Plateau in s.-cent. Tex. and in the e. part of that state, the loss of young livestock to vultures has been a severe problem. Parmalee suggested that this resulted from rapid expansion of the livestock industry 35–40 years earlier. More food became available to the vultures, their numbers increased, and then the food supply dwindled. This decline resulted from the burning or burial of livestock carcasses, declines in home butchering, and sanitation laws that eliminated open disposal of offal and chicken remains from poultry processing plants. Both vultures had been effective sanitary engineers, although there had been implications that they carried anthrax (Bullock 1956), in addition to fouling livestock water supplies.

Black and Turkey Vultures are wary if trapped and released, being difficult to retrap (Olson et al. 1967, P. and B. Parmalee 1967). On the other hand, Black Vultures seemed to anticipate when a trap was to be baited and would gather there daily for a week or more ahead of time (McIlhenny 1940). Unlike the submissive Turkey Vulture, a trapped Black flaps and struggles continuously, bites when handled, and, while shaking its head from side to side, almost invariably regurgitates (Olson et al. 1967).

McIlhenny (1939) described cooperative killing of a skunk and opossums. The vultures surrounded the skunk and attacked it, hooking their beaks into its skin to tear the victim apart. If a carcass needs further division, a vulture hops on it, balances with its wings, and hooks its beak into the flesh almost between the bird's feet. With strong, rapid jerks, it tears off the meat. In the instance of the skunk, 25 or more birds eventually assembled at the kill. According to P. and B. Parmalee (1967), the killing and eating of skunks is common; in dry spells in autumn when carrion was scarce, the birds would congregate in areas where skunks were numerous. The more powerful beak of the Black Vulture, compared with the Turkey Vulture, contributes to the greater effectiveness of the former as a predator. It always attacks in groups. Dead livestock is fed on at body openings, unless the carcass has rotted sufficiently for the skin to be ripped.

Thermoregulation   Black Vultures spread their wings in various postures as the sun shines on them in early morning, evidently to use solar energy to raise the body temperature (Kushlan 1973). As an evaporative cooling mechanism (as in our other vultures), they defecate on their legs (Kahl 1963). In Panama, taping shut the beak of an unruly captive was believed to have disrupted temperature regulation through the mouth so that the bird died by overheating (Olson et al. 1967). Mahoney (in Wilbur and Jackson 1983) concluded, as a result of experimental studies, that the Black relies on panting and excreting on its legs (urohydrosis) to maintain body temperature in hot environments.

Based on experience in Sonora, Mexico, van Rossem (MS) noted that this bird has good **night vision.** In Sonora, Black Vultures flew and maneuvered well along a dark cliff when a light was shined at them (J. T. Marshall, A. R. Phillips). In Ga., Stoddard (1978) reported 2 observations of Black Vultures feeding on dead hogs by moonlight.

Black Vultures were reportedly seen drinking salt water at Mazatlán, s. Sinaloa, Mexico (S. Bird 1941).

The Black Vulture recently has extended its breeding range n., but not as much as the Turkey Vulture. Reasons for the expansion and differences between the species are unknown but may reflect food availability or climate or may possibly be somehow related to the extinction in Precolumbian times of *C. occidentalis*.

Although its range has expanded, **winter counts** in our area have shown a steady

decline in numbers from 1952 to the 1970s (W. Brown 1976). The Black is more plentiful near coasts and near human habitations where, evidently, food is more plentiful. It shows little fear of close and continuous contact with man, as at cattle ranches and tropical marketplaces. Much more than the Turkey Vulture, it is commensal with man, perhaps even mutualistic—a close relationship that surely existed aboriginally. Declines noted in vulture populations in Mexico in recent decades may be attributed to pesticides (A. R. Phillips).

Folklore McAtee (1955) summarized a great deal of se. U.S. folklore about vultures. The species usually was not indicated and much of the material undoubtedly applied to both Turkey and Black Vultures (see also under the former). The following were mentioned. If you see a lone vulture and make a wish before it flaps its wings, your wish will come true. Some believe that if the bird flaps, the wish will come true; if it does not flap, it will not. If a vulture flies over your house, you will get a letter or hear good news. If you see a vulture's shadow without seeing the bird, an unexpected visitor will arrive. A rather specific portent is that if a vulture flies over a house at noon, some member of the family will die at four. Wearing a vulture feather behind the ear prevents rheumatism.

JEROME A. JACKSON

FOOD Of the species. Mainly carrion; preferably large carcasses, but of any size. At times a menace to newborn livestock, especially pigs. Other live items include turtles and their eggs, the eggs and young of birds, iguana eggs, and fishes. Vegetable matter is taken regularly at some localities.

Animal Excrement of mammals (Maynard 1881, McIlhenny 1939). Dead catfish in Tex. (Van Tyne and Sutton 1937); evidently, freshwater fishes in Miss. and Fla. (J. Jackson et al. 1978, Kushlan 1973); dead marine fishes in Panama (A. Wetmore 1965). Newly hatched leather-backed turtles in French Guiana (Mrosovsky 1971); newly hatched Ridley turtles in Costa Rica, where they also pecked their way into adult Ridleys overturned on the beach in a melee of mass nesting (D. Hughes 1973). Frequently kills and eats young pigs and lambs (Baynard 1909, 5 later authors). Stated to tear the eyes from newborn calves and from cattle in weakened condition (Figgins 1923, later authors). Skunks and opossums in La. (McIlhenny 1939). Known winter foods include shrews and moles, perhaps gotten at carrion. It robs traps, destroying mammal pelts in La. (A. Bailey and Wright 1931, later authors).

Destructive to eggs and young birds, especially of colonial nesters: cormorants, ibises, herons, and anhingas (Audubon, later authors). (Under a large heronry, e.g., dead and injured birds lie on the ground; their removal may be useful sanitation.) Young chicken taken from yard (Barnard 1909). On Barro Colorado I., Panama, where eggs of *Iguana iguana* were concentrated by these reptiles for burial, a surplus was pushed into the open; these were eaten by Black Vultures, who splashed and wasted much of the contents (Sexton 1975).

In Veracruz, Mexico, vultures that die are not eaten by other vultures or mammals, thus leading the Indians to say that their flesh is poisonous; the vultures are eaten by insects (Lowery and Dalquest 1951). (Many N. Am. Indian tribes regarded raptorial birds as unfit for human food.)

Vegetable Sweet potatoes eaten in La. (McIlhenny 1945). Meat of opened coconuts in Trinidad (Junge and Mees 1961); coconut meat and African oil palm fruit in Dutch Guiana (Haverschmidt 1947) (the Palm Nut Vulture of Africa also eats the latter); scraps of coconut meat and the oily pulp covering the seeds of pulp between the tough rind and the rock-hard seed of the coyol palm in Veracruz, Mexico (Lowery and Dalquest 1951).

Plastic objects Plastic, rubber goods, and other synthetic materials are swallowed, perhaps where natural foods are scarce.

JEROME A. JACKSON

TURKEY VULTURE

Cathartes aura

Medium-sized Am. vulture or condor. Skin of head and upper neck red (black in younger birds), naked except for some black hairlike bristles, with transverse folds, wrinkles, and wartlike growths in N. Am. populations. Beak short, stout, whitish, the nostrils broadly oval and perforate. Feathering dark with undersurface of wing lighter. Longest primaries of folded wing extend beyond secondaries; rounded tail extends more than ½ its length beyond folded wing. Sexes similar in appearance and essentially so in size, but separable by discriminant analysis using multiple characters (Gaby 1982).

Length 25–32 in. (63–81 cm.), wingspread to about 6 ft. (1.8 cm.), usual wt. about 3–4 lb. (1.4–1.8 kg.).

Six subspecies, 3 in our area.

DESCRIPTION *C. a. septentrionalis* unless otherwise indicated. One Plumage/cycle with Basic I earliest definitive (there may be minor differences between early and later Basics). Inadequate data on molting.

▶ ♂ ♀ Def. Basic Plumage (entire feathering) ALL YEAR, acquired by protracted molting from late winter through summer into fall, all flight feathers of wing evidently not renewed in a single year. **Beak,** head, and upper neck—see above; **iris** medium brownish; most **feathering** very dark, blackish with bluish gloss when new but soon fades to blackish brown or lighter. **Tail** very dark above and toward slaty brownish below. Legs and **feet** flesh colored to various deep reds, but usually appear whitish because of defecation on them—urohydrosis (van Rossem 1946); claws dark. In the **wing,** edges and tips of secondaries pale; undersurface of flight feathers progressively paler toward their bases, and shafts of quills white. Pterylosis was described by H. I. Fisher (1943).

Molting   The Stresemanns (1960) stated that primaries are renewed in irregular sequence, but molting is serial (inner to outer), beginning over again (inner) before the outermost is renewed; this is especially evident in fall; all primaries apparently are renewed in a single year in wild birds, although some inconsistencies may mask the pattern. Chandler (Rea, in Wilbur and Jackson 1983) followed secondary and tail molting of captives; he found, counting from outer to inner secondaries, foci at #1 and #5, with a tendency for a focus at #11, although #9 and #10 were independent of these foci. Sequence of tail molting was #1 (central pair), #6 (outermost), then #2, #3, #4, and #5. There are no data on contour feathers.

AT HATCHING   Beak stubby; much of head bare and blackish; white down is short on the head and much longer on the body (J. D. Ligon 1967), with a narrow bare ventral area (ventral cervical apterium); legs and feet black. There are no data on succession of downs, which are white.

▶ ♂ ♀ Juv. Plumage (entire feathering) worn for ABOUT A YEAR; essentially as Basic. It begins to emerge by 18 days posthatching and may be complete by 60 days (Ritter, in Wilbur and Jackson 1983). Some down may be present on the head past 88 days (Kempton 1927). **Beak** tipped black at first (Mossman 1976), becoming white later. A. Wetmore (1965) noted that "immature" birds in Panama have an irregular whitish mark on either side of the nape. Legs and **feet** lighten considerably (are not black). **Wing** undersurface almost uniformly dark—that is, flight feathers much less pale basically than in Basic Plumages.

By Oct., the dark **head** begins to develop traces of "adult" color, but remains mostly gray until late winter or spring.

Juv.   Basic

Molting The Juv. Plumage is succeeded gradually by Basic I beginning in late winter or spring of 2d calendar year of life; all primaries are renewed in Prebasic I molting.

Color phases None. More or less albinistic individuals have been reported at least 4 times, beginning with Alcott (1870).

Measurements Of e. U.S. birds: 43 ♂ WING across chord 509–545 mm., av. 526, TAIL 250–288, av. 267; and 35 ♀ WING across chord 518–552 mm., av. 535, and TAIL 255–292, av. 275 (Wetmore 1964).

Weight 2 Minn. ♀ (stomachs empty) 3 lb. 14 oz. (1,758 gm.) and 4 lb. (1,814 gm.) (T. Roberts 1955). In fall in Mo., birds with full crops: ♂ 2,180 gm. and ♀ 2,347; and birds shot at a roost at dawn (before having eaten): "adult" ♂ 2,079 gm. and ♀ 1,990, plus a Juv. 2,387 (D. Hatch 1970). In Fla., mean and standard error: 15 ♂ 1,426 ± 10 gm. and 5 ♀ 1,589 ± 118.35 (Hartman 1961).

Hybrids None. An individual, alleged at the time (McIlhenny 1937) to be a hybrid with the Black Vulture, proved to be the latter when red paint that had been applied to it wore off its head (E. P. Walker).

Geographical variation In size and color in this species, variation is rather slight. Birds are somewhat larger in e. N. Am. than w. and s., including s. through the W. Indies, Mexico, and Cent. Am. Birds of e. S. Am. are smaller yet, but those in a w. coastal zone from about Ecuador s. (also in and near the Falkland Is.) are about the size of e. N. Am. birds. Some birds from sw. Mexico (van Rossem 1946) s. to include tropical S. Am. have some color (yellow, white) besides red on the bare skin of head and upper neck. Darkness of feathering shows some geographical variation. Downies are white in N. Am., but are said (Cawkell and Hamilton 1961) to be pale gray in the Falklands.   JEROME A. JACKSON

SUBSPECIES Have been discussed by Friedmann (1933), Hellmayr and Conover (1949), again Friedmann (1950), then revised by A. Wetmore (1964), and discussed in some detail by Amadon (1977). Wetmore is followed here and his meas. are given.

In our area *septentrionalis* Wied—descr. and meas. given above. Breeds in e. N. Am., w. into e. and s. Ont., s. Minn., and into Kans., Okla., and e. Tex.; s. to include almost all of mainland Fla. (no data from extreme s. mainland and keys) and in places nearly to the U.S.-Mexican boundary. Northerly birds shift s. to winter from s. Ohio and Md. s. to the Gulf of Mexico and s. Fla.

meridionalis Swann—25 ♂ WING across chord 487–528 mm., av. 509, TAIL 237–268, av. 253; and 16 ♀ WING across chord 499–526 mm., av. 511, and TAIL 245–272, av. 259. The type is a N. Am. migrant taken in S. Am., and this name antedates *teter* of Friedmann. Breeds in N. Am. w. of the preceding subspecies and s. through Calif. (except lower Colo. R. valley) to s. Baja Calif. Mostly migratory. Recorded from s. Fla. Large numbers reach S. Am.—to Colombia, cent. Venezuela, parts of Ecuador, and s. Brazil. There is increasing size from somewhere in Cent. Am. or Mexico n.; division is arbitrary so as to define the nominate form thus:

aura (Linnaeus)—21 ♂ WING across chord 462–495 mm., av. 478, TAIL 226–249, av. 238; and 12 ♀ W WING across chord 471–495 mm., av. 482, and TAIL 231–251, av. 241. Breeds from lower Colo. R. valley, much of Ariz., s. N.Mex., s. Tex., and possibly extreme s. mainland Fla. (and keys?), s. to Panama, and on various is.—several in the Bahamas and continuing so as to include Jamaica. Hispaniola—formerly occurred? Puerto Rico—introduced.

Extralimital A recent useful reference is E. R. Blake (1977). *ruficollis* Spix—dark birds with pale nape and some coloring (additional to red) on head; from Panama (n. limits in Cent. Am. not well known) and s. into much of tropical S. Am.; *jota* (Molina)—Andean S. Am. and continuing s., where it is also a lowland bird; and *falklandica* (Sharpe)—the Falklands and some adjacent mainland.　JEROME A. JACKSON

FIELD IDENTIFICATION **In our area** The Turkey Vulture has a wingspread of nearly 6 ft. (1.8 m.), dark brownish feathering in all flying ages, whitish beak, head and upper neck red after early life (when it is blackish becoming grayish), and tail comparatively long and rounded. In contrast, the Black Vulture has a wingspread of 5 ft. (1.5 m.), more or less, black feathering and head–neck in all ages, and comparatively short, squarish tail. The anterior neck is naked in the Turkey Vulture; the nape is usually feathered in the Black Vulture. In flight, the Turkey Vulture's feet do not protrude beyond the tail, and it appears to have no neck.

Juvenal birds are "blackheads," and "adults" are "redheads."

The Turkey Vulture soars gracefully in circles, teetering gently in response to any slight change in air currents. Once aloft, it flaps leisurely and seldom. The Black has a more squat shape and shorter, broader wings and tail; its flapping is more frequent and seemingly hurried, as though some effort were suddenly required to stay aloft. Viewed from below, the flight feathers of the Turkey Vulture wing are increasingly light (silvery) toward their bases (to a lesser degree in Juv. birds), giving the appearance of a broad palish stripe the length of the wing. The Black Vulture's wing has a palish area, but it is in the outer primaries, toward the end of the outstretched wing. A soaring or gliding Turkey Vulture's wings are held in a shallow V or dihedral; they are relatively horizontal in the Black Vulture.

The much larger and very different California Condor has a very limited distribution; compare with that species. Compare also with the Zone-tailed Hawk, which is easily confused with the Turkey Vulture.

Our 2 common Am. vultures show very small heads in flight; the comparatively large, conspicuous heads of eagles and hawks, their sustained and vigorous wingbeats, and numerous other characteristics distinguish them.　JEROME A. JACKSON

VOICE Although lacking a syrinx (Miskimen 1957), a number of different sounds have been attributed to the Turkey Vulture. Many authors have described a long, threatening hiss given by adults disturbed at the breeding site. Coues (1874b) likened it to the "seething noise of a hot iron plunged in water." Other vocalizations described include a raucous growl or snarl reminiscent of vocalizations of larger herons (Pearson 1919); a "subdued croak" (F. M. Bailey 1928). A food call is a repeated short staccato *tschuck* of shorter duration in young than adult and somewhat like the clucking of a domestic hen. When a bird took flight it was heard and was followed by several whining notes (Allard 1934). A low-pitched nasal whine, uttered with closed beak, has been heard from perched, departing, and circling birds. It is said to resemble the whine of a puppy (Pemberton 1925).

Young from 1–2 days posthatching to flight age lower the head, extend the wings slightly, and give an inhalant hiss when disturbed. Vogel (1950) described it as resembling human snoring, noted that it constantly rose in pitch, lasted 5–6 sec., and was repeated frequently. Mossman (1976) described it as increasing and then decreasing in volume, lasting 3–5 sec., and being "low-pitched and throaty." A. Wetmore (1965), in Panama, referred to it as a "peculiar cat-like hiss" that can change abruptly to a "rough growl." Intensity of hissing increases as a chick is approached. Ritter (in Wilbur and Jackson 1983) described a "rattle" sound, similar to the buzz of a rattlesnake, given by 2-week-old young.   JEROME A. JACKSON

HABITAT   The Turkey Vulture can be seen almost anywhere within its range, but it is a much less urban bird than the Black Vulture today than it was 80 years ago, when it was so common about the Charleston, S.C., market that the city became known for its vultures (Sprunt, Jr., and Chamberlain 1949). Abundant sources of such food sources as open garbage dumps and landfills, fish kills, and animals killed by vehicular traffic attract them now; before modern environmental laws, the offal at slaughter houses and the like was a prime attractant. The Turkey Vulture seems to be more numerous in lowland areas, perhaps because of a greater abundance of thicket and hollow tree breeding sites. Roosting congregations are generally near stable food sources, near or over water, and often include hundreds of birds. Some have been also reported on sandbars in rivers, some on buildings. Many roosting aggregations are temporary, the birds dispersing in a few days, but others are used for years.

In Fairfield and Hocking cos., Ohio, where there are numerous deep valleys, there was only 1 breeding site per side of valley regardless of length (V. Coles 1944). In Md., there were 7 pairs on 2,656 acres of mixed forest, brush, scattered agricultural areas, and deserted farmland; there were 7 pairs on 11, 520 acres of "general farmland" with little woody cover (R. Stewart and Robbins 1958). Also note high nesting densities mentioned below under Reproduction.

This vulture may be more of a cold-country bird in s. S. Am. than anywhere in N. Am.   JEROME A. JACKSON

DISTRIBUTION   (See map.) This vulture can now be found breeding throughout most of N. Am. to at least lat. 50° N. Throughout most of this range it is migratory. Populations are more or less continuous through the Caribbean and Cent. and S. Am. to Tierra del Fuego and the Falklands. In N. Am., it has not always been so widespread, having expanded its breeding range n. during this century, most dramatically between the 1920s and 1950s. The most plausible reasons suggested for this expansion include a warming climate and the availability of road-killed animals for food.

The population dynamics of the Turkey Vulture through time are not well quantified, but some trends are evident (Wilbur, in Wilbur and Jackson 1983). The species seems to have been widespread and numerous in the 1800s, declining in numbers with declines in populations of the bison and other large herbivores, increasing with increased availability of road-killed animals as automobiles and highways become more prevalent, and again decreasing as forest breeding sites were cleared, organochlorine pesticide contamination increased, and environmental laws required burial of animal wastes.

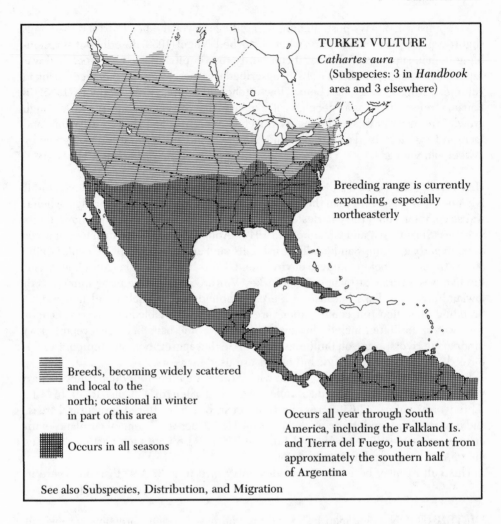

TURKEY VULTURE
Cathartes aura
(Subspecies: 3 in *Handbook*
area and 3 elsewhere)

Breeding range is currently
expanding, especially
northeasterly

Breeds, becoming widely scattered
and local to the
north; occasional in winter
in part of this area

Occurs in all seasons

Occurs all year through South
America, including the Falkland Is.
and Tierra del Fuego, but absent from
approximately the southern half
of Argentina

See also Subspecies, Distribution, and Migration

In several Mexican states, vultures and Caracaras decreased or disappeared locally some time between the 1950s and 1970s, this believed (A. R. Phillips) to be due at least partly to pesticides. Wilbur (1978b) also suggested that pesticides, which caused eggshell thinning, were responsible for vulture declines such as noted by Oberholser and Kincaid (1974) in Tex. W. H. Brown (1976) analyzed Christmas counts 1952–1975 and reported relatively stable winter numbers in the U.S. until the late 1950s, followed by a steady decline. In regard to n. expansion, numbers passing at Braddock Bay (near Rochester, N.Y.) in spring have increased "rapidly and steadily," tripling in the past 8 years (L. and N. Moon 1985).

Breeding   In this century, n. limits and numbers have expanded dramatically. The Turkey Vulture nested in Ont. at least as early as 1901. Northern populations have increased, especially since the 1950s, in the n. U.S. and in Canada at least from Alta. e. to Ont. and Que. No current summary of this expansion exists, but it was detailed earlier for the Great Lakes region by deVos (1964) and for New Eng. and e. Canada by

A. M. Bagg and Parker (1951, 1953). Eaton (1914) reported this bird to be only a summer visitor in warmer parts of N.Y.; it was first found breeding there in 1925 (Howes 1926) and made a "phenomenal advance" in all parts of the state (Eaton 1953). By 1930 it had bred in Conn., by 1954 in Mass., by 1981 in N.H., and by 1982 in Maine.

There are large areas within n. breeding limits where this bird evidently does not nest. There may be a dearth of suitable breeding places or, where there are fewer roads and less traffic, a scarcity of road-killed animals.

Summer–fall Turkey Vultures continue to be reported at locations n. of known limits of breeding. Yet not all boreal records are recent; see A. M. Bagg and Parker (1951). Early examples: Moose Factory on James Bay in 1898 and Nfld. in 1905. The 1941 record from Nain, Labrador (G. Sutton 1942), is apparently the most northerly.

Winter Northward occurrence is probably restricted by snow (which covers food) and low temperatures (frozen carrion is not easily dismembered; soaring conditions may not exist). In the w. U.S., most birds that remain are in coastal Calif.; there is much migration via Cent. Am. into S. Am. The e. N. Am. birds shift s. within their overall breeding range, but some (as evidenced by banding data) from latitudes as far n. as Ohio remain more or less locally all year. A few have been seen in midwinter as far n. as n. Calif. and s. Oreg., s. Wis., s. Mich., and s. Ont. There are notable winter densities between Del. and the Chesapeake Bay, along the Gulf coast from e. Tex. to s. Fla., and n. to Va. In the Fla. Keys they are abundant in winter and numerous in other seasons (Hundley and Hames 1960). In s. Fla., wintering migrants feed at urban landfills and roost on buildings in Dade Co.; resident birds rarely frequent those areas (Gaby 1982).

Islands There is a record for Bermuda and several for the Dry Tortugas. Distribution in the W. Indies is spotty: Bahamas (resident on Grand Bahama, Andros, and Abaco), casual on Bimini and Jamaica (where it decreased greatly because of predation at breeding sites by the introduced mongoose—W. Scott 1892). In these is., also the Caymans and elsewhere, known as "Jim (or John) Crow." It has only recently been known from the Dominican Republic and Haiti. There are recent sightings on St. Croix, Virgin Is. There are no reports from the Lesser Antilles and Tobago, but it is now a common resident in Trinidad. It is resident far s. in the Falklands. Common in the Tres Marias Is., w. Mexico.

Introduced Sw. Puerto Rico about 1880 (Danforth 1935); "less successfully" in the Bahamas (C. H. Blake 1975).

POSTSCRIPT For a history of this vulture in the Greater Antilles, with discussion of possible introductions, possible natural spread, and with emphasis on Puerto Rico, see Santana C et al. (1986).

Reported as **fossil** from the Pleistocene of Calif. (6 localities), Nev., Ariz., N.Mex. (2), and Fla. (4); also Brazil (2), Argentina, Ecuador, and Peru. Found in **prehistoric sites** in Oreg., Calif., Ariz., Tex., Iowa, Wis., Ill., S.D. (several sites), and Fla. (From Brodkorb 1964, with additions.) JEROME A. JACKSON

MIGRATION Emphasis on N. Am. data. Most migrants travel in loose associations. The Turkey Vulture and Swainson's Hawk occur at times in the same "kettles" and along the same aerial routes, both being long-distance soaring migrants. They are funneled through Cent. Am., where they pass in thousands, separate or intermixed with other migrant raptors. The vultures migrate by day, roost at night, and await favorable air currents before continuing in the morning. They travel great distances without eating, yet in spring are said to feed to some extent in N.Y. (L. and N. Moon 1985), and A. Wetmore (1965) stated that they pause along rivers to drink in Panama. They are generally lowland migrants and travel fairly low, but at times they ride thermals to at least several thousand ft. To cross narrow expanses of water (they generally avoid wide ones), they circle high over land, at times out of sight of the unaided eye, before gliding to the opposite shore. Repeated attempts may be made at different altitudes before suitable air currents are found. Then they leave, strung out, toward their destination. They breed on Vancouver I., hence a water crossing (island-hopping?) from the mainland; in fall they cross Almirante Bay, nw. Panama, in enormous numbers.

Spring In e. N. Am., migration is essentially a shift within overall Canadian–U.S. breeding range; this is supported by limited banding data (P. Stewart 1977). There is no reliable evidence of birds crossing the Gulf of Mexico, yet the distance separating Fla. and Yucatan is less than from the Argentine mainland to the Falklands, where Cawkell and Hamilton (1961) reported this species flying toward the latter place. Darrow (1983) suggested that some e. birds reach Latin Am. via the Fla. Keys, Cuba, and Yucatan, but there are almost no records from the Dry Tortugas or elsewhere to support this idea.

In the e. U.S., a shift n. begins in early Feb., especially in mild seasons; in s.-cent. Wis., Turkey Vultures arrive in numbers during the last week of Mar. (Mossman 1976); migrants reach s. Canada and n. New Eng. by early Apr. or earlier. There is much movement in middle U.S. latitudes from mid-Mar. through Apr. (a peak usually the last week in Mar.). Older birds (breeders) perhaps precede younger ones (pre-breeders) by a considerable span of time, which may account for prolonged overall movement.

Of anecdotal interest, the town of Hinckley, Ohio, celebrates the Sunday after the Ides of March as Buzzard Day. Turkey Vultures are said to have arrived there on Mar. 15 for many years (although dates elsewhere in Ohio begin at least as early as Mar. 3). Thousands of people gather to celebrate their return, traffic is tied up for hours, and days are required to clean up after the event. The Hinckley birds are believed to winter in the Okefenokee Swamp, Ga. (Frank 1979), but also in Fla.

In w. N. Am., the birds presumably migrate to Mexico, Cent. Am., S. Am., or a combination of these. Large numbers pass through Panama from late Feb. to early Apr.; Chapman (1933) reported them flying at 4,000–5,000 ft. over Barro Colorado I. At that season they pass mainly along the Atlantic slope of Panama (Loftin and Olson 1963). At a Panama location on Mar. 1, 1950, A. Wetmore (1965) estimated that about 15,000 passed in the hour before sunset. In Costa Rica there are great concentrations in Feb., ahead of the main hawk flights. In Guatemala on Mar. 23, Hundley (1967) saw them (and Swainson's Hawks) migrating in numbers. In n. Yucatan there were small flocks and individuals Mar. 26–27 and, during Mar. 31–Apr. 2, individuals and a flock left Yucatan headed n. out of sight over the Gulf of Mexico (Van Tyne and Trautman 1945). They might well have turned back unseen.

Migration in Veracruz, Mexico, is pronounced from about mid-Mar. to mid-Apr., sometimes with spectacular numbers of these birds in sight at once. Thousands were seen Mar. 27, 1966 (Bussjaeger et al. 1967), and Mar. 22–26, 1970 (Purdue et al. 1972). Along the Mexican–U.S. border, migration peaks in the last ⅓ of Mar.; n. it peaks in Mar.–Apr.

Fall Migration seems to be associated with a drop in temperature. In mild seasons, many n. birds remain within their summer range until very late, and some may not leave at all. A shift s. from s. Canada evidently begins by some time in Aug., but some migrants commonly linger at least into Oct. At the w. end of L. Superior 1951–1963, the peak was Sept. 15–28, and numbers declined to zero by Oct. 20 (Hofslund 1966). Throughout much of the U.S., movement is generally noticeable from early Sept. to well into Nov., yet in Mexico, Amadon and Phillips (1947) reported a gathering of about 1,000 (migrants?) in Durango as early as Aug. 25. Along the Pacific slope of Panama in Oct.–Nov., scattered individuals, then flocks of thousands, followed the lay of the land w. toward Colombia (Loftin 1963).

In Fla. Bay about 50 exhausted Turkey Vultures landed on a ship in fog on Nov. 2, 1968 (Mote 1969). Almost surely they found no thermals and could not attempt a water crossing.

There is an enormous amount that we do not know about migration of this species, for example, whether the schedules of prebreeders differ from those of breeders. It appears that many of the birds that breed in Mexico are migratory; it is possible that, at least at lower latitudes, prebreeders migrate, and breeders, by and large, do not. For numerous dates (without details) for both spring and fall in the U.S. and Canada, see Bent (1937). JEROME A. JACKSON

BANDING STATUS By Aug. 1, 1952, a total of 1,381 Turkey Vultures had been banded in the U.S. and 103 had been recovered (Parmalee 1954). Main places of banding: Minn., Ohio, N.J., Tex., N.C., and Calif. Recoveries of birds banded in N. Am., available to Oct. 13, 1976, totaled 131, banded as follows: Va. 48, Ohio 27, Md. 21, Ont. 5, Mo. 4, plus 1 or 2 from 14 other states (P. Stewart 1977). Most recoveries showed n.-s. migration within e. N. Am., but one had traveled some 3,300 km. from Wis. to Brit. Honduras (Mossman 1976). Through Aug. 1981, the total number banded was 2,474, with 158 recoveries (6.4%) (Clapp et al. 1982). Banding records suggest that Turkey Vultures make occasional erratic movements, particularly in winter (R. Stewart and Robbins 1958).

Band encrustation resulting from urohydrosis (defecating on the legs) has restricted circulation, causing loss of use of the foot or leg (Henckel 1976). Larger bands did not solve this problem, and the Bird Banding Laboratory suspended all vulture banding activities. To facilitate population and behavior studies, vultures now are marked with patagial tags. For example, sightings of tagged birds by Gaby (1982) indicate that Turkey Vultures wintering in s. Fla. come from Ont. and the e. third of the U.S. JEROME A. JACKSON

REPRODUCTION **In our area** Age when this vulture **first breeds** is unknown— perhaps at least several years. Few data indicating territoriality exist, although V.

Coles (1944) found only a single breeding site in one side of any valley in Ohio and felt that the birds defended a territory around it. Work and Wool (1942), however, observed several "adults" near active breeding sites without any indication of territorial defense.

Although the Turkey Vulture seems to be primarily a solitary breeder, there are records of up to 12 breeding sites/acre beneath a heronry in cent. Alta. (G. Moore) and of sites quite close together in cottonwood areas of e. Mont. near bison slaughters (Cameron 1907). In such cases it seems that a concentrated food supply may have facilitated increased nesting density, that is, this overrides any territoriality or any attachment to formerly used scattered sites.

Pair formation   Activities leading to this may begin before return to breeding areas among more migratory birds. At about this stage the birds perform a ritualized CIRCLE-DISPLAY (T. Roberts 1932, V. Coles 1938, Loftin and Tyson 1965). They gather on the ground in a cleared area and make a series of hops with wings spread and drooping. One bird hops toward its neighbor, which in turn hops until it approaches a third, and so on. According to Tyson (Lofton and Tyson 1965), this chasing is done with lowered head. Individuals drop down from trees nearby and join in, while other dancers break away. On a sand flat in a Fla. river in early Mar., Loftin and Tyson noted that vulture tracks formed 2 contiguous circles, together forming a figure-8. One was about 6 ft. in diam., the other 8. There were marks of trailing wings at the periphery. Each trail of tracks was about 15 in. wide, and the participants kept to these circles. Turkey and Black Vultures sometimes participate in the same dance (Coles, Loftin and Tyson).

Pair bond   Sustained or renewed from year to year; may be life-long for some individuals. Long duration is necessitated by long parental dependence of young. Family groups have been seen almost up to the time the adults begin the next year's reproductive cycle.

Deborah Davis (in Wilbur and Jackson 1983) described a conspicuous aerial display that takes place 2–3 weeks before incubation. Its most noticeable feature is FOLLOW-FLIGHT, in which one vulture precisely follows the other at an altitude of 20–50 m. for up to 2 hrs. or more. At times it seems like a game of tag in which there is much flapping and the following bird dives at the leading one. One marked ♀ was the leading bird in 82.1% of Follow-flights. Davis never observed vultures strike one another during Follow-flight dives, although she did during hostile encounters. V. Coles (1938) saw birds strike each other in their dives.

Copulation   Wilbur and Borneman (1972) noted no display preceding it, but Deborah Davis observed a SPREAD-WING display by the ♂ preceding 6 of 18 mountings. It was similar to the posture of a sunning bird except that primaries were pointed downward, "wrists" more elevated, and the posture was held for only a few sec. immediately before or during mounting. Davis observed a marked ♀ give this display on 2 separate occasions—once before and once after copulation. Such displays seem to occur in all Cathartidae, but with least frequency in the Turkey Vulture (Davis, Koford, 1953).

As the ♂ mounts the ♀, her legs are flexed and head is low. The ♂ may use his outspread wings for balance, but in 12 of 18 mountings, Davis also observed the ♂ flap his wings rhythmically while on the ♀'s back. Both birds often poked and nibbled at

34

each other's head with their beaks during mounting. Sixteen mountings lasted 3–130 sec. (mean 38.9) and the mean for 4 mountings when cloacal contact was observed was 64.3 sec. (range 36–79). J. Schmitt (see Davis, in Wilbur and Jackson 1983) observed copulation 3 times, each lasting approximately 7 sec., during a 35-sec. mounting. After dismounting, members of a pair often perch side by side for several min.

Laying site   Once a site for the eggs has been selected, the pair may perch together nearby for several days to weeks before laying (T. Jackson 1903, D. Davis 1979, J. Jackson). Sites consist of little more than a cleared, trampled area within some relatively dark recess. Kempton (1927) reported that a bird in a hollow tree pulled at rotten wood, then shredded it for use at the site. In our area, the site is usually at ground level, although some are in higher tree cavities, in caves, under rocks or ledges on cliffs, in upper rooms of old buildings, or even below ground level in caves.

J. Jackson (in Wilbur and Jackson 1983) summarized data from 899 laying sites. Of these, 76.9% of 324 w. of long. 100° having adequate data were in caves, and another 9.9% were on cliff ledges or among rocks. East of 100°, sites were quite different, with 34.5% of 418 in hollow trees, stumps, or logs, 27.8% in thickets, 12.9% in caves, 7.6% on cliff ledges or among rocks, and 5% in buildings. Fewer than 5% were in any other type of site. Exceptional sites, including some in heron nests up in trees, are quite unconcealed. Some sites are known to have been in use for several years; others are used irregularly or perhaps in alternate years.

Jackson divided his data set by time as well as by longitudinal subsamples and demonstrated significant differences in laying sites between a set of 164 reported to 1920 and a set of 282 reported beginning in 1921. Since 1920, significantly fewer (22.3% vs. 53%) have been found in tree cavities, and significantly more (38.3 vs. 11%) have been found in thickets. These changes may be attributed to clearing of old-growth forests, shorter rotations in modern forests, control of fire in forest areas, and proliferation of such exotic vines as honeysuckle and kudzu. To the extent that thicket sites are less protected from predators and flood waters than are tree-cavity sites, declines in breeding success of Turkey Vultures may be expected in the e. In se. Ill., Buhnerkempe and Westmeier (1984) noted an apparent shift from natural "nest" sites to abandoned buildings.

Egg laying   Occurs late Apr.–mid-June at the n. limits of the species's range and becomes progressively earlier at more s. lats. down to about lat. 30° in the e. and 34° in the w. (Jackson). At these lats. the range of egg dates is greatest, extending early Feb.– mid-May w. of long. 100° and from early Feb. to early June e. of 100°. South of these lats. early egg dates become progressively later (to at least lat. 26° in the e. and 28° in the w.), and the length of the laying period decreases.

Replacement clutches   No documented records of 2d clutches in Turkey Vultures, but at lower lats. there is ample time for one if the 1st is lost, and late egg dates undoubtedly represent 2d clutches. When an egg in a clutch of 2 was destroyed, a 3d was laid; later, 1 of these 2 was destroyed and no more were laid (Maslowski 1934).

Clutch size   Usually 2 eggs, occasionally 1, and rarely 3. There were 4 (in 2 pairs) in a N.J. site, probably from 2 ♀ ♀ (Bent 1937, photo). One to 3 days can elapse between deposition of eggs in a clutch (Kempton 1927, V. Coles 1944).

One **egg** each from 20 clutches (Calif. 6, Tex. 4, Pa. 5, and 1 each from Va., Ohio,

Md., and Kans.) **size** length 70.55 ± 3.13 mm., breadth 48.48 ± 1.28, radii of curvature of ends 17.89 ± 2.07 and 13.30 ± 1.66, **shape** oval to elliptical, elongation 1.45 ± 0.058, bicone −0.064, and asymmetry +0.141 (F. W. Preston). Other series: 52 av. 71.3 × 48.6 (in Bent 1937); 15 from Ohio av. 70.1 × 47.2 and av. wt. was 82.1 gm. (V. Coles 1944). The shell is smooth, ground **color** whitish gray, sometimes faintly bluish or greenish, with brown blotches concentrated around the larger end; pale lilac markings are similarly concentrated. Within a clutch, eggs commonly vary—the first usually more blotched, the second more speckled.

Incubation Presumably begins on completion of the clutch, though direct evidence is unavailable. The ♀ and ♂ incubate alternately (Kempton 1927, V. Coles 1944, later authors) for periods of about 24 hrs. The **incubation period** has been reported as 28–41 days depending on author, but supporting data suggest that the higher figures are more convincing. For example, Buhnerkempe and Westmeier (1984) recorded incubation periods per egg of 34 and 35 days. While one bird is on the clutch the mate often perches within view of the site.

V. Coles (1944) had difficulty catching an adult on the site if its mate was circling overhead, but no signaling was apparent. Work and Wool (1942) always found an adult on the breeding site, but Coles noted that both adults invariably were absent in morning when vultures in the area were sunning and again in evening when birds were preening and sunning before roosting. Adults do not aggressively defend the site from humans. If possible, an adult will try to escape; otherwise it may give an exhalant hiss and/or vomit.

Hatching The 2 eggs in a clutch can hatch on the same day (Kempton 1927) or up to 3 days apart (Prill 1931). For the first few days after hatching, the brooding parent remains with the chicks even if a human visits the site. Some workers report having to move the passive adult aside in order to view the nestlings only to have the adult return immediately. One ploy used at this stage is "death feigning," although the eyes are kept wide open and watchful (Vogel 1950). The site is clean and has relatively little odor; V. Coles (1938) thought that this might reduce predation there. Later it is soiled by excrement of the young and probably during feeding.

V. Coles (1938) and Deborah Davis (in Wilbur and Jackson 1983) found that **young** were brooded by a parent for about the 1st 5 days, at which time they seemed to be relatively thermally independent. In contrast, Gardner (1930) felt that full thermoregulatory ability was not achieved until about 2 weeks of age, and Lynch (1984) noted that young were brooded continuously during the 1st 2 weeks. Davis noted that after 5 days posthatching the parents spent increasingly less time at the laying site and that by 2 weeks posthatching they visited only briefly during the day to feed the young. Lynch reported that during the 3d week the young were sometimes unattended.

The young are nourished by regurgitation of semiliquid food, which they obtain from the throat of a parent or from where it was dropped on the ground or floor of the site (Work and Wool 1942, Vogel 1950). Davis found the frequency of feedings to vary from 3 in 3 hrs. to none in 26 hrs.

Ritter (in Wilbur and Jackson 1983) estimated hatching weight of Calif. birds at about 60 gm. and found that chick growth followed a sigmoid curve that most closely fits the logistic equation described by Ricklefs (1967). Half the asymptotic wt. of 1,754 gm. was reached in 21 days, and the asymptote was reached by about 40 days.

The young are noisy from birth, producing a warning hiss if disturbed; at an early age they regurgitate and peck when handled; after about 2 days they tend to hide in dark areas near the hatching site. They back toward a vertical surface when defecating, so that the walls at the laying site are "whitewashed." They can run at 6 weeks and climb well a week later.

A defensive action of young older than 2–3 weeks was termed "scare rush" by Work and Wool (1942) and "scare jump" by Mossman (1976). It is a lunge at an intruder, sometimes accompanied by hissing and by flapping the wings.

Captive young kept by Roddy (1888) drank water freely, preferably when flowing from a vessel with a constricted mouth, and they liked to thrust the beak into the opening in a partly closed hand (as a young one thrusts it into a parent's mouth when feeding). They were fond of being handled, especially when feeding, and they soon followed persons like dogs. They expressed pleasure by a low hiss, displeasure by a forcible one.

Age at first flight About 9 weeks; it was given as 62–65 days by Work and Wool (1942), but possibly the young departed somewhat prematurely. In Panama, a hand-reared bird flew at 70 days (McHargue 1977b). The young are fed and tended for a time thereafter, and the family may continue together into the following year. See Description, above, for some changes in appearance during nest life. For useful photos of preflight young, see W. B. Tyrell (1938); for tabular and photo documentation, see Ritter (in Wilbur and Jackson 1983). In s. Calif., **flying young** continue to interact with parents, chiefly by follow-flight, until at least onset of fall migration; siblings generally remain together and in the vicinity of their laying site until at least the onset of migration in the fall of the year after they hatched; some continue to return to their breeding site area for up to 2 years after hatching (Abbors 1979). JEROME A. JACKSON

SURVIVAL   Few data. Of 19 recoveries of birds killed or found dead after having been banded in first year of life, av. annual mortality rate was 21.5%; see table in P. Stewart (1977). A banded individual lived 16 years, 10 months (Clapp et al. 1982).
JEROME A. JACKSON

HABITS   In our area unless otherwise indicated. Turkey Vultures fly and perch singly, in pairs, and in groups of various sizes—but most commonly alone or in small numbers except in migration and at some roosts.

Flight   At least in the U.S. and Mexico, soaring groups, wheeling overhead, formerly might contain dozens of individuals, but such grouping is more typical of the Black Vulture. A soaring assembly may contain both species. Occasionally the birds disappear into the clouds. Flapping rate was 2.7/sec. in Fla. (C. H. Blake). Broun and Goodwin (1943) recorded a flight speed of 34 mph for a Turkey Vulture, but speed undoubtedly varies greatly with air currents. An unusual altitude record is that of a Turkey Vulture hit by a military jet aircraft at 12,000–14,000 ft. over Blythe, Calif. (R. Laybourne).

Search pattern   The Turkey Vulture flies low and singly over the ground at a good speed; even through forest. The Black seems incapable of this type of flight. Close observation of a fairly narrow strip of terrain permits the Turkey Vulture to locate small food items, often where there is considerable vegetation. It can thus feed without competing at larger carcasses with the Black Vulture. The Black often flies above the Turkey Vulture and seems to take advantage of the latter's carrion-finding ability. (So also does the King Vulture, and so did the California Condor.) When food is found and both species are present, the more aggressive Black dominates the Turkey Vulture, which must wait its turn. The Caracara will displace Turkey Vultures at food and chase them until they regurgitate, whereupon the Caracara steals the vulture's meal (Glazener 1964).

A debate over which sense, sight or smell, is most important in finding food has been in the literature since at least Audubon's day. Sight is obviously important, since the birds often find fresh rather than rotten and odorous meat. They also watch each other and other scavengers that have located food: Black Vultures, Com. Crows, and Com. Ravens. Evidently they may be aided by watching cats and dogs (P. Stewart 1978), and they either see or smell remains of prey at entrances of fox dens (T. Scott 1941). On the other hand, high-flying Black Vultures watch the lower foraging flights of Turkey Vultures and are led to food.

Unlike most birds, Turkey Vultures have a well-developed olfactory sense (Stager 1952, Bang 1960). For example, they have been captured in traps baited only with scent (E. L. Tyson); in Cuba, apparently they are attracted to a plant (*Stapelia nobilis*) whose flowers smell like carrion (D. E. Davis 1941). Controlled experiments show that the Turkey Vulture can detect concealed food (Stager, Owre and Northington 1961). Unlike our other vultures, it forages efficiently beneath the forest canopy. Sixteen or more Turkey Vultures dropped down a fissure from which they could not escape, presumably having smelled food there (Parmalee and Jacobson 1959).

Feeding behavior Having weak claws and beak, they are obligate carrion eaters. Cathartid feet cannot be used for predation (H. Fisher 1946). The beak lacks the strength to rip the fresh hide of larger dead mammals. Thus, at times, the Turkey Vulture must depend on the more powerful Black Vulture or on mammalian scavengers to do the ripping—or wait until the carcass is decayed.

A Turkey Vulture does not have to move quickly to catch prey; it only has to locate it

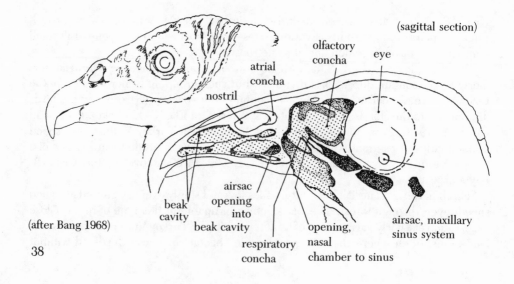

(after Bang 1968)

38

and make sure it will not move. No need to hurry, so the bird reconnoiters. Tyler (in Bent 1937) described the fate of the carcass of a young pig killed by an automobile on a southern road. The vulture behaved warily until assured the pig would not move, then stepped on it, and extracted and swallowed an eyeball. Next the skin was torn or pulled back. Three times, Tyler saw Turkey Vultures make the 1st incision in the upper shoulder area and then devour the underlying muscle before eating anything else except the eye. The bird's actions were deliberate, "like a skilled workman," and it reacted with threat if another approached. Prather et al. (1976) found that maintenance diet for caged birds was approximately 140 gm. of carrion/day, about ⅒ the wt. of the bird.

When one bird locates food, it is soon joined by others, including Black Vultures. If the carcass is so fresh and firm that it cannot be dismembered, the flock may stand on the ground, perch in trees nearby for hours, or even roost in the area. They also tend to perch near carrion after a full meal while digesting.

If a bird is surprised at carrion, it will sometimes pick up food and fly off with the food dangling from its beak. Generally it is not carried very far; sometimes it is soon dropped.

Live prey Most accounts of killing by Cathartid vultures likely refer to the Black, but a few cases are documented for the Turkey Vulture. Near Ft. Myers, Fla., Turkey Vultures not only killed newborn pigs, but Hamilton (1941) was also assured that it was no uncommon occurrence. Lovell (1941) suspected they were Black Vultures, but Hamilton (in Lovell 1952) maintained otherwise. In the Falklands (where the Black does not occur), the Turkey Vulture is continually persecuted "for its attacks on sheep" (R. W. Woods 1975). In Jamaica, "young and weakly chickens, etc." are consumed (W. Scott 1892). In Wis., Mueller and Burger (1967b) saw one kill a tethered sparrow; vultures also attacked a tethered Rock Dove and a Sharp-shinned Hawk that was enmeshed in a trap. A penned vulture killed and ate a Curve-billed Thrasher (B. and C. Glading 1970). Another penned captive captured, killed, and ate the flesh of several young Ringed Turtle-Doves (S. A. Smith 1982). In Glades Co., Fla., one waded into water, stabbed with its beak, and came up with a fish (J. Jackson et al. 1978). In Ohio in mid-Aug., 4 Turkey Vultures attacked a lone "adult" Great Blue Heron on a nest high up in a tree in a heronry (Mehner 1952). Also in Ohio, a parent Turkey Vulture got food for its 2-week-old young by beating nestling Great Blue Herons and causing them to disgorge their food (Temple 1969). Vultures themselves disgorge indigestible portions as castings or pellets of a characteristic shape; see Rea (1973) for details of size and of some of the contents.

In Everglades Park, a Turkey Vulture, "in the manner of an eagle" (!) seized a live Am. Coot, lifted it out of the water, then dropped it when a boat approached (V. Gilbert 1955). If seized in the beak, this seems possible; S. A. Smith (1982) saw a vulture thus transport a live dove. On the other hand, Varona's (1976) account of one seizing, lifting, and quickly dropping a dog in Havana, Cuba, seems fanciful, since the bird cannot grasp and transport anything in its feet. Possibly it was an incomplete observation—the dog might have jumped at an attacking bird.

Roosting Late in the afternoon Turkey Vultures perch to sun and preen much as they do in the morning before leaving the roost. In se. Wis. there were 2 general feeding periods—midmorning and late afternoon (Thiel 1976). Roosts are often near or over water. In spring and summer, some roost singly and even move away if Black Vultures attempt to join them (P. Stewart 1978). Others roost in aggregations year-round, often with Black Vultures. Roosts of hundreds to more than a thousand vultures have been reported at sites where the birds are not molested—as at an ammunition plant in Va. (Prather et al. 1976) and on an abandoned nuclear reactor at the Savannah R. Plant, S.C. (Jackson). At the n. limits of the species' winter range, birds may roost in caves and sheltered places. In rainy or bad weather they may remain at their perches for at least as long as 2 days, foregoing meals because of their incapacity to fly under such conditions (D. Hatch 1970). Roosts can be temporary (at a food supply), seasonal (spring–fall), or permanent (peak numbers in early winter).

Although Turkey Vultures leave the roost earlier than Black Vultures, they often remain long past sunrise. This may be for thermoregulatory reasons as well as to await favorable winds or updrafts for flight. Rabenold (in Wilbur and Jackson 1983) found that 89% of Turkey Vultures left the roost 3.5–5 hrs. after sunrise. Roost departure is correlated with ambient wind speeds (Abbors 1979) but not with temperature or cloud cover (Davis, in Wilbur and Jackson 1983). Keeler (1893) remarked that the dark color of vultures makes them visible at a great distance against the sky; thus color may have adaptive value in assisting the congregation when a bird's actions reveal that food is discovered.

Use of water The Turkey Vulture drinks by dipping the beak into water and then raising its head, not throwing the beak up, in order to swallow (A. Wetmore 1920). A captive was kept in good health for a year without drinking water (D. Hatch 1970). In Ariz., Turkey Vultures flew to open perches to get wetted by a rainstorm (McKelvey 1965). The Black Vulture has been seen drinking brackish or possibly salt water; see Food, below, for both species eating salt.

Thermoregulation Turkey Vultures can lower their body temperature markedly at night, thus reducing energy expenditures (Heath 1962). They often perch in sunlight at or near their roost, wings outspread, feathers raised, and backs to the sun for ½-hr. or longer in the morning, a behavior that may facilitate a return to normal diurnal body temperature (Heath). To thermoregulate at high temperatures, they stand erect and excrete on their legs, 1 at a time; this lowers body temperature through evaporative cooling (Kahl 1963, D. Hatch 1970).

Livetrapping Olson et al. (1967) had ample experience with the subdued temperament of the Turkey Vulture as compared with the Black. When approached in a trap, the former squatted motionless with folded wings and hanging head and could be picked up without the slightest resistance. It vomited rather passively at first and afterwards left its beak gaping until it was released. It made no attempt to bite.

Versus disease Some ranchers in Tex. have credited vultures with polluting water places by defecating and by regurgitating food (Parmalee 1954). Yet it is of interest that neither of our 2 common vulture species is a proven harborer or transmitter of any disease. It was formerly thought that vultures might carry hog cholera and/or anthrax, but the only evidence is a second-hand report of anthrax cultured from excrement of vultures that had fed on anthrax-killed sheep (Bullock 1956). Turkey Vultures do not harbor botulism and appear to be highly resistant to both oral and injected doses of this bacterium (type C) as well as to injections of types A and B (Kalmbach 1939). It is remotely possible that migrants from Cent. Am., for example, might carry infection on their feet and transmit it by later bathing, but there is no evidence.

Human food   Young vultures were eaten in Tex. a century ago (Benners 1887).

Folklore   Since the 2 common vultures are ubiquitous in warmer parts of our area, it seems surprising that they have not generated more recorded folklore since European settlement. (They are not differentiated in some folklore; see American Black Vulture.)

The Cherokee were impressed with the buzzard's immunity to disease, offensive odors, and corruption; drinking its blood was said to give temporary immunity from all endemic diseases. A dead buzzard hung near a home was thought to have a similar effect. In a conjurer's formula, buzzard down was prescribed as a dressing for shot and arrow wounds. (From Witthoft 1946.) Buzzard feathers were used in cleansing wounds; a feather was displayed by a shaman to indicate he could cure such wounds (Swanton 1946). Among plains tribes, the Mandan disliked the Turkey Vulture and Raven because they fed on human bodies placed on scaffolds; this information dates from Maximilian Wied-Neuwied's travels in the early 1830s. In the sw., the Turkey Vulture had prominence, being the "bird of purification" and as such rating a chapter in H. Tyler's *Pueblo Birds and Myths* (1979).

In an account published in London in Dec. 1693 the Rev. John Clayton noted that in Va. the fat of this bird "dissolved into an Oil, is recommended mightily against old Aches and Sciatica Pains" (M. and S. Simpson 1977).   JEROME A. JACKSON

FOOD   Primarily in N. Am. Turkey Vultures are primarily carrion feeders, and the diversity of their diet reflects the diversity of available carrion. Some preferences are suggested: they seem to prefer smaller carrion than does the Black Vulture (A. Wetmore 1943, later authors); they eat snakes, perhaps sometimes taken alive; and they prefer fresh meat to putrified. Two ate skunks, but not the scent gland (Florence Merriam 1896). Insects are sometimes consumed (includes beetles in dung), and vegetable matter under some circumstances. Also recorded eating salt. Live prey is often young or incapacitated.

Animal   They prefer fresh meat (W. Scott 1892, V. Coles 1938, Owre and Northington 1961). Pearson (1919) reported the killing of young colonial birds by "vultures." Vultures have picked out the eyes of a cow or horse mired in a bog (Wayne 1910). They take shrews and moles, perhaps at carrion. Mammals, birds, turtles, and snakes killed on highways and in fires (A. H. Howell 1932, Rapp 1943, others). At lakes, rivers, and oceans, dead fish (various authors); in Fla., live fishes (J. Jackson et al. 1978) and dead tadpoles in a drying-up pond (in Bent 1937). Seen feeding on dead pelicans, ducks, and seabirds (various authors), a dead alligator (Wright and Harper 1913), a dead whale (Jewett 1916), and sea lion excrement (F. Beebe 1974). Seal excrement and dead seals in the Falklands (R. W. Woods 1975). Occasionally human fecal matter in Mexico (A. R. Phillips). Cow dung, from which they may derive some benefit from beetles it contains. Occasionally grasshoppers (Dawson and Bowles 1909, Crafts 1968) and apparently Mormon crickets (La Rivers 1941).

Vegetable   Sixty-two birds ate pumpkins in s. Ohio when hard pressed for food;

pumpkins that were soft after a frost were reduced to shreds (J. Green 1927). In winter in Jamaica, over 100 instances were noted of feeding on coconut from rotting piles of opened and discarded nuts; the texture is similar to that of rotten pumpkins (Crafts 1968). (Carrion is scarce in Jamaica.) The fruit of palm trees has been reported as common fare of Turkey Vultures in Panama (A. Wetmore 1965). On the peninsula of Madre-Deus, Bahia, Brazil, the farmers know when palm nuts are ripe because Turkey and Black Vultures begin to visit and perch on the palms (Pinto 1965). Paterson (1984) found a high incidence of plant material in Turkey Vulture pellets in Va., but much of this could have been extraneous material rather than plants ingested as food.

Mineral   In Pa. in Nov.–Dec., a total of 22 Turkey Vultures on 6 occasions and 9 Black Vultures on 4 occasions were seen eating salt from a block in a pasture. Even when the block was moved 100 m., they persisted (Coleman et al. 1985). (See American Black Vulture for that species possibly drinking saline water.)

JEROME A. JACKSON

CALIFORNIA CONDOR

Gymnogyps californianus (Shaw)

Very large diurnal raptor; length 46–55 in. (117–134 cm.); wingspread about 9 ft. (2.7 m.)—greatest of any living N. Am. landbird. Feathering dark except: wing-lining, which is dark or more or less white to (definitive stages) partly white; and greater upper wing coverts, which vary with individual and age from part of them narrowly edged whitish to at least most of them rather broadly edged white (narrow edging typical of certain predefinitive stages). Face elongated, the eye being well behind midpoint between tip of beak and rear of head; most of head–neck bare in downy stage and again after early flight age; an erectile ruff around lower neck, its feathers and some venter feathers elongated, very narrow, and tapering; a reddish patch of bare skin ventrally along and below neck ("ventral cervical apterium"); folded wing reaches to or beyond tip of gently rounded tail; claw on pollex ("thumb") present from downy stages onward, curved and about 30 mm. long in adults. Sexes av. about same size. Weight usually 20–23 lb. (9–10 kg.) and may exceed this, but reports to 31 lb. are suspect.

No subspecies. A temporal precursor is mentioned beyond (see Distribution, below). Closest living relative, based on DNA hybridization studies (C. G. Sibley), is the Andean Condor (*Vultur gryphus*).

DESCRIPTION   There are 4 predefinitive Plumages; definitive feathering is not attained until at least age 5–6 years (Koford 1953), and birds evidently do not breed until past this age. There is a prolonged period of molting annually, Feb./Mar.–Nov./Dec. (and sometimes winter molting), not all feathers being renewed in a single period; that is, at least wing and tail require 2 such periods. For details of feather distribution, see A. Miller and Fisher (1938).

▶ ♂ ♀ Def. Basic Plumage (entire feathering), renewed as indicated above (incubation plus nestling periods occur within the molting span); heaviest molting (includes some primaries) occurs in midsummer.

Most of **head–neck** bare, color varying from yellowish through orange to vivid reds; **beak** silvery gray; **iris** brownish red surrounded by bright red sclera; some bristly black feathers on forepart of head, extending down onto cheeks; neck more muted than head, the skin toward grayish with violet-magenta patch on underside. Color of head–neck during breeding season was more vivid on some days than others (Koford 1953); in a zoo bird it changed from palish yellow to "dark crimson" in the morning when the bird faced the sun with spread wings—but only seasonally (M. Davis 1946); when a captive was excited, the head-color became more intense (F. Todd 1974). **Body** feathering blackish or sooty, the distal feather margins on dorsum edged paler; feathering fades toward brownish; ruff at lower neck can be elevated until it conceals most of neck; bare ventral skin reddish and most conspicuous when crop is distended. Legs and **feet** slaty grayish with small reddish patch at "knee," prominent early in the breeding season; they commonly appear white in life, being coated with excrement. **Tail** as dorsum. **Wing** flight feathers nearly black, except most of wing lining and axillars white; in a zoo bird the definitive white underwing was acquired by the 6th year (F. Todd 1974).

AT HATCHING   Down is short and white; head–neck, part of belly, and underwing bare; skin yellow-orange sometimes with purplish undercolor on body (W. Toone). Beak and iris dark, legs and feet yellowish with dark claws.

The above describes down-A; down-B is long, woolly, and dark gray. There is more gray than white down at age about 29 days; the long, gray down-B is well developed at age about 42 days (Koford 1953, photos). A stubby gray down, distinct from downs-A and B, develops on the head–neck by 50 days; the skin underneath is pale flesh color. The first Juv. down (it pushes out down-B) appears at about 18 weeks and is visible first on upper- and underwing. It is snow white interspersed with the emerging Juv. contour feathers and soon is covered by them (W. Toone).

44

2 weeks or slightly older

Twelve young hatched at the San Diego Zoo in 1983 and 1984 weighed 156.6–205.7 gm. (mean 185.3) (C. Kuehler, P. Witman). Four of these young in 1983 weighed 628–771 gm. (mean 701) at day 15, 2.2–2.7 kg. (mean 2.4) at 35 days, 4.1–5.6 kg. (mean 4.8) at 60 days, 6.7–8.8 kg. (Mean 7.3) at 93 days, and 7.6–9.5 kg. (mean 8.3) at 134 days (W. Toone).

▶ ♂ ♀ Juv. Plumage (entire feathering) begins to appear at age 8 weeks, forms a fairly complete covering at 18–20 weeks, and his fully developed at 24–25 weeks (W. Toone). Color of head skin changes from fleshy to slate gray at age about 18 weeks, although the head sometimes is already quite grayish at hatching.

Head–neck Largely covered with gray down; iris brown; ruff on lower neck well developed. Many of the blackish **body** feathers, especially on dorsum, have paler, brownish, terminal margins. **Tail** tends to be slightly wedge shaped (central feathers longest), not smoothly rounded as in most older birds (it is slightly wedge shaped in some). **Wing** tips of at least several inner (and usually almost all) upper greater secondary coverts pale gray, forming a line; a distinctive scalloped pattern on trailing edge of secondaries, resulting from somewhat pointed ends of the feathers; wing lining predominantly white but irregularly mottled dark brown in a dark spot near the axillars.

Subsequent predefinitive Plumages From field observations, Koford (1953) and later researchers recognized 3 in this sequence: "black," "ring-necked," and "subadult." Transition from one to another is gradual, through prolonged molting. The underwing is mottled white throughout, perhaps with least in Basic I.

▶ ♂ ♀ Basic I Plumage acquired beginning in LATE SPRING of year following hatching and continuing until 3D SPRING. Skin of **head**–neck dark, with more or less dark down; **iris** dark olive-brown; **wing** has indistinct light margins on ends of upper greater coverts; lining varies from mostly blackish to (in a captive) white mottled dark, including axillars.

▶ ♂ ♀ Basic II Plumage acquired gradually beginning in 3D SPRING following hatch-

45

ing. Skin of **neck** becomes pink, beginning at base of bare portion, forming more or less a colored ring, which is frequently hidden by the ruff but is visible when neck is extended and often when bird is soaring. The pink increases gradually and head colors start to develop; the down disappears from the **head.** There still are indistinct light ends on upper greater **wing** coverts and amount of white in underwing may be reduced. The ring-necked condition generally continues through 4th spring–summer after hatching, becoming more conspicuous in this year, then diminishing as head colors become more prominent. Although F. Todd and Gale (1970) reported development of some neck color in a captive in its 2d summer after hatching, this is not obvious in photographs taken of this bird, and it appears that this characteristic does not normally become clearly visible until birds reach their 3d spring–summer. Finley (1908) reported that a captive at age approaching 3 years showed no color on the head–neck and that the head still was covered with short gray down.

▶ ♂ ♀ Basic III Plumage worn ABOUT A YEAR following Basic II (normally through the 5th spring–summer after hatching). Ring-necked condition no longer distinct and **head** color evolves to definitive during this period; small dark bristly feathers on crown, occiput, and other areas give an irregular sooty appearance; neck pink. **Feathering** as definitive, but white of underwing may have a dark area or dark streaks within it near axillars; white bar on upper surface of wing becomes prominent. One bird observed in the wild 1980–1984 retained some dark streaking in underwing triangles for at least 4 years beyond attainment of definitive head coloring.

NOTES There are other changes before the bird is fully definitive. The sclera of the eye surrounding the iris changes from a pale pink at age 1 year to a distinct reddish color at about 2 years. Iris color begins to change from drab olive-brown of the Juv. stage to a more orange-brown at about age 3 years, gradually evolving thereafter to a brownish-red "adult" coloration. Beak color of Juv. birds is dark gray but gradually evolves to the silvery gray of "adults." F. Todd (1974) reported that the puffy condition of cheeks and chin developed in a zoo bird during its 6th year and that the red, wrinkled, ventral cervical apterium became conspicuous at about that time.

A large molted primary meas. 65.6 cm. (25.75 in.) across chord of arc and, when flattened, 69 cm. (L. Miller 1937).

Molting Primaries are numbered from inner to outer, secondaries from outer to inner, and tail feathers from middle pair outward (but numbering herein is indicated only for the primaries). Primary molting was described by N. Snyder and Johnson (1985) and N. Snyder et al. (MS). Obviously there are several foci or "molt centers" in the secondaries, but details are not ascertainable from photographs of wild birds in flight.

Birds of all ages have a general tendency to molt low-numbered primaries earlier than high-numbered ones (e.g., #3 and #4 tend to molt earlier than #5 and #6 in any year, etc.), but there are many irregularities in the sequence that become more prominent with age.

Yearlings in their first primary molt tend to renew primaries sequentially, starting with #1 and #2 and finishing with #5 in first molting period, following with #6–#10 in the next year (F. Todd and Gale 1970), but even yearlings vary enormously. Some individuals have gotten as far as #7 in the first period while others have not gotten past

dark-headed
young

molting

broken
primaries

Def. Basic
Plumage

J. Schmitt, del.

#2 or #3, and the pattern has not been strictly sequential. Often, before high-numbered ones are dropped, the bird again has begun to renew the lower-numbered ones; by the time a bird is 3 or 4 years old, almost all vestiges of sequence have dissolved into the irregular pattern seen in older birds.

Which primaries were molted in any year, hence the order in which they were replaced, was different for every bird observed in the wild population. As a general rule, about ½ of the 8 "fingerlike" primaries (#3–#10) were renewed each year, and the other ½ the following year, but the particular feathers replaced differed even for each wing of an individual and, on av., there were about 2 instances for each bird each year in which a bird molted the same feather that it molted the previous year or failed to molt it even once in a 2-year period.

Although primary molting normally begins in Feb. or Mar. and finishes in Nov. or Dec., some individuals have delayed onset until May or June and others continue overwinter. Primaries dropped in late fall or early winter characteristically are not replaced until the following summer—a much longer span than the usual 3½–4-month period from loss to full growth of a replacement occurring in the "normal" molting season. A bird at its breeding site was photographed while pulling a presumably loose primary until it became detached; then it was dropped.

Each wing has 22 secondaries. The gently rounded to slightly wedge-shaped tail consists of 12 rectrices. A zoo bird studied by F. Todd and Gale (1970) molted no rectrices and essentially no secondaries as a yearling; then it molted nearly all secondaries and rectrices the next year. Photographic studies of wild birds, however, clearly indicate that at least some individuals molt some rectrices and secondaries as yearlings and that renewal of all of them is not completed within a single year. Because rectrices and secondaries (in photos of flying birds) overlap considerably, it has not been possible to apply numbering to these feathers. Whether the molt cycle of rectrices and secondaries normally requires 2 years for completion, as it does for the primaries, is probable but not established from data at hand.

Body molting is prolonged, but details are lacking.　　　NOEL F. R. SNYDER

FIELD IDENTIFICATION　Great size; relatively small, orangish head; under-wings with elongated triangular white areas (widest next to body) extending almost to leading edge; and short tail are diagnostic of definitive Plumages. Younger stages: head–neck gray, to ring–necked (bare portion basally encircled pinkish), to blotched with orange, and white of underwing varies from mottled dark to nearly all white. In flight, the much smaller Turkey Vulture is more buoyant and tilts during soaring; the Golden Eagle is relatively larger headed and with longer tail. Golden Eagles when young have some white in the wing but not in distinctive elongated triangles along leading edge of lining. Predefinitive Bald Eagles, which occur in winter within recent condor range, are the most similar species in size and proportions; some have irregular white underwing triangles reminiscent of those of condors. At a distance, they are often difficult to distinguish from condors.

The condor soars in slower, larger circles than the Turkey Vulture, Red-tailed Hawk, and Bald and Golden Eagles. Condors generally complete a circle in 16–17 sec., Bald and Golden Eagles in 12–14, and Redtails in about 8–10. Condors rarely flap except when taking off or landing. Their normal body weight is at the limit proposed by Pennycuick (1969) for sustained flapping flight (about 10 kg.), and condors with full meals exceed this limit.

Viewed head-on, the inner half of the wings of the condor are decidedly arched (concave), and, distally, they curve upward with the primaries bent toward vertical; in the Turkey Vulture and Golden Eagle the inner half is straight and the outer has less upward curve. During soaring, condors perform a characteristic wing movement in which the tips are flexed downward and backward and quickly returned to the original position in a single continuous movement. These distinctions can be noted at a great distance when size or color patterns cannot be ascertained (R. S. Woods 1929, Koford 1953).

From the descriptions given earlier, it is evident, as discussed by Wilbur (1975), that age classes often may be recognized in the field, but one must be aware of the

48

possibilities of variation. Yearlings generally exhibit primary molting concentrated between #1 and #5, weak and erratic flight, difficulties in landing, close association with parents, proximity to places of hatching, and relatively pointed tails. At close range, one of the most reliable yearling field marks is the distinctive regular scalloping of the trailing edge of the secondaries. Two-year-olds often can be recognized by their dark heads and primary molting concentrated between #6 and #10. Three- and 4-year-olds are characteristically ring-necked, although the "ring" is often hard to detect in 3-year-olds, and birds of this age can sometimes be confused with 2-year-olds. Five-year-olds generally are predefinitive in head coloration and feather characteristics.

Condors usually perch erect in trees; their heads may appear very light to black, depending on the angle of sunlight; on ledges and on the ground their stance is more horizontal. Track is up to 7 in. (18 cm.) long with a span between tips of lateral toes of up to 5 in. (12.5 cm.). NOEL F. R. SYNDER

VOICE Usually silent. Perched condors of various ages make a sound like a suppressed human belch or low gurgle; this was heard from captives at the San Diego Zoo only during urohydrosis or defecation (W. Toone). Adults may hiss when disturbed at breeding sites. Grunting sounds when feeding have been reported. "Immatures," when fighting, make snarling, grunting, and hissing noises.

A day-old **young** made a wheezing hissing note; from age 2 days a hiss-growl was elicited by either departure of an adult or arrival of man, and at 4 weeks hisses lenthened. Hissing continued with age and was heard from large nestlings threatened at breeding sites. At 15 weeks, young gave a hoarse growl when handled and, when an adult flew nearby, a series of grunts. Still later, the young's grunts became throaty and staccato at a rate of about 2/sec. Also occasionally a short grunt in manner of older birds (Koford 1953). The bird aged about 19–20 days studied by Finley (1908) uttered a "crying note most peculiar for a bird, for it sounded exactly like the hoarse tooting of a small tin horn." It uttered this note a few times, then began hissing.

A captive in its 1st 6 years was never heard to vocalize (F. Todd 1974). This same bird, however, now (at age 19) gives a variety of hissing and grunting vocalizations (C. Cox).

Mechanical sounds The swish of wings flapping on takeoff can be heard up to ½-mi. In soaring flight there is a "steady hissing whistle," probably from the emarginated primaries, at times audible up to 100 yds. (Koford 1953). NOEL F. R. SNYDER

HABITAT Current (mid 1980s) breeding and foraging habitats of the condor are separate, and the birds commute between them during the breeding season. All recent laying sites have been located in pine- or chapparal-covered mountainous regions of the Los Padres, Angeles, and Sequoia natl. forests in San Luis Obispo, Santa Barbara, Ventura, Los Angeles, and Tulare cos., Calif. Recent foraging areas have been predominantly grassland or oak–savannah-covered private ranchlands in the foothills surrounding the s. San Joaquin Valley, principally in San Luis Obispo, Kern, and Tulare cos. Most foraging habitat is at lower elevations than most breeding habitat, although there is considerable overlap. Roosts are located in the vicinity of most breeding areas and most important foraging areas. Those in breeding areas are on cliffs or trees, especially dead snags of big-cone Douglas fir (*Pseudotsuga macrocarpa*). Roosts in the vicinity of foraging areas usually have been on trees rather than on cliffs. Long flights between foraging and breeding areas characteristically follow major ridge lines or proceed from one mountaintop to another. Condors were formerly known to forage along coastal shorelines and rivers, apparently using more varied habitats than they do presently.

Although most known breeding sites are 20 mi. (30 km.) or more distant from the principal foraging grounds, the birds cover such distances quickly and do not appear to suffer significant penalties in foraging efficiency as a result. Curiously, no condor breeding sites have been recorded from certain mountainous areas close to the foraging areas in the San Joaquin foothills, although caves are available in these areas. Possibly the absence of breeding condors from these regions is a reflection of greater densities there of natural enemies such as Golden Eagles and Com. Ravens.

NOEL F. R. SNYDER

DISTRIBUTION   (See map.) The mid-1980s range of the California Condor is J-shaped, surrounding the s. San Joaquin Valley n. of Los Angeles, Calif. The inner border of the J is the primary foraging range in the San Joaquin foothills, while the outer portion includes the mountainous breeding regions, a number of roosts, and foraging areas of lesser importance. Condors rarely move into the valley proper, possibly because an absence of topographic relief creates poor soaring conditions. Condors that move from one part of the range to another almost invariably follow the foothills around the valley, even though this entails a longer journey.

The geographic range of the condor formerly extended from the lower Columbia R. drainage in s. B.C. (into the 1800s) discontinuously s. into n. Baja Calif., Mexico, where the species was last recorded in 1937. Historical records, some of doubtful validity, exist for Ariz. (in A. R. Phillips et al. 1964). It is probable that condor remains will be found farther s. in Mexico than presently known.

The remains of *G. californianus* (sometimes including nestlings) have been found in **prehistoric sites** in Oreg. (2), Calif., Ariz. (several), and Tex.; and as **fossil** in the Pleistocene of Nev. and N.Mex. (2 sites) (references in Brodkorb 1964).

Other fossil remains, from the Middle and Upper Pleistocene, and at localities from Fla. to Nuevo León, Mexico, and Calif. are of birds that av. larger but may be separable (H. Fisher 1947) on skull characters. These [= *G. amplus* L. Miller] are "probably only a temporal subspecies" of *G. californianus* (Brodkorb).

A recent find of *californianus* is a humerus and coracoid from the lower stratiigraphic unit of a site 15 km. ne. of Batavia, N.Y.; wood, associated with mastodon remains at this site, was radiocarbon dated at 10,450 ± 400 years B.P. (D. Steadman et al. 1986). In the time of the Condor, the area was spruce and jack pine forest or parkland.

Recent finds of excellent material in limestone caves of the Grand Canyon have been dated at more than 11,000 years old, except a complete skull from more than 12,000 years B.P. (Emslie 1986). No dating from the sw. states (except Calif.) is more recent than 11,000 years B.P.

In Cuba in the late Pleistocene there was a vulture the size of the Andean Condor (Arredondo 1976).

NOEL F. R. SNYDER

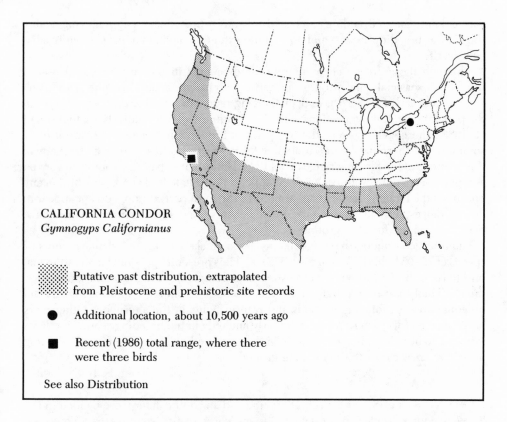

CALIFORNIA CONDOR
Gymnogyps Californianus

Putative past distribution, extrapolated from Pleistocene and prehistoric site records

Additional location, about 10,500 years ago

Recent (1986) total range, where there were three birds

See also Distribution

MIGRATION AND OTHER MOVEMENTS   Recent intensive studies based on photographic identification of individuals and radiotelemetry have revealed that all remaining wild condors use nearly the entire primary foraging range of the species in the foothills surrounding the s. San Joaquin Valley (N. Snyder and Johnson 1985, J. Ogden et al. MS). Nesting pairs commute mainly between their nesting areas in the mountains and the nearest portions of the foraging range in the foothills where they concentrate their foraging activities; they also wander to some extent throughout the foraging range, especially when not breeding. Unpaired condors, in contrast, tend to wander more extensively, basing their activities first in one part of the foraging range, then in another. All individuals living in the wild probably see each other at least several times a year during their movements through the foraging range; there is no clear evidence for the subpopulations proposed by Wilbur (1978a).

During the breeding season in spring and summer it is relatively common for prebreeders and other nonbreeders to visit breeding areas throughout the range. Breeding birds that have lost their mates have been observed remaining in their breeding areas when they are not foraging, patrolling them possibly in hopes of encountering and attracting replacement mates. Possibly most new pairs are formed as wandering nonbreeders come upon such unattached territorial individuals. One distinctive unpaired adult of 1982 was photographed visiting 4 different nesting areas and engaging in PAIR-FLIGHTS with resident adults in 3 of these areas. Very likely this bird

51

was seeking a mate. Breeding pairs have only rarely been documented moving among the various breeding areas—and only to the extent of moving into immediately adjacent territories.

Although there are no clear migration movements in the current population, a number of seasonal concentration patterns are characteristic of recent years: each summer and early fall there have been foraging aggregations consisting of most birds in the population in the sw. portions of the San Joaquin Valley foothills (E. V. Johnson et al. 1983); the heaviest use of the ne. parts of the foraging range has been in early summer; and there has been a tendency for prebreeders to spend large fractions of their winters in the foraging range ne. of Bakersfield. These patterns should be viewed as tendencies—not absolutes—since it appears possible to find almost any bird in any portion of the foraging range at any time. For the most part, condors do not appear to defend ranges, although some intraspecific chases of possibly territorial nature have been seen on the foraging grounds.

Radio-tagged condors have commonly been tracked in extended movements at speeds of 70–95 kph. (J. Ogden et al. MS), and it is presently possible for an individual bird to cover the entire range of the species in a single day's flight. With some pairs, the usual daily pattern throughout the year has been morning commuting flights from breeding areas to foraging grounds and return flights in the afternoon. Other pairs have followed this pattern more irregularly and only in the breeding season and have returned to breeding areas only rarely in the nonbreeding season, commonly roosting instead in areas closer to the foraging grounds.

NOEL F. R. SNYDER

BANDING STATUS   Five preflight young and an adult condor were banded in the Sespe Sanctuary region in the late 1930s and early 1940s. None was recovered, although Koford had resightings of 1 bird a year after banding. No birds have been banded in more recent studies, primarily because of the risks of build-up of excrement on bands for species that defecate on their legs, or practice urohydrosis. Since late 1982, 9 free-flying condors (7 ♂, 2 ♀, 3 "immature") have been trapped and marked with numbered patagial tags with attached radio transmitters. Seven of these birds were still alive as of late spring 1985; 1 of the 2 that disappeared was recovered by radiotelemetry and found to be a victim of lead poisoning. Other information derived from radio-tagged individuals is discussed in other sections herein.

NOEL F. R. SNYDER

REPRODUCTION   **First breeds** apparently at age 7 years for a ♂ (no other extant data on wild birds). California Condors build no nest in the conventional sense, being cavity-dwellers like other cathartids. **Sites** range from potholes or other kinds of caves in cliffs to crevices among boulders on steep slopes and, occasionally, burned-out holes in giant sequoia trees (*Sequoiadendron giganteum*). Usually, sites are caves in cliffs, but it appears that individual condors are flexible in this regard, since a bird that laid in a giant sequoia in 1984 was associated with a cliff pothole in earlier years. For a photograph of this tree site, see N. Snyder et al. (1986).

Site elevations   A study of 72 recent and historic sites indicates a range of 460 to

1,830 m., with preponderance of sites about 600–1,000 m. above sea level. Most have been located in the Upper Sonoran Life Zone, although a few have been as high as the Transition Zone. Sites at low elevations tend to face n., and those at high elevations s., as also has been noted in one study of Golden Eagles (Mosher and White 1976), but overall distribution of orientations has been random. Differences between orientations of high and low sites either may relate to temperature regulation or may serve only as a function of site availability.

Entrances   Exceedingly variable in size, the only obvious restriction being that it must be large enough to permit entry. Heights have varied from 30 cm. to 5.5 m. and widths from 20 cm. to 2.4 m. Depths have varied from 60 cm. to 14.6 m., with most sites about 1.5–2.0 m. Eggs generally have been placed as far back in the cavities as there has been a suitable, fairly level substrate and an adequately high ceiling. The lowest ceiling recorded at the egg position was only 38 cm. above it; the distribution of ceiling heights at egg position peaks strongly between 50 and 75 cm.

Not all egg substrates have been level. Six sites with bottoms sloping more than 5° have been located. An egg at one of these accidentally rolled out of the entrance and over the cliff edge in 1982. Evidently the degree of slope at egg position is important but not always fully appreciated by the condors.

Substrates   At the egg position, commonly surfaced with small chunks of rock and debris; it is clear from direct observations that the adults deliberately pick up these chunks in their beaks from the vicinity of the chamber and place them close to the egg. Thus condors do modify their sites to a limited extent and appear to prefer to rest their eggs on substrates of coarse gravel. Any adaptive significance of this is unknown, but it may in part be related to advantages in damping uncontrolled egg movements. Condors frequently have been observed kicking an egg clumsily while attempting to settle on it, a tendency that poses apparent risks of damage if the egg is free to roll easily. Since condors have been observed egg laying from a standing position, loose gravel substrates may also be advantageous in absorbing some of the shock that eggs experience when they drop. Other possible advantages of such substrates include reduction of contact of eggs with soil pathogens, partial protection from flooding of the site, and enhanced gas exchange.

In addition to small chunks of rock, substrates commonly include abundant wood rat (*Neotoma*) droppings, twigs, leaves, acorns, and, to a lesser extent, bone fragments, mollusk shells, trampled pellet material, and tiny eggshell fragments. Human artifacts occasionally have been found—bottle caps, pull-tabs from aluminum cans, broken plastic combs, and other plastic and metal items. It is likely that most such items had been brought into the sites by adult condors in misguided attempts to satisfy calcium needs of growing young, much as has been noted in Cape Vultures (*Gyps coprotheres*) by Mundy (1982). Substrates of cavities in sequoia trees have included sequoia cones, twigs, bark, and, surprisingly, gravel. Presumably the gravel came in as part of the crop contents of adults.

Six occupied sites examined by Snyder et al. contained Turkey Vulture eggshell fragments in addition to condor eggshell, indicating some overlap in site use between the 2 species. Another 5 sites contained wood rat nests, 1 an old Red-tailed Hawk nest, another an old Common Raven nest. Six sites had honeybee (*Apis mellifera*) hives nearby—at 1 (active in 1984), the hive entrance was only 56 cm. from the condor egg. Another recent site had a colony of bumblebees (*Bombus* sp.) on the cavity ceiling. Other coinhabitants include parasites. Mexican chicken bugs (*Haematosiphon inodora*) and ticks (*Argas reflexus*) were found by Koford (1953) in several sites. In addition, 3 species of bird lice have been found on California Condor specimens (K. C. Emerson): *Colpocephalum californici, Cuculiphilus alternatus,* and *Laemobothrion glutinans.* Of these, the 1st listed has been found only on the California Condor; the others also have been found on other cathartids. It is likely also that a species of *Falcolipeurus* may be confirmed for the condor, since this genus occurs on other cathartids.

Of the 72 sites studied by Snyder et al., 24 were accessible to man without climbing aids; 16 were easy walk-ins. In spite of relatively frequent use of such sites, no clear cases have been documented of predation on eggs or young by terrestrial predators (see Koford 1953, N. Snyder 1983). In 1983 a black bear (*Ursus americanus*) attempted to reach a roped-in site containing a nestling but failed. In 1982 a pair of condors harassed a bear that came within 100 m. of, but did not discover, a walk-in site.

Condors defend their sites vigorously from Common Ravens and Golden Eagles and, less consistently, from other condors. Ravens are a strong threat to condor eggs and probably also to small nestlings; Golden Eagles have been observed attempting to take older young that have come out to site entrances. Condors generally chase eagles away with vigorous flapping flight, lunging repeatedly with their beaks until an interploper is driven a km. or more away. Ravens are also chased off with vigorous flapping flight, but the chases are far less effective in keeping this species distant from breeding sites.

Territorial defense   Intruding condors are sometimes tolerated to the extent that resident pairs allow them to stand in the site entrances, but in other cases there has been vigorous defense. Two pairs in 1982 chose sites only 2.6 km. apart and established a sharply defined territorial boundary between them, maintained with repeated aggressive encounters. Yet 1 of the 2 pairs once was observed allowing a 3d pair to approach its breeding site closely and even copulate in its vicinity. Koford (1953) observed very few signs of intraspecific territoriality. Reasons for variability in territorial behavior toward conspecifics are unknown.

Alternative sites   All condor pairs observed over a period of several years have had more than 1 breeding site; in general, at least in recent years, pairs have changed sites in successive breeding attempts, whether successful or failed. While most sites examined have shown evidence of repeated use, many years often pass between years of occupancy. Alternative sites commonly are not in view from one another and often are in different canyons. The long distance between sites, coupled with the strong tendency for condors to move between successive breeding attempts, explains why laying a **replacement** "clutch" (single egg) was not known for this species until recently, although doubtless it has been occurring for millenia (see Koford 1953, E. Harrison and Kiff 1980, N. Snyder and Hamber 1985).

Prelaying behavior   Knowledge of condor reproductive behavior is based primarily on intensive study of 1 pair in 1939 (Koford 1953) and 9 between 1980 and 1985 (by N. Snyder et al.). In general, mated condors fly as pairs throughout the year except when dividing incubation and brooding duties, although a pair studied in 1983–1984 showed little tendency to keep together outside the breeding season. Pairs usually begin to make occasional breeding-site inspections in fall and early winter, but this activity usually does not become intensive until mid- to late winter, just before laying. Both adults participate in site inspections, alternately or simultaneously entering, lying down, and moving substrate around with their beaks for periods of several min. to an hr. or longer. Interspersed with these activities are preening and "courtship" behavior. Pairs frequently fly from one potential site to another, often km. apart, commonly making repeated inspections at 6 or more sites before settling on the one where laying will occur.

Time of laying As this nears, pairs tend to focus more and more on a single site, but in several cases the birds have switched at the last moment to another one. It appears that ♂ condors are not always aware of which site a ♀ ultimately chooses; ♂♂ have been observed flying off to forage at egg-laying time, then returning and flying systematically from 1 site to another in an apparent effort to locate their mates.

Before laying, pairs begin to roost consistently near the laying site. Often they begin the day with inspections, then fly off to forage, and return later for more inspections in the afternoon before roosting. The pattern is variable—morning inspections, afternoon inspections before roosting, or even foraging during the middle of the day may be omitted. The entire day may be spent in site inspections and associated activities.

Displays Long periods are often spent by the pair in aerial cruising over the breeding place, presumably in territorial advertisement. As laying time approaches, the birds are often seen in characteristic PAIR-FLIGHTS in which members keep close together, often side by side, synchronously turning and twisting. Display is conspicuous at perches. CIRCLE-DISPLAY: the ♂ extends his wings, generally facing the ♀ 1–2 m. away. With greatly exaggerated, slow, strutting footsteps, he circles and sways around the ♀ if there is space, generally keeping his ventral surface toward her but sometimes rotating so that his back is toward her. After some time, generally about ½ min., the ♂ usually moves around to one side of the ♀ and attempts mounting by stepping onto her back. There is irregular wing-flapping as the ♂ attempts to position himself properly. Cloacal contact usually occurs about 1 min. after mounting, lasts only a few sec., and is followed by immediate dismounting. Females normally react submissively, hunching over during mounting, but may reject a **copulation** attempt by biting repeatedly at the head of the ♂. Copulations sometimes proceed without prior Spread-wing display of the ♂ (Wilbur and Borneman 1972), and on occasion, ♀♀ give partial wing-out displays before mounting. Most displays and copulations observed have been on perches in the near vicinity of the laying site, but some have occurred inside the breeding cave and others have been seen at remote locations—even on the foraging grounds.

Interspersed with bouts of display, copulation, and site investigations, pair members also commonly engage repeatedly in mutual preening, especially of the head region (Koford 1953, photo).

Aberrant pair-bond Two pairs believed to consist of homosexual ♂♂ were observed closely between 1981 and 1983; in each pair, both members performed simultaneous Spread-wing displays to each other. Although dozens of mounting attempts were observed and the identity of which bird was on top was inconsistent in at least 1 pair, no mounting attempts led to cloacal contact, and all broke off in beak jabbing between the birds.

Laying and incubation Laying has been documented as early as the last week in Jan. and as late as May 7 (late spring dates are probably all cases of replacement eggs or delayed laying because of the presence of flying young of the previous year in the breeding area). Normal **dates for egg laying** extend from early Feb. through mid-Mar. Bent (1937) gave 38 dates for presumably viable eggs in Calif. as Feb. 17–May 28 (19 of them Mar. 23–Apr. 25); these are dates of collection, not of laying.

One **egg** per clutch (invariably). Egg **size** 46 measure length 102.4–120 mm., av. 110.2, and breadth 62.9–71, av. 66.7 (Bent 1937). Bent's maximum length was exceeded by an egg 131 mm. (5⅝ in.) long (in Koford 1953). Twelve eggs taken from the wild in 1983 and 1984 (for incubator hatching): length 91.6–120 mm., av. 108.9, and breadth 62.5–68.3, av. 65.7. Egg **shape** variably oval; the shell finely granulated, without gloss (when fresh), some with surface excrescences. **Color** whitish or very pale bluish or greenish when fresh.

Egg weight The dozen 1983–1984 eggs just mentioned at laying (calculated) weighed 210.4–299.6 gm., av. 266.7.

Since 1982, 10 cases of **replacement clutching** have been documented (N. Snyder and Hamber 1985), mostly as a result of taking eggs for artificial incubation. Three ♀ ♀ even demonstrated a capacity to lay 3 eggs within a single breeding season. Replacement eggs were laid 27–40 days after egg loss, with weak correlation between length of recycling time and length of prior incubation. Except for a case noted by E. Harrison and Kiff (1980), in all known instances of relaying, pairs moved to new sites.

Pairs may lay on an annual or biennial basis. Twice pairs have laid in 2 consecutive years with concurrent survival of young from the 1st year; in both cases, young attained flight early (Sept.) in the 1st year and laying was late (about Apr. 1) in the 2d year (N. Snyder and Hamber 1985). In previous cases of apparent annual laying, survival of young from the 1st year through the laying season of the 2d was not definitely established. F. Sibley (1970), for example, reported young (presumably all produced by the same pair) attaining flight in 4 consecutive years from the same site, but fates of the young after flying were unknown. In other recent cases, pairs did not lay on an annual basis and tended their strongly dependent young through the laying season of the 2d year.

The first clear sign of imminent laying is that the ♀ remains in a breeding site rather than flying off to roost at night. Laying typically follows within a day. Females also usually fill their crops with water about a day before laying. Actual **laying** has been witnessed on 2 occasions and was preceded by about 2 min. of tremors in the ♀. In both instances, the ♀ stood facing into the site and the egg was laid from a standing potition; each ♀ inspected her egg closely, touched it with her beak, and commenced incubation within a few min. Males generally have not been observed in company of laying ♀ ♀, generally being away foraging, then returning 1–3 days later to take their 1st turn at incubation.

Incubation Shared by the sexes; length of incubation turns av. 3.8 and 2.3 days respectively at 2 sites observed throughout the entire incubation period. At both, ♀

turns (4.3 and 2.6 days respectively) av. somewhat longer than ♂ turns (3.4 and 1.9). At a 3d recent site, incubation turns of up to 9 and 10 days were observed. The birds sitting for such long spans ultimately abandoned their eggs and departed, presumably to forage, but their mates soon appeared and resumed incubation. The pair observed in 1939 by Koford (1953) had relatively short incubation turns, av. 1.3 days (see J. Ogden 1983).

Changeover Variable; often the incubating bird leaves on approach of its mate, and they circle together overhead, sometimes out of sight into adjacent canyons. After a few min., the incoming bird arrives to commence incubation. In other cases, the birds have not left the egg untended—the incoming bird has walked into the site as the outgoing bird has flown off toward foraging areas. Some apparent exchanges turned out to be false; the bird that left the egg to circle overhead with its mate was the same that returned after a few min., while the mate departed alone.

Changeover does not always proceed smoothly; aggressive interactions, with ♂ ♂ usually dominant over ♀ ♀, have been noted with most recent pairs. In 1 pair observed closely since 1980, fights over access to the egg were chronic and long lasting, resulting in long periods of egg neglect and reproductive failure.

Incubating birds spend long periods of sleeping, interspersed with spells of preening, standing to gather substrate to place around the egg, rolling the egg with the beak, or changing incubation position. The egg is maneuvered into position on top of the inner toes, and commonly the parent kicks it accidentally while attempting to slide its feet underneath, sometimes even causing the egg to roll up to 0.5 m.

Although incubating birds sometimes take breaks to come to the entrance and look outside, usually they do not leave except during changeovers or, more rarely, to get a drink from a nearby stream or pothole. The birds using a sequoia tree cavity in 1984 sometimes drank from a water-filled cavity higher up in the dead treetop.

Data from a telemetered egg placed at a site for a week in 1983 indicated an av. duration of steady sitting of 59.8 min. Breaks occurred somewhat more frequently at night than in daytime (1.2 v. 0.8/hr.). Breaks were less frequent at the site studied by Koford.

Incubation period Approximately 56 days—one instance in the wild determined with any accuracy. It was 54–58 days in 12 incubator-hatched eggs (C. Kuehler).

Hatching and preflight period Hatching, closely observed twice, occurs about 2.5 days after the egg pips, judging from data on artificially incubated eggs (C. Kuehler). Adults appear to be unusually attentive at this time and, at one site, were observed actually picking away eggshell from the piphole. At the other site, hatching of the well-pipped egg was "assisted" by an adult standing on it, which caused the shell to separate in halves. The young hatch with their eyes open and, although not strong enough to hold their heads up except briefly, take food readily right after hatching.

Rate of changeover Increases dramatically at hatching, from once every 2–4 days during incubation to almost daily during the first weeks of the young condor's life. Frequency of visits then diminishes gradually during the remainder of the preflight period. In general, each parent makes about 3–5 feeding visits each week.

In the early phase the adults take turns brooding the young condor. Thus brooding is continuous for about 2 weeks and less so over the next 2, finally ceasing after about 4 weeks, when both adults begin to leave the breeding site at the same time and the young condor is alone at night. Attentiveness at 2 recent sites was 100% and 98% for the 2 weeks posthatching. Brooding is initiated either by the young crawling under the parent or by the latter rolling the young under its breast with the beak. Sometimes preflight condors appear to resist brooding and crawl out after having been drawn in.

During early stages, an adult typically sits or lies close to the the young condor and watches it when not brooding. Parents occasionally preen the young's down and sometimes snap at insects near it. The young sometimes pick up such objects as leaves and molted feathers and attempt to manipulate them; the attending adult occasionally takes these objects from the young and discards them out of its range.

The **young condor** is fed by regurgitation. The adult faces it, and it puts its head most of the way into the adult's mouth and begins swallowing food rapidly from the proximal area of the adult's tongue. With newly hatched young the feeding process apparently is initiated by the adult, which lowers its face to the young's level and either presents the side of its beak or opens it and takes the young's head in its mouth. A young condor may not start begging until a feeding is underway, when it begins beating its tiny wings stiffly during breaks in the meal. An older preflight condor begs before and during feedings by loosely flapping its opened wings, which are held out horizontally with tips dragging on the ground. Its whole body shakes with the effort.

Begging flaps are probably especially important in helping parents locate young that have wandered some distance from their natal caves onto ledges or into other sites or who have made early flights away from the breeding site. A band of white down on the upper wing surface of older young contrasts with the black feathers and makes begging movements conspicuous even at long distance.

During the 1st 2 weeks, preflight condors at 2 recent sites received about 6 feedings/day (in daylight), the rate gradually declining to about 1.2/day by the time of attaining flight. In the mid- to late nestling period, a visit to the nest by an adult usually begins with a feeding consisting of several bouts of contact interspersed with breaks. During breaks, adults sometimes temporarily restrain a frantically begging young by placing a foot on its neck and thus clamping it to the substrate. Also during breaks, adults often appear to bring food up to their mouths, reverse peristaltic movements sometimes being visible in the adult's breast and crop area. Adults sometimes toss their heads up and down in what appears to be a pumping motion before initiating feeding bouts. Feedings end with the parent raising its head or beginning some other activity, such as looking around or cleaning the beak and head region by rubbing on the substrate. Generally, a period of social interaction follows during which adult and young lie down in contact and preen each other, twining necks together and rubbing heads and necks over each other's bodies. Sometimes the adult becomes aggressive, directing nips, then blows, to the young and preening it with increasing roughness. During visits the adults also perform maintenance activity by digging with the beak through various areas of substrate to a depth of several in., much as during incubation.

Older preflight young   Spend most of their solitary daytime hrs. sitting, awake and alert. The next most common activity is preening and other self-maintenance, while a 3d is sleeping. Preflight condors spend lesser amounts of time picking up and manipulating objects such as sticks, feathers, stones, bones, and leaves. They dig and sort through material at the site and ingest light-colored objects selectively when they find them, probably as a means of obtaining calcium. A 5th activity category is exercise. Preflight condors perform bouts of wing flapping, leaping around, rapidly turning while jumping, capturing objects in the beak and then whirling around and carrying them away, and so on. A mock foot-capture behavior is similar to that seen in other nonscavenging falconiforms, except that in condors the foot stabs out to clamp objects to the floor of the site without gripping them. The presence of this behavior in young condors (but not adults) suggests that ancestors of condors may have had predatory habits.

Condors less than age 2 months appear to avoid spending much time in brightly lighted areas and generally retreat to the darker parts of their natal cavity as morning advances. Some young condors sun and exercise in early morning before retreating. Avoidance of sun may aid thermoregulation and reduce conspicuousness to predators.

Depending on the structure of the site, young condors may begin to wander outside the entrance as early as 6 weeks old. They are clumsy and suffer frequent slips and falls. A preflight condor found dead below a site in a cliff in 1966 may have fallen there (F. Sibley).

Attaining flight and subsequent dependency   First sustained flights have been observed at about age 5–6 months, and distance covered was 20–300 m. The young are exceedingly clumsy at first, gradually acquiring greater facility on the wing and in alighting, and they move progressively greater distances from their natal sites to land on ledges and slopes. Early attempts to alight appear to be uncontrolled; sometimes a young bird plunges deep into a clump of springy brush and disappears from sight.

Three young in recent years were not observed to attempt flight again for several days after their initial one but instead moved around on foot. First flights of all 3 occurred in the absence of adults. In 1, the young condor flew and landed on a rocky knob. When the adult returned, the young condor begged strongly and the adult alighted next to it, but the young refused feeding and continued to do so for 4 more days. Eventually it made a short flight back to near its natal cave, alighted on the ground and ran toward the cave, then begged as an adult alighted near it, and finally fed.

First flights have been seen as early as Sept. and as late as Nov. in recent years, and young have remained completely dependent on their parents for about ½ year thereafter. One that flew relatively early on Sept. 22, 1982, was first seen following its parents to foraging grounds on Feb. 1, 1983. During Mar. 1983 its parents became increasingly aggressive toward it and drove it from the breeding area, finally beginning a new cycle by laying an egg about Mar. 31.

Whether adults ever initiate breeding attempts in years following late attainment of flight of their young (Nov. or Dec.) is unknown. As adults have been seen feeding Juv. birds on the foraging grounds in summer and fall, it appears that partial dependency on adults continues in some cases for as long as about a year after they first fly. A captive at the Los Angeles Zoo exhibited begging behavior until its 5th spring after hatching (F. Todd 1974).

Breeding success   California Condors have generally reared young to flight age from about 40–50% of eggs laid, and there is no clear evidence that success dropped

59

significantly during the 1950s and 1960s (N. Snyder 1983). Three of 8 undisturbed nesting attempts since 1980 have produced flying young, a rate similar to the historical one. Since the success rate of the condor closely resembles that found by Jackson (in Wilbur and Jackson 1983) for Black and Turkey Vultures and by Mundy (1982) for various African vultures, and since there is good evidence that most adult condors have been attempting breeding, at least in recent years, it seems unlikely that the population decline of this bird has been primarily a result of poor reproduction.

Breeding failure Causes are, for the most part, poorly known, although it is clear from the historical data that most failures have occurred at the egg stage (N. Snyder 1983). In recent years, several instances have been observed of attempted and successful predation on condor eggs by Com. Ravens; condor eggshell fragments have been found in a number of old raven nests. As almost all condor breeding sites have resident ravens nearby, it is plausible that a large fraction of the historical cases of breeding failure may trace to this species—a hypothesis supported by the vigorous aggressive responses of breeding condors to ravens when close by.

Other documented causes of failure in the condor include an egg that rolled out of a badly sloped site, another crushed by a falling rock fragment, a young condor that apparently fell out of a site on a precipitous cliff, and eggs that probably would have chilled if they had not been brought into artificial incubation. All the cases of egg neglect were associated with a single pair, mentioned earlier. A chick studied by Koford (1953) apparently succumbed to a broken wing (cause unknown) shortly after attaining flight. In addition, aggressive responses of condors to Golden Eagles and black bears suggest that they are potential predators.

Condor eggshells were much thinner than normal during the DDT era, 1947–1972, but rate of eggshell breakage did not show an obvious increase and the breeding success rate did not show an obvious decline (Kiff et al. 1979, N. Snyder 1983). Therefore, strong evidence is lacking that the condor was seriously affected by DDT contamination. Recent eggshell thickness has been close to the historical mean.

NOEL F. R. SNYDER

HABITS **Daily routine** Nonbreeding condors generally spend most of each day perched at roost sites or foraging over rangelands. Birds often wait 3–5 hrs. after sunrise before leaving a roost and commonly return to roost anywhere from 2–5 hrs. before sunset. The actual amount of daytime spent at a roost seems to depend primarily on weather conditions (they may not fly at all on foggy or rainy days), hunger, and strength of winds. Condors normally fly only when there is enough breeze to give them lift over topographic features. On days immediately following a full feeding, a condor may only soar for a few midday hrs., either locally in the vicinity of a roost or in a round trip, out 20–30 mi. to foraging sites, without alighting (J. Ogden et al.).

After sunrise the birds generally shift on their perches and engage in comfort movements—stretching, shaking, turning, preening, and so on. When the first direct rays of the sun strike them, commonly they adopt a sunning posture with outstretched wings, facing either toward or away from the sun. Sunning bouts generally last several min. and end as the wings gradually sag and are pulled in toward the body. Full body shakes often indicate that a bird will take flight within a min. or 2. The birds appear to be excited if they see others soaring and often launch into flight. At times apparently they test the breeze before attempting to fly in calm air; they hold their wings arched and may wave them slowly; they bow-stretch and frequently take off from this position. In a take off from a level surface the birds generally make several running hops and flap for a while before shifting to soaring flight. Although birds that have eaten a full meal sometimes walk uphill before launching into flight, they seem to have no difficulties becoming airborne under most conditions. Flapping rate is 2–3 wingbeats/sec.

In roosting and foraging, paired adults often, but not invariably, travel together. Condors are also somewhat social with other condors that are not mates or close family members, joining them at roosts, carcasses, and in flight in an irregular fashion. Nonfamilial groupings, however, do not tend to be stable or long lasting, and the birds separate to go their own ways after variable lengths of time.

Condors generally fly within 1,000–2,000 ft. of the ground and often sail along level with the tops of high ridges or mts., although occasionally they soar to great heights. A mountaintop observer may spend as much time looking down on condors as up at them.

Unwariness   In the air, condors often are fairly tame and inquisitive, circling low over human observers, even changing flight direction markedly to approach and inspect groups of people closely. They seem attracted to groups of cattle on the range in a similar manner and may scan all sorts of mammalian groupings for moribund individuals. On the ground, condors seem more ill at ease and sensitive to man; birds may flush quickly from a carcass when a single person approaches within a ½-mi. Sometimes they are disturbed easily by noise and movement at roosts; when this occurs late in the day, it may disrupt roosting. Finley (1906) and others found that birds attending active nests sometimes are exceedingly bold on approach by humans. The young bird that Finley reared was playful and friendly toward him. It had a retentive memory. It was transferred to a zoo on Sept. 29, 1906, visited that Dec., and not visited again by Finley until Dec. 6, 1908, when it was "friendly and affectionate as ever" and nibbled his coat buttons and wanted to be petted. Records also exist of young that recently had attained flight approaching hikers to be fed such items as banana peels and peanut butter sandwiches. The general perception of the condor as an extremely wary creature, unable to suffer any human intrusion without irreparable psychological damage, apparently deviates somewhat from reality.

Feeding habits   Although they are carrion eaters, like other N. Am. vultures, condors prefer fresh meat—as clearly shown by Finley's young captive and by more recent field studies. The birds eat rapidly, often spending no more than 20–45 min. at a carcass. Whether a condor alights at a carcass and how long it feeds, may depend on such factors as location and condition of the carcass, hunger of the bird, and presence of other condors and other birds. When a number of condors are present at a carcass, a dominance hierarchy is common, possibly based on such factors as age(s) of the birds and proximity of the carcass to breeding territories of the various birds.

Condors almost certainly use other species as visual cues, especially Com. Ravens, Golden Eagles, and Turkey Vultures, as a means of locating food, and no satisfactory evidence exists that they use anything other than vision in foraging, unlike the Turkey Vulture. Condors generally displace Com. Ravens and Turkey Vultures at carcasses,

61

Turkey Vultures (foreground)

but their interactions with Golden Eagles are variable in outcome. The eagles often are able to exclude condors, and the latter wait patiently, a few yds. away, until the eagles are sated. On other occasions, possibly involving hungrier condors, the condors forcibly eject the eagles. It is rare today to see more than 1 or 2 condors, or a condor and an eagle, feeding together at a carcass, although several Com. Ravens may crowd around while a condor is feeding. Historic motion picture footage by E. Harrison and J. R. Pemberton, however, illustrates a massed, frenzied feeding by a large group of condors on a sheep carcass, a scene similar to that still observable today of large assemblages of African vultures.

Although a condor will drop to its "heels" to gain more leverage (F. Todd and Gale 1970), apparently it is incapable of ripping tough mammal hides, and this affects the way it removes flesh from some carcasses. Entrance is gained through body openings. In addition to native wild mammals, from the 1700s cattle have served as condor food. In earlier days, injured or diseased cattle were left to die on the range. After droughts in the 1860s and 1870s, there was a transition to sheep ranching, and again much food was available to condors. At a still later time, land increasingly was withdrawn from ranching and livestock were tended more carefully, yielding some declines in presumed food availability (Koford 1953, Wilbur 1978a). During the 1980s, cattle, especially calves, have been the most important food source, with native deer still seasonally or locally important.

Feeding frequency of individual condors appears to be highly variable and apparently depends on whether the birds are breeding, on weather conditions, and on other factors. Breeding birds with small young commonly bring in food on a daily basis, and their feeding frequency remains high throughout the nestling period. It is much lower during incubation; on 2 occasions, incubating birds have been known to go as long as 9–10 days without food. Nonbreeders probably feed on av. between 2–3 times a week.

Four captive condors at the San Diego Zoo in 1983, at 2 days of age and mean wt. of 193 gm., consumed 35–60 gm., av. 47, of food. At 7 days and mean wt. of 324 gm., they consumed 92–129 gm., av. 111; at 14 days and mean wt. of 654 gm., 180–360 gm., av. 267; and at 21 days and mean wt. of 1,224 gm., they consumed 225–674 gm., av.

440 (W. Toone). Average consumption rates of full-grown captives have ranged 570 gm.–1 kg. daily (F. Todd and Gale 1970; W. Toone and C. Cox). The crop capacity of a captive adult ♂ has been measured at about 1.4 kg. (M. Wallace). If this is typical, captives apparently need the equivalent of at least one full crop every 2–3 days to maintain their wt. Because of their greater activity, wild adults probably need to feed more frequently. There is no firsthand evidence that condors ever gorge themselves to the extent of being unable to fly.

A certain amount of indigestible material in the food, principally hair, is disgorged as pellets or castings. The rate at which condors disgorge these, however, does not appear to be nearly as high as in many accipitrids, probably because much condor food is soft tissues—generally they do not ingest the hides of mammalian carrion.

In recent years there has been no clear evidence of inadequate food supplies for the remnant population, and many carcasses observed on the range have not been exploited by condors or other scavengers (J. Ogden et al.).

Although R. Cowles (1968) speculated that condors might be having difficulties in procuring enough calcium, there has been no evidence of deficiency; the same problem has been suggested for certain African vultures, yet Dobbs and Benson (1984) questioned the likelihood of calcium problems in the Cape Vulture.

Drinking, bathing, and thermoregulation Condors have frequently been observed drinking and bathing in the wild. Koford (1953) gave detailed descriptions of heavily used sites; most were shallow pools that the birds could wade into without going in over their heads. Favorites are pools at the tops of waterfalls that allow ready access and unobstructed takeoff. Condors have also been seen drinking and bathing in many other sorts of sites, including temporary pools in potholes, along the shores of large lakes, and in cattle tanks and troughs. One apparently drowned in a cattle tank (Koford). The abundance of condor bones in the La Brea tar pit deposits could, in part, have resulted from birds wading into oil seeps, mistaking them for water sources (see H. Howard 1930). Bathing is normally followed by sunning with outstretched wings. F. Todd (1974) reported that a captive at the Los Angeles Zoo usually bathed daily.

Condors typically cleanse themselves after feeding by rubbing their heads and necks on whatever substrates are available nearby. The naked skin of the head region is normally kept in immaculate condition.

F. Todd (1974) discussed 3 ways in which condors may reduce body temperature in hot weather: panting, inflating the air sacs of the head region, and excreting a chalky residue on their legs (urohydrosis)—an evaporative cooling mechanism shared with other cathartids and the storks. In addition, condors may thermoregulate by moving to areas having favorable temperatures. Traditional midsummer use of high-elevation roosts on Mt. Pinos, for example, may be a function primarily of cool conditions there. In cold weather the birds elevate their ruff feathers to enclose the neck and part of the head.

Ceremonial use Keeping condors for ceremonial purposes was an ancient and widespread practice. The condor was prominent in Indian legends; Koford (1953) referred to totemic affiliation and a condor song, dance, and story in different parts of Calif. The condor-killing ceremony (sometimes a Bald or Golden Eagle was substituted) was probably the main reason for having captive birds—the California Condor in N. Am. and the Andean Condor in S. Am. A prolonged and rather gruesome ceremony, loaded with symbolism, involved the physical abuse of the victim until it was exhausted, then ritually killing it without shedding its blood. The condor represented a person who had been transformed into a bird. The symbolism varied in different cultural contexts, and ceremonies evolved to fit the circumstances of changing times. H. Harris (1941) referred to the "cosmogoic significance" of the bird to aboriginal man. At least in S. Am., a condor ceremony has persisted to recent times. The reader who wishes to pursue this subject beyond what is given in Harris may consult references to Bancroft, Gifford, Kroeber, and Parker, listed in Wilbur (1978a); Scott (in Bent 1937); and especially the chapter on condors and humans in prehistoric w. N. Am. by Dwight Simons (in Wilbur and Jackson 1983). For the Andean Condor, J. and L. McGahan (1971) is a useful introduction.

Condor quill   In former times, and apparently not as a general practice, miners used the basal portion of condor primary feathers as containers for gold dust; a quill, when tested for volume, held 10 cc. of fine sand (L. Miller 1937). A container was figured by H. Harris (1941).

Numbers   Long recognized as a vanishing species (J. G. Cooper 1890, later authors), the California Condor must have been reasonably plentiful over a considerable area until after the arrival of Caucasian man. For example, there are early reports of large assemblies at carcasses of stranded whales; the birds may have gone to the coast in numbers, more or less seasonally. The condor's history to 1900 was treated thoroughly and in a most readable form in "The annals of *Gymnogyps*" by Harry Harris (1941); for other history, see Koford (1953) and Wilbur (1978a). It is evident that the condor population began its drastic decline at least as early as the 1840s.

It is futile even to speculate on the actual size of the condor population until fairly recently. Because of the mobility of individuals and the inaccessibility of much of the species' range, *Gymnogyps* has always been difficult to census. Estimates of a total of 60 and 40 birds by Koford (1953) and A. Miller et al. (1965), respectively, were based on a number of questionable assumptions and probably underestimated condor numbers significantly (N. Snyder and Johnson 1985). An annual simultaneous count (Oct. survey) was begun in 1965 and led to a consensus that there still were about 60 birds in the mid-1960s (Mallette and Borneman 1966, F. Sibley et al. 1968). Yet totals of the Oct. surveys varied greatly over the years, leading to considerable debate as to their accuracy and significance (Verner 1978, Wilbur 1980). Nevertheless, there was an unmistakable overall decline during the 17-year period of the surveys, and by 1978 Wilbur (1980) estimated only 25–35 birds left in the wild.

In 1981, efforts were begun to use photographic identification of individuals as a basis for generating population estimates (N. Snyder and Johnson 1985). These revealed that differences in primary feather molting and damage give a highly reliable means for recognizing individual condors through time. Analyses of thousands of photographs from throughout the range of the species led to late summer population estimates of 21–24 individuals, including 7 "immatures," for 1982; also 19–22, including 5 "immatures," for 1983; and 15–18, including 2 "immatures," for 1984. By May 1985, only 9 wild condors could be found in greatly intensified efforts to photograph the wild population, and only 1 breeding pair could be found of the 5 pairs known in

1984. Of the remaining wild individuals, 5 were known to be ♂ ♂ and 4 believed to be ♀ ♀, based on blood sexing and reproductive history, from techniques reported earlier (Biederman and Lin 1982, A. Kumamoto).

Wilbur (1978a) gave a "chronology of significant events" in his history of the California Condor, beginning with the first known written record in 1602. Many of the events, regardless of their motivation, seem not to have materially altered man's direct and indirect impact on the condor. Causes of overall historical decline undoubtedly have been diverse and mostly a result of man's activities. A great many condors have been shot wantonly especially with rifles, increasingly available since the 1890s. Others succumbed to poisoned carcasses intended to eliminate grizzly bears from the region in the latter part of the 19th century. Some have been caught in various traps set for large mammals. Collecting for museums and private individuals had its effect in the past—a minimum of 288 birds and 71 eggs are known to have been removed from the population between 1792 and 1976 (Wilbur 1978a).

In recent years, at least, the decline has been caused primarily by mortality factors, as reproductive performance has been about what might be expected from comparisons with some other avian species. Quantitative assessment of the latter is not yet possible. In recent decades birds have been found dead from shooting, poisoning, collision with overhead wires and objects, drowning in cattle tanks, and so on, but causes of death have not been determinable for the vast majority of condors found dead because of their state of decomposition. Furthermore, biases in the way dead condors have been located do not allow safe generalizations about significant mortality factors. Of 2 found dead in 1983–1984, 1 was a victim of apparent cyanide poisoning from a coyote trap, the other of lead poisoning from an ingested bullet fragment (M. Anderson).

To some extent, the decline of the wild population since 1982 can be attributed to taking some birds to establish a captive breeding population. Two birds were taken captive in 1982, and all eggs and nestlings were taken in 1983 and 1984. Assuming 2 young might otherwise have attained flight to the wild in 1983 and 2 in 1984 (rate of attaining flight seen in 1980 and 1982), 6 birds were effectively removed from the wild population during those years, of which 4 might be expected to be alive at time of writing, on basis of recent mortality rates. Since the wild population declined by more than 12 birds between 1982 and early 1985, the taking of captives accounts for only about a third of the decline.

Meanwhile, because most birds kept captive have been from eggs produced by deliberate multiple clutching of wild pairs, more captives have been gained than birds have been lost from the wild population. From 1 captive ♂ in 1982, the population at the San Diego and Los Angeles zoos rose to 16 individuals (10 ♀ and 6 ♂) in 1984, yield a minimum total wild and captive population of 32 birds in that year and an overall increase of about 10 birds since 1982. However, with the heavy mortality in the wild and losses of breeding pairs experienced over the winter of 1984–1985, only 2 young were produced in 1985 and the total number of condors as of late spring 1985 stood at 27 individuals (18 captives, 9 in the wild). In July 1986 there were 3 condors (all ♂) left in the wild and 24 in captivity (9 ♂, 14 ♀, and a yet unsexed hatchling).

Although the decline of the wild population still projects to extinction within a very few years, recent progress toward establishment of a captive population and prospects for captive reproduction and for releases to the wild offer some hope that the wild population ultimately can be saved or at least recreated if it disappears in the years immediately ahead. The species now is so close to extinction that its fate is very much in doubt. [The last remaining bird in the wild was taken into captivity on April 19, 1987.—Ed.]   NOEL F. R. SNYDER

FOOD   Mainly carrion of land mammals, marine mammals, and fishes. Nearly all domestic animals of Calif. were listed by Koford (1953). Wild mammals, including those killed by hunters and trappers: mule deer, elk, coyote, bobcat, cougar, grizlly bear, jackrabbit, cottontail, and ground squirrel. Apparently prefers deer and young calves—preferably fresh. In 2 instances, 28 condors were seen at a deer carcass (C. Robinson 1940, Koford 1953). Four condors dragged the body of a 200-lb. young grizzly for a distance of 200 yds. downhill (Heerman 1859). Formerly fed extensively on dead fish, especially salmon along the Columbia R. (Audubon 1839, others); also dead whales (Gambel 1846, others). Reputed to attack severely wounded animals (Douglas 1829, others), but pursuit of small live animals not established. Bones and shells also taken in apparent drive to obtain calcium.   NOEL F. R. SNYDER

Def. Basic

KING VULTURE

Sarcoramphus papa (Linnaeus)

Large, robust, broad-winged black and whitish vulture. Length to about 32 in. (81 cm.), wingspread to about 70 in. (180 cm.). Sexes essentially alike in size and appearance; definitive condition described here. Head–neck largely naked except for hairlike black feathers (mainly on sides of head), naked skin brightly colored various reds, orange, bluish; lobed caruncle or comb on top base of beak; iris whitish. Most of body and smaller feathers of wing variably creamy or palish buff, nearer white on underparts; remainder of feathering blackish—enlarged ruff (feathers whitish basally) around neck, primaries, secondaries, tertials, primary and greater coverts, rump and upper tail coverts, and tail. Naked crop pendant and reddish. Legs and feet rather stout, mixed yellowish and dark neutral shades.

DESCRIPTION ♂ ♀ Def. Basic Plumage ALL YEAR as above. Molting of flight feathers of the wing apparently is in stepwise mode and rather prolonged.

AT HATCHING Down whitish, head naked and black, iris dark, feet dark; photo of young still largely in down in Lundy (1957).

Juv. Plumage—head–neck naked and dark; caruncle rudimentary; iris dark; all feathering variably blackish.

Other predefinitive stages—few data. Beginning at some stage, more or less of the underparts become whitish, under wing coverts mixed whitish and dark, axillars white.

Measurements Ten ♂ BEAK from cere 32.1–38.8 mm., av. 35.2; WING across chord 490–525, av. 503, and TAIL 207–227, av. 215; and 2 ♀ BEAK from cere 33.5–34

67

mm., av. 33.7, WING across chord 490–497, av. 493, and TAIL 213–217, av. 217 (A. Wetmore 1965).

Weight Usually about 3 kg.; a "young" zoo bird: 3,780 gm. (W. Fischer 1963).

RALPH S. PALMER

DISTRIBUTION **In our area** William Bartram (1791) either possessed or closely examined a specimen, taken somewhere along St. John's R. above L. George, Fla., in 1774 or 1775; see especially Harper (1936). Bartram's description, evidently prepared for publication long after the event, is detailed and correct—except for the tail. Much ink has been spilled because of this slip, some authors and the 1983 AOU *Check-list* having attempted to discredit this valid record.

"Rio Verde, Ariz.?" (Coues 1866); reaffirmation of belief that the bird entered Ariz. occasionally (Coues 1881); accidentally to s. Ariz. (Rio Verde) (Friedmann 1950). This all came about because Coues put too much faith in the word of a local naturalist. **Erroneously listed** Tex. by W. Fischer (1963).

Occurs Central Mexico s. to lat. of n. Argentina. Trinidad—1 shot April 18, 1942, is most recent record. RALPH S. PALMER

OTHER TOPICS Young birds in all-dark feathering conceivably might be mistaken for one of the smaller dark vultures. The California Condor is larger than the King Vulture, comparatively narrow winged, and varies from all dark (young) to same with white wing lining (older stages).

The single **egg** apparently was 1st described by J. P. Norris (1926); **size** length av. about 90 mm., breadth 64 mm.; **shape** oval or slightly toward pyriform; shell considerably pitted, **color** white; these data confirmed from zoo layings. The egg is laid on the ground or very near it, in the forest, and captives deposit theirs on the floor rather than on an elevated "nest" platform. Incubation probably by the sexes in turn; period 56 and 58 days in captivity in the boreal winter (Heck 1963) and probably somewhat shorter under other circumstances. One hatched in captivity on May 11 was fully feathered July 28 and tended by both parents (W. Fischer 1963).

The King Vulture is a bird of tropical lowland forests, over which it flies with heavy wingbeats and short glides. Destruction of Mexican forests has eliminated much of its preferred habitat, and it evidently does not now occur anywhere near our area.

Almost surely it hunts by scent (see Stager 1964) when low over the treetops, but when soaring at a great altitude presumably it is watching smaller vultures below to see

Mayan glyphs of King Vulture head; stages in reduction (Tozzer and Allen 1910)

68

what they will find. (Locating food by olfaction has been questioned recently, from experiments with caged birds [D. C. Houston 1984].) It is powerful and conspicuous, dropping from the sky at tremendous speed and with noisy wings, and is dominant over the smaller vultures at carrion. It was the commonest—at times and places the only—vulture in many wooded parts of Cent. Am. Food of the species: carrion, including dead snakes and fishes. Newborn calves seized by the umbilical cord and killed, so their mothers place them between their feet for protection (Orbigny 1835). Attacks newborn mammals and small live reptiles (Swann 1930).

This strikingly handsome bird has long been of interest to man; it commonly appeared in Mayan codices and was often noted by early explorers. RALPH S. PALMER

Family ACCIPITRIDAE (first part)

Osprey
Kites
Bald Eagle and allies
Harrier
Accipiters
Buteo allies

OSPREY

Pandion haliaetus

Fish Hawk and Fishing Eagle are misnomers, since the Osprey is neither a true hawk nor an eagle.

Rather large (size intermediate between large buteos and eagles) narrow-winged fishing raptor; distinctively and contrastingly patterned—almost or all of venter white, also most of head–neck and much of wing-lining. Very stout tarsi, covered with projecting scales; outer toes reversible (as in owls), their undersides with pointed prickly scales or spicules for retaining grasp on slippery fish; talons long, strongly and evenly curved, equal in length. Feathers dense and firm, not elongated (even on thighs), and quite uniformly distributed (especially on head–neck), mapped and described by Compton (1938). Third visible primary from outer (8th counting from inner) is longest, the 2 adjoining ones nearly equal in length; 4 or 5 long outer primaries have narrowed outer webs, the 3 outer with inner webs abruptly and deeply narrowed and the 4th slightly.

Sexes and all flying ages similar in pattern. Sexes overlap in size (♀♀ av. perhaps 10% larger); combined meas.: length about 17–22 in. (43–56 cm.), wingspread to about 56 in. (167 cm.), usual wt. of ♂ 2⅜–3¾ lb. (1.1–1.7 kg.), and of ♀ 2⅝–4⅜ lb. (1.2–2 kg.); av. difference between sexes about 7 oz. (200 gm.).

Nearly worldwide range; 4 subspecies recognized here, 2 in our area.

DESCRIPTION   *P. h. carolinensis.* Basic Plumage (entire feathering) acquired from about MID-OCT. through WINTER plus (after an interruption) from about JULY to SEPT., and retained a YEAR. Basic I is earliest definitive. For molting, see below after Juv.

▶ ♂ **Beak** black, cere bluish gray; **iris** sometimes stated as yellow, but color photos of

73

mates at nests show orange-yellow or orange in some ♂♂ (also see Ogden, in J. Ogden 1977). **Head–neck** white with more or less small black forehead patch and a larger one toward top rear of crown; a wide blackish brown stripe or band extends through eye and along side of neck, merging into dark of back; feathers on rear of crown and upper nape attenuate and erectile; more or less rusty coloring, especially hindneck. **Upperparts** including upper wing coverts blackish brown (purplish sheen in new feathering), the very margins of the feathers variably paler (and may wear off). **Underparts** white, indication of a breast band (some dark feather shafts and spotting in some), others plain; rusty tinge on some feathers. **Tail** feathers, as seen from below, with 5–7 blackish bars on white, the distal dark one often less well defined and much the widest; the very tips are narrowly white. Legs and **feet** pale bluish, talons black. **Wing** In the underwing all except several outer primaries have more or less evident dark barring on white inner webs (fewer and wider bars than in Juv.); smaller under coverts and axillars white, occasionally streaked dark and/or tinged rusty; the median coverts mixed dark and white; longer ones barred dark brown, but some may be white; the under primary coverts tend to be spotted dark (but much white shows), the carpal patch ("thumb mark") generally solid blackish and conspicuous.

▶ ♀ Basic Plumage as ♂ except **iris** variably yellow; more or less incomplete darkish band on **upper breast** (except rarely?) of dark shaft-streaks that tend to broaden into spots.

NOTE There is need to examine the tail pattern of birds of known sex and age. Some breeders have all tail bars of equal width (as Juv.) but few in number (as Basic); in others with few bars, the distal one much the widest (as Basic) but sharply delineated (as more typical of Juv.).

AT HATCHING Already patterned (foreshadowing the later pattern of head and back), the down very short. Head palish brown with paler streak down nape; a darker patch through eye; dorsum muted darker brown, mottled buffy, with conspicuous pale brownish stripe down middle; underparts a slightly grayed buff, grading toward tawny on breast and thighs. At about 10–11 days another down appears, soon forming a thick woolly covering; it is browner than the earlier covering, with back-stripe still conspicuous.

NOTE Nestling Ospreys differ markedly in appearance from all other Falconiform young, and their ontogeny deserves further study. Possibly there is a short down-A, those just described being downs-B and -C; see Witherby (1924, 1939) as opposed to Bent (1937). L. Jones (1907) figured the "natal down" attached to the tip of a pennaceous feather.

▶ ♂ Juv. Plumage (entire feathering) fully developed at age about 60 days. Pattern essentially as older stages. Differences: **iris** evidently orange-yellow in both sexes; top and upper sides of **head** mixed dark and light, becoming all white above cheek stripe; feathers of nape comparatively short and with rounded tips (not attenuated and pointed); hindneck often buffy or rusty; dark feathers of **dorsum** plus upper wing-coverts have sharply defined conspicuous buffy-tan to buffy to whitish ends (which tend to wear off); **underparts** plain white (invariably?), some with buffy or rusty tinge. **Tail,** as seen from below, white crossed with up to at least 9 dark bars (more, and narrower, than in later life), the distal one not wider, and the white tips fairly wide. On the **wing**

74

undersurface the secondaries and most primaries are barred dark on light (more bars than in Basic), extending across both vanes; axillars dark ended; smaller coverts white or some tinged rusty; proximal large coverts tend to be white, the others barred or with much dark; the primary under coverts are barred, and the feathers of the dark carpal patch ("thumb mark") are light-ended, that is, the patch much less conspicuous than in older birds.

▶ ♀ Juv. Plumage as ♂ except feathers of **upper breast** have (invariably?) dark shaft streaks that widen distally; **crown, nape, venter,** and **wing lining** quite often strongly tinged cinnamon-buff or rusty.

Molting   Timing is presumably about the same in both sexes. The schedule here applies to birds of n. temperate climates (spring–summer nesters) and needs adjustment for nonmigratory and/or s. birds. Juvenal birds migrate to winter range in calendar year of hatching and remain s. throughout the following year, during which they molt into Basic I and then start molting into Basic II before their first n. migration. The following is adapted from Prévost (1983)—based on a few retrapped marked birds and on museum specimens. (In considerable measure, it is an extension of earlier work by Carl Edelstam.) Treatment is in reverse order, older birds (migrants) being discussed 1st.

1   Basic to Basic molting tends to be in 2 active periods and slowed or interrupted in between—that is, part occurs principally (on winter range) before spring migration and the other (on summer range) before fall migration. Combined, there is renewal of all (or essentially all) feathering in approximately a 12-month period—about mid-Oct. to following mid-Oct. This is accomplished without impairing flight significantly through stepwise molting of the wing, starting at several foci or "centers" (see below) and later continuing where it was interrupted. Molting of primaries counting from inner is #1–#10; after some feathers are renewed, molting ceases, then it resumes later where it left off; also, a new wave starts at #1 before the preceding wave reaches #10. (The number of primaries renewed in a period of molting is less from Prebasic II onward than in prior Prebasic I.) Secondaries and tail begin molting after primaries have begun. Head–body may be undergoing renewal during the periods of flight-feather molting, or perhaps occurs in between on summer range (no details).

2   Prebasic I (Juv. to Basic I) molting. Assuming 1st flight about Aug. 1, the innermost primary is dropped approximately at the very end of the year (after s. migration). The primaries molt (outwardly) at a rate of about 1 feather/month. Tail molting soon starts, central pair of feathers 1st, then outward (some variation in latter) with completion at age about 14 months (on winter range). Secondaries start molting at age 6–9 months (later than primaries), at #1 (outermost) and #5, progressing inwardly (toward body) and at innermost (progressing outwardly). Combining the 2 wings, up to 16 (of 36) secondaries may be growing at a time. The head–body also molt into Basic I in winter (details not known). Before the end of the calendar year after hatching, the young Osprey is in complete Basic I—earliest "adult"-appearing Plumage. There is some overlap in its completion and in initiation of molting into Basic II (especially inner primary) toward end of the year. Then the 1st period of acquiring Basic II Plumage occurs before first n. migration.

Rate of growth of individual flight feathers, as determined from retrapped marked

Ospreys, was: primaries 5.5 mm./day, secondaries 3.1, and tail feathers 3.2 (Prévost). An Osprey may retain a few feathers long after their "normal" time of molting.

Color phases   None.

Measurements   Here from Friedmann (1950), but see beyond for larger series with WING meas. flattened.

Fifteen ♂ BEAK from cere 31–34 mm., av. 32, WING across chord 462–498, av. 477.4; and 11 ♀ BEAK from cere 32–36 mm., av. 35, and WING across chord 488–512, av. 503.7.

No series of meas. of Juv. birds are available, hence no information as to whether wing, and especially tail, av. longer than in Basic (as is well known in some other raptors).

Weight   Few available N. Am. data; these are for summer "adults." From ne. U.S. (live birds): 7 ♂ 1,218–1,534 gm., av. 1,437; and 10 ♀ 1,628–1,966 gm., av. 1,798 (MacNamara, in J. Ogden 1977).

Hybrids   None.

Geographical variation   Appreciable in the Osprey—a bird of apparently ancient lineage. Northerly birds are larger with more dark on head and breast band more often present, more extensive, and larger (see above). See the next section for variation in amount of white, and so on. Because of its morphological and behavioral characteristics, the Osprey has been rearranged in various classifications and now (Brown and Amadon 1968 1) is positioned near kites.   CHARLES J. HENNY

SUBSPECIES   Four, as in Prévost (in Bird 1983). Comparative meas. are from the same source, the BEAK meas. from cere and WING flattened—from museum skins— sample sizes and averages plus 1 standard deviation. Subspecies cannot always be discerned from skins because of overlap in size and presence or extent of breast markings. Ospreys in Juv. feathering apparently are nearly similar in pattern, sex for sex, worldwide. The sequence below places all New World birds 1st, for convenience, although placing nominate *haliaetus* of Eurasia 1st might be a more "natural" arrangement.

In our area   *carolinensis* (Gmelin)—described earlier; large in size; blackish crown-patch essentially similar in ♂ and ♀; breast markings reduced in area, often only dark shaft streaks and spots, there being a more or less incomplete band in the ♀ and the ♂ often plain; underwing as in Eurasian birds except larger coverts barred dark brown. Cool to warm temperate N. Am. Migratory, except resident in s. Fla. (where varies toward *ridgwayi*), perhaps on parts of the Gulf coast, and nw. Mexico (including some is.). Perhaps the birds that were breeding on the Pacific coast of Guatemala in 1863 were of this subspecies (Land 1970) or, possibly, *ridgwayi* (Griscom 1932).

Forty-nine ♂ BEAK 32.5 ± 1.2 mm., WING 485 ± 12, and TAIL 212 ± 8; and 47 ♀ BEAK 34.6 ± 1.3 mm., WING 507 ± 10, and TAIL 228 ± 6. The tail of the ♀ is longer than in the ♂, with some overlap, yet MacNamara (in J. Ogden 1977) found none in 7 ♀ and 10 ♂ in Mass., N.Y., and N.J.

ridgwayi Maynard—small in size; markings on crown, especially, and side of head– neck greatly reduced (some Bahamian Ospreys have hardly any black on side of head; beak relatively large and swollen; seldom any markings on white of breast; even so, morphologically closer to those adjoining it in this list than to the last one listed. Resident in a small total land area: Bahamas, cays off n. and s. Cuba, Virgin Is. (at least St. Croix, George Dog, Anegada), the e. coast (only?) of the Yucatan Pen. and adjacent is., and coast and is. of Belize. See Sprunt IV (in J. Ogden 1977) for 1971 survey results from e. coast of Mexico and Belize. (For possiblity of having bred on the Guatemalan Pacific coast, see *carolinensis*, above.)

Bahamas: 4 ♂ BEAK 33.5 ± 3 mm., WING 461 ± 7, and TAIL (no data); and 3 ♀ BEAK 36.1 ± 1.7 mm., WING 492 ± 26, and TAIL 225 ± 12.

Elsewhere *haliaetus* (Linnaeus)—size nearly identical with the 1st listed above; crown-markings also similar in the sexes; over ½ of the ♀ ♀ have a complete brownish breast-band, and others (both sexes) have more or less of it (♂ rarely plain); in the underwing the larger coverts are ½ rufous-brown and ½ white (not barred). Except for small resident e. Atlantic populations (Canaries, C. Verdes), breeds across cool to warm temperate Eurasia to Kamchatka, Japan, and Taiwan and is migratory. Small samples indicate some unique discrete breeding units. Synonyms include *friedmanni* Wolfe and *mutuus* Kipp (both of e. Asia).

Palearctic specimens: 72 ♂ BEAK 31.4 ± 1.2 mm., WING 474 ± 11, and TAIL 210 ± 9; and 77 ♂ BEAK 33.6 ± 1.5 mm., WING 496 ± 15, and TAIL 210 ± 9.

Cape Verdes: 7 ♂ BEAK 33.1 ± 1.3 mm., WING 479 ± 14, and TAIL 218 ± 7; and 4 ♀ BEAK 33.3 ± 1.4 mm., WING 490 ± 10, and TAIL 241.

Red Sea: 5 ♂ BEAK 30.8 ± 1.3 mm., WING 464 ± 16, and TAIL 199 ± 10; and 3 ♀ BEAK 33.8 ± 2.6 mm., WING 477 ± 20, and TAIL 219.

cristatus (Vieillot)—the most distinct subspecies; smallest in size; reduced dark on head–neck (reduction on crown not quite as extensive as in *ridgwayi*); ♂ ♂ have significantly darker crown than ♀ ♀; brown breast band, av. larger in ♀ ♀; underwing coverts nearly all ashy brown; tail and wings short. Resident so far as positively known. Although geographical variation in size is demonstrable (smaller n.), included here are the birds of Tasmania, Australia, and w. of Sumatra, n. to include the Philippines— thus including *melvillensis* Mathews and *microhaliaetus* Brasil.

Forty-two ♂ BEAK 30.4 ± 1.2 mm., WING 418 ± 17, and TAIL 181 ± 8; and 50 ♀ BEAK 32.8 ± 1.4 mm., WING 442 ± 15, and TAIL 195 ± 10.   CHARLES J. HENNY

FIELD IDENTIFICATION   **In our area**   Larger than any of our hawks; smaller than our eagles; decidedly long-winged with typical crook at "wrist." None of our other raptors, except the little Black-shouldered Kite and the dry-country White-tailed Hawk, has underparts almost completely white—to which add most of head–neck and much of wing lining. Even so, at long distance when pattern is not evident, could be mistaken for a large gull—especially since it flies with wings angled back somewhat. Powerful, steady wingbeats over a shallow arc, interspersed with soaring or gliding. Like a kingfisher, it hovers, then plunges right into the water with heavy impact to catch fish, whereas fish eagles (e.g., the Bald) normally snatch fish in passing on the surface or descend gently, like a parachute.

Under favorable conditions the sexes of birds in definitive feathering may be distinguished—usually the ♀ shows more darkish band on upper breast than the ♂, who may lack it entirely.

Birds beyond the Juv. stage have a sharply contrasting pattern; for example, the white in the underwing extends out to a sharply defined solid black carpal patch. The Juv. underwing has a more diffuse pattern, often with rusty coloring; the under coverts are mixed black and white, and the less clearly defined carpal patch appears grayed because of light feather ends. In the Juv., upper sides and top of head are streaked dark and light (appear darkish), not clearly white with some black. The Juv. dorsum has fairly conspicuous light feather ends that wear off. The Juv. tail has 6–10 dark bars on whitish background, the distal one same width as the others; older birds generally have fewer and wider dark bars, and often the distal one is much wider.

CHARLES J. HENNY

VOICE   Usually a series of plaintive, shrill, staccato whistles, gradually rising in pitch, often by only a quarter tone at a time. Occasionally slurred final notes, either upward or down. Ordinarily, about 7–20 calls (av. 14); duration 2–6 sec. May call when perched or flying. Calls often delivered after catching a fish or after unsuccessful dive. Can be imitated by human whistle and the bird answers and flies toward the observer (A. A. Saunders). The calls of the ♀ are lower pitched.

More or less within the above framework, possibly a dozen variants in vocalizing may be identified and presumed functions or motivation assigned. Perhaps of main interest are the following:

In HIGH-CIRCLING display and evidently from the ♂—screaming *cree-cree-cree* more or less continuously for fully 15 min., and "wholly different" from ordinary call (Brewster).

SKY-DANCE: much as above but apparently more variable; shrill and prolonged; by both sexes, but mostly ♂.

Softer calls, usually single notes, uttered by ♀ when ♂ approaches with nesting material or food, before copulation, and in other situations. The ♂ may reply variously—usually single chirps, but may be drawn out.

The ♀ on nest, on approach of observer—a low explosive grunt as if exhaling, seemingly modified from within the terminal series of extended alarm calls.

Nestlings peep at first. Their food call gradually evolves from a series of *tuck* or *yeep* sounds to become quite adultlike but shriller by about age 5 weeks.

Further information in Abbott (1911), Brewster (1925), Bent (1937), and especially Ames (1964).   CHARLES J. HENNY

HABITAT   **In our area** and nearby. Cool temperate to subtropical areas. Dependent on water—fresh, brackish, salt—where it can obtain fish. Absent from some apparently suitable inland areas, perhaps due to low dispersal potential (discussed below). Although generally a tree nester, will use sites of almost any height, natural or man-made, ashore or in water; where relatively free from persecution, as on is., even on flat ground. Although generally it nests close to water, it may travel 10–20 km. to forage. F. Beebe (1974) summarized the species's fundamental requirements as "**1** fish that move slowly near the surface of water, **2** an ice-free season sufficiently long to permit reproduction, and **3** elevated or inaccessible sites for nest-building, or alternatively, isolation from most possible sources of possible molestation." In migrations, tends to follow waterways and also readily crosses large bodies of water but may be seen almost anywhere—even over deserts.   CHARLES J. HENNY

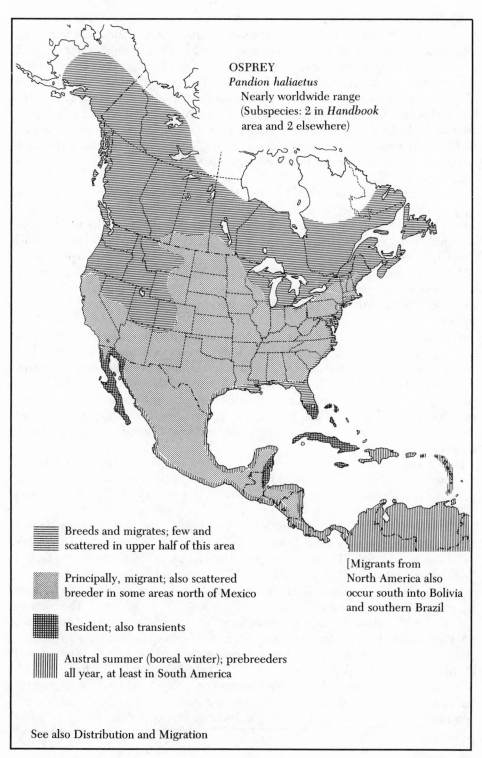

OSPREY
Pandion haliaetus
Nearly worldwide range
(Subspecies: 2 in *Handbook*
area and 2 elsewhere)

Breeds and migrates; few and
scattered in upper half of this area

Principally, migrant; also scattered
breeder in some areas north of Mexico

Resident; also transients

Austral summer (boreal winter); prebreeders
all year, at least in South America

[Migrants from
North America also
occur south into Bolivia
and southern Brazil

See also Distribution and Migration

DISTRIBUTION   (See map.) The pattern of the species is as follows: **Migrants** breed 1 in temperate N. Am., and 2 at about the same latitudes across Eurasia, leapfrogging over more s. resident birds to winter range in 1 Cent. and S. Am. and various is., and 2 from Europe to Africa (has **bred** in S. Africa) and from much of Asia to the Indian subcontinent, se. Asian mainland, and Sumatra, Borneo, and other is. The **resident** birds of N. Am. that are, for the most part, bypassed, are 1 in nw. Mexico, s. Fla., the Caribbean, and the e. side of the Yucatan Pen. and adjoining Belize, and 2 in Eurasia (aside from the few residents in the Canaries and C. Verdes) in the w. Mediterranean, Red Sea, Persian Gulf, and a portion of mainland China opposite Taiwan. 3 There are **resident southerly** birds in Australia, and northward e. of Borneo across the equator to include the Philippines.

In our area   Concentrated as **breeder** along and to some distance inland from marine coasts and in the Great Lakes region; thinly scattered or absent from large areas elsewhere (e.g., Mississippi drainage). Nesting numbers in the coterminous U.S. numbered (ca. 1981) about 8,000 pairs (Henny, in Bird 1983). Five regional populations exist (in order of abundance): Atlantic coast, Fla. and Gulf coast, Pacific NW, w. Interior, and Great Lakes. The Chesapeake Bay (Md.–Va.) area now has the largest known concentration of nesting Ospreys in the world (about 1,450 pairs in 1973). Beginning with Alexander Wilson's *American Ornithology* (the relevant vol. appeared in 1812), the Ospreys of Gardiner's I., N.Y., have figured prominently in the literature. Wilson noted that at "least three hundred nests of fish hawks that have young" were present according to Mr. Gardiner, proprietor of the island. It is 11 km. from end to end and, in the middle, a third as broad, with an area of about 1,600 ha. Chapman (1908) concluded that a similar number nested there about a hundred years later. There were some 300 nests in the 1930s and 1940s, before the biocide era. Biocides severely impacted the populations in the n. portion of the Atlantic coast (Boston to C. May) including Gardiner's I. and the Great Lakes, but populations now are recovering.

During recent decades in the West, especially in the interior, reservoirs have been responsible for a range expansion and, perhaps, a population increase. Ospreys of s. Calif. and the Channel Is. were extirpated early in this century and have not returned (Kiff, in Power 1980).

A discussion of past numbers and a U.S. summation, by regions, of counts that include those made during the biocide-related crash are by Henny (in Chancellor 1977, also in Bird 1983). The nesting population in adjacent Baja Calif. and the Gulf of Calif. was estimated at 810 ± 55 pairs in 1977 (Henny and Anderson 1979).

In Alaska in 1984 there were 88 known nests, and it was estimated that there were no more than 200 nesting pairs in the state, probably fewer (P. F. Schempf). There are no overall Canadian data, but population segments were investigated in n. Que. (Bider and Bird, in Bird 1983), Labrador and ne. Que. (S. Wetmore and Gillespie 1976a), the Maritimes (Prévost et al. 1978; Stocek and Pearce, in Bird 1983), B.C. (Kemper and Eastman 1970), and Sask. (Houston et al. 1977). Breeders are thinly scattered in such n. areas as most of Alaska, part of the Ungava Pen., Nfld., and Que., with perhaps higher densities in the Maritimes. Based on land area, however, considerable numbers probably nest in Canada. For example, Bider and Bird estimated that about 2,000 pairs may nest in some 500,000 sq. km. in n. Que. Stragglers occasionally are seen in summer beyond the known limits of nesting.

Boreal winter/austral summer A few migrant birds remain as far n. as cent. Calif., the U.S. Gulf coast, cent. Fla. (overlapping **resident** birds in s. Fla.), occasionally farther n. in mild winters, and occasionally in Bermuda. Main occurrence is from within Mexico (principally along coasts) through Cent. Am. and in S. Am. (including Trinidad and Tobago) into n. Argentina and, on the Pacific side, to cent. Chile. Furthermore, many banded Ospreys "wintering" in S. Am. have been found inland along major river systems (Henny and Van Velzen 1972). There is a high concentration around L. Maracaibo in nw. Venezuela. A few n. migrants "winter" on is. in the Caribbean. Thus there is some overlap with the warm-climate residents.

NOTES A strong fidelity to ancestral breeding areas (short dispersal distance) has slowed range expansion into newly created habitat, such as reservoirs in the Mississippi drainage.

Restocking Introductions (via so-called hacking) to distant reservoirs or elsewhere (from breeding populations) were being made in 5 states in 1984.

See Migration, below, for discussion of prebreeders remaining on "winter" (austral) range.

Ospreys reportedly were breeding in 1863 along the Pacific coast of Guatemala from Soconusco to San José (Land 1970).

In all probability, an abundance of Bald Eagles in the nw. U.S. and beyond into Alaska has a limiting effect on breeding distribution of the Osprey. Toward the tropics, Magnificent Frigatebirds probably function similarly; a confrontation in Fla., and death of the Osprey, was described by Lancaster (1886).

Oceanic/Atlantic Some records: As seen in daylight, the Osprey travels over the sea by flapping flight, which is energy consuming; it is capable of foraging (catching food and eating it) in the ocean, but it may become exhausted and be forced down in rough weather. GREENLAND 1 in fall in 1872 and in 1918 (from N. Am.); ICELAND rather rare vagrant (from Europe); FAEROE Is. 2 records. AT SEA data at hand certainly do not include all instances of Ospreys taking refuge aboard oceangoing ships or being found adrift—6 recorded (Aug.–Sept.) within 200 mi. of U.S. Atlantic seaboard (Scholander 1955), 19 in Sept.–Oct. and 5 in May–June recorded at sea (av. 118 km. from land) along U.S. Atlantic seaboard (Kerlinger et al. 1983). BERMUDA few but not regular in most seasons and even fewer in summer; BAHAMAS/CARIBBEAN scattered records of mainland birds (plus resident *ridgwayi*, e.g., J. Miller 1978); AZORES a few records; MADEIRA recorded; CANARIES resident (only a few pairs); C. VERDES last estimate was about 50 pairs (and, at least until recently, eggs and young taken for human consumption); off s. Africa recorded foraging at sea (Hockey 1981, Elst 1982).

Oceanic Bering/Pacific Some records: COMMANDER Is. regular spring–summer visitor from Kamchatka; outer ALEUTIANS (Amchitka) Oct. 1957; PRIBILOF Is. July 1960; QUEEN CHARLOTTE Is. occurrences but no breeding record; HAWAIIAN Is. (Kauai, Niihau, Hawaii) seen in various years beginning in 1939; PHILIPPINE SEA migrants occur on various is., to at least the e. edge; GUADALOUPE I. (off Baja Calif.) recorded; TRES MARIAS Is. (cent. w. Mexican coast) recorded on 4 is., 2 nests (in 1860s?), but P. Grant and Cowan (1964) found no breeding, 1957–1963; REVILLA

GIGEDO group (off cent. w. Mexico) winter; COCOS Is. (sw. from Costa Rica) boreal winter; CLIPPERTON ATOLL (mid. e. Pacific) 1 in Oct. 1957, and, starting from about 65 km. ne. of there, 1 hunted from aboard a ship for nearly a week in Oct. 1976; GALAPAGOS Is. boreal winter, irregular.

Comments on Palearctic Ospreys In Great Britain this species was exterminated as a breeder by persecution (including egg collecting); last nested in Scotland in 1908, with a single bird there until 1913 (P. Brown 1979). In 1929 four young birds were transplanted from Gardiner's I., N.Y., and released at the loch in Invernesshire where the species last nested (C. W. R. Knight 1930, 1932). This attempt failed. Natural recolonization began in the 1950s, and successful nesting dates from 1959; details in P. Brown (1979). In 1981 the expanding population had reached 25 pairs (22 laid eggs) that reared 42 young (Dennis, in D. Bird 1983). In Europe there now are 3 separate breeding populations: 1 Scotland, 2 nw. Europe (about 3,000 pairs excluding USSR), and 3 w. Mediterranean (about 50 pairs) (Cieslak 1980). The major nw. breeding area is in Sweden, about 2,000 pairs in 1971 (Österlöf 1973); followed by Finland, about 900–1,000 pairs in 1971 (Saurola 1976); with remainder in Norway, Poland, and E. Germany. European Ospreys migrate to Africa, almost entirely s. of the Sahara; reports of their having bred in boreal winter s. of Somalia–C. Verdes were rejected by L. Brown et al. (1982); there are at least 2 authentic breeding records for S. Africa (Dean and Tarboton 1983).

Reports of the Osprey as fossil from the Pleistocene and bones from prehistoric sites were compiled by Brodkorb (1964), summarized here, with additions. **In our area** it is known as **fossil** from Fla. (4 localities) and from Crooked I. in the Bahamas; and from **prehistoric sites** in N.S. and Calif. To this list add S.D. Recorded in error from Fossil L., Oreg. **Elsewhere** recorded as fossil from England, Denmark, Switzerland (2), Germany, and Italy; and from 2 archaeological sites in Denmark. To this list add Ukraine (2 archaeological).

Another Osprey species has been described from the Miocene of Calif. (Warter, in Olson 1976).   CHARLES J. HENNY

MIGRATION In N. Am. *P. h. carolinensis* is migratory except the s. breeding segment (s. Fla.–Mexico). In Belize, *ridgwayi* is resident in coastal and insular areas (E. R. Blake 1977). Further discussion is limited to the n. migratory segment of *carolinensis*. Ospreys do not migrate in flocks when southbound or northbound (F. Beebe 1974).

Fall R. Kennedy (1973) indicated that most birds from Md. and Va. in their first autumn of life remained within 160 km. of nesting sites until the last week of Aug., then started s.; by Sept. 15, most had left the U.S. Migration of Ospreys near Fisher's I., N.Y., began about Sept. 1, but some birds were seen as late as Nov. 22 (A. and H. Ferguson 1922). Most young banded in N.Y. and N.J. had left the state in which they were banded by Oct. 31 (Henny and Wight 1969). The greatest numbers of Ospreys passed through C. May, N.J., during the 2 middle weeks of Sept. (R. Allen and Peterson 1936). Ospreys from more ne. states begin migrating about 1–2 weeks later; young Ospreys from N.S. begin migration in mid- to late Sept. (Prévost et al. 1978).

New Eng. and mid-Atlantic state Ospreys migrate on a broad front—from Appalachian Mt. ridges to the coastline (Henny and Van Velzen 1972). In Europe, similar broad migrations occur, the adults preceding young of the year by perhaps 2 weeks (Österlöf 1977). N. Am. Ospreys arrive in Cuba in Sept. and usually remain only a short time (Barbour 1943). Atlantic coast Ospreys migrate through the W. Indies en route to and from S. Am. with no banded birds reported during the migration period in Mexico or Cent. Am. R. Kennedy (1973) indicated that most young birds from Md. and Va. reached S. Am. by Oct. 15, but a few Ospreys winter in the W. Indies.

In such mild winters as 1982–1983, a few Ospreys remain in coastal areas as far n. as Oreg. and Wash., and a few remain in the interior. Easterly, a few winter in Fla. (in range of resident birds) and around the gulf coast.

Migration routes from the interior of N. Am. are less understood, but the timing is similar to the Atlantic coast. Band recoveries suggest a general movement s. to the Gulf of Mexico, then toward S. Am. via Mexico or the W. Indies (Henny and Van Velzen 1972).

In the West, Ospreys leave n. Idaho throughout Sept. and early Oct. (Melquist et al. 1978, Melquist and Johnson 1984). Apparently they move s. rapidly; banded Ospreys were reported from s. Tex. as early as Oct. 4 and from cent. Mexico as early as Oct. 14. A few Calif.-banded birds have been recovered far down the w. coast of Mexico.

Austral summer Northwest S. Am. and Panama are the primary "wintering" localities for mid-Atlantic coast Ospreys. R. Kennedy (1973) noted that most birds from Md. and Va. "wintered" in Colombia, while Henny and Van Velzen (1972) reported that birds hatched in N.Y. and N.J. "wintered" primarily in Colombia, Brazil, and Venezuela. Some, however, "wintered" as far s. as Argentina, s. Brazil, and Peru. In boreal winter, few bands are recovered from interior N. Am., but birds banded in Mich. and Wis. were found in nw. S. Am. (Colombia and Ecuador) and Panama. Also, 3 banded in Sask. were found in Colombia and Ecuador (F. Scott and Houston 1983). The w. population apparently does not migrate to S. Am. Recoveries of birds banded in n. Idaho and e. Wash. suggest that they spend the austral summer in Cent. Am. (Melquist et al. 1978, Melquist and Johnston 1984).

Spring Henny and Wight (1969) showed that no banded birds in 3d calendar year of life and older were found in S. Am. after Feb., implying that breeding-age birds leave S. Am. by the end of the month, some perhaps earlier. Migration in Mexico is apparently on a broad front. Near the city of Veracruz, it extended Apr. 6–May 6, 1968, with peak Apr. 6 and rapid decrease after Apr. 20 (Thiollay 1979). Yet Ospreys arrive on N. Am. breeding grounds from mid-Mar. (midlatitudes) to early May (w. Canada and Alaska). Over a 30-year period, Ospreys 1st arrived at C. May, N.J., Mar. 9–30, av. Mar. 21 (W. Stone 1937). Migration at the se. corner of L. Ontario occurs late Mar.–early May and peaks the last week of Apr. (Haugh and Cade 1966). Hughes (in Ladd and Schempf 1982) reported nests in Alaska occupied by May 1 (earliest arrival Apr. 24).

Location of yearlings during the breeding season Swedish Ospreys did not leave the "wintering" area in Africa in the year following their year of hatching (Österlöf 1951); likewise, the migratory birds from N. Am. did not leave S. Am. or the W. Indies (Henny and Wight 1969). As a result of not returning n. during spring of the year following their year of hatching, the young Ospreys evidently spend at least 16 continuous months s. of the U.S. border. Numerous authors, writing about Cent. and S. Am. Ospreys, have noted that some (presumably yearlings) remain through the period of the boreal summer but do not nest.

Location of 2-year-olds during the breeding season   The majority of those birds in their 3d calendar year of life are randomly distributed s. of their natal area but all return n. (Henny and Wight 1969). Henny and Van Velzen (1972) attempted to further refine the distribution of this age class. They estimated that 25–54% return to their natal areas (state or adjacent state in the U.S.) and represent about 5–10% of Ospreys present on the breeding grounds. It still is not definitely known whether this age class has some relationship with nests. Most nesting studies show a small percentage of birds associated with nests but not laying eggs; their age remains a question, and investigators are urged to record these birds as nonegg-laying pairs in nesting studies.

Location of 3-year-olds and older during the breeding season   It appears that nearly all (90%+) of birds in their 4th calendar year of life and older return to the breeding areas (Henny and Van Velzen).

Dispersal   In N. Am., Ospreys have a low potential to pioneer into suitable habitat beyond 125 km. of their birthplace (summarized from Henny, in Chancellor 1977; Spitzer et al., in D. Bird 1983). Henny's review of 32 band-recoveries showed that most 3d year and older Ospreys were located within 30 km. of their birthplace during the nesting season. Another 25% were at 30–125 km., and only 6% were more distant. Spitzer further showed that ♂♂ (his sample size was 33) did not move beyond 37 km., but that 10.3% of 39 ♀♀ moved beyond 200 km. The information agrees with Greenwood's (1980) statement that ♀♀ usually disperse more than ♂♂. Ospreys disperse farther in Europe; only 43% nest within 50 km. and 59% nest within 100 km. of their places of birth; 19% move beyond 1,000 km. (Österlöf 1977). Spitzer et al. (1978) suggested that reduced density caused by the effects of DDT may reduce pressure for dispersal in the population they studied; many of the data analyzed by Henny, however, were recorded before population declines and show similar results.

Charles J. Henny

BANDING STATUS   Osprey banding in N. Am. began in the 19th century. Chapman (1908) interviewed Mr. Gardiner (owner of Gardiner's I., N.Y.), who told of his grandfather having placed a metal band on an Osprey (evidently in the 1800s) that occupied a certain nest for many subsequent seasons. Henny and Van Velzen (1972) analyzed the 649 band recoveries available through Dec. 16, 1971. Throughout N. Am., 15,984 were banded through Aug. 1981; there were 1,188 recoveries (7.4%) (Clapp et al. 1982). Recovery data has been extensively used in many publications. Main places of banding have been along the Atlantic coast from N.Y. to throughout the Chesapeake Bay area. Several hundred have been banded in Mexico.

Charles J. Henny

REPRODUCTION   N. Am. data unless otherwise stated. Age when **first breeds** reported as 3 years in N. Am. (Henny and Wight 1969), as had been reported earlier in Sweden (Österlöf 1951). There is an indication that not all birds in the area from N.Y. to Boston breed at 3 years, some waiting 1 or 2 extra years (Spitzer 1980). Interestingly, a ♂ mentioned by Spitzer bred as a 2-year-old. The whereabouts of prebreeders was discussed earlier.

Displays Related to pair-formation (or re-formation). Field observations in Europe suggest that the 1st-arriving bird may be of either sex— ♂ first in 9 of 15 seasons (R. Green 1976). Without presenting data, Bent (1937) stated that ♂ ♂ precede ♀ ♀. Older pairs arrive earlier and lay sooner than younger ones. Displays, evidently based principally on remating activity when 2 birds are present at the nest, may be characterized briefly as follows. In HIGH-CIRCLING, the 2 birds circle and soar, often high overhead, the presumed ♂ at times swinging close to or seemingly swooping at his partner. His high-pitched calling was described by Brewster (see "Voice"). In some situations, several couples soar more or less together and drift apart, as though there were some social connotation to this activity. A 2d display is the undulating "plunge and rise" (F. Beebe 1974) of the SKY-DANCE. This ♂ display (so far as known) may be brief or may cover considerable distance, but it tends to begin and end close to the nest. Often the bird carries a fish, occasionally a stick. At times this seems to be a solo activity (to advertise ownership of a site?); at other times it is directed toward a perched ♀. His calls are high pitched and frequent. A 3d activity, which is an exaggerated derivation of food getting, is HOVER-FLIGHT. F. Beebe noted it as a slow, almost hovering, display in what appears to be an excessively labored flight with body tilted tail down head up at a steep angle. The bird appears to be stalled and having difficulty recovering flight. This seems to be a ♂ display; typically he carries a food object (fish) and calls as though greatly excited. As with the preceding, there are variants. One example may be wing waving and calling from a nest, evidently to attract his previous mate or to acquire a new one. From such liveliness and calling, it is evident why Bent (1937) referred to displays as "an expression of joy" or "an exhibition of exuberant spirits."

On arrival or very soon after, the birds inspect their old nest and begin refurbishing it. One, presumably the ♀, stands on it and receives and arranges material gathered by her mate.

Pair bond Ordinarily continued seasonally as long as both members survive, but there are exceptions. Bent believed that Ospreys remained mated until one of the pair died and noted several cases where one was shot and the survivor secured a new mate. Detailed work with marked birds by Poole (in D. Bird 1983) showed that 2 ♂ and 2 ♀ changed mates between seasons. The ♂ brings food to the ♀ ("courtship feeding"); a poorly fed bird is less willing to copulate and is less faithful than a well-fed one (A. Poole 1985). Spitzer (1980) reported 132 of 136 banded adult Ospreys were at their same nest sites, typically for several successive years, or at one within 2 km. the following year. The 4 nesting adults that moved traveled 6, 8, 8, and 18 km. between breeding seasons. The fidelity to specific locations by previously nesting adults is high. (Further, the birds have particular feeding areas in winter and at times are seen there in twos.) As inferred earlier, gene flow in Osprey populations would be facilitated primarily by dispersal of prebreeders (especially ♀ ♀).

Species with long migrations and extended breeding seasons must begin the reproductive cycle quickly, so that the young have sufficient time to complete their development. This point is emphasized by the observations of Ospreys incubating at a frozen lake at high elevation in Calif. (Henny 1977a). Since mates return to the previous year's site at nearly the same time, mated Ospreys could eliminate some of the early phases of the reproductive cycle, which is one of the advantages of long-term monogamy (Levenson 1979). Minimizing the time spent in display might be particularly critical in areas with climatic extremes; the preincubation phase at Eagle Lake, Calif., was about 13 days shorter than in climatically moderate coastal Humboldt Co., Calif. (Levenson).

Polygamy Occurred in Mass. during the early 1970s (J. and G. Fernandez, in J. Ogden 1977), associated with an excess of ♀ ♀. They recorded 5 trios (1 ♂ : 2 ♀), each at an active nest. These occurred in 10 of the 18 nestings at Westport in 1971. Of the 10, 5 failed, of which 4 were double failures for the ♂ ♂ concerned. Spitzer (1980) believed the distorted sex ratio resulted from long-distance dispersing of ♀ ♀ from more productive areas (see Dispersal, above), in association with continued low production in Mass., which seems logical.

Nest site Described in general terms under Habitat, above; typically varies from region to region. The majority of Ospreys in N. Am. nest in marine areas, but many also nest inland along large rivers, lakes, and reservoirs. Bent (1937) and W. Stone (1937) indicated that many nests are located in the largest trees (live and dead; species dependent on region) and generally not far from water where fishing is good. Some, however, occasionally nest 3–5 km. from water (Henny 1977a; Flook and Forbes, in D. Bird 1983). Trees with broken or dead tops are used frequently. Male Ospreys spend most of their nonflight time at a perch site in one or two specific trees that protrude above the canopy. Many early records exist of Ospreys nesting on telegraph, telephone, or power poles; old chimneys, windmills, and other buildings; and nest sites provided especially for them. The early adjustment to manmade structures undoubtedly has played an important role in the Osprey's continued existence in many places. For example, large trees no longer are available in portions of the Chesapeake Bay area, but now only 32% of 1,450 pairs are tree nesters (Henny et al. 1974). The others nest on channel markers (22%), offshore duck blinds (29%), and miscellaneous structures (18%). Manmade structures have not been as important in the Va. portion of the bay as they have been in the more heavily populated Md. portion. The crossed poles at the top of the framework of an Indian tepee in n. Que. (DesGranges 1978) and an unexploded 1,000-lb. bomb on an island in Chesapeake Bay (Henny et al. 1974) are perhaps the most unusual sites. Trees were still used by more than 90% of Ospreys nesting in the Carolinas (Henny and Noltemeier 1975). Nesting on artificial structures is uncommon in Fla. but may be increasing in some areas (R. and E. Schreiber 1977). In heavily populated coastal N.J., Del., Md., and Va. (excluding Chesapeake Bay), only 26% of nests were in trees, with 28% on duck blinds, 11% on channel markers, and 34% on miscellaneous other structures (Henny et al. 1977). In the West (Idaho, Calif., and Oreg.), most Ospreys nest in trees (84%, 92%, and 95%, respectively) (Melquist and Johnson 1975, Henny et al. 1978).

The lack of trees in nw. Mexico has resulted in Ospreys nesting on cliffs (59%), on cacti (26%), on the ground on small is. in lagoons (7%), in mangroves (3%), and on miscellaneous structures (4%)—including pilings, channel markers, debris washed ashore, boats (sunk or aground), road signs, or power poles (Henny and Anderson

1979). Sometimes the rocky cliff sites consist of large pinnacles or stacks, but sandy cliffs are used in some areas. In flat terrain, Ospreys nest primarily on various species of tall cacti. Nesting above ground level is critical for Ospreys on the mainland where mammalian predator access is likely. Ground-nesting in Mexico (e.g., Scammon's and San Ignacio lagoons) and the U.S. (e.g., Great I., Conn.; Gardiner's I., N.Y.) is restricted to small is. Over-water nesting sites also afford protection from land preda-tors, and therefore height is less important (e.g., nests in shoreline trees were much higher than those in cypress growing in water at Orton Pond, N.C.—Henny and Noltemeier 1975). Nests on over-water channel markers and duck blinds used along much of the Atlantic coast likewise are not high.

Criteria that make reservoirs especially suitable for nesting were best evaluated at Cascade Reservoir, Idaho (L. and H. Van Daele 1982). The reservoir was created in 1948 and by 1978 supported about 50 nesting pairs. It was large (area 11,452 ha.) and shallow (mean depth at high water 7.6 m.) and contained an abundance of warm-water fish. When water levels in the reservoir were raised for irrigation, trees were killed near the shoreline. These snags and those on steep hillsides provided Ospreys with nest sites; some live conifers and man made structures also were used. All Ospreys had a relatively unobstructed view of the surroundings from their nest site; all had at least one nearby perch site, used by the ♂.

Nest-building   Ospreys visit nest sites soon after arriving in the breeding area and begin building nests or refurbishing old ones. They are prodigious builders, and the nest is composed primarily of large sticks—usually 0.5–1.5 m. long. The nest may be small for a few years, but a new layer is added annually; nests nearly 2 m. high have been noted in the U.S. (C. S. Allen 1892). In Mexico, at Kino Bay, Sonora, in 1977, nests were supported between 2 or 3 arms of cacti and were up to 4 m. high, with many 2–3 m. high (Henny). When building a new nest, Van Daele (in R. P. Howard and Gore 1980) reported an av. of 30 sticks and 10 items for nest lining brought in each day; at this rate the nest was ready for eggs in 3 weeks.

Sticks are added to nests throughout the breeding season; they are picked up from the ground or dead limbs are broken from trees by the Osprey in flight grasping them in its talons, as noted at Gardiner's I., N.Y., by Abbott (1911). In Va., most sticks were pulled from trees (Stinson 1976). Levenson (1979) and Jamieson et al. (1982) noted that the ♂ brought more sticks than the ♀ during the preincubation and incubation peri-ods. Generally, nest maintenance was minor during incubation. Soon after the eggs hatched, large amounts of nesting materials again were brought to the nest—primarily by the ♀ (Levenson 1979, Stinson 1978). Delivery increased until the young were about 3 weeks old, then decreased during the remainder of the nesting cycle (Van Daele, in R. P. Howard and Gore 1980). In Va., material (usually clumps of eelgrass picked up from the shore) was also brought to the nest throughout the summer, just as other raptors continue to deliver **greenery.** In other locations, the bowl was lined with moss, lichens, grass, bark, and even mud.

Nest   Ospreys build their nests at the apex of the chosen site—that is, when in trees, in the very tops. Nests are exposed to the open sky, and access from above is easy. Because of their position, however, they are more subject to destruction by wind than are most other raptor nests. In an extreme year in Idaho, 33% of 166 nests were

87

blown out by winter storms (D. Johnson and Melquist 1973). Nest losses due to wind ranged from about 7–10% during a study in Minn., including losses during nesting (Dunstan 1968). In a Mich. study, nestling losses were reduced from 28% to 7% by the provision of stable platforms (Postupalsky and Stackpole 1974).

The sometimes enormous nests are made mainly of large sticks, as previously noted; mixed in is sod and almost anything that the birds can pick up (Bent 1937). C. S. Allen (1892) and Abbott (1911) provided long lists of materials found in nests; many others have noted unusual objects. On an Indian Ocean is. the birds gathered what was available, including corpses of shearwaters and terns (Warham 1956). A moderate-sized nest from Gardiner's I., N.Y., weighed over 400 lb. (180 kg.) (Abbott). Several nests were in continuous use for at least 40 years (Bent).

The sides of massive Osprey nests sometimes are used by smaller birds to construct their own homes, such as Com. Grackle, House Sparrow, House Wren, and even Black-crowned Night Heron, as basement tenants (Chapman 1908, Abbott 1911). Small passerines are usually ignored, but C. W. R. Knight (1932) reported an Osprey killing a night heron. The E. Kingbird, Com. Tern, and Red-winged Blackbird—obviously not Osprey tenants—harass and pursue their larger neighbor. Erratic movements by an Osprey that was pursued in flight by small birds moved so erratically that it pierced its wing with a talon and broke its humerus (R. Hughes 1941). Reese (1977) discussed nesting associations on offshore duck blinds in Chesapeake Bay and reviewed the literature in detail: Green-backed Herons, Mallards, Black Ducks, Barn Owls, Barn Swallows, House Sparrows, and Com. Grackles share the blinds with Ospreys. Ducks nest either inside or on top of the blind; owls inside; swallows on the roof or floor joists; herons, grackles, and sparrows usually in brush covering the outside (grackles and sparrows sometimes in Osprey nests); and Ospreys on the highest part. Ospreys occasionally "stooped" on Green-backed Herons flushed from the blind, and heron young, scurrying across the top of the blind, were sometimes killed. Diurnally flushed Barn Owls were attacked severely. Reese believed that some negative influence on Osprey nesting success may have resulted from interspecific strife at nest sites.

Nests may be refurbished and reused, or there may be several nests close together with only 1 active—which may indicate that **alternative nests** were constructed within the territory over a period of years. Postupalsky (in J. Ogden 1977) provided definitions for active nests (in which eggs were laid) and alternative nests (1 of several structures built within a pair's breeding territory), the latter including "frustration nests" (defined below). Alternative nests may be on adjacent trees or stubs or, in absence of suitable nearby support, as much as a mile or more apart. The habit of building frustration nests is well known in the Osprey. After failing to rear young in the original nests, a pair may build a new one later in the season; as a rule they do not lay in it, undoubedly because the season is well advanced. "Frustration nest" connotes a particular category of alternative nests, and no implication relative to psychological state of the birds is intended. Postupalsky's review of nesting terminology is important reading for serious investigators of Ospreys.

The spacing of occupied nests cannot be generalized; occasionally there are **loose colonies,** but elsewhere pairs are **solitary.** Abbott (1911) reported occupied nests at

Gardiner's I. spaced at intervals varying from 10 to 300 m. Colonies occur on small is. and sometimes at reservoirs or lakes that offer special protection and have abundant food and nesting sites. Colonial-nesting Ospreys may hunt over communal feeding areas in nearby coastal bays and marshes (Abbott; Parnell and Walton, in J. Ogden 1977). Other large concentrations have been reported in Fla. Orton Pond, N.C., a narrow lake 11 km. long where 61 pairs nested in 1974 (Henny and Noltemeier 1975), perhaps now contains the highest nesting density in N. Am.

Nesting and hunting areas Undoubtedly vary in size. Males do all of the hunting except early in the preincubation phase and just before the young attain flight (Jamieson et al. 1982); during the latter period, ♀ ♀ accounted for only 7 of 115 fish brought to nestlings. The high nesting density at Orton Pond presumably is related to the location being protected (private land) and the proximity of the C. Fear estuary, where the Ospreys fish.

Territoriality Generally appears weak. There may be implications of it, however, in records of a ♂ Osprey pursuing a strange Osprey that ventured near the former's nest in Idaho (G. Schroeder and Melquist 1975). In 7 days of observations, 16 instances (including a ♂ from an adjacent successful nest) of intraspecific, apparently hostile, behavior were observed. In Scotland combat between ♀ ♀ was fatal (Cash 1914). Yet breeding Ospreys may fly through what appears to be the airspace of others to go fishing.

Copulation Ospreys arrived in N.S. Apr. 16–21 in a 5-year study (Prévost et al. 1978). Repair of old nests began within a few days of arrival and copulatory behavior was observed as early as Apr. 23 in 1975; each year, it continued throughout the laying period. Jamieson et al. (1982) reported copulation continuing during the incubation period and noted that, except once when a pair copulated at a regularly used perch, all copulations were on nests. There was a delay of about 2 weeks between spring arrival and onset of egg laying in N.S., but the span seems to vary among locations. Four instances of precopulatory behavior were similar: ♂ ♂ were on nest rims and facing away from ♀ ♀ on the nests. Each ♂ partly extended his wings and lowered his head for 5–7 sec. Then he flew, immediately turned, and hovered over the ♀. The ♂ the alighted on the back of the ♀ and remained there 7–10 sec. For excellent photos from Corsica, see Saïller (1977).

Laying interval In the wild reported as 1–3 days in Europe (Siewert 1941) and 2–3 days in N. Am. (A. Poole 1982b). In N. Am., hatching dates of chicks in a brood may be spread over as long as 10 days for a 4-egg clutch but av. 3.9 days (range of 1–8) for 3-egg clutches (A. Poole 1982b).

One **egg** each from 20 clutches (2 N.J., 14 Md., 4 Va.) **size** length 59.47 ± 2.46 mm., breadth 44.99 ± 1.30, radii of curvature of ends 17.61 ± 0.99 and 13.20 ± 1.04; **shape** elongation 1.32 ± 0.063, bicone −0.09, and asymmetry +0.13 (F. W. Preston). For comparison, 312 eggs av. 61.0 × 45.6 mm. (Bent 1937), or slightly larger.

Osprey eggs usually are more elongated than those of some other diurnal raptors, but they vary greatly in **shape**. Ground **color** usually is a creamy white, sometimes so evenly overlaid with pigment as to give a buffy or otherwise altered appearance. Sometimes a uniform cinnamon-rufous or a rusty color is present throughout. The eggs are usually heavily blotched and spotted with dark rich browns, reddish browns, or various drab shades; rarely only drabs; often browns and drabs. The markings some-times are concentrated at one end or form a "wreath," leaving much of the ground color exposed (modified from Bendire 1892 and Bent 1937). The volume of individual eggs decreased through the laying sequence: the 2d, 3d, and 4th egg av. 2.1%, 5.6%, and 8.2%, respectively, less than the 1st (A. Poole 1982b).

Clutch size Usually 3, occasionally only 2, seldom 4 (Abbott 1911, Bent 1937). Average clutch sizes for geographical localities, based on museum collections, range from 2.7 to 3.2 with the smallest in the sw. U.S. and Mexico (Judge 1983). A 5-year study in Chesapeake Bay (Reese 1977), based on 513 nests with eggs, showed that av. clutch sizes in different years were 2.9, 2.8, 3.0, and 2.9. Influences on clutch size still are not entirely clear, but several are known (A. Poole, in Bird 1983): **1** there is significant repeatability in an indivudal ♀'s clutches, suggesting some genetic control; **2** there is a tendency for young ♀♀ to lay 4-egg clutches; and **3** the mean size of clutches shows much stability within populations and year-to-year, strengthening the assumption that variation in so-called "courtship feeding" and local food supply are unimportant influences in clutch size. Females arrive on the breeding grounds nearly ready, if not ready, to lay; thus their own foraging skills and their wintering areas probably are important in determining their breeding condition.

Dates for presumably viable eggs (From Bent 1937): Que.—35 records May 24–June 28 (18 in the span May 28–June 8); N.Y. and New Eng.—48 records Apr. 25–June 18 (24 in span May 6–18); Md. and Va.—90 records Mar. 10–May 30 (45 in span Apr. 29–May 8); and Fla.—19 records Dec. 4–Apr. 28 (10 in span Mar. 13–Apr. 10). Laying typically begins on inland lakes in the n. U.S. and Canada soon after ice has melted. Earlier nesting in more s. latitudes is readily apparent. Egg laying was ex-tremely early in the nonmigratory birds of s. Fla. and ranged late Nov.–early Mar., peaking in Dec.–Jan. (Ogden, in J. Ogden 1977). In Gulf of Calif. (Mexico), laying continued early Jan.–early Mar. (Judge 1983). Jehl's statement (in J. Ogden 1977) regarding Ospreys in Mexico is typical for s. populations: "nests there contained all stages from fresh eggs to flying young." Generally, the nesting cycle is much more synchronized (onset of laying varies over about a 3-week span) in n. latitudes, which simplifies studies of nesting birds.

Incubation Primarily (about 75%) by the ♀, **period** about 38 days (D. Garber and Koplin 1972, later authors); it begins with laying of the 1st egg, hence subsequent asynchronous hatching. A. Poole (1982b), however, noted that "consistent" incubation usually began with the 2d egg. The ♀ incubates at night. The ♂ may do a large percentage, in 1 instance almost all, of observed daylight incubation (Grover 1984). In Scotland, incubation av. 37 days (range 34–40) (R. Green 1976). Eggs must be kept at 29–36° C to remain viable (Spitzer, in Temple 1978); the temperature of an incubated egg av. 35.9° C (range 34.7–37.9) (Stinson et al. 1976). Levenson (1979) reported that eggs were incubated 96.1% of daylight hrs. at a successful nest; L. and H. Van Daele (1982) reported successful nests incubated 99.5–100% of daylight hrs.

Hatching success Adversely influenced in many locations by the widespread use of DDT and other biocides since 1946. Many nesting studies have concentrated on number of young attaining flight per occupied nest (using Postupalsky's 1974 termi-nology, which includes a few nests without eggs laid) rather than checking nests many

90

times to determine the number of eggs hatched. A notable exception is the large series of data gathered by Reese (1977) in Chesapeake Bay, 1970–1974. The percentage of young hatched each year was: 43%, 42%, 51%, 54%, and 50% (av. 48%). For these years, the percentage of eggs yielding young reared to flight age were 38%, 33%, 39%, 50%, and 43% (av. 41%). The av. brood size was: 1.9, 1.7, 1.9, 2.2, and 1.9 (av. 1.95). Number of young that attained flight per occupied nest was: 1.04, 0.86, 1.11, 1.43, and 1.23 (av. 1.14). These values were among the highest in N. Am. at the time. For a general review of productivity studies throughout N. Am., see Henny (in Chancellor 1977). Stocek and Pearce (in Bird 1983) listed a number of nesting studies in e. Canada. Low rates of production were reported from the Great Lakes states and along the n. and mid-Atlantic coast during the 1960s and early 1970s.

In Idaho, Van Daele et al. (1980) reported that, although most nests were on snags (66%), the productivity of these was the lowest of any structure. Productivity was high in live trees, even higher on power poles and nesting platforms. Productivity was significantly higher on artificial sites (poles, platforms) presumably because they were more stable. (See also Habits, below.) Distance to fishable water or to other active Osprey nests was not related to productivity, but distance from human disturbance was. Nests more than 1,500 m. from disturbance were more productive (less than 500 m., 1.36 young/active nest; 500–1,500 m., 1.13; and over 1,500 m., 1.92). Similarly, in another forested region with little human use until June 15 (Yellowstone L., Wyo.), Swenson (1979a) reported that nests beyond 1 km. from campsites were more successful than nearer ones.

A relationship between productivity and "water clear of ice" was found in Labrador (S. Wetmore and Gillespie 1976a). In the more n. breeding areas, it appears that late springs have a negative effect on nesting success.

Rearing period The ♀ remains in almost constant attendance for about 30 days while brooding young. They are susceptible to direct sunlight, and, in view of the usually unsheltered situation at most nests, shading by the ♀ and keeping the young dry on rainy days is important--especially for the 1st 5–6 weeks (R. Green 1976, Jamieson et al. 1982). In Mich. on a hot day, the observer got the ♀ off the nest by his approach. She flew down to the surface of the water and dipped her breast feathers in it 5–6 times (like a dragonfly laying eggs), then flew to the nest, opened her wings, and hovered over the panting chicks, her feathers in contact with them (Nickell 1967). The ♂ does all the hunting for the family at this time and brings fish to the nest that the ♀ tears into small pieces and, usually turning her head on one side, offers to her young. In the half-downy half-feathered stage and subsequently, it is remarkable how young Ospreys resemble the surrounding nest. They lay prone in the presence of intruders so that it is almost impossible to detect them. Thus, accurate counts from fixed-wing aircraft are nearly impossible! The young, at 20–30 days old, begin to exercise their wings while standing on the nest. The first feathers become visible through the down at about 30 days; from about the 42d day onward the young are increasingly active and, when largely feathered, begin jumping up and down while wing exercising. The ♀ does not leave the nest until her mate arrives to relieve her. After the young are about 35 days old, the ♀ leaves more frequently and watches from some nearby perch (usually within 100 m. of the nest). She continues to feed the young regularly up to 42 days, and irregularly thereafter, even after the young leave the nest (L. Brown and Amadon 1968 1). Large young usually take the prey and feed themselves.

Wilcox (1944) reported that 3 eggs weighed an av. of 71.1 gm. A just-hatched young weighed 54.1 gm., at 7 days 216.4, at 14 days 595.1, at 21 days 1,000.8, at 28 days 1,298.4, at 35 days 1,433, and at 42 days also 1,433 gm. At age 49 days this young bird flew out of the nest, but its 2 siblings remained until 52 days old. For additional data on wt. gain of nestlings at 3 colonies, see A. Poole (1982b). Stinson (1977a) noted an inverse relationship between brood size and wt. of young at 1st flight. The av. time required to grow from 10% to 90% of the asymptotic wt. was 36.7 days. The "rank" of the young, judged by its wt., often fluctuated during the brood-rearing period. The growth rate of Ospreys was at the lower end of the spectrum of growth rates for falconiform birds but was consistent with the inverse relationship between body size and growth rate found by Ricklefs (1968).

Predation on nestlings In a tree nest by a raccoon for 3 successive years documented in N.Y. (R. Latham 1959) and in Md. (Reese 1977). Raccoons in Md. took eggs primarily from land-based nests as opposed to over-water structures. Common and Fish Crows in Md. were suspected of taking a few eggs. Both Kenyon (1947) and Jehl (in J. Ogden 1977) mentioned coyote depredation of ground nests on small is. in Mexico.

Sibling aggression Despite the asynchronous hatching of eggs, which results in size differences of young, a number of long-term field studies have yielded no observations of attacks by a sibling that were believed to be harmful or threatening to a young (Ames 1964, R. Green 1976, Stinson 1977a). Elsewhere, however, intensity of aggression at 3 colonies was inversely proportional to daily food-delivery rates (A. Poole 1982b). A. Poole (1979) noted that aggressive behavior by a bird in Fla. resulted in a differential growth rate; unfortunately, the study was terminated before flying age was reached. Jamieson et al. (1983) reported sibling aggression in 6 of 8 nests under observation in N.S.; however, except for a young that disappeared, all young in the nests (av. 2.8) attained flight. They noted that most aggression occurred in 3-young broods, but, based on their observed production, aggression had little or no influence on brood reduction. The latter observations might be considered "normal sibling rivalry." Sibling aggression is related to food availability (Hagan 1986), but severe shortages appear to be rare at established nesting localities. A. Poole (1982b) argued that egg-size variation and hatching asynchrony are consistent with the idea that brood reduction is an integral part of the Osprey's breeding strategy. As with other raptors, sibling aggression at times of food shortage would be an adaptation to ensure the successful rearing of at least a portion of the brood during periods of food scarcity. See discussion related to fish fluctuations, below.

Age at first flight Usually about 52–53 days, as a rule without parental coaxing. Specific data: Md.—48–59 days, av. 54 (Stotts and Henny 1975); Va.—44–59, av. 51 (Stinson 1977b); Scotland—49–57, av. 53 (R. Green 1976). Length of 1st flight varied according to distance to nearest acceptable perches—that is, from a few to 1,000 m., the majority 200–300 m. The young returned to their nest, albeit awkwardly at times. After all of the brood is flying, the nest and adjacent vicinity still are used for feeding, loafing, and roosting. During this period some young flew to nearby nests, begged for food, and were fed by other adults (A. Poole 1982a). In Va., Stinson concluded that the period of postfledging dependency ends by the time the young are about 93–103 days old. It may be shorter at higher elevations and more n. latitudes (F. Beebe 1974, Henny 1977a). Fishing behavior of the young is innate and not taught, contrary to Meinertzhagen (1954) and others.

The Osprey is **single-brooded.** Some have laid replacement clutches if the 1st was lost or taken early in incubation (W. B. Tyrrell 1936; Ames and Mersereau 1964; Kennedy, in J. Ogden 1977; Postupalsky, in Temple 1978; and others); this most likely explains some known late nestings. The nesting cycle requires in excess of 4 months.

CHARLES J. HENNY

SURVIVAL   N. Am. Data. Clapp et al. (1982) listed the oldest Osprey record for a banded wild bird at 21 years, 11 months (a retrapped bird, released). Spitzer (1980) recorded a 25-year-old Osprey recaptured alive at Gardiner's I., N.Y. Henny and Wight (1969) estimated from band recovery data an annual adult mortality rate of 16.2–19.6%, whereas 1st-year mortality was much higher (51.5–57.3%). Based on mathematical modeling, they estimated that 0.95–1.30 young must attain flight per breeding-age pair/year to maintain a stable population (they assumed all birds aged 3 years and older attempted to breed). A combination of slightly lower mortality rates (e.g., band loss could account for a high bias in Henny and Wight's original estimate), and some birds delaying 1st breeding until later in life also could yield a stable population with the same production requirement. A great many Juv. birds die heading s.; numerous breeders die soon after their long journey n. Observed production rates in most stable populations were within the range established by Henny and Wight. Spitzer, however, modeled the nesting population in N.Y. and vicinity (same basic model) with known production rates and rates of population change. He estimated that 1st-year mortality rate was 41% and adult mortality rate was 15%. The population was greatly depleted during this study (10–15% of pre-DDT era numbers) and probably had a skewed age distribution due to low production for many years. Increased postfledging survival seems likely to have occurred under these circumstances, although Henny and Wight's mortality rates (as mentioned earlier) may be slightly high. In the future, as numbers, it is hoped, continue to increase, annual rates of population change should be evaluated in relation to observed production rates.   CHARLES J. HENNY

HABITS   N. Am. data unless otherwise stated. **Unwariness**   Adaptability of Ospreys to man is readily apparent from their successful nesting under many circumstances. Typical examples include nests on channel markers in Chesapeake Bay with constant boat traffic nearby (Henny et al. 1974) or a nest in a parking lot at Conn. amusement park (A. Poole 1981). In contrast, Swenson (1979a) showed that an abrupt increase in human activity around nests at the midpoint of incubation in wilderness areas significantly lowered nesting success compared with undisturbed nests. In nw. Calif., productivity declined with increasing levels of human activity (Levinson and Koplin 1984). L. and H. Van Daele (1982) reported that Ospreys nesting near humans eventually tolerated their activities, whereas those nesting farther from humans were less tolerant. Concerns about disturbance at nests or activity around nests and the wariness of the species have led to varying conclusions depending on the local situation. The degree of habituation of individual Ospreys to man at each location probably has led to the varying opinions. A. Poole (1981) concluded that careful short-term visits by researchers have a negligible impact on Osprey production.

Hunting methods Highly specialized; the Osprey is the only living bird that has combined the plunging technique with a raptorial foot. To accommodate this, as indicated earlier, the feathering is closely imbricated, compact, and oily. (The Fishing Buzzard [*Busarellus*] of the Neotropics has spiny feet but lax feathering; it is not a plunger.) The Osprey also bathes by plunge diving.

Food consists almost entirely of fish captured by plunging feet-first into water to a maximum depth of about 1 m. The Osprey cruises about 15–30 m. overhead and looks into the water at an angle of 45° or less. Flapping rate in "ordinary flight" is 2.5 ± 0.2 wingbeats/sec. (C. H. Blake) and 2.6/sec. when hovering (C. H. Blake 1948). When it sees a fish it maneuvers to be as nearly above it as possible. It attempts to hold this position, hovering if necessary, watching for the fish to come close enough to the surface to be within its range of water penetration. Thus the plunge may be preceded by either a long glide or a brief hover (adapted from F. Beebe 1974). T. C. Grubb (1977b) noted that, under all weather conditions, dives from hovers were 50% more successful than dives from interhovers. As the Osprey enters the water, the wings are extended upward and back so that their tips extend past the tail. Just before entering, the feet are swung forward beyond the head. The bird strikes the water surface at a velocity of 30–70 kph and has been known to break a wing in diving (A. K. Fisher 1893). The bird may stay underwater for 1 sec.; the wings are brought forward and down with a powerful stroke that raises it to the surface and breaks it clear of the water. The fish is then adjusted in flight so that the head points forward. Rüppell (1981) provided excellent drawings and descriptions of the dive and prey catching based on slow-motion photography. When a fish is dropped from a perch or over the edge of a nest, the Osprey makes no retrieval attempt. When fish are found beneath a nest it is possible that some were alive when delivered and flipped over the edge, as commonly happens with the Bald Eagle.

Fish up to about 1 kg. generally are taken (see Food, below). Many early authors (Studer 1881, Abbott 1911, Farley 1924, others), some perhaps reporting the same observation, mentioned that Ospreys sometimes miscalculate the size and wt. of fish: the Osprey drives in its talons and, being unable to loosen its hold, is drawn underwater and drowned. Farley's record was of a salmon found dead with the Osprey still attached. Meinertzhagen (1959) discussed a photograph of a large carp (about 4.5 kg.) caught in Saxony (W. Germany) to which was attached an Osprey skeleton. A reported Osprey skeleton attached to a fish (Ferguson-Lees 1968a) proved to be *Buteo buteo* (G. Cowles 1969). The reliability of fish/skeleton records is questioned. An Osprey carrying a 680-gm. bream (*Abramis brama*) was knocked down by a train near Wroxham, England (Ferguson-Lees 1968b).

Ospreys had little difficulty in locating and capturing prey in n. Calif.—523 of 834 dives (62%) resulted in captures (Ueoka and Koplin 1973). In fact, in 2 instances, an Osprey captured 2 fish, 1 in each foot, in a single dive. The av. length of time spent foraging from first sighting until the capture of prey for the 523 successful fishing efforts

94

was 11.8 min. Also, as demand for fish by the growing young increased, av. foraging time decreased.

A number of studies evaluated physical variables affecting Osprey foraging, including tides and weather, and the dive success of adult and Juv. Ospreys in the same area (see citations in Swenson 1979b). T. C. Grubb (1977a), for example, noted that cloudy weather and rippled water acted independently to reduce the Osprey's catch per unit of time. Reduced visibility is the likely common denominator. Decreased capture rates were not caused by significant drops in success of dives but rather by significant decreases in dives initiated. A synthesis of 13 studies reporting dive success and prey species captured under natural conditions was provided by Swenson. Dive success (the proportion of the observed dives that were successful) was used as a measure of Osprey foraging success, because it measures the relative ease of capture. Then a "prey species foraging index" was calculated for each area. This index grouped fish into 3 categories according to foraging behavior: 1 benthic feeding, 2 limnetic feeding (excluding fish), and 3 piscivorous fish feeding. The prey species foraging indices accounted for about 74% of the observed variation in dive success among areas. Benthic-feeding fish were most vulnerable; their morphological and behavioral adaptations related to procuring food from the bottom may limit their ability to perceive attack from above.

Austral summer territories   Marchant (1958) noted that in Ecuador Ospreys may establish a territory, defending a stretch of coastline against others. This is a fertile area for research.

Communal roosting   The only mention found is a secondhand report by Jerome (in C. S. Allen 1892) who claimed that fully 2,000 roosted nightly at Plum I., N.Y., and that over 500 nests had been built there. Allen later (in Bent 1937) said the number was half that. This record apparently reflects colonial or semicolonial nesting rather than communal roosting.

Relationships with other birds   Passerines and other birds nesting in close association with Ospreys are discussed above. Interactions between Bald Eagles and Ospreys have been reported for several centuries. For example, Wm. Bartram (1791) wrote: "This princely bird subsists entirely on fish which he takes himself scorning to live and grow fat on the dear earned labours of another; he also contributes liberally to the support of the Bald Eagle." The Bald behaves aggressively toward Ospreys nesting nearby and occasionally robs them of fish. Meinertzhagen (1959) and L. Brown (1976) noted that the Osprey is often pirated by the African Fish Eagle (also a *Haliaeetus* eagle). L. Brown and Amadon (1968 1) concluded that piracy attempts by *Haliaeetus* eagles are often unsuccessful and that the Osprey does not seem to suffer from this mild parasitism.

F. Beebe (1974) noted that piracy is usually occasional, but when the reproductive timing of the 2 species coincides, it may be regular. In the n. portion of N. Am., Bald Eagles nest much earlier than Ospreys. In Fla., the establishment of a breeding pair of Bald Eagles led to the relocation of nest sites and to reduced breeding success by Ospreys. J. Ogden (1975) attributed the lowered success to harassment, but T. C. Grubb and Shields (1977) suggested that direct interference at nests could be also

95

involved. On the other hand, Ogden suggested that eagles only exhibit territorial behavior toward Ospreys the 1st year present and that adjustments are made later as the pairs learn to recognize each other through site tenacity and pair fidelity of both species. In n. Sask., Gerrard et al. (1976) suggested that Ospreys gradually may be replacing Bald Eagles as the region becomes more developed. They reported that 1 in areas of high-quality Bald Eagle nesting habitat, where human disturbance is minimal, nesting Ospreys are relatively rare; 2 in areas with considerable human influence (roads, powerlines, dams) Ospreys may be relatively common; and 3 Ospreys may be present in areas of marginal Bald Eagle nesting habitat. They hypothesized that the observed nesting distribution may result from 1 a virtually complete eagle dominance over Ospreys (see also J. Ogden 1975, above), and 2 the Osprey's greater toleration of human disturbance, which is generally accepted. The scenario would have Ospreys claiming areas after human development, which results in Bald Eagle population declines. The authors noted that habitat and prey-availability and/or changes also may explain present distributions. Perhaps it is worth noting that Osprey numbers are few in Alaska and nw. Wash., where Bald Eagle numbers are high.

Prévost (1979) reported that Ospreys and Bald Eagles tolerated each other at a common foraging site in N.S.: 1 eagles attacked Ospreys with fish; 2 eagles approached Ospreys with no fish; and 3 Ospreys attacked Bald Eagles. The eagle chases were short and intense (av. 60 sec.), with the eagle approaching to within a few m. of the Osprey while the latter tried to escape with violent maneuvers. When the Osprey dropped the fish, the eagle recovered it before the fish hit the water on one occasion and lost the fish on another. The consequences of food robbing were minimal to Ospreys in the N.S. study area; only 2 of the 1,793 observed captures were lost because of Bald Eagle attacks. Usually there was no intense pursuit when Bald Eagles approached Ospreys that had not captured a fish. When Ospreys attacked eagles, 4 of the 19 Osprey attacks involved reversal of roles—the eagle having first been the aggressor. Usually, the Osprey only swooped at a perched eagle.

In N.S., Ospreys drove Red-tailed Hawks away from their nests, but Great Black-backed and Herring Gulls and Great Blue Herons were not pursued (Jamieson and Seymour 1983). Ospreys responded to Common Crows near the nest but chased the intruders more often during the nestling stage than during incubation. Other authors have also mentioned interactions with crows.

In Mass., a Golden Eagle captured an Osprey after it dove into the water; as the Osprey spread its wings to take flight, the eagle seized it, dragged it ashore, and fed on it for several days (LaFontaine and Fowler 1976). Food for an eagle was scarce there.

Nest sites used by Ospreys in previous years are sometimes usurped by earlier-nesting species. In Labrador, Great Horned Owls nested in 35 out of 648 Osprey nests checked by aircraft (S. Wetmore and Gillespie 1976b). The owls were incubating or brooding prior to the beginning of Osprey nesting. Yearly fluctuations (0% to about 9%) in the owl's use of Osprey nests may relate to their nesting in response to prey availability. In Alta., McInvaille and Keith (1974) reported that, as a Great Horned Owl population increased in number and in rate of nesting in response to prey, the population usurped an increasing number of Red-tailed Hawk nests—forcing the hawks to build new ones. In Oreg., Osprey nests have been used by Redtails and

Canada Geese (Henny et al. 1978). Tree-nesting Canada Geese occur at several locations in Oreg.; the precocial goslings usually hatch and depart in time for the Osprey to use the nest the same year. In B.C., however, a tree nest contained both Canada Goose and Osprey eggs (Fannin 1894). In Mont., Ospreys sometimes evict Canada Geese, especially during late springs, which cause overlap in nesting cycles (Flath 1972). In Kans., an Osprey killed and ate a 2-week-old Canada Goose (Layher 1984).

Versus fish fluctuations   As indicated above (see Reproduction), clutch size in the Osprey shows much stability, evidently unaffected by local food supply. A. Poole (1979, 1982b) studied the relationship of nesting success to food delivery in Ospreys nesting near Flamingo, Fla. He found that young Ospreys on Fla. Bay received less food per day than those in N.Y. Furthermore, he found that greater nestling mortality coincided with a reduction in food delivery, which resulted in nestling starvation. As a result of these observations, it appears that the current low productivity of Ospreys in Florida Bay is due to food stress (Kushlan and Bass, in Bird 1983). Because these Ospreys, which nest in the N. Am. winter, have fewer hunting hours available to them than do more n. birds nesting in summer (Poole 1982b), even small reductions in abundance or availability of prey in Florida Bay may have a drastic impact on nestling growth rates and survival.

Biocides   Ospreys are a terminal link in an aquatic food chain and hence are susceptible to persistent bioaccumulative pesticides. Organochlorine pesticides (primarily DDE) have been correlated with eggshell thinning, poor reproduction, and severe population declines in several Osprey populations in N. Am. Reproduction was the weak point in the life cycle that was adversely influenced by organochlorine pesticides. Not one N. Am. raptor population exhibiting 18% or more eggshell thinning has maintained a stable self-perpetuating population (Lincer 1975). It is difficult to determine specifically what residue concentration of DDE, or any other chemical in Osprey eggs, results in reduced hatchability or production of flying young. This can only be understood from a large series of egg-residue data and the associated production. The limited information suggests that somewhere above 10 ppm DDE (wet wt.) in Osprey eggs greatly reduces production, but even lower levels may cause losses. The Black-crowned Night Heron provides a better understood example of a species with DDE residues, because a single egg was collected from each of 220 nests (Henny et al. 1984b). As DDE residues increased, productivity progressively declined; less than 4 ppm, 79% of nests successful (1 or more young left the nest); 4.09–8 ppm. 73% successful; 8.01–12, 58%; 12.01–16, 55%; 16.01–25, 45%; more than 25 ppm, 22%. The eggshell thinning for the respective categories was 3.3%, 8.0%, 13.1%, 14.5%, 20.0%, and 16.7%. Although egg sensitivity to DDE varies from species to species, it is difficult to determine the amount of residues that will affect eggs of a given species based on small series of eggs. Critical residues of other pesticides in Osprey eggs are understood even less.

Evidence of pesticide contamination in Ospreys exists primarily from the n. Atlantic coast populations; extremely low reproduction also was reported from the Great Lakes region. Some populations in other areas were affected to a lesser degree. D. Anderson and Hickey (1972) reported that Osprey eggs (a small series) collected in Conn., N.J., and Md. in 1957 had shells 18–21% thinner than museum eggs collected before 1947 (the pre-DDT era). In the late 1960s, eggs from Conn. had shells 15–18% thinner than pre-1947 samples, while Md. eggs showed only 10–12% thinning. Maryland eggs placed in Conn. nests in 1968 and 1969 hatched at rates comparable to the source areas, supporting the hypothesis that their lower DDE contamination was the reason for higher viability (Weimeyer et al. 1975).

Improved Osprey production during recent years has paralleled the decline in use of DDT and other persistent chemicals (reviews: Henny, in Chancellor 1977; Spitzer et al. 1978). Spitzer reported geometric mean concentrations of DDE in Conn.–Long I. eggs declined fivefold between 1969 and 1976, while PCBs (polychlorinated biphenyls) showed no change. Osprey production (no young attaining flight/occupied nest) for a number of locations showed improvement that began in the late 1960s or early 1970s. DDT was banned in 1972, but domestic use dropped nearly 50% between 1958 and 1966. N.J. Ospreys, like those in N.Y., Conn., R.I., and Mass., suffered extremely poor production; a long series of nesting studies (Henny et al. 1977; N.J. Div. Fish, Game & Wildl.) now shows a pattern of improvement (number of young attaining flight / occupied nest): 0.22–0.32 in 1968–1971, 0.26–0.81 in 1972–1975, 0.85–0.97 in 1976–1979, and 1.02–1.22 in 1980–1983. Some extremely high residues of DDE (up to 40 ppm) were present in N.J. eggs in the early 1970s (Wiemeyer et al. 1978), but the population increased since 1975 (68 pairs in 1975, 85 pairs in 1979, and 98 pairs in 1983). Spitzer and Poole (1980) presented detailed data for the coastal population between New York City and Boston that shows similar improvement in productivity with associated population increases (109 pairs in 1975 to 138 in 1979). The N.J. counts represent occupied nests, while Spitzer and Poole refer to active nests (those known to contain laid eggs). The number of pairs from 1975 to 1979 increased 25% in N.J. and 26.6% from New York City to Boston. The future looks promising for depleted populations. In direct contrast to the low production in N.J. through the mid-1970s was the normal production recorded across Del. Bay in adjacent Del. (Henny et al. 1977). DDT was used for mosquito control in coastal N.J., 1946–1966, but in Del. only 1947–1956. Since the 2 populations share common migration routes and wintering areas, only local DDT use could be responsible for the N.J. problem. Also, the strong fidelity to breeding areas and short dispersal distances are prerequisites for the dichotomy in Osprey population variables observed between the 2 states. For productivity data from other more stable populations, see Reese (1977, 1981) for Chesapeake Bay, as given under Hatching success, above, and other studies summarized by Henny (in Chancellor 1977). A severe food shortage, especially during the rearing period, can result in reproductive failure.

Declines in Osprey numbers were related primarily to poor productivity. Little evidence of direct mortality to adults from pesticides was available, although dieldrin apparently killed a ♂ in Conn. in 1967 (Wiemeyer et al. 1975). The Conn. population declined faster than expected, based on the reduced production alone. The Conn. R. population declined from 71 pairs in 1960 to 31 pairs in 1961, an unprecedented rate. Hurricane Donna in Sept. 1960 (the migration period) may explain this excessive loss or a portion thereof. The population continued to decline, however, from 31 pairs in 1961 to only 5 in 1969, which was still in excess of the annual rate of projected decline based on known production. Therefore, additional postfledging mortality (probably pesticide related and including adults) was implied for that population. Wiemeyer et al. (1980) necropsied and analyzed 33 Ospreys found dead or moribund in the e. U.S. between 1964 and 1973. Organochlorines were detected in the following percentages: DDE 100%, PCBs 96%, DDD 92%, dieldrin 88%, chlordane 82%, DDT 65%, and heptachlor epoxide 38%. An adult ♀ from S.C. may have died from dieldrin poisoning. Arsenic may have contributed to the death of a 1st-fall bird in Md.; an adult ♀ in Fla. contained potentially dangerous levels of mercury. Mercury shows up in feathers of young (Hakkinen and Häsänen 1980) in Finland.

Conservation/management At many locations within its breeding range, even while other raptors were suffering heavy persecution, the Osprey was protected by public opinion. Yet it continues to be shot in migration and on winter range.

The provision of safe nest sites (platforms) has improved the breeding success of some populations by 1 enabling certain pairs to move to places safer from human disturbance, 2 reducing losses to predators, 3 eliminating and replacing defective nest sites subject to blow-down losses, and 4 eliminating the limiting role of nest sites (Postupalsky and Stackpole 1974; Postupalsky, in Temple 1978; Eckstein et al. 1979; Hallberg et al. 1983). In Idaho, N.Y., and Fla., artificial sites used by Ospreys produced about twice as many young per nesting attempt as did natural sites (2.17 v. 1.28, 1.38 v. 0.58, 1.48 v. 0.71 (L. and H. Van Daele 1982, A. Poole and Spitzer 1983). One of the best examples of attracting Ospreys to a location with nest structures occurred on a refuge in the Chesapeake Bay area (L. Rhodes 1972). Ospreys have the highest success rate using platforms of any raptor; occupation of sites may be related in some measure to visibility of one from another.

Most Osprey nests encountered during logging operations are normally at locations remote from human disturbance. These nesting pairs are likely to be sensitive to disturbance. Attempts should be made to minimize intensive logging operations within 500 m. of any active nest from April to Sept. and have a no-cut zone within 100 m. radius of active nests (Van Daele et al. 1980). This activity distance is in general agreement with Adams and Scott (1979) and is intermediate between recommendations of Lind (1976) and Melo (1973). A summary of other management options, primarily relating to forested lands in the West, were given by Henny (in Chancellor 1977). Reintroduction of 6-week-old Ospreys to localities with depleted populations or to newly created habitat is another option being used.

Literature on the Osprey In the New World, exceeds some 500 significant references. Some 372 (worldwide) were listed in pt. 3 (1970) of the R. and S. Olendorff raptor bibliography. A later extensive listing is in Evans (1982). Many papers (among the 164 cited herein) date since about 1960. Useful photographs of young: W. B. Tyrrell (1936); fine color plates of Ospreys: R. T. Peterson (1969).

CHARLES J. HENNY

FOOD Ospreys feed almost exclusively on **live fish,** but dead ones are taken occassionally (Dunstan 1974, Nesbitt 1974). The Osprey has a remarkably long small intestine, of narrow diam., probably related to fish-eating (P. Mitchell 1901). Seasonal changes in diet and hunting areas occur in some localities. In N.S., early in the breeding season, Ospreys captured anadromous fish during spawning runs (alewives and suckers) in coastal rivers but in July, when these fish were less available, shifted to winter flounder in coastal estuaries (Prévost et al. 1978). Ospreys nesting inland then had farther to fly for food in the coastal estuaries with a possible negative impact on production of young. Green et al. (in Bird 1983) also discussed coastal Ospreys in N.S. flying up to 10 km. inland to hunt for spawning alewives in early spring.

Scattered reports of other prey (a small proportion of intake) were summarized by J. Wiley and Lohrer (1973); the list is diverse. General food habits were reviewed by Sherrod (1978); Swenson (1979b) summarized 12 quantitative studies of fish species in the diet (excluding species comprising less than 5%). The following is from Swenson unless otherwise stated.

Saltwater fishes Western N. Am. Mouth of Usal Creek, Calif.—surf smelt and night smelt 98%. **Eastern N. Am.** Antigonish Harbor, N.S.—winter flounder 90+%; Seahorse Key, Fla.—speckled trout 64%, striped mullet 27%, sea catfish 8%.

Freshwater fishes Western N. Am. Flathead Lake, Mont.—largescale sucker 59%, whitefish 26%, unidentified 11%; Crane Prairie Reservoir, Oreg.—salmonidae 57%, tui chub 43%; Eagle Lake, Calif.—tui chub 43%, rainbow trout 34%, Tahoe sucker 18%; Yellowstone R., Wyo.—cutthroat trout 90%, longnose sucker 10%; Yellowstone Lake, Wyo.—cutthroat trout 88%, longnose sucker 7%, unidentified 5%; Corn Creek Marsh, B.C. (Flook and Forbes, in Bird 1983)—black bullhead 83%, punkinseed 10%, yellow perch 7%; Cascade Reservoir, Idaho (L. and H. Van Daele 1982)—brown bullhead 38%, salmonidae 21%, northern squawfish 19%, yellow perch 12%, largescale sucker 11%. In the latter study, comparing Osprey captures with net captures, the birds caught significantly more bullheads and salmonids and fewer squawfish, perch, and suckers than were netted. Fish in the 11–30 cm. range constituted the bulk (89%) of the diet in the Idaho study. **Great Lakes** Minn. (Dunstan 1974)—bluegill 35%, black crappie 31%, yellow perch 13%, largemouth bass 10%. **Eastern N. Am.** Newnans Lake, Fla.—gizzard shad and threadfin shad 73%, sunfish, black crappie, and largemouth bass 15%, unidentified 12%; L. George, Fla.— mullet 52%, crappie 48%; Paynes Prairie, Fla.—sunfish 95%.

Other items captured In N. Am. (from summary of J. Wiley and Lohrer 1973): mammals—marsh rabbit, rice rat, cotton rat, and unidentified small mammal; birds— crow, Black-crowned Night Heron, chicken, N. Cardinal, Mallard, Wood Duck, and young Canada Goose; reptiles—turtle, snake, water snake, painted turtle, Fla. red-bellied turtle, and alligator; amphibians—frog. In other parts of the world: mammals—ground squirrel, mice, steppe vole, rabbit, and rat; birds—storm petrel, sandpiper, Jackdaw, duck, Herring Gull, coot, Lapwing, grebe; reptiles—sea snake; invertebrates—crustacean, sea snail, beetle. Of particular interest is preying on mating frogs in Finland while lakes still were covered with ice (Hildén and Linkola 1955).

Reasons suggested for taking prey other than live fish include scarcity of fish, murky water and inclement weather, lack of fishing skill due to youth, and attraction of easily captured crippled, captive, or concentrated nonfish prey. Wiley and Lohrer believed that some inland nesting pairs actually exploited such abundant alternatives as cotton rats. The capture of birds or mammals by migrants (documented at several localities) may be explained by either scarcity of fish or unfamiliarity with fish at the location.

Away from water, in w. Mont., a storm had stopped n. migration; the mammal taken was not identified (Henny).

Food requirements   In Idaho, adults brought an av. of 4.6 fish/day to a nest with 2 young, and 5.6 fish/day to a brood of 3 (L. and H. Van Daele 1982). This delivery pattern was similar but consistently higher than in n. Calif. (D. Garber 1972) and Scotland (Waterston 1960/1961). In Norway, a nest with 2 young received 6.5 fish/day (Nordbakke 1980). Lind (1976) calculated that adult Ospreys required 286 kcal./day and young at age of first flight 254 kcal./day. Assuming that fish contained 1 kcal./gm. of body wt., a nest with 2 young and 1 adult ($\delta\,\delta$ rarely ate at the nest) required 794 gm. of fish/day at time the young attained flight, and a brood of 3 plus 1 adult required 1,048 gm. In the Van Daele study the calculated minimum requirement was achieved before the young first flew. Nordbakke (1980) reviewed the European literature, which suggested that daily food requirements were slightly higher (300–400 gm.) and which concluded that an Osprey pair (in Norway) raising 2 young consumed about 170 kg. of fish during the breeding season.

Fish in the 11–30 cm. size class constituted the bulk of the diet (89%) in Idaho (L. and H. Van Daele 1982), but the 20–25 and 34–38 cm. size-classes comprised the largest portion in Norway, with a pike 52 cm. long (1,000 gm.) representing the largest prey (Nordbakke 1980). The av. wt. of prey fish in Norway was 200–300 gm.

CHARLES J. HENNY

melanistic

HOOK-BILLED KITE

Chondrohierax uncinatus

A slender-bodied, weak-footed, broad-winged, diurnal raptor slightly longer than the Broad-winged Hawk. Beak variably (to extraordinarily) large and laterally compressed; slitlike nostril overlaid by a broad membrane; cere yellow; naked skin from cere to eye variable—greenish, bluish green, yellow (Basic Plumage), more or less yellow (Juv.); no bony shield projecting above eye. Iris white (Basic) or brownish (Juv. only?); head smoothly contoured (not crested); blackish tail crossed by 1–2 (Basic) or 2–4 (Juv.) broad light (to white) bands. Two **color phases** with great individual variation in other than melanistic individuals. In general, ♂ ♂ are variably gray in Basic and ♀ ♀ variably brown, but neither exclusively so; in the Juv. stage both sexes in light phase are rather similar to brown ♀ ♀ in Basic.

Females av. slightly larger than ♂ ♂. Sexes combined: length 15–18 in. (38–46 cm.), wingspread in the larger ♀ to 38 in. (97 cm.), wt. about 8–12 oz. (225–353 gm.).

Three subspecies: 1 mainland (s. Tex. to n. Argentina) and 2 is. (Cuba; Grenada).

DESCRIPTION   Abbreviated treatment of mainland birds, which have tremendous individual variation. There is concealed white at rear of head (occipital spot) in both phases and sexes and all flying ages. No data on molting.

▶ ♂ Def. Basic Plumage (entire feathering) **light phase: head** cap gray; neck lacks "collar" (which is present in ♀). **Breast** with highly variable gray barring, from dark and bold to thin and hardly evident; **upperparts** also gray (usually deep or dark). **Tail** dark, narrowly tipped white, and crossed by 2–3 wide bands of pale buffy to white; **wing** underside of primaries barred light and dark, wing lining barred buffy gray on dark. **Melanistic** sooty black without barring; tail with single broad white band and narrow white tip.

▶ ♀ Def. Basic Plumage (entire feathering) **light phase: head** cap dark brown, remainder buffy brown; a broad buffy rufous "collar," which extends from back of **neck**

102

around on each side. **Underparts** breast barred brown, usually a deep brownish red; **upperparts** brown, usually dark and muted. **Tail** very dark, tipped white with 2–3 light grayish brown bars; **wing** underside of primaries banded dark and light, lining pale with dark brownish barring. **Melanistic** as ♂ described above. For further details, see Freidman (1934, 1950).

AT HATCHING   Beak and iris black, cere greenish yellow; down rather long, white with reddish tinge on crown and upperparts including wings (Haverschmidt 1964). No data on later down(s).

▶ ♂ ♀ Juv. Plumage (entire feathering) **light phase** as light-phase ♀ in Basic except **cap** black, barring on **breast** may be complete or vary to nearly absent with only faint buffy brown bars on white; **tail** has 4 palish brown bars. **Melanistic** as Basic except tail has 2–3 narrow white bars.

Color phases   See above; light-phase Basic is extremely variable, hence arbitrarily divisible ("varieties" of Friedmann 1950), a preponderance of ♂ ♂ being gray and ♀ ♀ brown.

Measurements   For many data, see Friedmann (1934, 1950), E. R. Blake (1977), and T. Smith and Temple (1982a). BEAK from cere of 347 specimens from all parts of species's range (sexes combined) 31.7 ± 4.3 mm.; for birds closest to our area (also not sorted to sex), WING across chord of 33 from e. Mexico 279 ± 12 mm., and 48 from w. Mexico 296 ± 12 mm. (T. Smith and Temple 1982a).

Weight   In Suriname 3 ♂ 251–257 gm., mean 253, and 3 ♀ 240–300, mean 255 (Haverschmidt 1962). Without localities or dates, and with standard error of mean, 4 ♂ 265 ± 11.6 gm., and 3 ♀ 296 ± 22.2 (Hartman 1961). A ♀ in Nuevo León, Mexico, shot near her nest with young, weighed 246 gm. after some dessication (A. R. Phillips).

Two young at flying age in Tamaulipas, Mexico, 200 and 205 gm. (T. B. Smith 1982).

Hybrids   None reported.

Individual and geographical variation   Whether Hook-billed Kites of the mainland comprise more than 1 species is an unsettled question. Amadon (1964) tentatively treated them collectively as the only species in the genus. Birds with beaks of assorted sizes are said to occur at the same locations throughout the mainland range—yet all presumably are alike in habitat preference, feeding behavior, and vocalizations; beak size is unrelated to overall body size, coloring, age, or sex.

One might postulate that, in some former time, there were separate populations (where?), differing in beak size, that now are joined and, although genetically intermingled, still vary enormously in individual beak size (this aligns with Amadon's 1964 comment on *"megarhynchus"*). Or one might postulate that beak size is related to variation in snail size, the former having evolved through "disruptive selection" where there were large and small snails (without intermediates), and that "directional selection" may have caused further specialization (T. Smith and Temple 1982a). Perhaps speculation may diminish when and if it is established whether individual kites have a preference for mates having similar-sized beaks. Such a polymorphism appears to be maintained in certain geographical areas through kites of different beak sizes feeding differently upon separate size classes of tree snails.

Chord of WING (used as an index of body size) differed slightly from region to region, but no pattern of variation within the overall range was discovered except that is. races are significantly smaller. Island races also differ from mainland birds in showing reduced variation in coloration of feathering (including no melanistic phase) and greatly reduced variability and lack of bimodality in beak size. (Based on Friedmann 1934, Amadon 1964, and T. Smith and Temple 1982a.)

Affinities No information.   THOMAS B. SMITH

SUBSPECIES All birds of the mainland and some adjacent is. are treated as 1 subspecies, varying little in size but with much color and pattern variation and remarkably large beak variation (length, area in lateral view). Two W. Indian subspecies, less well known, have reduced variation as mentioned above.

uncinatus Temminck—includes *aquilonus* and *immanus* of Friedmann (1934); descr. and meas. of n. birds are given above; larger- to smaller-beaked birds are said to occur throughout; a small percentage is melanistic. Extreme s. Tex. through Cent. and S. Am. into Argentina, on some adjacent small is., and (at least formerly) Trinidad. For further meas., see Friedmann (1934, 1950), E. R. Blake (1977), and T. Smith and Temple (1982a).

wilsonii (Cassin)—pale yellow upper mandible is diagnostic (Friedmann 1934); ♂♂ appear light gray, ♀♀ light brown, and both sexes have very narrow barring on breast. No melanistic phase known. Beak size less variable than on the mainland, lacks bimodality. Local in e. Cuba; last confirmed sighting in 1974 near Moa, Province de Oriente (Garrido 1976). Status: endangered (W. King 1978). For a few meas., see Friedmann (1950); mean length of WING across chord of 12 birds (not separated by sex) 255 ± 12 mm. (T. Smith and Temple 1982a).

mirus Friedmann—described (1934) as having seemingly arrested development of coloring—a tendency toward ♀ feathering in ♂♂ that has apparently become fixed; reduced variation in size of beak; no melanistic phase known. Lesser Antilles: Grenada—last documented sighting in 1980 (T. Smith and Temple 1982b). Status: endangered (W. King 1978). For meas. of a few specimens, see Friedmann (1950); mean length of WING across chord of 20 birds (not separated by sex) 253 ± 8 mm. (T. Smith and Temple 1982a).   THOMAS B. SMITH

FIELD IDENTIFICATION **In our area** and nearby. Trimmer than the slightly shorter Broadwing, its buteo-shaped wings narrowing greatly at the body; tail wedge shaped. Underwing, breast, and primaries usually with heavy gray (♂♂) or brown (♀♀) barring; dark dorsum with 2–3 contrasting wide white bars. Great individual variation—see Description, above. Beak remarkably large and individually variable in size, larger than that of any similar-sized hawk. Lower mandible may appear white. Melanistic birds are known from fairly near our area. In vicinity of nests, kites have feeding perches where they bring and extract tree snails from their shells, which are damaged in a characteristic way (see illus.), so that accumulations of these indicate the presence and identity of this hawk. Seldom perches in the open. Has flap-glide flight and sometimes soars; most often flies within the forest canopy.

Melanistic birds could possibly be confused with ♂ Snail Kite, but latter is very slender billed and its tail coverts (both upper and under) plus basal portions of tail are combined in a large white area.   THOMAS B. SMITH

VOICE   A loud rattling alarm call, descending in pitch (Fleetwood and Hamilton 1967). Nest defense call very similar to N. Flicker (*Colaptes auratus*) but more intense (T. B. Smith 1982). In Aug. in Guerero, Mexico, it attracted a collector's attention by its soft conversational *hu-ey* or *huey*, not whistled or hawklike; irises white (A. R. Phillips). Musical oriolelike whistle; harsh chattering and screaming when chasing a hawk of another species (L. Brown and Amadon 1968 1).   THOMAS B. SMITH

HABITAT   Tropical to warm temperate forest. A hawk of the lower canopy and understory, up to 3,000 ft. in Mexico and to 8,000 ft. in S. Am. In Mexico it is found most often in tropical deciduous or acacia thorn woodlands. Also occurs in rain forest and in high-altitude cloud forest in the Andes. Most important factor determining habitat is an abundance of tree snails.   THOMAS B. SMITH

DISTRIBUTION   Within overall range of the species there are large areas whence no records. **In our area** present all year (breeds) in a small portion of extreme s. Tex. Photo of small-billed ♀ at Salileno, Tex., Feb. 16, 1986, in 1986 *Am. Birds* **40** 300.
    Elsewhere   The mainland form occurs on some adjacent is. Example: occurs and may breed on Maria Magdalena, Tres Marias Is., w. Mexico (P. Grant and Cowan 1964). For the Panama region, see A. Wetmore (1965). TRINIDAD no record for over 100 years (J. Bond 1979); now very rare (Herklots 1965); CUBA known only from the e. part of the island; GRENADA on verge of extinction (J. Bond 1979), but see above for 1980 sightings.
    Recorded as **fossil** from the Pleistocene of Brazil (Winge, cited in Brodkorb 1964).
                                                                THOMAS B. SMITH

BANDING STATUS   None banded in our area.

REPRODUCTION   SOUTHERN TEX.   In Hidalgo Co. s. of Alamo on May 3, 1964, a shallow nest was found 22 ft. (6.7 m.) up and 10 ft. (3 m.) out from the main trunk of a black willow (*Salix nigra*); it contained 2 young, which were missing 2 days later (Fleetwood and Hamilton 1967). In the same area 2 pairs were seen from Dec. 16, 1975, onward until only 1 pair after the end of Apr. 1976. In early May in a Tex. ebony (*Pithecollobium flexicaule*), 2 eggs in a nest 6.5 m. (21 ft.) from the ground; they were newly hatched June 6; a chick disappeared later, but the other attained flight and was last heard away from the nest on July 10 (Delnicki 1978). In June 1978 there was a nest on the Santa Ana Natl. Wildl. Refuge; the ♂ had been seen carrying nesting material earlier, on Apr. 29; the nest with 2 half-grown young was discovered later (1978 *Am. Birds* **32** 1183); for photo of chick and parent on this nest, see 1979 *Am. Birds* **33** 878. The latter reference included these 1979 data: ♂ seen below Falcon Dam Apr. 7 and ♀ on nest downriver in Starr Co. on May 8; pair at Rancho Santa Margarita, w. of Roma,

Starr Co., May 4; adults and a "juvenile" Aug. 19 at Santa Ana Natl. Wildl. Refuge (possible duplication in these reports). In 1980–1981, as in previous 2 years, a pair at Rancho Santa Margarita, and a pair was presumed nesting in the Anzalduas unit of Rio Grande Natl. Wildl. Refuge (1981 *Am. Birds* **35** 957). "Recently reported annually and nesting" (1982 ABA revised *Checklist*).

Elsewhere These data are from 2 Mexican states abutting Tex. TAM-AULIPAS Clutches of 2 on May 14, 1908, and May 2, 1910, being reidentified eggs (Kiff 1981). Six pairs of these kites constructed nests in huisache trees (*Acacia farnesiana*) at heights of 5–7 m. Each was in an open portion of the tree, having minimal obstruction to aerial approach. They were composed of so few sticks that an observer could see the contents from underneath. A typical nest was about 11 cm. deep, 30 cm. in diam., and contained as few as 80 twigs. On June 18, 1979, 1 of these nests contained a single young aged about a week less than flight age. On June 21, 2 additional nests were located within 2 km. of the 1st; 1 contained 2 young about the same age as the chick just mentioned, the other a downy chick similar to the 2 described by Haverschmidt (1964) in Suriname. On June 23 a 4th nest was located, containing 2 eggs, and on the same day in 1979, and on June 2, 1980, 2 additional nests were identified—both empty (T. B. Smith 1982). NUEVO LEÓN E. of Monterrey there was an unsuccessful nest in 1975 and 2 pigeon-sized young in a nest in June 1978—the ♀ parent collected on July 21 (F. Montiel, A. R. Phillips).

In this species **clutch size** is more often 2 than 3. Six **eggs size** length 42.5–46.9 mm., av. 44.6, and breadth 35.3–37.6, av. 36.5, as calculated from Kiff (1981); **shape** nearly elliptical; **color** unglossed white, heavily marked with chocolate (tiny spots to large irregular blotches) scattered overall—unlike any of our other kites (see comparison photo in Kiff 1981).

Farther afield, in OAXACA, 2 eggs (undamaged one slightly incubated) May 27, 1966, and the attending ♂ had an incubation patch; for further details, including description of nest and eggs, see Rowley (1984).

The species is a late breeder, as all above data indicate.

In S. Am. this kite has been found nesting in Suriname in Apr. and Oct.–Nov.; both sexes build, and evidently both incubate; there is a laying interval and a consequent hatching interval (Haverschmidt 1964). In Costa Rica the ♂ was seen incubating repeatedly at a nest (Orians and Paulson 1969). Incubation period, age at 1st flight, and subsequent dependency period all unknown, except that a family group of 4 remained all winter in extreme s. Tex. (1982 *Am. Birds* **36** 310). This species is also reportedly seen in groups of 3s, which could indicate prolonged family bonds (T. Smith and Temple 1982b), but Hook-billed Kites may assemble in flocks. On Sept. 2, 1978, Paulson (1983) observed 25 kites soaring together near San Francisco de Apure, Apure, Venezuela. THOMAS B. SMITH

HABITS This kite has an interesting mixture of characteristics—lack of a bony shield over the eye (as in Swallow-tailed Kite), bare lores (as in Snail Kite and some *Buteogallus*), flap-glide flight (as in accipiters), and so on—adaptations to preying on snails.

Although published knowledge that this kite eats snails dates back at least to Gundlach (1876), actual observations of **foraging** are scarce. In Grenada, a ♀ walked along a limb, searching; on finding a snail she jumped to a small branch, hung upside down, removed the snail from a limb with her beak, and flew to a feeding perch (T. Smith and Temple 1982b).

Snail extraction All kites of this species, irrespective of beak size, remove snails from shells in the same manner. After a kite gets a snail, it flies to a branch and transfers it from beak to left foot. Bracing the shell against the perch (it may use both feet if the snail is large), with aperture of the shell facing the beak, the kite pierces and removes the epiphragm (a dried membrane covering the aperture), then wipes its beak several times on the perch. Then the shell is chipped to enlarge the aperture, and the kite inserts its upper mandible and breaks the inner whorls of the shell by driving the tip of the beak toward the apex of the spire of the shell. By breaking each consecutive inner whorl with the tip of the beak, the snail is freed and swallowed whole, leaving behind the shell with very characteristic damage (see illus.). This description is based on observations of over 60 extractions in which little variation in method was observed (T. Smith and Temple 1982a).

Parasitism? On Barro Colorado I., Panama, Van Tyne (1950) saw an adult ♂ being followed closely by 5 toucans (*Ramphastos sulfuratus*). As the kite went from tree to tree, the toucans watched intently. Van Tyne suspected that the toucans took advantage of the "phenomenal ability" of the kite fo find snails, then robbed this "rather sluggish" bird.   THOMAS B. SMITH

FOOD   Terrestrial and tree snails, although other organisms reportedly have been found in digestive tracts.

Tree snails This compilation is believed to include all snails eaten by this kite and reported through 1982. TEX. *Rabdotus alternatus* (small snail). TAMAULIPAS same. NUEVO LEÓN "snails." Colima, Jalisco, and elsewhere in W. MEXICO: *Orthalicus ponderosus* (has large- and small-sized age classes) and *Dryameus colimaensis* (small). GUATEMALA *Pomacea* in 1 instance (this is the main food of the Snail Kite). CUBA *Polymita picta*. GRENADA observed eating *Bulimulus wiebesi* (small); shells of *Endolichotus grenadensis* (small) showing kite damage were found; was not found eating *Strophocheilus oblongus* (has large- and small-sized age classes), which previously was

107

reported as food by J. Bond (T. Smith and Temple 1982b). In S. AM., in Suriname and other countries: *Strophocheilus oblongus*.

Other prey   According to Brown and Amadon (1968 1), this species eats frogs, salamanders, and insects, including caterpillars.

That its food in Grenada is "land snakes" (Curry-Lindahl, in Chancellor 1977) is a misprint for "land snails."   THOMAS B. SMITH

AMERICAN SWALLOW-TAILED KITE

Elanoides forficatus

Medium-sized black and white "kite"—wings long, tail long and deeply forked (more than any other raptor). Beak and feet small. Sexes alike, except ♀ av. perhaps minimally larger and heavier. Length about 19–24 in. (48–60 cm.), wingspread to about 50 in. (127 cm.), wt. about 13–18 oz. (365–500 gm.). Generally placed in the raptor subfamily Perninae, but has little external resemblance to other genera in that group. Two subspecies, 1 in our area.

DESCRIPTION   *E. f. forficatus.* Def. Basic Plumage (entire feathering) ALL YEAR, renewed by molting in summer–fall.

▶ ♂ ♀ **Beak** mostly black, its base, the cere, and eyelids black with bluish cast; mouth lining cobalt; **iris** dark brownish, perhaps varying toward a reddish brown; **head** and neck white. **Upperparts** of body black; white basal portions of feathers usually concealed, sometimes exposed as broad white band across lower back. **Underparts,** including tibial and tarsal feathers and under tail coverts white, often stained. **Feet** tarsus and toes pale bluish gray, talons grayish brown. **Tail** black, very long (outermost pair of feathers, 32–37 cm.), somewhat spreading at tip, and deeply forked—outermost feathers more than twice as long as middle pair. **Wing** long, narrow, pointed; 2 outer primaries (#9 and #10) deeply emarginated on inner web, the others tapering; primary #8 (or #8 and #9) longest; the primaries and upper wing-coverts black; secondaries white for basal ⅔ (this concealed by overlapping feathers), black for distal ⅓; tertials white or black tipped, the white partly concealed by black scapulars; axillars and wing lining white.

All black areas show purplish, violet, greenish, and bronzy iridescence, its extent and color depending somewhat on light. Purplish gloss is most pronounced on upper middle wing coverts, scapulars, and interscapulars. In life, the black areas have a "beautiful grapelike bloom" (Bent 1937); it soon disappears in prepared specimens.

The appearance may be caused by powder down—"a film of powder down" spread over the water surface around one that was shot and fell into a lake in Panama (A. Wetmore).

There are few data on molting. Bent found none in flight feathers of 5 birds taken in Aug. and inferred that molting occurred after departure on fall migration. As in various raptors, however, undoubtedly it begins in the breeding season, since individuals lacking remiges and rectrices have been seen in s. Fla. (W. B. Robertson, Jr.) and Costa Rica (A. F. Skutch) as early as late May.

AT HATCHING Covered with white down; later another down, longer and also white. By age 26 days a preflight bird had "lost every trace of down" (I. Sutton 1955). Also see below.

▶ ♂ ♀ Juv. Plumage (entire feathering) begins to appear at age about 2 weeks and is fully developed at about 40 days.

At about 2 weeks the black primaries, secondaries, scapulars, and tail begin to emerge; at 3 weeks, buffy contour feathers appear on head and foreparts, scapulars are solid black, but folded wings still a mixture of black and white; at 5 weeks, wings solid black, and buffy (Juv.) of head and breast are beginning to disappear, especially on head (incoming streaked white Basic I); about 40 days, buff largely replaced by white, tail distinctly forked but much less than in Def. Basic (based on N. Snyder 1974).

Head Base of beak and cere dull bluish gray; **eye** dark brownish with small dingy area around it; **light areas** of feathering buffy, varying from vivid rufous-buff on crown, nape, hindneck, throat and breast to pale buffy wash on rest of underparts and wing lining; **dark areas** most remiges and wing coverts have small whitish or buffy tips; scapulars and interscapulars narrowly edged buffy; **feet,** including exposed tarsus, whitish gray; **tail** abbreviated and shallowly notched.

Young a week out of nest—that is, aged about 47 days, had lost much buffiness from head and underparts (M. J. and W. B. Robertson, Jr.), indicating either extensive feather wear or fading.

▶ ♂ ♀ Basic I Plumage of authors, or else the fully developed Juv. Plumage, may begin to appear on head and foreparts in the preflight stage. Duration of molting unknown, but the Plumage evidently is retained into the following late spring–summer. Said (Forbush 1927, Bent 1937) to be like definitive except: **dark areas** have brownish cast; **iridescence** mostly greenish; white tips on some contour feathers; dusky **shaft streaks** on crown and breast. Three Mar.–May specimens from s. Fla., otherwise apparently "adult" (gonads in breeding condition, feathering unworn, no molting) retained dark shaft-streaks on crown, hindneck, throat, and upper breast (W. B. Robertson, Jr.).

Measurements Eight ♂ BEAK from cere 19–20 mm., av. 19.5, WING across chord 423–436, av. 431.3, and TAIL 328–343, av. 334.4; and 12 ♀ BEAK from cere 19–21 mm., av. 20, WING across chord 436–445, av. 440.3, and TAIL 343–370, av. 355.6 (Friedmann 1950). N. Snyder and Wiley (1976) gave mean meas. as: BEAK from cere in 22 ♂ and 22 ♀ 19.9 mm. each; WING across chord in 22 ♂ was 420.8 mm. and in 23 ♀ 428.4. Sexes nearly identical in size.

Weight Few data; these vary widely and do not show sexual and subspecific differences. *E. f. forficatus* ♂ Dade Co., Fla., with full stomach 475 gm. (J. C. Moore);

♂ Collier Co., Fla., stomach nearly empty 422.7 gm. (D. R. Paulson); S.C. (netted and released) ♀ 510 gm., probable ♀ 490 gm, probable ♂ 440 gm. (Cely and Sorrow 1983); ♀ Bermuda, stomach contents not stated, found dead (and emaciated?) Mar. 17 weighed 12.5 oz. (about 354 gm.) (Gross 1958). *E. f. yetapa* ♀ Petén, Guatemala, full stomach and egg ready to be laid 500 gm. (Van Tyne 1935); ♂ Panama, stomach contents not stated, 445 gm. on Mar. 1 (Natl. Mus. Nat. Hist. 472,092); Suriname, no data on stomach contents, 2 ♂ 390 and 407 gm., and 4 ♀ 372–435 gm., mean 399 (Haverschmidt 1962); ♂ no data given 505 gm. (Hartman 1961).

Two chicks on day of hatching weighed 26 and 30 gm., and the larger weighed 66 gm. at 5 days and 220 gm. at 12 days (N. Snyder 1974).

Geographical variation Slight; s. birds reportedly are smaller with green, rather than purplish, gloss on scapulars and interscapulars.

WILLIAM B. ROBERTSON, JR.

SUBSPECIES **In our area** *forficatus* (Linnaeus)—descr. and meas. given above. **Extralimital** *yetapa* (Vieillot)—reportedly smaller; see Friedmann (1950) for meas.; s. Mexico to n. Argentina and se. Brazil. Validity sometimes doubted; considered "scarcely separable" (Swann 1921) from the n. subspecies.

WILLIAM B. ROBERTSON, JR.

FIELD IDENTIFICATION Not readily confused with any other bird. Medium-sized "hawk" with long tail forked for more than half its length and long pointed wings. Black and white pattern in both sexes: head, neck, underparts, and wing lining white; remainder (except lower back may be white) evenly black. Young recently out of nest have tail shorter and narrowly notched, black areas dullish, and white areas more or less buffy (this most pronounced on head and foreparts). Young in 1st fall still recognizable as such by shorter tails and less agile flight.

Highly gregarious in all seasons. Not especially vocal, except when disturbed; seldom heard before it is seen. Largely aerial; seldom seen perched, except in rainy weather or near nest. Form and flight somewhat suggest a giant black-and-white Barn Swallow, but it is a far more versatile aerialist. Frequently soars high, hovers, engages in intricate solo and communal acrobatics, and quarters both open fields and forest fringes in slow hunting flight.

Only remotely similar species in our area would be an "immature" Magnificent Frigatebird. Confusion might be possible at a great distance, but frigatebird has twice as much wingspread, black underwing, and is primarily coastal and pelagic.

WILLIAM B. ROBERTSON, JR.

VOICE Calls of ♂ and ♀ sound alike to the human ear, but N. Snyder (1974) reported that frequency of the various ♂ calls av. about .5 kHz lower than the ♀ in the pairs he recorded.

Usual call a shrill, high-pitched whistle or squeal, 3 syllables (A. Howell 1932). Has been likened to calls of Spotted Sandpiper, Crested Flycatcher (I. Sutton 1955), Broad-winged Hawk (May 1935), and Osprey (A. Howell). Variously rendered *peet-peet-peet* (D. J. Nicholson), *kii-ki-ki* (E. G. Holt and G. Sutton 1926), *we-we-we* (Bent

111

1937), *wheet-wheet-wheet* (I. Sutton 1955), and *klee-klee-klee* (N. Snyder 1974). Loudness varies; sometimes rather feeble but of piercing quality audible at considerable distance. Varies 1–4 (usually 3) syllables; occasionally given as widely spaced single syllables (see below) rising in pitch and of thinner, more nasal, quality (the Robertsons).

Above apparently functions as an alarm call and as a contact call between individuals. In s. Fla., uttered by a group of 3 that probably were migrating (Christy 1928), by birds hovering over 2 that had been shot (in Bent 1937), by birds at nest when intruders approached, by adults with food for young when arriving and departing nest, to large young on adults' first morning flight over nest (Robertsons), and by pairs in pursuit-flight, believed to be part of display (D. J. Nicholson).

There is an *eeep* call, spectrographically similar to a single *klee* (mentioned above), repeated an indefinite number of times; uttered when food is passed between adults, also at changeover at nest.

A call that sounds disyllabic *gee-whip*, accented on 2d, may be repeated 5–8 times (the Robertsons). Evidently this is the *kees-a-wee* call of N. Snyder (1974); it appears to be built of 2 rising-falling notes, and emphasis changes from 1 to the next. Apparently, it is given only in presence of other adults (the Robertsons). Snyder reported it as used by either sex at approach of mate, by ♀ after copulation, and occasionally during diving-swoop interactions. A phonograph recording of it is captioned "adult at nest."

Soft twittering notes have been mentioned by authors but inadequately described; possibly they represent another call.

As is usual in raptors, there is no alarm call from the nest when a predator approaches; the bird flies off silently, then begins calling (N. Snyder 1974).

Nestlings Cheeping cries, uttered more or less continuously during daylight hours. At 1 week they cheeped when Great-crested Flycatchers called *weep*, but by 2 weeks they no longer responded. They reacted at first when large birds passed overhead, but—unless responding to flying kites—they ceased at about 3 weeks. Adults respond to chicks' food calls only when the former have food (Wright et al. 1970). At 5 weeks, young distinguished between kites carrying food or having none and usually called only to the former. Most data from N. Snyder (1974), which see for sonagrams of the various calls.   WILLIAM B. ROBERTSON, JR.

HABITAT Of the species. Diverse vegetation types, but primarily a forest-edge bird. Requires trees—usually tall ones—for nesting and relatively clear areas for hunting. These requirements are satisfied in a variety of habitats: open forests, patches of dense forest in open country, large areas of dense forest with openings. Seldom found within closed forest. It feeds mainly above the forest crown, along such natural edges as shores of streams and lakes, and around clearings.

E. f. forficatus In s. and cent. Fla. inhabits most sizable wilderness areas regardless of vegetation. Habitats include: tropical and s. temperate hardwood forest, pine woods, cypress, and mangrove swamps. Largely absent from the Everglades (few suitable nest sites?), but commonly hunts over marshes and wet prairies adjoining or interspersed in forested country, and may nest in tree-islands within wide expanses of marsh. Typical nest sites: in interior s. and cent. Fla.—in pine or cypress near or just within edge of dense cypress swamp (D. J. Nicholson), also in pines well within extensive pine forest; along coast of sw. Fla.—in mangroves usually near a stream or tidal channel. Often hunts below treetop level in open pine or cypress forests.

Elsewhere in s. and se. U.S., now restricted to less disturbed areas of lowland forest, mostly near larger rivers. These include cypress swamps and floodplain forests of sweet gum, magnolia, oak, ash, elm, and other hardwoods, and some pine. In some areas hunts (or formerly did) over rice plantations (Wayne 1910), hayfields (Murphey 1937), and other open country near edge of swamp forests.

In most of former range in cent. U.S., from cent. Tex. (G. Simmons 1925) and coastal prairies of sw. La. (McIlhenny 1943) to Ill. (Ridgway 1873), s. Wis., Iowa (J. A. Allen 1868), and Nebr. (Aughey 1878), nested in riparian timber belts and prairie groves, and fed over adjacent prairies. In n. Minn., also inhabited North Woods section (T. Roberts 1932). Here mainly in deciduous forests of white birch, poplar, sugar maple, also tamarack swamps; sometimes nested in deep woods well away from lakes (P. Hatch 1892, J. Preston 1886).

E. f. yetapa In humid lowlands, chiefly forest borders. Absent from Brit. Honduras pine forest (S. M. Russell). In more arid lowlands, as ne. Venezuela (Friedmann and Smith 1950), restricted to belts of forest along streams. In Colombia ranges from tropical forests and savannas near sea level to the Paramo Zone, but apparently most common in Subtropical Zone oak forests (F. C. Lehmann V). Usually nests near streams in primary forest. Where forest disturbed by man in Costa Rica (Ridgway 1905, Skutch 1965) and e. Nicaragua (Huber 1932), found nesting near edges and in isolated large trees left standing in pastures and fields.

Ranges into highlands of s. Mexico–Cent. Am. to elevations of 5,000–6,000 ft. Has nested at 5,400 ft. on Caribbean slope of Costa Rica (Skutch 1965). At higher elevations in Chiapas, Mexico, found in remnant cloud forest of sweet gum with understory of tree ferns and palms (L. I. Davis 1954), also in pine-oak forest (Amadon and Eckelberry 1955). On Azuero Pen. of w. Panama, carried nesting material from grassland with patches of cloud forest at about 3,000 ft. to tropical forest in river valley below (Aldrich and Bole 1937). In Suriname, in all kinds of forest, seldom seen in open country (Haverschmidt 1962). In n. S. Am., occurs from sea level to at least 10,000 ft. in Colombia (Chapman 1917) and to at least 3,500 m. in Venezuela (Swann 1921).

WILLIAM B. ROBERTSON, JR.

DISTRIBUTION   (See maps for our area.) The known breeding range of this kite embraced diverse forest and forest-edge habitats in continental areas of the New World from about lat. 48° N in nw. Minn. to about 30° S in se. Brazil. The principal environmental factor that limits distribution seems to be aridity. Range apparently was limited by extensive dry plains to the w. in cent. N. Am. and to the s. in s. S. Am., and the species is absent or almost so from more arid regions of the Neotropics, such as the Yucatan Pen. (Paynter 1955).

Many published accounts and maps of the distribution (including some of recent date) seem to err in various particulars (see below). Apparently, no accurate comprehensive map of present and former range has been published. Comments below address questions of distribution in various areas.

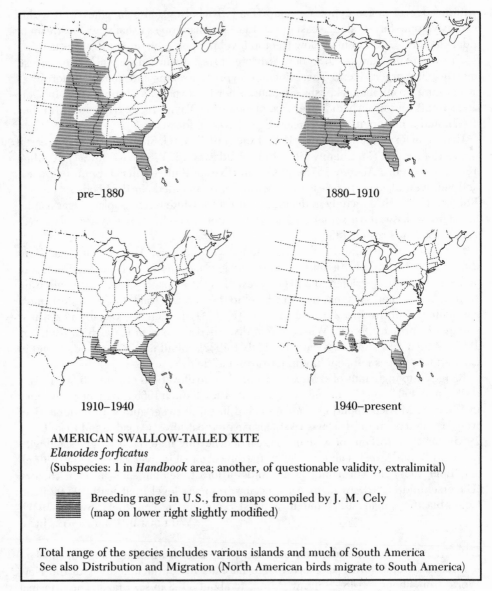

pre–1880   1880–1910

1910–1940   1940–present

AMERICAN SWALLOW-TAILED KITE
Elanoides forficatus
(Subspecies: 1 in *Handbook* area; another, of questionable validity, extralimital)

Breeding range in U.S., from maps compiled by J. M. Cely
(map on lower right slightly modified)

Total range of the species includes various islands and much of South America
See also Distribution and Migration (North American birds migrate to South America)

U.S.: The original breeding range probably included parts of 21 states—N.C., S.C., Ga., Fla., Ala., Miss., La., Tex., Okla., Ark., *Tenn.*, Ky., Mo., Kans., *Nebr.*, Iowa, Ill., *Ind.*, *Ohio*, Wis., and Minn.—but those in italics may not indicate definite observations of nesting. In addition, the species has been reported from all the remaining states e. of the Mississippi R. except Me. and W. Va.; from N.D., S.D., Colo., N.Mex., and Ariz. w. of the breeding range; and from the Canadian provinces of Sask., Man., Ont., and N.S. Alleged occurrence in several of these areas rests on single sightings or on old and somewhat uncertain reports. Except in cent. and s. Fla., the

114

breeding range apparently had a more or less dendritic pattern associated with riparian forest belts. Along the Atlantic and Gulf coasts it follwed river swamps inland as far as the fall line (w. to the Balcones Escarpment in Tex.—Oberholser and Kincaid 1974), and throughout its extensive Mississippi Valley range it seems to have inhabited mainly bottomland timber bordering rivers and lakes.

The species quickly disappeared from much of its U.S. range as the country was settled (reviewed by Cely, in Forsythe and Ezell 1979). Dates of reported decline in states where it was extirpated as a breeder were: OHIO gone from the ne. by 1838 (Kirtland 1883), from the entire state before 1860 (L. E. Hicks 1935); s. WIS., N. ILL., and IND. scarce by the late 1840s (E. W. Nelson 1876, Kumlien and Hollister 1903); s. ILL. and MO. persisted locally in fair numbers into the 1880s, then declined rapidly (Ridgway 1889, Widmann 1907); IOWA and MINN. fairly common to 1880, rare after 1900 (T. Roberts 1932, Dumont 1934), probably last nested in Minn. in 1907 (J. C. Green and Janssen 1975); KANS. largely absent as a breeder by the mid-1880s (Goss 1891), last known specimen 1914 (Johnston 1960); OKLA. probable last nesting 1902, last record 1910 (G. Sutton 1967); TEX. last reported nesting, Harris Co., 1911–1914 (Oberholser and Kincaid 1974). Marked reduction of breeding range also occurred in s. states, where remnants persisted in the larger coastal swamps: SW. LA. common when heavy settlement began in the 1880s, gone by shortly after 1900 (McIlhenny 1943); s. and NE. LA. fairly numerous in some areas to the early 1900s (Beyer et al. 1908), considered very rare throughout La. by the 1930s (oberholser 1938); ALA. common in river swamps of the upper coastal plain in 1858 (Gosse 1859), only a rare straggler there after about 1880 (Golsan 1939); upper Savannah R. valley, GA.–S.C. common in the 1890s, becoming rare by the early 1900s, only occasional after 1915 (Murphey 1937); N. FLA. population reduced to scattered pairs (Baynard 1914). At its nadir around 1940, this kite, while still numerous at that time in the s. half of peninsular Fla., was reduced elsewhere to small isolated populations in a few coastal swamp forests as Santee R. delta and environs, S.C.; Okefenokee Swamp, Ga.; along Apalachicola, Aucilla, and other rivers, n. Fla.; upper Mobile Delta, Ala.; Pearl R. swamp, Miss.–La.; and Atchafalaya Basin, La. (Cely, in Forsythe and Ezell 1979).

The species thus lost most of its U.S. breeding range in a period of little more than 50 years. Direct human persecution of a conspicuous, notoriously unwary bird whose original numbers in many areas may have been relatively small seems the most likely cause of the rapid decline. Authors have suggested lumbering and drainage as possible contributing factors, and Cely (in Forsythe and Ezell) correlated regional dates of disappearance with increase in the extent of improved farmland.

Reports (principally from *Aud. Field Notes/Am. Birds*) suggest that a modest recovery, first evident in the area from La. to n. Fla. (e.g., about 100, Choctaw Bluff, s. Ala., Apr. 1960–Imhof 1962), began in the 1950s. It appeared initially that greater effort by observers might account for the apparent change, but continuation of the trend leaves little doubt that a real increase has occurred. Reported observations outside known breeding range av. about 4/yr. from a total of 10 states in the 1960s; about 9/yr. from 21 states plus Ont. in the 1970s; and about 15/yr. also from 21 states and Ont. in the 1980s to date. Rapp (1944) listed a total of 33 occurrences in the ne. states (N.J., Pa., N.Y., and New Eng.) from earliest records through the early 1940s; observations in the

115

decade 1974–1983 equaled that number. Reports outside s. Fla. of aggregations larger than family groups (5 or more individuals) also appear to have increased. In 1963–1972, 9 such groups with av. size of 7 were reported from n. Fla., Ala., Miss., and La.; in 1973–1982, there were 21 groups with an av. size of 21 from S.C., n. Fla., Ala., Miss., La., and Tex. Notable among these reports were unprecedented numbers of spring migrants in coastal Texas in 1981 (1981 *Am. Birds* **35** 841) and assemblies of up to 100 individuals (far exceeding the known local breeding population) in S.C. in July 1982 (1983 *Am. Birds* **37** 168). Although no major extension of breeding range has occurred, it seems possible that the U.S. population of this kite may be entering a phase of accelerating increase similar to those of the Black-shouldered and Mississippi Kites in recent decades. Now increasing as a nester in n. suburban Fla. Keys.

An attempt to reestablish the species in former breeding range in Kans. by cross-fostering eggs and nestlings from Fla. in nests of Mississippi Kites was begun in 1982 (J. W. Parker, F. Williams).

MEXICO   With few exceptions, published maps and descriptions of the distribution show the breeding range as a continuous belt along the Gulf coast from the U.S. through e. Mexico. In fact, there are few records from e. Mexico, mostly at dates when spring migrants bound for the U.S. might be expected. On present data, a hiatus of at least 1,500 km. exists between nesting records in s.-cent. Tex. (Oberholser and Kincaid 1974) and in s. Mexico, where the species is fairly common in Chiapas (M. Alvarez del Toro). It also is said to breed in Campeche and Quintana Roo, but the basis for these assertions is not entirely clear (see Paynter 1955). The extreme scarcity or absence of this kite as a breeder in much of humid se. Mexico—for example, in such a relatively well studied area as the Sierra de Tuxtla, s. Veracruz (A. Wetmore 1943, Anderle 1967, others)—is not readily explained.

There remains an enigmatic record of possible nesting in n. Mexico based on a specimen in the Thayer coll. (#9708 = MCZ 309,708), a ♀, Apr. 8, 1908, Saltillo, coll. by James E. Johnson; specimen tag marked "parent of a set of eggs in my collection." The eggs are no longer in the collection, but Thayer's catalog entry mentions a set of 3 collected by Johnson, Apr. 6, 1908, "100 miles north of Saltillo, Mexico" (D. O. Hill). There is no clue to Johnson's identity, and discrepancies of date and locality may be transcribing errors, as it was Thayer's practice to replace collectors' labels with his own (R. A. Paynter, Jr.). The specimen is referable to subspecies *forficatus* (D. O. Hill), thus the record, if valid, would extend the subspecies' breeding range about 400 km. to the sw. In bounding the species' breeding range, Bent (1937) cited "Nuevo León (Saltillo)," presumably from the present record. Later authors have mentioned Nuevo León only in discussion of migration through e. Mexico. Saltillo actually is located in the state of Coahuila, but a collecting locality n. of Saltillo could be in Nuevo León.

Various authors have placed a zone of intergradation between the 2 subspecies (*forficatus* and *yetapa*) as crossing s. Mexico or n. Cent. Am. as far s. as Nicaragua (1957 AOU *Check-list*) or even Costa Rica (Bent 1937). It appears likely, however, that present breeding ranges of the 2 subspecies are disjunct and that the division between them coincides with the wide range gap in e. Mexico.

CENT. AM.   *E. f. yetapa* is apparently an uncommon breeder in n. Cent. Am., becoming more numerous s. from s. Costa Rica. In Brit. Honduras, 1 or 2 were seen per 10–14 days in suitable habitat (S. M. Russell). N. of cent. Costa Rica it seems to be largely absent from the more arid Pacific slope (Dickey and van Rossem 1938, Monroe 1968, Land 1970), but published accounts and maps of the overall distribution often do not show this.

S. AM. A useful generalized map of occurrence was given by E. R. Blake (1977), but it may be doubtful that the breeding range includes all of arid ne. Brazil. The species is evidently absent from trans-Andean S. Am. s. of Ecuador. The breeding range reaches n. Argentina and probably extreme se. Brazil (Belton 1973), but it is uncertain whether it extends into Uruguay. Most (at least) of the kites of N. and Cent. Am. migrate into S. Am., and within S. Am., the species withdraws in the local winter from at least its s. range limits and (more irregularly) from seasonally arid sections. Occurrence patterns of these migrant populations in S. Am. are almost entirely unknown.

W. INDIES Some earlier accounts (as Bent 1937) indicated that this kite probably bred in w. Cuba, but the Cuban and Jamaican records apparently pertain to migrants (J. Bond 1971). While some 15 records scarcely justify belief that it "occurs regularly" (1983 AOU Check-list) in migration, observers in the area are few, and migrants in rapid flight at considerable altitude often may pass undetected. Elsewhere in the W. Indies the species is unreported except for a recent sighting on Grand Bahama (1981 Am. Birds 35 866–867). Bent also included the is. of St. Bartholomew in the range, but the basis for this is obscure. On continental is. of the s. Caribbean, the species is known to breed in Trinidad and has been seen at least once on Tobago (ffrench 1973).

Elanoides has no known fossil record (Brodkorb 1964), but remains of *E. forficatus* has been recovered from **archaeological sites** in Ohio (Goslin 1955) and Ill. (Parmalee 1958, 1967) that date back to approximately A.D. 1000. The species presumably is Neotropical in origin, and its much more extensive former range in the Mississippi Valley than along the Atlantic coast suggests that the U.S. was colonized from the sw. via Mexico. WILLIAM B. ROBERTSON, JR.

MIGRATION May travel singly or in pairs; where numerous, more often in groups of 5–30 with flocks up to 500 reported. Flocks are loosely organized; they continually separate into smaller units, then drift together again. T. Davis (1954) mentioned the "purposeful direct flight" of presumed migrants in Guyana; but, as seen in the U.S., movement often seems leisurely and devious. They soar and feed as they go and may linger for a week or more where food is plentiful. However, presumed fall migrants in s. Fla. have also been observed flying s. rapidly at an estimated altitude of about 1,500 ft. (J. C. Ogden). Migrants travel early in both spring and fall and, so far as known, only by day. In Colombia a flock thought to be migrating roosted in late afternoon in large dead trees and moved on the next morning (F. C. Lehmann V).

The subspecies *forficatus* winters in S. Am. at least to Bucay, Ecuador (Chapman 1926), but there are few certain records s. of the breeding range. A nestling banded on Key Largo, Fla., June 17, 1965, was shot in se. Brazil at 24° 02′ N, 50° 27′ W on Dec. 22, 1965 (Mager 1967). The subspecies *yetapa* also is migratory at its range extremities, leaving s. Mexico and Cent. Am. n. of Panama during the N. Hemisphere winter (Skutch 1965, other authors), and n. Argentina (L. Brown and Amadon 1968 1),

117

Paraguay (Bertoni 1924), and s. Brazil (Pelzeln 1871, Belton 1973) during the S. Hemisphere winter. Migrants presumably withdraw toward equatorial S. Am., but no data are available. L. Brown and Amadon suggested that birds appearing in Trinidad in Aug. might be migrants from Argentina, but the species breeds in Trinidad, and migrants from N. Am. also may occur. Formerly said by various authors to be resident in Cent. Am., but most of those reported there in winter probably were early spring migrants. The subspecies appears to be permanently resident in w. and cent. Colombia (R. M. de Schauensee, F. C. Lehmann V), parts of Venezuela (W. H. Phelps), Suriname (Haverschmidt 1977a), doubtless other more humid sections of equatorial and n. S. Am., and possibly in Panama e. of the Panama Canal. It tends to leave more seasonal environments within this region during the drier months, however, and is largely absent from Trinidad, Sept.–Feb. (ffrench 1973), from ne. Venezuela, Oct.–Feb. (Friedmann and Smith 1950, 1955), and from interior localities in coast regions of Guyana, Oct.–Dec. (T. Davis 1954). Except in Apr.–July, most observations s. of the U.S. may refer to either (or both) subspecies.

Spring   South of the U.S., kites return to nesting areas as follows: PANAMA early Jan. (Ridgley 1976); S. COSTA RICA earliest Jan. 8, usually 2d half of Jan. (Skutch 1965); HONDURAS first noted Apr. 14, 1963, Apr. 1, 1964 (Monroe 1968); GUATEMALA earliest Jan. 26 (Land 1963), usually Mar.; BRIT. HONDURAS earliest mid-Feb. (S. Russell 1964); highlands of Chiapas, MEXICO arrives Mar. (Alvarez del Toro 1962). The sequence of dates suggests n. movement through Cent. Am. to s. Mexico. Spring migration in n. S. Am. and in Cent. Am. seems to extend 2–3 months. Flocks of probable migrants were seen: Mazaruni Station, GUYANA Feb. 27 through Mar. (T. Davis 1954); Pearl Is., PANAMA Mar. 13 (A. Wetmore 1947); PANAMA at large, Feb. 10–Mar. 18 (A. Wetmore, notes), late Jan.–Feb. (Ridgley 1976), "I have seen indubitable migrant flocks . . . as late as April 1, 1967" (E. Eisenmann); E. GUATEMALA mid-Mar.–mid-May (Griscom 1932); BRIT. HONDURAS Mar. 24, Cockscomb Mts. (S. M. Russell), and 200 on Apr. 16 at Manatee Lagoon (S. Russell 1964); Campeche, MEXICO Feb. 25 (Traylor 1941).

Otherwise unattributed U.S. records below are from *Aud. Field Notes*, now *Am. Birds*.

Regularly first reaches U.S. in C. Sable area of s. Fla. in last week of Feb. Average of 19 arrival dates 1952–1982 was Feb. 23, earliest Feb. 16 (W. B. Robertson, Jr.). Farther n. in Fla., usually arrives late Feb.–mid-Mar. Earliest reported: near Gainesville (wintering?) Feb. 6 (T. W. Hicks 1955); near Kissimmee about Feb. 10, St. Marks Feb. 21. Usually reaches coastal areas of Ga. and Carolinas latter ½ Mar.–mid-Apr., but recorded in S.C. as early as Mar. 5 (Sprunt, Jr., and Chamberlain 1949) and on outer banks of N.C. as early as Feb. 27. Returned to former nesting range in middle Savannah R. Valley, Ga.–S.C., Apr. 12–20 (Murphey 1937).

Migration tends to be later on w. side of the Gulf of Mexico. This kite reportedly has arrived in Tex. as early as Feb. 1 (in Bent 1937), but most arrival dates are mid-Mar. or after. The period of spring migration is given as: lower Rio Grande Valley—mid-Mar.–Apr. 24 (Griscom and Crosby 1925); Austin area—Mar. 22–early May (G. Simmons 1925); Tex. at large—Mar. 13–May 28 (Oberholser and Kincaid 1974); 58 spring reports from Tex. coastal plain localities 1940–1982 ranged Feb. 25–May 28 (1 in Feb.,

13 Mar., 34 Apr., 10 May); early authors gave the arrival date in La. as end of Mar. or early Apr., but more recently it has reached s. La. as early as Feb. 28 (Lowery 1960); s. Ala.—Mar. 1, and Fla. panhandle—Feb. 21. The tendency for later arrival dates eastward and many direct observations from Audubon's time (see Bent 1937) to the present indicate a w.–e. movement along the n. Gulf coast in spring. At Pensacola, Fla., it is seen most often in Mar. (earliest Mar. 8) moving e. within 30 mi. of the coast (F. M. Weston). This flight apparently continues across the Fla. panhandle with usual mid-Mar. arrivals at Choctawhatchee Bay (Worthington and Todd 1926) and St. Marks ("Williams" 1916, other authors).

North of s. Mexico the spring migration route of U.S. birds is uncertain. Migrants presumably reach Tex. by overland flight along the coast, but these kites evidently are rare in spring in e. Mexico (Loetscher 1955, Thiollay 1979), where known from fewer than 10 reports. No records are known from the Gulf of Mexico (Lowery and Newman 1954), and H. Stevenson (1957) considered the species a circumgulf migrant. Consistently earlier arrival in s. Fla. than in Tex., and dates of spring reports from W. Indies (Barbour 1943, Garrido and Garcia M. 1975, J. Bond 1971) and Fla. Keys suggest possible migration from s. Mexico via w. Cuba into Fla.

Reached former nesting range in Mississippi Valley usually Apr. 25–May, but recorded Mar. 20 in s. Minn. (T. Roberts 1932). First arrival dates (Fish and Wildlife Service files): Mo.—7 of 9 dates were Apr. 10–May 31, plus 2 in Mar.; Iowa—14 of 17 dates, May 1–28, 3 in Mar.; Minn.—13 of 16 dates, Apr. 29–May 29, 2 in Mar., and 1 on Apr. 6.

The species tends to **wander** extensively at the time of spring migration. More distant vagrants include: Grand Bahama I.—Mar. 6, 1981 (1981 *Am. Birds* **35** 866–867), and Bermuda—Mar. 17 (Gross 1958); allegedly England—Apr. 1853 and May 25, 1859 (Bent 1937, Alexander and Fitter 1955), but these were not likely natural occurrences. A partial summary of spring–early summer occurrences (number and inclusive dates) outside present known breeding range in the U.S. shows: MIDDLE ATLANTIC N.C., about 30 reports, Feb. 27–June 5 (includes Pearson et al. 1919, B. R. Chamberlain); Va., 7, Apr. 11–May 6 (includes J. J. Murray); Md., 7, May 3–June 24; Del., 4, May 11–27; N.J., about 20, Apr. 20–June 24 (includes Rapp 1941a); Pa., 4, June 7–15; N.Y., 7, Apr. 16–June 12 (includes A. Cruickshank 1942); NORTH-EAST Conn., 5, May 24–June 16; R.I., 1, May 27; Mass., 8, May 6–June 12 (includes Griscom and Snyder 1955); Vt., 2, Apr. 26 and May 26; N.H., 2, May 5 and May 15–25; Ont., 3, Apr. 14–June 24 (includes Baillie 1953); MIDWEST (since about 1920) Tenn., Apr. 10; Ohio, May 26; Ind. 1, May 31; Ill., 1, May 7–10; Wis., 2, May 15–17 and May 31–early June; Minn., 1, Apr. 29 (Faanes 1981); GREAT PLAINS Colo., 2, Apr. 24 and May 30; inland Tex., 4, Apr. 9–May 15. Also reported in spring from interior uplands of s. states, where it still nests in riverine swamps near the coast: S.C., 2, Mar. 10 (Sprunt, Jr., and Chamberlain 1949) and Apr. 24; Ga., 3, Apr. 22–29; Ala., 3, May 11–20. The number of spring records apparently has increased in recent decades, especially in mid-Atlantic and ne. states (see Rapp 1944). In fact, listings both above and below will be out of date when published.

Gathering in numbers larger than family groups and local movement away from breeding areas occurs regularly in s. Fla. in the 2d half of June. **Postbreeding dispersal** to n., ne., and w. includes both young of the year and adults (data from specimens). Of 62 such reports in U.S. and s. Canada outside the then known breeding range (mostly from Fish and Wild. Service files): 14 in July, 27 Aug., 12 Sept., 6 Oct., and 3 Nov. Records include N.S., Aug. 1905 (Godfrey 1966). Since about 1960, 34 late summer–fall occurrences w. and n. of known breeding range have included reports from 14 states and Ont., July 11–Oct. 12 (4 in July, 21 Aug., 7 Sept., 2 Oct.). The s. subspecies *yetapa* apparently has a similar postbreeding dispersal s. of its breeding range in n. Argentina (Pereyra 1950).

Fall In our area most migrate s., mid-July–early Sept. Apparent migrant groups heading s. or se. are seen annually in s. Fla., especially around the w. and s. shores of L. Okeechobee. The highest reported short-term counts in this area were 237 on July 16–20, 1959 (Horel 1960, F. Ligas, R. Mumford) and a premigration roosting assembly of 684+ at Moore Haven on July 26, 1986 (1986 *Am. Birds* **40** 1195), but flights commonly persist over a period of a month or more (extremes July 7 and Sept. 3) and thus conceivably include much of the breeding population of the se. U.S. Observations from the Fla. Keys (Aug.–early Oct.) and w. Greater Antilles (Aug.–Oct. 27) and reportedly sometimes numerous in w. Cuba, at least formerly (Gundlach 1876, Barbour 1943), suggest that migration continues directly s. across the Caribbean Sea. J. Bond (1971) wrote: "North American individuals migrate to South America via Cuba and Jamaica." It is uncertain to what extent late July–early Oct. observations in Trinidad (Léotaud 1866, Belcher and Smooker 1934) also may relate to migration of N. Am. birds.

Part of the U.S. population apparently also migrates s. via Tex. and Cent. Am. In Tex. in fall it is more frequent inland than along the coast (Oberholser and Kincaid 1974). Reports since about 1960 include 8 from coastal plain localities (Aug. 19–Oct. 11) and 16 from interior Tex. and (1 each) Okla., N. Mex., and Ariz. (Aug. 2–Oct. 12, including R. and J. Johnson 1968). As in spring, few fall reports from e. Mexico. In s. Mexico and Cent. Am., latest reports in various areas were: Chiapas, MEXICO early Sept. (Alvarez del Toro 1952); BRIT. HONDURAS late July (S. Russell 1964); Tikal, GUATEMALA early Aug. (Smithe 1966); s. COSTA RICA 2d half of July–Aug. 15 (Skutch 1965). Flocks of apparent migrants (possibly both subspecies) were reported: HONDURAS 30, Aug. 15 (Monroe 1968); E. NICARAGUA daily in flocks of 15–30, Aug. 5–27 (T. Howell 1957); Costa Rica—most southbound flocks seen in Aug. (Skutch 1965); PANAMA—migrant flocks with Mississippi Kites, Aug. 13–Sept. 6 (Eisenmann 1963a), and late July–early Sept. (Ridgley 1976). Christmas bird count records (*Am. Birds*) indicate that this kite may be resident in e. Panama. In 1974–1983, none occurred on 49 counts from the Atlantic slope of Cent. Am. (Mexico, Brit. Honduras, Costa Rica) or on 14 counts from Trinidad and n. Venezuela, but a total of 69 was reported in late Dec.–early Jan. on 9 of 30 counts in the area of the Panama Canal, with the most regular occurrence (6 of 10 counts) on the Atlantic side.

This species is scarce in the U.S. after Sept. 15, but stragglers have been reported even far n. in Oct. and Nov.: E. N.D. Nov. 14 and Nov. 17 (Talbot 1882); MINN. Duluth, Oct. 19 (Kuyava 1958) and, latest for state, Oct. 25 (T. Roberts 1932); MICH. specimen, Ypsilanti, Oct. 4 (Hankinson 1925); S.C. Charleston Co., Nov. (Sprunt, Jr., and Chamberlain 1949); ALA. Autaugaville, Nov. 24 (Imhof 1962); TEX. Austin, 2

(after N. Snyder 1974)

moving s. ahead of a "norther," Nov. 14 (G. Simmons 1925). Early reports of **wintering** in N.D. evidently were in error (Bent 1937, Friedmann 1950), and some doubt attaches to most alleged Dec. and Jan. occurrences in the U.S. About 10 such reported sightings exist from Ga. (Greene et al. 1945), Fla. (about 5 reports), La. (Oberholser 1938), and Tex. (Fish and Wildl. Serv. files) and Jan. 26, 1921, record from Geneva Co., Ala., is said to be supported by a specimen (Brannon 1921, Imhof 1962).

WILLIAM B. ROBERTSON, JR.

BANDING STATUS   Few banded in Fla.

REPRODUCTION   Age when **first breeds** evidently 1 year; several kites collected in spring in s. Fla. were in breeding condition yet still retained some predefinitive characteristics of feathering.

Pair formation   As seen in s. Fla., may occur in migrating flocks (N. Snyder 1974) but may also occur after birds arrive in nesting areas (W. B. Robertson, Jr.). Two birds often fly together at the time they arrive, but chases and elaborate aerial maneuvers (by 2 birds or pairs within groups) also are seen and are presumably associated with pair-formation.

According to Snyder, in the early stages of residence in Fla., the kites spend much time soaring. In a pair in which the sexes were identified, the ♀ cruised higher than the ♂ for reasons unknown. Commonly, one soars high, then swoops down within a meter or so of another with much vocalizing. At some point, perhaps when a bond has been formed, the ♂ frequently feeds the ♀. In 83 of 84 feedings noted by Kilham (1980), the prey was a chameleon (*Anolis carolinensis*) 6–7 cm. long; once a ♀ appeared to refuse a small frog offered by the ♂. In French Guiana in late Jan., a kite in a special flattened posture attempted to present a stick to another, which remained impassive, then dropped it (McGillivray and Brooks 1979). Such ritualized use of nest-building materials may relate to formation or maintenance of a bond or may perhaps be

121

an attempt by the ♂ to initiate nest construction (compare with Black-shouldered Kite).

Pair-bond form is at least **seasonal monogamy;** whether a bond is maintained in winter is unknown. Some migrants are seen traveling in twos.

Copulation Six instances in s. Fla.: on open perches in dead or living trees or on the nest (Nicholson 1928c). In 1 instance (Stephanic 1953), the ♂ hovered before the ♀ and presented a small snake before copulation; afterwards the pair (joined by another individual) soared, the ♀ carrying the snake. In yet another reported variant (in Bent 1937), the ♀ of a perched pair turned under a small limb, the ♂ meeting her from above. Copulation occurs repeatedly, beginning early in the day and mainly in the nest-building period, but it continued into early incubation at one nest (N. Snyder 1974, with photographs). Snyder's observations of 3 pairs were as follows: The ♀, on an exposed branch, faces the wind; the ♂ flies silently to another perch. Then, as he approaches the ♀, she bends forward, facing away, with wings slightly extended. The ♂ lands directly on her, balancing, with his wings drooped over hers, for as long as 30 sec. Then the ♂ positions his tail under the ♀'s and brings his beak down onto her back. Soon he flies forward over her head calling *klee-klee-klee,* while she remains perched calling *kees-a-we.* Mounting plus copulation in 8 instances lasted 28–37 sec. An unmated ♂ observed in s.-cent. Fla. (Kilham 1980) persistently interfered with copulation attempts and courtship feedings of a mated pair over a 10-day period.

Territory Not sharply defined; pairs with young in s. Fla. ranged over a large area, but took much prey within 200 m. of the nest. In S.C., 3 nesting adults fitted with radios confined about 75% of their activities to nest-centered areas of 330, 1,900, and 1,960 acres (132, 760, and 793 ha.) but made occasional forays to areas up to 15–20 mi. away (Cely and Sorrow 1983). Adults were captured near their nests when they attacked a Great Horned Owl tethered to a perch in front of a mist net (Cely and Sorrow).

The immediate area of the nest is defended vigorously by both ♂ and ♀ against large birds of other species, as Red-shouldered Hawk (I. Sutton, others); Great Egret (Wright et al. 1970); Bald Eagle, Peregrine, Great Horned Owl, Barred Owl, Com. Crow, and raccoon (*Procyon lotor*) (N. Snyder 1974); also humans, including attacks on observation blinds erected near nests (Wright et al. 1970, N. Snyder 1974). In Costa Rica (Skutch 1965), an incubating adult left the nest to chase a soaring Barred Hawk (*Leucopternis princeps*) and White Hawk (*L. albicollis*). The birds call loudly; they repeatedly dive near, but rarely strike, the intruder. As many as 8–10 other adults may join in alarm. There seems to be little territorial defense against other members of the same species, but C. Singletary several times saw both adults at a nest with young swoop on other kites that flew within about 20 m. of the nest tree. N. Snyder (1974) saw kites from elsewhere forage unopposed within 100 m. of an active nest; nesting pairs of kites also joined others nearby in foraging groups. He saw as many as 18 together, hawking dragonflies over a swamp.

The birds often return to nest near the site of the previous year, but apparently there is no record of a nest having been used more than once.

Nest site Near the top of a tall, often slender, tree at the main stem or on a horizontal branch. Reported height of most nests of this species is 18–60 m. (60–200 ft.), but in s. Fla., the kites sometimes nest in tops of much smaller trees, as low as 7.5–9 m. (25–30 ft.). The nest site is usually near the forest edge, in an isolated tree in the open, or in the crown of a tree that projects above the forest canopy. Requirements include a space for unobstructed landing at the nest with perhaps a suitable perch, usually a projecting dead limb, close by. Trees used for nesting: along coast of sw. Fla.—black mangrove (*Avicennia*), buttonwood (*Conocarpus*), Australian pine (*Casuarina*); interior s. and cent. Fla.—usually pine or cypress; in former range in Tex. to Midwest prairie borders—pine, cypress, cottonwood, elm, hackberry, sycamore, basswood, pin oak, hickory, pecan; in former Minn. range—white birch, maple.

As with other kites, this species is a somewhat **social nester.** In sw. Fla., "several pairs will nest within a few hundred yards" (Nicholson 1928), or 2–3 pairs within a ½-mi. radius (F. Phelps 1914). In the summer of 1960, 2 pairs nested on an is. of about 4 acres in Barron R. at Everglades, Collier Co., Fla. (J. Best). In Lee Co., Tex., in 1881–1882, 10 or 12 pairs nested within a radius of several mi. (Nehrling 1905). Nests often are well concealed from the ground, but in sparse pine forest of sw. Fla. the white head and breast of birds sitting on nests was conspicuous from a distance (D. J. Nicholson). Construction begins soon after the kites arrive, at times within less than a week (N. Snyder 1974).

Both sexes **build,** but roles vary. One bird may bring sticks while the other arranges them, or both may carry and place nesting material. They build most actively in early morning, but sometimes also in midday and afternoon (Dilley 1953). At one nest the ♂ brought food to the ♀ during construction, passing it from beak to beak; the ♀ postured when he flew in, just as when he joined her to copulate, and there was considerable calling (N. Snyder 1974). Building may consume weeks (in Bendire 1892) but at times is rapid, as eggs hatched May 12 in s. Fla. in a nest partially built Apr. 4 (I. Sutton 1955). In Tex., a nest begun Apr. 6 was completed 2 weeks later (Nehrling 1905).

Nest construction Some other dates for this or for completed empty nests are as follows: COLOMBIA Dec. (F. C. Lehmann V); SURINAME Mar. 6 (Haverschmidt 1977a); PANAMA Mar. 11–14 (Aldrich and Bole 1937); COSTA RICA at different localities, construction dates varied from Jan. 23 to 1 in period May 6–12 (in the former they were feeding nestlings on Mar. 7). It nests later in Costa Rica than most hawks, the late Jan. to late May–June breeding season apparently being timed to coincide with greatest abundance of insects and nestling birds (Skutch 1950). A nest found Apr. 17, 1965, in the Northern Range, Trinidad, was "built in a large bromeliad near the top of a 100-ft. tree" (ffrench 1973). In s. FLA. 12 nests Mar. 10–May 20 (various authors); CENT. FLA. Apr. 25, May 7 (A. H. Howell); N. FLA. Apr. 14, May 4 (C. J. Pennock); LA. Apr. 25 (Lowery 1960); TEX. May 26 (in Baird et al. 1874); KANS. May 18 (Goss 1891); MINN., Becker Co., began in late May (J. Preston 1886).

Greenery According to Ivan Sutton (1955), occasional twigs and bits of moss were added until about 2 weeks before the young attained flight. N. Snyder (1974) noted, during the 4th and 5th weeks of nest life, renewed activity fetching the lichen *Usnea* (probably *Ramalina usnea*, see B. Moore 1968). The young he observed did not defecate over the nest edge but dribbled, soiling the nest. The *Usnea* formed a compact layer, covering this excrement, and thus was important in nest sanitation. On

123

the other hand, and also in Fla., Wright et al. (1970) observed "normal" raptor defecation—that is, fecal matter ejected clear of the nest.

Nest material   Gathered in flight. It is seized by the feet and broken after a barely perceptible pause. Only small brittle twigs can be taken. In s. Fla., usually cypress, also pond apple (*Annona glabra*) (Dilley 1953), seldom pine (D. J. Nicholson). Skutch (1965) pointed out that gathering material requires great skill. That is, the twig is broken by the momentum of the flying bird; if it grasps one that fails to break, the kite might dislocate a leg or entangle its long wings in branches. A great many twigs are dropped, perhaps because they are too small. Having gotten a suitable one, the kite carries it in the feet, then transfers it to the beak during the approach to the nest. Sometimes this is difficult because the twig must be grasped at its balance point in order to be carried in the weak beak; this involves trial and error, the twig being passed back and forth between feet and beak; details in Skutch (1965). The kites may travel long distances bringing nesting material. In Becker Co., Minn., 400 dead tamarack branches were carried to a nest, 1 per trip, from a swamp a mile distant (J. Preston 1886). In s. Fla., the birds brought Spanish moss (*Tillandsia usneoides*) (a lichen, not a moss) to a nest, and the nearest known supply was about 2 km. away (N. Snyder 1974).

Aside from the lining, most nest material used is dead, but the nest may include small live brances of cypress with green needles. Nests vary in size and construction. Some are compact and symmetrical with a well-cupped central depression; others are little more than rough platforms. In Tex., 1 was 10 cm. thick with top dimensions 60 × 30 cm. and "perfectly flat on top" (Benners 1889); another, 30 cm. thick and 60 cm. in greatest diam. with central depression 7.5 cm. deep (Pope 1913). A nest in n. Fla. was 37.5 cm. in greatest diam. and 30 cm. thick with central depression 15 cm. in diam. and 10 cm. deep (in Bendire 1892). The exterior of the nest often is draped with Spanish moss. The lining is sometimes scanty, sometimes copious. Materials include: Spanish moss, pine needles, fine twigs, strips of inner bark of cottonwood tree (Goss 1891); also a spongy green lichen that is common on cypresses in Fla. (D. J. Nicholson). In La., one contained a snake (*Coluber*) skin (in Bendire 1892). As construction advances, so does the proportion of *Usnea*/"moss" or other lining materials.

In s. and se. U.S. and in parts of Cent. and S. Am., Spanish moss apparently is very important in nesting. Kites are said to have left some sections of s. Fla. after hurricanes destroyed the "moss" (in Bent 1937). Exceptionally, nests are composed entirely of Spanish moss or a matrix of it with a few small twigs (Benners 1889). Elsewhere kites use materials of similar texture. In Minn., the lichen *Usnea* (in Bendire 1892). On the Caribbean slope of Costa Rica, Spanish moss, but at El General (where this "moss" has not been found) a beardlichen, probably *Usnea*, was carried from areas "several miles away" and 1,000 ft. higher (Skutch 1965). In some coastal areas of s. Fla. where Spanish moss is scarce, kites use a similar lichen, *Ramalina usnea*. In our area, however, kites also have nested at localities where no obvious substitute is available. Spanish moss and other lining material often is carried long distances to nests. The erratic distribution of Spanish moss in s. Fla. may be due largely to transport by kites.

Clutch size   Usually 2, occasionally only 1 (complete?), rarely 3 or 4. Forty-three clutches in Fla.—2 (of 1), 35 (2), 6 (3); 34 clutches in Tex.—3 (of 1), 27 (2), 4 (3); 14 clutches in Iowa—13 (of 2), 1 (3) (Peck 1913, 1924). There were 3 young in a nest observed in June, 1935, in Santee Swamp, S.C. (Sprunt, Jr., and Chamberlain 1949). Clutches of 4 reported in La. (below) and Minn. (T. Roberts 1932). Audubon (in A. K. Fisher 1893) is said to have seen a nest with 4 young at the falls of the Ohio R. in 1820. Reports of clutches of 6 (Singley 1886b, Goss 1886, P. Hatch 1892) are surely erroneous.

Completed clutches Dates of those considered "fresh" or "unincubated" by collector: s. Fla.—5 clutches Mar. 14–Apr. 16 (various authors); n. Fla.—Apr. 11 (in Bendire 1892); Tex.—9 clutches Apr. 16–May 19 (various authors). Dates for viable eggs in nests: Tex. to Fla.—81 records Mar. 10–May 18 (but a set of 4, incubated a week, collected June 16, 1889, at Milton I. in L. Pontchartrain, La.—Bendire); 41 (of the 81) records Apr. 7–26 (Bent 1937). In Iowa, in Black Hawk Co.—May 22–June 17 (various authors); Minn.—May 15–June 16 (T. Roberts 1932).

Replacement clutches No data.

One **egg** each from 20 clutches (Fla. 17, Tex. 2, Minn. 1) **size** length 47.54 ± 2.37 mm., breadth 37.53 ± 1.56, radii of curvature of ends 15.73 ± 1.23 and 11.26 ± 1.04; **shape** between elliptical and short subelliptical, elongation 1.26 ± 0.048, bicone −0.085, and asymmetry +0.151 (F. W. Preston). An egg of E. f. yetapa, ready to be laid when taken from a collected ♀, meas. 46 × 37 mm., wt. 35.3 gm. (Van Tyne 1935). The shell is smooth, not glossy. Ground **color** white or creamy with dark brown to reddish brown markings—their extent highly variable; most eggs are heavily and irregularly blotched and spotted, or markings may be concentrated around the larger end; some are evenly spotted or sparingly marked with fine dots.

Rate of laying apparently unknown, but eggs in a clutch sometimes differ in extent of incubation, and sometimes the chicks differ in size—indicating that incubation may begin with first egg.

Incubation Shared by the sexes, but predominantly by the ♀. At 3 nests studied by N. Snyder (1974) incubation stints of ♀♀ av. 151 min., those of ♂♂ 98 min. Incubating ♂♂ have been collected from nests in Tex. (Singley 1887b) and sw. Fla. (A. H. Hardisty). In the latter case the ♀ also was collected 20 min. later as she came and settled on the eggs. At nest relief (changeover), the incoming bird (either sex) often brings greenery; the departing bird performs an AERIAL-SHAKE—dives toward the ground for a few meters with wings held in close, shaking its feathers, then extends its wings and soars onward (Snyder). Said (in Bendire 1892) to alight by hovering over the nest and lowering gradually and to leave by rising straight up "as if it were pushed up by a spring." In sw. Fla., D. J. Nicholson observed an adult fly to a nest and its mate fly away, the change of incubating birds being accomplished so quickly as to give the impression of a single individual in uninterrupted flight through the cypress swamp. At 2 s. Fla. nests in 1969, ♂♂ fed incubating ♀♀ about once per 2.5 hrs., but feedings were much less frequent at a 1972 nest (2 per 85.3 hrs.) when food was scarce due to drought; ♀♀ were not seen to feed incubating ♂♂ (N. Snyder 1974).

Incubation period Surmised to be about 4 weeks (in Bendire 1892), or possibly 21–24 days (in Bent 1937), "approximately 28 days" (N. Snyder 1974). In sw. Fla., 2 eggs hatched within 24 hrs. (I. Sutton 1955); at another s. Fla. nest, 1 egg hatched May 15, the other May 17 (C. Singletary). A ♀ was seen apparently eating eggshell fragments and other waste (Snyder).

Nestling period Data for s. Fla. are summarized here mainly from I. Sutton (1955), M. Wright et al. (1970), and N. Snyder (1974). At first, the ♀ remains more or less continuously, brooding, and feeding the young with prey brought by the ♂. During the first week the ♂ occasionally brood the young, but later his role consists of fetching food. Young are brood at night for about 3 weeks, only occasionally thereafter. The young are fed for the first time at 12–24 hrs. posthatching. Prey is dismembered for them by the ♀; she meticulously preens them after feeding them (C. Singletary). After about 3 weeks food is merely left at the nest or offered whole by either parent. Apparently the most available prey is fed with little change in fare as the young grow. The role of the sexes and feeding rate evidently varies, perhaps in part according to number of young. At a nest with 2 young (but only 1 in last 2 weeks) watched by I. Sutton, all feeding was by one parent, individually recognizable and presumably the ♀. For the 1st 3 weeks the presumed ♂ brought most of the food; later his mate did nearly all hunting and feeding. The presumed ♂ once landed at a perch near the nest and gave food to his mate, who came to the nest and fed the young. The av. feeding rates at s. Fla. nests watched at intervals through the entire nestling period were: 1.25 trips/hr. in 38 hrs. observation (I. Sutton); 1 trip/hr. in 23 hrs. at a nest with 1 young, and 2.24 trips/hr. in 34 hrs. at a nest with 2 young (Snyder); and 1.6 trips/hr. in 30 hrs. at a nest that had 1 young after the first week (C. Singletary).

At another s. Fla. nest, studied by M. and W. Robertson, both adults fed 2 young in the last week of nest life at an av. rate (observation for 21 hrs.) of 9.4 trips/hr. At times feeding was very rapid; one adult made 7 trips with food to the nest in a 14-min. period. (M. Wright et al. [1970] also observed bouts of rapid feeding of an older nestling: 12 trips with food in 23 min. at 36 days, and 27 trips in 3 hrs. 22 min. at 40 days.) Adults sometimes brought 2 smaller food items (insects, frogs) per trip, one in the beak, one in talons. The first food was brought to the nest at 0656 hrs., 0702 hrs., and 0652 hrs. (3 consecutive days). (Adults at a nest with 1 young aged 17–39 days [Wright et al. 1970] began feeding much later, 0819 to 0935 hrs. [av. 0852 hrs., n=8].) Latest food delivery was at 1820 hrs. Adults invariably landed at the nest in delivering food. Prey was delivered dead. Larger snakes were killed in the air by the adult biting the head. No more than 2 adults definitely were known to have taken care of young. The dominant nestling several times gave food to its nestmate.

Snyder's experience was much the same as the Robertsons'—that is, both sexes brought prey and fed the young. As noted earlier, Sutton once saw the ♂ pass food to the ♀ away from the nest; then she brought it to the young. Other observers have not seen this, although it may have occurred.

Various s. Fla. studies noted that mosquitoes were a constant irritant to preflight young when the air was calm; Snyder suggested that nesting in crowns of trees may, in part, be an adaptation affording some protection from these insects. However, the exposure of nests apparently also contributes to losses of eggs and young during storms (authors), a major suspected cause of nestling mortality.

At age 20 days the young called as parent approached with food; they preened at 24 days; at 26 days they stretched flat on the nest with neck extended when alarmed. In S.C., adults of 2 pairs that had large young regularly roosted 1–2 mi. away from their nest site (Cely and Sorrow 1983).

Age at initial flight In 1 instance, 35–39 days (I. Sutton 1955). It was estimated as 37–42 days by M. Wright et al. (1970). At 1 nest it was between 26 and 39 days, and at another it was 39 for 1 young and 41 for the other (N. Snyder 1974).

126

After first flight   Both parents feed young—back at the nest or perched in trees nearby—at same rate as before (the Robertsons). Young did not return to the nest the first night. First flights were mostly wild flapping, and often the young landed in places difficult for adults to approach with food. Four days later the young still were near the nest and still being fed. Short flights, within 50 m. of the nest, became more frequent. The young became much steadier on the wing—less flapping, brief soaring, using the tail to bank—but landings still were clumsy. They attempted to catch insects while flying.

Family groups   May stay together for most of the summer. One flying young, observed for 2 weeks, was fed by both parents at perches within 200 m. of the nest (M. Wright et al. 1970). In s. Fla., an adult was seen feeding a young out of the nest as late as Aug. 3 (W. G. Atwater). Feeding of flying young by adults has also been observed for *E. f. yetapa* in Colombia (F. C. Lehmann V).   WILLIAM B. ROBERTSON, JR.

SURVIVAL   No useful information.

HABITS   Data mostly from our area. This kite is **gregarious** at all times. Most often it is seen in groups of 4–20, but larger aggregations are not infrequent on migration or even during the nesting season at favorable feeding places. On May 22, 1943, a flock of 250–300 was seen in Collier Co., Fla. (Woodmansee 1944). In late July 1986, nearly 700 were seen at a premigration assembly area sw. of L. Okeechobee, as noted above. Flocks of up to 500 have been reported in Colombia (F. C. Lehmann V). There is little apparent organization in the flocks, but mated pairs and family groups may tend to keep together. There is, however, concerted flock action in harassing such potential predators as Bald Eagle, Great Horned Owl, raccoons, and humans (N. Snyder 1974).

Daily activity   Begins rather late and ends rather early; in cloudy weather they may hunt all through the day. The usual pattern in middle Savannah R. valley of Ga.–S.C.: they appeared at feeding areas about 0700 hrs.; they roosted until the dew dried and the insects became active about 0800 hrs.; they foraged continually until early afternoon; they soared in flocks for about an hour; and they then returned to the forest along the river (Murphey 1937). In s. Fla., a nesting pair was active as early as 0624 hrs. and as late as 1860 hrs. (the Robertsons). Birds watched in Suriname, however, seldom left their roost before 0800 hrs., even later on dark or rainy days (Haverschmidt 1977a).

Communal night-roosting   Occurs at times even during nesting (Wright et al. 1970, N. Snyder 1974) and seems to be an important element in the species's social behavior. In Suriname, a group of up to 9 birds used the same roost over a period of about 18 months (Haverschmidt 1977a). Most roost in conspicuous dead trees. Haverschmidt once saw kites sunning at a roost in early morning—wings out from the body, their tips vertically downward, and tail fully spread—apparently the only report of this behavior.

Their graceful, somewhat swallowlike, **flight** has drawn highly poetic descriptions from many authors. See especially that of Coues (1874, quoted in Bent 1937). It is characterized by buoyancy and great maneuverability, assisted by movements of the deeply forked tail. Seldom is it direct or sustained at high speed. Facing a strong wind

127

birds can hang motionless in midair for many minutes. Their **hunting** and feeding are almost completely aerial, with several distinct types of hunting flight.

Sometimes they quarter open fields in harrier fashion, taking prey on or near the ground. One, when hunting grasshoppers, "went over the ground like a well-trained pointer" (Baird et al. 1874). The kite is said also to alight and walk in pursuit of insects (Forbush 1927), but this must be rare. In Suriname, Haverschmidt (1962) never saw it on or even close to the ground. In s. Fla., kites several times have been seen to alight briefly on the ground, but they did not walk. Commonly they maneuver among treetops or low shrubs and along forest edges, seizing prey from foliage, exposed outer branches, and tree trunks. For an excellent description of this in Costa Rica, see Skutch (1965). In the above circumstances, flight often is slow, near stalling, with intricate twists and turns and sudden bursts of speed; it is rather labored; they flap and sail, with rapid, deep wingbeats; sometimes the kite hovers briefly to take prey or to inspect areas more closely. It hovers on rapidly beating wings close to nests of small birds to take nestlings (Skutch 1945a, 1965). Less frequently, it hunts while soaring, gliding down or diving at extreme speed to trees or near ground. Having taken its prey at bottom of the descent, it rises lightly to regain a soaring posture. Sometimes it pursues elusive prey, such as dragonflies, to a great height (in Bent 1937). Other kites often unsuccessfully pursue one that has taken prey (Skutch 1965). In Fla. kites congregate at wildfires to catch insects driven out by flames (Baynard 1914). In se. Brazil they forage in mixed groups of raptors; for example, some 75 with equal number of Plumbeous Kites, for flying grasshoppers, to a height nearly beyond human vision (C. M. White).

Flight speed Of foraging birds, timed roughly by auto on several occasions at about 40 kph. (N. Snyder 1974).

Individuals and groups frequently soar to 1,000 ft. or more. In **soaring** they associate at times with other large birds of similar flight habit, particularly the Mississippi Kite (in S.C., n. Fla., La.; formerly in Kans., Ill.); also the Plumbeous Kite (Friedmann and Smith 1950), and—ins. Fla.—White Pelican, Magnificent Frigatebird, Wood Ibis, and Turkey and Black Vultures. Presumed migrants in Cent. Am. have associated with flocks of Plumbeous Kites, probably Mississippi Kites, Broad-winged Hawks, and Swainson's Hawks (E. Eisenmann). Various forms of aerial "play" have been observed. Individuals soar, trailing streamers of Spanish moss. Pairs and small groups engage in rapid chases high in the air or darting among trees near ground. Repeated headlong diving from 200 to 300 ft. (60–90 m.) to treetops and midair somersaulting have been reported (Wayne 1910, A. Wright and Harper 1913, F. Phelps 1914). Sometimes they harry other birds, on occasions not involving defense of their own nests. Examples: in s. Fla.—Turkey Vulture (W. B. Robertson, Jr.), Brown Pelican and Barred Owl (E. G. Holt and G. Sutton 1926); Tex.—Crested Caracara ("McL." 1887); Chiapas, Mexico— Turkey Vulture (Amadon and Eckelberry 1955); highlands of Costa Rica—Red-tailed Hawk (Skutch 1965).

Seizes prey With beak or talons, large flying insects commonly with the latter. Such prey as larger snakes usually are carried in talons, smaller prey in either beak or talons. Adults feed mainly in flight from prey held in the talons. A foot is thrust forward and the head bent down to take either a bite or, if small, the entire prey. From this habit feathers of the underparts often are soiled and bloody or (Murphey 1937) stained brown from body fluids of grasshoppers. In Costa Rica this kite has been seen several times to carry away nests of small birds containing nestlings; a nest is held in the talons, the nestlings are extracted, and the nest is dropped; full details in Skutch (1965).

The Swallow-tailed Kite is apparently recognized **as an enemy** by small birds and is often pursued by more aggressive species: in s. Fla. by the E. Kingbird, Gray Kingbird, Mockingbird, Com. Grackle, and Red-winged Blackbird. In Costa Rica, Tropical Kingbirds lose no opportunity to harry the kites in spectacular aerial pursuit, often appearing to strike their backs (Skutch 1965). In Panama, a Gray-capped Flycatcher vigorously attacked a hunting kite (A. Wetmore, notes). Despite their agility of flight, the kites do not easily escape pursuit. P. Hatch's (1892) account of a kite having seized and borne away a tormenting blackbird or Purple Martin is unique. On the other hand, a kite was found immobilized by a snake (*Opheodrys aestivus*) that had wrapped itself around one wing (Tomkins 1965).

This kite **drinks** in flight from the surface of running or standing water, including small pools. One flew back and forth over Deep Lake, Collier Co., Fla., for 10 min.; sometimes it bowed its head and drank, sometimes it brushed its belly across the surface or trailed its entire underparts and tail in the water (Nicholson 1928). A description of birds drinking from a pool at Tikal, Guatemala (Smithe 1966), is almost identical.

This kite is usually **tame**—often excessively so—but individuals vary considerably. It may quickly desert a new nest if it is discovered before the eggs are laid (J. Ellis 1918, D. J. Nicholson); however, it nested successfully within 50 ft. of a busy highway in s. Fla. (Robertsons). It reportedly hunted around houses in n. Fla. and over the lawns of hotels and summer cottages in Minn. (in Bendire 1892). In Ga., it hovered above mowing machines in hayfields to catch insects (Murphey 1937). It is inquisitive. Kites in Colombia came readily to imitations of their calls (F. C. Lehmann V). Sometimes a kite quietly follows a man walking in the vicinity of the nest (D. J. Nicholson). In Venezuela, 1 was decoyed within range by repeatedly discharging a shotgun into the air, the bird dropping lower to inspect the spent charge (Friedmann and Smith 1950). Such unwariness doubtless contributed to rapid disappearance from large parts of the former range in U.S., but, with change in attitudes toward hawks, it also offers some hope for recovery. In s. Fla., for example, these kites commonly hunt, and occasionally nest, in suburban areas that most raptors avoid. (Robertson 1978, Lohrer and Lohrer 1984). WILLIAM B. ROBERTSON, JR.

FOOD   Determined by the almost wholly aerial mode of hunting and feeding. In its hunting style it is primarily a searcher that expends more energy in locating prey than in capturing and processing it (N. Snyder and Wiley 1976). The "stomach wall" of this kite was "thicker and more spongy" than that of any other raptor examined (Voous 1969).

Animal   Large to fairly small insects and insect larvae, frogs, lizards, snakes, nestling birds, and rodents (rarely?). Sometimes called "Fish Hawk" from its habit of skimming the surface of ponds and streams, but not known to take fish, though at times it may attempt to do so (L. Brown and Amadon 1968 1), and a captive readily ate several small minnows presented to it (Tomkins 1965).

Vegetable Flesh and seeds of fruits of various trees in the tropics.

E. f. forficatus May (1935) summarized literature reporting contents of 30 stomachs: all contained insects, none birds or mammals; 12 included other vertebrates. Five papers cited in the present account were summarized by Sherrod (1978). Apparently this subspecies was more insectivorous in its former cent. U.S. range, taking more vertebrate prey in the South.

Three stomachs from e. Nebr. contained a total of 129 Rocky Mountain locusts, 83 other insects (Aughey 1878). A ♂ from Cedar Rapids, Iowa, Sept. 20, had 117 insects (Hemiptera, Orthoptera, Coleoptera, Hymenoptera) plus a mass of insect fragments (B. H. Bailey 1918); another Iowa specimen contained 5 frogs (Henning 1896). A vagrant from s. Mich. had remains of crickets and beetles (Hankinson 1925). In Ohio said to have fed commonly on garter snakes (Kirtland 1883). In Richland Co., s. Ill., fed on insects and small snakes (*Opheodrys, Thamnophis*) (in Baird et al. 1874). In Tex. a ♂ had eaten 6 green snakes (largest 22½ in. [57 cm.] long), 1 large larva, and 2 beetles; another had eaten a 19-in. snake, 6 lizards, 4 large beetles, and 2 reptile eggs (in A. K. Fisher 1893); still another (Natl. Mus. Nat. Hist. #455,004) coll. June 2, 1901, contained "24 grasshoppers, 10 water beetles, 5 yellow hornets, 4 large beetles, and a mass of smaller bugs and insects." Also in Tex., especially fond of the larvae of wasps (Dresser 1865) and said to feed upon "field mice" (G. Simmons 1925).

In Fla., takes dragonflies, beetles, grasshoppers, flies, lepidopterans, and wasp nests (it extracts the larvae), but also feeds extensively on small arboreal reptiles and amphibians—particularly anoles (*Anolis carolinensis*), rough green snakes (*Opheodrys aestivus*), both first reported by Bartram (1791), and green tree frogs (*Hyla cinerea* and probably *H. squirella*). Three stomachs from Fla. had wasps, bugs, grasshoppers, beetles, 7 anoles, 3 *Hyla cinerea*, and 9 hairy caterpillars (A. Howell 1932). A ♂ from Florida City, Dade Co., contained 3 anoles, 1 rough green snake, 1 large beetle, and 1 large grasshopper (J. C. Moore). A ♂ from Marco I., Collier Co., has 2 curculionid beetles (*Rhynchoporus cruentatus*) and bones of a small tetrapod (D. R. Paulson).

Food brought to nestlings In s. Fla. types differed considerably between habitats. At 4 nests in mangroves in Collier Co. studied by I Sutton (1955—48 prey items) and by Snyder (1974—3 nests, 30, 83, and 16 items) insects (including wasp nests) 13%, 3%, 6%, and 0; tree frogs (*Hyla*) 33%, 64%, 47%, and 0; lizards (*Anolis*) 38%, 20%, 33%, and 31%; snakes (*Opheodrys*) 0, 0, 0, and 6%; nestling birds 10%, 3%, 8%, and 57%; mammals 2%, 0, 0, and 0; unidentified 4%, 10%, 6%, and 6%. At 3 nests in pine forest in Dade Co. studied by the Robertsons (194 items), Wright et al. (1970) (98 items) and C. Singletary (50 items): insects 43%, 32%, and 58%; tree frogs 25%, 20%, and 10%; lizards 2%, 0, and 6%; snakes 5%, 1%, and 12%; nestling birds 3%, 7%, and 0; mammals 0; unidentified (most items were small, almost certainly insects) 22%, 40%, and 14%. N. Snyder (1974) noted that adults seemed to take more insects than they brought to nests, but elsewhere (above) insects were the food items most commonly fed to nestlings. Of 31 insects identified to Order (Wright et al. 1970), 2 were

Odonata, 3 Lepidoptera, 6 Diptera, 8 Orthoptera, and 12 Coleoptera. Overall, feeding by nesting adults appears highly opportunistic, but Snyder (N. Snyder and Wiley 1976) considered that tree frogs and lizards were the primary diet of nestlings and recorded lengthened intervals between feedings in a year when tree frogs were scarce.

E. f. yetapa In Chiapas, Mexico, feeds mainly upon lizards and small snakes; items identified from stomachs were lizard (*Gerrhonotus*) and snake (*Adelphicus*) (M. Alvarez del Toro). In Guatemala, kites fed on a swarm of bees (Owen 1860), and a ♀ from Petén had eaten beetles and a large lizard (Van Tyne 1935); in s. Costa Rica mainly takes insects caught high in the air, nestling birds, and occasionally lizards, but not observed to feed on snakes (Skutch 1965). S. Am. birds perhaps are largely insectivorous. In Suriname, hemipterans were found in stomachs, but one kite's gizzard was full of flying ants (Haverschmidt 1962); a ♀ from ne. Venezuela contained large beetles (Friedmann and Smith 1950); in Colombia, preyed chiefly on beetles and caterpillars, especially a green scarab beetle that infests new foliage of *Quercus*, and never seen to take snakes (F. C. Lehmann V).

Both subspecies usually were said in the earlier literature not to feed upon birds or mammals, but the **nest-robbing habit** now is well known. Reported victims: in Fla., Mourning Dove (H. Stevenson 1958), probably Mangrove Cuckoo (I. Sutton 1955), "almost surely" a Red-bellied Woodpecker (N. Snyder 1974), Mockingbird (many observations), Loggerhead Shrike (Lohrer and Winegarner 1980), and Eastern Kingbird (Lohrer and Lohrer 1984); in Tex., Mockingbird and Painted Bunting (Pope 1913, G. Simmons 1925); in Costa Rica, Golden-masked Tanager, Clay-colored Robin, and Tropical Kingbird (Skutch 1954, 1965, 1981). Probably they prey upon nestlings of most small and medium-sized species that nest in relatively open situations. Birds brought to nests were often not readily identifiable, because they were very young nestlings as yet unfeathered (N. Snyder 1974) or were plucked (M. Wright et al. 1970). Kites may take 1 nestling and return later for others until the nest is emptied (Skutch 1965, 1981, Lohrer and Lohrer 1984, J. C. Ogden). Or, as observed in s. Costa Rica (Skutch 1965) and at Tikal, Guatemala (W. B. Robertson, Jr.), entire small nests may be seized and carried aloft. Mammals apparently are taken much less frequently, and reported instances perhaps should be considered inconclusive.

Vegetable Known only from the tropics. Guyana—seeds of *Loranthus* and other plants (Chubb 1916). Costa Rica—several were seen feeding on the fruits of a tree (*Matayba oppositifolia*) (Buskirk and Lechner 1978). The birds glided upward into the wind, stalled, plucked the fruits with their talons, and "processed" them in flight, removing and ingesting the beanlike seed and fleshy aril. Colombia—on 2 days in Mar., groups of 3 and 5 kites flew to or into the crown of a rubber tree (*Castilla elastica*), broke off the fruit clusters with their feet while in flight, fed in flight, and dropped the remains (Lemke 1979). Fruit may be consumed more commonly during dry periods when arboreal animals are less available.

Doubtful food items reported include whole eggs of a Gray Catbird (Forbush 1927), a tree snail (*Liguus*) in s. Fla. (C. Phillips 1939), and "rabbits" in S.C. (Giraud 1844).

WILLIAM B. ROBERTSON, JR.

131

Juv.

Def. Basic

Def.
Basic

pellet

BLACK-SHOULDERED KITE

Elanus caeruleus

White-tailed Kite (New World) or sometimes Black-winged Kite (Old World). Small-ish, light-colored hawk; sexes similar in size (♀ av. slightly longer beak) and color (♂ perhaps av. slightly paler dorsally). Length about 12½–15 in. (32–38 cm.), wingspread to about 39 in. (100 cm.), usual wt. about 9¾–11 oz. (275–310 gm.). Wing lining white or nearly so—much lighter than underside of primaries—being plain in Eurasia / Africa and with black spot or patch distally in New World and Australia. The outer primaries are emarginated on inner web and are nearly equal in length (next to outer usually longer), the 3d counting from outer nearly the same length; next to outermost pair of tail feathers longest, with outermost shorter than central pair. Our only diurnal raptor having underside of talons flat or rounded outward (not hollowed). It also has true powder-down patches (as in *Elanoides, Circus,* and *Buteogallus*).

One subspecies in our area and 8 elsewhere (nearly worldwide).

NOTE   For those who would treat the Am. birds as a separate species, earliest valid name is *Falco glaucus* Bartram (1791: 290); in any event, the Am. type locality is about 8 mi. s. of St. Augustine, Fla. (see Harper 1942: 212).

DESCRIPTION   *E. c. majusculus* of N. and Cent. Am.
▶ ♂ ♀ Def. Basic Plumage (entire feathering) ALL YEAR; acquired by prolonged molting in summer–fall or perhaps extending later; primaries renewed from inner to outer. **Beak** black with yellow cere; **iris** scarlet or even toward ruby. **Dorsal surface** of

132

body some variant of medium to dark blue-gray, this paling to white on crown or forehead; much of **head** and all of underparts white, except black encircles the eye narrowly and then widens to a patch anteriorly. **Wing** most of upper surface more or less as dorsum, except smaller coverts from a black patch (it may be blackish gray in some ♂♂); wing lining very light gray, generally with small black patch distally; underside of primaries dark gray, secondaries paler. Legs and **feet** variably yellow, talons black. **Tail** Central pair of feathers variably whitish gray, the others predominantly white tinged gray.

AT HATCHING Covered with short down, variably reported in N. Am—grayish, whitish tinged buff on crown and dorsum, or light tan. In a week another down, which is much longer and medium gray, is well developed. Eyes light brownish at first, beak black, mouth lining pink, legs and feet pale pinkish.

▶ ♂ ♀ Juv. Plumage (entire feathering) well developed by age about 40 days; at age about 100 days, evidently a gradual and prolonged molting (except of wings and tail) into Basic I begins.

Definitive pattern but with various browns and spotting. **Beak** black; cere and edges of gape vivid yellow; **iris** dark brown. **Head** forehead and chin mostly white, remainder mostly buffy tan, grading into dark gray on nape; a dark area around eye. **Dorsum** muted brownish or sepia, most feathers darker subterminally, smaller ones having tawny and others having white distal margins. **Wing** lesser and middle coverts nearly black (brown may be intermixed) and longest ones with whitish ends; greater coverts dark gray with white ends; primary coverts blue-gray with white ends; primaries same, their ends narrowly margined white; secondaries like greater coverts; wing lining white with dark spot distally, the axillars white. **Underparts** vary from largely white to white with much pale to vivid tawny, which, on some individuals, tends to form a band across upper breast. Legs and **feet** orange-yellow, talons black. **Tail** medium gray with fairly distinct darker subterminal band; more forked than in succeeding Plumages. For further details, see Moore and Barr (1941); for an excellent color photograph, see Waian (1976).

▶ ♂ ♀ Basic I Plumage (all feathering except Juv. wing and tail) acquired beginning at age about 3½ months and extending to age 6 months or possibly much longer. Molting begins on head, then mantle; the later renewal of Juv. wings and tail is either a postponement of part of molting out of Juv. or signifies onset of molting into Basic II. The **eyes** are scarlet-orange at about 6 months and vivid scarlet or deeper red some time later. **Head–body** as in later Basics, except acquired perhaps more gradually—a bird in Basic I may appear as Def. Basic but lack Basic wing / tail (Juv. still retained).

Measurement Fourteen "adults" BEAK from cere 18–19 mm., av. 18.7, WING across chord 302–328, av. 314, TAIL 174–186, av. 181.6, and TARSUS 36–39, av. 37.8 (Friedmann 1950).

In Calif., 9 ♂ BEAK from cere av. 18.5 mm., WING across chord 309, TAIL 184, TARSUS 42.5; and 7 ♀ BEAK from cere av. 19.2 mm., WING across chord 307, TAIL 183, and TARSUS 41.3 (Hawbecker 1942).

See also Oberholser and Kincaid (1974) (but sample size and how WING meas. not stated). The following includes some of the birds meas. by Friedmann, and figures given are the mean: BEAK from cere 19 ♂ 19.1 mm., and 15 ♀ 19.5; WING across chord 20 ♂ 316.4, and 15 ♀ 318 (N. Snyder and Wiley 1976).

Weight Presumably Calif. (from specimen labels), 2 ♂ 311 and 322 gm., 5 ♀ 332–375, mean 350 (Dunning 1984); 6 unsexed, livetrapped and released in Calif., Nov. and Jan.: 315–330 gm., av. 322 (P. Bloom). In Surinam, 3 ♂ 250–297, mean 273, and a ♀ 307 (Haverschmidt 1962).

Geographical variation Around the world, principally in presence or extent of black in underwing and in shade of upperparts.

Kites with black "shoulders" have been divided into as many as 5 species, but are reduced here to 2 as proposed by Parkes (1958) and further discussed by Husain (1959); on the other hand, what might be termed the status quo of maintaining 4 species (Americas 1, Australia 2, elsewhere 1) was the alternative of Brown and Amadon (1968 1); yet another is treating all except *scriptus* of Australia collectively as a so-called superspecies. Husain theorized as follows: *Elanus* probably originated somewhere in s. Asia or in Africa. It spread to Australia, where it evolved into present-day *E. scriptus*, which has the most black in underwing. Concurrently, the black in underwing was diminishing in Afro-Asian birds. Much later, the latter stock reached the Americas (*E. "leucurus"* of authors) and again invaded Australia (*E. caeruleus notatus*). The earlier and the later arrivals in Australia overlap in distribution, but they differ morphologically and coexist as separate species. The wing lining is all white in Europe, Africa, and beyond e. into the Philippines; it has a black patch or spot distally in Australia and the Americas. The other species (*scriptus*) in Australia has axillars and stripe within the wing-lining completely black. RALPH S. PALMER

SUBSPECIES **In our area** *majusculus* Bangs and Penard—as described above; N. and Cent. Am.; reportedly somewhat larger and longer-tailed than in S. Am.

Extralimital *leucurus* (Vieillot)—parts of n. and much of s. S. Am.; whether separable from those of N. and Cent. Am. is not satisfactorily resolved; *caeruleus* (Desfontaines)—Iberian Pen., much of Africa, and Madagascar; *vociferus* (Latham)—s. Asian mainland; *sumatranus* Salomonsen—Sumatra and nearby smaller is.; *hypoleucus* Gould—Borneo and Celebes to Philippines; *intermedius* Schlegel—Java primarily; *wahgiensis* Mayr and Gilliard—e. and cent. New Guinea highlands; *notatus* Gould—Australia except interior deserts. RALPH S. PALMER

FIELD IDENTIFICATION **In our area** Recognizable when far away—appears wholly white at a distance.

Distinctive flight as compared with our other raptors, the wings at a slightly upraised angle, their tips downcurved. Brief or extended hovering, the legs often dangling, then a glide; repeated over and over. Has been compared with a harrier (as when gliding), an Am. Kestrel (as when hovering), a Barn Owl (the head is large, the body stocky and pale), but, considering its light coloring and buoyant flight, it is better likened (Bent 1937) to Bonaparte's Gull or a Kittiwake.

When perched, this kite shows its black "shoulders" plainly; the wing tips extend beyond the tail, which is squarish when spread, and this birds has a habit of cocking the tail up and down somewhat after the manner of a Kestrel. Young birds may show more or less brownish and be less adept on the wing (which is somewhat more rounded at first) but, in general, appear so much like older ones that distinguishing them is not easy. Singles, scattered pairs, small loose groups and, at roosts, sizable assemblies (e.g., to 200 in Orange Co., Calif. (P. Bloom)). Sexes apparently not usually distinguishable afield. See Habits, below, for description of pellets. RALPH S. PALMER

VOICE   Usual call a more or less plaintive whistle, reminiscent of the W. Meadowlark or a distant Osprey. A higher-pitched rasping note, as when alarmed. Both have variants.

In Calif., "no apparent sexual difference," and 2 types of calls: 1 low, rounded whistle or chirp, soft or variably accented, to announce presence to mate and under various other circumstances; and 2 *eee-grack* or *whee-grack*, first part high pitched and thin, the last low, guttural, and raspy. Each may be used separately, or one or both in multiples. For example, a series of *eees* (probably by both sexes) as ♂ approaches to copulate; after he mounts, *gracks* and *eees* alternate; a similar change occurs when ♀ receives mouse from ♂ in midair. These data are condensed from F. Watson (1940).

A chittering sound by the ♂ during flight display (the Dixons 1957). A pair in Portugal were described by England (1963), who noted some apparent sex differences; for example, a rapid series of *chuck* notes to call the ♀ off the nest, but also used by the ♂ at nest when he fed her. Near Nairobi, Kenya, at least in certain circumstances, the calls of the sexes differ (van Someren 1956).

Nestlings have a forerunner of the whistle and, in "intimidation" behavior, a harsh scream resembling the rasping call of the Barn Owl, according to Pickwell (1930), who also summarized earlier authors. It is more falconlike than hawklike (the Dixons 1957). It is a "horse dry hiss" (Colar 1978), used as greeting to parent or among the brood.

RALPH S. PALMER

HABITAT   Worldwide—a preference for open, often semiarid, terrain with at least some arborescent growth and ground cover that supports an adequate supply of one or more diurnally active rodent species of a size the birds can manage. Often rolling country where any breeze or wind facilitates soaring. A preference for the vicinity of water may be explained as a preference by rodents and other small animals for nonagricultural grassy and marshy places. Where there are no trees the kites perch on posts, rocks, or the ground.

In Calif., Waian (1976) described the following events. By the mid-1800s, overgrazing by livestock nearly eliminated native perennial grasslands, which were prime vole/kite habitat. This was especially severe in moister areas, which were ideal for the California vole (*Microtus californicus*). Later, fences were erected to keep cattle off croplands, and fence lines provided vestiges of grassland where the kite could hunt. Then wetlands were drained, filled, or dyked, converting much terrain into crop fields. On the other hand, some habitat was added through irrigation projects. The house mouse (*Mus musculus*) had been introduced early to Calif., and it spread throughout all types of grassland areas and thus became an alternative prey of the kite, probably sustaining it when voles were scarce. All these events occurred in a period when kite eggs were sought in excessive numbers by collectors and the birds were reduced severely by shooting. They are easy targets, especially when coming to or leaving their communal roosts.

Well into the present century there was reasonable doubt that the kite could survive in Calif. (or elsewhere in N. Am.). However, the elimination of egg collecting and shooting, and the occurrence of grasslands now dominated by annuals that support voles and mice, favor an increase in kites. Land speculators, who buy up tracts that are kept fallow until sold for development, also favor the kites—temporarily. In opposition there is the enormous human population growth, especially since World War II, which eliminates kite habitat. Again on the favorable side is fire—natural and planned— in the vast areas of chapparral in coastal regions and inland ranges; this fosters a rodent/kite-favorable stage of vegetational succession. At present, legislative protection and a favorable public attitude toward this harmless bird, plus certain land-use patterns, including controlled burning of chaparral communities, augur well for an expanding number of kites. This is, however, the short-term outlook: 20 years hence the kite again may be endangered, its only remaining habitat being parks and military reservations.

Pieces of the above picture, or comparable situations, definitely apply elsewhere throughout the kite's range worldwide. That is, if the bird is not molested by man, it does best in environment that is disturbed or manipulated by human-related activities. The most detailed documentation from an area outside the U.S. is that of Schlatter et al. (1980) for cent. Chile.   RALPH S. PALMER

DSTRIBUTION   This kite is often regarded as very local in its movements. Yet in the ancient past, probably in periods of dry climate, it spread through the vast Indo-Pacific region, invaded Australia, and colonized the Americas. Viewed in this perspective, and considering that it has a high reproductive potential and actually does disperse or wander far to forage, its recent dramatic spread through Cent. Am. is more comprehensible.

In our area   (See map.) Nearly extinct by 1930 or earlier; has since reoccupied former principal range—even exceeded it—and its habit of turning up in distant places is not new. This kite was on the increase when almost all of our other raptors were decreasing due to pesticides. Numbers have declined from a peak in Calif. (see below) and seem to be very unstable in the Pacific Northwest; widely scattered occurrences continue to be reported. Such matters await later evaluation.

Most reports on recent increase come from Wash., Oreg., Calif., Ariz., Tex., and Fla. For many data, considerable analysis, and full documentation, see Pruett-Jones et al. (1980), principally for 1964–1978. The following depends in part on that source and adds some information, but it not exhaustive coverage of all states. The sequence is as in Pruett-Jones et al.

CALIF. apparently never abundant historically (Bent 1937) may be a misstatement; old nesting records extend n. to about Eureka; very scarce by the 1930s or earlier; considerable increase in 1940s (sizable roost, Jan. 1946); rapid increase and spread beginning in about the 1950s—details in Waian and Stendell (1970). Increased to 1,437 birds reported in 1975, but a decrease to 797 in 1978 (Pruett-Jones). OREG. for earlier records, see Laval (1948); an increase in reports began about 1970; first recorded breeding in 1977; winter roost in early 1980 and no reports of summer occurrence that year. WASH. earliest sighting July 1975; first evidence of breeding in 1982.

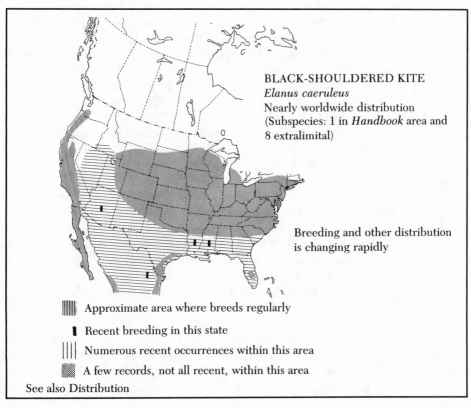

BLACK-SHOULDERED KITE
Elanus caeruleus
Nearly worldwide distribution
(Subspecies: 1 in *Handbook* area and
8 extralimital)

Breeding and other distribution
is changing rapidly

▥ Approximate area where breeds regularly

❚ Recent breeding in this state

▥ Numerous recent occurrences within this area

▦ A few records, not all recent, within this area

See also Distribution

IDAHO earliest unquestioned sighting may date July 31, 1980. NEV. sightings 1971–1975, none reported since. ARIZ. evidently no early records; occurrence reported beginning in 1972, but first documented recrod in 1978; a dozen or more records by the end of 1982; bred in 1983. N. MEX. at least 5 sightings from the 1960s through 1982. TEX. nested principally near coast and in lower Rio Grande valley (apparently earliest recorded breeding was inland in 1890); was extirpated along the coast, but a few remained inland; increase began in 1960s (193 reported in the state in 1978), with breeding again principally in coastal counties, but scattered occurrence of kites elsewhere. Records through 1972 were listed and mapped by Oberholser and Kincaid (1974); see Larson (1980) for 1944–1978 summary. LA. 1 shot in 1890; 3 sightings and a nesting attempt in 1970s; clutch of 4 eggs, May 26, 1983. MISS. Several recent records; nesting in 1983; see Toups et al. (1985) for details. ALA. Occasional in fall. FLA. various early records (e.g., nested Kissimmee R. in 1887); old and recent data were discussed and mapped by Kale (1978); an "immature" bird seen in 1972 suggests nesting; almost all records are for s. half of peninsular Fla. and show no seasonal pattern. Small resident population in s.-cent. Fla. Several pairs bred in Broward Co. in 1986.

Here are further data, mostly recent, for various states, listed more or less from w. to e. WYO. Aug. 20 and later, 1982. S.D. 1979. NEBR. Early 1982. MO. 1976. OKLA. ♀ and her clutch taken May 9, 1860. ARK. 1976 and 1978. MINN 1977. WIS. carefully studied June 6 onward, 1964 (Frances Hamerstrom 1965). MICH. 1978 and 1979 reports (Bent 1937) regarded by D. Wood (1951) as based on inadequte evidence. ILL. reportedly a pair, summer of 1863 or 1864 (Bent 1937). IND. Apr. 18, 1981. MISS. 2 or 3 in 1982; nest with eggs 1983. ALA. 1962 and 1965. GA. 1962. S.C. Audubon's records, other than for breeding, are acceptable; next record is May 27, 1929 (Sprunt, Jr., 1936); 1974 and 1979 sightings. N.Y. young bird, Dutchess Co., late Mar. 1983. MASS. seen on Martha's Vineyard, May 30, 1910 (Fay 1910). Except where otherwise indicated, these data are from *Am. Birds*.

Elsewhere MEXICO this species disappeared from portions of its range; it returned to Baja Calf. (where it had been unrecorded since about 1903), and elsewhere it now occurs generally throughout on suitable terrain (see Reproduction, below, for early winter nesting in Nuevo León).

CENT. AM. records of occurrence begin in the early 1960s (Eisenmann 1971); 1st seen in Panama in 1967; common in parts of that country less than a decade later (Ridgley 1976). Apparently there is no evidence, pro or con, that the birds spread from Tex. or the Mexican gulf coast s.; it was assumed (Eisenmann) that they spread from Calif.; it is obvious that a wide increase occurred rapidly. Although open areas had existed, the removal of forests and attendant changes throughout Cent. Am., which occurred at an accelerated rate after World War II, vastly increased habitat usable by this kite. See Eisenmann's paper for details.

In S. AM. this kite's range is extensive, as mapped by E. R. Blake (1977). Trinidad—occurs (but not reported from nearby Tobago). Bolivia—for 1st records, see Remsen and Ridgley (1980). Brazil—unrecorded before 1960; now common in cleared areas of Rio Grande do Sul; range evidently expanding (Belton 1972 *Am. Birds* **26** 565). Apparently, at least in n. S. Am., there is an expansion of range rather than merely better reporting.

ELSEWHERE This kite nests in much of Africa, excepting barren deserts and continuous forests, including areas bordering w. on the Mediterranean. North of that sea it nests locally in Portugal and Spain. There are scattered occurrences elsewhere in countries n. of the Mediterranean—even some well up into Europe. It is absent from most of the Middle East, then occurs farther e. and throughout the Indian subcontinent and the s. Asian mainland, also in a small portion of the Chinese mainland (n. of Taiwan), and on various is. from Sumatra to the Philippines and s. to include less arid parts of Australia.

Fossil record None; in N. Am., has been found in the La Brea tar pits in Calif. and in a cave deposit in Nuevo León, Mexico; references in Brodkorb (1964).

RALPH S. PALMER

MIGRATION No satisfactory evidence. Slud's (1964) report of migrants in Costa Rica has been questioned by Eisenmann (1971); Short and Crossin's (1967) statement that mainland Mexican birds are migratory lacks solid support. Reportedly migratory in parts of S. Am., but the evidence is not clear. This kite tends to move seasonally, at least in temperate N. Am., and is seen traveling and showing up at new localities in spring and fall. This might be emigration, since we do not know that those engaged in such movements also travel in the opposite direction in the opposite season. In a sense, it appears to be an incipient form of migratory movement as a result of a tendency to wander being more pronounced seasonally.   RALPH S. PALMER

BANDING STATUS   To Aug. 1981, the number of banded (mainly in Calif.) was 458, with 22 recoveries (Clapp et al. 1982). A few have been banded in Tex.

                                                                        RALPH S. PALMER

REPRODUCTION   Calif. data unless otherwise indicated. Age when **first breeds** unreported but probably 1 year for at least some individuals. In Calif. sometimes double brooded (during rodent plagues in S. Africa, many pairs double brooded and a few triple brooded—authors cited in I. Newton (1979).

Annual grass seeds begin to germinate after the 1st major fall rains, but growth is usually slow during the short days of winter. Grasses grow rapidly by late Feb.–early Mar., and vole numbers increase from fall to spring as their forage becomes increasingly available. In line with this, the majority of successful kite nestings in Calif. occur during spring (Waian 1976). Worldwide, in cooler parts of the species's range, it begins nesting in spring. In warmer climates, nesting usually begins at start of the dry season but may occur practically all year.

Unpaired individuals begin **pair-formation** activities by some time in Jan., but they continue to use a communal roost at night until the beginning of nest construction. WINGS-UP display: the ♂ establishes a territory and flies there in the near presence of the ♀ in a peculiar manner, wings in an upward V, rapidly vibrating, while he utters his chittering call continuously. Often he flies to where the ♀ is perched, fetching her a vole or mouse. Or the 2 fly together and the prey is transferred during flight, the ♀ adroitly snatching it by tilting upside-down beneath the ♂ as he hovers and dangles the vole or mouse in his talons. When the 2 birds perch and forage near each other, pair formation is completed. What began as symbolic feeding continues, as a part of the reproductive routine, throughout nest building and often into incubation. That is, the ♀ does not hunt but instead is fed by her mate during this span.

Another activity, which probably signifies that a nesting site has been chosen and that its whereabouts must be advertised, is HIGH-SOARING in which the pair soars high over the area, wings stationary, at times fluttered, one bird (♂?) occasionally diving as though in halfhearted pursuit of the other. As observed in Australia, there is a spectacular undulating flight or SKY-DANCE; the presumed ♂ dives and the ♀ turns over and presents her talons, and occasionally the birds even grapple and whirl some distance downward together (Brown and Amadon 1968 1). This may be seen outside the breeding season.

In S. Africa, ♀♀ joined ♂♂ as mates after moving around between territorial ♂♂ (there always being more resident ♂♂ than ♀♀). Unpaired kites held smaller territories than other residents. Males usually established territories when occupied areas fell vacant, and ♀♀ usually paired when most others were starting to breed. Both sexes abandoned territory when food supply was poor, and more nomads visited the area when feeding/breeding conditions were good. Most kites were resident for periods under 100 days, and ♀♀ spent either most or very little time breeding. The number of birds studied varied 19–35 (mean 26), and the turnover was 13% each half-

139

month. Males, after leaving territory, usually became nomads; ♀ ♀ probably moved to new territories. (From Mendelsohn 1983a.)

Onset of breeding   Indicated by a single kite using the same perch during certain hours day after day; this has been observed as early as Nov. 10 and as late as Mar. 10. Soon a 2d kite appears, and both hunt together. Then the ♂ attempts to copulate and is, at first, repulsed by the ♀. Concurrently, he endeavors to select a nest site and even goes through the actions of building, but this is apparently unacceptable to the ♀, who chooses the actual site (the Dixons 1957).

Near Santa Barbara, Calif., in 1965–1966, several successful nests were started within a mile of the roost that the kites had been using. The ♀ remained at night at the nest site much earlier in the breeding season than the ♂. After incubation had progressed some time or after the eggs hatched, the ♂ remained at the site during the night (Waian and Stendell 1970).

Although the Dixons saw no fighting, F. Watson (1940) reported that the kites are **territorial** and defend against neighboring pairs. The birds stayed on their own territory, even to forage. Both sexes defended it, presumably to guarantee a food supply. Often they nest near one another (Waian 1976), which probably reflects a local abundance of voles or mice. In San Diego Co., 2 pairs were evicted from their nesting territories by neighboring pairs (B. A. Wright 1978).

Again in San Diego Co., in a study of 26 nests the number of eggs was related to the mean number of active vole runways (prey density) in the kites' hunting areas. Further, the number of successful nests and number of young raised was related to the percentage of voles in the kites' diet (2,579 pellets examined). Rainfall flooded one area; this decimated the voles, and, as their numbers decreased, so did the number of kites (B. A. Wright 1978).

Copulation   Occurs at the ♂'s perch, within site of the nest tree, both birds calling continuously. In one pair it was noted over at least 22 days (including 15–20 days before incubation), and F. Watson (1940) referred to it as inefficient and compensated for by frequency.

Nest site   In the crown of a tree, usually 20–50 ft. above ground, extremes being 6 ft. in a bushy tree and 59 ft. in an oak. The grove or tree may be on a slope, on flat terrain, or even in a marsh or swamp. Live oaks commonly are used, but authors list a variety of deciduous species—any suitable tree near a food source (Hawbecker 1942). Unlike many raptors, kites do not build on a firm base such as where limbs fork but instead on slender branches in the very crown. Thus the nest is concealed from below but fully exposed from above, which allows easy access but also exposes it to such aerial predators as crows and certain hawks. It is made of dry sticks and twigs, then lined with such finer material as grasses, straw, weed stems, and the like, including Spanish moss. Nests appear flimsy, but most are well designed. A "typical" nest: outside diam. 21 in., depth 8; bowl diam. 7 in., depth 3½; one was on an old crow nest, and another on a Cooper's Hawk's (the Dixons 1957). One nest was so frail that an egg partially fell through it, another so compactly built that it held water (Ray, in Bent 1937). Generally speaking, a new nest is built for each clutch; in Suriname, however, the same nest contained eggs in Jan. and again in May (F. Haverschmidt). A past year's nest is rarely

140

refurbished and used again. Barlow (1897) removed a nest from a tree, and the following year, another nest was built on the exact site. The 2d nest of the season is as well built as the 1st.

On Masira I. in the Arabian Sea, this kite nests in caves for lack of trees; 5 nests each contained only a single nestling, which suggests that scarcity of food (there are no rodents) limits brood size (C. Green 1949).

With the beginning of copulation the ♀ pays no heed to the ♂'s attempts to "build" and selects and starts construction on the site to be used. Most material is gathered and brought by the ♂, who presents it to the ♀ at the site, and she does the actual building. Exceptionally, the ♂ builds briefly during the absence of the ♀.

Construction May continue as long as 2–4 weeks (the Dixons 1957), but evidently many nests are built in 7–10 days. The ♂ has been seen to fetch material and put it in the completed nest (F. Watson 1941), but he evidently does not continue to bring greenery throughout the cycle as do some raptors. A ♀ kept adding twigs during the early part of incubation (Watson). As noted earlier, the ♂ continues his display-flight, after which he returns to his perch and soon goes hunting. This Wings-up display, visible from a distance, is useful in locating nests (the Dixons 1957).

In S. Africa, both sexes collected nesting material. A kite would alight on a branch and search for a suitable twig, which was broken off with the beak or, on the ground, would hop about searching for suitable material. Material was carried only in the beak, and both birds "invariably whistled sharply when leaving a collecting site." Defended areas had a radius of 800–1,000 m. around the nest, and both sexes tail-wagged on approach of an intruder, but only the ♂ attacked (van der Merwe and Heunis 1980).

In Calif., the ♀ keeps constant watch at the nesting area, especially against buteo hawks; the Turkey Vulture, N. Harrier, and Cooper's Hawk are not attacked (the Dixons 1957). Lists vary with author. Crows are attacked but may persist in their persecution of the kites (Peyton 1915). Many kites nest within ¼ mi. of nesting buteos and eagles and are successful even though their nests are plainly obvious even to humans (P. Bloom).

The ♀ may go to the ♂'s perch tree and call him to bring her food, or the ♂ may fetch quarry and the ♀ arrives later. He takes wing and she flies beneath him, turns over, and extends a foot upward to grasp the food. She may eat it at his perch, deliver it to her brood (later in the cycle), or even decline it. The ♂ may fly near the nest and the ♀ fly out to meet him and take the food. If she declines, he eats it or stores it nearby in a hollow limb or wedged in somewhere until needed (the Dixons 1957). In S. Africa, during a plague (abundance) of rodents, several freshly killed mice were stuck in forks next to a nest from which 4 young had just flown (Malherbe 1963).

The eggs usually are laid at about 2-day intervals.

Replacement clutches In Calif., on Mar. 17 a nest contained 4 eggs, slightly incubated, which were taken; on Apr. 5 there were 3 eggs in this same nest and 5 eggs on Apr. 9; another nest on Mar. 14 contained 4 eggs, which were taken, and in 3 weeks this pair began a new nest nearby, which contained 1 egg on Apr. 12 but was destroyed by a predator (Barlow 1897). In Portugal, 3 eggs were laid alongside an earlier clutch of 4, presumably from the same ♀; none hatched (Collar 1978).

One **egg** each from 20 clutches (Calif. 17, Tex. 3) **size** length 42.5 ± 1.46 mm., breadth 32.67 ± 0.62, radii of curvature of ends 12.84 ± 0.72 and 9.49 ± 0.75; **shape** between short subelliptical and oval, elongation 1.29 ± 0.041, bicone −0.110, assymmetry +0.124 (F. Preston). This is remarkably similar to Bent (1937)—50 eggs av. 42.5 × 32.8 mm. Larger and smaller eggs are reported from other parts of the species's range (except no S. Am. data). They are among the most beautiful and richly colored of any hawk's (Bent). **Color** Although occasionally unmarked creamy white, usually this ground color is heavily blotched, spotted, or even entirely overlaid with various warm to deep reddish browns. Some are spotted over a lighter color that varies to include palish purple (ultramarine-violet). They are smooth, without sheen. According to Hawbecker (1942), eggs that have chocolate markings when fresh fade to mottled brown or tan during incubation.

Egg dates In Calif. earliest was 2 in a nest Feb. 6 (but earlier laying indicated by twice finding young at least 10 days old on Feb. 22), and latest was 4 in a nest July 10 (the Dixons 1957). Since some pairs are double brooded, at least in some years, the season is long. Winter nesting is known from near Monterrey, Nuevo León, Mexico. Most notable of 5 nests studied was a nest found Dec. 13, 1975, containing 2 young a week old or less; 1 nestling was dead Dec. 20; the other (banded) attained flight but was shot a km. away on Jan. 30, 1976, by a farmer "because they eat chickens"(!) (Monteil de la Garza 1978).

Some other indications of breeding season or its length are as follows: Portugal—1st eggs 2d week of Feb.; copulation noted as late as July (Collar 1978). S. African tropics (Zambia)—2 main periods, early and late in the dry season (C. W. Benson et al. 1971). Suriname—presumably viable eggs Jan.–May and Oct. (Haverschmidt 1959). Australia—eggs found May–Sept. and Oct., later in W. Australia (Brown and Amadon [1968 1], which see, also Baker-Gabb [1981], for additional information). Time of breeding can be adjusted more or less to coincide with an abundance of prey which, in turn, increases local nesting density.

Clutch size In Calif., 124 nests: 1 (of 6), 15 (5), 106 (4), and 2 (3); of 15 5-egg clutches, 8 were found in a season of vole abundance (the Dixons 1957). In San Diego Co., mean size of 20 clutches was 4.0 eggs (B. A. Wright 1978).

Incubation Begins with the 1st egg or soon after and hatching of an average clutch requires about a week. The ♀ incubates, taking brief absences from the nest (F. Watson 1940, Hawbecker 1942, the Dixons 1957). The ♂ remains close by at his perch when not hunting or fetching food for the ♀ at the nest or in flight. In Portugal, changeover at the nest was observed, and, in this instance, it was reported (England 1963) that the sexes spent about equal time incubating.

Pickwell (1930) believed that the **incubation period** was not less than 30 days, and Hawbecker (1942) gave 30–32 days as an estimate. It seems more likely that the period for each egg is about 26 days, the overall span of the clutch being 32 days or longer depending on laying interval and clutch size. Larger nestlings are not aggressive toward smaller (later-hatched) ones; in Portugal, however, Collar (1978) reported an unproved instance of suspected cannibalism or fratricide.

The ♀ broods the **young**. Since each adult requires several voles (or the equivalent) daily, the needs of both parents and brood keep the ♂ busy. When the chicks are

142

young, the ♀ tears the prey to pieces and feeds them; later prey is dropped to them, and they are able to dismantle it themselves, although they become very soiled as a result. They spend long periods cleaning themselves and are expert at it (R. Moore and Barr 1941). At a nest in Spain the young were mostly brought birds by both parents (Suetens and Groenendal 1977). The ♀ sometimes removes pellets and other waste from the nest.

Growth Two African young were graphed by von Michaelis (1952), who reared them. The ♀ was heaviest at 27 days, then fluctuated to 40 days (end of graph) but still was above "adult" weight; the ♂ was heaviest at 30 days, then fluctuated to 40 days, again, above "adult" weight. From day 12 onward the ♀ was the heavier bird. Feathering was fully developed at 40 days, with no visible down.

Nesting success In 23 nests in Calif. (included 2 second nestings), 94 eggs were hatched and 74 young **survived to flight age** (the Dixons 1957). The following are from Hawbecker (1942): 5 clutches av. 4 eggs, an av. of 3.2 eggs/clutch hatched, and an av. of 1.9 young/nest survived to depart. Four pairs produced 15 young in 1939, 2 produced 6 in 1940, and the same 2 produced 5 in 1941; that is, 1.6 young per adult per year. In San Diego Co., 17 of 20 nests with eggs produced a mean of 1.9 young reared to flight age (B. A. Wright 1978).

The **brood departs** in stages, the oldest nestling (according to Hawbecker 1942) being the 1st to fly, and the others following within a day or 2. Age at 1st flight is somewhat variable; in Calif., close estimates range 30–35 days (commonly) to longer. In Rhodesia (now Zimbabwe), 35 ± 1 day (Brooke 1962). On Masira I. in the Arabian Sea, it exceeds 40 days even with minimal brood size, evidently from scarcity of food (C. Green 1949). There is some indication that the parents discouraged the presence of the young, which still were present when another nest was started (Pickwell 1930). With at least the 1st brood of the season, the parents have been seen to terminate the family bond by flying at the young and driving them from the nesting area (the Dixons 1957). Yet in some circumstances, for a time the young return to the nest at night to roost and often in daylight to be fed. Even so, the 1st cycle may be completed in less than 100 days.

When **double brooded,** the 2 cycles may overlap. R. Moore and Barr (1941) saw a pair copulating at a perch within sight of their nest, which contained young; there was no preliminary display. Hawbecker (1942) thought it likely that the 2d nest (in the same territory) is built more rapidly than the 1st. He was attacked by a pair still feeding a brood that had started constructing a 2d nest. The ♂ tries to hasten the ♀ into the 2d cycle by seeking another nest site, by repeated copulations, and by abortive nest construction (the Dixons 1957).

Single-brooded parents possibly associate longer with their young, or the latter may at least roost with other nonbreeding individuals. Even those that are double brooded, however, have a span of free time, about Aug.–Dec., when they are seen singly. Yet they appear to be mated and still to be loosely bound to their nesting site—that is, sometimes 1 bird at the site, at other times both. Some pairs remain around the site all winter. More commonly, they reoccupy their territory in Feb. In winter, 1 bird is not seen to feed the other. (Summarized from Hawbecker 1942.)

RALPH S. PALMER

SURVIVAL   Oldest recorded in our area was aged 5 years, 11 months (Clapp et al. 1982). In S. Africa, Mendelsohn (1983b) concluded that causes of death often may be linked to food shortage—"probably the most important ultimate mortality factor."

RALPH S. PALMER

HABITS   Calif. data unless otherwise indicated.

The **history** of decline in numbers and recent recovery of this attractive little raptor has been discussed repeatedly—see especially Bent (1937), Hawbecker (1942), Waian and Stendell (1970), Eisenmann (1971), Warner and Rudd (1975), Waian (1976), and Pruett-Jones et al. (1980). (See Distribution, above.) In 1957 the Calif. legislature gave this kite fully protected status comparable to that given the California Condor. There was a parallel decline and recovery in Texas. In Fla., A. C. Bent never saw this kite, but records have increased markedly beginning in the 1960s.

Flight   A cruising kite flies with slow wingbeats, reminiscent of an Osprey, usually 20–70 m. above ground. That is, it hunts lower than buteo hawks, abut the same height as the Am. Kestrel (*Falco sparverius*). At times, however, wingbeat is quite rapid, like a nighthawk; at still other times, as when beating into a rather strong wind, the kite makes shallow strokes. When hunting it hovers a great deal, the wings angled upward, and its descent begins rather slowly before gaining momentum. It pounces with wings upward; rarely (B. Thompson 1975) are they closed during the terminal phase of descent. The legs commonly dangle during hovering and often during descent. Hawbecker believed that they do not have the speed to capture birds and various other open-ground diurnal inhabitants regularly, but this is not entirely so.

R. Moore and Barr (1941) described the "kite maneuver," participated in by 2 individuals. It occurs in a steady wind. Both birds ascend to perhaps 100 m., then they turn into the wind with a peculiar fast wing motion for about 1½ min. during which they seem stalled, motionless. Then there is a violent shaking, as though the bird were coming apart, after which the kite ceases seeming disorderly behavior suddenly and raises its wings straight upward, holding them perfectly still. The upward "kite" position is held 5–15 sec.; then the bird resumes more usual flying behavior. This presumably is a territorial display. The V-position has been likened to the display-glide of the Rock Dove.

Kites studied near Davis, Calif., by Warner and Rudd (1975) usually **hunted** within 1 km. of their perches. A hunt lasted 6 min. (205 observations) in both sexes and did not vary in length with success or season. Search time (hovering) and transport time (flying between hovers) were analyzed. There were 16 brief hoverings/hunt, and 39% of their strikes at prey all year were successful. They did not store food, as had been reported by the Dixons (1957). Hunting occurred at all temperatures recorded but was most frequent below 20° C. They hunted during high or gusty winds but rarely in the rain. (In Africa, kites hunted from perches 70% and from hovers 30% of the time [Tarboton 1978]; they spent 3% of their time soaring. The energy required in hunting equals the energy supplied by mammalian food [Koplin et al. 1980].)

Kites often descend high, so as to swoop down on buteo hawks. The latter, not greatly disturbed, move on. They may attack other large birds, but authors agree that they do not molest the Turkey Vulture. In the Palearctic they have been observed soaring at considerable heights.

In a breeze when coming to a slender perch, the kite approaches very gracefully with legs dangling; it may make contact, then be blown clear, and then return and settle on it. In such maneuvers the bird seems almost weightless.

Tail bobbing when perched May be a signal to other kites or may be related to maintaining balance; it is more conspicuous than in either the Am. or Eurasian Kestrel.

Kite roosts Although a pair bond is likely maintained, kites usually hunt solitarily in winter and spend the night at a communal roost. They come in toward evening and alight on the highest branches of trees, facing the wind; they are early risers, and most are gone by 0600 hrs. (the Dixons 1957).

Roosting was studied in the Goleta Valley near Santa Barbara by Waian and Stendell (1970). In Oct. 1965, the roost was in a mixed oak-willow grove on extensive grassland; then the birds shifted about ¾ mi. to a dense stand of live oaks close to a housing development and ranch buildings; still later (Dec. 23) they moved sw. 330 yds. to a small clump of eucalyptus trees. In the 2 following winters a similar pattern of shifts occurred.

The birds began communal roosting in Oct., and numbers gradually built up to a peak at the main roost in early winter. In mid-Jan. numbers began to dwindle, because kites remained away at nesting territories; all were gone in late Mar. As the build-up in numbers proceeded in fall, an increase in singles and pairs on territories throughout the valley occurred. Occasionally kites occupied a territory for a few weeks to several months, then moved elsewhere in the valley.

The kites arrived at the roost in a 35–45 min. period generally between sunset and dark. There was first considerable aerial activity nearby, such as hunting; at dark activity diminished, and within 2–3 min. all the birds disappeared into the foliage. When they left territories to go to roost, they occasionally went together but more often went singly.

In Tanzania in Mar.–Apr., Black-shouldered Kites were present in large numbers on open grasslands. At least 80 roosted in a small, isolated tree, only about 10 ft. high and with a 6-ft. crown diameter, that appeared at a distance to be covered with snow. In addition to the birds, the quantity of their excrement added to this effect. They sat almost wing-to-wing and could be approached very closely (Morgan-Davies 1965).

In Rhodesia (now Zimbabwe), Brooke (1965) found kites roosting in small flocks in reed beds and found 5–30 birds in a grove of young trees.

In Calif. the kites are up early, hunting voles and mice; the voles are active again as the day wanes and the kites correspondingly so. Occasionally the kites hunt in groups (Waian and Stendell 1970). Mean wt. of a Calif. vole is about 41 gm. and of a house mouse 29 gm. (Meserve 1977). A kite needs, roughly, the equivalent of 3 voles/day. E. Stoner (1933) found 5 house mice in a kite, and L. Miller (1926) found a shrew and 4 voles in another. In Chile, the primary rodent prey is *Akodon olivaceus*, mean wt. 29 gm. (Meserve); in s. Africa, it is *Rhabdomys pumilio* (Siegfried 1965), and so on. In Calif., evidently about the largest prey that this little kite can manage is a young rat

145

(*Rattus*) or, rarely, a young ground squirrel (*Spermophilus*), or something of comparable size (see Hawbecker 1940); evidently the smallest prey is large insects, but their role in kite nutrition usually is minor. The matter of prey size vs. habitat in Chile was reported in detail by Schlatter et al. (1980). The prey is carried in a foot and held close to the body until the kite approaches a perch or nest, when the feet are extended downward. It is surmised (England 1963), but not clearly established, that small insects are sometimes carried in the beak. Rodents and birds are commonly decapitated before delivery to a nest.

In Kenya, a 7-week-old captive ate 4 small rats/day (van Someren 1956). In Calif., a ♂, where voles were abundant locally, caught 3 in 8 min.; the 1st was delivered to a young bird, the 2d to his mate, and he ate the 3d (the Dixons 1957).

R. Moore and Barr (1941) thought that the **pellets** this kite ejects were extraordinarily large for the size of the bird—as described and illus. by Hawbecker (1940). Being rounded in shape, they are more owlish than hawklike. Waian and Stendell (1970) measured 523 pellets: length 25–43 mm., av. 32, and breadth 15–24, av. 18. A ♀ was seen to remove a pellet from a nest (R. Moore and Barr 1941).

Evidence of predation on this kite is scant. Great Horned Owls occasionally take nestlings—1 instance out of approximately 100 owl nests (P. Bloom). Since nests are in the very crowns of trees, R. Moore and Barr (1941) suspected that many young are blown away. M. S. Ray (in Bent 1937) reported that jays, magpies, and crows puncture kite eggs. According to the Dixons (1957), crows exploit every opportunity to scavenge from the kites; one crowded a kite on a limb to make it drop its food.

In Kenya, van Someren (1956) found that older young were delightful pets that would adopt and brood other birds.   RALPH S. PALMER

FOOD **In our area** unless specified. Small rodents, a few ground-dwelling birds, occasionally shrews, snakes, frogs, lizards, and some insects (generally large). Long known to be a specialist in small diurnal grassland rodents. In Calif., principally vole (*Microtus californicus*) and house mouse (*Mus musculus*). A shrew (*Sorex ornatus*) (L. Miller 1926). Also ground squirrel (*Spermophilus*) (Barlow 1897, Pickwell 1930, Hawbecker 1940). Hawbecker added harvest mouse (*Reithrodontomys*), pocket gopher (*Thomomys*), wood rat (*Neotoma*), and young cottontail (Sylvilagus). In Fla., a cotton rat (*Sigmodon*) (Bonaparte 1828); in Tex., cotton rats, a small shrew (*Cryptotis*, and a tiny mouse (*Baiomys*) (McKey and Fischer 1972). Less definite but probably reliable are reports of birds (Audubon 1831, Cooper 1870) (a Brown Towhee in a nest [P. Bloom]), snakes, frogs, lizards, and insects (beetles, crickets, grasshoppers) (Audubon 1838, Dawson 1923).

Hawbecker (1942) regarded the kite as being as nearly dependent on voles as is the Snail Kite on snails. Other prey species, especially the introduced house mouse, are very important—the more so if available when voles are scarce. In a period of vole scarcity the kites must capture other prey, go elsewhere, or work harder. At the Hastings Reservation in Monterey Co., where there was no other available small diurnal mammal, the kites adopted the 3d above alternative (Stendell and Myers 1973). In San Diego Co., B. A. Wright (1978) examined 2,886 pellets containing 3,276 animals: *Microtus* 2,759 (84.5%), *Reithrodontomys* 344 (10.2%), *Mus* 143 (4.4%), and

146

other organisms 30 (0.9%). There were only 5 birds and neither reptiles nor inverte-brates.

Nine studies (8 Calif., 1 Chile) were compared by Meserve (1977); this included analyses of over 7,900 pellets from Calif. Each study revealed a predominant (primary) prey species—vole or house mouse—and secondary prey in the different studies were vole, house mouse, harvest mouse, or pocket gopher. In Chile a small rodent, *Akodon olivaceus*, was primary, the introduced house mouse secondary. For comparison of prey taken in 2 different Chilean habitats and other details, see Schlatter et al. (1980).

Elsewhere Data from other parts of the vast range of this kite are not summarized here; the general pattern is that primary prey is a small diurnal grassland mammal. There are exceptions. In Costa Rica, a kite captured a Squirrel Cuckoo (*Piaya cayana*) (Slud 1980). At a nest in cent. Spain, small birds were the main prey (Suetens and Gronendal 1977). In Portugal, a breeding pair fed fairly regularly on Corn Buntings (*Emberiza calandra*), evidently taking ♀♀ from their nests (Collar 1978). Also in Portugal, tiny food was brought to the nest; England (1963) suspected it was cock-chafers. Records of capturing small lizards are widely scattered geographically. On Masira in the Arabian Sea, C. Green (1949) found 11 pairs of these birds and, excepting a single pair of Black Kites, no other raptors (including vultures). The avifauna was confined largely to littoral areas. He saw no sign of rodents, but there were a few lizards and snakes. The kites sought these, but their main food was small dead fish discarded from nets by local fishermen; for these, the kites competed with gulls.

RALPH S. PALMER

SNAIL KITE

Rostrhamus sociabilis

Formerly Everglade Kite. Medium-sized kite with smallish body in proportion to wing area; beak very slender, long, and downcurved; the 2 longest primaries (3d and 4th counting from outer) about equal in length, and the 4 outer emarginated on inner web; tail squarish (slightly indented); talons long, slender, and curved. The ♀ av. slightly larger and heavier than the ♂. Combined sexes: length 17–19 in. (43–48 cm.), wingspread to about 40 in. (102 cm.), wt. about 10½–14½ oz. (300–410 gm.). Sexes strikingly **dimorphic** in color and pattern. Definitive ♂ blackish slaty gray with white base of tail and tail coverts; ♀ very muted dark browns, paling to light brownish forehead and throat, the pattern at the base of tail as in ♂. The Juv. stage is quite like the ♀, and the early Basics (see below) are constrasting and progressively more dimorphic.

Three subspecies, 1 in our area.

DESCRIPTION *Rostrhamus s. plumbeus*. Def. Basic Plumage (entire feathering) renewed by gradual molting, in Fla., probably beginning during or soon after initial nesting (scant information); primaries molt from inner to outer.
▶ ♂ Def. Basic Plumage; **beak** black; cere nearly to eye, gape, and mandibular rami yellow to (in breeding season) scarlet or ruby; **iris** brownish red to ruby. There is a light area on the occiput, present in all flying ages and ordinarily concealed or inconspicuous. **Feathering** blackish slaty, becoming black on flight feathers; smaller wing coverts sometimes tipped muted brownish (typical of younger birds); all with

148

chalky bloom (lost from museum specimens); **tail** coverts and base white, remainder black except very tips of feathers light brownish gray to white. Legs and **feet** approximately match cere in color, talons black. Useful color photograph: Kern (1978).

▶ ♀ Def. Basic Plumage (entire feathering), probably renewed beginning in or after initial nesting. **Beak** black; cere to eye yellow, seasonally orange; **iris** more or less orange. **Head** partly buffy browns—forehead, line over eye, the cheek and upper throat white—with most of remainder of **feathering** variably buffy tan but so heavily marked and streaked with muted dark browns as to appear blackish brown; on the wings this combination forms a finely barred pattern; **tail** pattern as ♂—that is, top base and adjoining upper and under coverts white, distal portion black with narrow whitish tip; the distal dark portion light basal portion of ventral surface has a brownish cast. Legs and **feet** approximately match cere in color.

AT HATCHING Down-A is short, rather coarse, and more or less muted buffy with darker patches (toward sepia or brownish olive) on crown, along side of head, on rump, and on upper surface of wings. Later Down-B is longer, denser, much darker, variably gray-brown.

▶ ♂ ♀ Juv. Plumage (entire feathering) fully developed at age about 4 weeks; how long it is retained, entirely or in part, is unknown. Various cinnamon buffs and browns (not white). **Beak** black, cere yellowish; **eye** at first very dark but iris later becomes yellowish or toward orange. **Head** rich buffs to yellowish brown, the crown heavily streaked dark; **upperparts** a mixture of browns, many feathers with dark (to nearly black) subterminal area and fairly wide tan distal margins; **underparts** buffy-tan, somewhat diffusely streaked and blotched dark (toward sepia); **tail** dark, paling to buffy basal area and adjoining coverts, very tip buffy. Legs and **feet** yellowish, talons black. Useful color photograph: Sykes (1979).

▶ ♂ ♀ Early Basic Plumages. Data from known-age birds are few. It is definitely known that there is an interim condition of feathering after the Juv. and preceding Def. Basic. The buffy-cinnamon of the Juv. bird has disappeared to some extent—that is, a white eye-stripe by 2 months after the young 1st fly (Beissinger). Assuming that wild birds have the same stages as captives, it would appear that there are 2 predefinitive Basic Plumages, each consisting of entire feathering and each retained a year. These early Basics are more contrasting than the Juv. stage—light areas are white or whitish (not buffs, tan, etc.), dark areas are very dark, the heavy streaking sharply defined.

The last predefinitive stage (presumably Basic II) in the ♂ apparently differs from its predecessor and matches the description by Haverschmidt (1970) of 2 birds from Suriname. They were dark chocolate brown (not slaty) above and below, upper and under tail coverts and base of tail white, secondaries and tail broadly tipped buff, and thighs barred rufous. Apparently there is marked sexual dimorphism before definitive feathering is acquired.

Since younger cohorts may contain the most birds within a population, and since the vast majority of these kites seen afield in Fla. are in streaked feathering, as in Suriname (Haverschmidt 1970) but a moot point in Cuba (Beissinger et al. 1983), such a ratio is evidence that a predefinitive condition continues for some time.

Measurements Florida specimens: 10 ♂ BEAK from cere 22–25 mm., av. 23.3, WING across chord 340–368, av. 356.7, and TAIL 170–191, av. 182.5; and 10 ♀ BEAK

149

from cere 22–24mm., av. 22.9, and WING chord 345–373, av. 361.5 (Friedmann 1950). Some of the above birds were also included in N. Snyder and Wiley (1976), who gave these mean figures: WING across chord 12 ♂ 354.3 mm., and 12 ♀ 357.6.

Florida specimens: 7 ♂ BEAK from cere 23–27 mm., av. 24.4, and WING across chord 340–376, av. 354; and 2 ♀ BEAK from cere av. 25.6 mm., and WING across chord av. 353 (Beissinger).

Weight No Fla. data; probably not much different from S. Am. birds (see Subspecies, below).

Geographical variation Slight—none reported in color or pattern, but some in length of BEAK and WING (Amadon 1975). Northerly birds are larger, those from Honduras s. smaller; in between, Mexican birds have comparatively long beaks. When more specimens are measured, it is possible that purported regional differences are even less than currently indicated. STEVEN R. BEISSINGER

SUBSPECIES Amadon (1975) is followed here; it has been stated (L. Brown and Amadon 1976 1) that subspecies are "doubtfully distinct."

In our area *plumbeus* Ridgway—descr. and meas. of Fla. birds given above; also includes Cuba and Isla de la Juventud [Isle of Pines]. An is. subspecies, *levis* (of Friedmann 1933), is not regarded as separable.

Elsewhere *major* Nelson and Goldman—se. Mexico down to Belize, then intergradation farther s. with the one next listed. Larger birds with longer beaks; for meas., see Friedmann (1950) and Amadon (1975). A young ♀ on June 4 in Brit. Honduras weighed 438 gm. (S. Russell 1964).

sociabilis (Vieillot)—much of S. Am. and up into Cent. Am. to Belize; only 2 recent (1959) records for Trinidad; smallest in BEAK and WING length. For meas., see Friedmann (1950) and Amadon (1975). Weight of birds from Suriname: ♂ "adult" nonbreeding 357 gm., predefinitive ♀, incubating, 393 gm., and predefinitive ♂ 360 gm. (Haverschmidt 1970). Averaging these with 5 others yields a mean of 368 gm. (Beissinger 1983). STEVEN R. BEISSINGER

FIELD IDENTIFICATION **In our area** Usually compared with the N. Harrier, a bird of open wetlands having a white patch on top base of tail. The kite, however, is easily recognizable—rather broad wings, much of feathering variably dark (to blackish), white (or light) area includes basal portion of tail as well as end of body. The very slender downcurved beak is visible at a considerable distance. The kite flies in desultory fashion, not vigorous and purposeful like most raptors, but a slow flapping and short glides with wings flat to slightly bowed. Often seen perching on stubs and dead limbs. When away from the nest it is easily approached. See above for sex and age differences.

Elsewhere Another very similar-appearing snail catcher—the forest-dwelling Slender-billed Kite (*Rostrhamus hamatus*)—is found within part of the tropical range of the Snail Kite. It is a comparatively stocky, slaty blackish bird, without white in and near the base of the tail; predefinitive stages little known. It seems unlikely that the Snail Kite could be confused with any age or phase (including black) of the much more stocky and variably heavy-billed snail eater, Hook-billed Kite (*Chondrohierax*), which has a barred tail and occurs in drier habitat. STEVEN R. BEISSINGER

VOICE   Many conflicting descriptions exist. Lang (1924) described a harsh *kor-ee-ee-a kor—ee-a* call uttered by perched kites in Guyana, but N. and H. Snyder (1969) detected no sounds resembling this description. Others have compared kite vocalizations to the cackling of an Osprey but "finer in tone and not so loud" (Nicholson 1926), bleating "very much like a sheep" during aerial somersault displays (C. W. Townsend 1927), and like the bleat of a goat or the call of the Fork-tailed Flycatcher (*Muscivora tyrannus*) (Slud 1980).

Four distinct vocalizations by adults, used in different contexts, can be recognized (Beissinger, N. Snyder). In Fla., Cuba, and Guyana, the general call resembles a harsh cackling *ka-ka-ka-ka-ka-ka-ka* or, to rephrase Lang's description, *kor-ee-a-a-a-a*. This, often repeated several times, may be uttered aggressively toward intruding kites or humans near nests or feeding perches. A 2d call is used in Fla. by perched ♀♀, often near or from a nest site, during pair formation to elicit "courtship" feeding by their mates. It resembles the sound of a watch being wound—hence "watchwind call." A 3d call *ker-wuck ker-wuck* is heard least often but in a variety of contexts, such as at evening roost sites, in ♂ aerial displays, or aggressively toward other kites. A 4th is a rattlelike gurgle, uttered by the ♂ during copulation (Haverschmidt 1970, Beissinger).

Nestlings give screams resembling those of adult Red-tailed Hawks, but much harsher and coarser. By age 4 months kites give calls that resemble the general adult call described above, but much higher and raspier. By age 1 year, voices and calls resemble those of adults.   STEVEN R. BEISSINGER

HABITAT   **In our area**   In Fla., kites are found in large, open freshwater marshes and at lakes. Vegetation is usually low (0–3 m.), sometimes dense, but with the extensive patchwork of open water areas without emergent vegetation required for foraging. Scattered small trees or shurbs, mainly willow (*Salix caroliniana*), wax myrtle (*Myrica cerifera*), and pond apple (*Annona glabra*), which serve as perches and nesting sites, may be present. These areas often include *Eleocharis* flats and sloughs of white water-lily (*Nymphaea odorata*) dispersed in a marsh of sawgrass (*Cladium jamaicense*) or cattails (*Typha*) where water depths vary from 0.2 to 1.3 m. (Sykes, in Kale 1978; Sykes 1979, 1983b).

Continuous flooding of wetlands is required to sustain populations of the apple snail (*Pomacea paludosa*), practically the sole food of this kite. During periods of dryness, snail mortality is very great as water levels drop and the snails estivate by burrowing into the mud. This results in large declines in snail abundance (Kushlan 1975) and extensive kite dispersal. Beissinger and Takakawa (1983) documented habitats used during regional drought conditions in Fla., including agricultural and urban canals, seasonal and permanent marshes, borrow pits, shell pits, lakes, ponds, and agricultural fields. From these results, it is not difficult to imagine how large-scale habitat alteration in the past, by drainage of the Everglades, could have resulted in massive decrease in snails and kites.

Tebeau (1971), Carter (1974), Sykes (1979), and N. Blake (1980) discuss the history of drainage of freshwater marsh areas in Fla. and water management practices. The greatest impacts probably occurred between 1925 and 1950. During this period, L.

Okeechobee was permanently diked and large drainage canals were completed, shunting water to the coasts instead of into the Everglades. This resulted in a permanent lowering of the water table by as much as 1.5–2.1 m. in some places, which simply eliminated most of the Everglades. These massive environmental perturbations probably were responsible for the vast changes in distribution and numbers of kites in Fla. (See also Distribution and Habits, below.)

Elsewhere In Cent. and S. Am. and Cuba, the Snail Kite is locally common in freshwater marshes and lakes with characteristics similar to those described in Fla. and, additionally, uses wet savanna (Haverschmidt 1970, Mader 1981, others). Although much of the coastal freshwater marshes have been drained and converted to rice and sugarcane cultivation, kites have been able to forage in these habitats (Haverschmidt 1970, Beissinger 1983, Bourne 1985). Sometimes large kills of Snail Kites occur in rice fields from extensive application of certain molluscicides (Vermeer et al. 1974). In addition to feeding in young rice fields, kites also use surrounding drainage ditches. In Suriname, after a sugarcane field is cultivated for several years, it is burned, plowed, and flooded, providing artificial lagoons where large numbers of kites feed until the water is drained a year or two later. In Guyana, as rice growth increased, kite numbers declined until no birds used these fields because the vegetation was too thick and high for the birds to descend through it to capture snails (Beissinger 1983). There, rice cultivation was highly snychronized, and large areas became unavailable for kites during some seasons. Later in the growing cycle, kites must leave these areas (Beissinger 1983); probably they move into wet savannas farther in the interior.   STEVEN R. BEISSINGER

DISTRIBUTION   (See map.) Tropical Am., Cuba, and Fla. See A. H. Howell (1932) for Fla. distribution in earlier times; it consisted principally of the headwaters of the St. John's R., the Everglades (L. Okeechobee s. to Fla. Bay), cent. Fla. lakes (at least on occasion), and irregular wanderings into the panhandle as far n. and w. as Wakulla Co. The range has shrunk vastly (Sykes 1979, 1983a). Only parts of the Everglades and L. Okeechobee are now used consistently by the kites. Greatest loss in range has been almost all of the Everglades. During droughts, range expansion occurs—especially into the cent. lakes region and toward a corridor of wetter areas along the se. coast (Beissinger and Takekawa 1983).

Elsewhere   Little information is available. In Cuba, many marshes were drained, and the kite's distribution probably became restricted to the Zapata Swamp and several other lake areas (Barbour 1923, Garrido and Montana 1975, Beissinger et al. 1983). Large-scale changes in land use in coastal areas, from freshwater marshes to agricultural and drained lands, in Cent. and S. Am. also may be affecting kite numbers and movements; no information presently exists. There is no firm evidence of drastic changes in numbers at present, since kites still are common (see Habits, below).

No archaeological or **fossil** record.   STEVEN R. BEISSINGER

MIGRATION   None reliably reported in this species, although it has been suggested that birds in Argentina withdraw n. (Grossman and Hamlet 1964) and those in n. Fla. head s. (Sykes 1983a) to escape the colder season. North of the city of Veracruz,

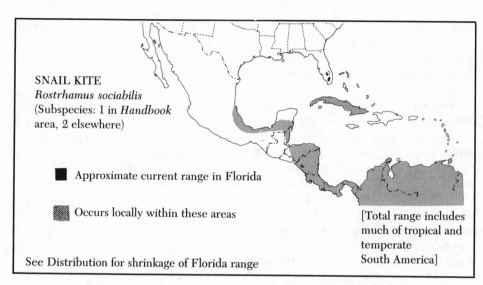

SNAIL KITE
Rostrhamus sociabilis
(Subspecies: 1 in *Handbook*
area, 2 elsewhere)

■ Approximate current range in Florida

▦ Occurs locally within these areas

[Total range includes
much of tropical and
temperate
South America]

See Distribution for shrinkage of Florida range

Mexico, Apr. 6–May 6, 1978, Thiollay (1979) saw 14 and estimated 20, which he termed migrants. This kite is nomadic, however, and moves in respose to changes in water level in search of snails. Data in Sykes (1979, 1983a) and Beissinger and Take-kawa (1983) substantiate the nomadic nature of the various age-classes in normal and drought conditions in Fla. In addition, Beissinger found a high degree of movement of radiotelemetered individuals between L. Okeechobee and Conservation Area 3A in the Everglades. A high degree of movement also has been noted at end of the nesting season (Beissinger et al. 1983).

Local movements   May include long daily flights, sometimes traveling high, at other times near the ground, between communal roosts and daily feeding or nesting areas (Haverschmidt 1954, Beissinger 1983). For example, Haverschmidt watched a flight to evening roost in Suriname that lasted from 1730 to 1845 hrs. during which the birds flew low, flapping slowly and alternating with short glides. He counted 712 kites—certainly not all of them.   STEVEN R. BEISSINGER

BANDING STATUS   In Fla., the number banded 1968–1977 was 64 (Sykes 1979), and from 1978–1983, 360 (N. Snyder, Beissinger), all but 10 as nestlings. A few have been banded in Brazil.   STEVEN R. BEISSINGER

REPRODUCTION   Fla. data unless otherwise stated. Recent studies have shown that age when **first breeds** in both sexes is 1 year—that is, yearlings are capable of reproducing successfully (N. Snyder, Beissinger, R. Chandler). Furthermore, Haver-schmidt (1970) collected a nesting pair in Suriname, and both birds, from his description, probably were between 1 and 2 years old.

Breeding season   In Fla., quite variable; nesting has been recorded in every month (Chandler, Snyder, Beissinger). In years of high water levels and snail populations, breeding may begin in Dec. and finish in Sept., whereas in drought years it may not begin until Mar., terminating by July. In general, the main nesting season is Jan.–

Aug., peaking Feb.–June. Little is recorded about the seasonality of nesting elsewhere, but it is probably related to length of rainy season. Nesting has been noted Jan.–Aug. in Suriname (Haverschmidt 1970) and Oct.–Feb. in Argentina (Martin R. de la Pena), when it is most rainy; in Venezuela kites nest in the wet season (Mader 1981).

Displays   Two main types are performed mostly by ♂♂ (Stieglitz and Thompson 1967, Beissinger 1984). SKY-DANCE: after a short rise, the kite closes its wings and descends steeply 2–4 m. before the wings are opened and the kite again rises. This is directed to **1** a ♀ during pair formation, **2** its mate or other nearby ♂♂ when returning to a nest site with a stick or snail in beak, and **3** other kites intruding near a nest site. In the 3d case, the swoops often are executed aggressively near the intruder. Sometimes the *ka-ka-ka-* . . . or *ker-wuck* . . . vocalizations are given during a dive. Swooping dives also have been observed in Suriname (Haverschmidt 1970) and Argentina (Weller 1967). The 2d display, DEEP-WINGBEATS, is used in the same contexts as Sky-dance and may also be used when chasing potential predators from the nesting area. During flight the kite gives very emphatic downward strokes of the wings, reaching well below the level of the body, during 5–20 m. forward progress.

There are several reports of groups of kites circling and darting at each other, somersaulting, and grappling with outstretched legs while vocalizing (C. W. Townsend 1927, Stieglitz and Thompson 1967). This has been observed rarely, shortly before onset of the breeding season; it may be a gregarious early stage of pair-formation behavior.

Pair formation   The ♂ dives or flies with deep wingbeats near a potential mate. Often these displays occur near future nest sites. Sometimes ♂♂ may begin nest building or defending a potential site from other ♂♂ before securing a mate. In either case, after initially attracting a ♀, a ♂ will capture a snail and feed it to her. The ♂ lands near a potential nest site with the snail and waits for the ♀ to fly a short distance to him to receive it. The ♂ may then fly off in search of nesting material and return with it shortly or initiate copulation. Nest building by the ♂ is interspersed with snail deliveries to the ♀. Once the ♀ chooses to remain with a ♂, the pair is formed, and she may spend most of the daylight hours perching on or near the nest (Beissinger 1984).

Males continue to "wait" on ♀♀ from pair formation through egg laying. Males provide an av. of 83% of the ♀'s food and 80% of the nesting materials and execute 75% of the chases of conspecifics or potential predators. By the end of egg laying, ♂♂ generally have invested more reproductive effort (energy and risk) in a clutch than ♀♀ (Beissinger 1984).

Pair-bond form is a type of **sequential monogamy**—"ambisexual mate desertion." The bond lasts only until the nestlings are 3–6 weeks old. Then, if food is sufficiently plentiful, one parent deserts its nest and mate; the deserted may attempt to find a new mate and renest while the parent that remains (the tender) cares for the chicks alone for an additional 4–5 weeks. Tenders almost always complete brood rearing without mortality of young. When snails are scarce, as in time of drought, no desertion occurs, and both parents continue to feed the young until they are independent. Larger broods are deserted later than smaller ones, probably because nestlings reach a late peak probability of survial due to greater age differentials caused by asynchronous hatching. Females desert smaller broods than do ♂♂; the cause is unclear.

154

The deserter usually, but not always, is the parent that invests less reproductive effort as measured by reproductive bioenergetics and time-activity budgets (Beissinger 1984). Deserters do not incubate, brood, or chase potential predators more or less frequently than tenders. Only provisioning the nestlings with snails, the most energy-intensive parental activity, differs significantly between deserters and tenders—deserters feed the young less often. Because mate desertion occurs so late in the nesting cycle, differences in reproductive effort between mates may be a less important determinant of which parent deserts than which one has the first chance to remate or which one recognizes the earliest possible moment to desert.

Mate desertion Functions primarily to allow deserters the opportunity to start new nesting cycles while their mates raise the offspring alone (Beissinger 1984). Since loss of young rarely occurs after mate desertion, kite clutch size must be selected to be smaller than 2 parents could raise together. Because Everglades water-level predictability and kite nesting success are low, kites do not respond to changes in snail abundance by adjusting clutch size but instead desert their mates facultatively, when conditions allow care by one parent to be as effective as biparental care.

Copulation In both Fla. and Suriname this may occur on the nest (whether under construction or finished), at potential nest sites, or on nearby shrubs or cattails (Haverschmidt 1970, Beissinger, N. Snyder). The ♂ hops onto the ♀'s back, attempting to twist his tail under hers and upward in order to contact her cloaca. The ♀ may throw her head upward and backward and peck at the ♂'s head. Usually he makes a rattlelike gurgling vocalization while copulating. The complete process lasts 10–20 sec. Immediately after dismounting, the ♂ usually departs and soon returns to the nest carrying a stick in his beak. A ♀ may control whether copulation attempts are successful by remaining upright, denying ♂ access to her cloaca, or by assuming a horizontal position, allowing cloacal contact (Beissinger 1984). Males do not appear to be able to force ♀♀ to a horizontal position, perhaps because ♀♀ are slightly larger than ♂♂.

Nests Bulky, somewhat flattened and elongate, resembling those of the Anhinga (Stieglitz and Thompson 1967). There are numerous pictures and/or descriptions; see, for example, Nicholson (1926), A. Howell (1932), Steffee (1966), and Sykes (1979). The base consists of woody branches and twigs, often willows in Fla.; the cavity is lined with dead herbaceous plants or vines. **Greenery:** a few green leaves may be added shortly before the eggs hatch. Two nests, meas. by Bendire (1892) and Nicholson (1926): diam. 13–16 in., height 8–12, and cavity depth 3–4.

Nests are always built over water in Fla., often in small shrubs or trees. Willows, wax myrtle, and pond apple are most common sites, but buttonbush, elderberry, and bald cypress have been recorded (Beissinger). Nests have also been built in sawgrass (*Cladium jamaicensis*), maidencane (*Paicum hemitomon*), and cattails (*Typha*); the last is used especially during low water conditions as they grow in deeper water. The **nest site** may be quite conspicuous or well hidden but typically is open overhead to permit unhindered aerial access. Sites usually are 1–5 m. above water, occasionally (A. Howell 1932, Haverschmidt 1970) up to 10 m. Nests in other parts of the species's range are similar to those in Fla. (various authors).

In Fla., sometimes nests are started, then work ceases, then a nest may be finished and occupied or abandoned (Chandler and Anderson 1974, Beissinger 1984). A delay of several days to a week can occur. One study (Chandler and Anderson) indicated that a nest may be completed in 6 days, but 2 weeks may be nearer av. (Beissinger 1984). Both sexes engage in building in Suriname (Haverschmidt 1970), but in Fla., ♂ ♂ bring nearly all the sticks—especially large ones (Bendire 1892, Beissinger 1984). A new nest is built each time a pair attempts to breed (Sykes 1979). Often, in renesting, the new nest is built in the general vicinity of its unsuccessful predecessor (Chandler and Anderson).

Although this kite typically nests in loose **colonies,** solitary nesting also is known in Fla. Colonies vary greatly in size and density. In Suriname in Feb., 51 nests were counted in a colony; the birds still were building, and in Mar., 90 nests were counted (Haverschmidt 1970). Recently in Fla., colonies have varied 5–20 pairs (N. Snyder, Beissinger, R. Chandler). Often these colonies contain nesting herons and Anhingas (A. Howell 1932). Colonies may form on the edge of tree-islands, in cattails, or in willowheads. In the Everglades, some willowheads are used by colonies several years in succession. Beissinger observed the initiation of several new colonies and found that they formed where a kite pair was already in process of nesting.

When Snail Kites nest in cattails during low water, nest failure is very high (Chandler and Anderson 1974). Because this weak vegetation substrate is destroyed easily by winds and the weight of adults and brood, artificial nest supports, consisting of shallow wire baskets on poles, were developed to reinforce and stabilize nests. Real nests were placed in these structures at risky sites, and the parent birds readily accepted this arrangement (Chandler and Anderson 1974, Sykes and Chandler 1974, H. Cruickshank 1977). Recent studies have shown that few nests without baskets are successful during low-water years, while basketed nests are highly successful (R. Chandler, Beissinger).

Eggs Laid at intervals of 1–4 days, usually 2 (Chandler and Anderson 1974, Beissinger 1984). Six days is probably the usual time for laying a 3-egg clutch. Contrary to Chandler and Anderson, incubation usually begins before the clutch is complete (Beissinger 1984). (See above on variation in length of breeding season for estimating dates for fresh clutches.)

Current clutch size In Fla., 2–3 eggs, the latter much more frequent (Chandler and Anderson, Beissinger, N. Snyder). Historical records commonly include clutches of 4, rarely 5, and once 6 (A. Howell 1932). Over 25% of the clutches in museums contain 4 or more eggs (Beissinger 1984). Large clutches declined in frequency to 9% in the mid-1900s and to only 2% of those observed recently. Because collectors of large clutches were reliable and because ♀ ♀ are not known to lay in nests of others (they are guarded continually during incubation), it is likely that a historical decline in clutch size occurred. Smaller clutches may be a response to Everglades drainage and unpredictable water levels, hence of snail numbers, which resulted in high nesting failure. A. C. Bent (1937), an astute collector, gave clutch size as 3–4 or sometimes only 2, and mentioned none larger. Six eggs in a nest at Tallahassee, carefully observed by H. L. Stoddard, Sr. (A. Howell 1932) probably were laid by a single ♀—possibly the only one in the region. There are few data from elsewhere in the range of the species, but clutches of 2–3 seem to be most common. Steffee (1966) reported a nest with 3 and another with 5 young in Suriname; Pereyra (1942) noted that a captive ♀ in Argentina laid 6 and 5 eggs in 2 consecutive years, some being relayings for earlier eggs that had broken.

One **egg** each from 20 Fla. clutches **size** length 45.22 ± 1.35 mm., breadth 36.21 ± 1.16, radii of curvature of ends 15.49 ± 0.82 and 12.34 ± 1.18; **shape** short elliptical, varying toward short subelliptical, elongation 1.24 ± 0.044, bicone −0.037, and asymmetry +0.109 (F. W. Preston). Bent's figures (1937) are very close: 65 av. 44.2 × 36.2 mm. Twelve of the Mexican race *major* av. 44.2 × 36.0 mm. (Kiff 1981). Thirteen in Suriname av. 44.6 × 34.6 mm., and wt. of 8 fresh eggs was 25.9–29.5 gm., av. 27.6 (Haverschmidt 1970); 16 in Fla. weighed 27–33 gm., av. 30.3 (Beissinger). Average energy content is 29.0 kcal/egg. The shell is smooth, without gloss; **color** white obscured by blotching, speckles, and washes of various very dark to palish warm browns, these sometimes entirely obscuring the ground color. A few are nearly immaculate, having only a few small light brownish spots or scrawls.

In Argentina, the parasitic Black-headed Duck (*Heteronetta atricapilla*) sometimes lays eggs in Snail Kite nests (Höhn 1975). Two of the 5 nests that Höhn found were parasitized, and another worker in the same marsh had seen over 30 kite nests, each with 1 or more duck eggs. Weller (1967, 1968) never reported this parasitism despite extensive studies where both kite and duck nested.

Incubation Shared by the sexes. Nests incubated predominantly by ♂ ♂ exceeds those by ♀ ♀ (Beissinger 1984). Often a parent will fetch a stick in its beak to place on the nest at changeover (nest relief) (Haverschmidt 1970). Incubation bouts range ½–4 hrs. with 1–1½ typical (Beissinger). **Incubation period:** 26–28 days (Chandler and Anderson 1974).

Preflight period Both sexes brood, ♀ ♀ mostly, and feed the young, but division of labor varies from nest to nest. The chicks are brooded until about age 2 weeks. They are fed snail meat, extracted from the shell by the parent (N. and H. Snyder 1969). Males feed young more often than ♀ ♀ during the first 2 weeks. By age 3–6 weeks, one of the parents has deserted—usually the one that has fed fewer snails. Around this time the parent may begin to bring whole snails to the nest (N. Snyder, Beissinger)—initially, with the operculum torn off and the columellar muscle cut; later, completely intact. After desertion, the remaining parent feeds the young at a rate similar to that of both parents before desertion (Beissinger 1984).

Age at first flight Various estimates are 23–28 days (Chandler and Anderson 1974) and 30 days (Nicholson 1926) to 49 days (Stieglitz and Thompson 1967). Disparity may exist because the young leave the nest at least a week earlier than they can fly and often continue to use the nest as perch, roost, or feeding platform long after they can fly. They leave at 4–5½ weeks but rarely are capable of sustained flight until age 6–7 weeks (Beissinger 1984, N. Snyder).

Flying young Fed by a single parent until age 9–11 weeks. By this time usually they are proficient in capturing snails on their own but still are clumsy and unskilled at extracting and eating them (Beissinger, N. Snyder). Sykes (1979) contended that learning to hunt snails is difficult for young kites and that, consequently, many probably die. Mortality at this age was very low during years when water levels and snail populations were good, but this period may be difficult for the young under poor environmental conditions. When parental care terminates, the young fend for themselves, continuing to develop their snail-handling skills. Young from several nests often join in a large group, feeding in the same area and roosting together, with or without adults.

157

In summary, a complete breeding cycle from earliest pair-formation activity to termination of parental care lasts about 4 months (Beissinger, N. Snyder).

Nesting success   In Fla., varies greatly from year to year depending on variation in weather and water levels. Sykes's tables (1979) give an impression of high success, av. over 54%, but this result was biased because the sample included many unstable nests that were saved by using nest baskets (mentioned above) and did not include some that failed before laying began (R. Chandler). Success (number of nests producing at least 1 young to flight age) of 331 unmanipulated nests, 1978–1983, varied annually 0–41% (N. Snyder, Beissinger 1984), overall averaging 33%. If humans had not intervened, a lower av. would have prevailed. On av., about 2 young attain flight per successful nest (Sykes, Beissinger).

Most nesting failure is caused by weather and predation. During severe drought, as in 1971 and 1981, few nests were initiated and even fewer were successful because more stable substrates (willows, shrubs, etc.) grow in shallower water, which dries out, forcing kites to nest in a poorer substrate (cattails). Most such nests fail when wind, rain, rapid water-level changes, and/or weight of the kites weaken the cattails, spilling eggs or young overboard (Chandler and Anderson 1974, Sykes and Chandler 1974). In one study over half the cattail nests were deserted even before eggs were laid, probably because they already were unstable (Beissinger 1984).

Nesting failure   Massive failure has been related to cold winter weather (D. Carey, N. Snyder, R. Chandler). Water temperature drops quickly as winds cool shallow waters, resulting in decreased apple snail activity. When a cold front stalls for several days over s. Fla., kite foraging success can decrease greatly, causing the adults to terminate nest building or incubation and to desert their nests.

The other major cause of nesting failure is predation. Raccoons (*Procyon lotor*), Boat-tailed Grackles (*Quiscalus major*), N. Harriers, cottonmouths (*Agkistrodon piscivorus*), and rat snakes (*Elaphe obsoleta*) are the most common predators (Chandler and Anderson 1974, later studies). Most unusual are the larvae of dermestid beetles (*Dermestes nidum*), which chewed crater-shaped holes up to 7 mm. diam. in the abdomen of nestlings in 11 nests in 1978–1979; the wounds usually healed, but death resulted in at least 1 instance (N. Snyder et al. 1984).

Infertile eggs sometimes are found in kite nests. Laboratory tests on 2 kites, a kite egg, and apple snails, collected in 1966–1967, showed very low levels of organochlorine pesticides (Lamont and Reichel 1970). These data, and no field evidence of broken eggs in nests (R. Chandler), would indicate no known failures due to eggshell thinning. As mentioned earlier, Snail Kites have died in S. Am. from eating snails in fields where pesticides had been applied.   STEVEN R. BEISSINGER

SURVIVAL   Although Snail Kites have a potential of being relatively long-lived, av. adult lifespan may not exceed 6 years. Maxima for known-age individuals in Fla. ranged 7–8.8 years (Sykes 1979) and 11–13 years (Beissinger, N. Snyder). Some captive individuals from Argentina were alive at 15 years (P. Sykes). Probably the main cause of adult mortality in Fla. is drought, which occurs every 5–7 years. For instance, the population declined from about 650 birds in 1981 to 250 in 1982 during a severe drought (Beissinger 1984).   STEVEN R. BEISSINGER

HABITS   The Snail Kite is best known for its specialized diet. Throughout its range it feeds almost exclusively on apple snails of the genus *Pomacea* (Haverschmidt 1962, N. and H. Snyder 1969, others). Its slender hooked beak, long curved talons, and buoyant flight are adaptations proficiency in capturing and eating this prey.

The kite's principal food in Fla. is the large apple snail (*Pomacea paludosa*), which feeds on vegetation such as bladderwort (*Utricularia*) and *Elodea*. It is an amphibious prosobranch snail that, for respiration, possesses a mantle cavity containing both a ctenidium (the characteristic molluscan gill) and another part that is modified as a gas-filled lung. The snail may be found 1 below but close to the water surface, where it ventilates its gas-filled lung and filter feeds (McClary 1964), 2 on plant surfaces, or 3 on the marsh bottom, where it grazes (N. and H. Snyder 1971). The snails are active both in daytime and at night, when they lay eggs after climbing emergent vegetation up to a ½-m. above water to deposit them (Perry 1973). During drought, the snails bury themselves in mud and can survive away from water for some months (Burky et al. 1972, Kushlan 1975). Currently, the apple snail occurs much more widely in Fla. than the kite; historically, their distributions were related more closely (Sykes, in Kale 1978).

Foraging   The kite forages by flying over a marsh, extending 1 or both feet, and seizing the snail near the surface of the water. Often it transfers the snail to its beak before returning to a perch, where it extracts the body from the shell. The bird does not plunge like an Osprey but descends only to the surface, plucking the snail from within 6–8 in. of the top. Its thighs may get wet, but its wings and tail remain dry. See Kern (1978) for excellent photographs of this behavior. Weller (1967) contended that, in Argentina, kites tested their captures in midair—that is, the shell was held in the kite's foot, sampled with the beak, and dropped if empty. No other observer has reported such behavior; kites usually drop empty shells shortly after capture without checking them in the beak (Beissinger 1983). More likely, the Argentine kites were repositioning the snail in the beak or initiating extraction procedure, perhaps by removing the operculum, since these birds occasionally eat snails in flight in Fla. (Nicholson 1926, R. Chandler).

Flight speeds   Vary from 8 m./sec. for sailing to 12.5 m./sec for flapping flight (Bourne 1983).

Hunting   Two main modes have been observed (N. and H. Snyder 1969, Haver-schmidt 1970: 1 still-hunting, in which kites visually search a marsh while perched, capturing a snail nearby after a brief flight; and 2 course-hunting, when a kite flies 3–5 m. above a marsh, usually facing the wind, and visually searches until it encounters a snail, whereupon it stalls and drops to capture it. In Guyana rice fields, both modes are employed about equally; in Fla., still-hunting is not used much by adults, although young kites may hunt in that manner (Beissinger 1983, D. Carey). Kites hunt through-out the day in Fla. and Guyana, but in the latter they were most active in morning (N. and H. Snyder 1969, Beissinger 1983). In Guyana, kites course-hunted more often in morning and still-hunted more frequently in the hotter hours.

A 3d hunting mode, robbery of snails from Limpkins (*Aramus guarauna*), has been observed only in Belize (Miller and Tilson, in press). By swooping in from behind and smashing into Limpkins, kites were able to steal snails from Limpkins' bills. The incidence of this parasitic behavior was related to an apparent decline in snail availability to kites; numerous Limpkins in the area still were successfully procuring snails.

When snails are available the kites have little trouble capturing them. For instance, Beissinger (1983) observed a 78% capture rate for hunting attempts in rice fields in Guyana. This is one of the higher values for avian predatory efficiency, similar to other invertebrate-eating birds (M. Collopy). In Guyana rice fields, hunting time to capture ranged 1–303 sec., av. 88, for coursing hunts where searching times could be measured completely (Beissinger 1983). When snail numbers are low, as during Fla. droughts, kites spend a much greater amount of time hunting and are frequently unsuccessful. Cold fronts can cause wave action from wind, which obstructs kite visibility, and the decrease in snail activity as water temperature lowers results in poor hunting success as previously noted.

Beginning with Lang (1924) there have been conflicting statements about the method whereby the kite extracts the fleshy snail from its shell. The matter has been settled by N. and H. Snyder (1969), Voous and van Dijk (1973), and N. Snyder and Kale (1983) by close observation of wild birds in Fla., Suriname, Guyana, and Colombia, and of captives from Argentina. The procedure is as follows: The kite flies to a perch, carrying the snail in its beak or feet. It holds the snail in one foot (sometimes both) against the perch and begins working on it with its beak. Usually the snail is positioned with spire pointing downward and aperture facing away from the perch. The kite works the tip of its slender upper mandible around the edge of the operculum until it locates a crack between operculum and shell. Then it removes the operculum by twisting it with both mandibles and tearing its attachment with the upper mandible. The detatched operculum is flipped aside, and the shell is repositioned so that its aperture faces upward and its spire points to the bird's left. Then, by thrusting its long curved upper mandible into the aperture and around the bend to the attachment, the kite cuts the columellar muscle (which attaches the snail's body to the shell) with a few strokes. Using both mandibles, the kite frees the fleshy snail from its shell and begins tearing the meat into pieces. The yolk gland is discarded, probably because it is noxious and distateful. Sometimes the digestive tract is discarded similarly. The kite usually eats the snail in several pieces, but sometimes swallows it whole. The extracted snail may held in the beak for a while, especially if it is to be delivered to nestlings. Shells are dropped before, during, or after ingestion of the flesh, and they accumulate under habitually used feeding perches. Unlike the Limpkin (*Aramus guarauna*), which may pierce the shell, the kite damages it slightly—if at all—at the lip.

In Guyana, the usual time required to extract and eat a snail ranged 21–200 sec., av. 69 (Beissinger 1983). On av., extracting and eating a snail took as long as finding one. In Fla., where the snails are larger, av. time required to extract and eat one was closer to 90 sec. (Beissinger).

From the above, it appears that Snail Kites are proficient at handling snails. No comparison has been made of the hunting and extracting ability of this specialist with more generalist feeders that also eat apple snails, such as Limpkins and Boat-tailed Grackles.

As a specialist, the Snail Kite rarely distinguishes between a number of food items to be included in the diet but must decide 1 among snails on basis of size, 2 whether to

search using the energy costs of flying (course-hunt) or from a perch (still-hunt), and 3 where (what patch) to search. Kites do select larger than av. snails but sometimes do not select the largest ones available (Beissinger 1983, Bourne 1985). Snail Kites did not require more time to capture larger snails than smaller ones and did not capture larger snails when course-hunting than when still-hunting (Beissinger 1983). Foraging behavior was influenced by changes in vegetation; the proportion of coursing-hunts increased and still-hunts decreased as rice fields grew higher and denser. Beissinger concluded that the most important decisions a foraging kite must make are what patch to search and for how long before abandoning one for another.

Bourne expanded on this work, using optimal foraging theory, and compared the profitability of several patch types in Guyana. He found that kites spend about 94% of their time in the most profitable patch but rarely switched patches in response to diurnal changes in profitability. In snail-size selection experiments in which kites were trained to feed from submerged pens, the kites took the larger snails more frequently (although this relationship did not always hold), and the kites seemed capable of using the density of snails as a proximate cue before selecting the larger individuals.

Although this kite is a *Pomacea* specialist, it will take such other foods as small turtles, crabs, and other snails—especially when apple snails are unavailable. (See Food, below.)

Snail Kites and Limpkins sometimes feed on snails in the same location and may compete for them. As observed in Belize, the kite robs the Limpkin of snails (B. Miller and Tilson 1985). A Limpkin diet generally includes several mollusk species, other invertebrates, and plant materials (Cottam 1936, N. and H. Snyder 1969), although in some areas they feed almost exclusively on *Pomacea* (Bourne 1983). Because Limpkins feed for snails by tactile search while wading, they must forage in shallow water; depth does not limit kites, which take prey in a different way. On the other hand, dense vegetation may hamper kite foraging but may encourage Limpkins, which require cover in areas where they are subjected to hunting.

In addition to habitat partitioning, it appears that snail-size partitioning may occur between Snail Kites and Limpkins. Two studies (S. Collett 1977, Bourne 1985) have shown that kites take larger snails than Limpkins in areas where they forage together, although overlap was high. While kites took snails that were larger than av. size

161

available, Limpkins selected ones that were smaller (Bourne). These differences may be due to antipredation behavior of the snails and to the modes of hunting of the 2 birds (Bourne). Snails can respond to mechanical disturbance created by wading Limpkins by burrowing but have no defense against aerial attacks by kites (N. and H. Snyder 1971). Thus, partitioning may be maintained more by snail behavior than by predator behavior.

Feeding on snails may pose a health hazard for kites; 7 species of trematodes (parasitic flatworms) and 1 parasitic protozoan are known from kites (Sykes and Forrester 1983); at least 8 other trematode species are described for *Pomacea*, and birds are definitive hosts in the 3 cases where life histories are known (see Beissinger 1983). If kites act as a host for hazardous parasites, snail parasite loads could affect snail-size selection. Since the parasite load increases with snail size (Hanning 1978), kites might avoid higher infection rates by not selecting the largest snails. Alternatively, the effects of parasites on snail surfacing behavior and vulnerability are unknown.

Snail Kites ordinarily do not defend an area away from the nest; rarely does **aggression** occur over a feeding area (Sykes 1979, Beissinger 1983). On one occasion, however, several nonbreeders were noted defending feeding territories along a canal in the East Everglades by chasing off intruding kites (N. and H. Snyder 1970). One defended an area of about 30 × 75 m. The Snyders concluded that apple snails were superabundant in a limited area and, hence, that defense was feasible in terms of time and energy; by contrast, when food is less abundant and feeding areas are large, a kite would be incapable of effective defense. Aggressive chases of this type also have been observed along canals during drought conditions when snails were scarce (Beissinger). Under such conditions the few good hunting spots may be small discrete patches, which may be more defendable than the larger heterogeneous feeding areas required when nesting.

No other instances of complete exclusion of other kites have been recorded. Occasionally, pairs nesting near one another will attempt to exclude each other from some hunting areas—usually unsuccessful in the long run—but in no way can this be considered strict territorial defense. In chasing, the aggressor usually pursues from below, occasionally rising up and bumping the intruder from underneath.

Communal roosts   Large flights (712 and 219 birds counted) have been observed in Suriname (Haverschmidt 1954, Vermeer et al. 1974). In Fla., roosts ranged from 2–200 birds (various observers); 1 in Cuba contained 25–45 kites (Beissinger et al. 1983).

Numbers   Although named from Argentina in 1817, this kite was not found in Fla. until the 1840s, since the Everglades were largely unknown and unmapped. The Fla. discovery site is located about 1½ mi. e. of Miami International Airport. Indications that this kite was numerous formerly were given by Nicholson (1926), A. Howell (1932), and Bent (1937). They indicated that, in the Everglades and St. John's marshes, scattered flocks of over 100 individuals could be found. Nicholson described, in a paper well worth reading, the difficulties encountered by the early naturalists, who had to travel by dugout canoe or afoot through the sawgrass to find the Snail Kite. All 3 authors noted a decline in kite numbers by 1930, and Nicholson warned that further drainage would cause further declines.

The 1st report that kites were in serious trouble in Fla. came from Sprunt, Jr. (1945), who believed that only 50–100 were left in the early 1940s. He had observed a steady decline in numbers at L. Okeechobee and a complete disappearance from the head-waters of the St. John's R. A decade later, Sprunt, Jr. (1954), estimated that only 50–75 kites remained in s. Fla., and Stieglitz and Thompson (1967) could find only 21. These were blind guesses, because most kite habitat was not easily surveyed.

The 1st thorough **censuses** were begun in 1967 (Sykes 1979). Using an airboat, Sykes was able to search most of the habitat available to the kites in s. Fla. The population reached its lowest in 1972—an estimated 65 individuals—and peaked in 1980 at 651 birds (Sykes 1983b), perhaps the largest number in Fla. since the 1930s. About half of the population perished during each of the severe droughts of 1971 and 1982 (Sykes 1979, Beissinger 1984).

All evidence points to habitat alteration as the main cause of kite endangerment and population decline; its range in Fla. has been dessicated by diking and draining the Everglades. Droughts and floods occurred naturally in regular cycles in Fla. In the past 75 years, natural cycles have been disrupted by management practices that diverted water to the sea and elsewhere, thereby shortening the wet cycles and changing the predictability of water levels, worsening the effects of droughts that always follow (Beissinger 1984). (See also Habitat, above.) Problems that might be associated with pesticides have not been detected in this kite in Fla. (Sykes 1985).

Two methods have been used to census Snail Kites in Fla. (Sykes 1979 and in D. Davis 1982). They may be counted either from standardized transects using an airboat or from birds flying into evening roosts from 1½ hrs. before sunset until dark. Each method has disadvantages. Transects are difficult to establish in the Everglades, and visibility from the airboat over the sawgrass varies depending on water level. Roost counts may tally individuals more than once, since kites may fly several mi. a day. When conducting roost counts, preliminary surveys must be made on several evenings to be sure that all roosts are located; if one is missed, the estimate may be greatly affected. In addition, the observer is often unable to sex birds during roost counts because of poor light, while this rarely happens during transect counts. In general, the roost count is probably the most efficient technique (Sykes, in D. Davis 1982), and repeated censuses on a roost during a period of stable water levels yielded little variation between counts (Beissinger).

Counts were conducted in Fla. in Nov. and Dec., when the kites appear to congregate more. Breeding, which would require 1 member of a nesting pair to remain at the nest to incubate at night (rather than going to a roost), does not usually begin during these months. Also, water levels are generally high enough at this time of year to permit both access to and good visibility of most marshes.

As Slud (1980) noted in Costa Rica, these kites are remarkably tame and easily shot. They often allow humans to approach closely before they fly away with low, seemingly indolent, flaps interspersed by brief glides. Shooting has occurred in Fla. (Sprunt, Jr. 1945, Sykes 1979), occasionally during the waterfowl hunting season. It probably occurs more often during regional drought, when the birds are forced to disperse from the Everglades wilderness into urban areas (Beissinger and Takekawa 1983). Even so, it is unlikely that shooting has been a major cause of kite decline in Fla.

Elsewhere No information exists on population trends, if any, in the Neotropical

163

range of this kite. It appears to be widespread and plentiful in Cent. and S. Am.; coastal wetlands there are shrinking rapidly by conversion to agriculture. Because the kite is a food specialist, it is extremely susceptible to habitat alteration and is thus a good indicator of environmental health. Tropical Am. populations should be monitored carefully.   STEVEN R. BEISSINGER

FOOD   Of the species. Almost exclusively large freshwater snails of the genus *Pomacea*. In Fla., almost entirely *P. paludosa* (A. Howell 1932, later authors), but recently has been observed to eat an introduced species—the little-known snail *P. bridgesi* (Takekawa and Beissinger 1983). In S. Am., 2 species are eaten, *P. dolioides* and *P. glauca* (Lang 1924, Haverschmidt 1962, later authors), but the latter is generally found in deeper water and is rarely taken. In Colombia, kites have fed on the larger *P. chemnitzi* (N. Snyder and Kale 1983).

Snail Kites must not be considered as strictly obligate feeders on *Pomacea*. They have fed on crabs (*Dilocarcinus dentatus*) in Venezuelan savannas (Mader 1981) and on a giant ramshorn snail (*Marisa conuarietis*) in Colombia (N. Snyder and Kale 1983).

The *Marisa* snails were taken in the same area that *P. chemnitzi* was taken preferentially (N. Snyder and Kale 1983). The kites had difficulty extracting *Marisa* from its snail, because the operculum is recessed and because the columellar muscle attachment of this snail is deeper inside the entrace—about as far as the long hooked bill of the kite can reach. Kites not only failed more frequently to extract *Marisa* than *Pomacea* but also got only about $\frac{1}{10}$ the energy value. Although Snyder and Kale found 10–20 times more *Marisa* than *Pomacea* in their backwater study area, they did not record capture times to assess relative caloric costs and benefits for capture and ingestion per species. They inferred that kites may be making mistakes in discriminating between the 2 snails when foraging on the wing because they look very similar when viewed from above and size difference is minimal.

Items other than snails   In Fla., nearly all such observations have occurred during times of food scarcity, mostly drought. The 1st observation was made in 1971 (Sykes and Kale 1974) when a kite was briefly observed feeding on a small turtle of undetermined species. A year later another kite fed on a small mammal, probably a rice rat (*Oryzomys*) or cotton rat (*Sigmodon*). Because neither bird was clearly visible when feeding, observations were limited. In both cases, however, the kite was observed tearing small pieces of flesh from its prey with some difficulty. Four kites of Argentine origin, however, lived "perfectly well" in captivity in Utah for 3 years on a diet of laboratory rats and day-old cockerels (C. M. White).

Observations by Beissinger during the severe 1981–1982 drought follow: small aquatic turtles were the most common items observed; of these, stinkpots (*Sternotherus odoratus*) and mud turtles (*Kinosternon subrubrum*) were by far the most numerous, but cooters (*Chrysemys floridana*), red-bellied turtles (*Chrysemys nelsoni*), and soft-shelled turttes (*Trionyx ferox*) were also recorded. Carapace length varied 30–90 mm. Turtles were killed and eaten in much the same manner that apple snails were extracted. The turtle was grasped in the kite's talons and held against the perch on its back with head nearest the perch and tail farthest away. The kite entered the turtle's body cavity through the right rear leg, which, from the kite's position, has the same circular shape as an apple snail's operculum. Small pieces of flesh were torn from the leg area and swallowed. Then viscera and organs were eaten. Head and forelegs were not consumed and feeding terminated, especially on larger turtles, before all of the body meat was eaten. Eating lasted 1–2 hrs.

At height of the 1982 drought, a Snail Kite may have fed for 6 weeks almost exclusively on a very small bottom-dwelling aquatic snail, *Viviparus georgianus* (Beissinger). It hunted on a large shallow mudflat that was exposed during low water. These snails are extracted easily by kites, Boat-tailed Grackles, or humans—the whole snail body comes free of the shell by pulling on the operculum. These snails, however, yield only about $\frac{1}{10}$ the dry wt. biomass of apple snails.

The only nondrought-related observations of nonsnail prey taken in Fla. occurred during colder winter months (Woodin and Woodin 1981, Beissinger). The prey items were a small shoft-shelled turtle and a small stinkpot turtle. Such observations of turtle predation in winter may be a response to low snail availability in cold weather.

STEVEN R. BEISSINGER

Juv.

ventral

MISSISSIPPI KITE

Ictinia mississippiensis (Wilson)

Smallish, sturdily built raptor, in general appearance more falconlike than hawklike. Length 14–15 in. (35.5–38 cm.), wingspread to 38 in. (96 cm.), and weight 8–13 oz. (220–390 gm.). Sexes nearly alike; the ♀ av. heavier, also darker anteriorly.

Upper mandible with fairly evident "tooth"; head–neck and venter vary from pale gray to, commonly, medium gray or darker; dorsum, including most of upper wing surface nearly black or black; secondaries pearly gray; counting from outer, the 3d primary is longest and 2d not much shorter; basal phalanges of inner toe fused to form a single functional unit; tail squarish to slightly forked, blackish and, in ventral view, plain or, rarely, with white or grayish areas on inner webs. Juv.: head–neck and venter heavily streaked and, on venter, also blotched with brown, gray, and black on white; mantle, wings, and tail (barred underneath) mostly muted dark browns to blackish; on tail feathers, the white areas on inner webs are extensive and form 2–3 (usually 3) broad transverse bars.

No subspecies treated here (but see below).

NOTE **Name priority** Arbitrarily retaining current practice herein conflicts with an earlier valid name: *Falco subcerulius* Bartram (1791: 290) [=*Ictinia subcerulia*], not

166

Falco misisippiensis [*sic*] of Wilson; type locality Oldtown on the Suwanee R., Dixie Co., Fla. (see Harper 1942: 212).

DESCRIPTION   In absence of adequate data on molting, the following is suggested tentatively: molting is principally on winter range, with renewal of flight feathers delayed, or "offset," until summer; Juv. wing/tail are apparently retained and worn with Basic I head–body; wings and tail are renewed as part of Basic II, which is earliest Definitive.

▶ ♂ Def. Basic Plumage (entire feathering) evidently acquired by protracted molting. Generally paler headed than ♀. **Beak** and cere black; sharply defined black patch on lores continues narrowly around eye; **iris** scarlet or ruby. On occiput a light spot or patch, only visible when feathers erected (present in both sexes and all flying ages). Dark of **dorsum** has a chalky bloom (lost in museum specimens); scapulars usually with light spots, which are concealed; venter variably gray. **Legs** short but stout and strong. Tarsus and toes some variant of scarlet-orange, rarely yellowish; remainder dusky to black; talons black. **Tail** varies from squarish ended to slightly notched (central pair of feathers to 1 cm. shorter than outer), usually black, but in rare cases faintly barred or washed light (to white). **Wing** long and pointed, except when soaring. Dorsal surface of secondaries pale velvety gray to silvery white, lighter near tips; both webs of some primaries and secondaries sometimes ventrally showing small patches of chestnut to dark brownish red, highly variable in extent. Area surrounding vent often stained dark by food remains carried in flight.

▶ ♀ Def. Basic Plumage (entire feathering), as ♂ except **head** usually somewhat darker. Decidedly larger.

AT HATCHING   Covered with white down except for dark gray to black eye-ring and lores. Faint areas of buffy reported by G. Sutton (1939) are rare, if ever present. Beak blackish, cere and rictus vivid to pale yellow. Iris dark brown. Feet and tarsi usually orange-yellow, perhaps very pale; talons gray. All nesting downs white. The egg tooth is retained to age 3–4 days.

▶ ♂ ♀ Juv. Plumage (entire feathering), its development for 1 individual described by T. Robinson (1957), in greater part confirmed by Parker. There are a few other data in Hardin et al. (1977) and S. Evans (1981). Tail and wing quills emerge at 10–12 days posthatching, when nestlings weigh about 100 gm. Feathers of other tracts except capital and ventral emerge about 12–15 days. All feathers grow approximately linearly to full extent. Juv. feathering well developed at age 35 days; retained for several months, then head–body begin molting gradually into Basic I, the flight feathers beginning later.

Head white streaked dusky, except chin and sometimes forehead nearly plain; **beak** black; cere bright yellow; **iris** dark brown. **Upperparts** blackish, some feathers distally edged whitish and others more or less reddish brown; scapulars broadly based white. **Wing** mostly black, various feathers with white tips, most pronounced on tertials and scapulars, but also prominent on greater coverts and flight feathers; wing lining more or less barred, alternating whitish and medium or darker brown. **Underparts** breast, abdomen, and flanks white to pale buffy, heavily streaked or blotched with brown,

167

rufous, and gray; area around vent similarly but less distinctly streaked. **Legs** and feet evenly orange-yellow, usually pale; talons black. **Tail** blackish with 3 white bars formed from white spots on inner vanes of the feathers, and tips narrowly white.

In general appearance Juv. birds vary from deep rufous toward blackish dorsally— latter as in Juv. *I. plumbea*. Color photos of nestling, Juv., and Basic Plumages: J. Parker and Ogden (1979).

▶ Basic Plumage (sexes alike?) consists of head–body (all of Juv. wing and tail retained); acquired probably beginning in winter when several months old, with molting often extending into midsummer. (Statements that Prebasic I molting begins in fall are evidently erroneous.) The new feathering presumably as definitive. Kites retaining a variable number of Juv. abdominal and wing lining feathers are not uncommon in June–Aug. (age 1 year), and, rarely, an individual may then have acquired only a gray head and upper breast. In most birds at age 1 year the **cere** is black, **iris** reddish brown to scarlet; some have begun to renew the long feathers of **wing** and **tail**.

Three captive yearling kites maintained by Parker on a simulated natural photoperiod grew all-black tail feathers at Prebasic I molt. Two others maintained on photoperiod of alternating 12 hrs. daylight and 12 hrs. darkness grew tail feathers barred white (as Juv.).

Color phases None.

Measurements Six ♂ BEAK from cere 14.5–15.5 mm., av. 15.1, WING across chord 286–305, av. 295, TAIL 149–166, av. 157.1, and TARSUS 35–37, av. 35.9; and 5 ♀ BEAK from cere (of 4) 15–17 mm., av. 16, WING across chord 300–315, av. 309.5, TAIL 154– 172, av. 163, and TARSUS 36.5–40.5, av. 38.3 (Friedmann 1950).

The above birds were probably included in these data from N. Snyder and Wiley (1976), the statistics being the mean: 20 ♂ BEAK from cere (of 19) 15.8 mm. and WING chord 294; ♀ BEAK from cere (of 13) 16.2 mm. and WING chord (of 14) 300.

Fitch (1963) gave overall LENGTH as follows: 7 ♂ 342–360 mm., av. 351, and 6 ♀ 348–370 mm., av. 361.

Weight Sixteen birds collected in Okla., May 9–June 12 (but mostly very late May–early June): 11 ♂ 216 gm. (stomach "not entirely full") to 269 gm. (stomach full), av. 245; 5 ♀ 278 gm. (stomach well filled) to 339 gm. (stomach contents 6.1 gm.), av. 311 (G. Sutton 1939).

Birds weighed by Parker during banding, plus museum data: "adults" 20 ♂ av. 266 gm. and 18 ♀ 324; yearlings 8 ♂ av. 269 gm. and 4 ♀ 341. Standard deviations are greater for ♀♀. N. Snyder and Wiley (1976) noted that this kite shows greater sexual size dimorphism than our other N. Am. kites—more than they expected in reference to a presumed 99% invertebrate diet. Based on a more accurate assessment (see Food, below), the difference is not unreasonable.

A large number of young, on day of hatching, weighed 12–20 gm. In a large sample of nestlings aged 30–35 days, most weighed 275–290 gm.

Hybrids None.

Geographical variation None reported in *I. mississippiensis*, but see below.

Affinities *I. mississippiensis* closely resembles the Plumbeous Kite (*I. plumbea*) of Cent. and S. Am. Little is known about the latter; see Skutch (1947). Primarily on basis of external characters, various authors (including G. Sutton 1944) have preferred to consider the 2 conspecific under *plumbea*. They will probably prove to be ecologically similar. The presumed pattern of molting, discussed earlier for the n. birds, would suggest that the 2 are genetically similar.

Sutton suggested that the range of *Ictinia* kites was once continuous but was later disrupted by events of the Ice Age and that the n. birds are now expanding their breeding distribution toward the tropical ones. The 1st proposal is reasonable; the 2d is possible and might be hastened by habitat alteration (see J. Parker and Ogden 1979). It is at least as likely, however, that the N. Am. gene pool derives its isolation from earlier geological and ecological events associated with the formation of the N. Am. Great Plains in the Miocene or Pliocene and that it is diverging from the Cent. and S. Am. gene pool. The 2 populations are reproductively isolated so far as known; hence, *mississippiensis* is retained here as a species, and the *Ictinia* kites are regarded as a superspecies. JAMES. W. PARKER

SUBSPECIES None as treated here. If *mississippiensis* and *plumbea* are treated as conspecific, then taxonomy would appear as in G. Sutton (1944): *I. p. plumbea* (Gmelin)—southerly; size about as in the n. *I. p. mississippiensis* (Wilson); generally darker overall and sexes more nearly alike; tail banded in all Plumages; in definitive feathering, rufous areas in wing larger and no silvery sheen or white tipping on secondaries; tail usually squarish ended and usually less than half length of wing chord; tarsi and feet more highly colored. Juv. more toward slaty. Evidently less migratory (in some areas sedentary?) For meas., see Friedmann (1950) and Haverschmidt (1962). In Suriname, 5 ♂ weighed 190–267 gm., mean 239, and 5 ♀ 232–272 gm., mean 255 (Haverschmidt). JAMES W. PARKER

FIELD IDENTIFICATION On the wing, often more or less resembles a falcon, but has slower, graceful, buoyant flight. When soaring, wings are distally rounded with slight slotting; flat dihedral. At times hovers like a kestrel and may stoop vertically at great speed for several hundred ft. After age 1 year: mostly various grays, head paler, dorsal inner part of trailing edge of wing pale silvery white, outer portion of wing and the tail black. Some reddish brown may be visible on wing. Juv. appears largely white faced, the head–venter heavily streaked darkish, dorsal surfaces black, wing lining mottled brown, white, and gray; underside of tail has wide white crossbars. Birds at age 1 year are identifiable as such afield—the head–body approaches definitive, but the Juv. wing, barred tail, mottled wing lining, and variable number of Juv. abdominal feathers are still present.

In our area No other raptor can be confused with the "adult" Mississippi Kite. A very inexperienced observer possibly might mistake it for a small gull or a Mourning Dove. Juvenal birds are more likely to be mistaken for young buteos, especially the Broad-winged Hawk, or perhaps a falcon. In Cent. and S. Am., confusion with the Plumbeous Kite is a major problem. G. Sutton (1944) and Eisenmann (1963a) have provided comparative descriptions (see also Subspecies, above).

This kite is gregarious and typically nests colonially in the w. parts of its range. It forages both singly and in small-to-large flocks. It perches alone or in groups, on power lines and in trees. It is not particularly vocal except when disturbed or in the near presence of a natural predator. Often abundant in urban areas. Despite local abundance it can be inconspicuous—hence easily overlooked.   JAMES W. PARKER

VOICE   Data from Okla., Kans., and Tex., which align with descriptions from elsewhere by S. Evans (1981) and Glinski and Ohmart (1983). Most common call, as between mature individuals, parent birds and nestlings, and on the wing, is a high, thin, pure whistle best written as *phee-phew*—first stated by G. Sutton (1939). Often repeated. First syllable short (¼ sec.) and may be clipped; 2d has downward inflection and is drawn out 2–4 times length of 1st, as described by Fitch (1963). Either may be emphasized. Parker and G. Sutton have noted that the *phee-phew* call is imitated by the Northern Mockingbird. Often it is replaced by a *phee-ti-ti-ti* (Parker), the final 3 or more syllables given in rapid succession; they may be soft or equal in intensity to the 1st. The call is usually given by especially alert or seemingly excited birds, as in "courtship" feeding. When harassed by predators, kites most often use particularly strong, emphatic renditions of the call 1st described. During aerial acrobatics of paired birds, "thin squeals and chipperings" (Sutton). There is no published sonagram except S. Evans's (1981) of *phee-phew;* only some sound libraries have recordings, none the complete repertoire.

   Nestlings   During their 1st week may utter 1 or more soft peeps; occasionally a very young chick may utter a soft rendition of the *phee-phew* call; by 14 days most make the "adult" call, but less loud, and also chipper loudly. When 1st venturing from the nest, the young may call frequently while awaiting arrival of a parent with food; on approach of the parent, the calls are given in rapid succession and slurred to a "high thin squablike squealing" (Fitch 1963). Mature birds are generally silent near nests unless disturbed.   JAMES W. PARKER

HABITAT   **As a breeder**   Woodlands for nesting; woodland edge, grassland, or savanna are preferred for foraging, although this also is done over the forest canopy. In e. U. S., for which Kalla (1979) and S. Evans (1981) gave detailed descriptions, most nest sites are in large expanses of tall trees, not far from woodland edge. Thus often riparian areas, although there is no reason to believe that the birds prefer such edge habitat to woodland–grassland areas. In the e. part of summer range this kite now is most common in mature, undisturbed stands of lowland and floodplain hardwoods s. of the fall line and along major rivers. Kalla stressed the current absence of nesting in smaller woodland areas. In e. areas these kites consistently prefer to nest in taller trees, not of any particular species. They have a clear tendency to nest in groups, but this is less pronounced in w. birds.

   Alteration by man of habitat in the e. apparently has not significantly changed the affinities of this kite. It is showing some tendencies, however, to colonize urban trees—as near Tallahassee, Fla., and Memphis, Tenn.—but not to the extent shown w. Lumbering, agriculture, and other activities requiring forest removal have increased the amount of edge habitat and opportunities to forage over low vegetation.

   Apparently the s. Great Plains were—are are—the stronghold of this species in terms of local density and (at least currently) distributional continuity. This suggests that this kite is better adapted to prairie riparian habitat and savanna than to the more continuously forested areas in se. U.S. (J. Parker and Ogden 1979). In the plains w. of the Mississippi, this kite originally was a bird of mixed riparian hardwoods (Probably often cottonwoods), as along the Medicine Lodge and Cimarron rivers today, and of oak savanna, such as that common in nw. Okla. Some nesting may have occurred in n. reaches of mesquite savanna in Tex.

Although still present in riparian areas, kites in the w. have shown plasticity in habitat selection and today are most common in shelterbelt (windbreak) plantings, established beginning in the late 1930s by the Federal Civilian Conservation Corps. These are linear patches of trees of several species planted in regular rows. Most are oriented e.-w. or n.-s., are about 0.5–1.5 km. long and about 20 m. wide, and have rows of cedar to windward and elms, the tallest trees, to leeward. In shelterbelts, density approaches 1 nest/ha., the majority of nests under 100 m. apart, with 4–8 nests not unusual in a single large shelterbelt, and colonies of 15 nests known (J. Parker 1974). Commonly, a shelterbelt with several nests will be near other belts of seemingly identical character—but without nests. Kites are also numerous in oak shrub prairie and savanna, over which large flocks sometimes form, and occur in lesser numbers in groves of mesquite trees. In both habitats nests are widely spaced, usually near edges (J. Parker 1974). Wide nest spacing is also characteristic in riparian cottonwoods today (M. Ports). Many nesting colonies are remote from water. The kites forage over the open prairie as well as near and over trees at the nest sites. In newly colonized areas in N.Mex. and Ariz., colonies are found in smaller riparian cottonwood areas, particularly those with introduced salt cedar (*Tamarisk*) (Glinski and Ohmart 1983).

A statistical analysis of prairie habitat and vegetation near colonies (D. Love 1975) confirmed J. Parker's assessment (1974) that no environmental features are crucial for, or predictive of, nesting unless it is the presence of healthy trees—preferably with other kites already there(!). Only the presence of snags, for perching, seems associated statistically with choice of area.

Habitat alteration on the Great Plains is continuing to have a positive effect on kite distribution and abundance (J. Parker and Ogden 1979). With Caucasian settlement, riparian forests were usually removed, and the kites were often probably displaced—many perhaps shot. Later land use practices on the Great Plains, primarily the establishment of shelterbelts and other tree plantings, which provide thousands of nesting habitat "islands," have resulted in a vast increase of woody vegetation. The n. expansion of mesquite woodland, a consequence of extensive cattle drives and overgrazing, similarly has provided new nesting habitat in s. plains areas. Extensive crop raising has probably increased insect populations; expanded woodlands on the plains have also enriched the environment by supporting larger numbers of tree-nesting songbirds and other vertebrates that these kites eat. An assertion that the kites shifted their nesting metropolis in a half-decade from the damp wooded East to the dry Great Plains (Oberholser and Kincaid 1974) is inaccurate. The plains of w. Kans., Okla., and parts of Tex. have probably always been rich in kites. Of late, however, they have become richer.

Most recently, kites have colonized literally hundreds of towns of all sizes throughout the Great Plains. In 1979, the 2,300 residents of Meade, Kans. (a town about 2 km. sq.), shared their lawns, parks, and golf courses with some 40 pairs of nesting kites.

171

Other colonized centers include: Wichita and Dodge City, Kans.; San Angelo, Tex.; Norman, Okla.; Roswell, N. Mex.; and innumerable smaller towns in these states. Residents in some of these places have indicated that the urban kites first became noticeable in the 1960s or early 1970s and that they saw them most often on golf courses and in city parks.

Migration and winter Environments must affect kite numbers, yet are relatively unknown. Three banding recoveries are from river floodplain areas in e., interior, and w. Guatemala and Honduras. The human population explosion in Cent. and S. Am. has resulted in agricultural expansion and forest removal on a grand scale; this has probably benefited the Mississippi Kite because it prefers to forage in open and edge habitats. Perhaps, in some measure, *mississippiensis* seasonally replaces *plumbea* (of which many also shift with the season) on the latter's breeding range, but it is more likely that the 2 share some areas during the boreal winter. If so, they probably mingle in social groups, especially when foraging. The n. bird probably occupies tropical savanna and grassland (J. Parker and Ogden 1979), although Meyer de Schauensee (1970) described austral summer habitat as pastureland and open shrub. Kalla (1979) concurred in offering the likely possibility that many "wintering" *mississippiensis* eventually might be found on the Grand Chaco of cent. and s. Paraguay and n.-cent. Argentina, and on the grasslands of w.-cent. Argentina. Some specimen evidence supports this suggestion. JAMES W. PARKER

DISTRIBUTION (See also Habitat, above.) Meaningful mapping of past and current distribution requires recognition of this kite's clumped, colonial nesting pattern in some areas plus the sometimes inconspicuous presence of sizable numbers at various localities. The latter is exemplified by Meade State Park and Lake, Kans., where more than 100 kites were once counted (J. Parker 1974) and flocks of 20 or more were common. Nevertheless, it was often difficult to find kites for periods of several days and depending on weather. In the Great Plains area there is evidence that entire colonies may occasionally relocate to another shelterbelt. This could be mistaken for a population decline; a similar phenomenon is probable in the East, where tall, dense forest canopy is a greater hindrance to observation than in the West. These concerns must also be weighed in attempts to interpret past records.

Breeding range See J. Parker and Ogden (1979) for a conservative determination of all counties for then-current evidence of nesting.

Knowledge of the species' early range is fragmentary, but, based on a 2d map in J. Parker and Ogden (1979), it probably resembled the current pattern in most respects. Before Caucasian settlement, this kite was probably rare n. of cent. Kans. to s. Ill., cent. Ala. to cent. S.C., and w. of w. Kans., Okla., and cent. Tex. Its w. range probably matched the river systems, but this is not true today in Kans., Okla., and Tex. Most current regional populations in Colo., w. Tex., N.Mex., and Ariz. are small and restricted to riparian areas, but some are in urban areas (e.g., estimated 30–50 pairs in San Angelo, Tex.—D. Shaw). Kites in these w. areas probably represent relatively new—since 1950—recolonizations (see Levy 1971), but it is equally likely that kites may have always existed there, at least intermittently.

J. Parker and Ogden (1979) analyzed past patterns of population change for the e.

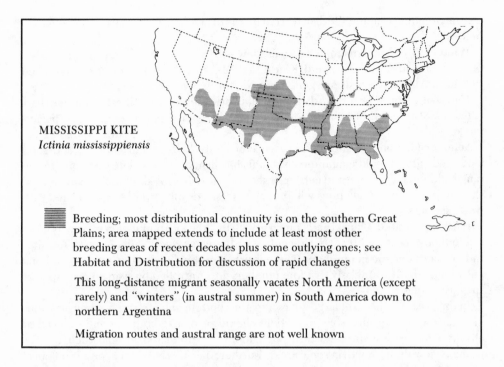

MISSISSIPPI KITE
Ictinia mississippiensis

Breeding; most distributional continuity is on the southern Great Plains; area mapped extends to include at least most other breeding areas of recent decades plus some outlying ones; see Habitat and Distribution for discussion of rapid changes

This long-distance migrant seasonally vacates North America (except rarely) and "winters" (in austral summer) in South America down to northern Argentina

Migration routes and austral range are not well known

and w. separately because they appear to be substantially different. In summary, in the East around the turn of the century, kites seem to have been extirpated where breeding density was low, as at many riparian sites, along smaller watercourses, and at range limits. Numbers dropped elsewhere to a greater or lesser extent. Because of inadequate documentation, shrinkage for some areas can only be surmised. For much of the region, an increase in kites and a reoccupation of areas was perceptible by the 1950s and led to today's situation: kites are widespread and numerous in many se. states.

Better documentation for w. areas clearly suggests no overall past decline in numbers, although this did occur locally; in some places the species has not yet recovered in numbers. Current abundance of this kite on much of the plains seems not to be a result of a recovery but an expansion of a population that escaped most negative impacts of Caucasian development and began responding positively to a number of habitat alterations.

Early declines can be associated with a number of probable causes: **1** in n.-cent. Okla. and ne. Tex., eggs were taken by collectors; **2** in the East, significant numbers of birds undoubtedly were shot from about the end of the Civil War onward for decades; and **3** much forest was removed, which Kalla and Alsop (1983) believed was as important as shooting. This last might often have produced only termporary disruption of nesting or colony relocation, judging from observations of the impact of tree cutting on the prairies.

Western kites were probably affected by the same factors, but to a much lesser extent because of sparse human population. The retention of much of the species'

173

central breeding range as "Indian territory" until nearly 1900 may also have acted as a buffer.

Winter Valid records in our area are few—1 in S.C. in Feb. (Sprunt, Jr., 1937), Tex. reports in Oberholser and Kincaid (1974), and a number of unsubstantiated sightings. Almost all birds are gone from N. Am. by Nov.

No **fossil** record. Two records from **prehistoric sites** (Ohio, Ill.); the former (Parmalee 1958) may indicate early nesting n. of the current extreme n. edge of the species' range.   JAMES W. PARKER

Some predictions Continued presence of shelterbelts and urban trees and good food availability should guarantee no significant shrinkage of the kite's current prairie range, although the aging and cutting of shelterbelts will probably cause frequent local shifting. Some sw. populations will probably persist despite problems associated with woodland loss.

It has been stated (Glinski and Ohmart 1983) that the kite population in Ariz. is more stable than that in N.Mex., but recent records suggest local shifts in breeding sites rather than a decline in numbers. There is urban nesting in N. Mex. but, as yet, none known in Ariz. It is unlikely that kite numbers are controlled by a single prey species such as cicadas.

In the East, retention of large areas of mature bottomland forest is not obligatory for kite nesting. Comprehensive predictions should recognize both this and reduced or absent shooting pressure. Eastern populations are predicted to hold their own or perhaps slow their growth in some areas. Further, biocides have not been a problem of recognizable consequence.

Overall, these kites will probably increase and their distribution will continue to expand more or less. For at least the past decade, kites—both adults and yearlings— have been reported beyond their usual range. May–June is the usual season; often more than 1 bird is reported. Thus, it is probably only a matter of time before breeding is documented at some of these locations—for example, in S.C. and near C. May, N.J. (nesting could be occurring already in the latter area, judging from frequency of sightings).   JAMES W. PARKER

MIGRATION In fall and spring this kite is often reported in loose groups of 8–20 birds, but groups of 200–300, or even more, are not uncommon. Many spring reports of flocks, in *Am. Birds,* are from s. Tex. The more numerous reports of flocks and movements in *Am. Birds* are from a wider area, including n. A group exceeding 250 birds was reported (Eubanks 1971) moving se. through Stillwater, Okla., on Sept. 4, 1971, apparently in response to a cold front moving from the ne., and assemblies of 78 and 121 kites passed through Hays, Kans., on Sept. 6 and 11, 1979, respectively. Other examples of spring and fall flocks are given below. Kites in larger groups seem to move as loose aggregations, usually flying at an altitude of 25–75 m. These kites and Broad-winged Hawks occasionally occur on the same route simultaneously, perhaps more often s. of the U.S. The kites presumably forage during migrations, especially if they encounter good concentrations of insects. They are long-distance migrants.

As previously noted, austral summer range is in S. Am.; see Eisenmann (1963a) for specimen evidence. A few reported boreal winter occurrences in e. or cent. s. states were apparently the basis of Bent's (1937) erroneous statement (often repeated since) that the species only withdraws somewhat from the n. part of its range. There are few winter records for our area (such as those in Oberholser and Kincaid [1974]), such individuals being far from their normal seasonal range. Further, it is unlikely that this kite is a regular "winterer" in Mexico or Cent. Am., since the increasing number of field workers have not reported it there in recent years.

Spring Southerly data are scant. Judging from the Paraguayan records, some birds still are that far s. until early Mar. In Panama, A. Wetmore (1965) reported a number of flocks in the span Mar. 20–Apr. 14 and regretted that he had no shotgun evidence to substantiate these sightings. From Costa Rica n., the birds probably follow an e. course and travel rapidly; the span of arrival dates for Fla. might possibly indicate that a few birds cross the Gulf of Mexico. North of the city of Veracruz, Mexico, Thiollay (1979) reported that migration extended through Apr. (peak in 4th week) into very early May; he saw 12,432 birds (but estimated 17,000); the daily maximum was 2,371 on Apr. 27, and the flocks flew low, rapidly. Most sources give earliest arrival dates for s.-cent. and se. parts of N. Am. breeding range as late Mar. or, more often, the 1st half of Apr. By late Apr. small numbers appear in Kans., Okla., and even n. parts of the species' e. range. By mid-May, most breeding colonies are probably reestablished. Some early dates (from *Am. Birds* 1981–1983): Tex.—Apr. 13, Mo.—May 7, Ga.— Apr. 23, Ala.—Apr. 24, S.C.—May 1, Tenn.—mid-Apr. and May 3, and Kans.— Apr. 28.

S. Evans (1981) and Parker observed that not all kites breeding at a particular locality arrive together; the bar-tailed yearlings apparently either arrive later than older age classes or move about while the latter are localizing their activity around nest sites. The kites seem to arrive in their historically new nesting areas (N. Mex., Ariz.), in re-claimed nesting areas, and in extralimital areas on about the same schedule as kites at comparable latitudes in parts of the original range. Thus, there are early dates, for example, for N.J., Pa., Mass., Ont., Minn., Nebr., and elsewhere. Similar occur-rences, some of flocks, continue into June and July.

Fall In n. breeding areas, small groups of kites assemble in premigratory flocks by early Aug. Presumably, they are composed of adults of both sexes plus that year's young. Ganier (1902) noted that they were often foraging very actively; a bird collected in late Aug. was fat. Postbreeding kites, perhaps individuals as well as flocks, seem to wander, probably seeking food. A Juv. banded in sw. Kans. was recovered 2 days later 45 km. e. A mature ♂ tagged in sw. Kans. was found a month later 145 km. directly n. Northerly or range-edge late occurrences, listed in *Am. Birds* for recent past years, include: N.J.—Aug. 14–16 and Sept. 19, Ky.—Aug. 23 and 30 (12 kites), Tenn.— Aug. 22, 26, and Sept. 18, Ill.—Sept 2 (10 kites), Kans.—Sept. 11, Okla.—Sept. 3 (132 kites), S.C.—Aug. 20, and Ariz.—Aug. 6. There is an old record (Chansler 1912) for a kite in Ind. on Sept. 18. A total of 121 kites were still at Hays, Kans., on Sept. 11.

Large flocks are usually seen well into migration. Typical examples from Tex., in recent volumes of *Am. Birds*, include: Johnson Co.—Aug. 30–Sept. 2 (138 kites), Corpus Christi—Oct. 2 (407) and Sept. 22 (200), Austin—Aug. 28 (100) and Sept. 16,

Falfurrias—Oct. 2 (500+), Denton—Aug. 28 (800+ passing in groups of 20+), Cambers Co.—Aug. 29 (1,000), Alice—Sept. 2 (65) and Sept. 9 (1,000+), and Brazos Co.—Sept. 9 (200). There are several comparable records from other s. states.

Recent information supports the generalization of most references—that the bulk of fall migration occurs late Aug.–Sept. There are a few more n. records of later dates, such as 5 kites in Okla. on Oct. 28 (DeVore 1977), but their paucity suggests that most kites are s. of the U.S. by mid-Oct. There is no solid evidence of fall migration over the Gulf of Mexico, although Kalla (1979) mentioned other observations of kites "heading out" over the Gulf.

There is not much documentation of s. movement beyond the U.S.; Eisenmann (1963a) summarized Mexican records for late Sept.–mid-Oct. A nestling banded Aug. 3 in Okla. was shot on Oct. 29 of the same year in Guatemala (J. Parker 1977a); another, banded July 16 in Ill. was recovered Oct. 10 of the same year, also in Guatemala. A Paraguayan specimen is dated Dec. 14. JAMES W. PARKER

BANDING STATUS   Since 1955, and excluding recent work by D. Shaw in San Angelo, Tex., 477 Mississippi Kites have been banded—416 (93%) of these since 1969, and 329 (74%) in Parker's study. By far the greatest number (422, 95%) were banded in w. states, primarily Kans. and Okla.; 359 (80%) were nestlings. Small w. samples are from Ariz. (15, R. Glinski and R. Ohmart), w. Tex. (D. Shaw), and se. Colo. (10, records from banding office). In the e., nests are usually 20 or more m. above ground, obviously a discouragement to banders; the most kites banded there were in Ill. (14, S. Evans 1981).

The largest number of free-flying kites (8 young of the year, 15 adults) was captured and color marked in Meade, Kans. In addition to leg bands, plastic wing-markers have been used (first by Parker in 1969) on 186 kites. Nestlings and older birds are resilient when handled and readily accept these patagial markers, but there is evidence of their removal. Parker was able to observe a large number of tagged nestlings, yearlings, and adults for various lengths of time after their release, but no kites tagged as nestlings have been resighted with markers in the breeding range in subsequent years.

There is a low rate of recovery. A nestling banded in Okla. in Aug. 1953 was recovered there the following June. Another nestling, banded in sw. Kans. in 1977, was recovered a year later at a colony approximately 50 km. e. of its origin. Six recoveries have been from the w. population, and a 7th was a nestling from Ill. Rate of recovery of patagial-marked kites (2.2% = 4 of 186) is twice that of birds banded but not wing marked (1.1% = 3 of 261 birds). JAMES W. PARKER

REPRODUCTION   Recent studies (J. Parker 1974 and MS, S. Evans 1981, Glinski and Ohmart 1983) provide data on reproductive pattern. Parker's work is based on over 1,000 nestings. Comparison of these data with 28 nestings over 5 years (S. Evans) and 63 over 4 years (Glinski and Ohmart) add geographical perspective. Full analysis of the data is needed.

Age when first breeds   Stevens (in Bent 1937) reported breeding by yearlings; J. Parker and Ports (1982) reported yearlings probably paired with "adults" at 35 of 209 (17%) of the nests where both individuals were identified. This estimate would be high

176

if some yearlings were helpers (see below). Glinski and Ohmart reported some un-paired "adults," but Parker detected few nonbreeders and concluded that most kites in "adult" feathering were reproductively active.

Parker and Ports observed **helping at the nest** by a yearling at each of 3 nests, judged it likely at 15 others (among 209 nests), and summarized observations by others that suggested the same phenomenon. D. Shaw (letter) noted a yearling at most of the 12 nests observed in tall trees in San Angelo, Tex., in 1983; in one case, 2 yearlings perched with 2 adults near a nest. She did not observe actual helping. S. Evans reported yearlings "closely associated" with adult pairs. Helpers observed by Parker and Ports, then later by Parker, participated in nest construction, incubation, brood-ing of a recently hatched nestling, and nest defense against predators. Higher success for nests with helpers suggests that this might be related to the additional defense provided. Since there is some biological advantage to helping, such behavior would appear to be adaptive for yearlings.

Displays   G. Sutton (1939), Fitch (1963), and others have described no displays and have implied or concluded that pair bonding occurs before arrival at nesting sites. Some pairs probably do continue some display activity during early summer. S. Evans, and Glinski and Ohmart, saw what they assessed as "courtship flights," but nothing further. The former described 3 instances of repeated swoop display (SKY-DANCE) by 2 adults. Parker saw ritualized posturing by 2 adults, perched on a dead limb, on May 23; the same has been seen by J. Stokes in his attempts to induce captives to breed.

Copulation   Described by Fitch (1963), has been seen on late spring and summer dates by several observers. It may occur without preliminaries between kites perched near each other or quickly upon arrival of a ♂, who may alight beside or on the ♀. Food offering by the ♂ is usual; copulation may be repeated often and at frequent intervals (S. Evans 1981). The ♀ shows no marked posturing, and copulation is brief.

Duration of the **pair bond** is unknown, but a strong year-to-year attachment to the nest site perhaps indicates that it may prove to be lengthy or permanent.

In shelterbelts on the plains and comparable habitat elsewhere the species shows a strong tendency toward **colonial nesting;** less than 10% of Parker's nests might be termed solitary, many being in small groves of trees, but most were in visual range of a colony. The largest shelterbelt colony was 15 nests with a density of 0.3 ha./nest. Density in shelterbelts with 2 or more nests was about 0.8 ha./nest and did not vary geographically. Colonies of 4–6 nests were common. Nests were usually either on the leeward side (n. or e.) of shelterbelts or within them, and distance apart av. 115 m. Many were much closer, as close as 13 m. Bent (1937) noted dense local nesting near suitable areas lacking kites, and Parker found large numbers of seemingly identical unused shelterbelts near colonies.

The largest colony of record is in cottonwoods and mixed woodland at Meade State Park and Lake, Kans. In the 1930s there was only a small colony in a few trees near an artesian well; it had grown to 100–150 kites by the early 1960s as estimated by Fitch (1963). He found over 40 nests and observed flocks of up to 44 kites. J. Parker's (1974) count of 24 nests in about half the woodlands there and a count of 108 kites at one time indicate essentially no change 10 years later. Nest density was similar to that in shelterbelts. A comparable but smaller colony has existed in cottonwoods near L.

177

Marvin, e. of Canadian, Tex. (Allan 1947, Parker). Other observations for the plains (Allan and Sime 1943a, Parker, M. Ports) indicate that kite nests in riparian woodlands are often spaced much more widely than those at Meade State Park or in shelterbelts. In riparian cottonwoods in Ariz., nests av. 550 m. apart; several were solitary and over 4 km. from others (Glinski and Ohmart 1983).

In shinnery oak prairies of w. Okla., where small groves of low oak trees are widely scattered, in oak woodlands and savanna farther e. (as in Wichita Mts. Wildl. Refuge), and in mesquite woodlands in n.-cent. Tex., kites tend to nest in more open aggregations, as in riparian cottonwoods. J. Parker (1974) calculated a density of 8.1 ha./nest with a mean nearest-neighbor distance of 188 m. in mesquite; A. Jackson (1945) suggested a density of 14.9 ha./nest in a 190+ ha. mesquite expanse. There is a puzzling account in Oberholser and Kincaid (1974) of about 100 nests in a 16-ha. mesquite area in Texas. No details were given, no kites were counted, and the report mentioned several nests in some trees. No one else has reported more than 1 active nest/tree, but fragments of old ones may be present.

Urban nests are often clumped. Four or 5 pairs nesting in a 3-block residential area in Newton, Kans., in 1983 is typical; large sections of urban area are often vacant.

Territorial defense Unknown against other kites of the same species. The close placement of nests, the many accounts of communal perching in nesting colonies by groups of assorted sizes, the group harassment of predators near nests, and the usually unmolested movement of adults near the nests of other kites all attest a lack of territoriality. The presence of yearlings at nests of adult pairs, sometimes as helpers, indicates that even the nest itself is not defended against other kites of this age class.

The vicinity of the nest is defended aggressively against predators by kites of both sexes and by flocks of as many as become aware of the intruder. Pursuit and repeated high-speed diving are accompanied by intensified 2-syllabled calling. Twenty or more kites may gather, some being attracted from a distance or considerable altitude. A. Jackson (1945) observed repulsion of a Cooper's Hawk; others have observed aggression toward Swainson's and Red-tailed Hawks, Am. Crows, Chihuahuan Ravens, and large owls. The owls harrassed are usually the Great Horned and Barn Owls, and kite response to the former is the most intense shown any predator. These owls are usually hit; Parker saw 1 forced to a violent crash landing by 2 kites. Oberholser and Kincaid (1974) reported kite harassment of Blue Jays.

Nest site G. Sutton (1939) and recent studies show that most nests are placed near woodland edge. Almost any tree species will serve, and nests are 2–45 m. high. Most shelterbelt nests are at 6–10 m.; in mesquite and oak habitat, 3–5 m. Plains nests were in 16 tree species (J. Parker 1974). Conifers were rarely used. Although uncommon in shelterbelts, the few cottonwoods present were often used. Five tree species are known to have been used in s. Ill.; conifers have been used more often in the se. than elsewhere. Old plus recent records in the se. indicate that the variety of tree species used merely reflects their respective abundance.

Nest construction Begins in early to mid-May, but kites may either add to or build new nests during June and even early July—depending on weather and early-season adversities. G. Sutton (1939) and S. Evans (1981) noted that building activity is often leisurely and protracted. The latter noted that an hr's effort, usually in early morning, sometimes added only 3 or 4 twigs. On several occasions, however, usually late in the season, Parker observed pairs building rapidly. Evans saw more ♂ ♂ than ♀ ♀ collecting materials and, in 1 case, saw a ♂ deliver twigs to a ♀ at a nest. Kites break twigs off with beak or talons while perching, during a plunging take off, or in short dives.

Nests Built of twigs, usually dead, they vary in size and sturdiness. There was no significant variation in nest structure in different plains habitats (J. Parker 1974). Most were in crotches with 3 or 4 supporting limbs. Average dimensions of 100+ plains nests were 27 × 24 cm. and depth 13 cm.—slightly smaller than the av. in S. Evans (1981). Smallest nest (with egg) 20 × 15 × 6 cm. (Parker). At least those on the plains often appeared flimsy. Nests in shelterbelts and cottonwoods tended to be much better shaded by foliage than those in mesquite and shinnery oak.

Greenery The nest bowl is quite shallow and is lined with a mat of green leaves of any of various tree species. Fresh "lining" material is added well into the nestling period; it forms a cushioning mat partly cemented together by, but usually covering, decaying food remains. Very young nestlings can be killed by arboreal ants, attracted to dead organic material, although this is uncommon (J. Parker 1977b). Addition of fresh foliage to the nest bowl may serve as a sanitary barrier.

Kites infrequently use nests previously built and occupied by other birds (Bent 1937, J. Parker 1974); they frequently reuse their own old nests. G. Sutton (1939) found more than half of 40 nests being reused. On the plains (Parker) and in s. Ill. (S. Evans), tenacity to old nest platforms and particularly to specific trees and limb forks was marked. Some years, over 30% of plains nests in shelterbelts and cottonwoods were in use for at least their 2d year. Reuse for a 2d or 3d consecutive year is the rule; rarely is the same structure refurbished and used a 4th or even 5th year. Some are built in limb forks where, some years earlier, a previous nest had existed. Reuse does not lead to significantly greater nest size and is probably limited by destructive weather.

Various birds, at least up to the size of Mourning Dove, share the same nest tree with this kite. Further, House Sparrows and wasps nest in niches in kite nests (J. Parker 1981). The proximity of other nesting species enhances defense against various diurnal predators.

Egg dates Most sources indicate that viable clutches are found in the latter half of May to mid-June. Bent (1937) gave extreme dates as Mar. 15 (which is suspect) and June 25, with about half of all records June 3–12. Fitch (1963) surmised that laying at Meade State Park, Kans., occurred in a period of less than 2 weeks around June 1. S. Evans's Ill. pairs laid eggs and began incubation May 20–June 8—2 weeks or more after arrival—almost exactly the laying period reported for Ariz. by Glinski and Ohmart. In 1969–1971, on the Great Plains, a large number of eggs were laid about May 10–June 20, with greatest frequency in late May the 1st 2 years and a week or so later in 1971. Laying date and latitude were clearly related for colonies from sw. Kans. to some 500 km. s., near Abilene, Tex., with southernmost clutches hatching earliest. Laying dates in a colony commonly spanned a 2-week period. In 1982–1983, laying dates in large samples of sw. Kans. nests were 2–4 weeks later than the av. for the late 1960s and early 1970s, associated with particularly late, cool, wet spring seasons (Parker).

One **egg** each from 20 clutches (Tex. 8, Okla. 7, Kans. 5) **size** length 41.20 ± 1.40

179

mm., breadth 33.68 ± 0.86, radii of curvature of ends 14.38 ± 0.49 and 11.41 ± 0.88; **shape** between elliptical and short subelliptical, elongation 1.22 ± 0.038, bicone −0.062, and asymmetry +0.108 (F. W. Preston). Fifty eggs av. 41.3 × 34 mm. (Bent 1937). Parker's data show that the 1st-laid egg is usually larger than the 2d. Shell smooth, without gloss, **color** white. Thousands of eggshells examined by Parker showed neither bluish tint nor any spotting (brown spots at laying might be traces of blood). Eggs occasionally become stained or caked with reddish brown mud, which is also sometimes seen on the legs and feet of these kites.

Clutch size Published statements are somewhat contradictory because of varying methods and schedules of examining nests. G. Sutton (1939) reported 38 clutches (of 2 eggs) and 2 (of 1). Stevens (in Bent 1937) found 2 eggs usual in about 500 nests, 1 occasional, and 3 rare (3 clutches only). Neither Parker nor More (in A. Jackson 1945) found a clutch of 3 when each examined over 1,000 nests. The only records of 3-egg clutches (the 3 from Stevens, also 3 others) are from egg collectors and are of questionable authenticity. McBee (1969) claimed a brood of 3, and Fitch (1963) speculated that a group of 4 nestlings might have been 1 brood. Both of these are undoubtedly misinterpretations from close proximity of broods.

Many pairs of kites eventually incubate a single egg. S. Evans (1981) documented this for 64% of her nest sample, but she, like many workers, was unable to make early and frequent examinations of nests. J. Parker (1974) found that nests with 1 egg approach 50% in some years; he presented evidence that most, if not all, of these were a result of partial loss of clutch and long interval between laying. Currently, data indicate neither geographical variation in clutch size nor limitation due to scarcity of food.

A. Jackson (1945) and T. Robinson (1957) reported **laying intervals** of 1 and 2 days; G. Sutton (1939) reported over 24 hrs. at a nest. For 61 broods of 2 monitored by J. Parker (1974) in 1969–1971, the mean period between hatching of 2 eggs was 3.8 days. Cranson (1972) and Parker have found nests with 2 nestlings that appeared to differ by almost a week in age. The interval between the laying of eggs apparently is often 2–3 days and may be longer.

Replacement clutches Apparently nonexistent, contrary to Bent (1937). Kites do renew nesting efforts after early loss of a single egg or even the same plus the nest. In some observed instances (Parker), the clutch is continued in the same or another nest. Kites obviously are single brooded; some individuals may build supernumerary nests after the brood is reared.

Incubation Begins with the 1st egg; nests with 2 similar-sized young have rarely been encountered—that is, virtually all reports of broods indicate that hatching of eggs is spaced a day or more apart. Incubation is shared by the sexes. G. Sutton (1939) mentioned an incubation patch on a ♀ but none on her mate. S. Evans (1981) observed ♀♀ on eggs for spans as long as 2–4 hrs.; she described vocalizing by the sitter and then, within 10 min., arrival of the mate (often carrying a leafy twig), occasional beak touching, and changeover. Usually the twig was added to the nest after the leaves were stripped off it and placed in the nest bowl. Adults were noticeably more restless just before egg hatching. There are no reports of a kite fetching food to the sitter. Either sex, when incubating, seems quiet, reclusive, and reluctant to defend against predators.

180

Incubation period   Twenty-nine to thirty-one days (G. Sutton 1939, later observers).

Nestlings   Attended by both parents; frequent brooding and shading when young are small. Early in the nestling period, S. Evans saw nearly continuous presence of at least 1 adult, for spans averaging 2.5 hrs. At 10 days ♀ ♀ spent twice as much time at the nest as ♂ ♂. Sometimes brooding continues late in the nestling period. Defense against predators increases markedly at hatching and intensifies as nestlings grow, ♀ ♀ usually more aggressive.

Both parents fetch food and feed the young; Glinski and Ohmart (1983) saw slightly more frequent delivery by ♂ ♂ at 3 nests. According to S. Evans (1981), very young nestlings were fed crushed food, probably primarily insects, carried in the crop and regurgitated into the nest. Dismembered prey were offered at 2–3 days; regurgitation was not seen after 11 days. Fitch (1963) wrote that most food was carried in the throat, but at nests with young of various ages Parker has seen only delivery in the beak.

Fitch reported food delivered every 8.5–12.8 min. (age of nestlings?) with majority of feeding visits lasting under 30 sec. S. Evans saw feeding of newly hatched nestlings about 3 times/hr. and, for 10-day-old young, 3–5 times/hr. She concurred that most feeding visits to older nestlings lasted less than 1 min. Fitch found no obvious trends in feeding time but observed feeding only between 1000 and 1700 hrs. S. Evans noted delivery most often during late morning and early to midafternoon.

Growth of nestlings   Much of the following is a tentative summary of Parker's preliminary analysis of data on some 300 nestlings. They weigh 12.8–21 gm. at hatching. Increase in wt. shows a general logistic pattern, reaching "adult" levels at 25–30 days, and younger nestlings in a brood showed slower growth. Average daily wt. increment to age 10 days, both for older nestlings in broods of 2 and for lone nestlings, was 7.7 gm.; for younger nestlings in broods of 2, 5.0 gm.

Growth meas. for BEAK from cere, TARSUS, MIDDLE TALON, and other meas. showed diminishing linear patterns and reached peaks generally before "adult" wt. was attained. Linear growth of most feather groups was not complete before 35–44 days—after nestlings were on the wing. T. Robinson (1957) suggested 2 growth periods: rapid wt. growth to 10 days and slower thereafter concurrent with feather growth.

For the 1st 7–10 days, nestlings are weak, quiet, and unaggressive but able to defecate with strong propulsion over the nest edge. After that, strength, coordination, and activity increase markedly; nestlings are soon able to grasp the nest firmly and to show hostility to intruders. They can stand well by 3 weeks and may move out onto branches and back by about 4 weeks. First flight can occur by day 34—probably often earlier, depending on wind, individual growth rate, and nesting events. Nestlings will jump from the nest as early as age about 25 days, and many are probably able to climb back. Older nestlings may vocalize aggressively while awaiting parents with food. Flying young are notably reluctant to take wing until about 50 days old, and they frequent the nest area, less often the nest. Family groups evidently join together in premigratory assemblages, but, in such gatherings, no evidence of family bond or feeding of young is reported.

Flying young   Fed until at least age 60 days, if not longer, receiving food while perched (S. Evans, Parker) and on the wing (Fitch). From lack of coordination, the young often drop food. Fitch, Evans, and Parker have seen them fed at a rate of about 6 times/hr. (intervals of 2–26 min., Evans), but small prey (as grasshoppers) may be delivered as often as 6 per 12 min. (Hardin et al. 1977). Presumably, both parents were feeding in this instance. S. Evans observed flying young attempting to capture insects (in air or on ground?) at age 50+ days.

Reproductive span Incubation and rearing total 65–70 days. The total commitment to reproduction, however, from early nest building to the time when the young can capture some prey, is probably at least 90 days.

Sex ratio In 120 "adults" in museums it was 1.4 ♂ : 1 ♀.

Reproductive rates Remarkably similar on the Great Plains (J. Parker 1974), in s. Ill. (S. Evans 1981), and in Ariz. (Glinski and Ohmart 1983). The percentage of nests producing young to flight age was 49%, 61%, and 54%, in that order, and 0.6 young attained flight per nesting attempt in each area. A. Jackson (1945) reported that a chick attained flight in each of 15 nests but may not have reckoned with probable early failure of others. See Parker for analysis of reproductive success in different years, colonies, habitats, and other matters relating to environmental and colony characteristics— especially predation and inclement weather. Evans also emphasized the importance of these. Parker, and Glinski and Ohmart (1983), reported much higher rates of nesting failure in the egg than in the nestling period.

Nest predators Confirmed and probable include fox squirrel, raccoon, bobcat, Am. Crow, Swainson's Hawk, and Great Horned Owl (various authors). Several species of snakes and a number of other birds and mammals probably also take kite eggs and/or nestlings. Fatality from ants was mentioned above.

Although the small clutch size of this kite might suggest natural selection by food limitation and the younger of twin nestlings grows more slowly, neither J. Parker's (1974) data nor other studies show significant food stress or starvation. In field experiments in 1976, 1977, and 1979 in which chicks were added to create trios in nests, many kites reared 3 young to flight age, and starvation was an inconsequential factor.

JAMES W. PARKER.

SURVIVAL Fitch (1963) estimated 10% of the Meade State Park birds to be yearlings; S. Evans (1981) estimated 15–30% yearlings at her Ill. study area, 1979–1981. Parker recorded flocks containing 25–50% yearlings (includes 13 yearlings in flock of 33 in June) but much lower percentages of yearlings at nests. Based on estimates of mortality rates and population age structure to 1971, life expectancy of kites in their 2d calendar year was estimated at 8–9 additional years (Parker). This may be conservative. Mortality rate in 2d calendar year of life was estimated at 50–60%.

JAMES W. PARKER

HABITS In N. Am. This handsome kite is highly **gregarious**, usually nesting in groups or colonies, engaging in joint attack against predators, foraging in flocks, and gathering seasonally at communal roosts. At least 200 roosted in Barber Co., Kans., on Sept. 1, 1951 (in Fitch 1963).

Mississippi Kites are **elegant fliers**, 2d only to Swallow-tailed Kites in grace and buoyance (Oberholser and Kincaid 1974). Audubon and, much later, Sutton expressed similar views. Fitch (1963) referred to their flight as "seemingly almost effortless."

They soar, drift, and circle at altitudes that depend on how high their insect prey is flying—that is, up to several hundred ft. They **catch their prey** so daintily and effortlessly by a slight sidewise, upward, or downward maneuver and rapid extension of the legs that it can be overlooked. Skinner (1962) described this as occasionally involving a few quick short wing strokes or half barrel roll, ending in a quick short turn at capture. The prey is usually held in 1 foot and often eaten in flight, the foot being brought forward and the head down toward the food as the kite soars slowly in a wide, level circle. Soaring and foraging can occur in the presence of other birds of prey.

Fitch saw kites perched near each other, and, in turn, glide down to skim the ground, capture insect prey, and return to a post to feed. Until recently it was thought that this kite rarely or never alights on the ground, even momentarily. Parker has seen large numbers of adults and yearlings alight repeatedly along an intermittent stream; they remained there for extended periods of time and walked along in shallow water, bathing, drinking, and possibly pursuing frogs. Ganier (1902) made 1 observation of a kite on the ground, and S. Evans (1981) saw this several times—usually a number of kites on partially flooded hay or fallow fields, where they drank and picked up items.

It is not unusual for kites to stoop in a rapid vertical dive to capture insects, and Parker has also seen them hunt by coursing rapidly and harrierlike across the prairie. "Cutting capers" in the air sometimes occur in competitive food chases or when a trio of kites contests ownership of a small snake (Parker).

Large mammals on the move often flush insects. Fitch noted kites feeding on insects disturbed by bison. Bent added a person, a horseman, and a team of horses, and A. Jackson (1945) mentioned deer and fire. Allan and C. W. Hibbard (see Fitch) fed cicadas to flying kites by tossing the insects into the air. Parker saw this in Meade, Kans., where the proprietor of a welding shop threw cicadas to kites that nested across the street.

At times the kites assemble where food is optimally available. A notable instance occurred in May 1892 near the Suwannee R. in Fla. (Wayne 1906): hundreds of this species plus a like number of Swallow-tails flew daily between the river and a large plantation, to which they were attracted by massive numbers of grasshoppers; they arrived with "greatest regularity" at 1150 hrs. and departed at 1408. A similar event occurred in the Savannah R. Valley (Murphey 1937).

Most foraging occurs either while soaring or by hawking from perches. The latter is most common early and late in the day and during inclement, becalmed or blustery weather. Kites may hawk after prey that is flying or on foliage. Glinski and Ohmart saw short hawking flights (less than 50 m.), usually from dead branches protruding above the canopy. Soaring increases as suitable air currents develop and is generally the common mode of foraging during the middle of the day.

These kites have been described as notably late risers, their activity increasing gradually after sunrise and tapering off again in late afternoon (Fitch 1963). Yet Parker has seen them foraging from perches at sunrise several times; once he saw a number foraging on insects (probably beetles and moths) attracted to street lights before dawn. S. Evans (1981) saw kites on exposed perches by 0630 hrs., preening, sunning, and casting pellets. She saw the greatest increase in hunting between 0800 and 1000 hrs.

Mississippi Kites may forage at a distance from nests, or at least from nearest

183

woodland. Fitch (1963) and C. W. Hibbard saw kites (3–20 in number) 4–5 and 5 mi. respectively from Meade State Park, and Parker had similar experience there and elsewhere. Kites leaving a nesting colony often rise together in tight circles to altitudes of several hundred ft., as if in a thermal, then strike out rapidly and purposefully together across country. At other times individuals move off alone, leisurely. In either case, they often return some time later on the reverse vector. Most prey, however, is probably taken relatively close to the nest. Various observers have reported repeated and protracted feeding within 0.5 km. of nesting areas. Glinski and Ohmart reported 96% of prey delivered from hawking within 150 m. of a nest.

Nesting kite reactions to intruders vary with individual bird and stage of breeding cycle. Some continue to sit on eggs until a predator has climbed within a few ft. of the nest. Then the bird departs, but abandonment is infrequent. At hatching or soon after, some swoop at the intruder at least once; others merely soar overhead, calling. Later, when nestlings are large, defense is most vigorous, and kites may assemble in some numbers; this may cause problems in urban areas (see below).

Available information indicates no need for concern about the welfare of this kite in most of its summer range, although it has attracted attention around the periphery. On the other hand, there is a concern over control of local kite numbers in many towns, at least in Kans., Okla., and N. Mex. This has arisen from what appears to be an increasing tendency for the kites to dive at and sometimes hit humans, particularly women and children, who unknowingly walk near nests. For an example, see Engle (1980). This situation first became newsworthy in the summer of 1978, when 28 kites were shot in a town in sw. Kans. by persons who overreacted to nest-defense diving. Since then, diving incidents have been reported annually throughout the region. Agencies and law enforcement authorities must respond to citizen requests for relief, particularly when incidents occur in public parks and on golf courses. Media reports become frequent and, at times, sensationalized.

Formal and informal strategies and public relations efforts have been developed on a small scale to deal with this phenomenon. In Kans., in cases where citizens could not be convinced to accept or at least tolerate diving behavior, nests were destroyed and the nestlings donated to foster parent kites elsewhere. In such cases, diving ceased, no kites were destroyed, and the offending pair was discouraged from renesting (as though a natural predator had intervened), and an opportunity was provided to educate the public about a wildlife "nuisance" problem with a sensible solution.

Overall, the **numbers** of this kite may remain much the same or perhaps increase; its distribution is predicted to expand. Almost annually for more than a decade, kites— yearlings and older birds—have occurred beyond their usual range limits, especially in May and June; often more than 1 kite is reported. It is probably only a matter of time before breeding is documented at some of these new locations (see Distribution, above.) Aside from the nuisance angle, there has been 1 attempt to manipulate local kite numbers; in 1983 Parker transferred nestlings from s. Kans. to w. Tenn. The ready availability of relatively robust nestlings in areas of high kite density, for transfer to foster parents of the same species elsewhere, precludes any need for captive breeding for other than genetic experiments.

NOTE   Many data given above and below are from near-annual field work by Parker from 1968 onward. Recent smaller studies by D. Love (1975), Kalla and Alsop (1983), S. Evans (1981), and Glinski and Ohmart (1983) have dovetailed with Parker's work and have been valuable in this review. Three of these studies were intended to investigate the species in areas where it is presumed to be, or may be, threatened. Some other information was derived from D. Shaw's continuing study in San Angelo, Tex.   JAMES W. PARKER

FOOD   In N. Am. Various large insects (it is not an obligatory insectivore); various vertebrates, some found dead.

Insects   Especially cicadas (A. Wilson and Bonaparte 1832 1, many other authors) and grasshoppers (Baird et al. 1874, many others); katydids and dragonflies. G. Sutton (1939) gave a long list of insects eaten in spring in Okla.—principally Acrididae, Carabidae, Dytiscidae, Locustidae, Scarabaeidae, Hymenoptera, and Lepidoptera. From sw. Kans., Fitch (1963) examined 205 pellets and nearly intact insects fetched by parent birds and dropped by the young. In pellets: Coleoptera (mostly unspecified, also Carabidae, Hydrophilidae, Scarabaeidae, and Silphidae), Orthoptera (mostly unspecified, also Locustidae and Tettigonidae), Homoptera (Cicadidae principally), and Lepidoptera (moth).

Vertebrates   In the older literature: a small fish (G. Sutton 1939); frogs and toads (Bent 1937); leopard frog and bullfrogs (T. Robinson 1957); toads (Rolfs 1973); lizards (Audubon 1840, others). Small snakes (Bent 1937, other authors), bats—probably *Pipistrellus* (Allan 1947), also intensive foraging by 15 kites on bats (*Tadarida brasiliensis*) (J. Taylor 1964); small rodents "probably" (Bendire 1892), and in 3 pellets "what seemed to be mammal hairs" (Fitch 1963); remains of mice and young rabbits found in nests with young kites (Stevens, in Bent), and Robinson found fragments of hindquarters of a rabbit (*Sylvilagus*) beneath a nest.

Most of the above reports, from examination of pellets or observations of foraging birds, show a wide variety of insect prey. The ejected pellets of indigestible material are roughly cylindrical, about 30 mm. long and 15 mm. in diam., and composed of crushed insect exoskeletons. No pellet examinations have disclosed bones or other material conclusive of vertebrates. This is not because they are not eaten, but because bones are not often ingested by adults (Parker) or are digested (as amphibians?). Only extensive examination of nest bowls and/or extensive observation of birds at nests or foraging will avoid a strong bias toward detecting only insect prey.

S. Evans (1981), Hardin et al. (1977), and Skinner (1962) reported no vertebrate prey, but their studies were not designed to encounter it. Other studies, at least in some areas, indicate a vertebrate component. J. Parker and Ogden (1979) suggested that this may be partly a result of an adaptive shift by kites in response to habitat change that has increased vertebrate prey availability. Glinski and Ohmart (1983) found 11% of 2,636 prey items delivered to 3 nests to be vertebrates, including toads, frogs, and pipistrelles. One ♂ seemed to prefer bats (54 delivered). Seibel (1971) and Waggener (1975) saw kites pursuing Chimney Swifts; Seibel found their remains at nests, and Waggener saw swifts hit. Parker saw protracted pursuit of Cliff Swallows and found their remains in and beneath kite nests. It has been fashionable to label this kite a "good" raptor that does not take small birds (Bent, Wolfe, others). Yet Parker has

185

found, in addition to aerial insectivorous birds, the remains of at least 7 passerine and 3 nonpasserine species at nests or being eaten; also ground squirrels, kangaroo rats, fragments of rabbits, deer mice, 3 species of lizards, including horned "toads" (*Phrynosoma*), small (intact) and road-killed adult box turtles, a snake, toads, and frogs. Many such were undoubtedly scavenged from roads. Juvenile House Sparrows were most common birds taken.   James W. Parker

COMMENTS   **Speciation:** Plumbeous Kite (*I. plumbea*) stock divided, a portion becoming highly migratory boreal breeders that return to the species' S. Am. ancestral range seasonally. The editor holds that the 2 stocks have not evolved into separate species—that is, are differentiated only as subspecies. **Food supply** through natural selection may well influence clutch size and number of chicks reared. Insects are marginal food for a kite-sized bird, hence almost constant foraging is required to sustain any young. Taking vertebrates is advantageous—perhaps necessary. Compare with the much larger Swainson's Hawk, which has greater energy requirements: although largely an insectivore, it is a seasonal carnivore in order to rear its young.

RALPH S. PALMER

BALD EAGLE

Haliaeetus leucocephalus (Linnaeus)

White-headed Eagle; White-headed Sea-Eagle; American Eagle. Very large diurnal raptor of the sea eagle group; a scavenger, predator, and pirate that occurs principally near water (coasts, inland) and feeds preponderantly on fishes. It "probably enjoys wider public recognition and popular concern" than any other species of animal (Robertson, in Kale 1978) since it is the national emblem of the USA. In all feathered stages the tail is rounded (not wedge shaped as in White-tailed Eagle, *H. albicilla*). At least half of the tarsus is naked after early life (one of many diagnostic differences from the Golden Eagle).

Definitive feathering (acquired as Basic IV in some and as Basic V generally): head–neck typically white (in its archaic variants, *bald* meant *white*, implying nakedness or without covering, as of feathers), body and wings very dark, tail and its coverts white.

Predefinitive stages: Juv. tends to be very dark overall, or showing little white. In succeeding stages the amount of white on the body increases, the head lightens (or stays the same with dark stripe through eye), and the tail lightens, basally at first. This picture is complicated by differing patterns at the same or different ages, by extreme bleaching, by abrasion of feather ends, and by prolonged molting. Then follows the distinctive dark/white definitive pattern.

Sexes similar in appearance, the ♀ larger (in any region, as far as is known, sexes overlap slightly in most meas., but in n. birds the av. difference in wt. is over 1 kg.). The sexes combined and geographical variation included (s. birds smaller): length about 28–38 in. (71–96 cm.), wingspread 66–96 in. (168–244 cm.), very questionably reported as greater. Usual wt. with empty digestive tract 6½–14 lb. (3–6.3 kg.).

DESCRIPTION   One Plumage/cycle, the molting of breeders beginning during incubation and continuing 5–6 months or longer. The timing of breeders of both sexes differs little, if at all, but perhaps prebreeders and nonbreeders begin and complete molting somewhat earlier. Almost all useful information is from n. birds, and the dating given here applies to them. For example, acquisition of new feathering begins some time in early spring in Alaska, Canada, and adjoining U.S. (but earlier—Nov. or Dec.—in Fla.). Portions of the wing regularly, and some wing coverts and a few other feathers usually, are retained longer than 1 cycle. The definitive condition is attained as Basic IV or V, depending on individual.

The following is based on known-age birds, a few of which were recovered, and 114 in the wild whose band numbers were read and of which various individuals were photographed (M. McCollough) during a span of up to several years. Data varies from the useful work of Southern (1964, 1967), whose sequence and age groupings were inferred from museum specimens (birds of unknown age). Bent's (1937) account was also based on supposition, as was Sherrod et al. (1976) and others.

▶ ♂ ♀ Def. Basic Plumage (entire feathering) achieved by some as early as Basic IV, acquired from early spring (of 5th calendar year of life) into fall and retained a year, but in others as Basic V (following year). **Beak,** gape, and cere yellow to orange-yellow; **iris** pale (usually) to buffy yellow. **Head,** neck, **tail** and all its coverts white; **other feathering** blackish brown, the margins of feathers (especially of dorsum and the upper wing coverts) distally yellowish brown (scalloped effect), more pronounced after wear and fading. Legs and **feet** deep yellow, talons black. The white tail and at least its upper coverts often have variable darkish areas or some mottling, usually basally (more or less concealed).

Variants   Birds with some darkish visible in otherwise white head and/or tail and coverts are well known. In the head this tends to be streaks scattered along feather shafts or more or less concentrated in a stripe or band through or from the eye backward—reflection of a pattern characteristic of certain predefinitive stages. A ♀ in the Jardin Zool. de Qué. showed more or less of this stripe in photos taken intermittently to age over 25 years (R. Cayouette). In another zoo captive this nonwhite finally disappeared when the bird was in its 11th year. Yet another. aged at least 18 years, still showed darkish streaking (Crandall 1941). A wild bird trapped when in definitive feathering had this condition and still had it when retrapped several years later (A. Harmata). A white-headed ♀ on Amchitka I. in the Aleutians in 1968 had a single dark feather in its tail and still had one in 1973 (C. White). Part of the reports, from Bendire (1892) onward, of nesting when in "immature plumage" quite obviously pertain to such variants. As long as such patterns recur, they tend to be similar.

Molting   Head–neck begins to molt in early spring, the body and flight feathers of wing begin later, and the tail begins in late July or Aug.; molting gradually diminishes and ceases by some time in fall. Primaries are dropped from inner to outer; the innermost secondaries molt outwardly (descending), the others from 2 "molt centers," beginning with the 5th functional one and the outermost, molt inwardly (ascending). This serial mode of molting of wing flight feathers and greater coverts ceases before all feathers are renewed—that is, in the next cycle, molting continues from where it had ceased previously and, at the same time, starts over again. Corresponding feathers in

188

the 2 wings do not necessarily drop simultaneously. (See also molting of the closely related and better-known White-tailed Eagle.)

In the tail (all feathers generally renewed annually at first, but perhaps usually not from later predefinitive stages onward), typically the central pair drops first, soon followed by the outer pair and the others in variable sequence. When some feathers are retained until the next molting period, the sequence presumably begins with their renewal; this could explain discrepancies in published reports. Tail feathers of some individuals are not fully grown in early Nov. A pause in molting extends through winter.

AT HATCHING In Sask., av. wt. of 6 nestlings on their 1st day was 91.5 ± 5.17 gm., or 79% of the av. wt. of fertile eggs (17 weighed 114.4 ± 10.59 gm.) near time of hatching (Bortolotti 1984c).

Natal downs The 1st, down-A (prepennae), is rather short, mostly under 2.5 cm. when fully developed, and off-white (toward gray-buff), palest on head and venter. (It is decidedly buffy in old museum specimens.) Dorsal distribution was well illustrated by Herrick (1932b, 1934). Southern young are darker dorsally, according to Bent (1937). There are hairlike structures in among this down, and this combination is the principal covering for 3 weeks. The entire tarsus becomes down covered, except for the underside (rear), which is naked (the lower half is completely naked later in the preflight stage).

Downy eaglets begin to thermoregulate at estimated age of approximately 15 days, when the amount of time at least 1 parent is at the nest declines sharply (Bortolotti 1984c).

Down-B (preplumulae) begins to appear at 9–11 days. It is darkish gray and basally white and much longer than down-A, which it largely conceals by 18–22 days (Bortolotti); it is very dense, like sheared wool—obviously excellent insulation. It bleaches and has more or less fallen out by the time the Juv. feathers cover the eaglet.

▶ ♂ ♀ Juv. Plumage (entire feathering) pushes out down-A on its tips (it also grows from other follicles), is nearly fully grown by flight age (about 10½ weeks), and is succeeded by Basic I during spring–fall of 2d calendar year of life. The 1st Juv. feathers appear in the "shoulder" area (scapulars) at 24–31 days, on head and upper back at 25–34 days, and on lateral underparts 26–45 days; feathers of the upper tarsus appear last, at 39–55 days (Bortolotti 1984c).

Beak and cere very dark, with small grayish area behind the cere; iris very dark brownish at 10–12 weeks. All feathering may be very dark (sometimes described as blackish), but there are many variants. Head–neck appear slim, the lanceolate feathers less than half as long as in definitive stages and often quite evenly dark; sometimes, however, cap is obviously darkest; sometimes some head feathers have white bases and/or all-white lanceolate feathers intermingle with the dark ones.

Basal portions of body feathers vary with individual from dark to variably light (even white) and sometimes intermingle with white feathers, especially on underparts. A few eaglets thus have mottled underparts while still in the nest. Because of subsequent fading and abrasion, some individuals under age 1 year have a largely white venter. Occasional birds have light buffy brown heads (like definitive-feathered White-tailed Eagles). Some have white axillars; at least most have more or less white in the wing

189

lining; some have whitish mottling either along the flight feathers of the wing or expanded to patches largely confined to the inner vanes of these feathers. **Tail** broadly rounded, the outermost pair of feathers squarish ended; often all are dark, but birds having white in underwing and on body may have considerably whitish rectrices. This tends to be concentrated in the midsection of the inner vanes so that, ventrally, the tail tends to appear light with terminal dark band (rather like Juv. Golden Eagle). Legs and **feet** yellow, talons black.

Estimating age of nestlings 1 Through the first few days posthatching, nestlings are perhaps best aged by changes in physical appearance. On day of hatching the area of attachment of the allantois is swollen, circular shaped, and somewhat protruding, and the chicks appear weak. Remnants of the allantois can be seen for up to 3 days, but it becomes threadlike. The loose, wrinkled, pink skin fills out and fades on the 1st day. Beginning usually on day 4 or 5 (but in some as early as day 2 or 3), the ventral skin, on close examination, is tinged blue; in the next 4–5 days it becomes mostly blue-gray (Bortolotti 1984e).

2 Nestlings 0–26 days old can be aged by BEAK from cere (culmen length), as graphed to 80 days by Bortolotti (1984d, fig.4), or refer to the equation in his paper. Sexes diverge with age; from about 40 days onward, presumed ♀ ♀ (larger) are clearly separable from presumed ♂ ♂.

3 Feather lengths are dependable estimates of age, for older nestlings, although primary and tail feathers are not easily measured when small. The increase with age of the LENGTH OF THE 8TH PRIMARY (3d from outermost) is largely linear (Bortolotti 1984e, fig.3) for both sexes aged 24–72 days. If the sexes of the young are unknown, a linear regression equation to determine their ages to ± 3 days is: 19.9 + (0.14 × 8th primary length). If sexed, young are best aged by substituting 19.2 (♂ ♂) and 20.6 (♀ ♀) for 19.9 in this equation.

After 72 days, growth rates of feathers, including the highly linear growth of the tail, decrease (Bortolotti).

Sexing nestlings If young are marked or banded early (hence identifiable as individuals) and measurements are recorded at intervals thereafter, the size of all is found to be quite similar at first and later separates into 2 divergent series—the ♀ ♀ larger. The earlier data on the marked individuals then also can be included on graphs, showing initial complete overlap of the sexes and their later difference. See Bortolotti (1984d), fig. 4.

DEPTH OF BEAK Increases at base of cere (bill depth)—very slowly in the last half of the nestling period. Measured in 1/10 mm., it begins to diverge by about age 20–24 days (Bortolotti 1984e, table 2), and the sexes almost never overlap thereafter. An easier method or a good double check, is to measure SOLE OF FOOT length by placing a ruler across the middle front and hind toes and neasuring the straightened pad (omitting talons); this becomes sexually size-dimorphic at 25–29 days. Mean changes from age 15–82 days for presumed ♂ and ♀ nestlings (Bortolotti 1984e, table 3) are: 15–19 days ♂ 87.8 and ♀ 88.6; 20–24, ♂ 109.2 and ♀ 110; 25–29, ♂ 114.8 and ♀ 125.1; 30–34, ♂ 126.2 and ♀ 134.5; 35–39, ♂ 129.3 and ♀ 142.7; 40–44, ♂ 130.3 and ♀ 146.4; 45–49, ♂ 132.4 and ♀ 146.5; and 50–82, ♂ 131.8 and ♀ 147.1.

Changes in weight and associated growth phenomena Complex matters; see Bortolotti (1984d) for details and photographs of known–age nestlings. The following points are of general interest:

The wt. of nestlings shows great sexual dimorphism but is not a useful criterion for sexing because so much individual variation depends on general health, the amount of food ingested, the time of day, and so on.

Daily wt. gain increases greatly, to as much as 150 gm./day in ♂♂ and 180 gm./day in ♀♀ at around age 35–40 days, and then declines.

Males (the smaller sex) develop feathers earlier and attain flight earlier than ♀♀, but grow at the same rate.

The age at which body feathers become unsheathed varies greatly, yet the growth of flight feathers varies little (they are largely independent).

Dimensions of tarsus and toes appear to reach "mature" size during preflight age, but such other linear meas. as length and depth of beak, lengths of feathers, and so on, do not.

▶ ♂ ♀ Basic I Plumage (entire feathering) acquired beginning in SPRING of 2d calendar year of life, retained through WINTER, and succeeded by Basic II in 3d calendar year. **Beak** medium to dark gray, usually grading to yellowish buff next to cere, which is somewhat lighter, with yellow showing and/or in the nostrils; **iris** at first variably brownish but may change toward creamy. Some individuals appear dark overall, but a somewhat blotchy or streaked appearance is frequent. **Head** crown frequently a light buffy brownish or tan; a darker band or line extends through eye and posteriorly. **Upper back** frequently has a whitish or buffy brown inverted triangle on an otherwise generally dark dorsum. **Underparts** vary from very dark to same with more or less white (basal portions of feathers) showing; **breast** darker than belly—a "bib." Belly varies from dark brown to nearly white, hence is often confused with both older and younger birds. Legs and **feet** yellow, talons black. **Tail** feathers still not as rounded as in definitive condition and still dark ended. **Wing** has some white mottling in upper coverts. Variable amount of wing lining whitish in known-age individuals.

NOTES   A young ♀ taken on Bering I., May 15, 1882, was evidently in Basic I or II; so much feathering was white that Ridgway (1883) named it as a previously un-described species, *H. "hypoleucus."*

A captive injured bird was in Juv. feathering in 1982; there was delayed molting into Basic I until winter of 1983–1984; it then proceeded directly into Basic II in summer of 1984 and into Basic III in summer of 1985. Color of beak, cere, and iris and the Plumage were a year behind wild birds of corresponding cohorts (M. McCollough).

Changes in shape and length, from Juv. stage onward, of the lanceolate head feathers have not been studied.

▶ ♂ ♀ Basic II Plumage (entire feathering) acquired beginning in spring of 3d calendar year of life and retained into the following year. These data on known-age wild birds may not encompass all individual variation. **Beak** a darkish gray with yellowish spot at its side base and extending as a line to nostrils or even along top of beak; cere mixed yellow and gray; **iris** usually cream colored, occasionally toward brownish. An in-creased lightening of the **head;** crown palish gray-brown, throat largely whitish, and a broad dark stripe through eye on side of head ("Osprey pattern" of Southern). The **dorsum** tends to darken, the inverted light triangle less prominent. **Underparts** breast

191

and belly darken toward a brownish olive, but occasional individuals have the belly mottled white. **Tail** typically has a variable amount of (usually much) white proximally with distal third dark. **Wing** upper coverts usually all brown, but some retain white mottling; wing lining typically more or less white.

▶ ♂ ♀ Basic III Plumage (entire feathering) acquired through SPRING–FALL of 4th calendar year and retained into the following year. There is individual variation in appearance, but typically a radical change to near-definitive feathering. **Beak** both mandibles yellow, usually with dark along top and extending down to nostrils; cere varies from mostly yellow mottled darkish to yellow; **iris** pale yellow. **Head** white with brown flecking on forehead and crown and usually a brownish or grayish line or stripe through and back from eye. **Body feathering** typically dark brown (as in all later stages), but there may still be a hint of an inverted lighter triangle on the upper mantle and some white flecking ventrally. Legs and **feet** yellow, talons black. **Tail** feathers largely white with some brown flecking proximally, the brown becoming heavy mottling toward the tips. **Wing:** upper coverts dark, occasionally with some white mottling; some white flecking in the wing lining.

▶ ♂ ♀ Basic IV Plumage (entire feathering) acquired through SPRING–FALL of 5th calendar year of life and retained into the following year. **Variable**—definitive in some and more or less like Basic III in others. **Beak** mostly yellow, cere yellow, **iris** pale yellow. **Head** white, usually with brown flecking, and rarely the eye stripe of "Osprey pattern" faintly indicated. **Dorsum** and upper wing coverts dark brown, the feathers scalloped or tipped a buffy brownish. **Tail** and its coverts white or flecked brownish, the former without terminal dark area.

▶ ♂ ♀ Basic V Plumage (entire feathering) acquired through SPRING–FALL of 6th calendar year and retained a year. **Definitive** Of the 5 known-age birds studied, 3 were indistinguishable from the 3 most "advanced" individuals in Basic IV. **Beak** and cere yellow, except 2 birds had light brown mottling at side base of beak or top of cere. **Iris** pale yellow. **Head** with faint gray flecking around the eyes. **Body** and **wings** dark brown, various feathers with scalloped buffy brownish edges. **Tail** feathers white with occasional dark flecks.

Two captives achieved completely white heads before the end of their 6th calendar year (Hulce 1886). An eagle at 6½ years had head markings as just described for some in Basic IV, but its head was pure white at 7½ years. Another at 7½ years had a brown smudge on the tip of the beak and extensive gray flecking on forehead, around the eyes, and on the auriculars.

Color phases None; a possible total of 3 "blond" individuals have been reported. A few birds in predefinitive feathering have shown so much white ventrally that they have been mistaken for albinos.

Measurements As previously noted, the ♀ is larger. In birds from any given area (thus excluding geographical size-variation), age for age, sexes evidently overlap slightly in overall size, but in certain meas. they are clearly separable.

Baird et al. (1874) gave meas. of 24 specimens. The birds were sorted in a table by sex and as "Ad." and "Juv." There was no overlap of the sexes in WING (across chord), and there was a slight overlap in BEAK and TAIL. The purpose of the table was "to prove the remarkable fact" that young eagles have longer wings and tails than older ones.

192

Primaries, secondaries, and tail feathers decrease in length through the early molts, with better evidence for ♂ ♂ than ♀ ♀ (Bortolotti 1984c). Juvenal ♀ ♀, therefore, have the longest wings and tails of any Bald Eagles.

Imler and Kalmback (1955) measured 108 Alaskan birds (in inches): "adults" 35 ♂ BEAK 2.44–2.69 in., av. 2.57 (65.2 mm.); WING across chord 21.7–24.1, av. 23.06 (585.7); and TAIL 10.8–11.9, av. 11.41 (289.8); and 37 ♀ BEAK 2.69–2.294 in., av. 2.81 (71.3 mm.); WING across chord 23.25–25.80, av. 23.61 (599.6); and TAIL 11.10–12.80, av. 11.97 (304). "Immatures" 18 ♂ BEAK 2.50–2.65 in., av. 257 (65.3 mm); WING across chord 22.62–24.70, av. 23.85 (605.8); and TAIL 11.50–13.50, av. 12.48 (317); and 18 ♀ BEAK 2.69–2.95 in., av. 2.79 (70.8 mm.); WING across chord 24.50–27.25, av. 25.68 (652); and TAIL 12.20–14.75, av. 13.43 (341). From these data, N. Snyder and Wiley (1976) gave the means in metric of WING (chord) as 35 ♂ 586.7 mm. and 37 ♀ as 624.8 mm.

Northern birds Friedmann (1950): 29 ♂ (Alaska to Va.) BEAK from cere 49-57 mm., av. 52.5, WING across chord 570–612, av. 588.6, TAIL 290–322, av. 309.7; and 42 ♀ (Bering I. and Alaska to N.C.) BEAK from cere 47–58 mm., av. 54.1, WING across chord 605–685, av. 640.2, and TAIL 300–365, av. 339.4.

Some indication of sexual dimorphism in eagles of all flight ages, from museum skins (Bortolotti 1984c): depth of BEAK at base of cere 63 ♂ 29.6–34.6 mm. (32.24 ± 0.136) and 45 ♀ 32.6–41.2 (35.97 ± 0.236); chord of BEAK from cere 76 ♂ 41.7–54.3 (50.81 ± 0.236) and 55 ♀ 50.4–60.6 (55.27 ± 0.333); REAR TALON (hallux claw) chord from base at top of toe to tip 77 ♂ 32.7–43.0 (39.65 ± 0.198) and 55 ♀ 41.2–48.9 (44.66 ± 0.254). In these meas., age classes lumped, sexes overlap somewhat; if only n. birds in definitive feathering are measured, there is apparently no overlap in BEAK from cere and WING chord.

Southern birds Smaller; Friedmann (1950) erred when he stated that the ♀ has the smaller beak. His other meas.: 16 ♂ (from Ga., Fla., and Baja Calif.) WING across chord 515–545 mm., av. 529.2, TAIL 232–264, av. 248.5; and 11 ♀ (Ga., Fla., La., and Baja Calif.) WING across chord 548–588 mm., av. 576.5, and TAIL 247–286, av. 271.2.

WINGSPREAD Reports of the span across the spread wings vary or are exaggerated. The largest of 18 "immature" Alaskan ♀ ♀ measured 95½ in. (242.6 cm.) and weighed 12.7 lb. (5.76 kg.) (Imler and Kalmbach 1955). In N. S., Gilpin (1873) claimed that a young bird "measured nearly 8 feet across, another 8½ feet [2.59 m.], exceeding some ["adult"] balds by over a foot." Twenty "immatures" in New Bruns. (might include s. birds that had flown n. in their 1st calendar year) had a wingspread of 5 ft., 6 in. to 7 ft., 6 in., av. 6 ft., 8 in. (203 cm.) (B. S. Wright 1953). Audubon's allegation that his Bird of Washington had a 10 ft., 2 in. wingspread may have come about from carelessness and faulty memory (see Mengel 1953).

Weight For Alaskan birds, Imler and Kalmbach (1955) fortunately gave wt. minus crop and gizzard contents: ♂ 35 "adults" 8.01–10.61 lb., av. 9.09 (4.13 kg.), 18 "immatures" 7.80–10.10 lb., av. 8.91 (4.05 kg.); and ♀ 37 "adult" 10.20–14.10 lb., av. 11.78 (5.35 kg.) and 18 "immature" 9.61–12.69 lb., av. 11.22 (5.09 kg.). Sexes overlap slightly. Seven other ♂ "adults" from Alaska weighed 9.3–12.4 lb., av. 10.7 (4.86 kg.) (Chura and Stewart 1967).

The largest individual weighed alive in Ill. by Southern (1964) was a 1st-fall ♀ in

Nov., at 12¾ lb.; it had a wingspread of 84.5 in. A ♀ in definitive feathering "found dead" near Rochester, N.Y., Mar. 31, 1965, weighed 14½ lb., was 34½ in. long, and had a wingspread of 84 in. (R. S. Palmer). Six of the "immatures" in New Bruns. (see above) varied 14 lb.–16 lb., 8 oz., av. 15 lb., 6 oz. (6.98 kg.). A captive young bird, "fed liberally with fish," weighed 17¾ lb. in early Nov. (Herrick 1933). One shot at Warsaw, N.Y., Oct. 1, 1876, weighed 18 lb., according to J. Otis Fellows (1876).

Brodkorb (1955) noted that the feathers of a yearling ♀ Bald Eagle weighed more than twice as much as its dried skeleton.

Hybrids None reported; the Bald would probably cross with the White-tailed Eagle, *H. albicilla*. As to fostering, in captivity a Bald Eagle was reared by a pair of Long-legged Buzzards, *Buteo rufinus* (Minnemann 1976).

Geographical variation Based on WING chord (an indicator of size), the birds become smaller going s., at least in e. N. Am.—this over some 2,750 mi. (40°) of N lat. There is no adequate evidence for assuming an even or an uneven size gradient (an even or a modified cline) over this distance. Birds from opposite ends of the range, when compared, are clearly quantitatively different, but when they are assigned names (as geographical entities) it raises the question of where, in between, to divide them. An arbitrarily assigned boundary has been shifted n. since Bent's (1937) day to lat. 40° N (Philadelphia, Kansas City, Denver, etc.).

Bald Eagles are big birds. In this context, their geographical size-variation seems moderate for so vast a breeding range. Since no satisfactory geographical subdivision is known, it is preferable to avoid categorizing the Bald Eagle into subspecies. Even so, possibly some biological basis (other than overall size, or egg size) for subdivision may be discovered. For example, there may be a definable cleavage between those that do and do not have extensive premigratory dispersal of younger prebreeders. In Mo., because of a difference in egg-laying dates (Nov. and spring), Griffin and Elder (1980) suggested that perhaps 2 subspecies nested there formerly.

In the present account, the Bald Eagle is referred to in both rather indefinite geographical contexts (n., s., etc.) and more definite ones (Alaska, Sask., Fla., etc.).

NOTES That the largest known individuals are from Bering I. (1957 AOU *Checklist*) is an error based on the size of young birds taken there.

In recent years many Juv. birds have been translocated long distances for restocking: for example, Canadian birds into n. U.S. and Alaskan birds to N.Y.

Affinities Among sea eagles, the White-headed (*leucocephalus*) of the New World and White-tailed (*albicilla*) of the Old are very close morphologically and in every other respect. In predefinitive feathering the only fairly obvious difference between them is the rounded versus the wedge-shaped tail. The head–neck of Old World birds in definitive feathering tends to be palish, a sort of predisposition toward the white of New World birds; some New World birds at some predefinitive stage have more or less brownish heads, perhaps reflecting an ancestral condition. In the long view, it appears that the New World bird is a recent derivative of the Old World eagle. The enormous ranges of each do not overlap (at least currently) except for occasional straggling in the N. Pacific–Bering area. In N. Am., the only *Haliaeetus* known from the Pleistocene and numerous archaeological sites is *leucocephalus*. The known fossils, from Calif. at

194

least, are of birds little, if at all, larger than large present-day n. Bald Eagles (H. Howard 1932).   RALPH S. PALMER AND JONATHAN M. GERRARD

FIELD IDENTIFICATION   Very large diurnal raptor—wingspread 6–7 ft. Bald Eagles are usually, but by no means always, found near water. They spend much time perched, and against a dark background young especially are not particularly conspicuous. Against the sky, or white-headed ones against dark foliage, they stand out. At times they soar and glide with flat wings (no dihedral) in thermals and updrafts. Flapping flight is used primarily for short distances, for carrying food, or for going to and from a roost. Singles, pairs, and small numbers are usual, but assemblies of scores, hundreds, even thousands (at an Alaskan locality) occur, especially in late fall and winter, at places where food is easily gotten (salmon run, fish die-off, abundant hares and rabbits, etc.). A few Goldens may intermingle.

In definitive feathering the Bald differs from the Golden in having white head plus tail and all its coverts, from the White-tailed bv having a white head, and from Steller's by its white head and lack of a white area on upper wing coverts. In flight, the head of the Bald protrudes the equivalent of more than half the length of the tail (but less than the Golden). The Juv. Bald tail, however, is longer than in definitive Plumage, so this feature should be used with caution when comparing with the Golden. White of wing lining of Balds of various ages appears as a line or a variably irregular stripe or area; in young Goldens it is distal—a basal "window" in the primaries. Some young Balds have much white in the tail plus a dark distal band; this is seldom if ever as clear-cut a pattern as in Juv. Goldens. The Bald has a larger beak and unfeathered lower legs—characters observable only at close range, where it may be noted that feathers from higher up may cover much of the legs.

Occasionally a Bald's new growing tail feathers are shorter laterally, so that the outline of the spread tail may vary from rounded (as Bald) toward wedge shaped (as White-tailed). In 13 seasons in the Aleutians and the Pribilofs, Kenyon (1961) once saw an eagle resembling the White-tailed that proved, on close examination, to be a Bald in "intermediate plumage." From these localities, he wrote, only occurrence of the White-tailed substantiated by captured birds should be accepted. (Occurrence now is documented by photographs and finding a nest.)

Among our raptors, the Bald Eagle is unusual in that we see many more birds in predefinitive than in definitive stages, since several years are required to attain the latter.

Field identification to Plumage/age class   In the Bald, high variability in predefinitive feathering tends to hamper assigning chronological age or Plumage reliably to individuals. It is further complicated by prolonged molting, abrasion of feathers, and so on. The following guidelines may be helpful under some circumstances: **Juv.:** Distinct from all others. Overall dark with underwing mottled white and dirty white tail with darkish terminal band; head relatively trim; trailing edge of wing serrated (not scalloped as in all succeeding Plumages); beak, cere, and iris dark. **Basic I:** Head–neck dark with tan crown; underparts variable, "bib" darkest; on upper back a mottled or lighter inverted triangle is common; secondaries often of 2 lengths, any retained Juv.

195

ones projecting well beyond the newer Basic I feathers; beak pales basally toward yellowish. **Basic II:** Head light with broad darkish stripe through eye; underparts variable; upper back may show inverted triangle indistinctly; most of beak still quite dark, cere may be yellowish, iris usually cream colored. **Basic III:** Radical change toward definitive. Head–neck, tail, and coverts predominantly whitish, and perhaps a dark stripe through eye; body essentially dark (as definitive); beak and cere sometimes yellow, otherwise partly so; iris pale yellow. **Basic IV:** Some are much as preceding, others definitive—that is, essentially white head–neck, tail, and tail coverts; beak and cere yellow; iris pale yellow. **Basic V:** Some are indistinguishable from predefinitive Basic IV, but most are definitive.

Nests Confusing Bald Eagle and Osprey nests may pose problems. Often the nest of the former is within the crown of a live tree and is somewhat irregular in shape. Ospreys tend to nest more in the open, and the structure is often flat topped and visible against the sky. Many Ospreys nest on man-made structures. Either species, however, may nest on or in any sort of low-to-elevated site and, where free of disturbance, on the ground. Hence, no firm rule exists—except identification of tenant. Even then there are problems, since promoters of the local scene may tell onlookers that Ospreys are "eagles."   JONATHAN M. GERRARD AND RALPH S. PALMER

VOICE   Often described as screaming, perhaps for want of a more fitting word. Hardly matches this bird's imposing size and presumed dignified bearing; many a listener has been disappointed. The following descriptions are appropriate. "Surprisingly thin, high, and weak" (E. G. Holt and Sutton 1926). "Weak in volume and trivial in expression," "snickering laugh" (Brewster 1925). It is mostly flat and dry, rather squeaky. Like the sound of clothesline pulley needing oil (F. Beebe 1974). Much Bald Eagle communication is visual, as when eagles circling overhead thus signal the location of food or a winter roost to others.

A sex difference in voice has been reported (Bendire 1892, later authors); in at least some calls, including the 1st listed below, the ♀'s voice is lower pitched.

Kah-kah-kah variable in duration and rate of utterance; the usual alarm of adults disturbed at nest. *Ye-ha-ha-ha* or *whee-he-he-he* repeatedly and with variants, the final syllables descending and uttered slowly; more often by ♀. Some resemblance to a horse neighing. Expresses annoyance, as when territory entered by another eagle, raven, or crow. Often joined or intermixed with more gull-like wail. Also uttered by ♀ when soliciting food from mate or copulating. Used by both sexes during pair formation and later, when it is uttered as head is thrown back in Head-toss display; this or a variant is used by mates "dueting" or as an early morning greeting during earlier phases of the reproductive cycle.

Contrary to the popular press, our eagles seldom give ear-splitting screams; the nearest Herrick (1934) ever heard from the Bald was a call uttered once or twice from a perched bird during Head-toss.

Captives during copulation: the ♀ uttered a soft, high-pitched note, repeated several times, very unlike other known calls; the ♂ called "loudly" (P. N. Gerrard et al. 1979).

Yaap-yaap-yaap or variant, having a wailing or gull-like quality, uttered in indefinite series by adults and older young in the nest. Mature birds use it during display, the young when hungry.

Chitter—really an intermixing of calls—by both sexes at changeover; also to announce change in actions, as when about to depart or return; when reconnoitering at the nest; when trespassers have departed (Herrick 1933); and during competition for food or for perch sites at a communal roost. On the Chilkat R., Alaska, "clear whistling notes continually uttered in the crisp air" (Rearden 1984).

Young Sonagrams were made of the voice of a captive-reared ♀ days 1–30 post-hatching. At first, single rising or rising and falling short tonal sounds were made; by day 30, a sharp *chirp* pulse at end of each note, giving a "quality very similar to adult call" (Gilbert et al. 1981).

In the wild, young make a thin peeping to express discontent or hunger; it later alters to a querulous *yeep*; when they are hungry or excited, it is given with rising inflection until it becomes shrill—a squeal or, still later in nest life, a scream (Herrick 1934). Shortly before and also after attaining flight, the food-begging call of the young is a variant of the gull-like wail described above.

Herrick heard peculiar clucking notes from both young and, he thought, from a perched adult. Nestlings, and adults showing anxiety, give a low repeated grunt.

A bird hatched in 1930 was kept in captivity; in early Sept., 1934, its voice changed— it still began its call with the "harsh notes of immaturity" but ended it with the "clear challenge of the adult" (Crandall 1941).   JONATHAN M. GERRARD

HABITAT   Bald Eagles usually inhabit coastal areas, estuaries, and unfrozen inland waters; in winter, also some arid areas in the w. interior. Generally speaking, a high amount of water-to-land edge, where prey is concentrated or generally available, is preferred. An unimpeded view is also important. Both horizontal and vertical aspects are used—a preference for margins of forest stands (horizontal) and trees projecting above the forest canopy (vertical). Where trees are low or absent, any location commanding a wide view.

Nesting   Trees selected (also for roosting and sometimes perching) are typically old growth, taller than their surroundings. Ideally, the nest lies below the top of the crown in a live tree, where the young are sheltered above from the elements and the parent birds have adequate aerial access. Of over 1,500 nests examined on the B.C. coast, in general, those that had an overhead canopy of foliage were more successful; those exposed from above were frequently abandoned or showed reduced nesting success (Hancock 1970). Of over 1,700 nest trees checked in se. Alaska, not one was in a stand of young timber (a 1972 USDA report). It is important not to cut, or at least not to clear-cut, old-growth stands of timber.

Although a great many tree species have been used for nest sites (12–15 in some areas), preference varies geographically about as follows: Maritimes—mostly hardwoods; n. New Eng.—white pine; e. interior U.S.—mature elm (now eliminated by Dutch elm disease), poplar, large hickory; Great Lakes states—white and red pines; Ont. w. across boreal forest of Man. and Sask. to NWT—aspen, pine; Chesapeake Bay region—loblolly pine; se. U.S.—various pines (commonly slash pine), also cypress in parts of Fla. mainland; Fla. Bay—dead stubs of hurricane-killed mangrove (in living ones, as many in red as in black mangrove), thus away from classic sites (big pine or cypress) where other conditions are favorable; La.—cypress in dense swamps; Rocky Mtns.—Engelmann spruce, lodgepole pine, Douglas fir; Calif.—Engelmann spruce, Douglas fir, ponderosa and sugar pines; Baja Calif.—1 in a giant cactus (others on cliffs); Pacific NW—Douglas fir; Alaska—Sitka spruce in coastal areas, cottonwood (and, where trees absent or too small to support a nest, shelves on cliff faces, pinnacles, islets, even nearly level ground).

Introducing foxes to the Aleutians and nearby may have brought change—that is, at present, easily accessible sites appear to be limited to is. where no foxes occur. In N. Am., away from marine is., ground nests have been few—perhaps mostly on is. in nw. Canadian lakes; A recent ground nest in the Fla. Bay area (Shea et al. 1979). Cliff and pinnacle nests are prevalent in Nfld. because of a lack of nest trees, and cliff nests have occurred w. across N. Am. Perhaps nearest to a natural cave would be a nest recessed in a perpendicular rockface on an is. in Pyramid L., Nev., reported in 1877; or a recess in Blue Ledge, 5 mi. n. of North R., N.Y., ruined by a rockslide around 1910. In Ont., at an unoccupied farm, a board was missing from a barn and the eagles had young inside on straw (Langille 1884). In the Southwest, some nest on cliff shelves and pinnacles. For Ariz. desert habitat, see J. R. Udall (1986).

A sentry perch commanding a view of the nest is a requisite, and a snag or a tree with open canopy is preferred. The eagle may perch as high as the limb will support its weight. Roost trees are various but, in breeding season, are not distant from the nest.

Occupation of nest-site habitat is seasonally discontinuous where waters freeze. Thus, in cold areas, nesting is concentrated near river rapids with an adequate supply of fish in early spring. On the other hand, in s. latitudes (and in such other areas as the Aleutians), sites get some use outside the breeding season as perches and feeding platforms. In the interior s. toward nw. Mexico, breeding is limited by lack of cool nesting sites; temperatures become high while the young are still flightless.

Some eagles can be quite persistent. If a tree dies, for example, the nest commonly continues in use. If a nest falls, it may even be used on the ground. Individual tolerance of human presence and activities varies greatly. Some become more or less habituated to a certain amount. Eagles have nested successfully in single trees isolated in a realtor's subdivision or on a golf course, but such nests usually go vacant as soon as something happens to a member of the pair. So long as the pair exists, abandonment may not occur as often as reduced breeding success or failure. Human behavior to which the birds are not habituated should be avoided. Recreational use of reservoirs, for example, almost surely prevents eagles from establishing nesting territory.

Winter Adequate food supply, usually at or in open water, is a requisite. Eagles are present at river rapids, impoundments, dam spillways, lakes, estuaries, and salt water, where they feed on aquatic-associated prey, including carrion. More birds seem to be remaining farther n. through winter than formerly, and large concentrations are reported.

Daytime perches are usually in open-branched trees that allow wide view. Dead trees, as well as live trees with broken tops are preferred. In treeless terrain, the birds may perch on rocky areas, turf, or, occasionally, artificial structures. Traditional night roost locations are known. Roost trees are usually the tallest in the stand and may be

198

coniferous for protection from the elements. In the arid w. interior, roosts up to 18 mi. from food sources are known.

Communal roosts are common, especially in winter, and protection from adverse weather—the presence of landforms (sheltered valleys, forested bottomland) and coniferous trees—is often an important criterion.   MARK V. STALMASTER

DISTRIBUTION   (See map.) The only sea eagle on the N. Am. mainland. General limits of occurrence are still about as mapped long ago by Oberholser (1906). Local changes in breeding distribution and, evidently, a long continuing reduction in numbers are nothing new. They have occurred throughout the past 250 years, although the rate accelerated as the country was settled (habitat altered) and as firearms became more numerous and efficient (shooting still continues). Decimation from pesticides and other pollutants, most evident from the early 1940s to the late 1970s, was severe. (See "some history," below.) Details of this reduction, by 1978 to "endangered" status in 43 coterminous U.S. states and "threatened" in 5 others, has been discussed numerous times. Aside from Alaska (pollution of eagles minor), common cause of all recorded cases of rapid decline was a lowering of reproductive potential. A nadir was reached about 1974. With the waning of the biocide era and with increased interest in and protection of the birds (bolstered to some extent by "recovery projects"), the situation has changed for the better at a rate hardly anticipated. There are perhaps as many eagles today as there were 50 years ago. A recent analysis (J. Gerrard, in D. Bird 1983) suggested about 48,000 eagles in Alaska and B.C. plus 22,000 elsewhere. (Later estimates are already higher.) Numbers could stabalize around these figures, but changes due to human impact on the environment are bound to continue. For example, the damage to or death of the fauna in lakes and streams from airborne pollutants certainly affects eagle numbers and distribution. Some birds die from ingesting lead shot in hunter-killed or injured waterfowl. On the other hand, ongoing habituation of the species to man (and vice versa) will contribute locally to the welfare of the Bald Eagle. Places already exist where, from conflict over ownership or use of terrain ("activity restriction zones" around nests), man—rather than bird—may regard himself as "endangered."

Changes in local distribution   Many; examples: recent absence as a breeder in large areas of the e. U.S., part of Calif., and so on, and the earlier vacating of various is. (as in the Aleutians) where foxes were introduced. Upper limits of wintering vary and depend on unfrozen water plus available adequate food (both are variable), but the species is basically food-limited in distribution. Habitat has been created by construction of dams and impoundment of other waters (unfrozen water, concentration of prey below spillways). Perhaps these mitigate slightly the changes caused by enormous reduction in salmon in parts of the Pacific NW. In Glacier Natl. Park, fall migrating eagles are attracted to Lower McDonald Creek by spawning kokanee salmon, introduced in 1916. An apparently recent phenomenon is winter roosts in such arid country as Utah and Colo., where considerable food is black-tailed jackrabbits (including traffic victims and hunter-killed individuals). This eagle now occurs in winter in n. New Eng. in much greater numbers than formerly, at present undoubtedly from artificial means—winter feeding programs.

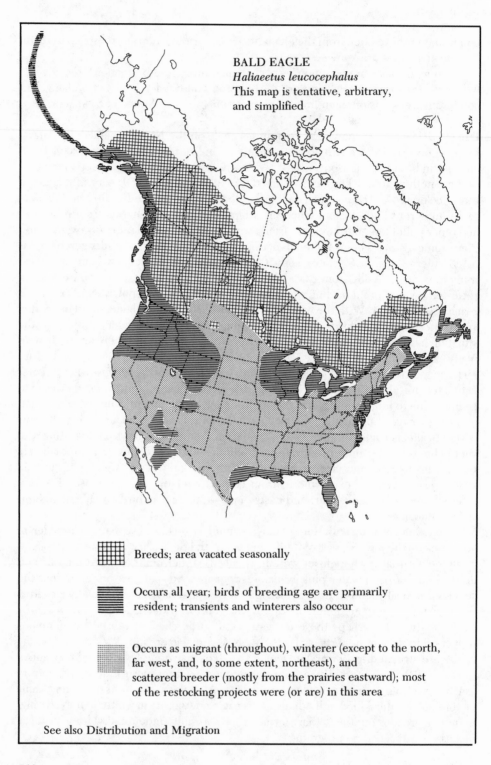

BALD EAGLE
Haliaeetus leucocephalus
This map is tentative, arbitrary,
and simplified

Breeds; area vacated seasonally

Occurs all year; birds of breeding age are primarily
resident; transients and winterers also occur

Occurs as migrant (throughout), winterer (except to the north,
far west, and, to some extent, northeast), and
scattered breeder (mostly from the prairies eastward); most
of the restocking projects were (or are) in this area

See also Distribution and Migration

Artificial repopulation efforts now seem almost routine. These consist of 1 "hacking"—rearing young birds to independence—in areas where the species had ceased to breed, 2 fostering—putting eaglets in nests where unproductive adults are present, and 3 translocation of viable eggs to nests where parent birds are contaminated and unproductive. The 1st method has had highest success, the 2d somewhat lower, and the 3d much the lowest. One Canadian province and 15 U.S. states have had hacking projects since 1976; over 300 birds had been hacked at over 20 sites through 1985. It is assumed that, with the waning of biocide contamination and the death of older birds, increased survivorship of and success by the "new" stock will result.

In 1975–1983, 156 eaglets from 5 Canadian provinces, Alaska, and several coterminous states, plus 63 captive-produced young were relocated in about a dozen states; various programs were expanding. In 1983 alone, 22 Canadian eaglets were translocated into the U.S. In 1984, 6 states planned to release some 70 young. The largest program has been the transfer in 1975–1983 of about 85 Alaskan eaglets to N.Y. and 33 more in 1984. At least half of the N.Y. eaglets have had good survival, a considerable number to breeding age by 1984 (1984 *The Eyas* **7** (1): 6).

Peripheral N. Am. records of occurrence CANADA Scattered records n. of known breeding limits; Old Crow (Yukon Terr.), Windy R. (Keewatin), Churchill (Man.), Moose Factory (Ont.), L. Mistassini, Knob L., and near Ungava Bay (Que.). ALASKA In the Aleutians, as far w. as Buldir I., and apparently now a rare straggler farther w. BERMUDA Four old records, fall–spring, 1 a capture (Reid 1884). PUERTO RICO Reportedly a sighting. Southernmost limits are somewhere in MEXICO, including Baja Calif. (breeds in vicinity of Magdalena Bay, probably elsewhere), s. Sonora (dispersal from Baja Calif.?), and Chihuahua (at least nw.).

COMMANDER IS. First reported by Steller long ago; over a century later, Stejneger obtained specimens, including a bird in predefinitive feathering (see Description, above); in the early 1930s Johansen (1961) had only reports from the natives and suspected their validity.

NE. ASIAN MAINLAND J. Koren, a field collector familiar with both White-tailed and Bald Eagles, saw the latter on several occasions and had other information on its occurrence in summer. Presumably it no longer occurs. Dementiev and Gladkov (1951, trans. 1966) mentioned 2 reports, perhaps from Koren's time, labeling them uncertain.

EUROPE Alleged records 1822–1865 can be faulted. Most publicized is a report of 1 said to have been killed in Sweden about 1850 (Bent 1937, Alexander and Fitter 1955, AOU *Check-list* 1957) and "apparently still extant about 1880" (Bent); it was taken in the Hebrides and was kept in Switzerland (R. Edberg, letter). (The diagnostic shape of the tail is unmentioned in the literature at hand; further, the White-tailed Eagle sometimes has a pale head–neck.)

Reported as **fossil** from the Pleistocene of Oreg., Calif. (4 localities), N.Mex., Nebr., Mich., and Fla. (3); and from prehistoric sites in Alaska (mostly in the Aleutians, 8 localities), Wash., Oreg., Calif., Utah, Ariz., S.D. (many sites), Iowa, Ill. (4), Ga., and Fla. (2)—from Brodkorb (1964) with additions.

NOTE HAWAII In some past time there was a native *Haliaeetus*; its bones have been found on Molokai and Oahu (Olson and James 1982a). RALPH S. PALMER

MIGRATION   Extant information, by no means all readily accessible, has expanded enormously in the past 15 years. These few pages attempt to present a general outline; of necessity, coverage is uneven, and generalizations have exceptions.

Bald Eagles that have nested tend to stay on or near their nesting locality around the year if food is available and the weather is bearable. In the Aleutians and vicinity, breeders, at least, remain through the seasons, often using their nests as roosts. In the n. interior they must vacate for the colder months, going whatever distance is necessary to find adequate food and shelter during severe weather. In Fla. (and to some extent n. to Chesapeake Bay and w.) young in summer of year of hatching and some older prebreeders go rapidly n. and then migrate s. in fall—as do some herons (see *Handbook* 1 430). Young birds hatched in n. latitudes (except perhaps some in the Canadian Pacific coastal region) are not known to go n., although there may be individual exceptions, before migrating in the opposite direction. There is extensive s. migration, some younger birds going from colder down to southernmost latitudes. Even so, and with extensive travel of thousands of individuals, the species in all ages and seasons is confined almost entirely within its breeding limits.

Especially in fall, Bald Eagles migrate throughout the warm hours of the day, without midday lull or cessation; Broun (1949) reported that they were active in late afternoon at Hawk Mt., Pa.

Migrating eagles often fly quite high, at times escaping notice. Generally speaking, young of n. birds go s. earlier and return n. later than older migrants. Perhaps older migrants tend to winter repeatedly in the same area, but at that season they are extremely mobile when seeking food. There is no definite indication that breeders behave as a unit, migrating and wintering more or less together. They seem to have the same goals but travel independently. As for the youngest cohort, perhaps some degree of interaction (visual contact?) may assist in holding to fairly definite flight paths to food sources along their routes. Breeders return to territories, and migrant or dispersed young to the vicinity of where they hatched, but again exceptions—some prebreeders go in almost any direction, and whether all return is a moot point. Since migrant eagles from different areas have wide distributional overlap in winter; this spreading might result in some individuals subsequently, in the opposite season, being found a distance e. or w. of where they originated. Some birds shift longitudinally within a season. One held captive for several years (did this affect its orientation?) was banded and released at Cortland, N.Y., July 4, 1831; on the July 11, it was shot near Dubuque, Iowa, thus having traveled an av. of over 100 mi. a day due w. (Herrick 1934).

The following pertains to a few large areas for which some information is at hand; within limits, one might extrapolate to get an approximation that would apply elsewhere.

Northern birds   ALASKA   Bald Eagles are resident on Amchitka (Aleutians), the only documented movement away being one seen 327 km. e. on Adak; when deprived of a usual source of food (garbage), some eagles died of malnutrition rather than disperse (Sherrod et al. 1976). In the n. Gulf of Alaska there is movement (probably not of local breeders) late Aug.–mid-Nov.; in Sept.–Oct., when light s. or w. winds prevail, scores pass e., soaring on updrafts; spring movement is apparent through Apr.–May (Isleib and Kessel 1973).

On the Chilkat R., in the rain forest n. of Juneau, there is an enormous assemblage seasonally. Because of an upwelling of warm water through gravel beds, the latest major run of chum and silver salmon in se. Alaska occurs here. The fish spawn and die. The water's warmth delays the time and extent of freezing, but many salmon freeze and then thaw during later warm spells, thus prolonging the availability of fresh food. Peak counts of eagles along several mi. of the river are around 3,500 (3,700 in Nov. 1981), but movement in and out may indicate a seasonal total of 4,500. Birds in predefinitive feathering arrive early (Oct.), and about late Dec. they diminish in numbers—heading s. Sudden cold causes numbers to decline rapidly; once, in the fall of 1980, some 2,000 departed in 1–2 days. Some have been sighted in B.C.; farthest was a bird in Wash.—1,100 mi. from its banding site. Birds in definitive feathering, which arrive later, begin to thin out in late Jan. as open water areas diminish and food becomes scarce. Evidently, these older birds go to the vicinity of river mouths from Juneau n. to Cook Inlet, where eagles occur in large numbers in winter–spring. There is a major concentration of eagles se. on the Stikine R. near Wrangell in Apr. (Postdating the above is an excellent report on Chilkat eagles by A. Hansen et al. [1984].)

PACIFIC NW The picture is complicated by residents, transients, and winterers, some young moving n. before migrating s., and by geography and local availability of food. Two radio-tagged young of the year moved in fall from n. Calif. n. into B.C. (W. G. Hunt). There is fall movement both down along the Pacific coast and out of interior w. Canada, some birds tending sw. over mountains toward the Pacific, others going more directly s. Many young birds inhabit coastal and insular B.C. and its s. lakes, Wash., and Oreg. in winter. Birds from Alta. to nw. Mont., stopping in fall at McDonald Creek in Glacier Natl. Park and then continuing to various destinations— Lower Klamath Basin, Idaho, Utah (Rush Valley), and Nev. Currently the largest s. wintering assembly (500+) is in the Lower Klamath Basin, just s. of the Oreg.–Calif. border. In spring birds gather in nw. Mont. and move onward on the e. side of the Rockies through s. Alta.; near Lesser Slave L. they divide, some going ne., others toward Great Slave and Great Bear lakes.

Data for the region are about as expected: s. Oct.–early Dec. and n. Mar.–early May.

Most birds at winter roosts in the arid w. U.S. interior evidently originate in the intermountain area; they are augmented by a few eagles that cross e. from Pacific areas.

SASK. Marked birds from the Besnard L. area. Beginning in Oct. the young move s. gradually, reaching their most s. av. latitude by early Feb.—having spread over an arc extending from N.Mex. and Ariz. to Tex. and even Mich. Observations suggest that older predefinitive-feathered birds may move first or go faster or farther than 1st-fall young. The birds tend to winter near inland waters, and there is some evidence that individuals use the same wintering area more than once. Saskatchewan supplies a large number of the eagles wintering in the midwest and s. to (and occasionally across?) the U.S.–Mexican border. Regardless of whence they come, most long-distance migrants are in predefinitive feathering; those reaching Ariz. arrive in late Nov. and depart in Mar.–Apr. Birds return to Sask. beginning in Mar.—the eagle month of the Crees—and continuing into May. The situation is the reverse of fall—old young

203

precede the youngest cohort. Unusual records: 1 banded as a nestling in cent. Sask. in 1973 was found dead near Juneau, Alaska, 3 years later; a Sask.-banded bird, at age 3 years, was sighted in Me. during the winter of 1984–1985.

GREAT LAKES REGION This contains more nesters than any other area in the coterminous U.S. Most migrants follow the Mississippi drainage, wintering in states on both sides of the river, but total lateral spread is from the Rockies to the Atlantic coast (Md. southward). In s. Wis. (where many winter), s. movement of transients reaches a peak in the 3d week of Dec., then declines to around mid-Jan.; n. passage is throughout Feb.–Mar.

MARITIMES AND N. NEW ENG. Some movement as early as late Aug. (but note below that some young Fla. birds are present), after the young are independent, and thereafter at least into Nov.; spring movement begins by early Mar., peaks in Apr., and ends in May. In Maine, breeders stay year-round; many are on territory through winter, especially on the coast. Birds in their 1st and 2d years disperse, then return to Maine. Experience with radio-tagged eagles aged 1–2 years reveals that they routinely travel from e. Maine to w. Conn. and back in a period of 3 weeks (M. McCollough). Winter spread is from seaboard and adjoining states and perhaps farther inland, s. into Fla. Birds at places where food was provided for them in Maine in winter, 1982–1985, included 2 from Upper Pen. of Mich., 1 from nearby Ont., 1 from Sask., 1 from S.C., 3 from Prince Edward I., 13 from New Bruns., and 14 from C. Breton I., N.S. (M. McCollough).

Young from Alaska, reared and released in N.Y., have been seen in various seasons as far away as Que., Mich., and Ala.

CHESAPEAKE BAY A large population of breeders are essentially resident. From few data, it appears that younger prebreeders may scatter in any direction (and probably return) and that various young eagles, even from a considerable distance, spend at least part of the winter in the bay area.

Southern birds FLORIDA C. Broley (1947) observed groups of eagles, thought to be premigration assemblages, on the w. Fla. coast in late Mar. Departure of young birds, recently independent of their parents, apparently begins about that time and continues into May. Observations reveal that many young remain near their nest for as long as 2 months after attaining flight, which would suggest that flying young depend on their parents for food for some time. Then their n. movement is rapid, and they spread out from near the Atlantic coast to inland well w. of the main axis of the Appalachians, with a tendency to occur about inland waters. Many young are more or less accustomed to people in Fla., so they are at a great disadvantage, being unwary when they go n. (Broley 1950); some have been killed in Canada 4 weeks after leaving Fla. Data on this movement are based on 62 (of 71) recoveries, Apr.–May. The s. return appears to be mainly in Sept.

The banding evidence (13 recoveries) of birds in their 2d calendar year indicates that a fraction of this cohort migrates substantially as do younger birds; there are few data for older cohorts of young; evidently some do move n., but perhaps not far compared with the youngest group.

There is some evidence also that 1st-summer birds from localities w. of Fla. also have a n. summer movement and that this pattern, in general, fits eagles as far n. as the Chesapeake Bay region.

Whether any Fla. breeders move n. in summer is unknown; if so, the number must be few. Occasional "adult" eagles taken in n. U.S. are rather small in size; whether they are s. birds or whether n. eagles vary more in size than is generally stated is unknown.

Field observations have revealed (contra Broley's belief) that breeders in se. U.S. (notably Fla.) remain at and near their nests through summer—that is, are there all year. As observed in s. Fla., they are quiescent much of the time, often perching in deep shade, where they are largely hidden; quite commonly, 1 or 2 "adults" are seen perched on the nest or using it as a feeding platform, and sometimes substantial repairs or additions to the nest occur in summer. There is some local movement, however, since the birds tend to assemble and scavenge at any attractive food source—especially midsummer–early fall. Breeders and older prebreeders then occur together at temporary roosts within commuting distance of these food sources.

The bulk of summer observations of eagles in s. Fla. believed (on characteristics of feathering) to be over a year old but less than definitive form night roosts ashore and on is. in nw. Fla. Bay; their near presence to established breeders probably accounts for the fairly constant summer attendance of the latter at and near nests. There is some evidence that a few birds in their 1st summer, rather than going n., join these older young at roosts, and there is more evidence that young late in their 1st calendar year, on returning to Fla., join these gatherings of older young. The largest number of prebreeders at a summer roost in s. Fla. is approximately 40.

Throughout the se. most young of the year disappear from nesting areas relatively soon, and virtually all band-recovery data indicate an extended n. movement such as Broley described from Fla. There are relatively few nesting Bald Eagles w. of Fla. to and including Baja Calif., and it is probable that the annual routine of the various cohorts is similar to that of s. Fla. birds just described.

Why an exodus of young eagles from the s.? They are reared in the cooler months, when food is plentiful; food is also plentiful for the others through the remainder of the year. The young, in their 1st calendar year, are dominated by older cohorts. By going n., presumably they can find room to feed where they are free of aggression from their own kind; those still surviving in fall return s. and enter roosting assemblies of other prebreeders—a better social situation that prevails until reproductive maturity, when the birds become territorial. The now-known pattern of occurrence of the birds of various cohorts that remain in the s. would seem to reduce aggression among them to more tolerable levels. (Based principally on MS from W. B. Robertson, Jr.)

As noted elsewhere herein, young in their 1st late summer–fall go n. from Calif. to food sources, then migrate south. RALPH S. PALMER

BANDING STATUS By Aug. 1981 the number of Bald Eagles banded was 7,571, and the number of recoveries was 499 (6.6%) (Clapp et al. 1982); main places of banding are scattered from Fla. to N.S. and Maine, thence w. and nw. to include Alaska.

Beginning in 1938, C. L. Broley banded nestlings, almost all on the gulf coast of Fla. from s. Hernando Co. to the vicinity of Ft. Myers, Lee Co. In 1950 he reported that he had banded 1,117; his final total was 1,168, and there are recovery data (last in 1960) on 108 (9.2%). Data given in the preceding section of this account, on migration of Fla. birds, include a recent study of the results of Broley's banding by W. B. Robertson, Jr.

In n.-cent. Sask., 1967–1975, 296 were banded mainly in the Besnard L. region; these were nestlings except for an older Juv. and a bird in definitive feathering (J. Gerrard et al. 1978). The work continues there, as elsewhere. Included in the total are the 65 mentioned by Houston (1970).

Fyfe and Banasch (1981) listed 99 banded 1973–1978 in w. Canada, with 6 (6.1%) recoveries.

In Maine, band numbers of many Bald Eagles have been read by using a telescope as the birds fed at winter feeding stations. From 1975 to 1984, 358 eagles were banded and 196 (54.7%) have been reobserved. Reobservation of birds banded in the 1981–1984 cohorts was 60–80% (M. McCollough).

Banding data have been used in numerous published sources. It is best to band nestlings at age 3–6 weeks (Broley 1947). In addition to banding results, information is now accumulating on tagged and radio-equipped birds.   MARK V. STALMASTER

REPRODUCTION   **Age when first breeds**   Of Alaskan eaglets, hand reared and released in N.Y. in their 1st calendar year of life, 3 "had begun breeding activity" at age 4, instead of the usual age of 5 (1983 *N.Y. Birders* 12 (1)); this is to be expected when there are no other breeders present to inhibit them. Some birds, when found breeding, have been regarded as showing "traces of immaturity" that may persist throughout life (see Description, above). A wild pair in Ga. were both "immature," the ♀ beginning to show white in the tail; they raised a brood (Hoxie 1910). There are some half-dozen records of nesting in Fla. (some successful) by pairs in which 1 member was not in "adult" feathering, and 1 record in which neither was "adult." These birds are obviously in predefinitive feathering, not individuals with some dusky in head–neck and/or tail, a condition fairly common among Fla. breeders and having little or no correlation with age (W. B. Robertson, Jr.). Several Aleutian pairs have nested in "immature plumage" (O. Murie 1959, C. M. White). Heinzman (1963) knew of 2 instances of "immatures" nesting but not producing young. Nicholson (1952) reported a breeding Fla. eagle in "immature plumage" (he suggested age 2 years but may have intended 3d calendar year). It had had a "full-plumaged" mate the previous year but had probably lost it. A captive ♀ 1st laid when at least aged 8 years and her mate was 3, but no young were produced until her 3d clutch, when the ♂ was aged 5 years (Hancock 1973).

From the above and other information: 1 at least some ♀♀ can produce a fertile clutch early (3d calendar year of life and later), and the ♂ is also fertile before attaining definitive feathering; and 2 a younger bird of either sex may be acquired as a mate or foster parent to replace a lost member of an established pair.

A high (saturated) density of established nesters in an area can inhibit breeding by others that have attained or exceed reproductive age. This is obviously so, for example, on the Chilkat R. in Alaska (Hansen and Hodges 1985). In n.-cent. Sask., of 5 marked birds that had acquired definitive feathering, none had acquired a breeding area and, of 3 at age 5, only 1 possibly was occupying such an area. One of these marked birds was resighted at age 6; it occupied a breeding area but did not raise a brood, which it did at age 7 (Remedios 1980, J. Gerrard). Many Bald Eagles probably first breed at age 7 or 8 years.

Not all mated pairs having a nest lay each year. The proportion of these has varied in different studies. Examples: Amchitka I., Alaska (about 1969) 19% (Sherrod et al. 1976); coastal B.C. (1980), at least 44% of "adults" were actually nesting (Hodges et al. 1984); San Juan I., Wash. (early 1960s), 4% (Retfalvi 1965); Man. and Sask. 4–23% (D. W. A. Whitfield et al. 1974); Besnard L., Sask. (1968–1981), 13% (J. Gerrard, in D. Bird 1983); Chippewa Natl. Forest, Minn. (1976–1977), 15% (Fraser 1981); and Maritime provinces (1974–1975), 12% (Stocek and Pearce 1978). On Amchitka it appeared that all white-headed territorial birds did at least some building or refurbishing but in many instances did not lay. Some may have been younger, not yet actively breeding, birds (Sherrod et al.); perhaps some lay in alternate years, or when nutritional levels are favorable. Of 96 nests (includes alternative ones) found in the Chilkat Valley, Alaska, fewer than ½, sometimes only ⅓, are active during the nesting season, and, for want of food, even these produce relatively few young (Rearden 1984). Nests are often abandoned. From much field experience in Fla., Bent (1937) stated that some birds do not lay every year; they refurbish nests and remain nearby. This had been the prior experience of Baynard (1913) and was the later experience of C. Broley.

Pair formation Timing is unknown, probably variable in length, and sometimes obviously has occurred before attainment of definitive feathering. Perhaps it may come about through protracted association of individuals in groups or larger assemblies of prebreeders. Birds in predefinitive feathering engage in High-soaring, Pursuit-flights, talon grasping, and related activities, by themselves or with older birds. Replacement of a lost mate can be very rapid.

Pair-bond form Believed to be lifelong monogamy, according to Herrick (1924b) and others; if a mate is lost, a replacement is found. A ♀ had a different mate each in 1924, 1925, 1928, and 1931 (Herrick 1932a). In Ga., a ♂ was killed Mar. 13 when the nest contained young; on the Mar. 16, the ♀ reportedly had another mate; on Mar. 17, an "immature" ♂ was feeding the young (Hoxie 1910). In Ont., when one of a pair was shot, the survivor got a new mate in 4 days (W. Saunders 1918). The most readily available replacement does not have to be white-headed, as Herrick noted. Ontario has fewer eagles nowadays, and those that lose their mates do not get a new one as soon as formerly (Weekes 1974). On Prince Edward I., N.S., a ♀ maintained a nest 1969–1978, and a mate was never seen (Nelson, in J. Gerrard and Ingram 1985).

In parts of the range where it does not become too cold and food is sufficient all year (e.g., parts of Alaska, B.C., Fla.), Bald Eagles remain on territory all year and probably year after year; no studies of marked birds, however, are available to confirm this. In part of the eagles' migratory range (Colo.), a close and consistent association of a few identifiable "adults" in pairs has been observed during winter (A. Harmata). Most, however, appear to be unattached then. (See also Duration of family bond, below.) In early spring, copulation of an apparently mated pair was observed, yet each of these 2 "adults" began its n. migration separately. The ♂ and ♀ of a previously mated pair may

207

arrive on breeding grounds separately (J. Gerrard) or may meet during migration and arrive together.

Both C. Broley and J. Howell reported that in Fla. eggs regularly were laid early in some nests and late in others, which is at least an indication that the same ♀ was at the same nest year after year. There are other indications of reoccupation of a nest by the same individual(s), which is expected in view of the long-continued residence of unmarked birds noted in recent years in Fla.

Soaring together, billing, stroking each other, joint nest-building or repair, sitting together on the nest, the ♂ bringing food to the ♀, and probably adults feeding each other (at least the ♂ feeding the ♀) on the nest have been described and presumably enhance bond maintenance (P. N. Gerrard et al. 1979, Remedios 1980).

Trio bond On Amchitka at 2 nests in 2 years and at 3 in 1, 3 white-headed birds were in attendance—often all on the nest together; sex of the "extra" birds could not be ascertained (Sherrod et al. 1976). In 1976–1978 there was a trio in n.-cent. Minn., and in 1980 there were trios at 3 sites on Amchitka (Fraser et al. 1983).

Displays Ordinarily employ much aerial space; it is not an invariable requisite for pair formation or successful breeding. The earliest reported captive breeding occurred in a 6 × 6 × 8 ft. slatted enclosure containing a nest box 3 ft. square, on a back porch (Bebe 1886, Hulce 1886, or as cited in Herrick 1934).

In early spring, where migrants are wintering, and during n. migration, birds may perform rapid chase or PURSUIT-FLIGHTS, or any number of birds may circle high up and some will dive at others—Pursuit-flights and HIGH-SOARING. This occurs in the prenesting period (late Sept.–Oct.) in Fla. (Pennock, in Bent 1937); Grimes (1944) even reported aerial evolutions above the suburbs of Jacksonville; in n. regions these actions occur in early spring. Birds in predefinitive feathering are included. An undulating SKY-DANCE, evidently to advertise territorial limits, occurs, as far as is known, after arrival but before intensive work on the nest. Immediately after arrival but before nest building, a ♂ was observed to FLY-AROUND extensively (A. Harmata), presumably to advertise his presence. In a spectacular "cartwheel" action, not often witnessed, 2 high-flying birds alternate in swooping very close together, in silence or calling; after sideslipping to avoid contact, they regain altitude rapidly. Then as one (♂) dives from high in the air, the other (♀) turns upside down, and the 2 birds interlock their extended talons; with wings spread, the pair falls earthward, rotating, and they separate when a crash (on land or water) appears imminent. Caged birds had "minor encounters" of talon grasping with "intense display and vocalization" (Price 1981). (Talon presentation or possibly grasping occurs in other seasons as an activity of birds of the same or mixed ages; see Habits, below.)

In the days (weeks, even months in nonmigratory eagles) before egg laying, ♂ ♀ commonly perch together; billing and mutual stroking occur (details for captives: P. N. Gerrard et al. 1979). On Amchitka, eagles frequently sit side-by-side on the nest in Dec., and in trio bonds, all 3 roosted there in early Jan. (Sherrod et al. 1976). Pseudoincubation occurs both in the wild and in captivity and can be misconstrued as evidence that eggs are present.

A HEAD-TOSS display is commonly observed. The bird is perched vertically and tosses its head backward, then forward and downward rather deliberately; loud calling

208

begins during the backward movement. On occasion it appears that the ♂ does this to elicit a response from the ♀, perhaps to initiate a duet. Mostly, however, it signifies either warning or concern, as in a human's approach. In a variant the bird's body is more horizontal and the call is uttered with head extended forward (a pose beloved by artists and designers of all sorts) and more or less raised or lowered. In autumn on the Chilkat R., an eagle displaces another at food, then Head-tosses (Rearden 1984).

High-soaring of flocks on warm days in at least the boreal autumn and winter constitute social behavior; whether this relates in any way to pair formation or bond maintenance is unknown. Descent to earth is extremely rapid, hence spectacular.

Nesting territory Usually located adjacent to or along a shore (of lake, river, brackish or salt water) or, in any event, within commuting distance of food. Islands are often preferred. In Alaska and Sask., 90%+ of nests are within 200 m. of water. Elsewhere, especially in areas where there is recreational or other human use of water, they nest farther back. The occupied nest and the perch trees from which it is visible more or less indicate the extent and shape of the defended area. Figures vary; examples: 1–2 sq. km. in Fla. (C. Broley 1947), Mich. (Mattsson 1974), and Minn. (Mahaffey 1981), to about 6 sq. km. in n.-cent. Sask. (J. Gerrard et al. 1980). At Karluk L. on Kodiak I., 14 territories were of 28–172 (av. 57) acres; smaller ones were usually contiguous and larger ones had unclaimed space between them (Hensel and Troyer 1964). At least from time of occupancy until the young are independent, the owners tend to defend against intruding members of their own species. On Amchitka, defense by resident birds is slight; an owner may vocalize but rarely takes wing, apparently paying little heed to others that fly through the territory (Sherrod et al. 1976). In situations like this, possibly the nesters sense that the other birds are headed elsewhere or at least are not motivated by territorial aggression. In Sask., breeders chase other eagles out of home territory, sometimes for a mi.; observations suggest that ♂ ♂ chase other ♂ ♂ and ♀ ♀ other ♀ ♀, but this needs confirmation (J. Gerrard).

Where there is year-round occupation of a site (for nesting; the nest used also as a rendezvous point, perch, or feeding platform), as, for example, in Fla., defense continues around the year and throughout the years of ownership. Numerous instances of eagles loath to relinquish a nesting territory are known. After a nest tree in Fla. was cut down with no suitable replacement, the birds remained for 2 years without nesting (C. Broley 1947). A poor or atypical site may be chosen over desertion. A case in Ohio was extreme; a pair chose to remain—and in 1976 built on the ground in a field of soybean stubble (Clark, in R. Knight et al. 1980).

Nest site In forests, usually in a tree, the more often-used species varying geographically (see Habitat, above), but conifers are favored over much of the range. The chosen tree is usually tall relative to surrounding trees, with a suitable crotch or branching to support a nest. This is built within the crown, and an easy flight-path or approach, generally from the direction of the nearest water, is essential. One or more lookouts or perch trees overlooking the site is very important, as is relative freedom from disturbance. Nests have been recorded at all heights from level ground to at least 60 m. up in trees. In treeless areas the nest is usually on a high place (see Habitat, above).

Bald Eagles have nested in heronries, a practice more common to Ospreys. In Fla., a pair nested near a piggery and took no young pigs; nor did eagles take a domestic fowl intentionally tethered below a nest, although they watched it (C. Broley 1947). No generalization can be drawn; some eagles do retrieve or catch live fish close to their nests. Where undisturbed, an eagle generally approaches the nest from high in the air. If distrustful, it keeps low, then swings up and goes over the nest edge rapidly (Herrick 1934)—like the usual approach of an accipiter.

Construction/refurbishing Limbs, branches, and assorted debris are gathered from the ground, transported in the talons, and put in place with the beak. Sometimes a bird flies (throws its weight) against a branch, grasping it in the talons and breaking it off, and then flies directly to the nest. Both sexes fetch material, but perhaps invariably the ♀ does the actual work of building. Captives: the ♀ usually initiated building activity; on several occasions, in soliciting posture, the ♂ vocalized close to the ♀, after which she would fly to the platform and work on the nest; then the ♂ would fly down, gather nesting material, and return and deposit it on the nest (P. Price 1981). In wild birds there is some indication that at least initial work on the nest tends to occur early and late in the day. The lining consists of finer items—sedges, grasses, seaweed, Spanish moss, anything convenient—and usually the cup or cavity meas. about 14 in. diam. × 4 in. deep (later, from actions of the young, the depression largely disappears and the nest becomes flat). Construction or refurbishing an existing nest can occur rapidly; Herrick (1934) mentioned a new nest, virtually completed in 4 days. Minimum usable size for a tree nest is probably about 50-in top diam. or larger. For a detailed and interesting description of construction, see Herrick (1932a) or as quoted in Bent (1937).

From his Fla. studies, Broley pointed out that a pair occasionally will repossess a nest it had abandoned (this not based on marked individuals). Sometimes owners desert for no apparent reason. As mentioned earlier, a nest may be refurbished annually and not contain eggs for some years. Or the birds may shift to an alternative nest. Occasionally they commandeer an Osprey nest. In Fla. Bay, conflicts between Bald Eagles and Ospreys apparently resulted in the latter sometimes relocating; J. Ogden (1975) suggested that, when the eagles exhibit territorial (aggressive) behavior toward Ospreys in the year in which the eagles first nest, they subsequently come to terms as pairs recognize adjacent ones.

Great Horned Owls regularly preempt eagle nests (owned and unowned); see, for example, data in text and table 4 in C. Broley (1947). The owls lay early, usually before the eagles but even alongside eagle eggs. The eagles seldom challenge the owls; they may build another nest but, if late in the season, seldom lay. In one instance an owl killed eaglets. Broley mentioned a preempted nest that the eagles frequently visited; they inspected the young owls in it but did not try to repossess it. There are at least 2 records of eagles incubating an owl egg.

Nests Those not many years in use are ordinarily 0.3–1 m. high and 1–2 m. in top diam. Although some material may be delivered sporadically around the year, there is a annual spell of refurbishing or building (new material added, old material reorganized), and the accumulated increments may eventually add up to a relatively enormous structure. Herrick (1924a) photographed one 12 ft. high and with a top diam. of 8½ ft. (nearly 57 sq. ft.); it weighed an estimated 2 tons and was felled by a storm in its 36th

210

year of occupancy. Broley (1947) described a Fla. nest that was 20 ft. tall and 9½ ft. in top diam. A nest in e. Md. that blew down in a 1933 hurricane consisted of 43 bushels and weighed 1,274 lb. (and some material did not fall). The variety of junk and clutter that turns up in nests is remarkable.

Sometimes the birds (both sexes) remove material from an existing nest for use in a new one. Nests on the ground, pinnacles, or ledges often consist of surprisingly little, coarse, material, but some are huge heaps of branches and debris. In Minn., when a nest blew down, an artificial one was substituted and used successfully (Dunstan and Borth 1970). For discussion of nesting on man-made structures and references, see Olendorff et al. (1980).

Most nests probably do not last more than a few years; the mean is 5 years in Sask. (J. Gerrard et al., in D. Bird 1983), but others may be used, continuously or intermittently, for decades. A partner may replace a lost mate, young reared locally may come back, or a site may be so favored by eagles that it is taken over by others if the owners relinquish it (J. Howell 1954). In 9 papers, 1937–1973, J. Howell reported on long-continued occupancy of some Fla. sites. See especially J. Howell and Heinzman (1967), but see also Herrick (1934) and Broley (1947). A nest at the uppermost of the 5 cataracts of the Great Falls of the Missouri R., seen in 1805 by the Lewis and Clark Expedition, was apparently occupied for more than 50 years (Herrick). In the Tongass Forest, se. Alaska, a tree known to have been used by eagles for nesting in 1907 was still in use in the early 1970s (C. M. White 1974). Some of J. Howell's nests, if still extant, have nearly a half-century of longevity. Eventually they fall from their accumulated wt., their support gives way, or they come down in a storm. In the damp Alaskan climate on the edge of the Pacific, older nests are more compacted and full of moisture, hence decompose, and remnants are scattered by the wind. Ground nests in the treeless Aleutians, if not in use, grow up rapidly to grasses and other vegetation.

Nesting density Very high if there is an occupied nest per 2 sq. mi. On Amchitka in 1972 the av. distance between nests was 2.7 km., the 2 closest active nests were 137 m. apart, and av. distance between nests successfully producing young was 4.5 km. (Sherrod et al. 1976). In Fla., C. Broley (1947) stated that 2 localities had 3 active nests within 1,000 ft. of one another. J. Howell (1937) wrote that they may be as close as a ¼ mi. apart there and that, when one is being examined, as many as 5 eagles soar overhead, calling in protest. Density is high on a section of the Chilkat R., Alaska, where abandonment is frequent.

Alternative or "extra" nests When a pair on territory has a nest and builds another, the new one is usually easy to find, not far away. In Fla., the distance between the various nests of a pair always is less than a mi.; of 12 pairs that each built 2 nests, 8 pairs built the 2d nest within ¼ mi. of the 1st, and all 5 nests built by 1 pair were within ¼ mi. of a central point (J. Howell 1937). In n. Calif., 42% of 54 territories contained alternative nests (Lehman 1979). There are supernumerary nests in nw. Ont. (Grier 1969) and elsewhere but evidently none on Amchitka (Sherrod et al. 1976). Of 233 territories visited in Sask. in 1969, only 27 had more than 1 nest (J. Gerrard). "Extra" nests, even if several, may be repaired and attended regularly.

Copulation The usual pattern (P. N. Gerrard et al. 1979), both in the wild and in captivity: mates perch together, then either may approach closer to the other and either may "solicit." With ♀ approach, or response, she lowers her head and spreads her wings and feet slightly, "bowing." Her call is low and distinctive, and the ♂ may respond initially by calling loudly, flapping his wings, and pumping his tail up and down or may proceed directly to mount the ♀. This occurs generally on the perch tree overlooking the nest but also on the ground (if the birds perch there) and on the nest. It is rather brief. Captives: most copulations occurred from 6 days before to 3 days after laying of the 1st egg of the 1st clutch; 3 pairs copulated after the 1st clutch was removed; they also copulated before and during relaying; and 2 pairs copulated after laying a clutch (which was removed) and did not relay (Wiemeyer 1981). Copulation occurs before, during, and after nest construction, occasionally even after hatching (Herrick 1932a, 1934). Afterward, mates perch together, and then, at least in captivity, they "rearrange" nesting material (P. N. Gerrard et al. 1979) and there is "intense" calling (P. Price 1981).

For annual cycle of the testes of captives, see Locke et al. (1966). Artificial insemination has been successful.

Laying rate Evidently variable; Herrick (1934), apparently backdating to estimated hatching date of small young and assuming a fixed incubation period, estimated a laying interval of 4 or more days. In captivity, the ♀ has laid an egg on successive days (Hancock 1973) or 2 and 5 days after the 1st (S. Gilbert et al. 1981). Laying is usually in the morning.

The ♀ is lethargic for some hours before laying an egg (only the 1st one?). As noted in captives, even before the 1st egg is laid, the ♂ or ♀ may sit in low posture as if incubating (P. N. Gerrard et al. 1979); this pseudoincubation in the wild was mentioned earlier. Incubation of the clutch ordinarily begins with laying of the 1st egg (Herrick 1932a, other authors), but this varies. Captives: incubation may start with 1st or 2d egg and is by both parents (Hancock 1973), but mostly by the ♀. Nicholson informed Bent (1937) that at every nest (in Fla.) that he visited after dark he found both birds present, 1 incubating or brooding, the other perched nearby. In captivity, on 3 occasions just before dark, ♂ and ♀ were seen side-by-side on the nest (P. N. Gerrard, in Maestrelli and Wiemeyer 1975). In very close confinement, the ♀ was on the nest constantly, fed by the ♂ (Hulce 1887). Captives nearly always began incubating after laying the 1st egg (Wiemeyer 1981).

Dates for fresh clutches Generally speaking, the Bald lays much earlier than the Golden Eagle. Data from various sources are given here, going from s. to n. for rather spotty coverage of the breeding range. There is a greater spread in s. U.S. (includes replacement clutches?) than to the n. The spans given in Bent (1937) presumably are for viable, not necessarily fresh, eggs. FLA.—Oct. 26 is earliest date, most clutches are completed Nov. 15–Jan. 15, and eggs in Apr. (replacements?) are known; at Tarpon Springs, most eggs laid Dec. 10–15. GA. mid-Nov.–late Mar. TEX. and sw. U.S. Nov. and later (in ARIZ. evidently late Jan.–3d week in Feb.); June 20 (Oberholser and Kincaid 1974) is very late for presumably viable eggs in Tex. BAJA CALIF. probably late Nov.–early Dec. TENN. Jan. or earlier. VA. most clutches completed by Feb. 10–15. CHESAPEAKE BAY last ⅓ of Feb.–Mar. OHIO Mar.–Apr. MINN. Mar. 16–Apr. 3. WASH. and OREG. coasts and vicinity: usually 1st 2 weeks of Mar. MARITIMES late

212

Apr.–May. NORTHERN NEW ENG. (Maine) early Mar.–Apr. N.-CENT. SASK. Apr.–early May. ALASKA on Kodiak I., late April, peaking in 2d week of May, and continuing to end of month; and on Amchitka, late Mar.–early May; in the Aleutians, eaglets still in preflight stage in Oct. (Dall 1874) would indicate a replacement clutch.

By adding 35 days (for incubation) and 77 days (nestling stage) = 112 days to the above clutch dates, one can arrive at approximate date(s) when young will attain flight.

Clutch size   Usually 2 eggs and more often 3 than 1; Bent (1937) reported 4 and thought perhaps they were the product of 2 ♀ ♀. Forty-six clutches on Amchitka in 1969—8 (of 1 egg), 34 (2), and 4 (3) (and 11[4] = error for 11 [0]) (Sherrod et al. 1976); these authors cited other Alaskan studies, the av. usually being close to 1.9 eggs/clutch. In Sask. at Besnard L. the mean of 33 clutches was 2.18 (G. Bortolotti). In Va., F. M. Jones (1940) reported that 12 of 15 clutches contained 3 eggs; one wonders if food was abundant. In New Eng.; 18 sets of 3 (F. Carpenter 1887) is exceptional if valid. In 91 nests that contained eggs in Fla.: 13 (of 1, with 6 probably incomplete), 77 (2), and 1(3) (J. Howell 1937). No Fla. records of 4 per clutch (Nicholson 1952).

For captives, the av. was 2.5 eggs for 1st clutches and 1.9 for relayings; 1 ♀ laid 3 eggs in each of 5 1st clutches (Wiemeyer 1981).

Northern birds   One **egg** each from 20 clutches (1 Labrador, 1 Nfld., 3 Maine, 1 Ont., 2 Anderson R., Canada, 12 Alaska) **size** length 75.38 ± 2.69 mm., breadth 57.46 ± 1.51, radii of curvature of ends 24.03 ± 0.92 and 15.73 ± 1.51; **shape** between elliptical and subelliptical, elongation 1.30 ± 0.036, bicone −0.088, and asymmetry +0.190 (F. W. Preston). Fifty eggs from Alaska and Arctic Canada: length 69.6–84.3 mm., av. 74.4, and breadth 53.1–63.4, av. 57.1 (Bent 1937). Fifty-seven from Karluk L., Kodiak I., Alaska, av. 73 × 53 (Hensel and Troyer 1964).

More southerly localities   Sixteen from s. Calif. and n. Baja Calif. av. "fully as large" as n. eggs—75.3 × 57 (Bent).

One **egg** each from 20 clutches (2 Ohio, 2 Md., 1 Pa., 2 Va., 1 Ga., 12 Fla.) SIZE length 71.51 ± 2.84 mm., breadth 55.20 ± 1.50, radii of curvature of ends 23.08 ± 1.46 and 17.02 ± 1.98; SHAPE as above, elongation 1.29 ± 0.044, bicone −0.058, and asymmetry +0.142 (Preston). Fifty from Fla. length 58.1–78.8 mm., av. 70.5, and breadth 47–57.6, av. 54.2 (Bent). Another Fla. series: 59 av. 69.9 × 54.1 mm. (E. Bagg 1889).

The **shell** is white, rather rough, without luster. From Karluk L., Kodiak I., the av. wt. of an unspecified number of fresh eggs was 130 gm. (Hensel and Troyer 1964). In captivity a ♀ laid 6 eggs, weighing 85–123 gm., av. 107—the 1st heaviest and 3d lightest (S. Gilbert et al. 1981).

In Fla., it was Broley's experience that early nesters are much more successful than later ones.

Replacement clutches   If the 1st is taken early enough, the ♀ may lay a 2d set after an interval of 4 weeks or more (Bent 1937). She may or may not use another nest. In Ohio, Herrick (1934) knew of 3 instances in which a bird was robbed early in the season and another set was forthcoming in the same nest. Also, 1 robbed of 3 repeated with 3 and 1 robbed of 4 repeated with 2. A zoo captive: each egg was removed on the day of laying, for a total of 7 eggs "in rapid succession" (S. Gilbert et al. 1981). Captives: 2d clutches were laid 9 of 11 times when the 1st were removed within 8 days of clutch completion, and the interval to laying of the 1st egg of the repeat clutch was 18–23 days (Wiemeyer 1981)—so-called double-clutching.

In Fla., after the great destruction of the Oct. 1944 hurricane, most nests were rebuilt in time for normal laying, but in 24 rebuilt nests no eggs were laid and eggs of 21 nests did not hatch although incubated for 2 months (C. Broley 1947). Poultry did not lay for 3 weeks after the hurricane; domestic hens appeared to have lost their desire to incubate; and no owls took over eagle nests that season. Observations there after severe storms in 1960 and 1965 show little agreement with Broley (W. B. Robertson, Jr.).

Generally speaking, if failure is early in incubation, the birds may work on an alternative nest and not lay; if failure is late in incubation or later, the birds have no residual nesting behavior that year.

In suitable quarters, captive ♀ ♀ evidently produce eggs annually as long as they live.

Incubation behavior   Similar for wild and captive birds, the sitter sits low on the nest. The idea that sometimes the eggs are covered with some material deliberately by the sitter before departure, even for a very brief absence (Herrick 1929), is repeated in several treatises. C. Broley (1947) reported it in Fla.; it has been reported to occur, but only occasionally, elsewhere; it is not known in the Aleutians (Sherrod et al. 1976). Captives: about once an hr. the sitter stands and turns the eggs. In the wild the incubating bird rarely departs before the mate arrives. In the wild in Ohio, the sitter utters a sharp chittering, the mate, if within hearing, comes to the aerie and moves up close, and the changeover is quick (Herrick 1929). Both sexes have an incubation patch. Captives: the ♀ did most of the incubating in daytime and either sex incubated at night. When the mate arrives at the nest, the incubating bird stands up and steps to the edge; the incoming bird steps, with balled feet, into the nest center (or first may walk a little or poke at the nest cup). The arriving bird pokes gently into the cup, grasps a firmly anchored bough as a pivot, rocks its body from side to side, settles down, and rakes surrounding material toward itself. Near sundown on 3 occasions, both birds were in incubating position on the nest, billing and stroking each other. The eggs were incubated almost constantly, the duration of brief absences being correlated with wind-chill index (very brief absences at higher wind velocities). (From P. N. Gerrard et al. 1979.)

Again captives: both adults carried materials to the nest during incubation (as in the wild), and there was some poking in the nest before a bird settled down. Twice adults poked hard at the nest center (this also seen in the wild), perhaps to alter an uncomfortable bulge or to drain a wet spot (P. N. Gerrard et al. 1979).

Greenery   The well-known raptor phenomenon of fetching some greenery to the nest, during incubation and much of the nestling period, is well exemplified by the Bald Eagle. In the Chippewa Natl. Forest, Minn., most nests contained a sprig of white pine; only that species of tree was delivered, even though red pine was up to 3 times as abundant (Mathisen 1970, Wechsler 1971).

Incubation period   In the wild in Ohio, closely calculated as 34–35 days (Herrick 1932a); in Fla., 36 days, evidently on authority of W. L. Ralph (A. K. Fisher 1893) and

214

35–36 days (Nicholson 1952); in captivity, 35–37 days (Hulce 1886, 1887); an egg in an incubator took 38 days (Price 1981). In an incubator (dry bulb 37.5°C, wet 30°C) the young was vocalizing in the egg on day 33 and hatched 35 days after laying, 24 hrs. after pipping (S. Gilbert et al. 1981). Figures sometimes mentioned—31–46½ days (F. Crandall, in Herrick 1934 and in Prestwich 1955)—were based on 3 clutches of disturbed birds in the Buffalo Zoo.

Hatching success Must be determined with care because the birds have a great susceptibility to desertion from human disturbance during incubation; various reported values may reflect such interference. At Besnard L., Sask., 1980–1982, 36 of 42 eggs (85%) hatched successfully (G. Bortolotti). on Amchitka in 1969, at least 1 egg hatched in 36 of 46 active nests (78%), and a total of 55 of 88 eggs (63%) hatched (Sherrod et al. 1976).

Eaglets The adults sit higher (brooding posture) on the nest after the eggs hatch. At least 1 remains in almost constant attendance for the 1st 2 weeks, then the amount of time gradually decreases. At this early stage, during the warm part of the day, the brooding parent (either sex) holds its wings apart to shade the chicks. Night brooding lasts 3–4 weeks, sometimes longer (Herrick 1932a). At first the young are in the center of the nest, but in the 3d to 5th week they move out and spend most or all of their time on the rim. At first they also use their wings for support when crawling; this ends in about a month as they begin more active flapping, and they exercise their wings progressively more as they get older.

During their 3d week the young spend much time preening as the longer, dark, down grows. This insulates the young, and the parent modifies its brooding to shielding, standing over the young with drooping wings. When the sun appears, the parent flies to a perch.

Food is brought by either parent. The bird fetches it in a foot, or in both if heavy, and a fish may be delivered alive and flop out of the nest (or a turtle may crawl out). Smaller items—small fish, tail of a large one—are sometimes delivered in the beak; that is, prey is shifted from foot to beak during flight (Herrick 1933). Often part of the prey is eaten beforehand, the head, especially, is removed as is done by many raptors. When the young are small they are fed immediately on delivery. The eagles studied by Herrick once delivered 3 fishes in 17 min. Prey may accumulate at the nest to great excess when the young are quite small (for Alaska, note fig. 9 in Sherrod et al. 1976), but if this is food caching, it is done only at the nest (Herrick 1934). The parents also brought grass, especially early in nest life, and seldom if ever removed anything (Herrick). Green branches, such as are brought during incubation, are also brought while the young are growing.

The parents initially tear off small pieces of fish and drop them into the open upreaching mouths of the young. By the 4th week the adults, with head sideways (horizontal, while a young's is vertical) offer the food so that the young usually have to reach for it. The young start to peck at fish on their own in the 3d or 4th week, but not until the 6th to 9th weeks are they well able to tear off pieces. Young at 1-young nests do so at an earlier age than those at 2-young nests (J. Gerrard). Herrick saw the ♀ tear off pieces of fish; then the ♂ took the food from her and "time and again" fed a young. Or both may rip off pieces and offer them to nestlings. After feeding comes brooding—

215

more constantly by the ♀. If the adults are away, according to Herrick, any sudden weather change would bring an old eagle to the brood.

For an excellent description of feeding partly grown young, see Herrick (1929) or as quoted in Bent (1937). In captivity the ♀ did the majority of feeding (Wiemeyer 1981); this is usual in the wild. The nestlings get no water to drink, but eaglets (age unstated) from a fallen nest "developed quite a fondness" for it (Stupka, in Bent 1937).

Especially when food is plentiful and living is easy, an eagle may spend hours at its perch. On warm days the wings may droop. Sometimes parents perch together. An eagle may spend much time preening; then it rouses and becomes quiet. It is often idle (Herrick).

The larger of 2 young usually gets fed first and, if food is scarce, may get all of it. If food is plentiful while the larger is manipulating and swallowing a piece, the smaller will be offered food (Herrick 1932b). A captive at 7–14 days was fed twice daily, 150–200 gm. (5.3–7 oz.); after 21 days it was fed once daily, gradually increasing the amount to a maximum of 772 gm. (24 oz.), but 336 gm. (12 oz.) seemed adequate for maintenance; it preferred fishes and birds to mammals (P. Stewart 1970). (The calculated age of this bird is in error [Gilbert et al. 1981].)

Siblicide occurs, but far less commonly than in the Golden Eagle. It usually happens when the young are small. Age for age, a ♀ soon becomes decidedly larger than a ♂. In Fla., interaction between young is common and results in substantial mortality (Robertson, in Kale 1978). At Amchitka, 1 eaglet repeatedly became larger and stronger and the other gained very little. The smaller one eventually disappeared. This usually happened between 3 and 8 weeks of age; apparently the stronger outcompeted for food, although a possibility may exist of some sickness differentially attacking the young (Sherrod et al. 1976). Herrick (1932b) graphically described an instance wherein the older (and larger) eaglet got almost all of the food and pecked the smaller sibling, then, after a day of bad weather, the smaller bird died and was trampled into the nest. Harsh treatment of the smaller one often occurred in absence

216

of the parent(s); yet it occurs as often when a parent is present, since the nest is rarely unattended when the eaglets are small. Survival of both young at nests containing 2 is frequent (e.g., 55% of successful nests on Kodiak I., Alaska) (Sprunt IV et al. 1973) and appears to depend on the ability of the parents to provide food. In a good year in Sask., as many as 7% of successful nests may raise 3 young (J. Gerrard).

Later nest life   The parents now spend progressively less time near their young. The latter are very aware of their surroundings, watching flies or any other living thing; they are strenuous in their play and are more bold and masterful generally. They perch on the aerie rim, whence they scan the ground below. They see, and evidently recognize, their parents at a great distance. An eaglet will feed, then suddenly jump sideways to the nest rim, lower its head, elevate its tail, and shoot liquid excreta clear of the nest. It may also back up to the edge beforehand. This tends to create a circle of "whitewash" below the nest tree. There is much flight preparation (flapping), also hunting play (jumping about, occasional treading movements as when controlling struggling prey) and fighting play (as when squabbling over food). In Ont., an eaglet twice made a "sham attack" on 1 of its parents (Weekes 1975). At intervals the young stand or lie peacefully, facing the wind. Or they may sunbathe, standing with wings outspread. They preen much of the time. Herrick (1924d) 3 times saw an eaglet offer food to a sibling, which accepted the items and deposited them at its feet. The recipient awaited its opportunity, then seized the whole carcass from the donor!

Herrick noted that older young were friendly, playing together, fondling one another, and showing "equable disposition." But among the young he had as captives, a 13-week-old ♀ killed her nest mate, and in another instance, 1 killed and ate its brother. Whether they were hungry "cannot be stated" (Herrick)—the eaglets were getting their daily food allowance. (Captive birds do not grow as well as those in the wild, and Herrick's weights are far below those of young wild eagles of similar age.)

Increase in DEPTH OF BEAK through base of cere during nestling life (♀ larger) was measured in n. birds and is an index of approximate age; see Description, above, for details.

Temperament of "adults"   Variable among individuals. Over most of the breeding range eagles rarely attack or feign attack when a nest is approached. Generally, they circle overhead, perch at a distance, or disappear, but after the eggs hatch 1 or both sometimes stoop close, and this can be very disconcerting; there are a very few reported instances of their striking a climber. In Alaska, a person was struck at a tree nest on Kodiak I. (T. G. Grubb 1976), and a considerable number do this at ground nests on Amchitka (Sherrod et al. 1976). At the latter place, some pairs are much more aggressive than others, a condition that seems to increase through most of the nestling stage and then wanes. They readily attacked helicopters. Captive eagles are very defensive in the breeding season, discouraging entry into the pens, and a few made entry difficult all year (Wiemeyer 1981).

Breeding success   In Fla. in a 14-year period, 345 of 735 "potential reproductive efforts" were successful, a rate of about 46.9%, varying in different years 37–60.8%. The 345 successful nestings included 135 broods of 2 (39.1%) and 9 of 3 (2.6%), for a total of 498 young that attained flight (about 0.68 young/active nest) and 1.44 young/ successful site (range 1.25–1.60). These data, from Robertson (in Kale 1978), suggest

217

that the Fla. birds were reproducing at a rate adequate to maintain population. The following 3 paragraphs list productivity data, variously defined, compiled from various sources:

The percentage of nests in which eggs were laid and from which young successfully flew has varied: n.-cent. Fla. (1973–1976)—72%, Amchitka I., Alaska (1969)—78%, and Besnard L., Sask. (1968–1981)—85%. For some areas the only data available are percentage of occupied breeding areas where young attained flight: Kodiak refuge, Alaska (1963–1970)—63%, Wis. (1962–1970)—66%, and Besnard L., Sask. (1968–1981)—73%. Lower values include Mich.—37% and Maine—26% in the 1960s, when the effects of DDT were severe. One could, of course, give a figure of zero where the birds were eliminated by biocides.

Number of young raised per successful nest has varied: Wis. (1962–1970)—1.24–1.69, av. 1.55, and Besnard L. (1968–1981)—1.36–1.88, av. 1.61.

Another measure is number of young per occupied breeding site: Ariz.—0.63–1.40, av. 0.80; San Juan I., Wash. (1975–1980)—0.62–1.02, av. 0.84; Wis. (1962–1970)—0.89–1.12, av. 1.02; Kodiak I. (1963–1970)—0.74–1.20, av. 1.02; and Besnard L. (1968–1981)—0.89–1.45, av. 1.17. These populations were apparently healthy; the value drops below 0.70 in areas adversely affected by DDT.

The young **attain flight** at various ages around 10–11 weeks (Herrick 1924d, later authors). Nestling period was 72–88 days in Sask. (Bortolotti 1984d). Departure may be sudden, final, and perhaps premature—the young may leave (or be frightened off the nest) in the 9th or 10th week and may spend time on or near the ground before flying well. Several such departures in Minn. were undirected and uncoordinated, usually a long downward glide (Kussman and Frenzel 1972); the young birds ended up remaining on or near the ground for some days, during which they were vulnerable to terrestrial predators. If departure is gradual, they make short forays to nearby trees or the perch site of a parent, finally leaving as late as the 12th or 13th week (Herrick 1934, J. Gerrard). In Ohio, the 1st to leave sometimes followed a parent back to the nest to be fed (Herrick). As soon as they can fly well, they often make the most of it, ascending to considerable altitudes. They kill without parental example (as in the case of "hacked" young).

Duration of family bond Variable in length. In Fla., the flying young soon seem to have lost all association with their parents and, in 2 months or perhaps often much sooner, they begin a long journey n. They remain in the vicinity of their nests for 6–9 weeks in n.-cent. Sask. (J. Gerrard et al. 1974), for 4.7–13.3 weeks, av. 5.9 in Minn. (Dunstan 1975), for 7–8 weeks in Maine (M. McCollough), and in Ohio were seen following parents until late Oct. and none was seen driven from parental territory (Herrick 1934). Rarely does a parent perch near a flying young. Observations early Dec.–early Apr. in Conn. (Faccio and Russock 1984) support the idea that 2 adults (mates) plus 1 or 2 young may be together and behave as a unit in winter. On Amchitka, at a nest with preflight young and a parent present, sometimes a presumed yearling or a 2-year-old was also in the immediate area—perhaps from that nest in a previous year (Sherrod et al. 1976). After dispersal or migrations, the usual pattern of birds aged 1–3 years is to return to the general region of their birth. Evidently, this occurs throughout the breeding range—that is, whether or not breeders are migratory. In Maine, 20–

50% of 1st-year eagles dispersed s. during their 1st winter, many into Chesapeake Bay and some as far s. as S.C. Most birds returned to natal areas during their 2d or 3d calendar year. Observations of an eagle from Ont. in Maine during its 2d, 3d, and 4th years and a 5-year-old eagle from S.C. in Maine suggest that some birds may not return to natal areas (M. McCollough). JONATHAN M. GERRARD

SURVIVAL   There are few firm data. Sightings and recoveries of 43 birds banded and marked as nestlings at Besnard L., Sask., suggest a minimum of 20% survival to age 3 years (J. Gerrard et al. 1978). These birds are migratory.

Sherrod et al. (1976) attempted to calculate mortality rates of eagles at Amchitka, in the Aleutians. They figured that, from nest leaving to acquisition of definitive feathering, the birds suffered 90+% mortality. They also assumed that 5.4% of definitive-feathered birds were lost annually. These authors believed that, on Amchitka and on Adak, starvation in winter was the single greatest cause of mortality. Cold weather must also be reckoned with; E. W. Nelson (1887) stated that many eagles were found dead in the Aleutians in winter and were too fat to have starved. These birds are not migratory.

There is various evidence that older birds are more successful at foraging and piracy than younger ones. Birds in definitive feathering are dominant and more experienced, hence more likely to survive. Highest losses are, as expected, in the youngest cohort, as evidenced by banding recoveries. (Some causes of mortality are mentioned under Habits, below.)

These data are based on reobservations of 196 banded and color-marked eagles in Maine and New Bruns. during 3 winters at feeding stations. Prefeeding survival rates were estimated to be 63% for 1st-year birds, 70% for 2d-year-birds, and a constant yearly survival of 91% for 3-year-old birds and older. A winter feeding program improved 1st-year survival to 73%, and 2-year birds to 84%; older bird survival rates remained at 91% (McCollough 1986).

Efforts to stem population declines   Largely directed at increasing reproduction. Advances in population modeling indicate, however, that augmenting reproduction rates is less effective than maintaining increased survivorship (Grier 1980). However that may be, programs aimed at benefiting the species include: transplanting eggs and young (to restore nesters where they had disappeared or to areas where birds are unproductive), restricting human activity (such as near nests), supplying nest platforms, enhancing food (such as providing winter food), enhancing habitat, rehabilitating and releasing injured individuals, breeding and releasing captives, restricting pesticide use, and so on. MARK V. STALMASTER

HABITS   Is the Bald Eagle majestic, noble, awesome? Or lazy, an "arrant coward" (Bent 1937), a thief? Are such attributes in the eye of the beholder? This eagle is our most-studied diurnal raptorial bird; it is also, figuratively speaking, the most often misquoted in the popular press. It would take a hefty volume to present all viewpoints on these matters, but at least some facets can be elucidated in the following pages.

Hunting methods   See Herrick (1924c) for description of the stoop, the feint, the true attack, and the crushing or suffocating method of completing the kill. The Bald

Eagle is a skilled maneuverer. In contrast to the Golden Eagle, a helicopter pilot stated that the Bald is almost impossible to shoot down: it can suddenly turn or double back, do an "Immelmann or split S" (Anon. 1971). Although most raptors are believed seldom or never to hunt close to their nests, the Bald Eagle fishes wherever the fishing is good. At Amchitka I., an "adult" left its nest to catch a young sea otter pup only 30 m. away (C. M. White). Prey brought from a distance is commonly beheaded (eaten by the eagle) before being transported to the nest, but some fish (and turtles) are delivered very much alive and may flop (or crawl) over the edge. They are not retrieved. Outside the nesting season or when foraging for itself, the eagle consumes small fishes during flight and carries large ones to a feeding perch.

In still- or perch-hunting the bird watches from a vantage point—a tree, cliff, or stack—and swoops down to seize its prey, braking as it nears the surface. This technique has a high success rate.

Hunting by flying or by circling overhead is not as successful as still-hunting, although special situations have an extremely high success rate. At San Juan I., Wash., the eagles sometimes coursed low over the water, snatching a fish without interrupting their flight. Sometimes a coursing bird made a powerful downward thrust toward the water, then suddenly changed direction in a half-somersault, and plunged headlong, yet terminated with only the legs getting wet (Retfalvi 1965). Both feet are used when transporting large prey.

Here is another example, from W. Townsend et al. (1980). On Dec. 23, 1979, 3 "adult" and 7 "immature" Bald Eagles were seen taking squid from the sea off Campobello I., New Bruns. The "immature" birds approached at a low glide and, when over the target, climbed steeply, hovered, and plunged. In most cases they alighted on the water with wings outspread—only their heads, the "wrist" area of the wings, and occasionally the tail, were above the surface. Even so, they had no difficulty with take-off; the body was clear of the surface in about 2 wingbeats, and after 5 or 10, they were comfortably airborne. Then they carried the squid in their talons to a ledge and ate them. Townsend thought that the eagles caught squid as soon as they hit the water but delayed their take off to avoid harassment by the abundant Herring Gulls. The "adult" eagles approached in a shallow glide, snatched squid at the surface, and ate them on the wing by reaching down with their beaks while extending their feet forward. C. Todd et al. (1982) reported a squid in and another under a nest nearby in coastal Maine and O. Murie (1940) listed squid among foods in the Aleutians.

Sometimes an eagle flies close to the sea, drops into troughs between swells, and thus takes seabirds, notably alcids, by surprise. Ashore, in the same fashion, they dip over the Aleutian tundra hunting ptarmigan in the manner of the Gyrfalcon.

There are several graphic accounts of hunting Am. Coots; this from Fla. (Batchelder 1881): The eagle swoops from its perch and the coots close ranks, appearing like a black mantle as they fly close together while striking the water with their wings. This mob action seems to baffle the eagle at first, but eventually some coots break away, and then the eagle always gets one. In another version, the coots dive and the eagle hangs over the spot and seizes one when it surfaces.

Ducks are hunted both from perches and from the air. If not caught on the wing beforehand, a duck may dive underwater; the eagle follows its course and, by forcing it

220

down whenever it surfaces to breathe, finally exhausts it, and picks it up. Some authors have asserted that ducks can escape pursuing eagles, which is true in some instances, but others point out that an eagle can be swift and maneuver expertly. Its ordinary flight seems labored, but this is misleading. In hunting geese and brant on the Va. coast, Cobb (in Brewster 1880) stated that the eagle overtook quarry on the wing, swept beneath it, turned over, and thrust its talons into the victim's breast.

In Utah in winter, according to C. Edwards (1969), the birds hunted by coursing 1–3 m. above ground, where jackrabbits were concealed in vegetation. This alternated with perching, so that some eagles were stationary while others were on the wing. The very act of alighting would cause a nearby rabbit to break from cover—that is, perching served as a flushing technique. The eagles would alight on the ground and even walk through low brush, like accipiter hawks, apparently attempting to flush prey; other eagles, in flight, then made kills. About half of the rabbits hardly covered 30 m. before capture when 2 or more eagles hunted cooperatively. The eagles perched on hummocks, sagebrush, even level ground, remaining there longer than on the wing. At least a major portion of a kill was transported to a nearby high spot; it was usually shared, at times with a Golden Eagle or with Com. Ravens. After feeding, an eagle might be quiescent for as long as several hrs., and then, in early afternoon, with slow, labored flight it would go to a communal roost.

Eagles are known to walk around in gulleries, seeking chicks. Their walking gait seems awkward; they can run rapidly for short distances. On an is. near Ketchikan, Alaska, Bald Eagles (mostly "immature") have been seen chasing storm petrels on the ground at twilight. Nocturnal seabirds were their principal prey; they even excavated shallow petrel burrows (DeGrange and Nelson 1982); see also Quinlan (1983). On another Alaskan is., "adult" eagles "rely on aerial prowess" to obtain food (seabirds), while "immatures" play a waiting game. One perches amid pupping sea lions or seals, cues in on a cow in labor, and inches closer. Patience is rewarded by acquiring the cow's afterbirth—"a highly nutritious meal" (Wehle 1984). (See also carrion as food, below.)

Where fish abound, eagles alight ashore and wade in, at times up to their breasts, and they may submerge their heads to capture fish. Such fishing, known at least since Audubon's day by dark-headed as well as white-headed birds, can be highly successful. A few times, Southern (1963) saw eagles stand on an ice edge and reach into the water with beak or talons. In season, dead and dying salmon are a staple food, and the ease with which they are gotten must be especially beneficial to the welfare of inexperienced young eagles. For example, on the Chilkat R. in Alaska, an eagle waded into the water until almost afloat, seized a dead or dying salmon with a foot, and with the other tugged the prey ashore (Rearden 1984). Bent (1937) stated that, on several occasions, Bald Eagles alighted on water, floated about as lightly as a gull, probably in pursuit of fish, then took wing with no great difficulty. In winter they walk long distances on the ice (Southern).

Cooperative hunting An eagle killed a cormorant in Fla. and tried to tow it ashore; 2 others joined in, and, taking turns, they managed to drag it to a place where they were about to eat it when interrupted (Worthington, in Bendire 1892). In Utah in winter, as noted earlier, eagles tended to hunt in small groups, cooperating in flushing

221

and killing jackrabbits. Sherrod et al. (1976) saw 2 or more eagles making sequential stoops at a duck on a lake, and 5 eagles taking turns stooping at a Least Auklet. There are various reports of cooperatively hunting waterfowl, especially ducks. Also, 2 sometimes cooperate in pirating fish from an Osprey, or several may "gang up" on a Golden Eagle to drive it from its quarry.

Eagle v. Osprey   Bent (1937) stated that the Osprey is "systematically robbed" of its fish, which should not be construed as indicative of a universal practice. For example, in an area in Minn., such piracy was not seen in 10 years (Rossman and Rossman 1971); in the Blackwater area of the E. Shore of Md., it was never seen (F. R. Smith 1936); and it is relatively uncommon in Fla. (Robertson, in Kale 1978). The eagle closes in from below on a fish-carrying Osprey, forcing it to fly higher and higher. The Osprey tries to keep above its tormentor and, of course, the fish, when released from a greater altitude, is longer in falling. The fish is dropped, and the eagle tries—usually successfully—to catch it during its fall. Nicholson (1952) may have been the first to describe 2 eagles cooperatively attacking an Osprey; 1 eagle turned belly up and took the fish from its captor.

When Ospreys and Bald Eagles nest in the same area, they seem to reach some sort of accommodation—perhaps 1-sided. J. Ogden (1975) suggested that harassment by eagles had a negative effect on Osprey reproduction in Fla. Bay. Ospreys will defend their nest, but an eagle did perch on an active one and was pursued out of sight by the ♂ Osprey when it departed (T. C. Grubb and Shields 1977). Ospreys regularly harass young eagles, especially if they enter Osprey nesting territories.

In ne. N. S., Prévost (1979) found the 2 raptors "tolerant" of each other. The eagles had little success in getting fish from Ospreys. The 2 raptors had different prey preferences. Eagles also approached Ospreys that were not carrying fish. Then an Osprey would cease hunting and begin soaring, the eagle below, forcing the Osprey upward, for reasons not clearly evident.

Other piracy   The evidence grows that experienced eagles are more successful pirates than younger birds. If some other species has possession of visible desirable food, in many circumstances an eagle will try to seize it. Thus, other raptors, burdened in flight with prey, may be forced to drop it—the Peregrine, various buteos, the Northern Harrier, and so on; see discussion by D. Fischer (1985). This might explain why the aggressive Red-tailed Hawk is decidedly antagonistic toward Bald Eagles. Near Helena, Mont., a Prairie Falcon dived at a yearling Bald Eagle, breaking its neck and killing it (1982 *Am. Birds* **36** 998). Long ago, Audubon reported that a vulture flying with horse entrails dangling from its beak was pursued and killed and that the carrion was eaten by the eagle. At carrion, the eagle is dominant over our common vultures, gulls, ravens, crows, and, reportedly, dogs. On Amchitka, where eagles were tame enough to take food from the hand, they would follow a person who was carrying fish. They rob sea otters of food and, apparently, foxes occasionally. An eagle and a river otter were found, both dead, perhaps having fought over possession of a fish (Rosen 1975). In Wis. in winter, otters in possession of fish were attacked by eagles; the otters dived, taking their fish with them (Beckel 1981). At the Amchitka garbage dump, eagles with food were chased persistently by others (Sherrod et al. 1976). When they assemble at carrion or other food, minor altercations can ensue, "adults" dominating "immatures." Aggressive displays are ritualized, so there is little or no physical contact. Where carrion is plentiful, eagles may feed alongside one another quite amicably, joined by ravens, gulls, crows, even magpies, which they usually seem to ignore. In Mo. in winter, in robbing another eagle, 1 or several approach the one flying with prey from the rear; then a pursuer flips over and takes the food from the carrier's talons or else dives repeatedly to force the carrier to drop its food, which the pursuer attempts to recover (Griffin 1981). Coyotes occasionally rob eagles of food. Numbers make a difference. Thus eagles are mobbed, but not always driven off, when they enter gulleries. In Nfld., they fled from Great Black-backed Gulls (Lien 1975). One attacked a loon, evidently for the fish it had just caught ("Roamer" 1875). In various places they keep an eye on either Common or Red-breasted Mergansers to rob them when they surface with fish.

Using a beater   Eagles often follow one another, the follower(s) seeking to be led to a food source. Eagles also use other species in locating food—gulls, crows, ravens, jays—but these scavengers, in turn, may benefit by taking food scraps; such relationships abound, but when food is scarce, the other scavengers may become prey. In B.C. in July, eagles evidently associated availability of prey with the presence of killer whales, which forced salmon to the surface, where the birds captured them (Ofelt 1976).

In Utah in winter, and with adequate food, the Bald seems to be more altruist than pirate. If 1 captures a jackrabbit, it may share its quarry with another, even with a Golden Eagle, and, commonly, ravens (C. Edwards 1969).

Upper limits of prey size   As previously indicated, the Bald Eagle often is misquoted. It is reported to have carried off a 30-lb. pig, a 50-lb. lamb, and to have eaten 40 lb. of flesh at a sitting (Imler and Kalmbach 1955). If one includes carrion, it has fed on sperm whale (Kenyon 1961)—the largest food so far reported. The heaviest wt. of prey caught and transported, and for what distance, remains in question. An upper limit has been played down—perhaps too far—by some eagle proponents to discredit exaggerated newspaper reports of human infants and young livestock being carried away. These reports also mention eagles weighing up to 50 lb. and having a wingspread to at least 15 ft. (L. and M. Walker 1940). Bent (1937) made a guess, stating an eagle "probably can lift" an object weighing as much as itself. The lamb episode (from J. West 1875) that Bent mentioned was as follows: Near the mouth of the Neuces R., N.C., an eagle was seen flying toward an observer. The river at this point is about 5 mi. wide, and the bird was becoming very exhausted and flew lower and lower, finally alighting on the shore within 20 steps of the gunner, who shot it. It was carrying a "little live lamb," which was unhurt. A. K. Fisher (1893) was the first to state that this showed that an eagle was capable of carrying a burden "fully equal to its own weight" a long distance. The little lamb may have weighed a lot less.

In Alaska, where eagles are large, the heaviest prey found in nests include Emperor Goose, Common Eider, cormorant, smallish Canada Goose, and Pelagic Cormorant; also sea otter pups. These are from Sherrod et al. (1976), who saw an eagle catch an adult Emperor Goose and fly with it to a sea stack. The goose may have weighed about 5 lb., a sea otter pup about 4 lb. In Fla., C. Broley (1947) found Brown Pelicans, Great Blue Herons, and a cormorant in eagle nests—that is, transported there. Even if the

223

eagles fed on these before delivery, the remains could be quite heavy. Robards (cited in C. Snow 1973a) estimated the weight of sticks carried to nests as not exceeding 3 lb. The largest healthy mammals captured (but not necessarily transported) are, perhaps, foxes or young pigs.

There are at least 9 published accounts of Bald Eagles catching or finding large prey (fish, birds) and towing it ashore. For example, Brewster (1880) stated that an eagle dragged a large goose nearly a ½ mi. through the water, and Hatler (1974) wrote of 1 killing an Arctic Loon—probably a weakened bird—and towing it ashore. But when a 4-lb. pickerel was tied to a 10-lb. submerged rock, an eagle managed to drag this combination only about 20 ft. (Casillo 1937). In B.C., an eagle swam 150 yds., towing a dead cormorant, then preened on a rock and flew away carrying its prey (Campbell 1969). In Alaska, Hehnke (1973) stated that eagles caught fish estimated to weigh 10 lb. (4.5 kg.) and dragged them ashore (did not fly with them). In Fla., Nicholson (in Bent 1937) mentioned catfish, "some up to 15 pounds in weight," found in eagle nests. Herrick (1924c) went the limit when he wrote of 1 carrying a carp "which appeared to be larger than the bird itself and to have weighed 6 to 8 pounds." In Norway, Willgohs (1961) witnessed a White-tailed Eagle (closest relative of the Bald and about the same size) pick up and carry a fish weighing 15 kg. (33 lb.)—surely an error for 1.5 kg.

Young Bald Eagles, especially, occasionally strike something either inappropriate or unmanageable. An eagle seized a rubber decoy (Wheeler and Raice 1967). One struck some object in the water, perhaps a seal, and was drawn below the surface (Boardman 1875). An eagle reportedly struck an infant and dragged it a short distance, then quickly departed, bearing a fragment of the child's garment (Wilson and Bonaparte 1832 2); this has often been cited. There is no certainty that a child has been carried to an aerie, as reported the same year by Nuttall (1832). Such reports are among the reasons why Herrick (1934) took note of the "great amount of rubbish" written about eagles carrying off children. Yet this idea has existed in various cultures. It was believed by the Inuit near the mouth of the Yukon (E. W. Nelson 1887).

On the basis of acceptable evidence, a Bald Eagle is doing very well when and if it lifts an object ½ its own wt. or transports prey more than ⅓ its wt. very far.

Use of water   Young in the nest get no water, except possibly when it rains. Swimming perhaps occurs most frequently after an unplanned fall into water or sometimes when towing prey. One reportedly entered the water and swam, searching unsuccessfully for a fish it had made an Osprey drop (Edscorn 1973). In Iowa one swam across L. Macbride (Kent 1978). At least in winter, bathing seems to be a social activity, usually done in groups. Wiemeyer (1981) reported that captives bathe frequently.

Play   At Buckeye L., Ohio, Trautman (1940) watched 6 eagles in Feb. They were grouped at a hole in the icebound lake. One, followed by 2 or 3 others, took a stick about 18 in. long and began to ascend in great spirals to an altitude at which the birds could barely be seen with the unaided eye. Then it dropped the stick, and the others stooped and tried to catch it before it struck the ice; the bird catching it began an ascent while vocalizing, followed by the others. After playing for over 10 min., the birds descended and stood about the hole.

Russoch (1979) described 17 soaring instances in w. Conn. in winter, 15 of 2 birds and 2 of 3 "immatures" (a lone "adult" was involved in only 3 bouts). The birds took turns chasing each other. Five of 14 bouts included transferring sticks in midair. Three times the "adult" chased an "immature," but the latter never chased the former.

In n.-cent. Mo., talon presentation (and clasping) occurs all winter, low and high in the air, but cartwheel display was not reported. When a diving bird nears a lower-flying one, the latter flips over, belly up, and presents its talons. There were no observations of an "adult" talon clasping with "immatures" (Griffin 1981), yet it is known in Fla. (B. King 1982) and occurs between the sexes and all ages in Alaska (Rearden 1984). Various other observations could be cited, showing that such activity is common.

An activity hard to classify but fairly common is flocks of smaller birds swirling around or seemingly following a raptor. Even flocks of ducks have been seen following the Bald Eagle in winter and spring in Ohio (Trautman 1942).

Interest in white objects In S.C., according to folklore, every nest contains a stone guarded by the bird—a water-worn white quartz pebble, for example (Hoxie 1888). Eagles bring white objects, including plastic items, to nests (J. Gerrard 1983). In the Chesapeake Bay area in summer, the birds "play" with white plastic bottles and with sticks, leaves, cow dung, and pine cones (Clark, in J. Gerrard and Ingram 1985). Clark has photographed an eagle manipulating a bottle with a foot and lifting it with its beak. In nw. Conn., white plastic bottles of gal. and ½-gal. size were deployed in appropriate places by D. A. Hopkins to determine whether eagles moved and "played" with them. Usually they did, and in various seasons. The bottles were checked about once a week. Beak marks were usually on the neck and handles, and talon marks were lower down. They also manipulated, pierced, and sometimes partly demolished thin metal 12- and 16-oz. beverage cans of assorted texture and colors.

Winter Social grouping may facilitate locating and acquiring food and may possibly aid in establishing or maintaining pair bonds. Daily activities are limited, and to minimize energy costs, flight occurs infrequently (Stalmaster 1983). Soaring and gliding are common since they require less effort than flapping flight, which appears labored and which requires a long clear path to become airborne. Feeding is most intense in early forenoon, and perching (or sometimes soaring) occupies much of the remainder of the day, although some birds may forage again well along in the afternoon. There are various activities during flight or feeding—aerial pursuits and talon presentation and clasping, with more or less calling; on the ground while feeding, aggressive behavior includes beaking, raising the wings, mantling over food, and so on. During severe weather, eagles may remain all day at sheltered roosts.

Although soaring in groups may occur in any season or time of day, it can be spectacular where many birds are at winter assemblies. Soaring in warmer weather may have a thermoregulatory function; if the temperature drops markedly, soaring decreases and foraging increases. In Oct. on the Chilkat R. in Alaska, more than a thousand eagles flap upward into afternoon thermals that carry them so high that they are visible only with binoculars. There is a good deal of play at this season, and the birds plummet back to earth at sunset (Rearden 1984).

Communal roosting Occurs widely in winter, in coterminous U.S. from Oreg. and Calif. to the Atlantic seaboard and to s. Fla. The usual pattern is about as follows:

225

A **night roost**, which may be composed of scores of birds, needs protection from the wind, adequate perches, and freedom from disturbance. In the arid w. interior, canyon roosts have a n. exposure and Douglas firs for perching. The perch trees are high up on the canyon walls, allowing easy access. First arrivals choose favorite trees and limbs, and later ones alight as close as possible. A tree may fill before an adjacent one is used. A few Goldens roost among the various cohorts of Bald Eagles, and any activity akin to hostility is limited to birds supplanting others. Young Goldens are more aggressive. The eagles are quite vocal. They also soar high over the roost on clear days, just after storms. (From C. Edwards 1969.)

Roosting trees vary in species depending on locality; usually they are in single-species stands and are past maturity; see, for example, table in Keister and Anthony (1983). In some localities, Douglas fir and ponderosa pine are favored. In the Chilkat Valley, Alaska, cottonwoods along the river are ideal for resting, perch-hunting, and night perches, but in cold weather communal roosts are in dense spruce and hemlock on an adjacent ridge (Rearden 1984). Proximity to food (usually much less than 15 km.) is a prime determinant in locating a roost.

As noted at a valley roost, as it becomes light, the birds that still are present turn toward the sun and preen; departures, however, begin as early as 1 hr., 50 min. before sunrise. There is no mass exodus. "Adults" fly directly out of sight, singly and in pairs, and any that linger had probably fed late the preceding day. "Immatures" take wing, only to return within a min.; they chase each other, then perch side-by-side. Sometimes 3 birds were observed in these "mock dogfights," and 3 times "immatures" were seen carrying large sticks and chased by another "immature." (From J. Platt 1976a.)

The birds return in the last 2 hrs. of daylight, alone or in small loose groups. Those already present utter a high-pitched chittering, and no real aggression is seen. "Adults" and "immatures" perch within a m. of each other, and Com. Ravens and Golden Eagles share the roost. The same perches were used at 4 different roosts, night after night, throughout the 6 years of study (Platt).

A day perch may be at a distance from the roost, must be close to food (the foremost requisite), is preferably in a tree, and is preferably on the edge of an open area that allows unobstructed access. Dead trees with sizable limbs are preferred at some localities. The birds tend to be more scattered than at night roosts, and they shift depending on weather, season, and food availability (Swisher 1964, later authors).

In s. Fla., where breeders occupy territories all year, assemblies away from territories usually contain well under 2 score birds—prebreeders, occasionally joined by very few breeders. In the Aleutians, birds of all ages intermix.

Some history The treatment of this essentially harmless bird since the arrival of Caucasians in N. Am. is hardly inspiring. On the one hand, its image, by being stamped or embossed on public documents and appearing on coins and paper money,has "multiplied and spread more widely over the face of the earth" than that of any other "living being" in world history (Herrick 1934). It has gone to the moon on spacecraft: "The Eagle has landed." On the other hand, its environment has been reduced and degraded, and the bird itself was listed or treated as vermin in the coterminous U.S., Alaska, and Canada for a century. In brief, as a direct result of human-induced mortality and drastic habitat changes as the human population increased, the Bald Eagle decreased in numbers in much of its range for many years.

In Alaska, a bounty was in effect, 1917–1945, and again, 1949–Mar. 2, 1953. Payment (per pair of eagle feet) went from 50 cents to a dollar and doubled again. The number of birds bountied has been given as 102,946 (Imler and Kalmbach 1955), 103,459 (Lincer et al. 1975), and "about" 128,273 (Robards, in C. M. White 1974). Sometimes it has been stated neatly (for shock effect?) as "over 100,000." Fox farmers and salmon fishermen traditionally shot eagles whether presented for bounty or not. Therefore, J. King et al. (1972) stated that as many as 150,000 may have been killed in Alaska during the inclusive spans of bounty dates. In B.C., there was a bounty on Golden Eagles, 1910–1924, and, after its cessation, eagles were "removed" by game wardens; misidentified young Bald Eagles undoubtedly were among the victims.

Perhaps the number of Bald Eagles in Alaska was reduced by the bounty, but this is not demonstrable, since there are no prebounty data on numbers. At the beginning of the 1970s, Robards (cited in C. Snow 1973a) estimated the number in Alaska at 35,000–40,000. In se. Alaska a 1977 census produced an estimated 7,329 ± 894 "adults" (Hodges et al. 1979). The overall Alaskan population was at a high level in the 1970s. A calculation, published in 1983, of 48,000 in B.C. and Alaska was mentioned earlier (see Distribution, above).

In the coterminous U.S., over many decades and in addition to the effects of biocides, the cumulative kill of Bald Eagles both in the name of defending young livestock and randomly and wantonly has surely greatly exceeded the number of birds bountied in Alaska. No neat figure is suggested. The point is that the greatest ignominy at the hands of modern humanity is not the publicized Alaskan bounty kill but in addition to it.

The use of agricultural and industrial chemicals was an ongoing practice when pollution of the environment became greatly complicated by the biocide era beginning in the 1940s. The occurrence of man-made chemicals and pollutants in the environment is implicated (or determined) in death, increased susceptibility to death, and diminished reproductive success. DDT and its metabolites, as well as other organochlorines, are well documented as causing eggshell thinning, breakage, and toxicity. Additional disturbance has resulted from the growing human population, including a great increase in outdoor recreation, timber cutting, and use of waterside areas as well as continued shooting. By the mid-1960s the decline in numbers of breeding eagles exceeded 50% in some areas, reached 90–100% in others, and was accompanied by nesting failures of 55–96% (Sprunt IV, in Hickey 1969).

The classic work, to go back some years, is that of Charles Broley in s. Fla., where he began banding eaglets in 1939. By 1947, 41% of the birds failed to produce young, in 1950 78% failed (46 pairs showed no breeding behavior), and in 1957 86% failed. Broley related the spraying of DDT to the decline. Eggshell thinning and related pathology were not known then, and so he believed that over 80% of the birds were sterile (C. Broley 1950, 1958). Numbers had declined by the mid-1930s (antedating Broley's work), and decline was drastic in many areas after the late 1940s. For various data, see references in Handbook 5 to J. C. Howell, Sprunt IV et al., and Robertson (in Kale 1978).

At Hawk Mt., ne. Pa., 1934–1975, numbers of migrants were rather low at first, then built up about 1945–1950, then declined steadily. As graphed by Nagy (in Chancellor 1977), the number of "immatures" was very low, much lower than

227

"adults," and reflected diminished production of young. Based on selected Christmas censuses in coterminous U.S., 1956–1970, numbers declined steadily (W. H. Brown 1975). It seems hard to imagine, but, at Derby Hill on se. L. Ontario, after a long decline, Bald Eagles were so few that they were scarcer than the Golden (G. Smith and Muir 1978).

Although the Bald Eagle is protected by the Migratory Bird Treaty Act (1913), the Bald Eagle Act (1940: full protection except in Alaska; strengthened 1971), and the Endangered Species Act (1966), on Feb. 14, 1978, its recognized status had become such that it was "officially" listed as "endangered" in 43 coterminous states and as "threatened" in 5 others (Mich., Minn., Wis., Oreg., Wash.). Before then, attempts had begun to redress past wrongs, the beginning of the period of so-called management.

The effects of the biocide era are waning. Bald Eagles entering the breeding population in the 1980s are far less contaminated than older birds, and various regional populations have already reached or exceeded a break-even point of producing enough young to maintain their numbers. Current threats include widespread acid deposition (it can eliminate the food supply) and lead shot in waterfowl carcasses (ingesting it can be fatal).

Some interrelations with man   In areas where Bald Eagles have little or no contact with man, human intrusion near the nest can be very disturbing. Where they are around some human activity, especially if it is repetitious, they become more or less habituated or conditioned to it. On Amchitka, where the eagles are not molested, the is. personnel formerly fed them, and the eagles would take food "greedily" from the hand (Sherrod et al. 1976). In Fla., an eagle was fed regularly by tossing fish to it in the air. At Bar Harbor, Me., the eagles use the breakwater and other vantage points as perches, keeping an eye on passing lobstermen; when a fisherman finds a sculpin in a lobster trap, he tosses it overboard and an eagle usually gets it. The eagles know the local boats and are much shier if unfamiliar craft come by. (This practice has now been outlawed.) At Reelfoot L., Tenn., in winter, commercial fishermen provide some fish for the eagles and have a protective attitude, since the 200+ birds are an attraction to visitors. On the Pacific NW coast the eagles get some waste from fishing boats and are dominant over the gulls. On the B.C. coast the eagles are unconcerned about boats passing near nesting trees but are very upset when people come ashore (F. Beebe 1974). On Mandarte I., B.C., more eagles were present on weekends, presumably because they were kept on the move inadvertently by people seeking recreation on the water. The eagles disturbed the cormorants there, so the crows got more cormorant eggs when the eagles were around (Verbeek 1982).

Two winter roosts in Utah were in valleys within 1 mi. of small rural communities, and both roosts were disturbed almost daily by the landowners. The birds seemed to become habituated to humans and their equipment. The eagles would take flight, but they waited longer and flew shorter distances than when flushed by strangers (J. Platt 1976a). In nw. Wash., wintering eagles can become habituated to routine human activities, but they are sensitive to human presence. Older birds flush first and young ones seem to react to them rather than to the observer; thus it is possible that young eagles are sensitized to human activity by their seniors (Stalmaster and Newman 1978).

228

In winter in N.Y., the eagles tolerated some vehicular traffic, but not people afoot. Overzealous birdwatchers appeared to cause the greatest disturbance (Nye and Suring 1978). In the Chilkat Valley, Alaska, roadside eagles become conditioned to auto and other traffic; the longer the birds remain through the season, the more tolerant they become (Rearden 1984).

In w. Ont., Grier (1969) did not find any measurable effect on eagle productivity from single climbs to band nestlings. This may be true, yet interference at nests containing eggs or young should be discouraged lest it lead to desertion.

Causes of losses have been alluded to elsewhere, but further listing may be in order. Shooting is demonstrably the most frequent single cause of death as determined from autopsied individuals (Coon et al. 1969, Kaiser et al. 1980). Young birds are more susceptible to shooting, probably because they are less wary of humans; in some parts of the country, Bald Eagles are also mistaken for another target—the Golden Eagle. Shooting continues by sheep ranchers, purportedly in defense of sheep, and by duck hunters, tempted by a large living target; an old prejudice against any bird of prey also lingers.

The Bald was once numerous in the Wichita Mts., sw. Okla., but had become almost extinct when J. H. Gaut visited there in early 1904. This was a result of persistent persecution by the Indians, who prized eagle tail feathers for manufacture of war bonnets. The 2 largest feathers brought a dollar each, the others 50 cents each (Oberholser 1906). A recital of similar examples would fill pages. Feathers, talons, beaks, and bones are used in the manufacture of native American artifacts; there is a lucrative market, at home and abroad. For this trade, in the early 1980s, 200–300 Bald Eagles were killed on and near the K. E. Mundt Natl. Wildl. Refuge in S.D. and Nebr. On June 11, 1986, the U.S. Supreme Court ruled that Indians may not kill Bald Eagles without being subject to federal prosecution. **Feather identification:** In some areas, white (or partly dyed) domestic turkey feathers have proven a satisfactory substitute for eagle feathers. This should be encouraged. The groove along the ventral surface of the shaft is V-shaped in Bald and Golden Eagle tail feathers; it is U-shaped in turkey feathers (R. Laybourne). Better to be caught with the substitute than face heavy fines and imprisonment for possession of parts of birds protected by 3 federal statutes.

Losses of eagles are caused by trapping, food poisoning (eating coyote baits), electrocution, lightning, collisions, and various accidents. Sherrod et al. (1976) were able to document starvation in the Aleutians, and no doubt it has occurred elsewhere, but emaciated carcasses are rarely found. Such deaths might be expected in winter when food is harder to obtain and adverse weather induces energy stress. In B.C., during intense winter cold, several were seen perched together in "such a benumbed state" that a man could shoot 1 without disturbing the others; one morning 3 were found "frozen stiff upon the ground where they had fallen from their perches" (E. W. Nelson 1887). The young are more susceptible. They are less experienced at finding food and in preventing piracy of their food by older eagles (Stalmaster 1981). Fowl cholera, trichomoniasis, and coccidiosis have been found in Bald Eagles; they are susceptible to parasites (for a list, see Tuggle and Schmeling 1982) and pathogenic agents.

Eagle management The subject is not treated separately here. There is an excellent summary in Olendorff et al. (1980), and this field continues to expand.

Attributes   Eagles—a semiabstract concept—have had what Herrick (1934) labeled an "extraordinary versatility" in acquiring human (and superhuman) attributes. The Phoenix and the Roc of early mythology are probably eagle-derived. Eagles are symbols of omnipotence, courage, freedom, independence, magnanimity, and truth; the eagle has been messenger of the king of Olympus and carrier of his thunderbolts, servitor of the sun, and bearer of the souls of emperors (ordinary mortals had to make do with loons). Eagles topped the standards of Roman legions, are pervasive in the military today, and are prominent in architecture and all forms of art. For further details, see Doherty (1982).

The extent to which eagles permeate our present culture may be indicated in many ways, but 3 will suffice. *The American Eagle in Art and Design* (Hornung 1978) depicts 321 selected examples of how an eagle's anatomy can be modified or stylized to fit almost any purpose. During the long (premargarine) era of the churn, the most popular butter mold produced the eagle in bas-relief. Among the 122 *million* McGuffey's Readers used in American schools between 1836 and the 1920s, the *New Sixth Eclectic Reader* (1857 onward) was a mainstay of hundreds of thousands of children year after year. It contained a story of an eagle (the bird is actually the Golden, the locale Scotland—a safe distance away). In this story, the bird seizes a child and flies to its mountain aerie. The child's young mother climbs the cliff (no man dares attempt to scale it), rescues the unmangled, untorn, still-swaddled babe, makes the impossible descent, and swoons. The onlookers kiss the babe while the minister eulogizes the power of mother love.

Native American symbolism   Eagle clans, totem poles, carvings, and a host of other applications of eagles, plus much mythology, are indigenous on this continent. Eagle bones are common in some archaeological sites—parts of 16 birds found in 1 (Parmalee 1958). Eagles, the Bald included, were admired and respected. The most elaborate physical expression of this were carvings and designs of the nw. coastal Indians. These have considerable realism—more so than the highly stylized (Golden Eagle-derived) thunderbirds of the Southwest. An eagle dance, today nearly extinct, occurred across at least most of N. Am. down to the Gulf of Mexico. Fenton and Kurath (1953) described it and its variants. Although eagles were regarded with esteem, their feathers and other physical parts were desired (consider the quantity in anthropological collections), and in early times the birds were shot over bait, using bow and arrow, or were taken by pit trapping and probably snared. The Bald Eagle was the symbol of the Iroquios Confederacy, and membership was indicated by wearing an eagle feather. (That one who *shows the white feather* is a coward is not Indian but is derived from cock-fighting.)

Inuit mythology about the eagle is widespread. Inhabitants of the Yukon Delta believed that eagles formerly were larger, possessed of many superattributes, and very fierce.

The numismatic eagle   Appears on all sorts of coins dating from long before the Christian Era and on paper money. The "American" eagle appeared on a coin, a Mass. penny, as early as 1776. As a numismatic adornment to fit the shape of a coin, the Bald Eagle's image has fared variously—an understatement.

The Washington eagle   The Bald Eagle arrived on the Great Seal of the USA,

figuratively speaking, over a bumpy road strewn with committees, discord, and designs of dubious merit. Benjamin Franklin was chairman of the 1st such committee, and a majority rejected his design, which may have affected his subsequent views. The Bald Eagle was finally adopted on June 20, 1782, some 5 years earlier than the Constitution. As is well known, Franklin asserted (and J. J. Audubon agreed) that the Bald Eagle was of bad moral character: dishonest, a coward, and so on. Franklin persisted in these views, for example, in a letter written to his daughter on Jan. 26, 1784. In a way he was sensible to prefer the turkey, and turkey promoters down to the present remind us of this. By a fickle twist of fate (as noted above), turkey feathers increasingly supplant eagle feathers. Herrick (1934), a true eagle man at heart, pointed out at great length that negative views are based upon "a complete misunderstanding of the facts." For the history of the Great Seal, see Gaillard Hunt (1909).

A famous eagle   In 1861 a Chippewa chief captured a nestling ♂ that was soon exchanged for a bushel of corn and later was bought by an infantry company for $5 (or maybe less). Known as Old Abe, he participated in 42 battles and skirmishes, became famous, survived the war (although once some of his tail feathers were shot off), and was saluted by Gen. Ulysses S. Grant. He died Mar. 26, 1881, after having inhaled greasy smoke, and his mounted remains were burned in a fire in 1904. For many further details and 2 photographs, see Carson (1979).

The culinary eagle   In June 1796, the explorer David Thompson and 2 Indian companions were near starvation and so ate 2 well-developed eaglets from a low nest between Black and Woolaston lakes in n. Sask. Allegedly as a result of eating the eaglet fat, Thompson and an Indian developed intense diarrhea and nearly died (J. B. Tyrrell 1916). Audubon, very likely from personal experience, once stated that the flesh of young eagles is very good and resembles veal. In the Blackwater area of the E. Shore of Md., the "colored people and some whites" regularly ate hawks and eagles and "declared them equal in flavor to ducks" (F. R. Smith 1936).

The 80th birthday of A.C. Bent (who is cited often in this volume) was celebrated in Boston, Nov. 25, 1946. In his earlier years he had done much collecting in Fla. in winter. R. S. Palmer attended the celebration and, having admired Bent's good health, later wrote and asked how he managed this. Bent's reply began as follows: "By all means have at least one eagle eggnog each year; but the trouble is to get the egg and be sure it is fresh!" Current self-proclaimed environmentalists take umbrage at this, showing little comprehension of the former abundance of eagles or the triviality of the taking of several eggs by this responsible collector.

An appraisal　The Bald Eagle was "well chosen to be the symbol" of the U.S., even though it has "none of the anthropomorphic characteristics ascribed to it" (C. Snow 1973a). A successful pirate, scavenger, and predator, in the eyes of some its image is tarnished, but its symbolic quotient and emotional appeal are pervasive. In an "afterword," Herrick (1934) noted that an eagle's life is no more sacrosanct than that of any other creature but that an emblem embodies an idea that, "if commendable, should be among a country's most treasured possessions." If a living emblem is "not too destructive to life more valuable than itself," then we "should be lenient in dealing with its shortcomings." The biology of this bird is now fairly well understood. No doubt eagles will continue to be shot, and losses of habitat are inevitable. It is hoped that in the long run bird and humanity will make significant accommodation to one another—provided the former is given a reasonable measure of security and freedom from disturbance. There is great public interest in the bird and its welfare, but constant effort and education are needed to maintain it.

References　Over 2,000 are listed in the bibliography by Lincer et al. (1979). Many were not consulted in preparing the present account, but items not listed therein and more recent material have been used. The journal papers by F. H. Herrick (1924a–1933) constitute a monograph, rewritten, with additions, as a book (Herrick 1934). The book by Myrtle Broley (1952) on her husband, Charles, contains a valuable list of banding recoveries, recently expanded and reanalyzed by W. B. Robertson, Jr. Friedmann (1950) gives technical descriptions and long lists of earlier references. An extensive, more recent list is by D. Evans (1982). C. Snow (1973a) gave a short summary of biology. Among the better color photographs are those of Truslow (1961) and Dunstan (1978). Steenhof (1978) is useful for winter habits and habitat. References to food are included below.　　　　MARK V. STALMASTER AND RALPH S. PALMER

FOOD　Items ingested or consumed by the Bald Eagle vary considerably. The bulk of its diet comprises fish (principally), waterfowl, seabirds, and mammals of assorted sizes. Since small items are known to be eaten during flight, and since some prey is consumed at feeding perches, observations at nests are necessarily incomplete. This bird eats an assortment of carrion, which renders uncertain whether some remains found in nests are of individuals that were taken alive. McAtee (1935) considered the Bald Eagle to be a vulture "in the guise of a hawk." Reptiles (turtles mostly), at least 20 invertebrates, and garbage are known foods. All this is possible through piracy, scavenging, and various methods of hunting. There is daily, seasonal, and geographical variation.

Food consumption　Varies depending on both the energy contained within the diet and the energy needs of the eagle. Daily consumption in captivity varies 5–11% of body wt. In a 90-day wintering period, the minimal gross energy requirements of a captive 4.5 kg. eagle at 5°C is predicted to be 13 chum salmon, 20 jackrabbits, or 32 Mallards (Stalmaster and Gessaman 1982). Winter food, energy, and prey consumption of free-living birds is approximately 10% greater than in captives, because of increased thermoregulatory demands due to wind, long-wave radiation, precipitation, and flight activity (Stalmaster 1981).

Bald Eagles are easily raised but require an "astonishing amount" of food (Bent 1937). Captive Alaskan birds, while being experimentally fed DDT, ate an av. of 274 gm. of fish/day, and, in relation to body wt., ♂♂ ate more than ♀♀ (Chura and Stewart 1967). A young bird in its 1st autumn was not fed for 16 days and lost 1,260 gm. of its original 4,508 gm.—that is, 27% of its wt.; the bird was returned to full feeding, and there was no indication of permanent harm (P. Stewart 1970). Lack of food "even for a considerable period" is apparently not a serious inconvenience; an individual was kept without food for 32 days (Oberholser 1906). A young eagle egested indigestible material 32–34 hrs. after ingestion, regardless of the amount of material involved; bones were digested completely (P. Stewart 1970).

Size of food   Upper limits were discussed above (see Habits); lower known limits are voles, small songbirds, and some invertebrates.

Lists of prey   Skewed from reality, because some items disappear entirely. Fish, especially smaller ones, may be digested in their entirety—that is, no evidence of them occurs even in ejected pellets. If amphibians are eaten, the evidence is missing. But mammals at least leave fur, and birds feathers. Fishes brought to nests are fresh or no more than very slightly stale; away from their nests, eagles may at times feed on fishes that are more decayed.

Preferences   As with various other raptors, an eagle is choosy. A captive ♀, offered pigeon, rabbit, fish, and beef, much preferred pigeon to all others (Hancock 1973). Another captive preferred fish first, then birds, then rats (P. Stewart 1970). Wild eagles in New Bruns., when offered Black Duck and hare, did not accept them, preferring the various fishes also provided (B. Wright 1953). At certain Fla. nests, waterbirds were apparently favorite foods (C. Broley 1947). In the Aleutians, 31 of 42 Fulmars during 1 season were at the same eagle nest (Sherrod et al. 1976).

Carrion   Probably, but not necessarily, more important in winter. The following gives some idea of variety. On Amchitka: whales, sea lions, seals, sea otters killed in storms, frequently the afterbirth of sea lions, and occasionally sea lion dung (Sherrod et al. 1976). Harbor seal placentas and dead pups are staple summer foods in some areas. Oberholser (1906) listed such items as cattle in the arid West, drowned squirrels in W. Va., and a sheep and the carcass of an ox in Fla.; sometimes an eagle routs vultures and dogs from carrion, keeping them at bay until its appetite is satisfied. In se. Alaska in early May, 30 eagles were "feasting" on the carcass of a bear shot the preceding day (Swarth 1911). Carcasses of elk in winter in Yellowstone Natl. Park (Imler and Kalmbach 1955). On is. in Prince Wm. Sound, Alaska, winter-killed black-tailed deer (Isleib and Kessel 1973). Dead deer are widely eaten. Sheep carcasses in winter, as a supplement to fish, on the s. Gulf Is. of B.C. (Hancock 1964). Dead lambs and the afterbirth of sheep on San Juan I., Wash., in nestling season (Retfalvi 1970). Offal from a fish processing plant at Port Moller, Alaska (Hehnke 1973). Discarded crippled and dead fish from commercial fishing boats in Atlantic and Pacific waters, and nonmarketable fish left for them at various places. Waste and regurgitated fish in a Fla. pelican colony (Imler and Kalmbach 1955).

Many tons of mammal carcasses have been put out for eagles at feeding stations.

The following major categories of food are listed in diminishing order of importance, based on extant knowledge:

Fishes If available in quantity, greatly preponderant in bulk and in numbers taken (to 90%, even 100%), both inland and at marine localities. The concentrations of eagles, especially at salmon runs or spawnings, or the same of various herrings, are impressive. See, for example, earlier mention of the enormous concentration on the Chilkat R., Alaska. On the lower Fraser R., B.C., over a century ago, J. C. Hughes (1882) counted "as many as a thousand in a distance of 3 miles," feeding on eulachon *(Thaleicthys pacificus)*. Even in the n. Atlantic area, where there are far fewer eagles, as many as 100 assemble in Mar. and Apr. and again in fall to feed on the herring run at Long Harbour, Nfld. (L. Tuck 1952 MS). A partial list of known fishes: eels, cod, various salmon, sculpins, various herrings, mullet, ocean catfish, red snapper, striped bass, mackerel, dogfish, sunfishes, yellow perch, suckers, pickerel, northern pike, trout, sheepshead, blue pike, carp (including goldfish), catfish (in Fla. and Ariz., notably *Ictalurus*), shiners, and (in winter) gizzard shad.

Birds Generally speaking, where waterfowl are abundant, an eagle's interest in healthy ones is minor if injured or dead ones (or fish) are more easily obtainable. In fact, where fish are available, ducks are not molested and show no evident fear of eagles (B. Wright 1953, Russoch 1979). Many waterfowl refuges attract eagles; where gunning is allowed on these, especially during and after the shooting season, the take of healthy birds is apparently very minor. Crippled and dead birds, mainly Canada Geese, are the prime winter food in n.-cent. Mo. at Swan Lake Natl. Wildl. Refuge— except when there are large die-offs of fish (Griffin et al. 1980, 1982). Waterfowl are the prime winter food at Bear R. Migratory Bird Refuge, Utah. The only significant count of domestic fowl reported was 12 in 1922 in Ohio (in Herrick 1924c); in examining some 800 Bald Eagle nests, almost all in Fla., C. Broley (1950) found domestic fowl only twice. The Cattle Egret, a newcomer to N. Am., is not disdained (C. Knight 1976, McEwan and Hirth 1980). Bald Eagles approach and enter bird colonies, including gulleries, and get chicks or occasionally kill gulls; but where fish are abundant and available, eagles and gulls feed close to one another with no observable hostility. Audubon (1831) stated that the Bald Eagle frequented the roosts and breeding places of the Passenger Pigeon to pick up young that had fallen from nests or old, injured pigeons.

Various raptors occasionally capture smaller raptors but, since the Bald Eagle readily takes birds as carrion, evidence that it may take live raptors is still circumstantial. Findings in eagle nests include: skull of a Red-tailed Hawk in Md. (F. Smith 1936); a N. Harrier in n.-cent. Fla. (McEwan and Hirth 1979); and 3 skeletonized Osprey legs in a nest on Mt. Desert I., Maine (Stupka, in Herrick 1934).

Over 75 species of birds are known food of the Bald Eagle. Among them: loons (2 species), grebes (5), storm petrels (2 or more), ducks (a long list), mergansers (2), geese

234

(2 or more), Brant, Am. Coot, Fla. Gallinule [Com. Moorhen], Sora, gulls (7 or more), herons (at least 6), Anhinga, cormorants (2 or more), pelicans (2), auklets (5), puffins (2), murrelets, guillemots, murres, Fulmar, shearwater, tern (1 or more species), oystercatcher, a grouse, ptarmigan, Wild Turkey, raven, flicker, longspur, rosy finch, and at least 3 species of sparrows. This list includes injured birds and carrion.

Mammals Important, especially in winter and especially in w. N. Am., probably reflecting their numbers, accessibility, and relative scarcity of other food. Feeding on mammals that fluctuate greatly in numbers raises some questions about switching to other prey or going elsewhere.

Among domestic mammals, probably the largest healthy individuals killed are young swine, often taken in the se. U.S. in former times—a subject dwelt on by several authors. C. J. Maynard (1896) saw 3 eagles attack young pigs that were "valiantly defended" by the sow; he intervened and the attack failed. Eagles feed on sheep carcasses and afterbirths, and very likely on sick lambs. It has been claimed that they take healthy ones (Oberholser 1906, later authors), but practically all of the evidence is circumstantial. In Utah in Feb. 1981, a pregnant ewe was unable to stand; she was fed on by several eagles and died in the night. See McEnaeny and Jenkins (1983) for this, perhaps the only, firsthand information and for discussion of earlier reports. In view of a low winterkill of deer, this ewe may have been an alternative food.

Bald Eagles are said to prey on fawns and, if hungry, to attack full-grown deer, particularly if wounded. One must keep in mind a possibility of "panic hunger"—a starving bird attacking a quarry that it cannot manage (compare with the Golden Eagle). When and if domestic mammals and other sizable quadrupeds are taken or fed on during the long nesting season, rarely is any portion transported to the nest; any bones or other evidence are almost nonexistent or may be carrion.

Dogs are "sometimes taken" (Oberholser 1906), but no documentation is at hand. A captive eagle in B.C. served as a "watchdog"—it was avoided by dogs and had torn several cats to pieces (*N.Y. Times* Aug. 23, 1953). When another captive was offered a choice of foods, it rejected a house cat (P. Stewart 1970). For a captive's method of killing cats, see Forbush (1927). Wild eagles are known to have taken cats occasionally, most recently noted (1983 *Am. Birds* **37** 280) in Conn. in Dec.

On Atka, in the Aleutians, an Indian shot 175 eagles one winter "to prevent their making depredations on the young of a colony of blue foxes" (A. H. Clark 1910). They also are said to take full-grown foxes in the Aleutians. On Amchitka, young sea otters were brought in, decapitated; at the nest, the eagles removed the flesh expertly, leaving skin and bones (Krog 1953). Kenyon (1961) thought that sea otter pups found in eagle nests had possibly been washed ashore dead. But the pups, left untended on the surface while the mother is diving, emit a bleating, often long repeated, scream. "We suspect" that the eagles are conditioned to associate this scream with food; they prey regularly on the pups, but adult sea otters are not afraid of them (Sherrod et al. 1975, 1976). Another important mammal food on Amchitka is the brown rat; it is crepuscular along beaches but abroad even at midday in winter (Sherrod et al.).

Muskrats, injured or dead in traps, are a locally common food; the eagles make off with both furbearer and trap, which was a cause of complaints on the E. Shore of Md. (F. Smith 1936). An Ohio nest contained 14 steel traps (Herrick 1932a). Exposed-bait traps for various furbearers are a known hazard, but burying the bait prevents this. Within its range in se. U.S., the round-tailed muskrat (*Neofiber*) is a minor food.

Even the porcupine has been attacked (Bent 1937, other authors); of late, one such unfortunate bird has been rehabilitated.

Other mammals taken include at least: opossum, skunk, prairie dogs, voles (*Microtus*), weasel, marten, foxes (3 species), cottontails (several species), jackrabbits, arctic hare, and tree and ground squirrels.

Reptiles Locally common in warmer months and inactive in colder ones, reptiles are seldom prey. Various authors list turtles, usually 1 or 2 individuals. Twelve shells, 14, or even 18, of the musk turtle in Bald Eagle nests (references in W. Clark 1982) are noteworthy. In the Chesapeake Bay area, turtles were found in 25% of successful nests (Clark), but if and how the birds derive any substantial nourishment from them is not explained. In Lancaster Co., Pa., the ground beneath a nest was strewn with land terrapins in various stages of decay; the eagles were thought to have brought them as food for their young and, on more careful examination, to have thrown them out of the nest (Ladd, in Bendire 1892). More likely, they were delivered alive, crawled out, and fell to their death.

Unlike the Golden, the Bald Eagle seldom preys on snakes. Barrows (1912) noted that the Bald is said to eat snakes; in Ohio, Herrick (1934) suspected an eagle of making off with a dead snake; in n.-cent. Fla., McEwan and Hirth (1979) reported a black swamp snake (*Seminatrix*) in a nest; a racer (*Coluber*) was identified in an eagle pellet from Blackwater Natl. Wildl. Refuge, Md. (Imler and Kalmbach 1955). A captive young eagle, experimentally offered snakes, declined them (P. Stewart 1970). They do catch and eat eels.

Invertebrates Some 20 species are known foods. At Fitzhugh Sound, B.C., at least 1 Bald Eagle gathered Japanese abalones (*Haliotis kamschatkana*) and carried them inland to a spot where it ate them (Hawbecker 1958). Also in B.C., crabs may form a good part of the summer diet (A. Brooks 1922). Freshwater mussels (*Anodonta*) are evidently consumed in quantity in winter in Coconino Natl. Forest, Ariz.; broken shells are abundant below eagle perches. The eagles evidently break the mussels, which are introduced, apart (T. G. Grubb and Coffey 1982). Grubb and Coffey summarized other reports of invertebrates as food: snails, squid (see under Habits, above), crabs, shrimp, and so on.

Garbage At dumps on Amchitka and Adak is. in the Aleutians. After a bad winter storm, about 85% of the Amchitka eagles were at the dump—even eating bread (Sherrod et al. 1976).

Vegetable matter According to Herrick (1933), leaves are occasionally ingested by both parent and nestling eagles, but whether for any alimentary function is questionable. The adults were also seen to gather clover and alfalfa and probably carried it to the nest, but evidently not to eat (Herrick 1934). In Fla., C. Broley (1947) found epiphytes, about the size of pineapples, in nearly every nest. He noted that the long leaves, especially at the tender base, were ragged and torn—they often looked as though the birds had been eating them. When a captive ate grass, it was egested later in pellets (P. Stewart 1970).

There are no data at hand on **pellet size**, other than that they measure up to 10×4 cm. (about $4 \times 1\frac{1}{2}$ in.).

Sources For further evidence that the Bald Eagle is a versatile opportunist, consult especially A. K. Fisher (1893), Oberholser (1906), Forbush (1927), Imler and Kalmbach (1955), C. Snow (1973a), Sherrod's (1978) summary of 11 earlier sources, and numerous journal papers from the early 1970s on.   MARK V. STALMASTER

WHITE-TAILED EAGLE

Haliaeetus albicilla

Sea-Eagle; White-tailed Sea Eagle; Gray Sea Eagle; Erne (Anglo-Saxon: *the soarer*). A large, heavy-bodied eagle—similar to Bald in size, but differs as follows: Tail wedge-shaped when folded or partly spread, less evident when fully spread; the wing appears more truncated (squarish) distally, but the primaries are similarly notched. In definitive feathering only the tail and its longest *upper* coverts are white or predominantly so; some individuals have palish head–neck (which evolved further, to white, in the Bald Eagle); predefinitive stages presumably parallel those of the Bald, allowing for differences in head–neck and tail coverts.

Sexes similar in feathering, the ♀ larger; combining them, in definitive feathering **length** about 27–36 in. (69–91 cm.), **wingspread** to 7 ft. (2.1 m.) or more; usual **wt.** of ♂ to about 10 lb. (4.5 kg.) and ♀ to 13 lb. (5.9 kg.), but heavier ones recorded. The ♀ weights about ⅕ more than the ♂ and is larger in various measurements (see table 1 in Love 1983). The ♀'s tarsus is some 14% larger in diam. (details in Helander 1981). Depth (height) of BEAK at base is greater in the ♀ with little, if any, overlap between the sexes. Birds in Juv. Plumage have longer wings and, especially, tail and include the heaviest individuals known.

Two subspecies are listed (but see below); **in our area** 1 extends peripherally from ne. Asia to the outermost Aleutians; the other is resident in sw. Greenland (from whence it may have straggled).

DESCRIPTION   Except for downies, the following is based largely on Forsman (in Stjernberg 1981) from Finnish and Swedish specimens and data on known-age individuals. Retention of portions of earlier feather generations is important in identifying age classes, at least from Juv. through Basic III. ABout ⅓ of the primaries and secondaries are renewed annually (Forsman: diagrams), also more or less of the tail. First molting (Prebasic I) begins in May–June of year following hatching and ends in Oct.–Nov.; succeeding molts begin earlier, in Mar.–Apr., starting in the flight feathers from the ones at which molting ceased the previous year and following a fixed sequence—stepwise mode of molting.

▶ ♂ ♀ Def. Basic Plumage (Basic V, acquired beginning in 6th calendar year of life, is earliest definitive according to Forsman, but Basic IV may sometimes be "final"). **Beak** entirely yellow, **iris** pale yellow. Almost all of **body** and wing coverts various browns to (especially when faded) yellowish browns; head–neck paler—sometimes nearly white and may appear so at a distance (see especially Waterston 1964, pl. 63). Longest **upper tail coverts** white; much of exposed portion of **tail** white, sometimes speckled or blotched dark and more or less of basal portion generally dark.

AT HATCHING   Down A is whitish gray, somewhat darker around the eyes and on dorsum (best illus.: O. and M. Heinroth 1927); the tarsus is bare the entire length of underside and the distal half of upper. Down B consists of short whitish tufts in among A, and down C, which is much longer, coarser, and dark gray, very quickly replaces B (Witherby et al. 1939) and is the woolly covering of older nestlings. (In Description of the closely related Bald Eagle, the above downs A and B are combined as A and the entire front of tarsus is downy at first.)

▶ ♂ ♀ Juv. Plumage (entire feathering) fully developed at about age 80 days and retained through WINTER into the following SUMMER, with molting from then into late FALL. **Iris** dark brownish, **beak** black. **Feathering** notably dark; on venter the whitish bases show more or less (spotty pattern). Head–neck plumes shorter and narrower than in all succeeding Plumages, and, when sleeked down, the head (especially of the ♂) appears smaller than in older birds. There is some white in the **wing lining,** especially in the axillar area, and this recurs in several succeeding Plumages. The Juv. **tail** feathers are muted brownish basally and up the outer web; the inner web tends to be light flecked dark; the tip is dark.

▶ **Feather generations** (Plumages). Definitive and Juv. are described above. **1** Juv. (to age over 1 year)—notably dark; secondaries and tail feathers longer than succeeding ones, also narrower and with more pointed (less squarish) ends. **2** Basic I (acquired beginning in May–June of year after hatching)—new feathers on dorsum and breast largely whitish with sharply defined contrasting dark brownish ends; new upper wing coverts more uniformly brownish; new flight feathers shorter, the secondaries and tail feathers with wider, more squarish, ends; adjoining feathers are retained Juv. ones. **3** Basic II (beginning in 3d spring)—has most white of any Plumage; new feathers of back, rump, and breast white with dark brown tips; some Juv. feathers still present, much worn and faded, also some Basic I. **4** Basic III (beginning in 4th spring)—beak still dark on outer half in spring, but turns yellowish from base outward; iris lightens; on underparts the white bases of new feathers are reduced (dark ends are more extensive), some new breast feathers are uniformly brown (as definitive); apparently, this is the last Plumage in which the tail feathers typically are dark across their outer ends. **5** Basic IV (beginning in 5th spring)—beak almost entirely yellow, iris more or less yellow; still some white in breast and underwing; tail feathers more or less white except for brownish bases. **6** Basic V (beginning in 6th spring) and succeeding Plumages are definitive—tail not invariably all white distally; ratio of dark base/white remainder in tail apparently constant through life of individual, but individuals differ.

Molting   The molt out of Juv. (Prebasic I Molt) begins in May or June and continues into late fall, thus being later and generally more prolonged than succeeding molts. It begins on head–body; almost immediately, flight feathers of wing and, soon, the tail follow. The inner primaries (#1– 3, also #4 sometimes) are renewed; secondaries start at the body (#17) and molt outwardly to #12; "molt centers" are also located at #1 (outermost) and at #5. The new secondaries are shorter and more squarly ended. Renewal of head–body feathering is perhaps never complete. In the tail, first the central pair drops, then usually the outermost pair, then the others randomly. The incoming shorter squarish-ended Basic I feathers contrast with the longer and rather pointed Juv. feathers, as long as any are retained.

Prebasic II usually begins in Mar. or Apr. and continues the stepwise mode. That is, primary molting continues from where it left off—renewal of #4, #5, and #6. In the secondaries: #2 and #3, and #11 and #10, and a new center begins with loss of #5 and #6; the 3 innermost (#17–#15) are renewed a 2d time.

In the next molt, Prebasic III, primaries #7 and #8 and sometimes #9 are renewed, and molting also begins again at #1. Thus, only the outermost (#10), or sometimes also #9, are still retained Juv. feathers, now much worn and faded. Secondary molting continues from the 3 centers, and soon all have been renewed at least once. (Based in part on Richter 1974.)

Stepwise molting continues throughout the life of the bird; each year, 3 or 4 primaries and 6 or 7 secondaries are renewed, as is more or less of the tail. Well-fed captives replace more feathers annually (have more complete molting) than wild birds, and molting is seldom, if ever, bilaterally symmetrical.

Albinistic individuals   Captured a few times in the past, mainly in Sutherlandshire, n. Scotland (J. Love 1983). Best known, however, was a ♀ on N. Roe, Shetland Is., whose mate was "normal" in color. The pair last bred in 1908, then the ♀ continued to occupy the site alone until shot in 1918. In flight she was "as white as a gull" on June 30, 1914, when last seen by G. E. Lodge (1946). For a photograph taken about 1912, see fig. 19 in J. Love (1983).

Measurements and weight   Of the various compilations, see especially tables 1 and 2 in J. Love (1983). It is possible that WING was not always measured similarly.

Geographical variation   Clinal (as in the Bald Eagle): increasingly larger size n. in Europe (includes Iceland), where the bird was formerly much more plentiful. Schiøler (1931), and Salomonsen from at least 1950 onward, maintained that the resident sw. Greenland birds av. largest of all (as Brehm had indicated a century earlier), and that this disjunct population qualified for subspecific recognition. As with the Mallard in Greenland (which differs markedly even from its Icelandic congeners), there may have been genetic isolation at least from the hypsithermal (warm) interval about 6,000–4,000 years ago—presumably time to evolve an indigenous subspecies. Salomonsen argued that a slightly longer av. WING length in this eagle is of less importance than greater length of breastbone, tarsus, and pelvis—Greenland birds are sturdier and more powerful, as befitting their rugged life. See Salomonsen (1979) for text, meas., and photos of breastbones. His arguments for greater av. egg size are weakened by recorded data (which he did not cite) showing complete size overlap with individual eggs from Norway and elsewhere. For geographical variation in egg size, see Bent (1937) and especially table 5 in J. Love (1983).

If one recognizes a Greenland race, perhaps there is need to reappraise the status of birds in e. Asia. They have been reported as smallest and subspecifically recognizable by some workers (examples: A. H. Clark 1910, Oberholser 1919) and, on very little material, not corroborated once (Hellmayr and Conover 1949), nor even mentioned by others (examples: Vaurie 1965, L. Brown and Amadon 1968 1). Treatment here aligns with Jourdain (in Bent 1937). Extant material may not be adequate for assessing individual variation, but some Far Eastern birds are the smallest. So also are their eggs (Mori 1980).

Affinities See under Bald Eagle. RALPH S. PALMER

SUBSPECIES *albicilla* (Linnaeus)—variable in size but av. smaller; vast Palearctic range; here tentatively includes small individuals of the Far East (*brooksi* Hume?). Works containing meas. of small series include Schiøler (1931), Witherby et al. (1939), Dementiev and Gladkov (1951, trans. 1966), and Vaurie (1965). There is a useful compilation in J. Love (1983).

groenlandicus Brehm—tentatively recognized here; av. longer WING and larger breastbone, tarsus, and pelvis, and in weight; essentially resident in sw. Greenland. For meas., see especially Schiøler (1931) and Salomonsen (1979).

RALPH S. PALMER

FIELD IDENTIFICATION **In and near our area:** When flying at a great height, might be confused with the Common Raven. The White-tailed differs from the Bald Eagle in having a tail that is almost always obviously wedge shaped. When a White-tailed in definitive feathering is overhead, the tail, with its feathers successively shorter laterally and their basal portions concealed by long dark under tail coverts, shows much less white area than the Bald (has white under coverts). Some White-tailed have a pale head–neck that, in some conditions of light or at offhand glance, might be mistaken for white. Caution is needed in identification. Birds in the various predefinitive stages are more of a problem, being very like Balds except in outline of tail. Sex for sex, the White-tailed is somewhat larger and much heavier than the Golden, which has smaller beak and head and pointed (not squarish) wing.

RALPH S. PALMER

VOICE Apparently as Bald Eagle. Aside from some common calls, the following, from Willgohs (1961), may be of interest. The ♀'s voice is lower pitched and hoarser than the ♂'s. Occasionally, when a person approaches a nest, a deep and not loud series of *ga* notes, resembling the deepest calls of the Great Black-backed Gull (*Larus marinus*). Loud shrill persistent series of *kee* or *klee* notes by local birds when another

241

of their kind intrudes; particularly characteristic of the ♂. A "duet" or "morning greeting," or sometimes the shriller yelping of the ♂. Similar calls preceding changeover at the nest—that is, when the sitter is approached. A drawn-out high-pitched "whimpering" by the ♀, with head lowered, on approach of her mate with food. A hoarse staccato call from the sitting ♂. Various calls, from high pitched and drawn out to brief when mobbed by gulls or pestered by the Peregrine or Com. Ravens. During coition, usually only from the ♂ but sometimes incessantly, a monotonous *kee* series, ending in *ka*; in one instance, more melodious and probably from both birds.

RALPH S. PALMER

HABITAT   Principally n. Temperate, but extends beyond into the Subarctic as well as s. nearly to some Subtropical areas. Primarily a bird of coasts and shorelines from areas of heavy forest to treeless tundra; the sea, estuaries, lakes, large rivers. According to Dementiev and Gladkov (1951), also steppe country far from water in nonnesting season and to considerable elevations, as in the Altai, Transcaucasia, and the Tien Shan. Palearctic counterpart of the Nearctic Bald Eagle.   RALPH S. PALMER

DISTRIBUTION   Resident (and to some extent wandering or seasonally migratory; see below) from sw. Greenland and nw. Iceland across Eurasia into the Pacific, n. in places to beyond treeline (Greenland, Iceland, Fennoscandia, part of USSR, Attu I.) and s. in warm temperate areas to latitude of the Baltic and Caspian seas with smaller disjunct fragments of range scattered considerably farther s. Useful recent map: C. Harrison (1982). Extirpated both indirectly (from loss of habitat) and directly by man from large areas, especially s. and w. Eurasian range. Example: last bred in Britain in 1908 (or 1911—see Leslie Brown 1955). In 1975–1985, 82 young from Norway were released on the Scottish is. of Rhum; nest was built in 1981, eggs were laid in 1983 and 1984, and a pair raised 1 young in 1985.

ICELAND   Perhaps 100–200 pairs in early times; now down to 10–12 pairs plus prebreeders, almost all northwesterly.

GREENLAND   Now reduced to perhaps 85–100 pairs in sw. coastal area n. to about lat. 67° N; contraction from s. (C. Farewell area) and n. ends, and breeders concentrated in Frederikshab region. Straggler n. of breeding range and to se. coast.

CANADA   Of the several reports, and a specimen said to have been taken on Vancouver I., none is a "completely satisfactory" record (Godfrey 1966). Most persistent (Bent 1937, Friedmann 1950, AOU *Check-lists*) and perhaps credible is alleged nesting across from Greenland in Cumberland Sound, Baffin I., in 1878. (A Juv. Golden Eagle from "Hudson Bay," in a 1743 illus., was misidentified as a "White-tailed Eagle" by Elsa Allen [1951].)

EASTERN U.S.   A bird in "immature plumage" flew aboard a Dutch vessel that was passing the Nantucket, Mass., lightship, Nov. 14, 1914; it was delivered alive to the N.Y. Zool. Soc. (Crandall 1915). Alleged sightings of "adults" in Mass. "lack the proof desirable for such a rare vagrant" (Griscom and Snyder 1955).

ALASKA   In the Aleutians on Unalaska a dead ♀ Juv. (there was down adhering to tips of the secondaries) was found Oct. 5, 1899 (Osgood and Bishop 1900)—often cited as 1895 from Gabrielson and Lincoln (1959). Various Alaskan reports are questionable because of possible confusion with young Bald Eagles. On Attu I. (westernmost of the Aleutians), up to 3 birds have been seen fairly regularly since May 1977. **Breeding** A nest was found on Attu I. on May 25, 1982, and a nestling was later seen in it; details in Balch (1982, with photographs; 1982 *Am. Birds* **36** 885, photograph); the same nest had at least 1 nestling on May 29, 1983 (1983 *Am. Birds* **37** 902).

In 1934, among bird bones found in an archaeological site on Kodiak I. by Hrdlicka, were those identified as of 3 (!) eagle species by Friedmann (1935); *H. albicilla* was represented by 2 metatarsi and a metacarpal from surface deposits.

NOTES   Beyond the Aleutians on the Commanders, Johansen (1961) reported this bird as only a straggler.

The White-tailed Eagle is protected legally throughout Greenland by an Act of Apr. 4, 1973. It has been legally protected in Iceland since Nov. 10, 1913, which slowed down serious persecution (although it did not halt until much later).

Prebreeders, especially, seem prone to wander—at times far over water. This eagle is reported, for example, in the w. Atlantic (see above), e. Atlantic (Canaries), Mediterranean (Malta, Cyprus), Persian Gulf (Bahrein), and w. Pacific (Ryukyus, Bonins, elsewhere). Baron Toll was reported to have seen it n. beyond the New Siberian Archipelago on higharctic Bennett I. (Uspenskii 1963).

For a compilation of **fossil** and **archaeological** localities worldwide, see Brodkorb (1964); later additions include (fossil) Romania and (archaeological) Ukraine (13 localities), Georgian SSR, Denmark, and Hungary (4). For British records in late glacial era and continuing to recent time, see J. iove (1983).

In a paper on evidence of wholesale extinction of birds by man in Hawaii in prehistoric time, Olson and James (1982b) mentioned a sea eagle. RALPH S. PALMER

MIGRATION   Like the Bald Eagle, breeders tend to remain locally all year, but in colder areas some are forced to move seasonally by freezing of waters and consequent scarcity of food; they may gather in groups elsewhere to feed at any acceptable food. In addition to dispersal of some prebreeders (they may go in any direction, including n.), others are seen regularly in passage in parts of Eurasia. Papers used in the next paragraph, but see especially Helander (1980), contain some information on distances traveled.   RALPH S. PALMER

BANDING STATUS   Fifty-four were banded in Greenland, 1946–1965, and 19 have been recovered (Mattox 1970). Much has been done in w. USSR and n. Europe in recent years, a development from early beginnings in Finland in 1913. The number banded (from J. Love 1983) to 1976, with recoveries in parentheses, is: Norway 264 (8), Sweden 138 (21), USSR 79 (9), Finland 54 (10), and W. Germany 35 (6). Color banding began in 1976. For an update and observations of marked birds, see Stjernberg and Saurola (in Bird 1983). At least some young birds released in Scotland wear patagial wing-tags.   RALPH S. PALMER

REPRODUCTION   Similar to the Bald Eagle. Principal literature: Norway (Willgohs 1961), Iceland (Ingolfsson 1964; Gudmundsson, in Kjaran 1967), Hokkaido, Japan (Mori 1980), and in general (J. Love 1983). A sketchy outline follows:

The **nest** and a perch fairly close by have unobstructed aerial approaches and command a good view from near the sea or other waters; where there is forest, the nest is typically close to the top of a tree—often a pine, mature or past maturity, the tallest one available. Other nests are on soil or rock. A nest may vary from almost nothing (at many ground and cliff sites and at sites where inexperienced young birds are preparing to breed) to a structure of large and increasing bulk, refurbished over many years. **Sites** in Iceland and Britain are known to have been occupied through a span of 150 years and 1,000 years is entirely probable. A **territory** often contains **alternative nests**, best known in Norway (mean of 2.5, max. 11), where 4 pairs had both a tree nest and a cliff nest (Willgohs). Resident birds in Norway and Japan bring material to the nest intermittently all year and at least 1 member of the pair brings fresh **greenery** through the nesting cycle. If a nest falls down or is destroyed, a new one may be built nearby, but no eggs will be laid until the following year. Some pairs build a new nest each year. The ♂ may initiate construction and even bring almost all nesting material, but both sexes work on the nest. **Laying** is early, beginning in Jan. or Feb. at s. places, as in the Near East, to late Mar. through mid-May in the n.; that is, over 3 months difference going from s. to n. Fourteen **clutches** in Iceland contained 1–3 eggs, av. 2.1; and 58 clutches in Norway: 5 (1), 40 (2), 12 (3), and 1 (4)—a mean of 2.16/clutch; very few 4-egg clutches are reported from elsewhere. Eggs are white and quite variable in **size** (1st egg largest), av. about 77 × 59 mm. **Incubation** begins with the 1st egg; the ♀ sits at night, the ♂ is on considerably in daytime, and (Willgohs) he may fetch food to his sitting mate. **Period** closely calculated (Norway) as 38 days/egg; in captivity (Gregory 1981) it "did not exceed" 37 days; in the wild or in captivity, 38 days (Fentzloff, in J. Love 1983). Hatching interval between eggs is usually 2–3 days, and often an egg fails to hatch. A **replacement clutch** is laid if the 1st is taken early.

In Iceland, 42 nests av. 1.38 young (mostly well feathered when counted), but commonly a single chick survives to flight age. Intermittent breeding is suspected there, and the number of young reared to flight per pair per year av. only 0.65. In 97 instances in Norway, the number hatched av. 1.6, and natural mortality apparently was low. For many additional data, see table 7 in J. Love (1983). Almost all extant data precede the worst of the biocide era. In Sweden in the 1970s individuals of this species had the highest levels of mercury known for any raptor. In Finland, post-1967 eggshells were significantly thinner than those laid before 1935 (Koivusaari et al. 1972), and in 1973, from 34 aeries, only 5 young reached flight age (Koivusaari 1973).

The ♂ not only brings food to the ♀ and **young** but also, at times, feeds and even broods them in daytime in absence of the ♀. When food is scarce (Japan), the smaller young may perish and be eaten by the larger one. The evidence summarized in J. Love (1983) indicates that a smaller, hence weaker, one may be removed to a site where it has siblings of like size, and then the foster young develops normally. This points to scarcity of food as the ultimate cause of sibling aggression. For useful data on **growth of nestlings,** see Mori (1980) for Japan and Helander (1981) for Sweden. **Departure from the nest** is at age 70–84 days, maximum (Japan) 90 days. The young may stay close for a while and may even return to roost or receive food. Some possibly are independent of their parents 5–8 weeks after 1st flight. In Japan, young stay with their parents through their 1st winter, then some leave but others remain through yet another winter. In Norway, young are tolerated in territories, even quite near occupied nests.

RALPH S. PALMER

SURVIVAL   Scattered information from Europe indicates approximately the following: from flight age through the following calendar year, mortality is very high, probably over 50%; then it declines; even so, less than 10% of those that attain flight live long enough to breed; thereafter, annual losses amount to about 30% of those surviving into any calendar year.

In E. Germany, Oehme (in Klafs and Stubbs 1977) examined 194 dead or injured White-tailed Eagles in 1947–1971; 39% had been shot, 6% met with accident, 7.5% were lost in territorial fighting, and at least 13% had been poisoned. There were 95 "adult" birds.

Artificial feeding programs, as in the Baltic area, may improve the survival rate of younger birds, but more time is needed to determine whether this practice will maintain or increase the number of breeders.

Maximum known age in the wild is at least 27 years, in captivity over 40.

RALPH S. PALMER

HABITS   Much **hunting** is done from a perch, where the eagle may remain quietly for hours. It is done also during low flight, when seeking fishes near the surface of the water (occasionally an eagle may even plunge until nearly submerged) and such carrion as dead fish and marine mammals or (ashore) sheep and whatever. Much has been written on **cooperative hunting**, especially of seafowl, usually the Com. Eider (*Somateria mollissima*)—the eagles forcing the prey to submerge repeatedly until too exhausted to dive again. The Puffin is taken in some numbers, but how it is captured is not reported. In Iceland, a pair was seen to maneuver a flying Fulmar within the confines of a fjord until one of them caught it (R. Clem), and Fulmars have been found in aeries. That this eagle, which seems sluggish at times, is "insufficiently agile" (Witherby et al. 1939) to catch flying birds needs modification. It pirates fish from the Osprey. It is commensal to a degree with the otter, or at least it profits from the otter's prey (R. Collett 1921, Willgohs 1961). Like the Bald Eagle, it watches or follows fishing boats, waiting for handouts of fish offal.

Agility   In nw. Iceland, 1 of a pair, probably the ♂, was flying quite high when a Gyrfalcon got above him and stooped hard. The eagle rolled sidewise to an inverted position and presented his talons. The Gyr sheered off and the eagle righted himself—not by turning back but by continuing his roll till the evolution was complete. Several times the Gyr stooped, and each time, the eagle made the same complete revolution ("E. Lewis" 1938).

Versus livestock   Hard evidence indicates that this eagle seldom kills healthy lambs or reindeer calves but commonly seeks out and eats dead ones. The bird has been much blamed and persecuted in the past as a consequence, and even to the present in Greenland. Much information on eagle v. sheep and reindeer was reviewed by Karlsen (1978). Allegations by sheep farmers caused delay in extending legal protection from part to all of Greenland. For the long and involved history of man v. eagle in Iceland, see Gudmundsson (in Kjaren 1967). In Norway, between 1953 and 1963, the average number of "eagles" (Golden/White-tailed) on which bounties were paid was 198 a year—a serious drain on their numbers. In the early days of sheep farming in n. Scotland it was stated that all would be well in the world "but for the Erne and Bonaparte" (Pennie 1962). After having placed a carcass nearby for bait, gunners hid in

245

After
B. Liljefors.

pits and waited in the Scottish rain and mist for the eagle to alight—to be shot; this particular method was described well by MacGillivray (1836). The demise of the natural population in Britain, and some of the reasons why, were presented in a most readable manner by Leslie Brown (1955) and have been gone over again at much greater length by J. Love (1983).

Interspecific relations   In Norway, White-tailed and Golden Eagles are largely separated ecologically—the latter inland—but there is some overlap (Hagen 1976, map 2) and some competition for food and nesting sites (Willgohs 1961). The same was true in Britain in earlier times, when the White-tailed Eagle is believed to have outnumbered the Golden. On Islay, Hebrides Is., it was said that as long as a pair of White-tailed Eagles remained, no Goldens were present; the former was destroyed or died, and the latter came at once ("E. Lewis" 1938).

Intraspecific relations   As with the Bald, the birds feed in close association where food, usually carrion, is plentiful.

Captivity   The Schönbrunn Zoo, Vienna, has the best known record of rearing this eagle. A pair of "immature" birds was acquired in 1955; from them, in 1961–1969, 12 eaglets hatched and 9 were raised; there were more eggs later, but the young did not survive, and the ♀ parent died in Mar. 1973. At the Kansas City Zoo, 1969–1981, eagles laid 32 eggs, of which 11 hatched and 9 young attained flight age. A few have been reared from the egg elsewhere—Heidelberg, Tel Aviv, and Tokyo—some the product of 2d-generation captives. In 1979, in zoos around the world, there were 20 potential breeding pairs in 17 collections; a total of 55 zoos had captives. (Based mainly on Gregory 1981.) Captive rearing, fostering, and other methods of maintaining and augmenting the population are treated fully by J. Love (1983). RALPH S. PALMER

FOOD   Carrion when available, but also has taken a long list of live prey. Earlier information was summarized by Uttendorfer (1952); there is a long list and full discussion of foods and of daily intake by J. Love (1983).

Mammals   From voles (exceptionally) to size of large hares, rarely the arctic fox (usually robbed from a trap); young seals, probably as carrion only; lambs and reindeer calves, for the most part dead or sickly.

Birds   In terms of numbers the most numerous prey species reported—in size from a few passerines to the largest sea ducks and occasionally, larger birds; Eurasian Coot (*Fulica atra*) in numbers, also many Com. Eiders (*S. mollissima*); remains of Com. Heron (*Ardea cinerea*) and Com. Crane (*Grus grus*) found in aeries.

Raptors found in White-tailed Eagle aeries include 2 Ospreys (1 a nestling), Red and Black Kites, a Peregrine, 1 of its own kind, and 2 Imperial Eagles (*A. heliaca*) (Uttendorfer).

Fishes   Compose almost all of diet in some areas (as Greenland) in the warmer months—lumpfishes, salmonids, cod and allies, sculpins, and so on; usually all remains are digested—that is, little or no evidence in pellets.

Invertebrates   Marine mollusks, freshwater mussels (*Anodonta*) robbed from crows; also snails, cuttlefish, crabs, lobster, starfish, and sea urchins.

Carrion   By preference, and **offal** as available. Also now fed by man, at least through winter, in the Baltic area.

For content, shape, and size of the large **pellets** egested, see photographs in W. Fischer (1952) and meas. in J. Love (1983).   RALPH S. PALMER

STELLER'S SEA-EAGLE

Haliaeetus pelagicus (Pallas)

Pacific or White-shouldered Eagle. Very large—length to 45 in. (114 cm.) and wing-spread to 9 ft. (2.7 m.); the latter is approximately the same as the California Condor. Many, however, are decidedly smaller. Among fishing eagles (*Haliaeetus*), this eagle's yellow beak is extraordinarily large and is laterally compressed; tail very markedly wedge shaped (outermost feathers about ⅗ as long as middle ones), of 14 feathers; 7th primary (3d from outer) longest.

▶ ♂ ♀ Def. feathering of **"normal"** phase brownish black, but the following areas are white: forehead, patch on crown (usually), alula and lesser and middle upper wing coverts ("shoulder"), more or less of wing lining, thighs, rump, upper and under tail coverts, and tail. **Dark phase:** a few s. birds retain most of the Juv. pattern, that is, are blackish but for a white tail and its undercoverts—photograph of a zoo bird in W. Fischer (1959, fig. 13). A zoo bird that remained dark otherwise attained the definitive condition of the tail "at the age of five years" (O. L. Austin 1948). This author managed to accumulate records of 18 black individuals: 17 from Korea and 1 from nearby Ussuria in the USSR.

No subspecies are recognized here; the few dark-phase individuals known to date were from the s. part of the former (and present?) breeding range where the "normal" phase presently occurs as a migrant if not also as a breeder.

DESCRIPTION   See above for definitive condition.

AT HATCHING   Down whitish except for black lores and around eye; the head and back are lightest (Lobkov 1978); for a passable photograph of a nestling at estimated age of 2 days, see Chernikin (1965). A young bird at age 25 days was in uniformly gray down (Lobkov) and undoubtedly had become so considerably earlier.

▶ ♂ ♀ Juv. Plumage, similar in both phases, is blackish brown with some light feather bases and light mottling in tail (which is longest in Juv. Plumage). There are at least 3 subsequently Prebasic Plumages, progressively approaching Def. Basic, which probably is attained as Basic IV in 5th calendar year of life, judging from fragmentary data on zoo captives.

Males are "considerably smaller" than ♀ (Dementiev and Gladkov 1951, trans. 1966). WING across chord of 2 ♂ 60–61 cm., BEAK from cere 63–65 mm.; 1 ♂ WING across chord 64.8 cm., BEAK 70 mm. (Friedmann 1950). Wingspread "about 2–2½ m. (Dementiev and Gladkov)—the larger figure being nearly 8¼ ft.; W. Fischer (1959), who was familiar with zoo captives, gave a spread of 280 cm. (9 ft., 2 in.!). Weight of an "adult" ♂ 7.5 kg., "young" 5–6 kg., and 2 "adult" ♀ 6.8 and 8.97 kg. (Dementiev and Gladkov). The larger figure for a ♀ is over 19½ lb.! A bird of unstated sex in the Berlin Zoo weighed 7 kg. (15¼ lb.) (Fischer). For a few additional data, see Hartert (1922).

RALPH S. PALMER

FIELD IDENTIFICATION   Once the birds acquire white "shoulders," they are unmistakable. The main problem is to separate younger cohorts, especially the Juv. (see above), from same of the White-tailed Eagle. Steller's Eagle has a massive beak, very wedge-shaped tail, more ponderous flight, and is generally darker. These also are characteristics of dark Steller's of any age.

RALPH S. PALMER

DISTRIBUTION   **In our area**   A rare straggler to the Pribilofs: ST. PAUL specimen Dec. 15, 1917; Aleutians; ATTU I. "immature" seen May 9, 1980, and UNALASKA I. seen May 26, 1906; KODIAK I. specimen Aug. 10, 1921; HAWAIIAN CHAIN, Midway and Kure atolls: seen early 1978, photographed on Kure in Feb.

Recorded from an **archaeological site** on Kodiak I. (Friedmann 1935).

Elsewhere   **Breeds** on the n. half of Sakhalin I. and clockwise on the adjacent mainland entirely around the Sea of Okhotsk; also n. into Koryakland, around the entire perimeter of Kamchatka (its main stronghold), and s. on some of the Kuril Is. Breeds or formerly bred in Korea and n. on the mainland coast (in former times probably extending n. continuously to meet the range just given). On some maps, that is, Dementiev and Gladkov, given as a **winterer** only from about mid-Sakhalin s. on the mainland and in the Japanese archipelago s. to s. Honshu. Also the Izu Is.

Many remain **all year** on breeding range where there is open water and food; others, especially the younger cohorts, migrate.

Straggler   E. Asia n. to Anadyr, w. to Yakutsk, sw. to Beijing, s. to the Ryukyu Is., and e. to Bering I.

RALPH S. PALMER

OTHER TOPICS   The numbers of Steller's Sea-Eagle are "quite satisfactory" (Lobkov 1978) in Kamchatka; in 1977 an estimated 480–520 breeding pairs plus perhaps 2,300 nonnesters (mostly prebreeders). On the e. side they nest principally within 30–50 km. of the sea, on the w. side within 50–80 km., some also along large rivers and at lakes. Much of the interior is the domain of the White-tailed Eagle (*H. albicilla*), but, although their diets are about the same and they may occur together (as at an abundance of spawning salmon), there is little observable conflict.

Beginning in Feb., on quiet sunny days, the birds form in small groups, are very

249

vocal, and circle over the forest. Construction and refurbishing of **nests** (they are used for years) occurs from the latter part of Feb. into Apr. They are built on trees (alder, poplar, birches) past maturity, usually having decaying crowns; rarely in healthy birches; sometimes on ledges. Some become relatively enormous in diam. and height (Dementiev and Gladkov). **Copulation** is on the nest. **Laying** occurs from about the 1st ⅓ of Apr.–late May. **Clutch size** is usually 2 eggs, occasionally 1 or 3; 4 av. 79 × 62.2 mm.; color white, at first with a greenish tinge (which fades). Earliest date: clutch of 3 on Apr. 12 in a year of early thaw. Incubation period unknown, except that it exceeds 34 days. Earliest young: May 13. Preflight young have been found into mid-Aug. and evidently occur into Sept. On the Kronotskii reserve (e. Kamchatka), in 6 years, only 4 of 13 eggs produced young to flight age. Losses were due to destruction of nests by man, other predation, toppling of inadequately supported heavy nests, and disappearance of some clutches for reasons unknown. Sometimes nests that are very close to marine waters are upset by heaving shore ice.

This eagle hunts on the wing, but mostly from such elevated perches as pinnacles and treetops, even sometimes low down near the surf. In the warmer months they feed to a large extent on such fishes as spawning salmon. They catch a few birds, up to the size of large grouse and ducks. They capture terrestrial mammals to the size of hares (and Steller saw one catch a fox, see Bent [1937]), also an occasional young seal, and a variety of marine invertebrates. Carrion—dead pinnipeds, offal left by hunters, and so on—is eaten readily, and up to 5 eagles feed together. Data are based mainly on Lobkov (1978), but see also Chernikin (1965) and Dementiev and Gladkov (1951, trans. 1966) for further information. RALPH S. PALMER

♂ Basic   ♀ "ringtail"

NORTHERN HARRIER

Circus cyaneus

Long known as Marsh Hawk in N. Am. (where it is the only harrier) and as Hen Harrier in Britain (where another species, *C. aeruginosus*, is called Marsh Harrier); the circumboreal distribution of *C. cyaneus* extends farther n. than that of any other harrier.

A medium-sized slender hawk with low wing loading, long wings, legs, and tail, conspicuous white rump, rather owlish face (narrow ruff of feathers with recurved ends extends from above the concealed ears downward and joins across the throat), and with bristlelike lore feathers that extend noticeably beyond the cere. These, all or in major part, are characteristics of all other harriers. The Northern has 4 long primaries (#6–#9 counting from inner, the 7th longest after age 55 days) with the adjoining ones (#5 and #10) much shorter and nearly equal in length. As in the Pallid Harrier of cent. Eurasia, the primary feather next to the outer one is emarginated or incised along its leading edge to so near its base that the proximal end of the indentation is concealed under overlying coverts. In flight 4 distinctly long flight feathers show. The Northern has broader wings than smaller harriers but narrower ones than the larger Marsh Harrier, thus appearing more bulky than the smaller species and more slender than the larger one. Its relatively (for harriers) broad wing with short tip may be an adaptation to rapid acceleration during high-speed bird chases (Nieboer 1973). (Differences within the genus *Circus,* in which the number of recognizable species may be debatable, are largely in size, proportions, coloring, and degree of sexual dimorphism).

In definitive feathering, *C. cyaneus* has great sexual dimorphism in color, pattern, and, in all ages, size. The definitive-feathered ♂ is largely gray dorsally and white with some rusty markings ventrally, the ♀ dark browns above and toward buffs or tawny with streaks below, and young of both sexes are quite ♀-like but overall darker and

251

ventrally less streaked. These dimensions are for N. Am.: length ♂ 17¼–20 in. (44–51 cm.) and ♀ 18¾–24 in. (48–61 cm.), wingspread ♂ 40–44¾ in. (102–114 cm.) and ♀ 43¼–54 in. (110–137 cm.); weight in breeding season ♂ about 10¾–13 oz. (300–365 gm.), usually about 12 oz. (335 gm.) and ♀ 16¼–24 oz. (460–595 gm.), usually about 18⅓ oz. (520 gm.).

Three subspecies—1 each in N. Am. and Eurasia (occurrence possibly overlaps in outer Aleutians), and one, the "Cinereous" Harrier, in part of S. Am.

DESCRIPTION   *C. cyaneus hudsonius.* In the ♂ in close view, the darker Basic I can be distinguished from Basic II, hence latter is earliest definitive. In the ♀, Basic I is richer, darker brown than Basic II, which is lighter and more toward gray. An occipital spot (of Hafner and Hafner 1977), largely concealed when head feathers are not raised, is present in both sexes and all flying ages.

▶ ♂ Def. Basic Plumage (entire feathering) late SUMMER to the following late SUMMER with molting from spring to early fall. **Beak** black distally, grading to bluish toward yellow cere; **iris** and edge of eyelid lemon yellow or varying toward orange-yellow. **Head** and **upperparts** in the light to medium bluish gray range (individual variation), except upper tail coverts and rump white. Males under ages 3–4 years tend to be somewhat darker dorsally than older birds and often are tinged with brown on nape, mantle, and scapulars. **Underparts:** gray of upper breast grades posteriorly toward whitish or white, which varies from plain (rarely) to, typically, more or less rusty markings (especially prominent in Basic I) that vary from fine to coarse and from longitudinal to—usually—transverse and are usually prominent on long feathers of flanks. **Wing** dorsally gray (like back but with somewhat lighter coverts), but secondaries distally blackish, then terminally edged white, and primaries distally ⅔ black; ventrally, inner webs of all flight feathers white (except for black of primaries and secondaries), and wing lining also white with some sharply defined transverse dark gray markings on greater primary under coverts. Legs and **feet** vivid yellow, talons black. **Tail** variably darkish blue-gray above, central pair of feathers darker and faintly barred, the several bars on the others progressively darker laterally; the most distal dark bar is widest, and very tips of feathers white.

Molting   Begins with renewal of primaries (inner to outer) and soon the secondaries (molt centers at least at 5th counting from outermost and at innermost—(Hamerstrom 1974, diagram), then greater upper coverts of flight feathers, and tail (inner to outer except central pair delayed). Very early in the process, new unfaded feathers appear on head and foreparts, later gradually elsewhere. In cent. Wis. most breeding ♂♂ begin molting primaries in late May–early June, approximately 2–4 weeks later than ♀♀ but the former molt faster, and most have renewed at least ½ their primaries by the end of June; the timing of molting was said to not be significantly correlated with nest brood events (Schmutz and Schmutz 1975). Molting evidently continues at least until early fall, perhaps with intervening slowdown or pause. There is some evidence that ♂♂ become progressively paler through several early molts (molts continued to about age 6 years in a captive).

▶ ♀ Def. Basic Plumage (entire feathering) SUMMER to following SUMMER. In breeding birds, molting begins earlier than in ♂ (see above), sometimes during incubation;

in Orkney, Scotland, never more than 2 remiges and several rectrices concurrently. As in ♂, molting is protracted into fall.

Beak blackish distally to bluish at cere, which is pale to vivid yellow; **iris** brown with yellow flecks in 1st-year ♀♀, usually at least 50% yellow in 2d-year birds, and mostly yellow by 3d calendar year. (In the Palearctic the change is from chocolate brown in nestlings to amber in 3d–4th-year birds, to yellow in 6th year.) **Head** has light bar extending from beak over eye; auriculars are tan streaked very dark brown, and have, at their rear border, a ruff of whitish feathers streaked very dark—the whole combination lending a particularly owlish appearance; feathers of crown and nape narrowly edged tawny; chin pale buff. **Upperparts** variably blackish brown, the feathers edged tawny, the upper tail coverts and rump usually plain white (sometimes faintly marked rusty). **Underparts** dark of dorsum sometimes extends down and across foreneck, but usually all of venter "dirty" white to warm tan; breast, sides, and flanks often with dark shaft streaks. **Wing** upper coverts as back; flight feathers appear mostly dark dorsally, but ventrally their inner webs are whitish—primaries with 4–5 dark bars and dark tips, secondaries with 3 bars (terminal one widest) and very tips tawny; wing lining mostly matches venter, axillars with warm tan or tawny edges and sharply defined midportion of same. Legs and **feet** yellow, talons black. **Tail** central pair of feathers gray-brown tipped tawny, others more toward buff, each succeeding pair (outwardly) increasingly darker, and all tipped tawny; all pairs except have 4 very dark bars (outer has 6 narrow ones).

NOTES   If eyes are yellow with no more than a hint of brown, a ♀ is probably at least 3 years old (Hamerstrom 1968). A captive had successively grayer rectrices and primaries at least through year 6. In the Palearctic, Balfour found much variation independent of age, but palest and most gray-brown ♀♀ tended to be among the oldest (D. Watson 1977).

AT HATCHING   The whitish or faintly pinkish-buffy down is densest on upperparts; beak blackish with white egg tooth, cere muted flesh color, eye (closed for a day or less) appears blackish gray, legs and feet flesh colored. In a week or less another down appears; it is long, some variant of smoke gray, paler on crown. Legs, feet, and cere yellow by 2d week.

▶ ♂ ♀ Juv. Plumage (entire feathering) begins to appear in 2d week posthatching, is essentially fully grown by about age 35 days (although young recently on the wing still have recognizably shorter tails and somewhat blunter wings). This Plumage is retained through 1ST WINTER into following late SPRING–SUMMER. Palearctic birds: key text on growth of young of this species is Scharf and Balfour (1971); also, pls. 6 and 147 in Heinroth and Heinroth (1927) are useful illus. for stages to about 8 weeks.

Beak dark; cere palish yellow, sometimes with greenish tinge; **iris** dark (lighter in ♂ and with grayish cast, chocolate to medium brownish in the ♀); much of **head** and **dorsum** blackish brown with some pinkish tan streaks on head; edge of facial ruff light tan and chin pale tan; lower rump and upper tail coverts white, some feathers with small faint tawny central mark; **underparts** vary with individual from overall deep rufous-tawny to palish tan (latter especially in late winter–spring when faded), the feathers with dark internal streaks on upper breast and elsewhere mostly fine shaft streaks except wider on flanks (more apparent by late winter after basal color fades).

253

Wing: upper surface like dorsum with narrow buffy margins on coverts, the very tips of secondaries and proximal primaries grading to whitish; most clearly shown on underside, the primaries are rather narrowly barred dark and white; greater primary under coverts mixed whitish, very dark, and some tan; remainder of wing lining buffy tan with streaky dark markings. Legs and **feet** vary with individual from pale to vivid yellow, talons black. **Tail** barred very dark, the intervening areas and tips buffy-tan (lighter centrifugally except on 2 central feathers where dark gray), paler on undersurface.

NOTES Nestlings can be sexed with confidence by age 2 weeks (especially if both sexes present) by eye color and relative size of tarsi. Weight shows considerable overlap until at least 3d week, when it, too, becomes diagnostic of sex. The smaller ♂ develops more rapidly; primaries are almost fully grown 4–6 days earlier than in the ♀, and flight is attained 3–5 days earlier (♂ 29–33 days, ♀ 32–38); at first the eye is very dark, but it lightens to grayish brown as early as age 10 days (and gray by late winter); tarsus comparatively small—#4 band fits nicely with almost no exceptions. The larger ♀ develops more slowly; her eyes are chocolate brown throughout nest life and later (typically still brown, but paler, at age 1 year); her tarsus is larger—ordinarily requiring a #5 band, a few #6 (Hamerstrom 1968). The idea that Juv. ♂ ♂ are lighter colored than ♀ ♀ is untenable. Much individual variation exists in this, especially on underparts, in some measure due to fading, which probably varies geographically with weather.

▶ ♂ Basic I Plumage (entire feathering), acquired by prolonged molting that begins (in 2d calendar year) in late spring or later; the new feathering retained ABOUT A YEAR. **Beak** black, cere yellow, **iris** usually changes from gray to yellow during summer of 2d calendar year. **Feathering** variable, typically differs from later (definitive) Basics thus: head darker and browner, dark ends of feathers of the occipital spot have tawny lateral margins; back darker, some feathers tawny, others margined tan or tawny; underparts more heavily marked, especially upper breast, which may be tinged with tawny; sides and flanks often heavily barred brownish sepia; wing has smaller upper coverts terminally margined buffy brown to tawny; undersurface of primaries usually have some dark barring or irregular marks, and the smaller under coverts have both horizontal darkish markings and some barring of same.

NOTES In the Palearctic, Prebasic I molting sometimes begins as early as Mar. (Witherby 1939); in a captive it lasted 3–4 months and was completed by mid-Oct. (Montagu 1802). In N. Am., partially molted ♂ ♂ with 2-toned wings (gray outer secondaries and inner primaries and brown remiges elsewhere) are frequent sightings in late summer–early fall, but most flight feathers of wing are gray by some time in fall of 2d calendar year.

The change in ♂ iris color from gray to yellow is approximately concurrent with Prebasic I molting, but a few individuals are precocious or tardy (Hamerstrom 1968).
▶ ♀ Basic I Plumage, mostly as succeeding Plumages, but somewhat darker with fewer tawny streaks on head, less tawny on upper wing coverts, and less gray on primaries. Iris still brown.

Measurements Livetrapped birds in Wis. (mean figures in parentheses), WING across chord: 1 spring migrants ♂ 21 Juv. 322–347 mm. (336.3) and 29 Basic 325–362

(344.5), and ♀ 23 Juv. 350–394 (377.4) and 52 Basic 372–406 (383.3); and **2** breeding birds ♂ 6 Juv. 325–342 (333.3) and 52 Basic 325–356 (342.5), and ♀ 24 Juv. 368–403 (375.4) and 88 Basic 361–410 (381.9). (These meas. from life are slightly larger than of museum specimens, usually cited.)

TAIL: **1** spring migrants ♂ 20 Juv. 190–218 mm. (206.4) and 29 Basic 193–224 (210.3); ♀ 23 Juv. 221–251 (235.7) and 52 Basic 210–258 (235.8); and **2** breeding birds ♂ 5 Juv. 197–213 (204.8) and 53 Basic 196–238 (208); ♀ 25 Juv. 194–249 (235.6) and 79 Basic 217–246 (234.6).

In the above sample there is no overlap in WING between the sexes in Juv. or in Basic feathering. As for TAIL, comparing the sexes by cohort, there is slight overlap but no significant age-dependent difference. The slightly longer WING of spring migrants compared with breeding birds is presumably a result of later feather wear (Bildstein and Hamerstrom 1980).

For other WING chord meas., see Friedmann (1950), Scharf and Hamerstrom (1975), and N. Snyder and Wiley (1976). For flattened WING, see Nieboer (1973) and Scharf and Hamerstrom (1975).

From Friedmann (1950) for birds in definitive feathering from all parts of N. Am. range: 48 ♂ BEAK from cere 15–17.5 mm., av. 16.1, and TARSUS 69.4–73.5, av. 72.8; and 54 ♀ BEAK from cere 17.5–19 mm., av. 18.5, and TARSUS 72–84, av. 79.5. Note that in BEAK the sexes just meet and in TARSUS the overlap is slight.

Weight Live birds (few with any food in crop) in Wis. (mean values in parentheses) **1** spring migrants ♂ 21 Juv. 305–384 gm. (341.2) and 29 Basic 297–469 (369.6), and ♀ 25 Juv. 443–594 gm. (511.2) and 52 Basic 466–752 (546); and **2** breeding birds ♂ 6 Juv. 337–363 (346) and 57 Basic 308–387 (336.5), and ♀ 24 Juv. 435–654 gm. (500.5) and 93 Basic 432–621 (513.1). Migrants in Basic (both sexes) weighed significantly more than migrating Juv. birds. But for both sexes migrant Basics precede Juv., and differences may be affected by weighing birds from early spring onward (Bildstein and Hamerstrom 1980).

Fall migrants at C. May Point, N.J. ♂ 191 Juv. 290–466 gm. (341.3) and 31 Basic 309–343 (371.6); and ♀ 121 Juv. 407–650 (502.4) and 27 Basic 420–621 (521.7) (W. S. Clark).

Albinism/melanism In the Palearctic at least 20 partly or wholly white examples were reported, and some figured, by D. Watson (1977); areas prone to whiteness are forehead and talons; included are both sexes and all ages. Watson also mentioned a few instances of melanism, including a dark young in an otherwise "normal" brood of 3. North Am. records of either type of variant evidently are lacking. (In the Palearctic, a melanistic phase of *C. aeruginosus* is known, and a small percentage of *C. pygargus*, in both sexes and all ages, is melanistic; in S. Am., the dark phase of *C. buffoni* is not rare.)

Hybrids None in the species, but suspects have been seen in the Palearctic region. Nieboer (1973) speculated that the Northern and the very closely related Pallid Harrier (*C. macrourus*), which he considered to be a specialized Northern, might cross.

Geographical variation There seems to be agreement that harrier stock originated in Eurasia/Africa; the following attempt to unravel the evolution of *C. cyaneus* is hypothetical. Antecedent stock crossed to the Americas, perhaps via ne. Asia and perhaps early in the Pleistocene. It evolved to species level in the New World (both hemispheres) and n. birds spread back to the Old. Part of the returned population became isolated in the w. Palearctic and adapted to arid conditions during successive glaciations, evolving into the present Pallid Harrier (*C. macrourus*). This would account for *C. cyaneus* in the Americas and for the presence of 2 very closely related harriers—Northern and Pallid—in Eurasia. These speculations are based in part on Moreau (1955) and Nieboer (1973).

The present *C. cyaneus* of N. Am. is larger and more richly colored than in Eurasia. North Am. birds in Juv. feathering have nearly unstreaked underparts, while Eurasian young are heavily streaked. Definitive-feathered ♀ ♀ are similar but darker in N. Am., and ♂ ♂ in N. Am. are more richly colored. The *cyaneus* stock that reached S. Am. (where *C. buffoni,* not reckoned with here, also occurs), perhaps relatively soon after reaching N. Am., is, at present, widely separated by present environment considered unsuited for harriers. The young are much like n. birds; in Basic feathering, ♀ ♀, especially, have underparts barred rusty. Some ♂ n. birds appear nearly as barred underneath, thus tending to bridge a hemispheric difference. Nieboer suggested that the S. Am. pattern is closer to the ancestral type.

Long ago, Ridgway (in Baird 1875) treated the S. Am. birds as a subspecies—*Circus cyaneus cinereus*—as later also Hellmayr and Conover (1949) and Nieboer (1973); some others, on basis of differences in Basic feathering, habitat, and the large distributional gap, have treated it as specifically distinct—that is, *Circus "cinereus"* (as by Amadon 1961a). In some measure this depends on one's concept of species. For the time being, including the S. Am. with the Holarctic birds seems preferable even though current genetic isolation eventually may result in progression from incipient to obvious speciation. When including the S. Am. birds (as *Circus cyaneus cinereus*) with those of the N. Hemisphere, a possible inclusive, or "umbrella," name might be White-rumped Harrier (of Meyer de Schauensee 1966)—but a white rump is not an exclusive trademark of these harriers. *C. cyaneus* is the northernmost-breeding harrier, no matter how far s. its range extends, and *Northern Harrier* is preferred.

There is not much information from the Falkland Is., s. S. Am. A ♂ specimen was small; Hellmayr and Conover (1949) thought that this might indicate a recognizable subspecies of *C. cyaneus,* namely *histrionicus* of Quoy and Gaimard (in Freycinet 1824). Nieboer's (1973) sample of 11 ♂ ♂ supports this, against the probability of gene flow from the continent. Falkland birds were included with mainland *Circus "cinereus"* in L. Brown and Amadon (1968 1). Cawkell and Hamilton (1961) presumed it still bred there.

RALPH S. PALMER AND KEITH L. BILDSTEIN

SUBSPECIES   Various raptors, including *C. cyaneus,* have discontinuous distribution and show geographical variation. That it is "by no means certain" that the Old and New World birds of the N. Hemisphere are conspecific (Amadon 1961a, L. Brown and Amadon 1968 1) is unlikely; a preferred evaluation is A. Wetmore's (1939) inclusion of them in a single species.

In our area *hudsonius* (Linnaeus)—N. Am., in migrations occasionally as far s. as S. Am.; larger-sized, with longer tarsus, larger feeding apparatus, and smaller tail/wing ratio; definitive-feathered ♂ usually with rusty markings on underparts; the bars on the tail of *hudsonius* are bolder than those on Eurasian birds, but the black wing tips are not as distinct; ♀ and Juv. of both sexes av. darker than Eurasian birds; young have reduced streaking (occasionally none) on upper breast; descr. and meas. given above.

Elsewhere *cyaneus* (Linnaeus)—Eurasian, some migrating to n. Africa; av. smaller than N. Am. birds and generally somewhat paler; ♂ definitive typically has unmarked underparts; young of both sexes have ground color of underparts heavily streaked darker, although there are reports from both Europe (van Kreuningen 1980) and e. Asia (Nieboer 1973) of Juv. birds with unstreaked underparts. Breeding birds in Basic feathering in Orkney, Scotland: 15 ♂ flattened wing 332.3 ± 10 mm. and 156 ♀ 374,3 ± 8.1 (Picozzi 1981). Weight of 53 ♂ 346.8 ± 19.6 gm. and 151 ♀ 520.1 ± 30 (Picozzi). For additional meas., see Schiøler (1931), Dementiev and Gladkov (1951), Scharf and Hamerstrom (1975), and especially Nieboer's (1973) large sample; for additional wt., see Glutz von Blotzheim et al. (1971) and Scharf and Hamerstrom (1975).

cinereus Vieillot—the birds of s. S. Am., including the Falkland Is., are discussed above; they are even smaller than Eurasian birds. See especially Nieboer (1973) for meas. KEITH L. BILDSTEIN

FIELD IDENTIFICATION   Since we have only 1 harrier in our area, identification is quite simple. (In Britain/Europe, for example, where there are several harriers, the brown-feathered ♀♀ and young of the various species can confuse even the experts.)

A fairly large slender hawk, usually seen in flight just clearing the highest bushes or other vegetation, over open terrain. It beats over the ground—on seemingly irregular, but often prescribed, course—rather leisurely, and during its fairly frequent short glides (its flight may be termed flap-sailing), the wings are decidedly angled upward. The white rump, present in all flying ages, is generally conspicuous because the bird is often well below the horizon. In comparison, the Black-shouldered Kite has black "shoulders" and white tail; the Snail Kite and most Rough-legged Hawks have white toward base of tail but differ greatly in all other respects. The kite and Roughleg, at least, are more likely to be seen hovering.

The ♂ harrier in Basic feathering is palish to medium gray dorsally, except for white rump and black primary ends and trailing edge of wings; much of venter and most of wing lining white (The pale "bloom" of the live ♂ is lacking from museum skins, which are decidedly darker.) Tail barring is inconspicuous, especially in older individuals. Hardly to be confused at a distance with any gray gull because of different profile and flight. Males in Basic I (approximately age 1–2 years) tend to have darker heads than older birds, some brown flecking dorsally, and more markings on the light venter; these are relative matters and not always evident.

Females of all ages plus Juv. ♂♂ greatly outnumber gray ♂♂ except in winter in some areas. They are very dark above, except white rump and, in some, a head streaked with buff; the tail has alternating blackish and fairly light bands—this plus the white rump that appears to ring the base of the tail has led to the British/European colloquial *ringtail* (applied collectively to several *Circus* species). Ventrally, the ♀ is variably tawny with rusty or reduced dark markings on body and wing lining; palest areas on a flying individual are basal portions of primaries, under tail coverts, and white rump. Juv. birds of either sex tend to be darker ventrally than older ♀♀. In spring (when approaching age 1 year), the Juv. breast and belly have faded, and it is often difficult to separate brown harriers—Basic ♀♀ plus Juv. ♂♂ and ♀♀—but Juvs. retain noticeably darker secondaries ventrally and are recognizable when captured for banding (Hamerstrom, in Hickey 1969).

Under very favorable circumstances afield or when handling birds for banding, **eye color** may be noted. If a bird has dark eyes, it is a ♀ and probably less than 2 years old; if it has grayish or yellow eyes and is still in dark Juv. feathering, it is a young ♂; if it is known to be a ♀ and has yellow eyes, with few exceptions it is aged 3 years or older (Hamerstrom 1968).

Comparison of pellets of this harrier with Short-eared Owl (*Asio flammeus*) is given under Habits, below.   KEITH L. BILDSTEIN

VOICE   Most vocal near the nest. Over a dozen Am. authors and more than 3 times as many in Britain/Europe have made very definite statements about the voice of this harrier. The calls are not readily categorized (although it has been done), there being much variation depending on context, motivation, and certainly the ability of the observer to record them. Obvious examples include the summary in Forbush (1927) quoted in Bent (1937) and in Cramp and Simmons (1980).

During display the ♂ usually utters abrupt *kek*, *quik*, or *ek* notes or variants in rapid series of from several to more than 10 dry notes. This is typical of him during Sky-dancing and sometimes occurs as early as late winter over communal roosts. In alarm or defense it becomes a more staccato, higher-pitched *ke* in rapid series, similar to the call of the N. Flicker (*Colaptes auratus*). This or a variant is uttered by both sexes. A number of European observers report it as lower pitched in ♂♂, despite the relatively smaller size of this sex, but spectrographic confirmation is lacking. The call occurs when ♀♀ are disturbed at their nest by ground predators, raptors, humans, or approaching ungulates and often attracts ♂♂, which join in calling and swooping on the intruder. It is also given at winter roosts in response to ground and aerial intruders, where it induces flight in birds roosting nearby and frequently results in assemblages of calling and stooping individuals (Mois 1975, Bildstein 1976).

The ♀, from the beginning of display through nesting, has a piercing, insistent, downward-slurred scream, *eeyah eeyah*, occasionally dropping lower to *eeeya*, usually repeated in couplets or triplets for up to 40 min. at a rate of 15/min. for brief periods. It is higher pitched than that of the Red-shouldered Hawk so does not sound like it. This is the ♀ call most often heard. She utters it both on hearing or sighting the ♂ approaching with food (and he utters a weak *kek* or *quip*) as well as when she approaches the ♂ perched near the nest in an apparent effort to induce him to hunt; also to "solicit" copulation and in other situations when mates are interacting. In addition, it is given by individuals protecting prey and by those recently displaced from it.

When a parent drops food to young on the ground, the latter sometimes answer with a sort of *preeeiii* (repeatedly), the voice sounding shaky. After the young can fly, they utter the "adult" scream *eeyah eeyah* as they approach parents returning to the nest with food as well as parents perched near the nest (apparently to induce hunting) and siblings with food.

In winter the scream is heard most often from birds of the youngest cohort, but in severe weather it is heard also from older ones. It is almost always directed at the latter. Most instances involve a calling individual approaching a bird with food and attempting to rob it. Calling individuals sometimes shadow hunting birds for long periods, and the call is also frequently heard in late afternoon at communal roosts, where calling individuals intercept and follow incoming birds for long periods of time.

Nestlings   A thin, almost lisping, *peep* uttered monotonously as a food call. Also a thin "distress" call and a prolonged series of *chit* notes, designated as "pain chitter" (F. Hamerstrom). As the nestlings get older, they hiss when approached and, evidently as threat or alarm, give a rapid series of *kek* variants. By the time they are on the wing, they have variants of adult-type calls, but their voices are still decidedly different.

KEITH L. BILDSTEIN

HABITAT   In N. Am.   In breeding season this harrier occupies a wide variety of open terrain, typically with herbaceous cover and often intermixed with woody growth. Although it is reported to prefer moist or wet areas in much of its range, it is by no means restricted to those sites. It winters in dry open areas if suitable prey is available and also breeds in these areas if relatively secure nesting sites—free from mowing—can be found. In Mich., "wet areas as of marsh, kettle, and seepage" were used more, and dry areas less, during spring–summer than in fall–winter (the Craigheads 1956), probably a result of nest-site selection. Choice of terrain is apparently less restricted in N. Am., however, than, for example, in parts of Eurasia where there are other—presumably competing—harrier species. At home and abroad there is niche overlap with the Short-eared Owl, but conflict is far from inevitable. Owls nest earlier and in drier, more open locations than harriers, and the 2 differ in habitat and periods of activity; owls tend to be crepuscular and harriers diurnal. But substantial overlap in most niche dimensions exists, and neighboring owls and hawks often maintain exclusive territories (Linner 1980); both in breeding season and in winter at communal roosts, hostile encounters and prey robbery occur sometimes, if not regularly (R. Clark 1975, Bildstein, 1976).

Harriers tend to avoid mountainous areas, but in Yellowstone, Wyo., they hunt open land at elevations to 10,300 ft. (Skinner, in Bent 1937). Abroad, *C. c. cyaneus* is the most abundant harrier in open areas of the Sikkim Himalayas, occurring to 8,000 ft., and on migration occurs to over 16,000 ft. in the Punjab Himalayas (Ali and Ripley 1968). In S. Am., *C. c. cinereus* occurs at over 12,000 ft. at several locations, including L. Titicaca (Amadon 1961a).

In parts of temperate N. Am., this harrier nests in marshes and swamps, with or without brush; in vast sagebrush-steppe areas of the West, it nests remote from water—in fact, may not be near it for months; it nests in swales on farmland and in cranberry bogs; other sites are lush growth bordering prairie sloughs, ponds, lakes, and sluggish streams; drier portions of estuaries (salt, brackish, fresh) grown to sedges, grasses, or especially cattails, often with much brush; hayfields, wheatfields, even, as in Wis. (Hamerstrom, in Hickey 1969) plantations of young conifers.

Northward into the boreal forest it nests in wetlands adjoining streams and lakes and, principally at lower elevations, occasionally where the forest recently has burned or been cut. Continuing n., they occupy muskeg from Hudson Bay w. across Alaska. As muskeg and bare uplands predominate and the forest is broken and restricted, harriers become few but conspicuous, and then none. There is room for speculation why this bird apparently does not breed in open places in the boreal forest of the Ungava Pen. and why there is a solitary nesting record for Nfld.

In Wis., nesters quit conifer plantations when the trees are aged 4–6 years (Hamerstrom, in Hickey 1969); in Scotland they occasionally remain until the trees are aged 14–15 years (D. Watson 1977). On the L. Ontario plains of N.Y., from loss of suitable marshland, the birds shifted to nesting in fallow fields, where serious nest-losses resulted from predation and human disturbance (Kibbe 1975). In the Cache Valley, Utah, they nested in cattail-bulrush marshes but preferred to hunt wet old fields and tended to avoid cultivated areas and grazed pastures (Linner 1980). In N.D., harriers breed on reclaimed coal mining areas where grazing is prohibited. In Calif., they breed in cultivated areas in the Mojave Desert.

Although the Northern Harrier is reported to nest on grass-covered sand dunes in Scotland (L. Brown 1976), there are no comparable N. Am. records.

In winter it is widespread on forested uplands and occurs on deserts (frequently in transit between moist valleys), on grazed terrain, and water expanses—Everglades, wetter estuarine areas, and other fluvial and tidewater areas. Some of the highest concentrations of wintering birds occur on the dry plains of the Texas Panhandle (Bystrak 1974). Also occurs in terminal drainage basins called playas (Schibler 1981); and, in Ga.–Fla., in round-tailed muskrat (*Neofiber*) habitat. In s.-cent. Ohio: croplands, especially hay and fallow fields rather than grazed, wooded, and residential areas; the bird-hunting ♂ ♂ over hillier terrain and corn stubble fields more often, and over fallow fields less often, than Microtinae-hunting ♀ ♀ (Bildstein 1978). Age and/or sex differences in habitat use occur also in S.C., where "adult" ♂ ♂ comprise a greater proportion of harriers inland than in coastal salt marshes (Bildstein), and on the Texas Panhandle, where Juvs. predominate (Schibler 1981). In Cent. Am., open lands from sea level to higher mt. elevations.

Except as a transient, the Northern tends to avoid areas of continuous forests. In s.-cent. Ohio, for example, wintering birds concentrate at high densities on open agricultural land along terminal Wis. glacial moraines se. of which lie the forested Appalachians (Bildstein 1978).

Abroad In mainland Britain now, principally on higher ground (moorland), but on n. is. on lowland equivalent. Also, to some extent (Scotland, Ireland), conifer plantations. At an earlier time it bred in fens and marshes, as it does today on the Continent, but it also nests elsewhere there, even among standing crops. KEITH L. BILDSTEIN

DISTRIBUTION (See map.) The most widely, also most northerly, occurring harrier. Although it is considerably an opportunistic feeder, its distribution seems to be

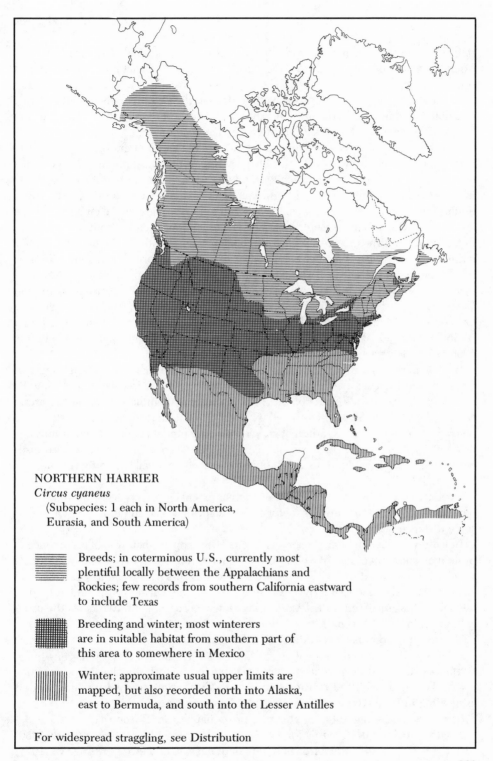

NORTHERN HARRIER
Circus cyaneus
  (Subspecies: 1 each in North America,
  Eurasia, and South America)

Breeds; in coterminous U.S., currently most
plentiful locally between the Appalachians and
Rockies; few records from southern California eastward
to include Texas

Breeding and winter; most winterers
are in suitable habitat from southern part of
this area to somewhere in Mexico

Winter; approximate usual upper limits are
mapped, but also recorded north into Alaska,
east to Bermuda, and south into the Lesser Antilles

For widespread straggling, see Distribution

tied closely to the presence of small diurnal, primarily grassland, rodents (principally Microtinae) and perhaps birds to some extent; this would restrict it from warmer arid regions, except in passage. Also, in the ne. Atlantic area, it is only a straggler to the Faroes (which lack voles, *Microtus*), yet plentiful in the Orkneys (where voles occur). It is doing well in Ireland (no *Mictotus* there). Except where otherwise indicated, the following pertains to the New World *C. c. hudsonius*.

As a breeder Especially before the great decline in numbers that began in the early 1950s (W. H. Brown 1973), this bird was apparently most plentiful in the continental interior—from the Appalachians and Great Lakes to the Rockies and approximately from the latitude of s. Colo. and Kans. n. to extensive coniferous forest. Upper limits of recorded breeding, from e. to w., are as follows: Single record for Nfld. (where few occurrences at any season); breeding range evidently ends about at the upper limits of agriculture in Que., where the spring thaw is late; limits are at a higher latitude w. of Hudson Bay across into Alaska (and thinly spread in much of interior Alaska, decreasing n. and w.). There is little satisfactory breeding habitat on the humid perimeter of the Gulf of Alaska on mainland or is.; to the s., 1st recorded nesting on Vancouver I. in 1967. Southern limits of known breeding in N. Am. in this century, based on a few scattered records, are approximately as mapped. Possibly bred on a coastal N.C. is. in 1981. Formerly bred in Fla. A nest in Ariz. in 1980 (see A. Phillips 1968 for the few earlier records).

Beyond breeding range Recorded as follows: Dead I. Harbor, Labrador; mouth of Great Whale R., Que. (se. Hudson Bay coast); Windy R., s. Keewatin; and Blow R. mouth, n. Yukon (Godfrey 1966). In Alaska, numbers dwindle to rare on the arctic coastal plain, on the Seward Pen., and w. beyond forest limits on the Alaska Pen.; see below for Aleutian records. South of known breeding range it has occurred in summer down at least to s.-cent. Fla., various Tex. localities, Ariz., and probably also elsewhere. In Fla., July sightings are thought to be of early fall migrants (Layne and Douglas 1976).

In migration Almost anywhere—even over extensive forests—to way above timberline on w. mts., the rainy perimeter of the Pacific in w. Canada and s. Alaska, and to some distance off coasts.

In winter Most birds are in conterminous U.S., approximately s. of occurrence of prolonged snow cover and of where waters remain frozen seasonally, and fewer birds beyond through Cent. Am. Yet some are scattered across frozen country n. to several areas in Canada, but regularly there only toward the Pacific coast, and recorded beyond on the rim of the Gulf of Alaska plus a few records for cent. Alaska. At the usual s. limit, in Panama, this harrier is "tolerably common" (A. Wetmore 1965). Recorded in S. Am. in Colombia (Nov., Mar.) and Venezuela (Dec.).

Atlantic BERMUDA occasional in autumn, formerly more or less regular in winter; BAHAMAS scattered occurrences, may be expected almost anywhere; see map for certain W. Indian is., PUERTO RICO few records; CUBA winter recovery of bird banded as nestling in Wis. (Hamerstrom); VIRGIN Is. rare in winter.

ICELAND Rare vagrant (A. Petersen), presumably from Europe.

Pacific ALEUTIANS records for Unalaska, Adak, Amchitka, Shemya, and (1980) Attu (Palearctic or Nearctic birds in outer Aleutians?); CLIPPERTON I. Aug. 12, 1958;

HAWAII Oahu (several, details unrecorded) and Midway—young ♀ collected Oct. 30, 1964 (Palearctic birds?).

Eurasian sightings and specimens of harriers purportedly resembling those of N. Am. are inconclusive evidence of occurrence abroad of the Nearctic race *hudsonius*.

Recorded as **fossil** from the Pleistocene of Oreg., Calif. (3 localities), Nuevo León in Mexico, and sw. Ecuador; and from **archaeological sites** in Calif. (2), Utah (7), Ariz., N.D. (2), and S.D. (18); references in Brodkorb (1964) with Ecuador added here. He also listed several European records for the species.

NOTES In N. Am. we have 1 harrier and useful information on changes in its numbers but very little data on changes in distribution. In Britain, where there are several harriers, there are known massive distributional changes, continuing to the present.

The early comparative status of British harriers is obscure, since originally all ♀ ♀ were presumed to be of 1 species—"ringtail." This matter was sorted out by Colonel Montagu (1802), but obscurity still surrounded migrants, breeders, and visitors. When they emerged from obscurity in the 1st half of this century, the Northern was in full retreat to the Orkneys (where there are voles and no predators of consequence except possibly Short-eared Owls and cats), and Montagu's (*C. pygargus*) was widely and thinly distributed in the s. As D. Watson (1977) put it, before 1939 the Northern Harrier's disappearance from most of the British Isles had the "same apparent finality" as that of the Osprey and White-tailed Eagle. The best chance of seeing it was in the Orkneys, the Hebrides, and possibly Ireland.

Since the 1950s the Northern has spread s. and is presently well established as a breeder in Wales and Ireland, while Montagu's has become just about the rarest breeding bird in Britain (but now is increasing in Scandinavia); in fact, the Northern is the "only raptor to increase in Ireland since the planting of conifers" (Bijleveld 1974).

These 2 harriers should have been affected about equally by the activities of game-keepers, by the reclamation of bogland, and by afforestation (which can be beneficial in early stages). Distributional changes appear to be related in some way to climatic change (D. Watson 1977). First the n. species was in retreat and was replaced by the s.—then vice versa. Yet another species, the Marsh Harrier, was widely distributed as a breeder in Britain in the 1st half of the previous century but ceased to breed by the end of the century; about 2 decades later it became reestablished, but presently there are only about a score of pairs. It has also had its ups and downs—mostly the latter—in various parts of the Continent. In the USSR its n. and s. breeding limits have moved n., and it now breeds w. to the Arctic Ocean but no longer in the Crimea and Caucasus (Galushin 1981). Although agricultural pesticides, large-scale farming, and the "exploitation of uncultivated land and moors" have all been linked to shifts in the distributions of European harriers (Bijleveld 1974), clearer understanding of such changes might help explain shifts occurring in N. Am.   KEITH L. BILDSTEIN

MIGRATION Data from N. Am. mainly. Judging from fragmentary data, the following are probabilities that need to be explored. Some of the more s. breeders tend to remain locally all year, provided that food is available and weather is not exceptionally severe. Northerly breeders "leapfrog" s. over some of the more s. ones. The birds migrate on a broad front; they occur in both inland ridge and coastal counts but rarely form more than a small fraction of reported raptors. Migrants primarily travel singly or at least widely scattered (Audubon stated otherwise), although Beske (1978, 1982), in an intensive study that employed radio telemetry, reported that a Juv. bird which he tracked dispersed from a nest in cent. Wis. and flew with other Juvs. (not siblings) for periods up to 1½ hrs. Although nominate *cyaneus* is said to be a gregarious migrant in the Old World (L. Brown and Amadon 1968 1), D. Watson (1977) reported only one "not wholly convincing" British record of a group of 10 migrants. At times harriers use thermals, like buteos, thus flying much higher than is usual except when displaying. Beske reported relatively direct, fast soaring (approx. 40 mph), interspersed with somewhat meandering, low-altitude, hunting flight and perching in Juvs. dispersing from nests; flights were "primarily down-wind but deviated slightly to follow drainages and marshes." Movement began after 0830 hrs. and usually ended 1–2 hrs. before sunset.

Occasionally harriers mix fortuitously in the vast numbers of migrant raptors that collectively occupy much airspace—for example, with Swainson's Hawks in spring in Cent. Am. Unlike buteos and accipiters, Northern Harriers cross water quite readily—that is, they do not concentrate around large expanses of water. There are reports of them crossing the mouth of the Bay of Fundy from s. N.S. to Mt. Desert I., Maine. Many island-hop across the inner Gulf of Maine. Kunkle (1976) reported them crossing Delaware Bay even in light winds in flap-glides at 50–200 ft., singly and in twos; but, while some apparently make water crossings of at least 30 mi., many (most?) follow bayshore marshes toward the head of the bay before crossing at much narrower expanses. Yet harriers have reached Bermuda, the Bahamas, and the W. Indies. In autumn, flights are deflected to some degree by the Great Lakes, and harriers tend to travel along the w. side (as near Duluth, Minn.). In spring at these lakes they tend to be deflected e. It appears that they migrate around, and only rarely cross, the Gulf of Mexico. Abroad, nominate *cyaneus* is regularly seen over the Irish Sea and crosses both the North and Mediterranean seas.

The Northern Harrier hunts while migrating—even over water.

When the young leave their natal locality they do so alone, sometimes late in the day. In cent. Wis., Beske (1978, 1982) found that they tend to depart toward the s. or se., but at least some apparently travel in almost any direction. He reported daily movements in the same general direction of 14–66 mi. "interrupted by the establishment of temporary home ranges" not more than 106 mi. (for 3 birds) from the nest in suitable habitat where the birds fed and roosted and from which they engaged in "exploratory" flights. Farthest total distance for a marked bird was to se. Fla. In spring they do not return to their natal area but scatter widely. In Britain most recoveries of nominate *cyaneus* before Nov. of year of hatching are less than 20 mi. from the nest (D. Watson 1977), and older birds are recorded to breed near birth sites.

The number of ♂♂ in Basic feathering that winter around the n. Gulf of Mexico appears to be disproportionately high; this may indicate that mature ♀♀, which are larger and can capture larger prey, tend to remain farther n. This partial seasonal sexual segregation apparently also occurs in Europe.

Spring   Migration lasts a month (Mar.) or more in Cent. Am. and is more extended in time progressively n.; mid-Mar.–Apr. in s. states (mostly before mid-Apr.), through Mar. into mid-May in n. coterminous U.S. and into Canada and se. Alaska (mainly last half of Apr. and 1st third of May), and through Apr. to end of May at upper limits of breeding in nw. Canada and Alaska. Although migrants are more numerous some days, unlike some other raptors there seem to be no great peaks in numbers. The movement of birds in Mar. all the way from Cent. Am. to Canada obviously indicates a shift of birds wintering in various latitudes.

Based on the Wis. studies of Hamerstrom (in Hickey 1969) and the Man. studies of Broley (in Bent 1937), in general, gray ♂♂ arrive earlier than brown ♀♀ and older ♀♀ precede yearling ♀♀. At se. L. Ontario the first arrivals invariably are gray ♂♂, who are preponderant for some time; after early Apr, browns outnumber them, and gray ♂♂ are infrequent (G. Smith and Muir 1978). Nominate *cyaneus:* in the Kiev region, USSR, ♂♂ precede ♀♀ (Dementiev and Gladkov 1951); in Orkney, where some of both sexes remain through winter, ♂♂ do not precede ♀♀ (D. Waston, 1977). In cent. Wis. wt. declines throughout spring migration (Bildstein and Hamerstrom 1980).

Summer   There is some postbreeding dispersal, at least by young of the year.

Fall   In general, Juvs. (♂♂ before ♀♀) precede older birds, all with overlapping dates. In the n. half of coterminous U.S. and occasionally farther s., some young of the year are already migrating by the 1st week in Aug. Migration is heavy and widespread through that month. Breeders evidently begin to vacate upper limits of range by early Sept., about the time ice first begins to form. Migration is protracted—in Canada and down to middle U.S. from some time in Aug. at least until late in Nov. As in spring, no big peak is evident, and relatively high numbers may be expected from mid-Sept. through the end of Oct.; peak movements at Hawk Mt., Pa., and San Francisco Bay, Calif., are mid- to late Oct.; in s. U.S. large numbers occur in late Sept. and around mid-Oct. The birds begin arriving in s. Cent. Am. late in Oct. As noted above, a few make long water crossings, as to Bermuda and Cuba. Older reports of ♀♀ preceding ♂♂ on fall migration were apparently the result of lumping 1st-fall birds of both sexes with older ♀♀. Banding stations in N.J., Ont., and Minn. report Juvs. (both sexes) preceding older cohorts (both sexes), and, at C. May Point, N.J., Juv. ♂♂ precede Juv. ♀♀ (K. Bildstein).

Winter   Evidently many harriers roost solitarily or at least widely apart. In areas of vole (*Microtus*) or cotton rat (*Sigmodon*) abundance, they assemble at communal roosts, which they occupy in middle latitudes of coterminous U.S. approximately from late Oct. until well into Mar. The number assembled may not be constant—that is, they shift in winter, probably depending on hunting conditions, but they are not as nomadic as Short-eared Owls. In Europe and beyond, where there is a general exodus of the n. limits of range for the winter season, the Northern is the least migratory harrier—last to leave in autumn and 1st to return in spring. Also, as in N. Am., they have communal winter roosts.   KEITH L. BILDSTEIN

BANDING STATUS   **In our area**   Errington banded 47 nestlings near Madison, Wis., and had 10 recoveries (G. Wagner 1933). Hammond and Henry (1949) reported

150 nestlings banded at Lower Souris Refuge, N.D., nearly all in 1937–1939, and listed 12 recoveries. In Sask., Houston (1968) gave details of 24 recoveries 1929–1961 resulting from 294 banded nestlings. For these studies, most recoveries were of birds shot outside the breeding season in the s. ⅔ of the U.S. e. of w. Tex. Beske (1982), using recovery data from Hamerstrom, reported 12 1st-winter recoveries of nestlings banded in cent. Wis. Most were toward the se. U.S.

Hickey (1952) indicated that earlier bandings had been done principally in Alta., N.D., Ill., and Ohio and that there had been recoveries in 6 Canadian provinces and 21 states. He did not report total number banded. Many have subsequently been banded, notably in Wis.; there is as yet no inclusive analysis of N. Am. data.

Hamerstrom (in Hickey 1969) reported 553 harriers banded 1959–1965 in 1 area in Wis.: 92 breeding birds, 217 nestlings, and the remainder migrants or birds apparently not breeding.

During 1971–1980 a number (mainly Juv.) have been banded in fall at C. May Pt., N.J. (415), Hawk Cliff, Ont. (433), Duluth, Minn. (370), and Kittatinny Mt., N.J. (38) (Bildstein).

The number banded in N. Am. to Aug. 1981 was 8,694 with 509 (5.8%) recoveries (Clapp et al. 1982). Banding localities: Wis. (by far the most birds), Ont., Sask., N.J., Minn., Alta., Mich., Calif., and a scattering elsewhere.

Elsewhere Many Northerns were banded in the Orkneys, Scotland, by the late E. Balfour and some subsequently by other workers; of these, 62% recovered outside Orkney were shot. Mead (1973) mapped recoveries over 100 km. in Scotland and, for Britain/Ireland, all those to and from abroad of over 250 km. The number is rather small. According to Spencer and Hudson (cited in D. Watson 1977), before 1974 a total of 1,544 had been banded in Britain/Ireland—all except 12 as nestlings—and there were 143 recoveries (9%). These studies reveal that, following range contractions elsewhere, the Orkney birds acted as a source for recolonization but that breeding stock immigrated to Orkney at the same time. Of 65 nominate *cyaneus* banded in Finland 1913–1962, 2 were recovered in Finland and 7 outside. Additional data are in Glutz von Blotzheim et al. (1971).

NOTE The netting of adults with nestlings but not eggs, if done by qualified biologists, does not significantly increase nesting failure. KEITH L. BILDSTEIN

REPRODUCTION For N. Am., some of the earlier literature is used, especially when it is supported by subsequent findings. The more recent data are principally from Wis.—the work of Hamerstrom and her associates. Included here also, for completeness and comparison, are data from the Orkneys and elsewhere in Scotland based on the work of the late E. Balfour and his successors and on D. Watson's (1977) monograph.

A few harriers (both sexes) **first breed** as yearlings, but most not until at least 2 years old. Hamerstrom (in Burke 1979) reported that, for known-age (banded) breeders, 13 of 168 ♂♂ (8%) and 39 of 198 ♀♀ (20%) were yearlings; in Man., 2 of 13 ♂♂ (13%) (R. Clark 1972a); and in sw. Scotland 4 of 47 ♂♂ and 13% for ♀♀ (Balfour and Cadbury 1979), and the number of 1st-year breeders falls below that expected based on banding results, indicating that social behavior (preempting of nesting areas by older breeders) may exclude some younger birds from breeding. In Wisc., the number of ♀ ♀, and to a lesser extent ♂ ♂, breeding as yearlings is correlated positively with vole numbers, and these young breeders are more successful during vole highs (Burke 1979). Polygamy is widespread in the Northern Harrier but rare among yearling breeders—especially ♂ ♂. In both Wis. and e. New Bruns., where polygamy occurs, no 1st-year ♂ ♂ were polygamous (Burke 1979, R. Simmons); in Orkney, only 1 of 33 breeding ♂ yearlings was a bigamist, while the majority of older ♂ ♂ were polygamists. There is a tendency in Orkney and elsewhere for yearling ♂ ♂ to mate with young (especially yearling) ♀ ♀ and for yearling breeders (especially ♂ ♂) to be less productive than older birds. Harriers that have bred in a previous year have unusually high breeding success (Hamerstrom, in Hickey 1969).

Although, in Britain, this harrier reportedly may migrate in small groups in spring (and roost communally at this season), in N. Am. there is almost no indication of the birds traveling other than singly. Males arrive in Man. in mid-Mar., as much as 3 weeks ahead of ♀ ♀ (Bent 1937). In Wis., ♂ ♂ arrive about mid-Mar. and ♀ ♀ 5–10 days later (Hamerstrom). Where winters are less severe, it is possible that they behave more as they do in Scotland—♂ ♂ or even pairs visit breeding areas increasingly in Feb.–Mar. and well may be the individuals that will breed there. In Scotland they may depart only to return later, or they may be gone for days in stormy weather (D. Watson 1977). Even this is not the full story. This harrier SKY-DANCES on migration over suitable nesting terrain as well as over eventual nest sites, and in Wis., Hamerstrom caught and banded as many as 11 ♂ ♂ and 18 ♀ ♀ passing by one small marsh; the last ones remained and nested. In Scotland, a ♂ may move from hill to hill and Sky-dance on each; the wings flap rather slowly and loosely "as if the bird were acting in a trance" (Watson 1977). It has been assumed that the ♂'s Sky-dancing (it is done occasionally by ♀ ♀ also) is a necessary component of pair formation. In Wis., however, during years of

heavy aerial spraying of DDT, some harriers nested—successfully—even though this display was essentially or entirely absent, and D. Watson (1977) reported an absence of Sky-dancing in especially sparse breeding populations in Scotland.

Male harriers, by Sky-dancing at communal roosts and while migrating, are evidently advertising for a mate in a suitable state of reproductive readiness (this display continues later also); they are not hindered by cold weather. That is, they are not necessarily advertising territory (Hamerstrom, in Hickey 1969). A ♀ may display with a ♂, especially when ♀♀ outnumber ♂♂ and polygamy occurs; Sky-dancing is most intense in clusters of polygamous groups (D. Watson 1977). Female displays, which tend to be less extensive than the ♂'s, are usually precipitated by displaying ♂♂. When the ♀ joins the display, sometimes she "turns over and presents her claws to his" (L. Brown 1976). In New Bruns., R. Simmons watched a ♀ display to 3 ♂♂ late in the season. She failed to mate with any of them and was even chased by one.

Breckenridge (1935), describing Sky-dancing in Minn., stated that the ♂, in a "very evident state of excitement," dived from a height of about 100 ft. at a precipitous angle for about 50 ft., then zoomed up again to near the original height where he turned over sidewise. He beat his wings 2–3 times in this inverted position, then righted himself by the same sidewise turn, and again dived repeatedly. While the ♂ is displaying, the ♀ usually perches or seems to continue hunting nearby. Broley (in Bent 1937) suggested the av. number of dives may be 25, yet he noted 71 in succession. In Orkney, Balfour noted 105. The most prolonged displays are by young unmated ♂♂ and by ♀♀ that have lost their mates (D. Watson 1977). Brown birds that Sky-dance include both sexes, but young ♀♀ are believed to perform less actively.

A. K. Fisher (1893) reported what now is a well-known variation. A bird at considerable altitude throws its wings over its back and, in falling, turns over and over much like a tumbler pigeon till near the ground, then ascends rapidly and falls again. Both Sky-dancing and TUMBLING are variable and they are bridged by intermediate actions, next described.

From the Palearctic, here is a translation of Hesse (1912): When the ♂ starts his display, usually after circling a short while, he flies with strong wingbeats steeply up to an appreciable height with his body almost in vertical plane; then, with wings held more or less close to his body and still beating, and "wrists" sharply bent, he lets himself fall; mounting again, he continues this flight display for a longer or shorter time. He flies in arcs with very steep, high, narrow curves. Behavior at the top of the curve varies; sometimes he flips over to start the descent while actually upside down, having made a half-somersault; sometimes he only tips sidewise, whereby the transition into the descending curve is less steep. There are variations and modifications; sometimes he is more on his back, sometimes more on the side. (All this fits well with observations in Wis.—Hamerstrom.) Zealously displaying individuals, in addition, frequently rotate their bodies 1 or more times on the upswing. (Is there a terrestrial counterpart, as when the ♂ turns his white rump toward the ♀ and bows repeatedly? See Dickson 1982.) The aerial display is accompanied by calling. New Bruns. data: The av. was 13 dives in 35 ♂ displays and 10 in 5 ♀ dives; it was 6.5 in 12 instances by yearling ♂♂ (R. Simmons).

Sky-dancing often continues until the clutch is complete and will recur if a nest fails and a 2nd clutch is laid (L. Brown 1976). In New Bruns., ♀ displays were most intense late in the season (Simmons).

In Wis., the high-intensity dance is as though the harrier were following the path of an invisible coil spring in the sky. Seen from the end of the coil, it is plain that the bird is looping-the-loop. One can see it twisting—upside down for a moment, like an aviator performing a barrel roll—at the top of each loop. High-intensity display seen from the side again resembles the path of a coil spring with the flash of the barrell roll at the top. Attempted, or low-intensity, dancing lacks the barrel roll at the top and simply undulates (Hamerstrom). Temme (1969) described display of a ♂ while 2 ♀ were below.

Pair formation Details are not entirely clear. Presumably, in spring, if a ♂ presents food to a ♀ and she accepts and they copulate, a bond has been formed for the season. Yet there is no certainty that harriers do not copulate promiscuously beforehand; Hamerstrom (in Hickey 1969) reported seeing a marked ♀, which had copulated with an unmarked ♂ 4 days earlier, "flying about with a different, and marked male." In the Orkneys, copulation follows almost every food-presentation until the sexual urge has been subordinated to that of "brooding" (Balfour 1957). At any rate, the ♂ that brings food to the nesting ♀ and/or defends the nest may be defined as the mate (Hamerstrom). There remains a possibility that some pairing may occur at winter roosts, where Sky-dancing has been reported.

In N.D., F. M. Bailey (1915) watched a pair that had 2-week-old young. They flew high, uttering "low squealing notes." Two days later they were sailing together high up, uttering "soft whistling screams," very different from their "distracted cackle" or their "quiet hunting calls." Forbush (1927) wrote that, when mated or mating, the birds are much together on the ground and in the air. When the ♀ alights, the ♂ follows and keeps close company; on the ground he "bows" to her and "swells with amorous ardor" (note display of rump, mentioned earlier).

In n. Scotland, Nethersole-Thompson (in Bannerman 1956) noted that before laying the birds often betray the nest location by their aerial acrobatics. Mates "ring up" so high that it is difficult to follow them, even with binoculars. Then the blue ♂ dives at his robust partner, buffeting her as she turns on her back at his approach. Or he glides smoothly over her, dipping as he passes, or he may tumble earthward like a raven. Mates may pass and repass in narrowing circles till they "seem knit as one." From time to time a sharp *kwee-ah* call is uttered as they answer one another. Then 1 or both come earthward, stalling their descent just above the heather.

Copulation Occurs regularly, from before nest construction until some time during incubation; it may promote the pair bond. In Scotland (Watson 1977), after a food pass, both birds are some distance apart on the ground. The ♀ "mantles" over the food, giving a "food" or "soliciting" call to the ♂. They copulate on the ground, near where the nest will be built or is already constructed. The ♀ has wings half-spread and tail raised, and the ♂ flaps to maintain balance. It can occur without food presentation; Balfour (1957) noted that the soliciting call is "sometimes heard time and again ringing out with a suggestion of petulant insistence. She will pester him by alternately chasing him from perch to perch, flattening herself on the ground and calling, until he either mates with her or flies away."

In Wis., Hamerstrom witnessed few copulations, probably because of the nature of the terrain. In Man., R. Clark (1972a) observed it off the ground once, on a post. At a nest in Nebr., Newell (1950) observed 2 copulations after the 1st egg was laid. In New Bruns., R. Simmons witnessed 11 copulations, 10 on the ground and one 10 ft. up in a tree. Females postured in a crouch, calling for up to 10 min., exposing their rumps and sometimes wagging their tails. Preening always followed.

Sexual nexus   When pairs nest solitarily, pair-bond form is at least **seasonal monogamy.** Forbush (1927) suggested that harriers mate for life, basing this on presumed mated pairs seen hunting in winter. Pair fidelity may exist, apparently rarely—at least in migratory N. Am. harriers. In Wis., none of 70 pairs in which both birds were color marked remated the following year despite a "strong tendency for successful nesters to return" (Burke 1979). On 3 occasions both members of a pair returned the following year to the 40,000-acre study area but did not remate. In only 1 instance did a ♂ and ♀ remate: a ♀ that mated monogamously in 1960 was not seen in 1961, but in 1962 she mated with a different ♂, who was a bigamist. In 1963 she returned to mate with yet another ♂ and in 1964 remated with the same ♂ she was mated with in 1962. In 1964 he was a trigamist.

There is a tendency toward colonial nesting plus a strong tendency toward **bigamy,** even **harem polygamy** (up to 7 ♀ ♀ have been reported) by older birds, especially in dense populations when voles are abundant. In Wash., a ♂ defended 2 nests 400 yd. apart with equal vigor on each of 6 visits; on May 7 (last day of observation) a clutch of 6 eggs was at least 19 days incubated and the 2d nest contained 3 fresh eggs (Yocom 1944). Similarly, Reindahl (1941) reported a ♂ defending 2 nests several hundred yd. apart. One of 4 ♂ ♂ studied by Linner (1980) in the Cache Valley, Utah, provided food unequally to 2 ♀ ♀ nesting 180 m. apart. In Man., a ♂ defended and fed young at 2 nests 0.4 mi. apart, favoring 1 nest in both actions; a 3d nest may also have been involved (Hecht 1951). In e. New Bruns., 4 of 21 ♂ ♂ were polygamists: 1 bigamist, 2 trigamists, and 1 attempted quadrigamist. Male polygamists, but not their ♀ consorts, were more successful than monogamists (R. Simmons). In cent. Wis. (Burke 1979), polygamy occurred in 12 of 21 years; at 263 nests there was either bigamy (20 cases) or trigamy (7 cases). Although occurrence of polygamy was not enhanced by a sex ratio skewed toward surplus ♀ ♀, it was correlated positively, along with increased nesting, with vole abundances. In 1979, 13 monogamous nests av. 624 m. apart, while 12 pairs of bigamist nests av. 260 m. apart, with the nearest nest outside the pair 513 m. distant. Similarly, in Orkney polygamous nests tend to be closer to each other (Balfour and Cadbury 1979). In Wis., 20% of the ♀ ♀, but none of the ♂ ♂, involved in bigamy were yearlings. Monogamous ♀ ♀ raised 2.3 young to flight age, while bigamist ♀ ♀ raised 2.0 and trigamist ♀ ♀ 1.7, but in 7 of the 12 years in which polygamy occurred, bigamous ♀ ♀ av. more young/nest than monogamous ♀ ♀. Polygamous ♂ ♂ were more successful than monogamous ♂ ♂ (2.3 young for monogamists vs. 4.0 and 5.0 for bigamists and trigamists). In New Bruns., 12 of 30 nests were polygamous in a high vole year and 2 of 22 in a low year (R. Simmons). Males had up to 4 mates. A ♀'s success depended on her position in the harem, with first-arriving (alpha) ♀ ♀ doing better than the others—even better than monogamous ♀ ♀ (av. 5.2 eggs in 5 nests of alpha

♀♀ v. 4.6 in 21 nests of monogamous ♀♀). Males delivered more food to 1st-arriving ♀♀ than to others in their harem.

Abroad, 5 of 70 ♂♂ were polygamists in ne. Scotland (Picozzi 1978) as were 2 of 47 in sw. Scotland (D. Watson 1977). Polygamy is also recorded for Sweden (Arividsson 1980) and for Holland (all but 3 of 38 nests in 1 location) (Schipper 1978).

A remarkable instance of polygamy is reported from the Dutch is. of Ameland (Van de Kraan and Van Strien 1969). There were 7 nests, distributed over 14 km. of dunes, and only 1 ♂—recognizable by a damaged flight feather. One nest failed; 6 reared 18 young successfully and, for the most westerly ♀, the authors reported that food was brought only until end of copulation. Without help, she reared 2 young. This documents the shortest possible effective **temporary monogamy**—for the duration of coition.

In Orkney, where there are nearly twice as many ♀ as ♂ breeders, 100 of 151 ♂♂ in Basic feathering and 34 yearling ♂♂ were polygamists (with up to 6 mates). Most (9 of 14) yearling ♀♀ were monogamists, but most older ones (76 of 99) were polygamists. Clutch size did not vary with mating type. Hatching success, but not attainment of flight, was significantly higher for monogamist ♀♀. (These differences, as well as those cited for cent. Wis., do not take into account that where both mating types occur, polygamist birds tend to be older than monogamous birds.) On a per ♂ basis the number of young reared to flight increased with the number of mates, at least through 4 ♀♀. Polygamy was less frequent before 1950 when the number of birds was smaller and the sex ratio less skewed. While the recent excess in ♀♀ may be a result of differential mortality, Balfour and Cadbury (1979) suggested that social regulation may be involved—especially if Orkney can support only a limited number of ♂♂.

In Orkney a nest with 10(!) eggs was shared by 2 ♀ and with no aggression; when the young were small, all food was provided by the ♂, and the ♀♀ cooperated in feeding them (Picozzi 1983a).

In almost all cases where polygamy has been studied in detail, ♂♂ tend to favor certain ♀♀, with regard especially to food but also to nest defense. In Wis., the nest of the less favored ♀ is apt to fail or to produce fewer young because the ♂ carries most of the food to the preferred ♀. Slighted ♀♀ sometimes attempt to rob prey from their mates who are en route to the preferred ♀. These "robber females" (Hamerstrom, in Hickey 1969) sometimes leave their nests—even in the egg stage—and perch for lengthy periods near the nest of the preferred ♀ (K. Bildstein). Although this tactic frequently enables such ♀♀ to secure food, time spent away from the nest almost certainly contributes to lower breeding success.

Based on his Orkney studies, Balfour (1957) stated that the chief cause of nest desertion appeared to be bigamy. He later wrote Hamerstrom that, with harrier numbers reaching a peak in 1949–1950, the sex ratio became unbalanced in favor of ♀♀, resulting in widespread bigamy by ♂♂ and considerable "emotional upsets" among ♀♀. There was desertion of nests at all stages; or a ♀ sometimes finished a clutch in a 2d, hastily made, nest; and ♀♀ made "frantic display flights."

That a large percentage of available breeders nest when voles are abundant is partially offset by nest failure of bigamists; on the other hand, more yearlings are mated

271

in such years, which accelerates reproduction (Balfour to Hamerstrom). The harrier-vole relationship is close but not obligatory; for example, the bird is thriving in Ireland (no voles there). A paucity of breeding ♂♂ may sometimes have been reported erroneously; it takes experience to distinguish between a breeding ♀ and a yearling ♂, and ♂♂ of all ages are more difficult to detect because of their lower, faster, hunting flight.

Nesting and hunting territories As previously noted, Northerns tend to nest in loose colonies—even when ample nesting grounds for wide dispersal are seemingly available. In ne. Scotland, however, Picozzi (1978) found an apparently "regular dispersion" of nests within the aggregation of those he studied, and L. Brown (1976) reported that in Britain harem ♀♀ tend to space themselves regularly within the ♂'s territory. Two or 3 nests may be within 400 yd. of each other. Polygamy need not necessarily be involved (Errington 1930), but the colonial tendency facilitates it. Nonbreeders have hunting territories (Hamerstrom, in Hickey 1969), and in Europe unmated ♂♂ sometimes construct "cock nests."

Nesting/hunting territories are usually established by the time of egg laying. In Mich., they varied 0.38–2.14 sq. mi., av. 1.3, in 7 pairs in 1942 and 0.9 sq. mi. in 9 pairs in 1948 (the Craigheads 1956). The area defended against humans in 10 nests in Man. av. 0.1 sq. mi. (Hecht 1951). Evidently this harrier was a solitary nester in Mich. (possibly as a result of habitat patchiness), where densities varied 0.24–0.14 pair/sq. mi. (3 and 2 years on two 36-sq.-mi. blocks (the Craigheads 1956); 1 pair/sq. mi. (2 years, 5 sq. mi.) in Sask. (Furniss 1938); 2–4 pairs/sq. mi. (8 years, 3 sq. mi.) in N.D. (Monson 1934). It appears to be colonial elsewhere, even within extensive tracts of apparently similar habitat—5 nests in 5 acres in Calif. (E. M. Hall 1947); 7 nests in ⅓ sq. mi. in Ohio (C. Walker and Franks 1928); 3 in a "triangular pattern" 400 yd. apart in N.D. (Duebbert and Lokemoen 1977); 2 nests 400 yd. apart on 80 acres in Wash. (Yocom 1944); av. 2.1 pairs/100 acres (5 years, 28 acres) in Wash. (Wing 1949); 5 nests in ¾ sq. mi. (Reindahl 1941); 6 nests in 1 sq. mi. in Man. (Hecht 1951); 15 nests 120–1,342 yd. apart in Man. (R. Clark 1972a); 3 nests within 400 yd. in Wis. (Errington 1930); 6 nests 40–200 yd. apart in N.Y. (Munoff 1963); 13 monogamous nests av. 625 yd. and 12 bigamous nests 284 yd. apart in Wis. in the year with greatest concentration of breeders (Burke 1979); 2 broods within 200 yd. in Minn. (Breckenridge 1935).

Abroad, in Orkney, 1.6 pairs/sq. mi. (4 years, 31 sq. mi.) with an av. distance to nearest nest 886 yd. (Balfour and Cadbury 1979). In a "sparse" population in sw. Scotland, nests were at least 500 m. apart even in polygamous groups (D. Watson 1977) but as close as 150 m. to a *C. pygargus* nest (Douglas, in D. Watson 1977). In Ireland, adjacent nests were closer when on opposite sides of a ridge (D. Scott, in D. Watson 1977).

In N. Am. and abroad there is marked overlap in "home ranges" or hunting areas, especially away from the nest. In Wis. (Hamerstrom and De La Ronde Wilde 1973) and ne. Scotland (Picozzi 1978), these areas are not hunted uniformly; the birds fly particular routes that enable them to surprise prey, sometimes hunting as little as 30% of their territory. The "daily censusing range" of a pair of radio-tracked birds in Wis. (Hamerstrom and De La Ronde Wilde) was 1¼ by 2¾ mi., with little overlap in areas of intense use. Females with nestlings tend to stay nearer the nest, hunting for short periods, when the young are 5–10 days old. Picozzi (1978) found that where nests with young were dispersed widely, home ranges of successful pairs were large and did not overlap much.

In Wis., a fence used for perching by the middle of 3 pairs separated it from the pair on one side, and a ditch, used by neither pair, separated it from the pair on the other side; the middle territory was 120 yd. wide and of undetermined length. Before establishment of territories, all 6 harriers were seen fighting together at one time (Errington 1930). Windrows and roads also serve as territorial borders; Bildstein was able to position his 8-ft. observation tower closer to nests when natural or man-made landmarks separated it from the nest. Overlapping of hunting territories, more so in this raptor than in some others, has been noted by several authors (the Craigheads 1956). In some cases, individuals from different pairs seemingly hunt side-by-side without aggression (Breckenridge 1935). Intraspecific interactions are greatest early in the nesting season (Errington 1930), when intruding harriers sometimes engage in high-speed pursuits and talon grappling (Geroudet 1965, later authors); it decreases as the season progresses to that by the time the young are on the wing they are not always attacked if they trespass. By midseason most intraspecific interactions consist of what Balfour described as "escorting flight," where the territorial owner (♂ or ♀) flies in a direct line to the intruder and then follows several m. behind and below (as if to prevent it from alighting) until both reach the edge of the territory. There are no reports of boundary displays in which ♂ ♂ fly slowly with wings held in "an exaggeratedly high angle and . . . tarsi thrust straight down," as occurs in the Marsh Harrier (Baker-Gabb 1981). In polygamous groups the ♂ defends 2 or more nests in this fashion and each ♀ defends a subterritory about her nest, often against harem mates.

Individuals vary in the extent to which they defend their nests against human intrusion. Upon flushing, some ♂ ♂ fly to a nearby perch, others fly off distress calling, while some circle over the nest calling, stooping, and sometimes striking the intruder. In Wis., the ♀ defends more strongly (possibly because she is usually closer to the nest) and persistently, but the reverse occurs at some nests (Hamerstrom). In Man., Hecht (1951) reported that 6 nests were defended largely by the ♀, 3 rarely by the ♂, and 1 almost entirely by the ♂. R. Clark (1972a) reported that the ♀ was most aggressive at 1 nest and the ♂ at another. In N.J., the ♂ was more responsive at all 3 nests (Urner 1925). Attacks on man, especially by the ♀, may be equal in intensity throughout the nesting period. In defense, if the ♂ is absent, after her initial response the ♀ may soar in circles, often at great altitudes—distress circling—so that the ♂ will see her and come to her aid (Hamerstrom, in Hickey 1969). In practice, other (sometimes mated) ♂ ♂ may come to her defense. Females begin circling the intruder and calling kek-kek-kek. Closer to the nest, they dive at and occasionally strike a person's head with their feet. Often they are accompanied by the ♂, who also may dive and strike. Occasionally a ♀ may defend against a person after the young have departed (Urner 1925). There is communal defense against the coyote (W. Powers et al. 1984). Hamerstrom (1963) found that, after the young are half-grown, some ♂ ♂ seldom—possibly never—come near the nest again. In both Wis. (Hamerstrom) and Scotland (D. Watson 1977), territorial defense is intensified against persistent human intruders, and, in Scotland at least, individual recognition of specific human intruders is maintained from 1 season to the next.

Harriers defend their nests in somewhat similar fashion against human intruders on horseback (Peabody 1900); crows and Herring Gulls (in Nieboer 1973); Turkey Vultures, Red-tailed and Swainson's Hawks, Golden Eagle, Prairie Falcon, and Long-eared Owl (Linsdale 1938); Peregrine (Urner 1925), which they often "escort" to the harrier's territorial boundary; and mammalian predators, including foxes, and domestic and free-ranging ungulates (latter presumably because of threat they pose in trampling eggs or young).

Nest site   On grassy ground, among low brush or close beside a bush or tree, or in mixed herbaceous/woody growth, in damp places and often near water; areas of cattail (*Typha*) are much favored; occasionally on a muskrat house in water or on accumulated floating vegetation. Eighteen upland nests in N.D. were in "tall, dense cover" (Duebbert and Lokemoen 1977). There have been high densities in *Salicornia*, in cranberry-*Sphagnum* bogs, virgin and once-cultivated prairie, *Phragmites-Fluminea* marsh, goldenrod and nettles, sweet clover, tumbleweed, and weed stalks. Also tidal marshes, marsh meadows, and upland sedge meadows along the coast, and, inland, in sugar beet, alfalfa, sweet clover, rye, and wheat fields. In cold desert sagebrush-greasewood steppe, its ground nests may be surrounded by larger sagebrush, the nearest water a remote pond or a stock-watering tank. Abroad, it also nests in corn and kale fields. In young stands of planted conifers in Wis., Scotland, and Ireland; in Mass., in cut woodlots "where sprouts are growing on the stumps" (Bent 1937). In N. Am., a report of nesting 20 ft. up in a willow in a Swainson's Hawk nest (Mann 1946); in Orkney in a dwarf willow 15–30 in. high (Balfour 1962). On a haycock (Bendire 1892). Scotland: generally on a gentle slope just above or in a gully, sheltered from the wind. A tendency to nest in densely vegetated areas within a field, but in Holland, Schipper (1978) reported a nest in which the incubating bird was "sitting not unlike a Lapwing fully exposed." (See also Habitat, above.) Where with Short-eared Owls, this harrier nests in wetter, less exposed sites.

In a 19-year 184-nest study in cent. Wis., Hamerstrom and Kopeny (1981) reported nesting in many types of vegetation, with a shift from *Salix*, *Populus tremuloides*, *Carex*, and grasses to *Solidago* and *Spiraea*, in part because of concurrent shifts in vegetation cover. By the time clutches were completed, most nests were well concealed (at least from the ground) in dense stands "not normally used as travel lanes by mammals."

According to Criddle (1912), the birds seem 1st to decide on a locality and then, flying to and fro, inspect every in. of the ground; gradually they choose the actual site. In cent. Wis., nests tend to occur in the same general location but not the identical spot, from year to year, even when the same birds are not involved (Hamerstrom). In the same study, successful breeders were more than twice as likely to return and breed on the 16,000-ha. marsh as were unsuccessful breeders. Returning ♂ ♂ nested an av. 546 m. from their previous sites, returning ♀ ♀ av. 1,092 m. away (Burke 1979). In Alta. and Sask. (Sealy 1967), the same nest sites are not reused, but nesting occurred "in the same clump of snowberry" 4 successive years. When the same nest is used for several years in a row, new materials are added annually (A. K. Fisher 1893). In

Orkney, Balfour (1962) reported that a ♀ returned to nest in the same location for 6 years and that some areas have been used for well over 30 years.

During this phase, the ♂ flies close and slightly above the ♀. Then both gather nesting material (usually within 200 yd.—L. Brown 1976). In New Bruns., ♂ ♂ always initiated nest building, usually in the presence of the ♀ (R. Simmons). But the ♀ does most of the gathering and all of the arranging at the site. Whatever the ♂ fetches he leaves or drops at the site. Sumner (in Bent 1937) reported a ♀ making 7 trips to the nest in 10 min. R. Simmons saw a ♂ make 20 visits in 30 min. Both sexes carry larger items (up to 3 ft. long: thin alder branches) in their talons, but such smaller items as strands of grass are sometimes carried in the beak. Material is occasionally dropped, apparently accidentally. In New Bruns., ♀ ♀, especially later in the season, do not always use the foundation built by the ♂ but build a new nest usually within 5–15 m. About the time building begins, the ♂ begins bringing food to his mate, who continues to do some hunting at least until laying begins. A Saunders (1913) first noted a pair in the vicinity of a nest 5 days before it was found with a fresh egg. In Nebr., a ♀ was at the nest 4 days before laying began (Newell 1950). Two days after a harrier had been seen in another area, an unfinished nest was found; 2 days later, an egg was laid, within a day of the addition of grass lining. Another ♀ spent a full week in construction. In Orkney (Balfour 1962), nest building takes from several hrs. to several weeks. When renesting is attempted, construction is brief. In New Bruns. (R. Simmons), late-arriving ♀ ♀ induce intense nest-building activity in the ♂, complete the nests rapidly themselves, begin laying 4–5 days later.

Greenery   Additions to nests, particularly of grass, are made after the structure is finished—even after the young are well grown (A. Allen 1929, Linsdale 1938, Sealy 1967). In visits to a nest when chicks were 2 and 11 days old, Shelley (1935) noted fresh green oak leaves in a nest even though such were not listed as occurring nearby. In Scotland, the ♀ continues to add material through the season (Watson 1977).

Nest   May be a hollow in the ground lined with grasses or, usually in damp situations, sticks or weed stalks. Diam. usually 15–18 in., occasionally to 30 in., especially in wet areas. Height of nest varies with height of water in tidal areas; a nest in a dry location was 1–2 in. high; 1 exposed to occasional flooding was 5–6 in., and 1 frequently flooded 15–18 in.; apparently these were original dimensions and not a result of subsequent enlarging (Urner 1925). Nests in wet areas often act as bulky, floating rafts (Sealy 1967). For excellent comparative photos of nests in wet and dry sites, see R. Clark (1972a). The nest bowl diam. usually is 8–9 in., and the nest is shallow or nearly flat; sometimes it is lined with grasses. It is trampled by the young before they reach flight age and is frequently difficult to locate long before then.

In Orkney (Balfour 1962), some ♀ ♀ start to build 2–3 nests. Elsewhere abroad, the ♂ sometimes builds extra "cock nests" but does not line them. A ♂ that had apparently lost his mate built such a structure. A ♂ added material to an old nest; he had no mate but displayed frequently; later a ♀ joined him but took no interest in his nest (D. Watson 1977); cock nests are unheard of both in Orkney (Balfour 1962), and here. In Denmark, ♂ Marsh Harriers (*C. aeruginosus*) regularly build cock nests without lining them and use them as eating and resting places (Weis 1923); in New Zealand, this harrier uses them for "courtship feeding" (Baker-Gabb 1978).

Nesting associates   In Sask., 18 duck nests of at least 6 species were within 10–100 yd. of a harrier nest (Houston 1949); crow and 3 Mallard nests within 50-yd. radius (Furniss 1938); duck nest 10 ft. away (Eastgate 1944). In Man., 21 duck nests of 6 species within hunting ranges of 5 harrier pairs (Hecht 1951). A Pinnated Grouse and a harrier incubating 8 ft. apart (Preston, in R. Anderson 1907), and another nest with eggs 50 ft. from a harrier nest containing young (A. C. Fox 1938). None of these authors reported any antagonism.

Urner (1925) reported harriers nesting close to Short-eared Owls; the owls attacked the harriers but not vice versa. In Utah (Linner 1980), harriers and Short-eared owls nesting within several hundred yd. had overlapping ranges but hunted at different times and over different habitats. The owls tend to nest earlier than the harriers (R. Clark and Ward 1974). In Wis., breeding harriers and Short-eared Owls that share hunting ranges rob each other of prey (Berger 1958, Bildstein and Ashby 1975). In Sweden, where Northern and Marsh Harriers are intermixed as breeders, they maintain interspecific nesting territories (Johannesson 1975). In France, Delamain (1932) described an instance of talon grappling between neighboring Montagu's and Northern Harrier ♂ ♂, and Schipper (1978) reported numerous "aggressive encounters" among Northern, Marsh, and Montagu's breeding in the same area in Holland; individuals of the smaller species initiated most encounters. In Britain, the same 3 species sometimes nest in "neighbourly association" (D. Watson 1977). In Orkney, there have been instances of close nesting association of Northern Harriers with Merlins, Short-eared Owls, and Eurasian Kestrels (Watson).

Linsdale (1938) described how blackbirds (mainly Red-winged) attacked in swarms, even preventing harriers from settling on their nests. In cent. Wis., 3 ♂ harriers, watched for 57 hr., were harassed by mobbing passerines (mainly Red-winged Blackbirds) more than twice each hr. (Bildstein 1982b). They were mobbed more frequently when carrying prey than when flying without it and were never mobbed when perched. Laine (1928) found a harrier incubating 12 "prairie chicken" eggs in Sask.; later there were only 5 and apparently only 1 hatched; the ♂ harrier was on guard at each visit.

Laying dates   Evidently laying can be delayed if the weather suddenly turns cold or wet. In w. Europe, Schipper (1978) found that laying followed warming trends by about 5–6 days. In most of N. Am. breeding range, nests with eggs are reported in May and June, seldom with adequate data to determine peaks. The following is a compilation of data for nests with eggs. Fla., La., and Ark.—Apr. 14–May 6 (4 nests); N.C.— May 20; New Eng. and N.Y.—Apr. 30–June 14 (30); N.J. and Md.—Apr. 18–June 23 (33); New Bruns.—May (25 clutches) and June (6); Ohio—May 30 (4) and July 5 (1); Wis.—June (4, but see below); Ind. to Iowa and N.D.—Apr. 16–June 30 (118); Kans.—May 1–10 (peak); Nebr.—Apr. 24 (1); Mont.—May 26–27 (2 nests, 1st eggs); Sask.—May 7–June 26; Man.—May 2–July 13 (15); Idaho—May 19 (earliest?); Colo., Utah, and Wash.—Mar. 16–July 18 (34); B.C.—May 10–June 5. In Mich., dates for earliest and latest laying were May 5–20, 1942, and Apr. 26–May 9, 1948 (the Craigheads 1956). In cent. Wis., over 16 years, laying peaked in mid-May (Hamerstrom). In N.D., Hammond and Henry (1949) found the spread in starting dates for 1st and last nests in 3 successive years to be May 13–22 (31 nests), Apr. 26–

May 30 (16), and May 7–June 1 (13). In N.D. more recently, Duebbert and Lokemoen (1977) reported laying early May–late June (18). In Orkney, where birds arrive on nesting territories as early as Mar., laying begins in late Apr. and 90% of 856 eggs were laid in May (Balfour 1957). In Scotland, Ireland, and Holland, laying begins in early or mid-Apr. (D. Watson 1977). For additional Palearctic data, see Glutz von Blotzheim et al. (1971).

Clutch size Usually 4–6 with full range of 2–10. N. Am.: 1–7 eggs (3.7 ± 1.7) in 428 clutches, and 1–6 nestlings (3.3 ± 1.4) in 349 broods (Apfelbaum and Seelbach 1983). Late clutches tend to be smaller than early ones. For example, in New Bruns., May clutches av. 4.75 (25) while June clutches av. 4.0 (R. Simmons). New Eng.: 18 clutches (of 3), 4 (4), 67 (5), and 11 (6), av. 4.7 (F. Carpenter 1887). Of 60 N.D. nests, there were 3 eggs (1 nest), 4 (in 12), 5 (31), and 7 (1), for a mean of 5.0 ± 0.77. Thirteen completed clutches in Mich. av. 4.3 (the Craigheads 1956). Thirteen in Man. were of 4–7, av. 5.07 (R. Clark 1972a). In Wis., 42 clutches av. 4.5 eggs (Hamerstrom, in Hickey 1969). In Sask., 21 av. 4.18; in Alta., 11 av. 4.45 (Sealy 1967). In New Bruns., 19 av. 4.95 in a high-vole year, and 12 av. 4.25 in a low-vole year (R. Simmons). Comparable synchronous shifts in vole numbers and clutch size were reported from Norway (Barth 1964). There is a photograph of a 9-egg clutch in Bent (1937); two 10-egg clutches were reported from Mich. and Kans., 1 included 3 infertile eggs and the other was "probably laid by two females" (Baumgras 1942, Johnston 1960). Up to 12 eggs have been found in Scotland—either the product of 2 ♀♀ (Balfour) or a ♀ laying a repeat clutch in the original nest (L. Brown 1976). In the Orkneys, where mean clutch size varied considerably from year to year, for 288 clutches it was 4.6 eggs, of which 60.5% hatched and 61.9% of the chicks were reared to flight age; the mean number of young reared in 223 successful nests was 2.5 (Balfour and Cadbury 1975). In sw. Scotland, nests in forests were more successful than those on moorland (D. Watson 1977). In ne. Scotland, mean size of 27 complete 1st clutches was 4.70 ± 0.24 eggs (Picozzi 1978). As in various raptors, paired ovaries are by no means rare; only 1 is functional.

One egg each from 20 clutches from widespread N. Am. localities (3 provinces, 8 states) size length 46.32 ± 3.04 mm., breadth 36.31 ± 1.54; radii of curvature of ends 15.59 ± 0.62 and 11.85 ± 0.88; shape between elliptical and short subellipitcal, elongation 1.27 ± 0.052, bicone −0.040, and asymmetry +0.128 (F. W. Preston). Bent (1937) gave meas. of 84 eggs: av. 46.6 × 36.4 mm., extremes of length 39.5 and 53, of breadth 34 and 41.4. For N. Am., Schönwetter (1961) gave data on 96 eggs: length av. 46.4 mm. (41.4–53) and breadth 36.2 (34–39.5). His figures for 160 eggs of nominate *cyaneus* from widespread Palearctic localities are very similar—av. 46 × 35.6 mm. In the Orkneys, Balfour measured 901 eggs, mean dimensions being 46.3 × 35.6 mm. (D. Watson 1977). Runt eggs occur occasionally. The shell is smooth with little gloss, if any; color very pale bluish, soon bleaching to white and the shell soiled; about 10% of clutches (Bent 1937) in N. Am. show scattered spots of very pale browns. At Churchill, Man., eggs (number unstated) weighed an av. of 30.1 gm. (Heydweiller 1935). In Altea., 5 weighed 36.9–38.9 gm., av. 38, and 5 others 28.9–33.9, av. 32 (B. Baker and Walkinshaw 1946).

Laying interval One to 2 days (usually 2) between early eggs of a clutch; may increase up to 8 days between later ones. Laying spans: 5 eggs in 7–8 days; 6 eggs in 10, also 6 in at least 10, 11, and 14 days; 7 in 20–21; 8 in about 17 (various authors). Eggs are usually laid in the morning.

Nesting failure Most scattered reports in N. Am. attribute it to predation by mammals, occasionally by snakes, trampling by cattle, and to plowing, haying, and flooding. In Wis., a pair deserted a nest that had contained 5 eggs after a predator took 4 (Bildstein 1970a); the pair did not renest in the area. In Mich., a pair **renested** after early loss of a clutch; the new nest was 0.75 mi. from the former one and clutch reduced from 6 to 4; there was no renesting after destruction of 7 other nests (the Craigheads 1956). In N.D., nests begun in late May and in June are presumably renesting attempts (N. Hammond). Purportedly (L. and M. Walker 1941), a robbed ♀ laid 3 clutches in a season. In the Palearctic, D. Watson (1977) reported completion of a clutch in a makeshift nest within 3 days following loss of the 1st nest. When an entire clutch is destroyed, a 2d, smaller 1 generally is laid in about 2 weeks at a new site (in Bannerman 1956). In the Orkneys, 1st-year birds are less successful at hatching young (Balfour and Cadbury 1975); in Wis., they are about equally successful (Hamerstrom).

Incubation By the ♀, usually begins when the 2d egg is laid but sometimes not until the 4th; the laying span is often longer than the hatching span. The ♀ is a close sitter. Several authors state or imply that the ♂ spends some time on the clutch, but apparently this occurs only in unusual circumstances. In 1 instance the ♂ shared in incubating addled eggs after they should have hatched; in another the ♂ incubated several hrs. after the ♀ deserted the nest. In Orkney, Balfour (1957) reported that ♂ ♂ sometimes defend a nest for several days after abandonment by the ♀ and that they occasionally try to cover the eggs in her absence. In Minn., in 75 flushings from 10 nests during incubation, only the ♀ was seen (Breckenridge 1935). In a long series of observations in Utah at 13 nests in 4 years, only ♀ ♀ were seen at nests with eggs or young (Linsdale 1938). Males have been reported at nests—but not incubating (example: A. Allen 1929, photograph). Newell (1950) stated that the ♂ usually visited the nest between 0900 and 1000 hrs. during a 14-day laying span and "sometimes settled momentarily on the eggs." The ♀ frequently leaves the nest in early morning to preen nearby (Hamerstrom). There seem to be no data on attentive periods. In Mont., the ♀ incubated almost constantly after the last (7th) egg was laid (A. Saunders 1913).

Incubation period Thirty to 32 days (Breckenridge 1935, the Craigheads 1956, Hammond and Henry 1949), with 30 days/egg a useful generalization and shorter stated periods probably erroneous. A. Saunders (1913) found that 3 of 6 eggs had pipped 1 evening and that all 3 young had emerged the next morning. After these, other young hatched about 1, 3, and 6 days later. Wilhelm (1960) found that 6 eggs laid in 10 days hatched in an 11-day span. But a number of Palearctic sources report closer synchrony in hatching than laying. If the weather is bad during the hatching span, the ♀ is reluctant to leave her brood, which need continuous brooding (Watson 1977). F. Wilson (1927) watched a ♀ fly away with eggshells from a newly hatched nestling in 2 trips. Sometimes, however, eggshells are either not removed or are eaten there by the ♀. In Scotland, a ♀ incubated at least 52 days on eggs that never hatched (D. Watson 1977), and L. Brown (1976) reported incubation for up to 70 days.

Hatching dates   Can be calculated by adding 30–38 days to time of 1st laying or 30 to onset of incubation. Larger broods usually hatch asynchronously, but small ones sometimes on the same day. Hatching of an egg requires about 24 hr., sometimes as long as 48 (Balfour 1957, Sealy 1967).

Young   Most observations in N. Am., until recently, have been made during projects involving serious disturbance, such as food habits studies or photography without use of a blind. Young are born with eyes closed, but they open in a few hrs. (A. Saunders 1913). In Scotland, their av. wt. is 19.8 gm. (Scharf and Balfour 1971). First, 2d, and 3d-hatched nestlings weigh significantly more than 4th and 5th-hatched ones, and birds weighing less than 18 gm. suffer a 92% mortality rate (Picozzi 1980). R. Clark and Ward (1974) suggested that very young harriers are more precocial than are young Short-eared Owls, even though the owlets leave the nest more than 2 weeks sooner than the hawks. Urner (1925) reported that young 1–2 days old are active, fearless, and noisy; he was squealed at and approached by a bird, estimated to be 2 days old, using its wings and legs for locomotion. Vocalizations at this age include a high-pitched *cheek-cheek-cheek* (Sealy 1967) and a twitter (Linsdale 1938), the latter reported from young less than a day old. The hunger call of the young (discussed below) is reportedly an auditory releaser. Young spend almost all of their 1st 4–5 days under the ♀, especially in cold, wet weather. In W. Europe, most ♀ ♀ protect young from rain for their 1st 3–4 weeks (Schipper 1978). Young less than a week old are apparently unable to discriminate between humans and their parents, as evidenced by begging (Hecht 1951) and approach behavior. Some details of this period were given by the Craigheads (1939), as follows: To shade the young, the ♀ would sometimes spread her wings but usually used her foot, held limp so as not to hurt her young; she would push them all together into the middle of the nest bowl, then stand over them. When they were only a few days old, the mother would push her beak down into the nest and dig 2 holes, 1 on either side of her young, then step into these and squat down to brood. The nestlings were usually lying on her talons so that, when she flushed suddenly, she threw them out of the nest up to 1 ft. away; 1 was injured in this way. Lumsden (1981) watched a ♀ retrieving 2 less than 2-week-old young that had crawled about a ½ m. from the nest. They were picked up by the down and/or skin of upper neck in a "slow and deliberate" movement; see Lumsden for an excellent photograph of the ♀ carrying a nestling.

The ♂ brings all the food at first. Typically, prey has been beheaded, sometimes eviscerated and, if a bird, usually more or less plucked. Not until the young are 5+ days old does the ♀ make brief hunting flights, at first near the nest (under 500 m.), then farther away as the young develop. Should someone approach, young over 5 days old usually leave the nest, retreating to a nearby nook, of which there is sometimes more than 1 per nestling; retreats are extended gradually up to 10 ft. (Hecht 1951) or farther; some nestlings have been found 20 ft. or more from a nest along a path trampled by observers on earlier visits (K. Bildstein); they often spend much time far from the nest (Peabody 1900). The nest is cleaner as a result of the young using these hideouts, which, at least later on, are often crude platforms. The young also leave the nest to seek shade in covered portions of runways. Almost invariably, they return to the nest when the ♀ returns with food. In some instances, 1 of the newly developed platforms is used by the ♀ as a distribution center for prey (K. Bildstein). Young at wet sites are less likely to leave the nest before they can fly (R. Clark 1972a). During the 1st several weeks before they are strong enough to stand, they sit on their tarsi, but by age 9–10 days they throw themselves onto their backs and strike with beak and talons when approached (Shelley 1935, Sealy 1967), using their wings for balance. Urner (1925) suggested that young ♂ ♂ were more "courageous" than ♀ ♀, attacking intruders more readily. F. Wilson (1927) described an incident in which a ♀ returned from hunting; her older young came from the weeds back to the nest, but the younger ones, being slower, were grasped by the ♀ with her beak just back of their heads and replaced in the nest, 1 by 1, with much squealing. Compare with Lumsden (1981).

In 7 days the young are about 3 times as large as when hatched; at about 16 days the legs and cere begin to change from light pinkish to yellow (A. Saunders 1913). Breckenridge (1935) found that early in life ♀ ♀ are larger than ♂ ♂ and have heavier bones—especially in legs and feet. (This now is well known; details in Scharf and Balfour 1971, Picozzi 1980.) By 3 weeks the young sometimes stand on their toes instead of resting on their tarsi (A. Allen 1929).

Weight In N.Y., Munoff (1963) studied the occupants of 6 nests and gave wts. for 4 individuals, sexes not indicated: age 1 day 21–27 gm. (av. 25), 7 days 87–108 (102), 14 days 247–312 (273), and 2 young at 28 days 423 and 597 (av. 510). His descriptive data show that beaks grow fastest in 1st week, wt. gain is most rapid in 2d, flight feathers grow most rapidly in 3d, and tail most rapidly in 4th—as others have noted. Most useful, however, are studies in the Orkneys by Scharf and Balfour (1971) and Picozzi (1980), the former with data from Wis. added by Hamerstrom. The size difference between the sexes, evident early, never obscures the size difference caused by asynchronous hatching. Weight differences in the sexes may be significant at day 15 (Picozzi). See both papers for full discussions of the development of sexual dimorphism in early life. Almost always, the lightest birds (♂ ♂) with well-developed wings **attained flight** 1st—between 31 and 34 days; all but 3 of 21 records of ♀ ♀ were between 35 and 38 days. It is of interest that the heavier ♀ ♀ were too heavy to fly before their 35th day; that is, there is a wt. loss before they are on the wing. A ♀ is often 100 gm. heavier than a ♂ at 1st flight (D. Watson 1977). At flying age, ♂ wt. is about 75% that of ♀ wt. (Picozzi). Young nestlings seldom recover from a period of wt. loss and weakness (Scharf and Balfour).

The following data on 3 captive young (Shelley 1935), after they had been taken at 10–11 days and put in a fenced yard, are confirmed by recent studies in the wild. Appetite was greatest during the period of greatest feather production, 2–4 weeks of age. Having obtained a morsel, "one would cover it with the wings, scold and complain, neck hunched for a possible fray, and at an opportune moment clutch the meat in the talons and carry it to a distance." Having lost innumerable feathers from attacks by the older bird, the younger ones learned to wait, complaining, until the former had gotten food and satisfied its wants. But soon they learned to spar back. At 3 weeks they began to tear up their own food and preferred to eat separately. Three pellets appeared within 24 hrs. after capture, all containing food obtained before capture. The 1st pellet from food obtained in captivity appeared more than 48 hrs. later. Five days after capture, a pellet appeared containing stones (the "rangle" of falconers) taken before capture, as well as later food. Young took stones for about 2 weeks after this and then ceased as bones apparently substituted for these. When about to eject a pellet, a bird would sit still and appear listless. Young were known to eat just before and after ejecting a pellet, which occurred early in the morning. A pellet usually contained a divisory line between items fed at different hours the previous day. Young 2 weeks old carefully watched black ants. After feeding, a young bird often grasped its own toes in an apparent search for food. Frequently, when a nestling's wing crossed its line of vision, it would grasp and bite it viciously. The nestlings soon learned what human whistling at various pitches and tones meant and responded accordingly. At age 3 weeks they began to exercise their wings by beating them as if in flight; thus, they could raise their bodies, but not their toes, clear of the ground. This was repeated many times daily. A variant was to run along the ground beating the wings above the back. They first perched successfully on branches at 4½ weeks. They seldom drank water when provided, but once they were flying out of the yard it became their habit to alight at a stream to drink after meals. When bathing there, "they invariably waded in even with the wings and dipped and ducked and spattered the wings."

During incubation and early brood life, the ♂ parent typically does almost all **food catching** and delivering. In 28 hrs. of observation at 2 nests, Breckenridge (1935) found that ♂♂ captured prey 43 times, ♀♀ 8 times. More recent data align with this. In Wis. (Bildstein), ♂♂ provided all of the food during incubation, but by the time the young were about 2 weeks old, ♀♀ were providing more than a third. By the time young attained flight (about 30–35 days), ♀♀ were providing more than half of it and, by the time they were dispersing from the nest, about 80%. The 8 nests varied considerably. Several ♀♀ supplied most, if not all, prey from about 25 days posthatching, while at several nests ♂♂ supplied about half almost until dispersal. Overall, monogamous ♂♂ tended to supply food for the nestlings longer than polygamous ♂♂, who often ceased prey deliveries to less favored nests. The same is reported in the Palearctic (Schipper 1978, Balfour and Cadbury 1979). In a number of instances in Wis., this led to ♀♀ attempts to intercept their mates while the latter were carrying prey to another ♀ and to piracy attempts between ♀♀ mated to the same ♂. Similar piratical behavior occurred among harem ♀♀ in New Bruns. (R. Simmons). In ne. Scotland (Picozzi 1980), the proportion of prey provided by ♂♂ decreased only slightly during the nestling stage, but in Holland, Schipper (1973) reported a dramatic decrease as nestlings grew, and in Orkney, 2 ♂ ceased to bring food at 22 days posthatching. A ♀ evidently raised 2 young by herself, at least from 5 days posthatching (Hecht 1951), and this also has occurred in the Palearctic. Caution: as ♂♂ sometimes transfer prey to ♀♀ far from the nest, observations may underestimate the role of the ♂ as a provider of prey late in the season.

When the ♂ fetches food, the ♀ usually flies up to seize it with her talons after he drops it, usually within 100 m. of the nest. In some instances, especially around hatching and soon after, during inclement weather, a ♀ may only jump several ft. above the nest to accept the transfer (D. Watson 1977). In 160 hrs. of observation at 3 nests with young, the ♂ landed at or near the nest with food 8 times compared with 146 landings by the ♀; if the ♂ arrived and found the ♀ absent he circled over the nest and

called for some minutes before landing; he left the food and immediately departed (Breckenridge 1935). Others have similar reports. In Scotland (D. Watson 1977), sometimes when the young are large, the ♀ seemingly ignores the ♂'s arrival, and he drops prey directly to the young. If the ♀ is killed or abandons the nest during this time, the ♂ may continue to deliver prey but does not feed the young (Hecht 1951, S. Thompson and Cornely 1982). This may result in accumulation of considerable prey when nestlings are too young to feed themselves (A. Beske). Selleck and Glading (1943) found that, if the ♀ was removed, the ♂ redoubled his efforts to keep the brood well fed in each of 3 cases. Based on 10 nests, Breckenridge concluded that the function of the ♂, once the young are hatched, was to hunt for food and to guard the nest from a nearby perch when the ♀ was feeding chicks and during her short absences to hunt; the ♀ guarded the nest from perches the remainder of the time and fed the young. Recent Wis. data are similar. While ♀ ♀ spent more than 80% of the time within 500 m. of the nest until the young were 25 days old, ♂ ♂ spent only about half the time there during incubation and very little time nearby thereafter. Females spent most of their time near the nest perched on fence posts less than 50 m. from their young (Bildstein). Several observers report that the ♂ may be chased by the ♀ from the nest vicinity in an apparent effort to encourage hunting. In Wis., 3 ♂ ♂ were chased from perches near nests 14 times in 45 hrs. by their then-incubating mates (Bildstein 1979a).

Hamerstrom (in Hickey 1969) described the classic **aerial transfer of prey** from ♂ to ♀ as occurring "with the ♂ flying high and dropping the prey to the ♀ who catches it in the air beneath him." It is not always so. When less-favored harem ♀ ♀ intercept prey-carrying mates, they may snatch prey from the ♂'s talons (Hecht 1951). Hamerstrom (in Hickey 1969) suggested that heavy pesticide levels may induce low altitude talon-to-talon transfers. Linsdale (1938) noted that extra-large prey was transferred at higher altitude than smaller prey. A variation in the transfer technique was for the ♀ to circle above the ♂ and dive straight down and take the prey released by the ♂ just before she passed him. In Wis., some transfers may occur over a km. from the nest (Bildstein), and the same may apply in the Palearctic (D. Watson 1977). If the ♂ brings prey in rapid succession, or if both parents have caught it simultaneously, the ♀ will sometimes accept another quarry while already clutching one. In the Palearctic, Picozzi (1980) reported that a characteristic call by the ♀ accompanies each transfer.

On receiving the prey, the ♀ will prepare it (if the ♂ has not already done so), return to the nest with it, and feed the young; sometimes she first eats a portion (Selleck and Glading 1943). The Craigheads (1939) described the feeding of very young harriers. The ♀ tore off tiny pieces of meat with her beak; then she turned her head sideways, opened her beak slightly, and let the young bird take the proffered morsel. If she tore off an entire leg, she would often start to feed it to a nestling and then, instead, swallow it. She always ate gizzards, feet, and pieces of skin and feathers. At about 3 weeks, ♀♀ fed roughage to the young and pellets first appeared. Urner (1925) found the nest to be scrupulously clean the 1st 3 weeks; afterwards, the young usually spent much time away from it, and less care was taken about sanitation. Jewett et al. (1953) stated that a nest with very young nestlings was clean; Shelley (1935) wrote that a nest with young 10 or 11 days old was "filthy with excrement and overrun with carrion beetles"; at this age the young discharged excreta to a distance of 2 ft.

Evidently, until the young are fairly well grown, the ♀ either eats the prey remains at the nest or removes them. Urner (1925) noted that, at about 4 weeks, pellets of fur and feathers with some bones began to appear at a nest. A. Allen (1929) reported this at 2–3 weeks; the ♀ may have removed them earlier. Wilhelm (1960), on the other hand, collected 63 pellets in daily trips to an Ark. nest for 33 days that included laying and incubation periods and that ended when 5 young were 1–9 days old.

In Orkney (Picozzi 1980), and allowing for daily fluctuations, 2–3 week old siblings received relatively equal amounts of food without regard to age or sex. Balfour and MacDonald (1970) reported that in a brood of 4 the quickest young often got food and the largest one got more than the others; when the oldest one was able to tear its own food, the ♀ sometimes distributed food among the remaining siblings only. Since the quickest individual is only infrequently the most recently fed sibling (at least among older nestlings and fledglings), prey distribution may be more equitable in the long run than is apparent. Hamerstrom (in Hickey 1969) suggested that a particular hunger call and display of white down of the least recently fed young might enhance its liklihood of being fed.

Adults leaving 2 nests in Minn. followed 1 of 3 fairly definite loops over about a sq. mi. of surrounding country (Breckenridge 1935). Definite flight paths to and from the nest were also noted by Hecht (1951). Breeders seemingly range over a limited portion of their hunting grounds at a time but work that portion thoroughly, going again and again over the same route. This results in a particular prey species composing a significant portion of the diet for a short period and then possibly not recurring (Errington and Breckenridge 1936).

A pair of breeding harriers in Wis. (Hammerstrom and De La Ronde Wilde 1973) abandoned their young but remained on territory after being radio-tagged. Their daily cruising range covered 1¼ × 1¾ mi., and within this each bird seemed to have its preferred hunting grounds. The ♀ was seen in the ♂'s hunting area only once, and the ♂ was flushed 4 times in hers. They flew more in A.M. than P.M. They roosted apart— up to 1.2 mi.—and neither ever used the same roost twice. Night roosts were in grasses and forbs with a scattering of *Spiraea*. In daytime they ceased flying for a while and went to day roosts. The ♂ preferred low brush or tall *Spiraea*. Daytime roosts seemed to be more open than nighttime ones.

Bildstein, who followed the hunting behavior of 3 ♂ ♂ and a ♀ at 3 nests for a total of 85 hr., found them using certain areas near the nest significantly more than others. The birds tended to depart in the same direction whence they had just returned with prey.

As the young become older, in some instances the parents catch larger prey. In Utah (Linner 1980), the rate of **prey delivery** increased through the 1st 5 weeks, decreasing markedly by the 8th week when the young were departing the area. Picozzi (1978) reported a similar increase through the nesting period in ne. Scotland. In Wis. (Bildstein) the rate of prey delivery was reduced by half during the 7th week; Breckenridge (1935) and Errington and Breckenridge (1936) described a "weaning" period coinciding with onset of hunting by the young.

Feeding rate In Minn., at a nest in which 5 young hatched and 3 attained flight was from 4 times daily at age 8 days to a peak of 24 times at 23 days, dropping to 6 at 34; total number of feeding in preflight stage was estimated at 388 and wt. of food 63 lb. (Breckenridge 1935). At 1 month, A. Allen (1929) reported that at least 3 voles or small birds per young/day were required. A captive young ♀ maintained in seminatural fashion outdoors consumed an av. of 112 gm. of small mammals and passerines daily during her 4th and 5th weeks and an av. of 102 gm. in 6th and 7th weeks before beginning to hunt for herself (Bildstein and A. Beske). At 4 Scottish nests in 130 hr. of observation, av. number of prey brought per chick in a 14-hr. hunting day was 3.2 (D. Watson 1977), very close to Schipper's (1973) data for Holland and Linner's (1980) for Utah. Different findings may reflect differences in prey and in ambient temperatures. Picozzi's (1978) impressions were the same as Schipper's—that the number of young that survive is, ultimately, related to number of prey provided.

Hunting Both sexes appear to hunt throughout the day (Picozzi 1980, R. Simmons, K. Bildstein), and, while some observers note A.M. and P.M. peaks and midday lulls (Hamerstrom, Watson 1977), others have found no peaks (Picozzi 1980) or, sometimes, a tendency toward a slight midday peak (Bildstein). Errington (1932b) found that the best times to find food in gullets of chicks were about 0900–1000 hrs. and an hr. before dark. In a multiyear multisite study in Holland, Schipper (1973) reported a variety of peaks in activity depending on both year and location that he attributed to the various activity periods of major prey species taken. Rate of prey delivery to young diminishes in rainy weather and, to a lesser extent, on windy days. Rates vary considerably from day to day, especially late in the season, when they may drop to zero for a day at nests with a few older young (Bildstein). In some instances, as many as 5 voles may be brought to a large brood in less than an hr. (Bildstein, R. Simmons); Simmons reported 2 deliveries in 2 min. at a nest in New Bruns.

Small rodents, young passerines, and, to a lesser extent, young galliform birds are most frequently reported as the main food of dependent young (examples: Errington and Breckenridge 1936, Randall 1940, Hecht 1951). In Utah, Linsdale (1938) found that food in the nesting season was almost entirely lizards and mammals. In Idaho, they switched almost entirely from rodents in alfalfa fields to lizards in sagebrush once alfalfa exceeded 46 cm. in height (J. Martin). In Calif., prey delivered by ♂ ♂ included passerines, quail, rabbits, and small rodents in that order (Selleck and Glading 1943). Some individuals evidently have their **preferences.** At 2 nests in Man. ½ mi. apart and in similar habitat, mammals made up 85% of 34 items at 1 nest and 47% of 32 at another; blackbirds did not appear at the 1st, but 7 were recovered from young at the 2d (Hecht 1951). Of 3 families studied on a sq. mi. in Minn., 3 of 5 pheasants and all domestic chickens caught were taken by a single pair (Breckenridge 1935). Selleck and Glading (1943) reported substantial internest differences in Calif. Similar prey types are reported from the Palearctic; ♂ ♂ tend to supply the more agile species (Schipper 1973, Picozzi 1978). In N. Am. and abroad, shifts in prey types taken through the breeding season indicate little preference for certain prey, with the most vulnerable types taken in large numbers. Pellets from young harriers are of aid in qualitative, but not quantitative, work (Errington 1932b). Based on 19 pellets from a captive young bird fed 22 days, Glading et. al. (1943) found that many items fed were not found in the pellets even as traces (compare with Rough-legged Hawk).

After the young are on the wing They continue for about 2–3 weeks to use the nest and nearby areas as a base of activity. Siblings tend to remain rather close to one another until just before they depart (Beske 1978, Bildstein). As soon as they can fly, they spend considerable time on elevated perches, and availability of such to a certain extent determines the location of young relative to the nest. As soon as they fly well, they play on the ground and practice diving at clumps of grass, clods of dirt, sticks, and sometimes insects; they chase one another in the air. L. Snyder and Logier (1931) described this period well. In Wis., Beske (1978) followed the movements of 7 radio-tagged young from 3 nests. All stayed close (under 1.4 km.) until just before they left the area, and they hunted very little—if at all. During their 1st week of flight none ventured farther than 91 m. from the nest. Usually they roosted within 18 m. of each other and within 800 m. of the nest. A Great Horned Owl killed 1 of them; 5 of the 7 left the area about 3 weeks after 1st flying, but 1 took 7 weeks. At least 4 departed alone. There was no indication that parents drove them away. Bildstein spent 800 hrs. watching flying young at 12 nests in Wis.; his impressions follow: The first flights are usually vertical springs several m. into the air as the parent returns with food. When the young first fly they tend to travel in short loops that end back at the nest area. Many of these occur as the ♀ returns with prey. Within several days of their 1st flights the young spend considerable portions of the day resting on elevated perches—usually fence posts and low bushes. In this period the parent normally returns to the nest with prey, and any young not already there return rapidly, sometimes uttering the begging call. Several days thereafter 1 or more of the siblings fly out to meet the parent (♀ usually) and escort it back to the nest or receive prey from it in an aerial transfer, as between adults. Later, all prey is transferred aerially and a parent rarely returns to the nest but frequently flies low over it. If a young bird misses or drops the prey and fails to recover it before it hits ground, the adult sometimes attempts to retrieve it. As a result of aerial transfers, location of the young tends to drift in the predominant direction of the parents' arrival. If, after delivering prey, the parent remains near the nest, it may be chased by unfed young. Parents almost always deliver prey to the 1st young encountered and very rarely return to the nest with prey if intercepted on the way. Recently fed individuals are less aggressive in pursuit of the parent; on several occasions a sibling pirated prey from another. Although there was considerable daily variation, prey appeared to be distributed relatively equally, and the most determined (hungriest?) chick usually received it. As Beske (1978) also noted, young do not follow their parents on hunting flights. In fact, the young fly very little during this period, and before their departure they are in the air less than 20% of daylight time; very few have had a flight exceeding 10 min. Flight duration can increase dramatically, however, on warm sunny days when some young soar. The same is reported from Ireland (Doran 1977). Throughout the period, young ♂ ♂ precede ♀ ♀ in age in occurrence of almost all activities and depart from the area several days earlier. Young with more than 1 sibling tend to develop faster than those with 1 or no siblings. No Juv. was seen catching vertebrate prey, although several apparently ate insects and chased small birds. Beske (1978) and Linner (1980) also reported a lack of prey captures, but Shelley (1935) mentioned a possible bird kill by a 5-week-old. When young depart they are receiving less food less regularly, but some are fed to the last day. The ♀ remains protective throughout and on occasion escorts foreign Juvs. and other raptors from the nest vincinity. A fledged young was killed by a Redtail, and another was eaten by an unknown raptor.

At this stage the young are still somewhat awkward in flight and are far from expert at making a living, as indicated by their frequent hunting throughout daylight hrs. while, at the same time, adults appear to be satisfying their own needs without much effort. Although none of the young harriers that Beske (1978) followed from the nest returned there, 1 of Shelley's hand-reared birds departed his hack site at about 8 weeks only to return 6 days later injured and emaciated. Carrion, large insects, and snakes are important to new-flying young (Errington and Breckenridge 1936). Cameron (1907) described a 10-oz. young attempting to disable a 1-lb. domestic chicken by pecking its head and striking it on the back with its feet while flying above the bird and following it around (compare with panic hunger of the Golden Eagle).

There is, as yet, no direct observation in N. Am. of a larger nestling killing a smaller nestmate, but several observers report siblings pecking the head of a smaller young that eventually died. A dead nestling is regarded as food and may be eaten. Several authors note **reduction in brood size** without adequate explanation. Hecht (1951) reported siblings eating a nestling, and Breckenridge (1935) saw a ♀ pick up a dead one, dismember it, and feed it to the remaining young. He felt that late-hatched, hence smaller, young could not survive in competition with older siblings. A. Allen (1929) reported 2 young eaten by 4 nestmates up to 5 days older. Hagen (in Bannerman 1956) noted 3 cases of "cannibalism" in Norway, either from partly eaten young in nests or from evidence in pellets. From the Orkneys, Balfour (1957) reported that a weakling in the nest, usually the last-hatched, almost invariably dies and may be eaten. Evidence for and against cannibalism was summarized by D. Watson (1977), and instances of it are on record in the Palearctic. In view of size discrepancy among broodmates, it would seem astonishing that the tiniest ever survives (Hamerstrom). Hamerstrom stated (in Hickey 1969) that a special call, the "distress cheep," is probably a survival mechanism; it causes older nestlings to scuttle away as though they cannot abide the sound. The mere presence of a very young harrier does not have this

286

effect. Balfour and MacDonald (1970) knew about this but did not observe it in Orkney.

Age at first flight   Young fly short distances at 30 days and well at 35 (Hammond and Henry 1949); 30–35 days (Urner 1925); av. 31 days (the Craigheads 1956); they learn to fly in their 5th week (Breckenridge 1935). In Scotland, the period varied 29–38 days, the shortest possibly due to disturbance; earliest was July 1 and latest Aug. 17 (Watson 1977). Males attain flight 2–3 days earlier than ♀♀, which are larger and develop more slowly, as is known from the Orkneys (Balfour 1957), where a ♀ first flew at 42 days while ♂♂ av. 32 days, and from Wis.—at 8 nests ♂♂ av. 29 and ♀♀ 32 (Bildstein). Singletons, possibly because they are overfed and hence too heavy, fly later (Scharf and Balfour 1971, Bildstein). Urner (1925) flushed newly flying young from a nest and was attacked by the ♂ parent; 2 young followed the ♂ in his attack, although they could not vocalize as he did. In Minn., until the young were about 8 weeks old, they spent nights in vicinity of the nest; then families seemed to break up and the young started out on their own (Breckenridge 1935, Beske—see above). This contradicts A. K. Fisher (1893), who, almost certainly influenced by Audubon, stated that several families unite and migrate. There is no recent evidence of this in N. Am., although young birds sometimes beg for food from nonparental adults through at least their 1st winter.

Breeding success   In N.D., eggs hatched in 72% of 60 nests in 3 years, annual figures being 66%, 70%, and 82%. Of 303 eggs laid, 58% hatched, annual figures 60%, 57%, and 53%. On av., over a 3-year period, each of 60 nests of 5.05 ± 0.77 eggs produced 4.07 ± 1.10 young less than 6 days old (43 nests) and 3.18 ± 1.08 young 30–35 days old (11 nests). Assuming no mortality among breeding adults and a different pair for each nest, the 3-yr. av. adult-to-flying young ratio was 1:1 (Hammond and Henry 1949). In a more recent study in N.D. and S.D. (Duebbert and Lokemoen 1977), eggs hatched in 48% of 27 nests. In Mich., 23 eggs produced 18 young of which 16 survived to fly in 1942, and all 33 eggs failed to hatch in 1948 (the Craigheads 1956). In Wis., in 99 nests in 1959–1965, at least 1 young survived to flight age in 65 nests, and total number of flying young was at least 212 (Hamerstrom, in Hickey 1969). On another area in Wis., 1963–1974, 59 of 79 nests hatched at least 1 egg, and 219 young attained flight (Follen 1975). In a 20-nest study in Wash., 27 young flew from the 6 successful nests (P. Thompson-Hanson). In Alta. and Sask., 25 of 40 eggs in 11 nests hatched and 15 birds attained flight (Sealy 1967). For a few nests in N.Y., see Munoff (1963), and in Utah, see Linner (1980).

Abroad, in a 101-nest study in Holland, 55% of eggs laid produced flying young (Schipper 1978). At 299 nests in Orkney, 1944–1956, 28% of eggs laid produced flight-age birds (Balfour 1957). In the same area, 1965–1973, at 223 nests, success increased to 37%, possibly because of fairer weather (Balfour and Cadbury 1975). Also from Orkney, Picozzi (1980) reported that in 1975–1977, 67% of 269 hatched eggs at 79 nests produced flying young. During the same study, survival was better in broods of 1–3 than 4–6, with 57% of in-nest deaths occurring within the 1st 5 days. During 17 of 25 years of study in Orkney, more ♀♀ than ♂♂ were produced—1.15♀:1♂—which differs significantly from 1:1 (Picozzi 1980). In ne. Scotland, young hatched in 28 of 35

287

nests and 57% attained flight; 17 nests contained 32 ♂ and 21 ♀; the mean number of flying young for 19 successful nests was 3.11 ± 0.26 (Picozzi 1978). In sw. Scotland, 34% of eggs resulted in flying young, forest nests tended to be more successful than moorland ones, and 33 of 52 flying young were ♀ ♀ (D. Watson 1977). In Norway, 142 young attained flight from 287 eggs laid in 69 nests (Barth 1964).

Some factors affecting nesting success In a 16-year intensive study in cent. Wis., harriers bred more successfully when meadow voles were plentiful: 83% of nests hatched at least 1 young during vole highs and 62% during lows (Hamerstrom 1979). Yet, in this study, number of young attaining flight per successful nest did not vary with vole fluctuations. An abundance of voles appears to trigger increased polygamy in cent. Wis. (Burke 1979). Number of young attaining flight is higher during vole highs in Orkney (Balfour 1957, Balfour and Cadbury 1975), sw. Scotland and Norway (D. Watson 1977), and Holland (Schipper 1978). Variation has also been linked to mating systems: polygamous nests produce fewer flying young than monogamous ones both in Wis. (Burke) and Orkney (Balfour). In Orkney (Balfour) and sw. Scotland (Watson), but not in Wis. (Hamerstrom), 1st-year birds have lower reproductive success than older ones. Cold, wet weather (Balfour 1957, Scharf and Balfour 1971, Schipper 1978) and snake, gull, and mammalian predation (Sealy 1967, Schipper 1978, Bildstein 1979a) also affect nesting success; Schipper reported a seasonal decline in Holland. In stressful situations the last young hatched usually is the 1st to succumb.

KEITH L. BILDSTEIN AND J. BERNARD GOLLOP

SURVIVAL Earlier N. Am. studies indicated that perhaps a third of the young that attained flight still were alive a year later. The percentage was much higher for older birds. There was enormous mortality from shooting, which now is both illegal and considerably out of fashion; hence, future studies will point more strongly to other influences affecting longevity.

In our area Near Madison, Wis., 47 nestlings were banded in 1931. Omitting 1 killed under experiment, there were 16 recoveries; all but 1 of these birds were dead in less than 8 months—6 killed at nests, others elsewhere. Nine were shot. Details in G. Wagner (1933).

Of 150 young banded at Lower Souris Refuge, N.D., 1937–1939 mainly, there were 12 recoveries 1937–1945; at least 10 had been shot, 9 before the end of 1940.

Hickey (1952) analyzed extant N. Am. data to some time in 1949. Of 102 birds shot in their 1st year of life, about 80% were killed in the first 5 months, with about 25% of mortality occurring between flight attainment and Aug. 1. The mortality rate was of the order of 60% the 1st year, and mean adult rate, based on a small sample, was 30%.

In Mont., the Craigheads (1956) suggested an 88% mortality of young birds and 12% annual rate for adults. They attributed heavy losses in the 1st months to shooting, starvation, malnutrition, and highway mortality.

The oldest bird in the wild thus far reported in N. Am., was 16 years, 5 months, based on recovery of a bird shot in Ont. that had been banded during its first year in Ohio (Clapp et al. 1982).

Elsewhere The long study in the Orkneys was reported on by Balfour and Cadbury (1975). Based on banding recoveries, only 32% of young that attained flight still were alive a year later. There was a 70% annual survival rate thereafter. This would indicate few birds surviving over 5 years, yet of breeding birds of known age banded since 1968, 42% of ♀ ♀ were at least 5 years old and a few aged 9 and 10 were present. The data also showed a low proportion of yearlings and of 2d-year ♀ ♀, which supports the presumption that social behavior may be influencing age-structure (younger birds excluded from breeding). As to causes of mortality, there was a "strong bias" toward human agency in various forms.

Table 8 in D. Watson (1977) showed mortality after attaining flight of 62% in 1st year, 11% in 2d, 9% in 3d, and much lower thereafter to age 12–13 (end of table). This included, and was a continuation of, Balfour's work. Later, mean estimated annual survival rates of observed marked birds aged 0–2 years were ♂ 14% and ♀ 29%, and for 2–6 years, 72% and 90% respectively (Picozzi 1984).   KEITH L. BILDSTEIN

HABITS   *Circus cyaneus hudsonius* of N. Am. unless otherwise stated. Our only raptor to habitually seek small and medium-sized prey by low-level lineal scanning; in this respect, and in manner of flight, it superficially resembles the Turkey Vulture (F. Beebe 1974), which has a sense of smell. Its search-pause-pounce technique is reminiscent of a fox; its closest avian counterpart as a hunter is the Short-eared Owl, which flies in silence and perhaps has even more sensitive hearing. Hunting flight is buoyant, sustained, and generally less than 3 m. above vegetation; the bird is intent on its search, flying over the terrain and, now and again, doubling back to reinvestigate a likely spot—as though it had second thoughts after scanning there the 1st time. Keeping the hawk in sight is not always easy; it may disappear briefly behind a bush or down over the crest of a knoll. As it goes up a slope, its flight often seems to become slightly labored, and the bird reminds one of a child's kite that has temporarily lost its sustaining airflow. Then, having reached the apex, the harrier seems almost to glide over the downward slope with a sudden increase in speed—again, somewhat like a child's kite plunging toward earth.

♀ Juv.

♂ Def. Basic

facial ruff
(as in owls)

In N. Am. (Bildstein 1982b) and Europe (Wassenich 1968, Schipper et al. 1975), distinct flight types are known. Although harriers do not typically hunt while soaring or gliding, they engage in both during migration and sometimes employ both when transporting prey. They are known to soar to great heights, as when mates are together in spring and as when young, soon after they can fly, soar together on fair days. Few of our diurnal raptors are as independent of rising air currents. At times harriers take advantage of a prairie wind and the vagaries of air currents to swoop and soar and sail with remarkable skill—as well described by Mrs. F. M. Bailey (1915, or in Bent 1937). They also are accomplished at fairly high and steady flapping flight, without zigzagging, as frequently on migration. This transect flight follows a rather straight line, often more than 5 m. above vegetation, with fewer than 5 sharp turns/min. It is typical of birds returning to and departing from communal roosts in winter and nests in summer. It is seldom used in hunting. Quartering, the flight type most often associated with hunting, can be characterized as flying to and fro over short distances, with more than 5 sharp turns/min. Despite numerous descriptions of quartering as a rather "systematic search for its prey" (e.g., Bent 1937), detailed observations over 4 winters in s. Ohio revealed that in most instances less than 20% of a field is hunted (Bildstein 1978). Many harriers that at first glance might appear to be systematically quartering fields (i.e., methodically searching most or all of the area) are in fact following prescribed hunting routes over only certain portions of it. These may be traversed repeatedly several times a day for several weeks; many include lengthy spans of border following. This is especially apparent during nesting (Breckenridge 1935, Doran 1976, Bildstein). Border following, an important but sometimes overlooked hunting flight type, is characterized as "powered flight within 5 m. of land type and/or vegetation type edges, such as fence rows, ditches, ditch banks, or roadsides" (Bildstein 1982b). In Europe, several authors report its frequent use by birds—in some instances at least, especially adult ♂ ♂—hunting along ridges and vegetation discontinuities in apparent efforts to surprise mobile prey. In N. Am., adult ♀ ♀ and Juv. birds of both sexes wintering in s. Ohio engaged in border following more than twice as often as quartering. In adult ♂ ♂ the ratio was skewed even more at 4:1 in favor of border following. In the same study, soaring and gliding composed less than 10% of air time (details: Bildstein 1978). The above flight types are quite distinct and, with little effort, easily distinguished.

Here (Bildstein 1978) and in Europe (Wassenich 1968, Schipper et al. 1975) ♂ ♂ tend to fly lower and faster than ♀ ♀. In Europe, harriers have been noted to fly lower and faster over sparse vegetation and to change flight speed more frequently with increasing wind speed.

Harriers quartering dense vegetation, especially in a mild breeze, often hover persistently. After quartering for some time they seem to stall in midair and drop lower, at the same time reaching down with their legs. Often they foot-stab in an apparent effort to force prey from cover. Such actions may last up to several min. or until the quarry makes the usually fatal mistake of attempting to break into the open. This technique is used against songbirds in brushy vegetation and rails hiding in wracks of floating detritus. Some individuals use the technique regularly. In S.C. salt marshes, harriers often fly from one stranded detrital wrack to another, hovering over and sometimes landing on them in what appears to be an attempt to flush prey (Bildstein). This harrier does indeed harry its prey. Seldom is there pursuit; if flying quarry is not taken immediately it is usually passed up, and the hunter moves on. Harriers often appear to "test" their prey by approaching and flushing them. Those unable to withdraw quickly are taken, while others are not pursued, as noted in Europe (Tamisier 1970). First-year birds are more likely to extend pursuits than older ones. In N.H. in Sept., a harrier (said to be ♀) chased a Belted Kingfisher in an erratic course some 200 yd. over water and then gave up after at least 5 attempts to strike it down (Perine 1931). An 800-m. unsuccessful chase after a small bird in Kent, England (Hodgson and Wyatt 1979), was exceptional.

Errington (1938) stated that the harrier's flight is slow enough that most birds can escape or even annoy it with safety but that it is "capable of remarkably quick maneuvering at close range." He stated that its grasp is a weak one for a large appearing raptor, the talons being adapted for seizing and holding rather than piercing. Thus, much actual killing is done by the beak, often incidental to eating the prey as the hawk feeds in the region of the neck and throat. Voles and small birds usually die quickly from talon punctures and beak wounds, but larger prey may remain alive longer until infliction of injuries causes death.

Because harriers fly low, they sometimes appear to overfly their prey before sighting it. Their momentum carries them beyond striking range and they double back to pounce—the resulting hook pounce is preceded by a ¾ turn of radius less than 1.5 m. Harriers also pounce without changing direction as well as after hovering. A 4th type of pounce, much slower and deliberate, is used on Microtinae nests. In 600 pounces over 4 winters in s. Ohio, harriers employed the 1st 3 types only 25% of the time but had higher success when they slow pounced on nests; 18% for hook pounces, 11% for hover pounces, 13% for straight ones, and 4% for nest pounces other than slow ones. Adult ♂♂ hook pounced less and nest pounced more than ♀♀ (Bildstein 1978).

There can be no doubt that this harrier's hearing, which is very acute, as Shelley (1935) noted in captives, is an integral part of the hunting pattern. Hunting "mouse" (vole) nests, first described by Rolfe (1897, or in Bent 1937), who watched an individual pick up 7 nests along a 2-mi. flight, appears to be an example of harriers using acoustic cues to locate prey. Rice (1982), in a series of elegant laboratory and field experiments, has confirmed this view. Harriers have an angular acoustic resolution along the horizontal axis of 2°, which is within the range of that known for owls and at least 4 times as great as that of "typical diurnal raptors." In the field, harriers are able to "locate vole vocalizations (squeaks) accurately and attack prey successfully without the aid of visual or olfactory cues." Thus, it can hunt in a manner known for the Great Gray Owl (and possible for the Roughleg).

Using a beater In Europe, harriers were reported "hovering over bands of reapers" (Muirhead, cited in D. Watson 1977). The reverse occurs—Peregrines "waiting on" hunting harriers and Merlins following the latter closely (Dickson 1984). (Other examples of using another species to obtain food are scattered through this section.) In Pa., breeding individuals tended to hunt newly mown hayfields for uncovered songbird nests (Randall 1940). In Miss., a ♀ focused her hunting efforts near a target in an active bombing range (J. Jackson et al. 1977). In Ohio, Bandy and Bandy

(1978) saw 2 harriers hunting in close association with a red fox. Robinson (in Bent 1937) detailed the activities of harriers along the edge of a prairie fire, a situation that attracts various diurnal raptors. Harriers also hunt while perched (usually on the ground). The Craigheads (1956) saw a ♂ alight frequently to watch for voles. In s. Ohio, only 1 of 601 pounces was made by a perched bird: an adult ♀ pounced from a fence post on a meadow vole 5 m. away, in a raging snowstorm.

In Mich., the Craigheads (1956) noted that time perched av. 57% of daylight hours. In Wis., during 55 hr. of observation, 3 ♂ that were procuring food for themselves and mates and, in 2 instances, offspring, spent 64–78% of time aloft. Of that time, about 3% was spent ferrying food to the nest (Bildstein 1982b). This harrier is inconspicuous on the ground and, except for newly flying young, seldom perches in trees and only occasionally on stumps and posts. Twenty-one percent of 1,024 winter harrier sightings in s. Ohio were of perched birds. More than 50% were on the ground, others (19%) on fence posts or (17%) in corn or wheat stubble. Average perch height was 0.6 m.; it was lower during high winds, when almost all perched birds were on the ground (Bildstein 1978).

Winter territory   In Mich., the Craigheads (1956) gave the ranges of 3 wintering individuals as a little over 0.5 sq. mi., of which certain areas were hunted more intensely than others. In both Mich. and s. Ohio, wintering birds hunt the same area for several days (in Wis., in summer nonbreeders hunted the same area day after day). In Scotland, D. Watson (1977) reported birds traveling the same route at approximately the same hour for days, and, on the Continent, Schipper et al. (1975) believed them to have "fixed hunting ranges in winter." Boedeltje and Zijlstra (1981) noted that 8 individually recognizable ♀ ♀ defended winter hunting territories and that av. size varied greatly—supposedly related to density of voles. A pair of radio-tagged breeders in Wis. had daily ranges of 1.25 × 2.75 mi.

As elsewhere, area was not used evenly, since each bird had its own favorite spots; most hunting was along drainage ditches (Hamerstrom and De La Ronde Wilde 1973).

In winter it is probable that some individual harriers hunt over portions of very large areas. In s. Ohio, those wintering at small-grain and livestock farms used cropland more than expected and grazed pastures less, based on relative availability. They tended to hunt larger fields and fields with fewer tree-lined edges than perch hunting Red-tailed Hawks and Am. Kestrels. Fallow fields were hunted more heavily and corn stubble fields less heavily by adult ♀ ♀ than adult ♂ ♂. The ♂ ♂ hunted hillier terrain. (See especially Schipper's papers for habitat use in W. Europe.) In the Tex. panhandle in winter, playas (undrained desert basins) are hunted more than are the surrounding agricultural fields (Schibler 1981). In R.I., where the only known winter comparison between this harrier and the Short-eared Owl was made, the former hunted tall shrub areas more and grassy ones less than the latter (S. Reinert).

In the Tex. panhandle in winter, Juvs. predominate and ♀ ♀ (Juv. and older) are more common (Schibler 1981) than ♂ ♂. On winter rangeland in Colo., 23 of 35 harriers seen were ♂ ♂ (Bauer 1982). In a 4-winter study in s. Ohio, of 893 birds of known age and/or sex, 29% were adult ♂ ♂, 32% adult ♀ ♀, and 40% unsexed Juv. (Bildstein 1978). In winter in Scotland, in upland habitats only 5 of 46 individuals were adult ♂ ♂ while along the coast 14 of 17 were adult ♂ ♂ (Marquiss 1980).

Daily hunting activity   Varies as a result of weather, competition, prey activity, and other factors. In Mich., the Craigheads (1956) found that time spent perched increased in rainy weather. The same appears true in sw. Scotland (Dickson 1974) and W. Europe (Schipper 1973). Harriers tend to switch to hunting birds when it is windy (Schipper), but especially windy weather may keep them on the ground (Wilkinson and Debban 1980), and, during periods of especially cold weather accompanied by snow cover, harriers may "either move locally, migrate or become less detectable." In s. Ohio, an especially severe winter with increased snow cover and low temperatures did not significantly affect the number of harrier sightings. Whether this reflects a constant population or a smaller, more visible, one is uncertain, but in severe winter harriers fed more on carrion and robbed prey significantly more often than in milder ones (Bildstein 1978). In England, D. Green (1980) saw a ♀ harrier hunting in Liverpool suburbs twice in cold snowy weather. In W. Europe, they hunt songbirds when voles are under heavy snow cover (Schipper et al. 1975).

In Ont., a ♀ struck, then seemingly drowned, a Com. Gallinule [Moorhen] in 2–10 in. of water. Over a 10-min. period the harrier stood on the submerged prey, occasionally bringing it to the surface. When it stopped thrashing, the harrier dragged it to ground close by and fed on it. Whether drowning was deliberate or the prey was held under until it was motionless is conjectural (Fitzpatrick 1979). A similar harrier–Blue-winged Teal incident occurred in a S.C. salt marsh (Bildstein). Both are somewhat reminiscent of E. R. Ford (1941), who saw a ♀ in Fla. feeding on a partly immersed scaup, which, "after vigorous effort," the harrier dragged from the water. In Sask., a ♀ was unable to pull a dead Am. Coot, which it had not killed, to shore (Millar 1964). In Wash., a harrier tried to snatch a young coot and was driven into water by the adults; then Ruddy Ducks and Eared Grebes surrounded the hawk, and it drowned after a 10-

min. struggle (1982 *Am. Birds* **36** 953, 998). In England, a brown harrier (♀ or Juv.) carried a live Eurasian Wigeon only 10 of 500 yd. toward shore before dropping it as a result of the duck's struggles and the presence of gulls (Griffiths et al. 1954). In Orkney in late Oct., 2 ♀ or Juv. birds hunted over the sea, repeatedly and unsuccessfully trying to capture migrating thrushes, *Turdus* (Beaman 1979).

In Conn., a harrier plunged Ospreylike and caught a 10-in. fish in a pool (Proctor 1973); a few traces of fish have been found in digestive tracts. In Britain, various evidence that it fishes, or at least tries to, and that it includes stranded dead fish among carrion it eats, was summarized by R. Rhodes (1979).

Capture rate   In s. Ohio in winter, harriers caught prey in 7% of 601 pounces, and success varied little with variation in vegetation. Juvs. had a 5% rate and adults 9%. All ages and both sexes pounced at about the same rate—0.6 pounce/min.—and it appeared that Juvs. were able to detect prey as well as older birds but were unable to capture located prey as efficiently (Bildstein 1978). In W. Europe, adult ♂ success rate was 6% and a "brown bird" 8%. In Utah, breeding adults caught prey (mainly Microtinae) on 30 of 77 strikes during 14.4 hrs. of aerial hunting, for a capture rate of just over 2 prey/hr. (Linner 1980). In Wis., breeding ♂ ♂ caught 39 prey items (3 passerines, 36 Microtinae) during 37.3 hrs. of hunting, for a capture rate of just over 1 prey/hr. (Bildstein 1982b).

Harriers vary their hunting technique depending on the situation. Example: mostly horizontal passes along the top of a stream of flying bats (Looney 1972).

Responses of potential prey to harriers also vary. Passerines and shorebirds flush in advance of the raptor (various authors). Harriers were useful in antebellum ricefields in the South: "As it sails low and swiftly over the surface of the field, it keeps the flocks [of Bobolinks] in perpetual fluctuation, and greatly interrupts their depredations" (A. Wilson and Bonaparte 1832 2). Other Icterids are similarly disturbed (G. Foreman). In N. Mex., 2 harriers flying over Lesser Prairie Chickens kept them in "a state of constant alarm and agitation" (H. Campbell 1950). Instances of Greater Prairie Chickens standing their ground against harriers were reported by Berger et al. (1963). In Wis., harriers encountering this species 886 times on their booming grounds were seen making only 1 kill. Some or all of the "chickens" flushed 69% of the time, squatted 11% of the time, and showed a weak response or none in 20%; ♀ harriers elicited a stronger response than ♂ ♂ (Berger et al.). Ring-necked Pheasants will stand their ground. In Nebr., a ♀ harrier was feeding on an 18-week-old ♀ pheasant; from 50 ft. away, 3 cock pheasants ran toward the raptor, forcing it to drag its prey into denser vegetation (Weigand 1967).

But harriers are also mobbed, even by passerines. A perched harrier is not mobbed, but whatever the harrier is carrying (prey, nesting material) seems to elicit mobbing, and mobbing induces the harrier to move on (Bildstein 1982b).

Aside from piracy, discussed below, some raptor interactions follow: At Chincoteague, Va., harriers avoided areas that hacked Peregrines haunted (1981 *Am. Birds* **35** 927 and 1982 **36** 963). In N.J., Urner (1925) noted that breeding harriers chased off Peregrines but not Short-eared Owls. Yet interactions with this owl appear to be common, probably due to similarity in niches and often roosting in the same fields. In winter in N.Y., R. Clark (1975) noted 47 owl/harrier encounters; in 39, the owl was the aggressor. Sometimes individual harriers were apparently singled out and harassed repeatedly while others were left alone. In 44 evenings at 8 harrier roosts in s. Ohio, Bildstein (1976) witnessed 19 owl-initiated and 21 harrier-initiated chasing and stooping interactions between the 2 species. Later (1978) he also reported 2 owl- and 2 harrier-initiated interactions between birds hunting and away from roosts. Other aggressively interacting raptors include the Rough-leged and Red-tailed Hawks (Bildstein 1976) and possibly the Great Horned Owl, which is suspected of preying on roosting individuals (Weller et al. 1955). In N.Y., a harrier chased both a Roughleg and Peregrine (Elliott 1941); in Calif., a Juv. Redtail and Juv. harrier soared together, "playfully" stooping on one another (E. Stoner 1936).

Social behavior is modified by abundance or scarcity of food. As noted earlier, harriers may hunt on parallel courses, one probably defending an invisible boundary from the other. If 2 come together, they may touch or grasp talons—the "crabbing" of falconers (Dickson 1974). Such interactions occur in any season. On the other hand, in winter in Scotland, an observer saw up to 5 harriers hunting on 2 kale fields of 85 ha.; in autumn and winter, when voles are plentiful, not uncommonly one may see 2 or 3 hunting in view at the same time (D. Watson 1977). In s. Ohio in winter, a Juv. was seen following within several m. of an adult ♀ several days in succession whenever the latter hunted a certain large fallow field (Bildstein).

Even when captured as adult, the Northern Harrier is easily tamed, although tethered individuals attempt to fly from their perches much more frequently than do raptors that typically hunt from perches. Although generally regarded as unsuited to hawking, and although F. Beebe (1974) stated that it has "no history of use by man," Blohm et al. (1980) mentioned that a trained ♀ in Wis. captured an adult Blue-winged Teal.

Nieboer (1973) suggested that the pale coloring of the ♂ is an advantage when hunting sharp-eyed prey on open terrain. (As stated earlier, he does most of the hunting during incubation and rearing.) In general, he takes more passerines than does the ♀ (Schipper 1973, Bildstein 1978). The ♂ pattern may have some sort of signal function—a possibility in a species that is much out in the open on rather monotonous terrain. The gray color might aid in spacing ♂ ♂ apart while informing others of the whereabouts of exploitable food. It is not essential for attracting mates, since some ♂ ♂ breed while still brown yearlings. The white rump, visible at a distance in all ages and both sexes, is probably a social signal and (see above) may have a use in display.

Communal roosting Known in at least 6 harrier species and 1st reported in the Northern Harrier in the 1830s (D. Watson 1977). It consists of assemblages of individuals roosting on the ground in open habitats. If reported accurately, thousands of Montagu's Harriers roosting in autumn in France (Dresser 1878) seems to be much the largest recorded gathering. In the Northern, as far as is known, roosts of 100–200 birds are exceptional, 1 to several score more usual. In the Old World, there are a few reports of more than 1 harrier species at a roost—Meinertzhagen's (1956) report of Montagu's and Marsh Harriers wintering together in Kenya is commonly cited. Short-eared Owls in Mo. and Ohio preferred drier sites with denser cover than did harriers. Individual harrier roosts can be distinguished from individual owl sites by the presence of green and pellet-like droppings (harriers) compared to black and string-like ones (owls) (Weller et al. 1955, R. Clark 1972b). Regurgitated pellets are diagnostic— harrier's are spongier and not nearly as firm as owl pellets (R. Clark 1972b). In sw. Scotland, D. Watson (1977) suggested that owls may use harrier roost-forms during the day; in s. Ohio, owl defecations and pellets from both species were found in a number of individual sites in communal roosts used by both species (Bildstein 1976). There is some debate why harriers roost in assemblies. It is quite clear that the birds have a social inclination that, in the near-presence of an optimal food supply, tends to over- ride territoriality. Individuals roost somewhat apart; in Miss., there was evidence of 300 sites within a 1.1-acre plot, but no more than 23 birds were seen on a single day (J. Jackson et al. 1972). At 2 roosts in s. Ohio, the av. distance between closest (but not necessarily concurrently occupied) sites was about 2 m. While some investigators have reported that harriers take flight singly if disturbed, long-term observations at numer- ous roosts in Scotland (D. Watson and Dickson 1972, Watson 1977) and s. Ohio (Bildstein 1976) indicate the opposite—alarm calling by a disturbed bird causing others to take wing and sometimes to stoop on the intruding human or fox. A Great Horned Owl that roosted within 200 m. of harriers was suspected of having killed at least 5 of them (Weller et al. 1955).

In N. Am., communal roosts have been reported from at least N.Y. across the prairies and down into Tex., in the se. to at least n. Fla. and cent. Miss., and in the Pacific NW in Wash. All were in the open, usually away from human activity. Some were in swamps or on is., which may hinder approach of ground predators. In Ind., they roosted in a wet 40-acre fescue field 150–300 yd. from the nearest road where vegetation was up to 3½ ft. high (Mumford and Danner 1974); in cent. Mo., usually in damp fields of mostly intermixed wheat stubble and ragweed (Weller et al. 1955); in Fla., in heavy broomsedge usually on an elevation (Stoddard 1931); in cent. Miss., broomsedge and silver beardgrass (J. Jackson et al. 1972); in Tex., in water-free areas of a playa covered with smartweed (Littlefield 1970); in Wash., in dry fields of cheatgrass, especially in depressions where forbs were thickest (P. Thompson-Hanson); in s. Ohio, in wheat and soybean stubble and in fallow fields not near roads (Bildstein 1976). Variation is roughly the same abroad.

Individual roost sites are well-trampled ellipses, in long dimension about 15–18 in. Some are very close and are interconnected by "runways." In s. Ohio, they varied from simple depressions in grass to "partially domed sites" (Bildstein 1976). In cent. Miss., vegetation at individual sites was "neatly clipped off 2–3 in. above the ground" (J. Jackson et al. 1972). There may be none to several pellets and little to considerable "whitewash." Whether individuals use an identical spot more than once is unknown. There are reports of ♂♂ using only certain areas of a roost.

In most locations in N. Am., communal roosting is limited to Oct.–Apr. or within that span. In Wis., Beske (1982) reported siblings resting within 18 m. of one another while still receiving food from their parents. They departed individually and roosted singly, at least for several weeks. A pair of radio-tagged breeders in Wis. roosted 0.2– 1.2 mi. apart on 3 evenings (Hamerstrom and De La Ronde Wilde 1973). In Europe, at most roosts brown birds (the greater portion of the population) greatly outnumber gray ♂♂, although there are exceptions in Belgium (Mois 1975) and Scotland (Marquiss

1980)—possibly from sex-dependent differences in habitat use. The ratio fluctuates at solitary roost sites within and between seasons, which may reflect differences in timing of migration. From his Scottish observations, D. Watson (1977) speculated that gray ♂♂ might roost singly more often than adult ♀♀ and Juv. birds of both sexes. In s. Ohio, this did not seem to occur; gray ♂♂ composed about a quarter of the harriers seen at roosts and hunting areas (Bildstein). At an Ind. roost, toward dusk the ratio of gray ♂♂ to brown birds increased (Mumford and Danner 1974). In Denmark, adult ♂ Montagu's Harriers roosted alone, separate both from adult ♀♀ and young of both sexes (Weis 1923).

From his s. Ohio observations, Bildstein (1979b) suggested that birds arriving on wintering areas first roost near their hunting places, but as the season progresses "the tendency to roost together leads birds to select communal roost sites equidistant from their hunting areas." Thus, by late fall–early winter, centrally located roosts are fewer but larger. This seems to be the case elsewhere. In Ohio, when most of the birds at a roost began to return from one direction, the roost decreased in size as another one, located in the direction whence most of the birds were returning, increased in numbers. Similar reciprocal fluctuations were reported from sw. Scotland (D. Watson and Dickson 1972).

In s. Ohio, the "overwhelming majority" of birds left the roost within 2 hr. after sunrise and returned during 2 hr. preceding sunset; at larger roosts, a few birds could be found throughout the day. Mean arrival time was 23 min. before sunset, and 77% of the birds arrived before sunset. Earliest arrivals usually flew about the roost before perching near its perimeter; later arrivals were more likely to enter the roost directly. At times, later arrivals were joined in flight over the roost by those perched nearby. By 45 min. after sunset most birds were at roost sites. In the morning, mean departure time was 25 min. after sunrise. "Birds usually became active singly; there were no mass flights over the roost as occurred in the evenings," and overall the roost appears less active (Bildstein). During high winds and low temperatures, preroosting birds perched on the ground more and on fence posts less than on warm, calm evenings. The birds came earlier and departed later on cloudy than on fair days. The same occurs in Scotland (D. Watson and Dickson 1972). In Ohio, the harriers interacted with others of their kind, and Short-eared Owls, Roughlegs, and Redtails during evening preroosting. "On many occasions, evening pre-roosting activity ended with a mass flight with seemingly every bird on the roost circling and swooping on conspecifics before finally settling down for the night" (Bildstein 1976).

Both here and abroad, preroosting behavior includes harriers attempting to displace one another from perch sites as well as both brief and prolonged aerial pursuits over the roost. Often these appear to be playful encounters, but British authors report that ♀♀ regularly displace ♂♂ from roosting sites.

Although some investigators have commented on a general lack of hunting in the vicinity of communal roosts, others have reported nearby captures—especially at time of evening preroosting. Overall, however, the vicinity of the roost does not seem to be more heavily used than distant areas. On a 36 sq. mi. area in Mich., the Craigheads (1956) saw more harriers in a 9 sq. mi. area in which the roost was located than in the other 3 quarters, but they reported several harriers flying "in a more or less straight line" to hunting ranges at least 5 mi. from the roost. Several other observers have followed harriers at least that far. In s. Ohio, most flights to and from roosts were at heights under 5 m. (Bildstein 1976).

Play objects   There is mention earlier (see Reproduction, above) of flying young harriers engaging in play or practice hunting—pouncing on inanimate objects or chasing insects. This is common before dispersal from the nesting area, a time when little—if any—serious hunting takes place. Two or more siblings may play with the same object, each in turn picking it up, manipulating it, and dropping it. Shelley (1935) reported that until the young were about 8 weeks old, his captives "spent a stated period of time" playing with bark or a piece of wood after each meal. Bildstein (1980) observed harriers, including adults, at communal roosts, singly and severally pouncing on, carrying, dropping, catching in midair, and apparently "eating" corn cobs of approximately vole (*Microtus*) size. He also saw them pounce on and carry clumps of dirt and grass, and sometimes they uprooted vegetation. Young harriers may go through the motions of "killing" the play object. (For very similar English data, see Shrubb 1983.) Rolfe (1897, or in Bent 1937) wrote of this harrier pouncing on and carrying empty "mouse" nests. In Merced Co., Calif., in July, E. Sumner (1931) saw a brown-feathered harrier drop, then pounce on, a still-alive Horned Lark. This was repeated 7 or 8 times. Eventually, after some other doings, the harrier ate it. Sumner called it "play" and added that he had reared young hawks and owls that "regularly exhibited" similar behavior toward real or mock prey. There are "playful" aerial encounters at roosts.

Piracy   Known in at least 3 harrier species. Flying young in the vicinity of the nest rob one another of food brought by the parents, who do not interfere. If a prey is dropped by the pursued flying bird, it may be lost to both. In the breeding season in Wis., Hamerstrom (in Hickey 1969) noted the occurrence of "robber females." At least some were 2d and 3d mates of a polygamous ♂—these ♀♀ sometimes waited near nests of their mate's consorts to intercept him (Bildstein). In other cases they were opportunistic, robbing ♂♂ that were passing over their nest. In Sweden, a ♀ Montagu's rose from a nest and took prey from a passing ♂ Pallid Harrier (Lundevall and Rosenberg 1955). Hamerstrom (in Hickey 1969) pointed out that aerial food transfers may not always indicate a mated pair. Throughout the year, this harrier and the Short-eared Owl rob one another—usually near nests or a roost. Usually the owl is the victim, although in most cases the potential pirate is unsuccessful (various authors). Harriers rob Eurasian Kestrels (D. Watson 1977) and, perhaps surprisingly, Peregrines. In Fla., Maynard (1896 and in Bent 1937) reported witnessing a harrier rob a Peregrine "repeatedly" of ducks; in N.J., Herbert and Hickey (1941) watched a Juv. unsuccessfully attempt to rob a Peregrine of a shorebird. The Peregrine was forced to flee and ate its prey on the wing. Harriers are often robbed, usually by such larger raptors as, for example, the Caracara (K. Hamilton 1981). A Peregrine knocked a harrier from a fallen duck that it was eating (Forbush 1927). In w. Nev., 1 or more Prairie Falcons were seen to watch and follow harriers, forcing them to relinquish their prey—not occasionally, but as a "systematic habit" at this locality (Ridgway 1877). Harriers can also force Prairie Falcons to leave prey they are attempting to kill (C. M. White). In e. N.Mex., Merchant (1982) watched Prairie Falcons flying "approximately 30–50 m. above and 5–100 m. behind" harriers 6 times but saw no prey caught. In Oct.

at Comox, B.C., a ♀ harrier passed overhead, accelerated, and then threw a small vole to 1 side; in an instant, a ♀ Prairie Falcon shot past and seized it in midair with a foot. Then an adult ♂ harrier swept by and struck at the falcon, which paid no heed and ate the vole while sailing along (H. Laing 1979). In Scotland, a Merlin followed a hunting harrier for a ½ hr., pursuing small birds that were flushed (D. Watson 1977). In S.C. in Mar., a white-headed Bald Eagle robbed a harrier of a Sora (Baldwin 1940).

In s. Ohio during 4 winters (Bildstein 1978), harriers attempted to rob Rough-legged Hawks twice (unsuccessfully) and other harriers 9 times (4 successful); most of the latter were attempts by Juv. harriers to secure prey from other Juv. or older harriers. In turn, Red-tailed Hawks attempted to rob harriers 6 times (at least 4 successful); Roughlegs attempted the same 13 times (at least 4 successful). Voles and several small birds were the quarry. During the 4 winters, harriers were seen to catch prey 80 times. On 28 of these occasions the harrier was chased by another raptor, and 12 times harriers were robbed (15% of their captures). In an apparent response to this, harriers ate their prey hurriedly and rarely hunted fields in current use by other harriers or buteos. In many instances harriers attempted to dislodge perched buteos from areas they flew into and, when unsuccessful, usually moved on. Frequency of both inter- and intraspecific piracy increased during severe weather. Whether harriers suffered substantially from this is unknown (Bildstein). In Mich., the Craigheads (1956) reported harriers avoiding areas in use by buteos but noted only "subtle" interactions among the birds and reported no instances of piracy; they stated that the birds had seemingly established a "hunting tolerance" of one another.

Effects on grouse   In a long-term study in Wis., 1,379 encounters between Greater Prairie Chickens (*Tympanuchus cupido*) and various raptors were seen on the booming grounds—in the course of which only 3 (♂) "chickens" were known to have been killed and circumstantial evidence of a few more (Berger et al. 1963). One of the 3, although very heavy prey, was killed by a harrier. The harrier is not a serious predator on adult prairie chickens, but there is considerable harassment. The prairie chickens respond differently—ordinarily more strongly—to ♀ harriers than to the smaller ♂♂. In se. N.Mex. in Feb., 1, at times 2, harriers constantly patrolled about a sq. mi., flushing flock after flock of Lesser Prairie Chickens (*T. pallidicinctus*). The "chickens" fed out onto a field toward evening and a harrier downed 1, which escaped (H. Campbell 1950). In Minn., the remains of 3 young Greater Prairie Chickens were found in pellets (Peabody 1900); in Mont., the breast bone of a young Sharp-tailed Grouse (*T. phasianellus*) (Saunders 1913). A harrier "family" took both old and young Blue (*Dendragapus*) and Ruffed (*Bonasa*) Grouse.

On a Scottish moor, 1970–1974, harriers were nesting at fairly high density, and grouse (*Lagopus l. scoticus*) were plentiful. Young grouse and lagomorphs were vastly preponderant by wt. in prey brought to harrier nests (Picozzi 1978). Other Palearctic data could be cited; in the long view, more young grouse are taken when readily available and other acceptable prey is less so; the same evidently applies to pheasants (*Phasianus colchicus*).

Food consumption   Breeding season data were given earlier (see Reproduction, above). In mid-June in Ohio, a ♂ delivered an adult E. Meadowlark (partially plucked?) to his mate, who ate it in 3 min., 10 sec.; she was not away from her nest over 5 min. (Trautman 1940). In s. Ohio, harriers carried 31 prey (usually voles) an av. of 68

m. from the capture site (Bildstein 1978). Eighty-five percent of 66 prey items were eaten on the ground, 14% on fence posts, and 1 while the harrier perched on corn stubble. Prey was eaten piecemeal, beginning with the head, and usually all was consumed except the gastrointestinal tract, "which they pulled from the visceral cavity with their beaks and dropped to the side"; they first plucked bird prey, "an exceedingly slow process," and usually only legs, sternum, and sometimes wings were uneaten. They consumed 22 small mammals in an av. of 3 min., 17 sec., and 7 small birds in an av. of 23 min., 35 sec. Larger avian prey are not always plucked; Blohm et al. (1980) described a N. Pintail kill from which back and breast muscle and the proventriculus had been partially consumed. From a decapitated Mallard the heart, esophagus, trachea, and much of the liver had been eaten. J. Jackson et al. (1972) noted that most feathers in pellets were from the head region of passerines. In N.S., Tufts (1962) saw a harrier feeding on a frog that had been "neatly and adeptly skinned." Nethersole-Thompson (D. Watson 1977) reported a similar observation. In N.Y., R. Clark (1972b) saw harriers stripping off and discarding the fur of voles, and Errington and Breckenridge (1936) stated that ground squirrel entrails containing a "large proportion of vegetable debris" were usually discarded. In especially harsh winter weather in s. Ohio, harriers discarded less and consumed more of the voles they captured (Bildstein). Consumption of the gastrointestinal tract may be related to specific dietary requirements (Hamerstrom).

Based on feeding captive birds, the Craigheads (1956) gave av. wt. of prey eaten per day by a ♀ as 100 gm. (♀ wt. av. 526 gm.) and of a ♂ in spring–summer as 47 gm. (♂ wt. av. 343 gm.). Since *Microtus pennsylvanicus* av. about 34 gm., one might convert consumption into some sort of vole units, but there are too many variables. For example, part of the material is ejected as pellets. An unrestrained captive young ♀ (4–7 weeks old), feeding on small mammals and passerines, consumed an av. of 107 gm./day (A. Beske and K. Bildstein). Up to 11 voles (size unrecorded) have been found in a harrier's digestive tract. As indicated earlier, some recent studies confirm that the larger ♀ tends to take fewer and larger prey than the smaller ♂.

Ejecta and excreta The pellets that this harrier ejects, of fur or feathers and bone, vary in shape—ordinarily 20–25 mm. diam. and 35–50 mm. long (sometimes to 65 mm.)—and can be misidentified as to origin. See, for example, pellets of various raptors in the Craigheads (1956: pl. 43). Because of similarity in habitat and pellet size, the most likely confusion is with the Short-eared Owl. Where prey was almost entirely *Microtus*, the harrier tended to break up the bones when feeding much more than the owl (R. Clark 1972b). The ratio of bone wt. to pellet wt. was much less in the harrier; as a consequence, when a pellet was squeezed between thumb and forefinger in the field, owl pellets were firm and the harrier's spongy. The disarticulation of small mammal skulls is more complete in harrier pellets. Fresh pellets also have less mucus than owl pellets (Shelley 1935). Harriers kept indoors and fed a diet of small mammals and birds cast 1, sometimes 2, pellets a day, the 1st usually in morning before feeding. Free-ranging birds in winter presumably would consume more and cast more pellets.

Winter excreta of the owl are black and stringlike, of the harrier green and pelletlike (Weller et al. 1955)—the latter especially so when the birds have not fed recently. Uric acid of the owl is generally buffy, of the harrier chalky white (R. Clark 1972b).

300

Numbers   Harrier counts in N. Am. have been made variously and are not directly comparable; they do add up to a great decline throughout the species' range over about 40 years, perhaps with slight improvement beginning in the late 1970s. Biocides are implicated, at least early on, but the evidence could be stronger. Loss of marshland and other nesting habitat has become a major factor, as were guns formerly, but harrier numbers have dwindled even in remote n. areas where man's impact is seemingly minimal.

Christmas counts in Ill., 1903–1955, did not show any appreciable change in numbers (Graber and Golden 1960). From analysis of Christmas counts in 45 states plus B.C., 1952–1971, W. H. Brown (1973) graphed a considerable decline and then some recovery, 1967–1970. The upturn was reported largely from Calif. but was followed by a decline. Christmas counts in the Carolinas, 1971–1976, failed to indicate any change (Bildstein 1979c). In Wis., 1960–1965, there was a prominent and continuous decline of 70% of spring migrants (Hamerstrom, in Hickey 1969). In Md. in autumn, comparing 1951–1954 with 1958–1961 revealed a 7% annual decline (Hackman and Henny 1971). Autumn counts at Hawk Mt., Pa., 1935–1965, showed no strong long-term trend but a slight increase (Spofford, in Hickey 1969); the birds are somewhat concentrated as migrants there. In N.Y., this bird "nearly disappeared" as a breeder during a time when annual fall counts at Hawk Mt. showed a "considerable increase" (Evenden 1968).

Hamerstrom (1979) reported a "damped" response to a vole high in the mid-1960s, when there was heavy use of DDT on the Wis. site, as well as behavioral abnormalities; in 1968, 87% of the harriers failed to nest. Since then the breeding population has rebounded, presumably a result of breeding stock migrating into the area.

D. Evans (1982) described the continental U.S. population as "stable or declining slowly," with greater declines in the E. In Canada, populations are currently declining in the Maritimes, stable in Ont. and Que. (but with marked decline in the Ottawa area and fluctuating widely in the prairie provinces and B.C. (Fyfe 1976).

Data for Britain and Europe are omitted here; see D. Watson (1977).

KEITH L. BILDSTEIN

FOOD   *Circus cyaneus hudsonius* has its preferences but exploits whatever readily available quarry it can capture—small mammals (especially voles and cotton rats), small and medium-sized birds (especially passerines, also small poultry, etc.), and some reptiles, amphibians, and large insects. It eats some fresh and, if hard pressed, not so fresh carrion.

In a 1954 MS, A. W. Schorger summarized 8 papers, further condensed here. McAtee's report (1935) on 601 "stomachs" was the largest sample, but other (mostly later) studies relate better to local conditions or seasonal changes. His report listed poultry in 20 crops, game birds in 51 (includes pheasants in 37), waterfowl and shorebirds in 14, miscellaneous birds in 265, lagomorphs in 62, voles (*Microtus*) in 173, house and "other" mice in 38, miscellaneous mammals in 60, snakes in 13, frogs in 15, fish and crayfish in 1 each, and insects (grasshoppers in 15, other insects in 24) in 39.

In Canada and the U.S., various studies to date reveal that small rodents usually predominate late fall–spring; that there is great variety in prey through spring, includ-

301

ing young mammals, nesting and flying young plus adult birds, and so on; and that in summer the harriers again exploit any acceptable food in good supply, such as voles, young and adult birds, young rabbits and ground squirrels, and grasshoppers. Good accounts of changes around the calendar include Randall's (1940) for Pa. or R. M. Latham's (1950) subsequent compilation.

Mammals The above-mentioned 8 studies include at least 21 genera and vary in size from small shrews (*Sorex*) to skunks, snowshoe hare, and jackrabbits. Except for young individuals, the larger species must usually have been found in traps, wounded, or dead (carrion).

R. Clark and Ward (1974) summarized 15 N. Am. studies (includes some of the above) and found that, by wt., mammals composed 58%, birds 34%, and other prey less than 9% of the diet; most prey weighed under 65 gm., and ♀ ♀ took larger prey. See Sherrod (1978) for a more recent compilation from 10 sources. In some areas breeding harriers are largely dependent on voles, in some other areas ground squirrels. The cotton rat (*Sigmodon*) is a regular winter food in s. regions. In some coastal salt marshes in se. U.S., marsh rabbits; in other marshes, Clapper Rails (Bildstein) are the most important. Especially in fall–winter, carrion can be essential; harriers have been seen both sharing it with crows (Long 1961) and at a carcass previously fed on by a falcon and a buteo (A. Cruickshank 1939); in N.S., Tufts (1962) disturbed 1 that had been eating a long-dead salmon. In s. Ohio (Bildstein 1978), the number of harriers seen feeding on carrion more than doubled (to almost 10%) during an especially cold winter with heavy snow; Juv. harriers fed on it more often than adults. In the same study, direct observations revealed that small mammals (mostly voles) composed 79% of prey captured; small passerines and Mourning Doves made up the remainder of noncarrion prey. Concurrent analysis of pellets from communal roosts in the same area tended to overrepresent small mammals (90%) and failed to detect carrion. Based on direct observations, birds were 40% of the prey taken by adult ♂ ♂ but only 4% of that of adult ♀ ♀ and 7% of the prey of Juv. birds.

On the Craigheads' (1956) study area in Mich., pellets indicated that voles made up more than 90% of winter diet; in summer, voles were more than 50%, and other items included rabbits, ground squirrels, and especially small and medium-sized birds.

Harriers tried unsuccessfully to catch bats (*Tadarida*) near a cave entrance in Okla. (Looney 1972). At a nest in se. Alta., nestlings were fed adult cottontails (*S. nuttallii*) (Sealy 1965). The domestic cat has been found in pellets (Randall 1940)—carrion?

Birds At least 80 species are known food in N. Am., in size mostly from smaller sparrows to Mourning Dove. Meadowlarks and flickers are relatively frequent. Evidently largest are several duck species and the Am. Bittern, perhaps mostly found injured or dead. Also, an "adult" ♀ killed a 5-week-old Sandhill Crane in Mont. (Genter 1985). There is an assortment of upland gamebirds, usually young individuals. See especially Blohm et al. (1980) and Wishart et al. (1981) for attacks on crippled and healthy ducks.

In Europe, this harrier is said to prey on eggs sometimes (Dresser 1878, Doran 1976).

Insects Several kinds of crickets, beetles, and so on, and especially grasshoppers. Some may have originated in digestive tracts of prey or (carrion beetles) at the prey.

302

Miscellaneous Prairie rattler, garter snakes, blue racer, leopard lizard (*Cro-taphytus*), fence lizard (*Sceloporus*), whip-tailed lizard (*Cnemidophorus*), horned toad (*Phrynosoma*), toads (*Bufo*), and frog (*Rana*). Fishing was mentioned earlier (see Habits, above). Spiders are listed.

Adults and young accidentally swallow plant material with their food. However, fleshy fruits of dogwood, blueberries, and raspberries in pellets of young just learning to fly strongly suggest that the birds were hungry and mistook them for animal food (Breckenridge 1935).

NOTES McAtee's list of harrier foods included these raptors: Short-eared Owl 1, Screech Owl 4, and hawks 5 (Sharp-shinned, Merlin, Am. Kestrel). Errington (1938) included "young screech owls." There are comparable reports from Europe. (See also Peregrine.)

McAtee's high count of pheasants was from migrant harriers killing game farm stock. Adult wild pheasants are usually safe, although younger birds are taken.

In the more arid W. and SW., jackrabbits and cottontails, usually those killed by motor traffic, are staple food at times. On Padre I., Texas, a harrier killed a large black-tailed jackrabbit that it could not lift; it skinned the belly and fed several times (1981 *Nat. Geographic* **159** (2): 160–161 [excellent photographs]).

Individual harriers show a predeliction for small poultry, as noted by several authors; see Breckenridge (1935); the fowl-eating harrier was not, so to speak, the nearest one to the chicken coop. Cameron (1907) said this bird was the common "henhawk" in e. Mont., inexperienced young harriers being especially persistent and unwary. In the Comox region, B.C., in the 1920s and later, harriers specialized in young waterfowl and grouse. This was discussed by A. Brooks (1928, and in H. Laing 1979) and caused considerable controversy because it did not match what was known elsewhere. In Mont., Hecht (1951) found that young muskrats (*Ondatra*) appeared "in a wave (July 6–19)" at 2 of many nests examined.

In Minn., young harriers supplement parental feeding with such slow, weak prey as they themselves can catch—as large insects. Garter snakes are probably among the first vertebrates caught by "clumsy juveniles." They also eat fresher grades of carrion (Errington and Breckenridge 1936).

In a Calif. study, Selleck and Glading (1943) found that prey fed to the young was principally House Finches, blackbirds (*Agelaius*), Calif. Quail, and brush rabbits. Most nongame birds were nestlings or newly on the wing; all quail were under 12 weeks old.

Comparing data from Britain and Europe with those of N. Am., it would appear that rabbits and grouse are more important in those areas abroad where they occur. There is an apparent tendency to feed on carrion more in N. Am., which may indicate greater availability of highway kills. KEITH L. BILDSTEIN

FOOTNOTE Sparrowhawk; Eurasian Sparrowhawk *Accipiter nisus* (Linnaeus)—**no satisfactory record** of natural occurrence. One reported at C. May, N.J., Oct. 24, 1978 (*Peregrine Observer* [Newsletter of C. May Bird Observatory] **2** no. 4; and C. Sutton, Jr. 1980). See Field Identification, below, under Sharp-shinned Hawk.

RALPH S. PALMER

SHARP-SHINNED HAWK

Accipiter striatus

A small forest hawk with broad rounded wings, long tail, and long legs. The diagnosis here fits the *Handbook* area, but elsewhere the species varies from having unmarked white underparts, to a variable amount of chestnut or rufous, to (one region) pale, rufous, and so dark overall that the blackish tail bars are nearly obscured.

Greatest sexual size-dimorphism of any N. Am. bird. Sexes combined: length 10⅛–13½ in (25.7–34 cm.), wingspread 20–27 in. 51–68.5 cm.), the ♀ markedly larger within these spans. The ♂ weighs 2.8–4.4 oz. (82–125 gm.) and the ♀ 4.2–7.4 oz. (120–210 gm.). That is, no overlap in length and almost none in wt. between sexes. Nearly featherless tibiae—*sharp-shinned* (tibiae feathered only on proximal anterior quarter in the Sharpshin, but on a third in Cooper's Hawk). Wing as Cooper's, but primaries with less brownish olive tinge; counting from innermost, primaries #6–#8 are nearly equal in length (#7 slightly the longest); #5–#9 emarginated on outer and #6–#10 on inner web; vestigial alular claw usually detached by preening; 14 secondaries, the inner ones and scapulars with some white spots, usually concealed. Tail more or less squarish ended (rounded in Cooper's). Sharpshin and Cooper's are different in proportion—for example, eye relatively larger and middle toe relatively longer in the Sharpshin.

In definitive stages in our area, dorsum variably bluish gray, venter whitish with much transverse rusty barring, under tail coverts white, and tail with several very dark bars. The Juv. pattern, with venter longitudinally streaked, is also much as in Cooper's, except for white under tail coverts (rarely a few dark streaks).

Tentatively treated here as a species with 10 subspecies: 2 in our area (1 very widespread), 5 in Mexico and Cent. and S. Am. mainland, and 3 on is. (Cuba, Hispaniola, P.R.).

DESCRIPTION   *A. s. velox* one Plumage/cycle with Basic I earliest definitive.

▶ ♂ Def. Basic Plumage (entire feathering) acquired beginning at about age 1 year and retained a year. **Beak** blackish distally and bluish basally, cere and side of gape yellow to greenish yellow, **eye** variable—light brownish red to dark scarlet-orange, occasionally quite orange. **Head** as Cooper's Hawk but sides more buffy or tawny; **upperparts** slaty bluish (as Cooper's); **underparts** as Cooper's but breast feathers often more heavily streaked transversely with rusty; the plumose under tail coverts white; legs and **feet** yellow, at times toward orange, talons black; **tail** not invariably squarish ended, with 3 or more exposed dark transverse bars (distal one wider) and very narrow whitish tip (it wears off). **Wing** as Cooper's, but less brownish olive.

▶ ♀ Def. Basic Plumage (entire feathering); as ♂ except top of **head,** the **dorsum, wings,** and **tail** with more or less brownish olive tinge; underparts less heavily barred rusty; coloring of soft parts more muted.

Prebasic molting   The ♀ begins probably when laying her clutch or soon after; molting slows down or ceases from soon after the eggs hatch until the young are flying, then continues at a slower rate to conclusion (all or almost all feathering renewed). Prebreeders probably begin somewhat earlier and may continue uninterruptedly. The ♂ starts about 2 weeks after the ♀, and molting slows or ceases entirely for much of the period in which he hunts food for the young before it continues. The total span for the sexes combined is from late spring or early summer into fall. Molting begins with innermost primary and soon some head–body feathering. The primaries are molted from inner to outer. In the secondaries there is a molt center at the outermost and, toward the body, others at #5 and #9 or a higher number (molting is inward from #1 and #5 and centrifugally from the innermost center). Tail molting begins sometimes (often late) during wing molting, central pair (#1) 1st, then outer (#6), then variable but usually ends with #2 or #5; sometimes a tail feather is retained. Sequence of feather renewal tends to be bilaterally symmetrical in the wings but not in the tail. The above is based in part on both J. Platt (1973) and Henny et al. (1985); see the latter for further details.

In Minn., 90 of 155 ♂ and 241 of 274 ♀ in Basics retained unmolted feathers in Sept. (most commonly secondaries, wing coverts, and especially rump); of the others, more ♂♂ than ♀♀ had finished molting (D. Evans).

Eye color   Changes from grayish (at hatching) to pale yellow to orange to scarlet to ruby. Timing varies, but in general the changes occur earlier in the ♂. Birds with irises deep orange or various reds can definitely be assigned to Basic II and older age classes; birds with light to deep orange eyes cannot be aged with certainty; 6 Juv. in spring of year after hatching all had light orange irises; so also did 3 of 4 ♀, and another one had yellow eyes (J. Roberts 1967, Mueller et al. 1979b). It has been hypothesized (N. and H. Snyder 1974a) that red eye color in parent *Accipiter* elicits feeding response of the nestlings.

AT HATCHING   Essentially as Cooper's Hawk (which see), including short whitish or white down; in somewhat more than a week, a longer white down begins to appear. A day's development in Cooper's is comparable to 0.73 days in the Sharpshin; for example, if a Sharpshin resembles a 14-day-old Cooper's, its age can be calculated as 14

× 0.73 = 10.2 days (H. Meng). Female young are obviously larger from very early in the nestling period.

▶ ♂ ♀ Juv. Plumage (entire feathering) begins to appear in 3d week of nest life and is fully developed at 38–40 days (Mueller et al. 1981a); it is retained through WINTER, then succeeded by Basic I beginning about very late May–early June in latitude of n. U.S. and is completed by early FALL (of 2d calendar year of life). As in our other accipiters, dorsal feathers are margined light and the whitish venter is longitudinaly streaked heavily with dark (except under tail coverts white). **Head** darker than Cooper's Hawk, the feathers on crown with or without narrow cinnamon margins; **dorsum** entirely muted browns and most feathers have clear-cut buffy or tan margins; underparts patterned as Cooper's, the streaks generally wider and lighter buffy tan to dark cinnamon; flanks usually barred; **wing** as Cooper's except distal edges of secondaries usually with narrow pale cinnamon margins.

Color phases None in N. Am.; problematical elsewhere. Whether *A. s. ventralis* (mts. of Venezuela; Andes s. to nw. Bolivia) varies continuously pale/rufous/melanistic or whether there are disjunct phases is unclear from available information.

Measurements BEAK from cere: the mean fig. for 20 ♂ is 9.9 mm. and 20 ♀ 12.7 (N. Snyder and Wiley 1976).

AUTUMN BIRDS IN WIS. Between 2 age categories (Juv./Basic), ♂ ♂ differ significantly from ♀ ♀ in every meas., and, within each sex, older birds differ significantly from 1st fall (Juv.) (Mueller et al. 1979b). Because of wear, both WING and TAIL are slightly longer when new (autumn) than when worn through winter into spring.

♂ Basic I and older WING across chord (of 437 birds) 161–182 mm. (171 ± 3.5) and TAIL (of 440) 115–143 (132 ± 4.0).

♂ Juv. (1st fall) WING across chord (of 493) 158–182 mm. (169 ± 3.7) and TAIL (of 494) 121–144 (134 ± 3.8).

♀ Basic I and older WING across chord (of 489 birds) 192–217 mm. (203 ± 4.3) and TAIL (of 492) 144–175 (156 ± 4.4).

♀ Juv. (1st fall) WING across chord (of 544) 183–213 mm. (200 ± 4.4) and TAIL (of 548) 146–174 (158 ± 4.2).

NESTING BIRDS IN NE. OREG. ♂ BEAK from cere (of 9) 9.2–10.4 mm. (9.8 ± 0.45), WING across chord (of 11) 167–177 (172 ± 3.26), TAIL (of 10) 127–136 (131.4 ± 2.55); and ♀ BEAK from cere (of 6) 11.3–12.8 mm., (12.1 ± 0.57), WING across chord (of 7) 184–210 (199.7 ± 9.70), and TAIL (of 7) 150–176 (161.6 ± 8.89) (Henny et al. 1985).

Weight On av., ♂ weighs less than Com. Grackle, ♀ more than Com. Flicker (Mueller et al. 1979a). The following is from Mueller et al. (1979b). Birds in 2d fall and older 435 ♂ 82–125 gm. (103 ± 6.4) and 487 ♀ 144–208 (174 ± 10.4); and in 1st fall (Juv.) 489 ♂ 80–116 gm. (98 ± 5.8) and 522 ♀ 125–197 (166 ± 10.3).

Nesting birds in definitive feathering in ne. Oreg., May 19–June 2: 6 ♂ 93–100 gm. (96.5 ± 3.3); and July 10–Aug. 3: 5 ♂ 90–101 gm. (95.2 ± 4.4); same early period 1 ♀ 147 gm., and late period 6 ♀ 152–225 gm. (183.7 ± 24.3). Heaviest ♂ weighed 101 gm. and lightest ♀ 147 (no overlap between the sexes). From Henny et al. (1985).

Five nesting yearling ♀ ♀ weighed in the later time period: 189.2 ± 9.8 gm. From Henny et al. (1985).

Mean figures from specimen labels: 98 ♂ 102 gm. and 92 ♀ 179 (N. Snyder and Wiley 1976).

Birds in Basic feathering have longer and wider wings (more area), higher wing loading (gm. of wt./sq. cm. of area), and so on; in the Juv. stage the birds weigh somewhat less and have longer tails (more area). The young are evidently adapted for greater maneuverability and probably require lower energy consumption than adults. Since hunting skill is attained with age, Sharpshins can evidently afford higher speeds, greater striking force, and higher energy consumption. Increased wt. with age is probably due to increase of flight musculature. For technical details, see Mueller et al. (1981b).

Geographical variation Rather complex and, in some measure, clinal. **Size** The birds are larger down through Mexico than either to the northward or southward; in W. Indies they are very small. **Color** In N. Am. darker on is. off the B.C. coast and probably adjacent mainland; in n. Mexico, heavily marked ventrally with thighs plain rusty or rufous; then paler down to the Isthmus of Tehuantepec; in n. and w. S. Am. montane environment, highly variable (pale to rusty or rufous to overall blackish brown); in se. S. Am., upperparts are very dark neutral and underparts have fine dark transverse markings; W. Indian birds are rather heavily pigmented rufous or rusty on sides of head and on venter. See also Wattel (1973).

Affinities *Accipiter* is of Old World origin. *A. striatus* of N. Am. and *A. nisus* of Eurasia are very similar and are ecological counterparts; obviously they are very closely related. Together, plus 1 species in Africa, 1 in Madagascar, and possibly others, they compose a group. See also Wattel (1973). RALPH S. PALMER

SUBSPECIES **In our area** *velox* (Wilson)—descr. and meas. given above; widespread across the continent from boreal forest s.; migratory; *perobscurus* Snyder— size about as preceding but darker, especially Juv. Plumage (L. Snyder 1938); Queen Charlotte Is., B.C., and perhaps mainland areas approximately from Yakutat Bay, Alaska, down into Wash.; apparently not migratory, but similar-appearing individuals occasionally occur widely.

Elsewhere (Presumably all resident) *suttoni* van Rossem—heavily barred rusty ventrally; occurs from s. of U.S.-Mexican border s. (not in our area, contra 1957 AOU *Check-list*), in winter into Sonora, Mexico; *madrensis* Storer—Guerrero and perhaps w. Oaxaca, Mexico; *chionogaster* Kaup—nw. Chiapas, Mexico, down through El Salvador; *ventralis* Sclater—mts. of w. Venezuela and Andes to Bolivia; *erythronemius* Kaup—e. Bolivia, se. Brazil, Paraguay, Uruguay, and n. Argentina; *striatus* Vieillot—Hispaniola; *fringilloides* Vigors—Cuba (local); *venator* Wetmore—P.R. (humid forest, local), color photograph 1985 *Am. Birds* 39 18. For further details overall, see Hellmayr and Conover (1949), Friedmann (1950), and L. Brown and Amadon (1968 2). See also especially Storer (1952) for Mexico, Wetmore (1914) and W. King (1981) for n. Greater Antilles, and E. R. Blake (1977) for S. Am.

RALPH S. PALMER

FIELD IDENTIFICATION Short, rounded wings—very unlike the pointed-winged Merlin (a falcon) of approximately similar size. **In our area** the main problem is to

307

distinguish the Sharpshin from Cooper's Hawk. All Sharpshins are smaller than all Cooper's, but afield a ♀ Sharpshin (the larger sex) approaches in size a small ♂ Cooper's (the smaller sex). The species are separable by size and size-related characters, which requires expertise. See full discussion under Cooper's, based on Mueller et al. (1979a).

In proportion to body size, the Sharpshin has larger wings and shorter tail. It is also smaller, appears more buoyant, and flies slower but flaps faster than Cooper's. Although the Sharpshin has a squarish or slightly notched tail (Cooper's is rounded), the tail is moderately rounded in some ♀ Sharpshins and can appear rounded in either sex when spread. All characteristics of Sharpshin and Cooper's feathering that can be seen afield overlap more or less; this applies to the streaked Juv. Plumage as well as to the definitive condition.

The Sparrowhawk (*A. nisus*) of Eurasia is alleged to have occurred in N.J. It is darker dorsally than e. Sharpshins, with more contrasting (darker) transverse markings ventrally. It is also a dark bird when in Juv. Plumage. If it should occur—naturally, escaped, or released—recognizing it would be a problem—except in hand. It is recorded in Iceland but not satisfactorily in N. Am.   RALPH S. PALMER

VOICE   Less known than that of the Sparrowhawk (*A. nisus*).

Adults are silent when hunting or distant from the nest. In general, similar to the Goshawk but thinner; with a little experience, recognizable from voice of Cooper's Hawk. Typical alarm notes are *kik-kik-kik-kik* (long series). Occasionally ♀ follows a series of *kiks* with several *cacs*. As to "wailing," in the Sharpshin the *whaaaaas* and *wheeeees* of our other 2 accipiters are supplanted by *keeeeeeeeps*. Some calling ends with falling pitch and downward-slurred syllables. Males are 2 notes higher than ♀♀.

Aside from difference in voice, the morning duet (early in the reproductive cycle) is similar to that of Cooper's Hawk.

When the ♂ arrives in nesting territory he utters *kip* . . . *kip* . . . (spaced out and clear-cut); sometimes the ♀ replies with several *keps* or a *keeeeep*. Both of these are lower than the *kip* of the ♂.

This is from a comparative study by N. and H. Snyder (1979). Our 3 accipiters have an alarm call consisting of a series of repeated short notes. This cackle, highest pitched in the Sharpshin, is the call of the ♂ when delivering food to the ♀. There is a "separate solicitation-type" call developed from the begging calls of the young uttered by ♀♀ and rarely ♂♂. Begging calls of chicks and solicitation calls of adults "sound identical." The solicitation call of the Sharpshin is a "high-pitched *ee*," used in various contexts and sometimes linked to other vocalizations. During copulation, Sharpshins are sometimes silent and at other times utter "weak cackles."

Calls of the young are similar to those of the better-known Cooper's Hawk. From D. Evans: a single *chip* is uttered by Juv. birds when hunting, especially at evening, during fall migration. So far, it is associated only with Juvs. and seems to be uttered more commonly during flight.   RALPH S. PALMER

HABITAT   **In our area**   In **breeding season,** seldom above the forest canopy except in display. The majority breed in boreal forest, nesting in stands of young or similar-aged conifers adjacent to clearings, brushy areas, or open deciduous woodland. Some preference for nearness to water (R. Reynolds et al. 1982). Small birds—their main prey—are more plentiful in mixed than in continuous stands. In w. and sw. U.S. they nest in groves of conifers on slopes above valley and canyon floors. They also occur higher up, nearly to timberline, still generally within coniferous stands in or near mixed forest. Occasionally in deciduous trees, especially if growth is dense enough to conceal the nest.

As a migrant   Almost any terrain, but tends to avoid extensive open areas (deserts, plains) lacking concealment; many are channeled via slopes on updrafts. Some make wide water-crossings, but seem hesitant to do so.

In winter   At lower elevations wherever small birds are plentiful, especially where there are trees, brush, or other concealment from which the hawk can strike suddenly at close range. The Sharpshin makes no friends by often taking up residence close to houses where food for songbirds is provided regularly.   RALPH S. PALMER

DISTRIBUTION (See map.) **In our area**   Complete overlap in breeding range with Goshawk, nearly complete with Cooper's Hawk.

This paragraph presumably pertains to *A. s. velox:* Some **n. records** of interest include Nunivak I., Alaska (Swarth 1934); Canadian arctic Victoria I. in Nov. 1979 (T. G. Smith 1981); and Churchill, Man., June 15, 1982 (1982 *Am. Birds* **36** 979). As a **migrant** or **straggler** has occured in BERMUDA (includes 2 banding recoveries); the BAHAMAS: sometimes fairly common (see Bent 1937); FLA.: Key West, secretive (few seen), records beyond for the Dry Tortugas; CUBA: a few from the mainland evidently reach there, 1 banding recovery (J. Bond 1978); YUCATAN PEN.: apparently rare migrant, also taken (M. Thompson 1962) offshore on Cozumel I. In **winter** irregularly n. in ALASKA to Copper R. delta and rarely in interior; also n. into s. ONT. and QUE. occasionally and in the MARITIMES. NFLD.: present all year (in winter at least in s. part of the is.); Hersey (in Bent 1937) recorded migration "still in progress" at C. Ray on Sept. 15, which would indicate that some birds attempt crossing Cabot Strait to the mainland. Southerly known limits of occurrence of *velox* are in s. BAJA CALIF. and in GUATEMALA, HONDURAS, NICARAGUA, COSTA RICA, and PANAMA—all except 1st and last of these based on recoveries of birds banded in Minn.

The species is recorded as **fossil** from the Pleistocene of Calif. (3 sites), N. Mex., S.D. (2), Va., Fla. (2), and Bahamas (2); and from **archaeological sites** in Ariz. (3) and P.R. (Brodkorb 1964, with additions).

A "small hawk (*Accipiter*)," somewhat larger than *A. striatus,* is reported from Hawaii by Olson and James (1982b), who included it in their definition of "fossil."
                                                                    RALPH S. PALMER

MIGRATION   *A. s. velox.* There has been considerable study, yet uncertainty remains about some matters. The attempt here is to cover the subject briefly and generally.

The Sharpshin largely vacates the upper portions of its breeding range (a few birds remain, often not surviving until spring) and in colder seasons is distributed mainly from more s. parts of breeding range s. through Cent. Am. (The Pacific NW birds have

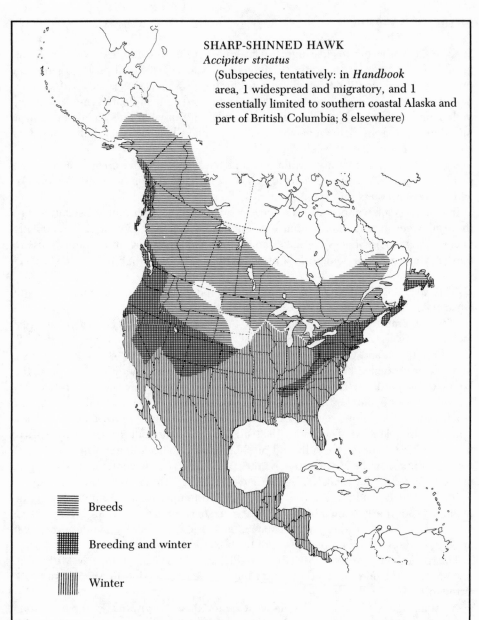

SHARP-SHINNED HAWK
Accipiter striatus
(Subspecies, tentatively: in *Handbook*
area, 1 widespread and migratory, and 1
essentially limited to southern coastal Alaska and
part of British Columbia; 8 elsewhere)

≡ Breeds

▦ Breeding and winter

▥ Winter

In *Handbook* area, occurrence as breeder and/or winterer and absence except as migrant (white areas) form a complex pattern across the continental interior; this map, therefore, is a generalized approximation of current status; numerous migrants go south of the U.S., into or via Mexico (absent from parts of the interior?) with numbers diminishing to the south; records extend to western Panama
There are resident populations outside the *Handbook* area, except Sharpshins of nw. Mexico may be more or less migratory
See also Subspecies, Distribution, and Migration

been considered local, but relatively dark individuals "suggesting origin in the Pacific Northwest" are captured and banded in fall near Duluth, Minn.—Evans and Rosenfield, in Newton and Chancellor 1985.) Even the most sw. nesters in the U.S. leave their nesting territories and vicinity seasonally but probably do not travel extensively, as do many n. breeders and young. Movement also occurs from higher elevations (summer) at least to lowlands and valley floors (winter).

There is still speculation about what influences the hawks to travel, although weather patterns play a definite role. It is known that the Sharpshin hunts early in the day, travels during the warmer hours of rising air currents, and hunts again toward evening. Many migrate fairly high at times, in thermals, beyond the range of unaided human vision; they descend to low levels on approaching water (its boundaries tend to funnel many through adjacent land areas). Migrants also commonly travel only 1–2 m. above ground or cover. Many pass along mts. and foothills where there are favorable updrafts.

Fall movement   The general pattern in cooler temperate latitudes is as follows: 1st-fall birds begin traveling first, well along in Aug., ♀♀ beginning before ♂♂, but soon the latter are moving and the sexes approach equal numbers of travelers at the time of the 1st peak; then numbers taper off gradually from around mid-Sept. to mid-Oct. Birds of all older cohorts start later; again, ♀♀ first, and numbers are low (especially of ♂♂) at the time the 1st-year birds reach and pass their peak; then the adults have a peak in about the 3d week in Sept., preponderantly of ♀♀; then numbers of ♀♀ decline rapidly, but ♂♂ continue in considerable numbers for about a half-month. Migration is essentially over for all Sharpshins in the 3d week in Oct. across s. Canada and the n. third or more of coterminous U.S. For a good example of the above general pattern, see Rosenfield and Evans (1980).

Mueller and Berger (1967c) made daily counts on 915 fall days, 1952–1964, at Cedar Grove, Wis., tallying 17,628 Sharpshins. There was a mid-Sept. peak (mostly Juv. birds) and another in mid-Oct. (largely older age classes). They suggested that weather conditions hundreds of miles n. may affect the flights at Cedar Grove. Most Sharpshins were seen on days of w. winds, within 2 days after passage of a cold front, often with a drop in temperature, and on at least partly sunny days. They suggested that the birds fly when weather is conducive to formation of updrafts and that wind drift (lateral displacement) concentrated the birds along the w. shore of L. Michigan. The Sharpshin does soar when migrating on favorable winds.

Direction and distance   The distribution of fall and winter banding recoveries of birds banded at Cedar Grove, as mapped by Mueller and Berger, show that the birds head approximately s. and then occur laterally both w. and e. of due s. At least many passing through Cedar Grove evidently winter in the s. U.S., but others elsewhere (1 recovered in se. Guatemala). Based on recoveries of birds banded in fall near Duluth, Minn., they leave in a se. direction and then veer sw. toward e. Tex. and Mexico—a pattern that corresponds to prevailing winds. The mean latitude of winter recoveries was ♂ 33°20′N and ♀ 24°50′N—a difference of over 900 km. In their 1st winter, ♂♂ tend to remain farther n. than ♀♀; in older cohorts, each sex evidently tends to winter farther n. than younger birds of corresponding sex. The categories overlap broadly. In spring they tend to retrace the general route taken in fall. (From Evans and Rosenfield, in Newton and Chancellor 1985.) A ♂ banded in Ont. in Oct. 1975 was recovered in Guatemala 3 years later (M. and D. Field 1980).

Reverse migration Good examples are known from the e. coast of Fla. where, for example, on Oct. 23, 1976, Sharpshins approached a large body of water, turned around, and headed n. in a stiff nw. wind (Simons 1977). They go down the Fla. Keys, then reverse direction (Darrow 1983). About 1,000 were seen flying n., Sept. 20, 1982, at Wellfleet on outer C. Cod, Mass. (1982 *Am. Birds* **36** 153).

Fall dates Sharpshins depart interior Alaska in large numbers in early Sept., the month of mass movement in s. Alaska and across Canada. At Hawk Ridge, near Duluth, Minn., the highest daily count was 1,510 on Sept. 22, 1970 (same day as maximum Broad-winged Hawk count: 24,300). This location is a modified funnel—Duluth at the tip—formed by the Sawtooth Range and the shoreline of L. Superior; other factors also contribute to concentrating the flight. See Hofslund (1966) for map of major fall concentration areas in e. N. Am. At Hawk Ridge in 1951–1963, 33,475 Sharpshins were seen in fall. On the n. shore of w. L. Erie at Point Pelee, Ont., there is a big Sept. flight of Juv. birds; see also below.

At C. Race, extreme se. Nfld., 45 Sharpshins were seen Oct. 11, 1984 (1985 *Am. Birds* **39** 26); do they winter there or head w. toward Cabot Strait?

In the ne. U.S., migration is on a broad front, s. and sw., often at relatively high altitude (observation is difficult); when the broad-fronted movement approaches such water crossings as Long I. Sound or the mouths of Del. and Chesapeake bays, a variable portion of the migrants descends to a lower altitude and is diverted, depending on wind direction and other local factors. At the e. end of Long I. Sound, many (almost entirely Juv.) Sharpshins cross from the mainland to Fisher's I., which has long been a notable place to observe them (A. and H. Ferguson 1922, Bent 1937). At C. May, N.J., when lateral winds are strong, the birds refrain from crossing the mouth of Del. Bay to C. Henlopen but instead reverse direction and cross inland at the head of the bay. The vast majority of those that cross over from C. May are 1st-fall birds; they continue down the coastal plain and may spread w. to some extent, but many migrate to peninsular Fla.

Again, the ne. region: migration begins in the 2d ½ of Aug., usually peaks in the 3d week in Sept. (mostly young birds) and again in early Oct. (older cohorts mainly), and ends with the last migrants the 1st ½ of Nov. Many island-hop in the inner Gulf of Maine. Along the barren e. edge of the Rockies, migration also extends from some time in Aug. to well into Nov.; apparently young birds start 1st and migrate over a long span, overlapping with adults, which peak in early Oct. Near the cent. Calif. coast, the birds begin moving about Aug. 1; there is a peak in late Sept., and some movement to about mid-Nov.

In interior w. U.S., migrants travel along ridges; most are concentrated rather narrowly.

The principal time of passage in the n. half of Mexico is apparently late Sept.–Oct.

Spring Concentrations are not as large as in fall. Sparse data for e. coastal Mexico indicate passage principally from late Mar. to past mid-Apr. (probably an early Apr. peak). In s. Tex., migration ends in last third of Apr. Whether s. birds leapfrog over migrants (and nesters) farther n. or whether all blend in spring movement is unknown.

312

There is movement in s. Canada from about Mar. 20 on. There are often peaks, varying in duration and quantity, depending on weather. There is some indication that older birds tend to precede yearlings and that older ♀♀ may sometimes arrive early on territories.

In the lat. of Pa. and Md., some movement is noted by very early Mar., most pass in the last 3 weeks of Apr., and movement ceases around May 10. At the same lat. in w. U.S., a few birds travel as early as Feb. and more in Mar., but migration is primarily in Apr., thinning out rapidly in early May.

Near the se. shore of L. Ontario, on av., migration lasts Mar. 20–May 25, with high numbers through much of Apr. into very early May. In spring of 1980 near Braddock Bay (s.-cent. L. Ontario shore), 6,271 Sharpshins were seen through June (1980 *Am. Birds* 34 893). Movement was great from about 0800 hrs. to 1200 hrs., again (fewer) at 1330–1500 hrs., and ceasing at 1600–1700 hrs. After passage of a cold front, when skies are clear and w. winds prevail, many Sharpshins may migrate (Haugh and Cade 1966, G. Smith and Muir 1978). At Whitefish Point (se. L. Superior), Mich., 3,000 were counted on May 5, 1982; the season total was 11,647 (1982 *Am. Birds* 36 855).

Across Canadian midlats. and s. Alaska, Sharpshins begin arriving by mid-Apr., and migration continues to about May 20; peak numbers are seen about Apr. 25–May 10 and, in interior Alaska, sometime in May. RALPH S. PALMER

BANDING STATUS   Many more Sharpshins have been banded than any other N. Am. raptor (closest runner-up is the Am. Kestrel). The total number banded to Aug. 1981 was 101,578 with 1,257 (1.2%) recoveries (Clapp et al. 1982). Main places of banding: the hawk-watching stations in the Great Lakes area and in N.J.-Pa.

At Hawk Ridge, near Duluth, Minn., 1972–1980, of 66,069 Sharpshins seen during fall migrations, 8,138 ♂ and 7,509 ♀ (total 15,647, or 23%) were captured, banded, and released. To 1982 there had been 73 (0.47%) recoveries—33 ♂ and 40 ♀ (Evans and Rosenfield, in Newton and Chancellor 1985). For their fate, see Survival, below.

At C. May Point, N.J., 1967–1982, the total number banded was 27,426 with 337 (1.5%) recoveries. For many details, plus maps of recoveries, by age and sex, from parts of e. Canada to s. Fla., see W. S. Clark (in Harwood 1985). RALPH S. PALMER

REPRODUCTION   *A. s. velox.* Some **first breed** as yearlings, but most when older. A. Brooks (1927) reported an adult acquiring an immature (yearling) mate after an adult mate had been shot. Bent (1937) stated that both sexes breed in Juv. Plumage—that is, as yearlings—undoubtedly basing this on reliable information of his own and from other egg collectors. Meng (1951) reported an adult-young nesting pair. At Baggs, Wyo., an "immature" ♀ reared 2 young in a nest that, earlier that year, had produced 3 Great Horned Owls to flight age (1982 *Am. Birds* 36 1001). Breeding pairs in interior Alaska, 1979–1981: ♂ "adult" × ♀ "adult" 8, ♂ "adult" × ♀ yearling 5, and ♂ yearling × ♀ yearling 1 (R. G. Clarke 1984). In Utah/Idaho: 1 member (either sex) has been "immature" in breeding pairs; also a pair in which both were "immature" (D. Fischer 1984). In ne. Oreg., 6 (of 10) nesting ♀ were Juv., and, based on limited data, there was no obvious difference in timing of nesting between birds in Juv. and in Basic feathering (Henny and Olson 1984).

The Sharpshin is the latest of our accipiters to arrive at breeding sites—many in Apr.–early May in temperate N. Am.—and the last to start nest building or refurbishing an old nest.

Territorial ownership   Advertising begins immediately or soon after arrival. There is considerable calling in spring, although quieter than our other accipiters, yet there is almost no information on displays, and this species is considered to be rather silent. C. W. Townsend (1920) clearly described both HIGH-CIRCLING and calling as well as the shallow undulations typical of accipiters and precipitous dive into the forest of the SKY-DANCE. Tail flagging (fanning-out of under tail coverts) has been seen in perched birds and occurs during High-circling plus calling (♂ at least). From rather cursory observations in N.Y., H. Meng (MS notes) was of the opinion that territorial and pair-formation activities are essentially as in Cooper's Hawk.

Nesting territory (defended) and hunting area   In Utah, Sharpshins regularly fly up to 1200 m. from their defended area to their hunting range and do not forage in the intervening area (J. Platt (1973). In N.Y., the ♂ defends an area up to about 75 m. in diam. and hunts elsewhere (H. Meng). F. Beebe (1974) stated that the Sharpshin is an opportunist, without the year-to-year fidelity to a specific nesting territory that characterizes our other accipiters. In Oreg., however, established areas contained more than 1 nest; that is, if a pair returned to a previously used location, a new nest was usually built within 100 m. of the old one (R. Reynolds and Wight 1978). One nest was used 2 years by Sharpshins and the following year by Cooper's Hawks. In Utah, traditional groves are commonly used and may contain as many as 5 old nests; if a pair nests in the same location and builds anew, it usually does so within 50–100 m. of the former nest (J. Platt 1973). There are a few reports of refurbishing and using last year's nest. Presumably, 1 member of a pair, and often both, returns to the former nesting area. That they may shift more than our larger accipiters may be a consequence of their probable rather short av. life span (rapid population turnover), shifting abundance and scarcity of food, and competition with earlier-nesting raptors (especially Cooper's Hawk) for living space. That they seem to form no enduring pair bond (F. Beebe 1974) is neither proven nor disproven; having mated and bred at a locality—although mates may be elsewhere and seasonally separated part of the year—both sexes probably tend to return to their former nesting location in succeeding years.

Total area used in Wyo. was approximately ¼–½ sq. mi. per pair (the Craigheads 1956); in Oreg., 4 pairs av. 2,750 ha./pair, and mean distance between nests was 4.3 km. (R. Reynolds and Wight 1978), but note in Reynolds and Wight, fig. 2, that active nests of Cooper's Hawk intervened.

Copulation   The pair mate repeatedly, more often in morning, away from the nest but within the defended area and in the same manner described for Cooper's Hawk. Shelley described it and the accompanying vocalizations well (in Bent 1937).

Nest site   Typically in a small stand of dense young conifers near a forest opening. Near Montreal, W. J. Brown examined over 200 nests, the majority in black spruces, a few in balsam fir, and very few in other conifers. They were 10–60 ft. above the ground on longitudinal branches, generally in a thick clump of spruce near a clearing or path. A few were built on nests of a former year. In Utah, the majority are in conifers, but some are in deciduous trees—cottonwoods, maples, oaks, and so on—and none in lone trees or open stands but characteristically in a densely foliaged conifer within a dense stand among taller deciduous trees (J. Platt 1976b). Others report similarly; apparently, concealment near a suitable hunting area is of prime importance to the Sharpshin.

Nest Newly constructed, a shallow platform, about 2 ft. in diam. and 6 in. thick, of interlaced dead conifer twigs. Both sexes fetch material, but the ♀ does most or all building (H. Meng). As in Cooper's Hawk, the **greenery** added is typically flakes of bark. Unusual nests include an old Blue Jay's nest 6 ft. up in a hemlock sapling (Bent 1937), 1 reportedly in a hole in a cave and another in a "hollow prong" of a broken sycamore branch (Audubon 1840), on high rocks in Pa. (Krider 1879), and on an old collapsed magpie nest in Colo. (C. F. Morrison 1887).

Clutch size Usually 4 or 5 eggs. N. Am.: 0–6 eggs (3.9 ± 1.3) in 37 clutches and 1–6 young (2.7 ± 1.5) in 31 broods (Apfelbaum and Seelbach 1983). New Eng.: 94 sets (of 4) and 37 (5) (F. Carpenter 1887). Pa. (Pocono Mts.), 61 first sets: 28 (of 4), 29 (5), and 4 (6) (Street 1955). Oreg.: mean number of eggs was 5 (in 3 nests, 1969), 3 (1 nest, 1971), and 5 (1 nest, 1972) (R. Reynolds and Wight 1978). Average clutch size in 34 nests in Utah was 4.3 (range 3–5) (J. Platt 1976b). Full range is 3–8 (Bent 1937).

If the 1st clutch is taken, the ♀ will lay again in a new nest nearby. A ♀ in Conn. laid 18 eggs as a result of repeated nest robbing (J. M. W. 1882).

Breeding season The period of rearing the young, when food demands are greatest, coincides with an abundance of nestling small birds and the young of small mammals that can be readily captured. The Sharpshin thus nests later than Cooper's Hawk and much later than the Goshawk. See fig. 11 in N. Snyder and Wiley (1976).

Egg dates Omitting full samples and giving the median group (for presumably viable eggs taken) from Bent (1937), dates are: Alaska to Que.: 108 (of 216 records) May 25–July 8; New Eng. and N.Y.: 74 (of 149) May 22–June 3; N.J. to Ga.: 14 (of 29) May 18–29 (and in the Poconos in Pa., av. date for clutch completion was May 25 [Street 1955]); Ohio, Iowa, Minn., and Colo.: 4 (of 8) May 8–June 2; and Wash. to Calif. and Utah: 13 (of 25) May 22–June 11. Ten nests in ne. Oreg.: clutches completed May 30–June 21 (Henny et al. 1985). Bent's compilation did not indicate state of incubation or whether replacement clutches were included.

Two records of other subspecies than *velox* may be of interest: Colima, Mexico, ♀ in "adult" feathering but with brown eyes was taken from a nest July 9 (Schaldach 1963); and in Las Vilas Prov., Cuba, 2 eggs taken Jan. 3 (Garrido 1967).

In equatorial P.R., the Sharpshin (*A. s. venator*) has a short breeding season (N. Snyder, in I. Newton 1979); also, 1–3 eggs or young in no less than 30 nests (Delaney 1982).

One **egg** each from 20 clutches (Canada 1, Maine 1, Mass. 1, Conn. 5, N.Y. 1, Colo. 1, Utah 3) **size** length av. 37.70 ± 1.34 mm., breadth 30.44 ± 0.91, radii of curvature of ends 12.84 ± 0.73 and 10.84 ± 0.63; **shape** short subelliptical to subelliptical, elongation 1.23 ± 0.050, bicone −0.037, and asymmetry +0.081 (F. W. Preston). Fifty-eight eggs av. 37.5 × 30.4 mm. (Bent 1937). They are among the handsomest of any N. Am. hawk and have an almost infinite variety of markings (Bent). Ground **color** whitish to pale bluish (it fades), overlaid with light to dark browns, some even with a hint of violet, in blotches, splashes, washes, and/or fine spots or dots; the pigment may be concentrated at either end or at widest diam.; occasionally an egg has almost no markings; usually there is a slight sheen.

Eggs are usually laid on alternate days, which would require 9 days for a 5-egg clutch, and they generally hatch in 2 or fewer days. The ♀ is probably on the nest at night before or from time of laying of the 1st egg, but continuous warming does not begin until about the time the 3d egg is laid (H. Meng) or until the clutch is complete (J. Platt 1976b). Some ♀ are close sitters (Tufts 1962). Although the ♂ is so much smaller than the ♀ that he could not cover a 5-egg clutch satisfactorily, he does sit occasionally while the ♀, nearby, is eating food he has fetched.

Incubation period   Hatching began 30 days after the last egg of a clutch was laid (Tuttle, in J. Platt 1976b); period assumed to be 30–32 days (R. Reynolds and Wight 1978); also given as 34–35 days (Nice 1954).

The ♂ at first roosts at night in a dense conifer within the defended territory but tends to remain away from it after the young hatch—except to fetch food. On these occasions, he sometimes remains for a while, particularly when his mate is in another tree eating the prey he has delivered to her. In Utah, during the rearing period, the ♀ remained in a nearby grove until the young were at least 10 days old, and it was not until they were 15 days old that she began to spend time away from the nest (J. Platt 1973). A study of 2 Ariz. nests (N. Snyder and Wiley 1976) indicated that, to midnestling stage, nearly all food eaten by the pair and offspring was captured by the ♂; then the ♀ began to hunt extensively and continued throughout the remainder of the breeding cycle. (See also these authors for prey size, capture rate, feeding rate, etc.)

Hatching success   Some data were tabulated by R. Reynolds and Wight (1978). In clutches in which some eggs hatch, it is probable that the number hatched is at least an egg less than the number laid. In Oreg., success was down to 69.9%—lower than in either Cooper's or the Goshawk—from infertility, death of embryo, and shell breakage, all presumably related to the very high level of pesticides in the Oreg. Sharpshins studied by N. Snyder et al. (1973).

Development of young   Little recorded information. A disparity in size between the sexes (♀ larger) is apparent from very early in nest life, and ♂♂ become feathered at an earlier age than ♀♀. Growth is probably similar to that of *A. nisus* of Eurasia, for which see Moss (1979).

Age at first flight   The young are developed sufficiently to move out of the nest (become "branchers") in Oreg. in 21–24 days (R. Reynolds and Wight 1976); in Utah in 24 days (♂♂) and 27 days (♀♀) (J. Platt 1976b); and in Ariz. a 4-week "nestling stage" (N. Snyder and Wiley 1976). The Juv. feathering is fully developed in 38–40 days (Camp, in J. Platt 1976b).

Breeding success   Some data were summarized by Reynolds and Wight (1976), indicating that 70–100% of hatched young survive to fly. In 1980 at Laurel, Md., 30 pairs raised 60 young to flight age, the highest success in a 10-year study (1980 *Am. Birds* **34** 883).

Reynolds and Wight regarded branchers as difficult to observe, but in Ont., Mueller et al. (1981a) watched a brood for nearly 2½ weeks and found that they, and even the ♀ parent, adjusted rather readily to the near-presence of the observers. In 120.5 hr. of observation there were 73 deliveries of food—40 by the ♂, 23 by the ♀, and 10 by undetermined sex. There were indications that most of the hunting was done more than 1.5 km. from the nest, although prey appeared to be abundant in the immediate vicinity. The young began predatory behavior at estimated age 40 days, when the parents were still delivering food quite frequently. There was a rapid decline in such deliveries when the young were 42–47 days old, even though prey was plentiful, which aligns with observations that the young become independent at about age 7 weeks (J. Platt 1973, N. Snyder and Wiley 1976). Mueller and Parker discussed fully the roles of both parents and the amount of prey available and captured and concluded that, apparently under most conditions, the ♀ could provide whatever prey the brood needed without having to be 1.7 times as large as the ♂ and capturing slightly larger prey.   RALPH S. PALMER

SURVIVAL   Of the records reported by Keran (1981), major identifiable causes of mortality were "road kill" and kill by predators rather than shooting. Of the 73 recoveries of birds banded near Duluth, Minn., 1972–1980, the major causes of recovery were: found dead, collision with windows, shot (12 of 13 s. of the Mexican border), and recapture at other banding stations. Juv. mortality was highest in fall–winter; almost 50% of mortality of older birds occurred in spring and within 700 km. of Duluth. Apparently the rigors of spring travel are mainly responsible for these losses—primarily of ♀♀. (From Evans and Rosenfield, in Newton and Chancellor 1985.)

Few Sharpshins live 5 or more years. Based on 92 recoveries plus 18 fall returns, figures are 19%, 24%, 25%, 15%, 10%, 5%, 2%, and 2% for calendar years 0–7; thus, 19% lived more than 3 years (D. Evans).   RALPH S. PALMER

HABITS   A. s. velox. The Sharpshin is an expert—numero uno—at sneak attack, lightning fast and at times reckless. From concealment in foliage it dashes out so fast that even the practiced eye has difficulty in following it, seizes a small bird, and vanishes. It usually hunts well up in the forest canopy. Another hunting method is to leave a sheltered perch with a fairly commanding view, drop close to the ground, and alternately flap and glide. On its course it takes advantage of any sort of concealment— bushes, stumps, fallen trees, fencerows—then, in an instant, drops or turns to grasp at a small bird or rodent. If it fails, it swings up into another tree from whence it soon makes another foraging flight.

The Sharpshin does not hesitate to pursue its prey closely through dense foliage or even to run after it on open ground or through weeds or bushes. In Calif., 1 left a perch on a fence, alighted on the ground, extended its talons in under a bottom rail, and dragged a chicken from its hiding place (G. Lawrence 1874). Its relatively long legs enable it to run rapidly, as one did on approaching a pond to drink (Marshall 1957).

As with our other accipiters, prey is squeezed, and the needle-sharp talons can penetrate and cause fatal damage. No doubt some prey is suffocated; very probably, the shock of being suddenly seized and squeezed is a major cause of death. The hawk flies off with its prey to a convenient perch nearby and begins tearing and plucking at the base of the skull; in the nesting season, prey is often beheaded before delivery to ♀ or nestlings.

317

Many persons who maintain feeders for song and other birds are thoroughly familiar with the accomplishments of this hawk. The slightest hint that a Sharpshin is in the vicinity causes small birds to vanish to shelter, and there is great hesitancy to come into the open until long after sundown. According to Gaddis (1980), 1 or 2 of the prey species in a mixed foraging flock utters a high-pitched alarm, and all react instantly; foraging flocks in Fla. were very irregular in movement and direction, which probably rendered predation on them more difficult.

Michener reported that one can trap and release the same individual repeatedly (1930), but D. Evans did not find this to be true. (Compare with Cooper's Hawk and note suggestions that banding them accustoms them to man, so that they are more easily shot.)

Much has been written about prey size v. size of the smaller ♂ and larger ♀; see especially Storer (1966), Mueller and Berger (1970), and N. Snyder and Wiley (1976). Based on various stomach analyses, major prey species of the Sharpshin are Am. Robins, Com. Starlings, Catbirds, House Sparrows, towhees, various native sparrows, and juncos. In general, prey tends to be smaller than that of Cooper's Hawk.

C. J. Maynard (1896) saw a Sharpshin strike down a Night Heron (*Nycticorax nycticorax*), but the heron recovered and flew into a thicket. Was this territorial defense or attempted predation on oversized "prey"? At least the ♀ Sharpshin is well able to capture species as large as the Bobwhite (*Colinus virginianus*), very young domestic fowl, and even the red squirrel (*Tamiasciurus*). On the small end, a Sharpshin, believed to have been a ♂, captured an Anna's Hummingbird (*Calypte anna*) that was perched when attacked (Peeters 1963).

R. B. Simpson (1911) saw one attack a Pileated Woodpecker (*Dryocopus pileatus*) that most obviously was trying to avoid the encounter, and Simpson shot the attacker. Kilham (1958) saw one make 7 attacks on a Pileated within 10 min. and was convinced that it was not play but that the hawk was trying to strike down the larger bird. In Fla., a Red-bellied Woodpecker (*Melanerpes carolinus*) gave "scream calls" and got free of a hawk's grasp (Saul 1983).

The Belted Kingfisher (*Ceryle alcyon*) is known to mob the Sharpshin repeatedly, just as it does Cooper's Hawk; it then escapes by flight or diving or both. The McCabes (1928), in a most interesting account, thought that the kingfisher enjoyed baiting the hawk, which it did daily. For more on this subject, see Bent (1937) and R. E. Kirby and Fuller (1978).

In cent. Nev. in May, in response to squeaks made by a man in an open field, a ♀ approached directly and was shot (Linsdale 1938).

In N.H. in early fall, woodchucks (*Marmota monax*) were shot and the carcasses left in a meadow; a pair of Sharpshins came there to feed, evidently on carrion-feeding insects. In due course, on hearing the report of a rifle, the hawks habitually flew overhead, watching the doings below (Shelley, in Bent 1937).

Numbers   Although past evidence is not accurate to the third decimal point, it is well known that fall migrants, concentrated at such places as Fishers I., N.Y., and Hawk Mt., Pa., literally were slaughtered from about 1880 on. This slowed down beginning in the early 1920s. Apparently Sharpshin numbers held up better in the West, where the birds were less concentrated for shooting. Then came the biocide era,

318

dating from the late 1930s, with eggshell thinning and other wasting effects. Later, N. Snyder et al. (1973) suggested that high levels of DDE in Sharpshins in the West suggested exceedingly high levels in the East. Various information could be mentioned, but the following is indicative: at a Md. location, in comparing fall numbers for 1951–1954 with 1958–1961, Sharpshins declined at an annual rate of 12–21%, more rapidly than the Peregrine (Hackman and Henny 1971). In our area generally, after the decrease to near-cessation of shooting, Sharpshins declined drastically from around 1940 on. Use of DDT was banned in the U.S. beginning in 1972, and numbers have since leveled off, and have possibly improved since the late 1970s. Westerly birds evidently continue to be exposed to persistent organochlorines, the use of which is increasing in Mexico and Cent. Am.   RALPH S. PALMER

FOOD   In N. Am. n. of Mexico. Small birds mainly, occasionally small mammals, reptiles, amphibians, and insects. There are important general summaries of data by Storer (1966) and Sherrod (1978); for ne. U.S., see R. Latham (1950); for part of Oreg. in breeding season, see R. Reynolds and Meslow (1984). S. Duncan (1980) gave data on 86 stomachs dated 1917–1941 and from throughout the area covered here. It is generally agreed that small birds make up over 90% of the prey captured.

Birds primarily   The 107 stomachs with food examined by A. K. Fisher (1893) contained birds of 46 species. In N.Y., A. and H. Ferguson (1922) reported that 483 stomachs contained 530 birds, 16 mammals, and 38 insects. Of 18 stomachs from Maine, birds (mainly sparrows) were in 16, frogs 1, mice 1, and grasshoppers 1 (Mendall 1944). McAtee (1935) found 20 families of birds in 944 stomachs: poultry in 2, gamebirds in 5 (Bobwhite 4, Woodcock 1), sparrows and finches 305, warblers 175, thrushes 116, vireos 44, swallows 29, mice 25, bats 2, and 1 each shrew, squirrel, rabbit, and lizard. Identified at a nest in B.C.: birds of 13 species, including young Sharp-tailed Grouse (*Tympanuchus phasianellus*) (J. Munro 1940). Of the 22 species of birds identified in 62 stomachs from Pa., the Robin and Rusty Blackbird were the largest prey (G. Sutton 1928). The Sharpshin attacks the Bobwhite with success (Stoddard 1931). In Ariz. in winter, a Sharpshin was seen feeding on a still-warm body of another Sharpshin (Ligon, in A. Phillips et al. 1964). Chief prey in the Fresno area, Calif.: Mockingbird, White-crowned Sparrow, Calif. Quail, and Say's Pheobe (J. G. Tyler 1913).

Mammals   Seen to snatch a red squirrel from a limb (Simpson 1911). Has also taken red-backed vole (*Clethrionomys*), meadow vole (*Microtus*), deermouse (*Peromyscus*), house mouse (*Mus*), rabbit (*Sylvilagus*), shrew, and bats (*Tadarida*, etc.).

At a Tex. cave, Sharpshins arrived to await the evening emergence of free-tailed bats (Sprunt, Jr. 1950).

Cold-bloods   A few frogs, snakes, and lizards are recorded.

Insects   Mostly grasshoppers, dragonflies, crickets, beetles, large lepidoptera, and caterpillars. Mormon crickets (*Anabrus simplex*) reported (La Rivers 1941). Some identified insects may have come from the digestive tracts of prey or may be carrion-eaters.   RALPH S. PALMER

COOPER'S HAWK

Accipiter cooperii (Bonaparte)

Smallish hawk (slightly smaller than Am. Crow) with rounded wings, long rounded tail, and long legs. Length 14¾–19¼ in (37.5–49 cm.), wingspread 35½–39 in. (90–99 cm.); the ♀ is larger within these spans (little overlap between the sexes); the ♂ av. over 12 oz., or about 340 gm., the ♀ over 20 oz., or about 560 gm. (no overlap between the sexes). The 5 outer functional primaries are notched on their inner webs; the outermost of these is longest and next outermost nearly as long. There is a slight difference in ratio of total length to wingspread in our accipiters (both sexes have similar ratio in each species), Cooper's having relatively longer tail and shorter wings. The upper anterior third of the tarsus is feathered in Cooper's (the anterior half in the Goshawk, the anterior quarter in the Sharpshin). The middle toe of the Sharpshin is relatively the longest, that of Goshawk shortest, and Cooper's intermediate. The eye, in proportion to size of head, is also intermediate in size in Cooper's, being relatively larger in the Sharpshin and smaller in the Goshawk.

After the Juv. stage: fairly well defined very dark crown (especially in the ♂), the dorsum quite dark and with or lacking bluish cast, the white underparts transversely marked with some variant of rusty, the tail broadly barred dark and light. The Juv. is dark above with much lighter feather margins, the pale venter is longitudinally streaked dark (rarely it is plain), and under tail coverts white (lack the arrowhead-shaped marks of young Goshawks).

No subspecies.

DESCRIPTION   One Plumage/cycle, sexes nearly alike, Basic I apparently earliest definitive; ♀ starts molting ahead of ♂; molting prolonged.

320

▶ ♂ Def. Basic Plumage (entire feathering) worn from late SPRING or later to following late SPRING or later. **Beak** blackish distally and bluish basally, cere greenish yellow; **iris** deep orange (rarely paler) to various reds depending somewhat on angle of view. **Head:** crown dark lead color, forehead feathers edged buffy cinnamon or lighter, occiput feathers white with narrow blackish tips ("occipital spot" when feathers raised); nape abruptly lighter than occiput; lores grayish; ear coverts and side of neck vary from white through palish grays to browns, finely streaked black; throat white, occasionally toward buffy, usually with blackish shaft streaks. Remainder of **upperparts** dark bluish gray (fading toward brownish), the feather shafts darkest; scapulars with concealed spots of white; upper tail coverts tipped white and often with a more or less evident single white band. **Underparts** white with fine black streaks and almost always with many transverse bars that vary with individual from rusty (usually) to tawny olive; barring varies in width, the white at times nearly obliterated on chest and flanks. Tibiae banded tawny or reddish brown; under tail coverts white. **Feet** tarsi and toes palish yellow. **Tail** variably very dark neutral colored above, becoming whitish toward bases of inner webs of outer feathers, the undersurface pale grayish crossed with 3 (a smaller 4th concealed) broad, sharply defined blackish bars, the distal one widest and very tips of feathers white. **Wing** dark (like back) above, the flight feathers white toward bases of inner webs; undersurface pale grayish, the feathers conspicuously barred and tipped darker; under wing coverts and axillars white, barred more or less reddish brown.

▶ ♀ Def. Basic Plumage (entire feathering) worn from SPRING to SPRING. As ♂ except no bluish cast to dorsum and a tendency to be less heavily barred ventrally.

Prebasic molting (in latitude of cent. N.Y.) begins during late Apr. or early May and ends approximately 4 months later. The ♀ ordinarily starts a week or 10 days ahead of the ♂. First to be dropped is primary #1 (innermost) and its greater covert; then the others are molted sequentially outward. A feather usually drops as soon as the adjoining new one is about half-grown. Secondaries, counting from outer to inner, #1, #5, and #13, and usually the central pair of tail feathers, molt next. About then, most or all secondary coverts are lost. From secondary #1 and #5, molting proceeds inward (toward the body), also from #13, and from #16 centrifugally. Secondary #4 is usually the last to drop, with #8 next to last.

Arrested molting (data from ne. Oreg.). At least sometimes, in nesting birds, molting ceases about the time the 3d primary is dropped and resumes after a considerable pause when stress of feeding the brood diminishes (see Henny et al. 1985).

In the Oreg. study, tail molting started with the central pair (#1) 28 times, the adjoining pair (#2) twice, and #3 once (Henny et al. 1985). The middle and lesser wing coverts are renewed somewhat irregularly and, generally, not all of them during the main span of molting. For example, one can often identify a bird as in Basic I by 1 or more persisting Juv. lesser wing coverts. A few dorsal feathers also are retained sometimes as is, occasionally, a flight feather of wing or tail.

The scapulars molt starting with median. The rump starts on each side and molting proceeds posteriorly to the upper tail coverts. The back begins between "shoulders." On the breast the upper lateral feathers are dropped first, with molting proceeding both medially and posteriorly. The 1st crural (thigh) feathers molted lie along the outer (distal) portion, and molting proceeds proximally and medially.

321

The last contour feathers to be renewed are at front of head, back of neck, center of back, median proximal parts of tibiae, chin, and middle of breast. Sequence is the same for both sexes and all molts; however, feathers of Basic Plumages are shorter than corresponding feathers of Juv. Plumage.

Eye color In Mar. or later of the year after hatching a pale yellow or orange tinge develops under the lower edge of the pupil. This gradually encircles the entire pupil. By the end of Sept., the irises are yellowish orange. They remain about the same during Prebasic Molt II, but the orange becomes somewhat more vivid in both sexes. During Prebasic Molt III the eyes of the ♀ do not change, but those of the ♂ turn scarlet-orange. A mated pair with clutch in Texas had yellow eyes (Van Tyne and Sutton 1937); in Ariz., some breeders have yellow eyes at presumed age of 2 years (N. and H. Snyder 1974a).

Tarsal scutes The tarsal scutes of two birds examined in N.Y. were so indistinct as almost to obliterate the individual scales. All scales on the front of the tarsus except the lower 4 and on all on the back except the lower 2 were fused. The small lateral scales were only slightly fused. Ragsdale (1894) examined a number of such birds and noted that some from Mass. had partially fused scutes, some from Minn. showed complete fusion, and a few from Texas had the scutes entirely obliterated.

AT HATCHING The eyes are open as soon as the nestling is dry; they are pale bluish gray with a faint brownish tinge. Beak pale brownish gray, cere pinkish. The nestling is covered with short creamy white down A (prepennae) that is later pushed out on the tips of the true feathers. There are short tufts in among A. Legs and feet nearly white. (See also Reproduction, below)

Soon a longer down B grows; by age 9 days, it has obscured all of A. It is white and varies from 6 mm. long on top of the head to 27 mm. on sides of breast and back. When the young hawks are about 11 days old, the pin feathers begin to break through their sheaths, carrying down A at their tips. At 21 days the rectrices and some of the scapulars and remiges protrude as much as 14 mm. out from down B. In the following week the feathers grow rapidly, and, by end of the 4th week, they completely cover the down except on legs, forehead, chin, and postauricular regions. From then until they depart, young lose much down, and often the nest is completely covered with it. Much down is picked or preened off. See Reproduction, below, for growth of nestlings.

▶ ♂ ♀ Juv. Plumage (entire feathering) fully acquired by late SUMMER of year of hatching and succeeded by Basic I beginning in late SPRING or early SUMMER of the following year.

On about the 51st day in ♂ ♂ and 53d or 54th in ♀ ♀, the remiges and rectrices reach full length; a few days later their bases become dry, and there is no further change in wings and tail until the following late May or early June. Head–body feathering grows to some extent after growth has terminated in wings and tail.

Beak more or less grayish, cere pale yellow; iris grayish, then pale yellow (see below). Top of **head** and the **dorsum** variably brownish black, the feathers on dorsum with sharply delineated palish brown margins. The feathers of the occiput are laterally and basally white (light area when feathers raised). **Underparts** palish buffs or browns with narrow longitudinal shaft streaking, but flanks and under tail coverts paler and unmarked. **Tail** dark above (inconspicuous barring), the feathers narrowly tipped white; on underside, 5 (and a partially concealed 6th) transverse dark bars on palish gray. The Juv. has more, and narrower, bars than Basic Plumages. Legs and **feet** pale yellowish. **Wing** dark above (the very dark barring inconspicuous), and the scapulars and inner secondaries have large whitish patches; underside shows the narrow dark barring on pale background, and the very pale wing lining has elongated dark markings or streaking.

The Juv. feathering is longer and more lax than in subsequent Basics (tail perhaps 4–5 mm. longer).

If a feather should be lost accidentally after it is fully grown (or "hard-summed," as a falconer would say, meaning fully cornified basally), the feather to follow will be of the next (Basic) Plumage. In 1st-winter birds these new feathers are easily seen. That is, many young birds have a few reddish breast feathers, the result of their precursors having been knocked out during dives through underbrush in pursuit of prey.

Eye color of young As the nestlings grow, the brownish tinge disappears except for a narrow band at edge of the iris. When the young are 4 weeks old, or just before they are ready to leave the nest, the pale brownish inner band has almost disappeared and the irises are slightly more intensely bluish gray than previously. The eyes retain some of this color until about the middle of July (age just over 1 year), when pale yellowish or orange appears around the iris. This ring gradually becomes more intense and radiates outwardly. The pale bluish gray of the iris is also diffused gradually by this tinge, and by late Aug. or mid-Sept., all of the bluish gray has been supplanted by pale lemon yellow or orange. This increases slightly in vividness during the next few months.

Measurements Birds in Juv. feathering have significantly shorter wings, longer tails, and weigh less than those in Basic feathering.

Estimated overall LENGTH: sexes overlap in fewer than 5% of individuals— ♂ 375–435 mm., av. 405, and ♀ 422–490, av. 455 (Mueller et al. 1979a, text and diagram). See McDowell (1941b) for additional data.

BEAK from cere of "adults" 34 ♂ 15–17.5 mm., av. 16.2, and 27 ♀ 17.5–21, av. 19 (Friedmann 1950); mean figures in N. Snyder and Wiley (1976) are very close.

The following, from Mueller et al. (1981c), all are for same time of year—birds trapped in **fall** at Cedar Grove, Wis., on the w. shore of L. Michigan:

Basic feathering ♂ WING across chord (of 48) 225–246 mm. (238 ± 5.4) and TAIL (of 51) 180–202 (191 ± 5.4); and ♀ WING across chord (of 56) 258–292 mm. (270 ± 6.6) and TAIL (of 58) 210–238 (221 ± 7.1).

Juv. ♂ WING across chord (of 52) 224–247 mm. (234 ± 4.5) and TAIL 185–207 (196 ± 5.2); and ♀ WING across chord (of 59) 254–275 mm. (266 ± 5.2) and TAIL (of 58) 210–238 (221 ± 7.1).

Mueller et al. also gave a table of **spring** meas. plus detailed analysis of all mensural data.

In ne. Oreg., in Basic feathering WING across chord 41 ♂ 214–233 mm. (223.5 ± 4.90) and 24 ♀ 237–265 (253.7 ± 6.70); TAIL 37 ♂ 171–189 mm. (178.7 ± 4.30) and 23 ♀ 190–216 (206.6 ± 7.18) (Henny et al. 1985).

Within each sex, Juv. and Basics differ significantly in every meas.; also, comparing Juv. with Basics, ♂ ♂ differ significantly from ♀ ♀ in every meas. Birds in ne. Oreg. in summer have shorter wing and tail than those in Wis. in any season; see Henny et al. (1985).

Weights   Birds with empty crops are preferable, since crop contents can equal ⅕ weight of a bird. Fall birds at Cedar Grove, Wis. (Mueller et al. 1981c):

Basic feathering 51 ♂ 297–380 gm. (349 ± 19.6) and 57 ♀ 460–588 (529 ± 36.1). Juv. 53 ♂ 292–389 gm. (335 ± 26.5) and 58 ♀ 413–598 (499 ± 39.8). The same authors also gave spring wt. plus detailed analysis of all data. Note that there is no overlap in wt. of ♂ ♂ of any age with ♀ ♀ of any age.

In ne. Oreg. (Henny et al. 1985): Basic feathering, "early" (May 14–June 14) 31 ♂ 235–300 gm. (277.3 ± 14.9) and 2 ♀ 439–480 gm. (459.5 ± 29); and "late" (June 28– Aug. 6) 17 ♂ 245–338 gm. (284.1 ± 24.4) and 18 ♀ 395–542 gm. (474.1 ± 42.6). Also 9 Juv. ♂ "early" 263.9 ± 10.9 gm. and "late" 318.5 ± 19.1; these prebreeders weighed less than older birds early and outweighed them later. Five ♀ Juv. (4 known to nest) in "late" period weighed slightly more than ♀ ♀ in Basic at the same time.

Juvenals apparently achieve "adult" wt. about the time of Prebasic I molt, that is, when approximately a year old. Females in both Juv. and Basic feathering weigh significantly more in spring than in fall, while ♂ ♂ of both categories are slightly lower.

Birds in ne. Oreg. in summer weigh significantly less than those in Wis. in fall; see Henny et al. (1985).

Hybrids   None; the *A. gentilis* × *cooperii* included in Suchetet (1897), cited by various subsequent authors, is very questionable (see under Goshawk).

Geographical variation   Cooper's was formerly listed by many authors as comprising an e. and a w. N. Am. subspecies; see literature citations in Friedmann (1950). The birds are evidently more variable westerly where the country is more open. There appears to be a gradual size increase from n. to sw., but differences in extremes are not great enough to warrant designation as 2 subspecies (S. Jones 1979). Based on WING chord meas. of birds trapped in Wis., Mueller et al. (1981c) suggested that larger individuals migrate earlier than smaller ones and breed farther s. Summer birds in ne. Oreg., weighed and meas. by Henny et al. (1985), were smaller than those in Wis. in any season.

Affinities   Cooper's is close morphologically to Gundlach's Hawk (*A. gundlachi*) of Cuba, the latter presumably being an isolated derivative of the former. In fact, in an earlier time (see Friedmann 1950), Gundlach's was treated as a subspecies of *A. cooperii*. According to J. Bond (1965), Gundlach's has close affinity with Cooper's and is very different from the Bicolored Hawk (*A. bicolor*) of s. Mexico to Tierra del Fuego. Amadon (1964) treated all 3 as composing a superspecies.   RALPH S. PALMER

FIELD IDENTIFICATION   **In our area**   Like the Sharp-shinned Hawk and Goshawk, Cooper's has a relatively long tail and short, rounded wings; its usual mode of flight consists of alternating several rapid wingbeats and brief periods of sailing. Distinguishing Cooper's from the other 2 accipiters has been discussed in detail by Mueller et al. (1979a) and W. Clark (1984); their findings, based primarily on migrating birds, are condensed here.

All 3 species are clearly separable by size.

The smaller, slower-flying Sharpshin beats its wings more rapidly than a rapidly moving Cooper's or Goshawk. The Sharpshin is more buoyant. The Goshawk is relatively long-winged and flaps more slowly. Cooper's is intermediate. All 3 have flap-glide mode of flight.

All Cooper's are larger than all Sharpshins and most ♂ Cooper's (the smaller sex) are considerably larger than most ♀ Sharpshins (the larger sex). Based on measured live birds, fewer than 5% of large Cooper's (♀ ♀) overlap in size with the smallest Goshawks (♂ ♂).

Attempts afield, indeed, at times in hand, to distinguish these species by characteristics of feathering can be extremely difficult. Cooper's definitely have more rounded tails than Sharpshins or Goshawks, but often the difference appears slight. Female Sharpshins have moderately rounded tail even when folded, and tails appear rounded in both sexes when spread, as when soaring. Also, shape of tail during molting can be misleading. The white terminal tail band (not including contiguous light gray or light brown) is relatively wider in Cooper's than in Sharpshins, but individuals may vary. In proportion to body size, Sharpshins have longer wings and shorter tail than Cooper's.

The Goshawk in definitive feathering has a barred gray breast; an occasional pale Cooper's, in poor light, can be confused with it. Goshawks in all ages have a light stripe over the eye, but in some (particularly Juv. ♂ ♂) it is obscure.

The rusty breast barring in definitive-feathered Cooper's tends to be uniform in width; in most Sharpshins, it is somewhat wider at the shaft. This requires an excellent view in the field.

The venter in predefinitive Cooper's appears more sharply and finely streaked than in Sharpshins. This might allow correct identification of 80–90% of the birds if one has excellent judgment of it and sees it clearly. Some Juv. Cooper's have narrow streaks of nearly uniform width, and some Sharpshins have distinctly teardrop-shaped marks. Sharpshins also tend to be somewhat buffier on the breast than Cooper's—and streakings tend to end somewhat higher on the belly in Cooper's than in Sharpshins.

Under tail coverts in Juv. ♂ Sharpshins and Cooper's are almost always immaculate; in Juv. ♀ Cooper's they are occasionally lightly streaked; in Juv. Goshawks they are always streaked or spotted.

The dark bars on a tail feather of a Juv. Goshawk have offset (unaligned) halves, but in Cooper's they are approximately transverse (aligned); thus, the young Goshawk has a zigzag tail pattern, while the banding is nearly even in Cooper's. In a good view of the spread tail this is readily apparent. The bands appear irregular in folded tails of all our accipiters.

There is disagreement over whether the head of Cooper's is proportionately larger than that of the Sharpshin and whether Cooper's head in definitive feathering has a clearly defined cap, that is, is darker than the back.

Summary Definitive-feathered Goshawks have barred gray-appearing venter, and the Juv. tail has zigzag barring. All other so-called field marks of our 3 accipiters show overlap between species of some sort, hence provide only a possibility of correct identification. Best are size and size-related characters, which require experience and skill on the observer's part. Cooper's and the Sharpshin are most frequently confused. Broad-winged Hawks are about the same size as Cooper's, and Juv. birds of the 2 species are quite similar in coloring, but the Broadwing lacks Cooper's heavy barring

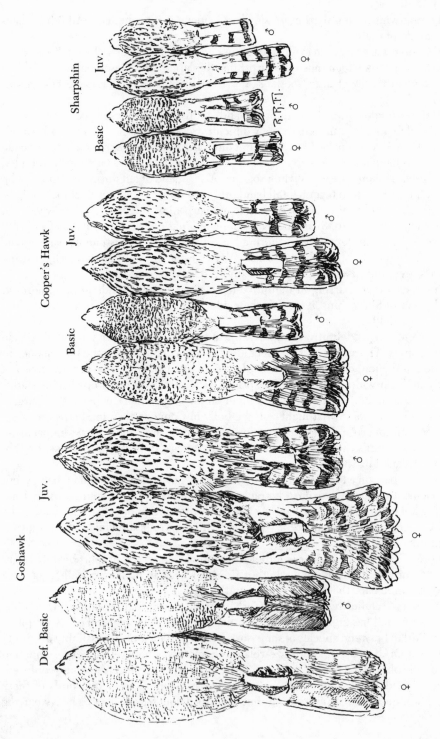

on underside of flight feathers of wing and only 3 outermost primaries are emarginated (there are 5 in Cooper's). When in doubt, one should list as an unidentified accipiter.

ROBERT N. ROSENFIELD

VOICE   Based on Meng (1951). (For brief comparison of vocalizations of our 3 accipiters, see N. and H. Snyder [1979].) Cooper's Hawks are silent much of the year, but with start of the breeding cycle, they become increasingly vociferous. As soon as actual nesting commences, the pair begins each day with a duet. They roost near one another, usually in a pine or hemlock stand, within about 100 m. of the nest. On awakening, the ♂ begins calling and "singing" and is likewise joined by the ♀. After incubation begins, the ♀ sleeps on the nest, but the ♂ still roosts nearby. As soon as dawn lightens the eastern sky, he starts calling; then the ♀ flies over to him and they both sing for 10–20 min. She then returns to the nest, but the ♂ continues singing for a while. As incubation progresses, the ♀ is increasingly reluctant to leave her clutch to join the ♂ in his singing, and by the 3d week, she leaves only to get food from him or to defecate. The ♂ gradually sings less and ultimately ceases. After the young are about 3 weeks old the ♂ sings only briefly, during midmorning and occasionally in late afternoon.

In addition to the various notes uttered during duets, the hawks have a great variety of vocalizations, heard most frequently after the young hatch. During 4 nesting seasons and at over 24 nests, all calls heard, along with the prevailing circumstances, were recorded. For most of them, function(s) could be assigned subjectively. Totals were: "adult" ♀ 42, "adult" ♂ 19, and young 13—probably more than recorded for any other raptor in the wild. Only a portion of this detailed record (from Meng 1951) is given in this volume.

In general, the ♂'s voice is higher than the ♀'s, also slightly faster and not as harsh, but certain calls are lower than hers. Fitch et al. (1946a) noted the same. The voice of older ♂♂ tends to be lower than that of younger nesting ♂♂, and the voice of older ♀♀ generally has a more rasping quality. Females nesting as yearlings have high voices, reminiscent of the young at time of first attaining flight. In general, their calls resemble those of older ♀♀ but are higher in pitch. Their typical alarm call could be written ki-ki-ki instead of ca-ca-ca; Bent (1937) described it as kak-kak-kak. The answer to the kik of the ♂ from older ♀♀ is whaar, but in yearling ♀♀ it sounds more like keea, wheea, or wheer and is quite flickerlike.

Voice of "adult" ♀   1 ca-ca-ca-ca (indefinite series): typical alarm when someone approaches the nest area; repeated often; many overtones give it a harsh quality. (The ♂'s is similar but lacks harshness and is generally 2 notes higher, although in some ♂♂, it is lower.) 2 As preceding, given while flying toward ♂ arriving with food and announcing this with kik. Suggests excitement; is faster and not as harsh as 1. Also uttered when the ♀ has finished her meal and is about to return to the nest to incubate. A sitting ♂, on hearing this, sometimes gets up from the eggs and watches for her to come; more often he just stretches his neck and looks about nervously; as soon as the ♀'s feet touch the nest, he executes a hasty dive out of the nest. 3 As 1 but much softer and clearer, a main component of the morning duet. 4 Series of about 8 ca notes, then a kik; as 1 but not as loud or harsh; indicates mild alarm or irritation. 5 caac whaar ca

327

(series), 1st note rising and 2d falling, given when coming to nest with food; the chicks call on hearing it. **6** *caa caa whaaaaa:* if the ♀ wants to know whether her mate is near, she gives this call. If he is within hearing distance, he answers *keee* (his **5**) quite a bit higher than the ♀'s call.

Voice of "adult" ♂ **1** *ca-ca-ca-ca* (long series): the ♂'s typical alarm note; not as piercing as the ♀'s **1** and usually 2 notes higher; sounds distinctly flickerlike, but sometimes lower and with reduced resemblance. Males heard uttering the higher version had paler irises and presumably were younger birds. A ♂ may dive at an intruder either silently or while giving this call. **2** The same, but slightly higher and faster, with very nasal quality like call of White-breasted Nuthatch; much lower than the ♀'s **1** alarm or **3** song, included in the morning duet and often followed by a couple of sharp *kik* notes. **3** Same, but softer than **1**, in flight when fetching food; after the ♂ alights, he follows it with a series of *kik* notes. **4** *cu-cu-cu-cu* (long series), under same circumstances as **3** but when ♂ is irritated. Uttered while burdened with quarry or chased by a Red-winged Blackbird or a Kingbird. **5** *keee keee:* higher than any of the ♀'s notes and given in reply to her **6**. **6** *kik* at 5–10 sec. intervals, the ♂'s most frequent note. Announces his arrival with food in the nesting territory. He calls a few times, then the ♀ flies to him, gets the prey, and takes it to the young. When young are 3 weeks old or older, the ♂ is often not inclined to deliver the food, and she sits idly by, 30–50 m. from the nest. The ♂ sees her there and may *kik* for as long as a ½ hr. before "realizing" that she wants him to take the food to the young. He then promptly does this but rarely, if ever, does any of the feeding. Sometimes this call is also given during the morning duet in an effort to lure the ♀ from the nest. Occasionally she is reluctant to leave her eggs, and if, after he has called about 40 times, she has still not come, he discontinues the *kik* notes and goes through the rest of his repertoire.

Voice of the young **1** *cheep* or *crirrp* occasionally audible when the eggs are pipped; a few hrs. before hatching, uttered quite loudly and can be heard from the ground on a calm day. The ♀ becomes more attentive and sometimes aids the young in getting free of the shell. Also uttered later on. Resembles note of hatching domestic fowl. **2** *eeeeeee* or *eeeeeeee-oo*, the latter with falling inflection at end; a squeal-like whistle; given when young are out of nest and anticipating or longing for food.

HEINZ K. MENG

HABITAT **Breeding season** In Mass., 27 of 48 nests (58.3%) were in white pine (Bent 1937); in N.Y., 14 of 36 (38.9%) in beech (*Fagus grandifolia*) (Meng 1951); in Md., 4 of 6 in oaks (*Quercus*); in Wis., 29 of 82 (35.4%) in white pine (Rosenfield and Anderson 1983); in nw. and e. Oreg., 17 of 18 (94.4%) in Douglas fir (*Pseudotsuga menziesii*) and 8 of 15 (53.3%) in ponderosa pine (*Pinus ponderosa*) respectively (R. Reynolds et al. 1982); in ne. Oreg., a preference for Douglas fir (K. Moore and Henny 1983); and in w.-cent. Ariz., in all conifer and riparian communities except mesquite-salt cedar and having a high density of "rather small, densely foliaged trees," usually nesting in the dominant species (Millsap 1981).

Meng (1951) reported that Cooper's nests in N.Y. were near forest edges or other clearings and that such edges were used as primary hunting sites by "adult" ♂♂. Rosenfield and Anderson (1983) noted that nests in Wis. were relatively close (av. 66.1 m., or 217 ft.) to forest openings. In Md., Titus and Mosher (1981) found no difference between distance from forest opening to nest and from random points to an opening. Yet site selection is evidently not random.

The importance of open water to nesting Cooper's Hawks is unclear. In the cent. Appalachians, Titus and Mosher (1981) found no evident relationship. In Wis., Rosenfield and Anderson (1983) suggested that water is not required, based on its relatively far distance from nests. R. Reynolds et al. (1982), however, suggested a preference for nearby water in Oreg. In Utah, av. distance from water was 224 m. (735 ft.) (Hennessey 1978). In w.-cent. Ariz., over ⅗ of 54 nests were within 1 km. of standing water (Millsap 1981), which may relate to occurrence of suitable nesting trees.

A dense canopy cover is a consistent vegetative characteristic of nest sites. On av., nests are higher up than those of the Sharp-shinned Hawk. Five studies (all cited above) reported av. percentage of canopy closure of 64–95.2%. Good vegetative cover probably protects the nest from adverse weather and predators (R. Reynolds et al. 1982). An alternative explanation is the *Accipiter*, having evolved in shaded forest or woody habitat (Wattel 1973), may have low tolerances for higher temperatures and direct sunlight (R. Reynolds et al., 1982). This also may explain why 2 studies in Oreg. and 1 in Utah reported a tendency for Cooper's to nest on n. and e. slopes, aspects that, due to various biophysical interactions, comprise more shaded stands than those with s. exposure. In the Appalachians in Md., however, sites were randomly oriented (Titus and Mosher 1981).

R. Reynolds et al. (1982) found a vegetative profile around Cooper's Hawk nests of trees 30–60 and 50–70 years old in nw. and e. Oreg. and of a tree density of 656/ha. (265/acre) and 1,159/ha. (469/acre). They also reported av. vegetative ground cover of 38% and 6% for nests in nw. and e. Oreg., respectively. There are further data for Oreg. in K. Moore and Henny (1983) and for Wis. in Rosenfield and Anderson (1983). Cooper's Hawk nests in Md. were in stands of larger overstory trees, denser understory, and denser ground cover in comparison with random plots (Titus and Mosher 1981).

Several authors have noted relatively open understories, which may facilitate approach to and departure from the nest.

K. Moore and Henny (1984) reported different nest-site habitat between younger and older Cooper's Hawks in Oreg. Yearling ♀♀ nested in younger successional stages or stands that had undergone recent selective overstory removal than did those of older age. They also reported that yearling ♀♀ used mistletoe as a nest structure significantly less often (50%) than older ♀♀ (70%). They suggested that, since mistletoe may provide concealment from predators searching for nests from the ground, and since the percentage of successful nests (96%) on mistletoe was higher than those elsewhere (86%), yearling ♀♀ were using lower quality sites—perhaps due to inexperience in breeding. This assumes that the ♀ selects the site; in N.Y., Meng (1951) reported that the ♀ selected it.

Exceptional situations Cooper's occasionally nests in small wooded areas and rarely in an isolated tree (R. Stewart 1975, Asay 1980) or an urban location (Stahlecker and Beach 1979, Rosenfield and Anderson).

Migrations and winter A preference for a mixture of habitats, commonly hunting on the perimeter of wooded areas. Migrants cross wider waters than the smaller Sharpshin; evidently they tend to avoid the Great Plains. Some winterers seem to have

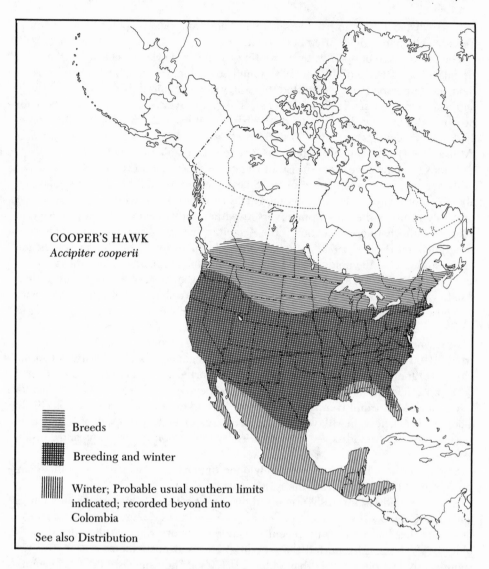

COOPER'S HAWK
Accipiter cooperii

≡ Breeds

▓ Breeding and winter

▥ Winter; Probable usual southern limits
indicated; recorded beyond into
Colombia

See also Distribution

an affinity for human habitations and suburbs, where Starlings, for food, are probably
the main attraction.   ROBERT N. ROSENFIELD

DISTRIBUTION (See map.) **Breeding**   Cooper's Hawk does not breed as far n. as
the Sharpshin, and it is more plentiful across coterminous U.S. than beyond in most of
its Canadian range. Seldom penetrates extensive boreal forest. Has benefited by man's
reduction of large forest tracts to discontinuous wooded areas and scattered tracts,
which seems to be the explanation of its recent extension of breeding range n. in
Canada e. of the Rockies; see especially J. Grant (1957) and Houston (1958). Has
apparently always been scarce in e. part of Canadian Maritimes.

330

It does not extend s. into the tropics. Absent or rare in some areas of s. U.S. (rare in s. Tex.), but has bred rarely beyond in Baja Calif. and across extreme n. Mexico e. into Nuevo León.

Winter Withdraws from n. range, including almost all of Canada and much of n.-cent. states in U.S. Most birds occur at this season within coterminous U.S., but they are also widespread in Mexico, where records decrease s. Recorded beyond in Guatemala, Honduras, Costa Rica, and Colombia.

Recorded as **fossil** from the Pleistocene of Calif. (3 localities), N.Mex. (2), Fla. (4), and from **prehistoric sites** in Calif., Pa., W.Va., and Ga. (Brodkorb 1964, with additions).   RALPH S. PALMER

MIGRATION Cooper's Hawks from the n. third or half of the breeding range are migratory, although some remain behind—a few even in Canada—through winter. More s. birds are locally migratory or more or less resident; they vacate snow-covered forests and canyons for desert valleys, low woodlands, coastal plains, and elsewhere. Much information has come from raptor migration lookouts; their locations and flights have been described in journal papers and by Heintzelman (1975, 1982).

Fall Birds of the year migrate earlier than older ones, and ♀ ♀ precede ♂ ♂ of each category by a minimum of several days; that is, there is overlap of these groups, but peaks are spaced over considerable time, as with the Sharp-shinned Hawk. Passage coincides with that of the hawks' main prey: medium-sized birds. Generally, fall movement in e. and w. N. Am. extends late Aug.–early Nov., with peak accipiter flights at most lookouts about mid-Sept.–mid-Oct. The av. overall distance traveled is probably greater for ♀ ♀ than ♂ ♂, although the latter have been taken far s. It is also of interest that, whereas falcons start flying very early in the day, accipiters are not seen in any numbers until the air has warmed and currents are prevalent, around 0900 hrs.; there is a lull at midday, and, along in the afternoon, the hawks are again flying. Cooper's begins its day's travel later in the morning than does the Sharpshin.

Important places to observe fall passage of accipiters include Hawk Mt. on Kittatinny Ridge in e. Pa., C. May at the s. tip of N.J., and Hawk Ridge near Duluth, Minn., at w. end of L. Superior. Of these, data for the longest period are from Hawk Mt., where 62 to 590 (av. 206) Cooper's have been counted 1934–1975 inclusive (Nagy, in Chancellor 1977). Relatively little has been published from the West, but it may be noted that winter comes earlier there (prey is scarce earlier), and so peaks of movements are apparently at least a ½-month earlier than corresponding eastern ones. Also, in keeping with the varied terrain, migration appears to be more dispersed; see Gullion et al. (1959) and Anderle (1966).

In e. N. Am., fall migrant Cooper's are concentrated on the periphery of the Great Lakes and along Appalachian ridges and are also funneled down such peninsulas as C. May, N.J., and Fla. From Hawk Cliff, Ont., the birds migrate w. along the n. shore of L. Erie and then disperse s. to wintering areas in the e. U.S. (B. Duncan 1981). Those going via more w. Great Lakes locations evidently have much lateral spread to the s. in winter. Birds from far w. in interior Canada may first head se. (toward Wis.) to avoid crossing the Great Plains (Mueller et al. 1981c), while those from the Rockies westward in Canada and the U.S. probably head fairly directly s. It seems probable that some birds traveling both e. and w. of the Great Plains pass the winter s. of the Mexican border.

Heavy autumn flights usually occur on days of nw. winds with clear to partly cloudy skies, which usually follow the recent passage of a low-pressure area (Haugh 1970). For example, these winds, blowing at right angles to the ne.–sw.-oriented Appalachian ridges, are forced upward, resulting in an ascending current of air at the top along which the hawk can glide with relative ease (Meng 1951). Cooper's crosses some waters but shuns wide ones. An extreme example would be groups seen circling over Key West, Fla. (Hundley and Hames 1960); there is no evidence that they continue out over the sea.

Spring   Sequence of travel differs from fall, because older birds than yearlings go first, ♂♂ preceding ♀♀ (peaks a few days apart), then yearlings in larger numbers (more ♂♂ than ♀♀ at first). Migrants seem to be more dispersed than in fall. In Wis., judging from meas. of WING chord, larger birds migrate earlier than smaller ones, suggesting that larger ones breed farther s., as previously mentioned. Since migration in the latitude of s. Tex. continues well into May (when some s. birds are nesting), it would appear that there may be an overall shift of birds in the same period on the continent since breeders in cent. N.Y. return to their territories from late Mar.–mid-Apr. (Meng's data).

Flight speed   Twelve records from Hawk Mt. in autumn ranged 33.6–88 kmh. (21–55 mph.); flapping flight was generally faster than gliding. The av. speed was 46.9 kmh. (29.3 mph.)—virtually the same av. ground speed (48 kmh.) as for 152 hawks of various other species (Broun 1949).

A Cooper's Hawk banded in Wyo. on Sept. 13 was recovered 480 km. (300 mi.) away in Colo. on the 30th—thus averaging about 26 km. (15–20 mi.) per day during fall migration (Meng 1951).   ROBERT N. ROSENFIELD

BANDING STATUS   To Aug. 1981 the number banded was 10,777 with 482 (4.5%) recoveries (Clapp et al. 1982). Main places of banding: Ont. and N.J. (mainly), also Calif., Wis., Pa., Va., Utah, and Oreg.

B. Duncan's (1981) paper was based on 960 Cooper's banded 1971–1980 at Hawk Cliff, Ont.   ROBERT N. ROSENFIELD

REPRODUCTION   Many data here are from cent. N.Y. (Meng 1951); where other information is given, the location is indicated.

Age when first breeds   Most individuals do not breed until they are at least 2 years old. A variable percentage—of ♀♀ (and ♂♂ rarely)—breed as yearlings, as noted from N.Y. to Alaska, Oreg., Calif., and Ariz. In the ne. U.S. and se. Canada, based on "adult" survival rates, 1941–1957, yearlings and older would account for 34–36.8% of a stable population (it was declining, however); it was estimated that about 19% of the yearling ♀ age class bred (Henny and Wight 1972). In Utah in 1973 and 1974, 20% of the ♀ breeding population were yearlings; this was attributed to high predation at nests, resulting in loss of older ♀♀ (Hennessey 1978). In ne. Oreg., 8 of 37 breeding ♀♀ in 1975–1979 were yearlings (K. Moore and Henny 1984). In w.-cent. Ariz., on 54 occupied territories, yearling ♀♀ were on 4 of 7 failed nests and at 7 successful ones

(Millsap 1981). In Wis., a breeding yearling ♂ had orange eyes (Rosenfield and Wilde 1982); these authors cited a reference to a yearling pair of breeders in Calif. In cent. N.Y., the occasional nesting yearling ♀ had not acquired fully "adult" voice (Meng).

There are some "adult" birds, and more yearlings, available to replace lost mates. In B.C., a ♀ was shot from her nest with eggs; some days later another ♀, also in definitive feathering, was incubating the clutch and was likewise shot; later, a 3d ♀, in streaked Juv. feathering, occupied this nest and raised the brood (Law 1919). In w. Pa., a ♀ disappeared just before her clutch was due to hatch; the ♂ hatched 1 of 2 eggs (2 others had been removed) and, before the nestling was 2 weeks old, the ♂ had attracted a Juv. ♀ as a new mate. She laid 2 eggs alongside the nestling but did not incubate them (Schriver, in Hickey 1969).

Pair bond Probably renewed in succeeding years, at least occasionally when both birds survive. K. Moore and Henny (1984) reported that 10 of 17 (59%) nest sites were reused in a following year—by the same ♀ in at least 3 instances. They also indicated that only successfully nesting ♀♀ returned to the same sites and that no 2d-year ♀♀ returned whether successful or not. Based on characteristics of feathering, Höhn (1983) suggested that the same ♀ bred in the same grove of trees in Alta. in 2 successive years and again 2 years later. Meng (1951) felt able to recognize nesting individuals by characteristics of voice and behavior; he suggested that the same birds were paired seasonally in more than 1 year in cent. N.Y.

Displays Cooper's ordinarily arrive at cent. N.Y. nesting areas during the last week in Mar., and they are occasionally heard calling at that time. Soon the ♂ begins defending an area of about 100 m. (300+ ft.) radius, and any prey that he captures is brought there; if the ♀ of his choice is present, he offers it to her—apparently as an inducement for her to remain. In Kans. 1 year, the bird that arrived 1st on territory did not obtain a mate for several weeks; then, on Apr. 1, 2 birds were seen in display flight, or SKY-DANCE. The ♂'s wings were raised high over his back, then moved in a wide arc in slow rhythmic flapping, his flight resembling that of a nighthawk (*Chordeiles*); once a presumed ♀ was seen to fly in this manner (Fitch 1958). Mockford (1951) saw a ♂ fly thus in Ind. and noted that the under tail coverts flared laterally (compare especially with the Goshawk). In B.C., F. Beebe (1974) also noted this spread during display. He further stated that displays were "brief," usually occurring on bright, sunny days at about 1000 hrs. and that they started with both birds soaring aloft (HIGH-CIRCLING) on thermals, followed by the ♂ diving down at and behind the ♀. Then a slow-speed, slow-motion chase developed, the birds moving with slow exaggerated wingbeats alternated with glides during which the wings were held in high dihedral. Berger (1957) observed nighthawk-flapping on 17 occasions in spring by migrants and once in fall; he questioned its purpose.

Nest site Tree species used are mentioned earlier (see Habitat). Average height above ground ranges 8–15.4 m. (26.6–50.5 ft.) and diam. at breast height 21.3–44.5 cm. (8.4–17.5 in.) (various authors). In Oreg., Cooper's was reported to nest in the lower portion of a tree, immediately below the crown (R. Reynolds et al. 1982), or in the crown (K. Moore and Henny 1983). Usually nests are built in a main crotch or on a horizontal limb against the trunk. Some are built on squirrel nests or on rubble in the fork of a tree, or they may be incorporated in masses of mistletoe (K. Moore and Henny

333

1983, R. Reynolds et al. 1982) or grapevines (Hamerstrom 1972). One was apparently built on a tree nest of a wood rat (*Neotoma*) (Fitch et al. 1946a).

Nest size Those in conifers are rather broad and flat, measuring about 64–76 cm. (25–30 in.) in diam. and 15–20 cm. (6–8 in.) in height. Those in deciduous trees are higher, measuring about 61 cm. (24 in.) in diam. and 43 cm. (17 in.) high (Meng 1951). The nest bowl is about 19 cm. (7–8 in.) in diam. and to 10 cm. (4 in.) deep (Meng).

Nest density and spacing In Mich., the Craigheads (1956) found 1 pair per 1,554 ha. (3,840 acres) in 1947–1948 and 1 per 1,166 ha. (2,881 acres) in 1942. Postovit (1978) estimated 10–12+ pairs on 23,310 ha. (57,598 acres) in N.D. One nest per 734 ha. (1,814 acres) was found in cent. Wis. in 1981 (Rosenfield and Anderson 1983). R. Reynolds and Wight (1978) reported 1 nest per 2,321 ha. (5,735 acres) during 1 year and the next year both 1 per 1,857 ha. (4,589 acres) in w. Oreg. and 1 per 2,200 ha. (5,436 acres) in e. Oreg.

Distance between nests has been reported as follows: 1.6 km. (1 mi.) in Calif. (Fitch et al. 1946a) and Ariz. (Brandt 1951, N. Snyder and Wiley 1976); 2.4 km. (1.5 mi.) in N.Y. (Meng 1951); 1 km. (0.6 mi.) in Kans. (Fitch 1958); 5 km. (3.1 mi.) (av. of 4) during 1 year and 5.5 (3.4 mi.) (av. of 5) the next in w. Oreg., also 3.5 km. (2.2 mi.) in e. Oreg. (R. Reynolds and Wight 1978); and 1.6 km. (1 mi.) (av. of 4) in cent. Wis. (Rosenfield and Anderson 1983).

Territorial defense As with our other accipiters, the nesting territory from which intruders are evicted if possible, has a rather small radius centered at the nest; the area hunted may be relatively large, show little overlap with nesting territory, or even be entirely separate. At beginning of Apr. 1951, a captive mature ♂ Cooper's was tethered near the tree in which a wild pair was building a nest. The wild ♂ flew at the "intruder" repeatedly, then alighted alongside it on the fallen tree on which the captive was tethered. From here, the wild bird attacked repeatedly. Finally, unable to evict the rival, the wild ♂ departed and the ♀ followed. The nest had not increased in size a week later, and a search revealed a new one about 100 m. (300+ ft.) away (Meng).

Cooper's v. Sharpshin There seems to be no record in e. N. Am. of these 2 accipiters nesting in the same woods simultaneously. In one instance a Sharpshin nested in an area previously occupied year after year by Cooper's. In 1948 a Cooper's nest was in a beech woods intermixed with hemlock. In 1949 Cooper's again nested in this woods, but in 1950 a Sharpshin raised her brood there. The following year Cooper's was back again. In Oreg., in the same year, 2 Sharpshin nests were approximately 300 m. (980+ ft.) from active Cooper's nests, and 5 Cooper's nests were 300–450 m. (980–1,470 ft.) from active Goshawk nests (R. Reynolds and Wight 1978).

Nearby nests of other birds In studying 30 Cooper's nests in cent. N.Y., distances from them to nests of other birds were compiled for 29 species. These nesters varied in size from the Great Horned Owl down to wood warblers and Wood Pewee. Examples: Red-shouldered Hawk—closest 87 m. (17 within 384 m.), Great Horned Owl—46 m. (2 within 411 m.), Barred Owl—69 m. (5 within 283 m.), Ruffed Grouse—57 m. (7 within 197 m.), Am. Crow—137 m. (21 within 439 m.), and N. Flicker—140 m. (17 within 457 m.). N. Flickers are not often seen in Cooper's nesting territory, but once 1 alighted 9 m. from a nest and "scolded" the hawk nestlings for 10 min. Its head swayed

334

in a wide arc with each call. Shortly after it departed, a plucked, headless, and eviscerated Flicker was delivered to the nest by the ♂ parent hawk. Scarlet Tanagers often sing close to Cooper's nests, especially during the latter part of the incubation period. The sitting ♀ hawk watches with apparent great curiosity but does not disturb them even if only 1.5 m. away. Birds that seem to show no fear of the nesting hawks are Red-eyed Vireo, White-breasted Nuthatch, and Veery. Whenever either parent hawk is on its way to the nest, 1, or even all 3 of these birds, "scold" very loudly and often dive at the hawk—even as close as 6 m. from the aerie.

Reactions to humans During nest building the hawks are quite shy and secretive and ordinarily will not dive or call when the nesting territory is entered or even if the nest tree is climbed. After the 1st egg is laid, however, the hawks are occasionally heard calling when one comes close to the nest. Throughout laying, the ♀ often dives and calls if a person climbs to the aerie, but the ♂, if he happens to be nearby, will sometimes dive without vocal utterance.

Throughout the 1st week of incubation, the ♀ usually flushes quietly when one enters the nest area or taps on the base of the nest tree, but she will occasionally call a couple of times when someone climbs to the nest. Not until she has incubated for almost 2 weeks does she occasionally make "half-hearted" dives at a climber. During the 3d and 4th weeks she becomes increasingly more concerned over the safety of her clutch and calls longer and comes closer during her ever more determined dives. Sometimes, however, she will flush and depart silently. Temperament varies in ♀♀; some are excessively shy and are almost never seen, while others start calling and diving when a human intruder is more than 100 m. away.

During the final week of incubation, and especially after the eggs are pipped, the ♀ usually screams violently and may come within 2 m. when one climbs to the nest. Once a ♀ got up from her eggs and focused her gaze on an ascending climber, Heinz K. Meng, then dove straight down without altering her course until the last fraction of a second. Meng continued climbing, and the ♀ flew back to the nest and repeated the performance with a great deal of cackling. Three of her 4 eggs were pipped.

After all young are hatched the ♀'s protective instinct lapses temporarily, and she usually only calls from a distance when someone climbs to the nest. If the ♂ happens to be near, he may also call for a short time. As the young grow older, the ♀ becomes bolder, and, after they are 3 weeks old, she often dives within a m. of an intruder's head, cackling loudly. The ♂, too, may dive and call, but he is less aggressive than the ♀, who has been known to strike and draw blood. Meng has been struck by Goshawks, Sharpshins, and Red-shouldered Hawks but never by Cooper's. Bent (1937) also found this species to be less aggressive toward humans than our other accipiters. N. and H. Snyder (1974b) reported both a ♂ and ♀ nesting Cooper's diving at and striking a climber.

After the young are on the wing, the ♀ parent may call when a person enters the nesting area and may fly closer for a better inspection, but she will not dive. The ♂, if he should be in the vicinity, leaves the area. From this time on, both adults become increasingly more wary toward humans and are seen or heard less often.

Relations with other predators In addition to humans, other species occasionally disturb nesting Cooper's Hawks. American Crows are not allowed close to the nest and are quickly and easily driven away if they venture too close; occasionally, however, a crow is able to steal an egg in an unguarded moment. Broadly speaking, relations with crows are somewhat at a standoff—see Mailliard (1908), Richardson (1957), and G. Sutton (1929). Richardson saw a young ♀ Cooper's in spring knocked down by 2 crows; it was on its back and fighting them off when he captured it, and it may have died from shock.

If a Great Horned Owl should come near a Cooper's nest in daylight, the hawk, chattering in extreme alarm, dives and strikes at it. Often several crows and 1 or 2 Red-shouldered Hawks are attracted and join in the attack. While the owl remains close, the Cooper's will concentrate on it and tolerate the crows temporarily, but as soon as the owl departs the hawk chases them away. The Great Horned Owl is a serious predator on nesting Cooper's and takes many incubating and brooding ♀ ♀ and some nestlings. Some of the owl/hawk literature is Errington (1932a), Gullion (1947), and Wiley (1975c).

When large quadrupeds walk through the nesting woods, the hawk gives her semi-alarm *ca-ca-ca-ca-ca-ca-kik* but does not dive at them.

Nest building and morning duet The nest foundation consists mainly of dead branches of about ½ cm. diam. These are broken from a tree by the wt. of the airborne bird and are transported in the feet. Later, thinner sticks, either broken off by the beak or by the wt. of the bird, are used. Often these are carried in the beak. Most delivery is by the ♂, but the ♀ occasionally brings a stick or flake of bark. A single item is brought at a time, and usually about 2 weeks are required to build the nest, but on 1 occasion it took only 4 days. As soon as construction has begun, the mates roost near the site, usually in hemlocks or pines. On awakening, they "sing" a duet of a great variety of notes. The ♂ usually starts 1st (his voice is generally higher pitched). The duet may last for an hr. At its conclusion the birds copulate and preen. On a sunny day they often fly separately to a pool in the woods and bathe; then they fly to a sunny perch to dry. They also, however, go through bathing motions when it is raining. Duets are heard throughout nest building and most of incubation.

At about 0630–0700 hrs. the ♂ starts building and the ♀ watches him from a perch

within sight of the nest. She utters a call every so often. Occasionally she flies to the nest, inspects it, and may rearrange a stick that does not suit her, but she seldom brings any nesting material. After a 2- or 3-min. inspection, she flies to a convenient lookout perch and continues to call occasionally.

In most woodlands it is much easier for a hawk to fly near the ground rather than up among interlacing branches. Thus, Cooper's can customarily be seen flying with considerable speed within 3 m. of the forest floor. Just before the hawk reaches the nest tree it beats its wings rapidly a few times, and the attained momentum enables it to shoot up almost vertically to the nest. While building is in process, the ♂ stays at the nest only long enough to place a stick in proper position. When leaving, he dives with partly opened wings down toward the forest floor and then, with legs partially extended, straightens out and flies among the tree trunks for another stick. At certain hours in the morning during the height of the building period, the ♂ may alight on the nest every few min., evidently securing all of the material within 100–200 m. of the nest. During building the ♂ comes to the nest more than at any other time. His actions are quick and nervous, and while on the nest he jerks his head around continually as though there were some danger nearby. Occasionally he may call *kik* at this time.

When the nest is almost complete, the ♀ sometimes comes to it with prey received from the ♂ and eats it there.

Nesting materials   A newly constructed nest is identified readily from the ground if freshly broken ends of sticks can clearly be seen. Sometimes there are a few dry leaves in the nest base; they are not brought by the hawks but may be the remains of an old nest of crow or squirrel or may merely have accumulated in that particular crotch.

The nest is entirely composed of clean dry sticks and flakes of bark; the latter line the nest bowl. Sometimes 1 or 2 green hemlock branches may be found in the body of the nest, having been added during construction. Usually, a day or 2 before the 1st egg is laid, flakes of bark—often oak, maple, or hemlock—are added to the lining by both birds, although the ♂ gathers the majority. They are about 3–8 cm. long and are broken off by either beak or feet. Hawks kill with their feet, hence are proficient "footers." Many seem to enjoy striking with their feet and, when not particularly hungry, occasionally jump up and strike at the limb on which they are perching or fly to the ground and strike at and clutch leaves or other debris. Bark flakes are broken off similarly. The perching hawk looks "keenly" about until it spies a suitable flake, then darts swiftly at it and clutches it as if it were live prey. After a flake has been "killed," it is brought to the nest. In rare instances the 1st egg may be laid in a nest that lacks flakes, but they are soon added. At first there are only a few flakes, but more accumulate each day, and by the time the eggs hatch there may be a layer about 8 cm. deep in the nest.

Greenery   In addition to bark flakes, green sprigs of hemlock or pine, av. about 13 cm. long, are brought to the nest by the ♂ or ♀. Usually only 1 or 2 sprigs "decorate" the nest during laying, but in 1 instance there were several sprigs around the rim, and once there were 2 birch sprigs with catkins attached. Bent (1937) mentioned a nest liberally lined with white pine sprigs.

In cent. N.Y. dried grass was not used as a nest lining. If grass is present, it is a crow's nest. Occasionally a Cooper's, in grasping prey in a grassy spot, also clutches a bit of grass and brings it to the nest. In Fla., a nest was made of Spanish "moss" and dead oak branches (Grimes 1944).

Little is added to the nest during incubation, but as soon as the eggs hatch 1 or 2 fresh conifer sprigs are again placed on the rim. Occasionally even a maple sprig with partially unfolded leaves is used, but never a profuse lining of fresh leaves, as is characteristic of some *Buteo* nests. When the young are about 2 weeks old, fresh conifer twigs are again sometimes found at the rim. These are brought by the ♀, since the ♂ is busy hunting, and when he arrives in the nest with prey, the ♀ usually receives the quarry from him and takes it to the young herself. On the few occasions that the ♂ comes to the nest during this time, he always carries prey in his talons and, therefore, cannot bring "nesting material." From about the time the young are 2 weeks old, space on the nest becomes crowded and the ♀ adds a few sticks daily; she discontinues this 2 or 3 days before the chicks attain flight.

Copulation   Occurs from the time nest construction starts until the end of egg laying. Several times each morning the ♂ interrupts his other activities to copulate on a horizontal branch some 20–100 m. from the nest. He leaves the nest and flies over the forest floor until almost underneath the ♀, then rises vertically and alights directly but gently on her back. She has taken a firm grip on the branch, is leaning forward, and has her wings and tail partly spread. He remains about 10 sec.; in this span the ♀, occasionally also the ♂, gives a long call *whaaaaaaaa*. Afterwards both birds perch and preen for a while, then the ♂ resumes building. He ends his nest building for the day about midafternoon and starts hunting. The ♀ may hunt also, but usually she is supplied food by her mate.

Laying   Eggs are laid on alternate days (except often an extra day between the 4th and 5th eggs), usually early in the morning but sometimes around 1830 hrs. The ♀ remains on the nest 10–20 min. at each laying.

Egg dates   In cent. N.Y., the date the 1st egg is laid is remarkably regular for any particular ♀; it can be found on almost the same date year after year, with variation of a day or 2 either way depending on whether the season is early or tardy. If variation is

much greater, the original ♀ has probably been succeeded by another. Two yearling ♀♀ started their clutches a week or 10 days later than the av. for older birds. In ne. Oreg. the mean lag for completed clutches of Juv. birds is about 5 days (May 26 v. May 21)—Henny et al. (1985).

In Ariz. and N.Mex., laying av. about 2 weeks later in 1971 than in the 2 previous years; this was associated with a severe drought and a dearth of both vertebrate and invertebrate prey. When a wave of migrant songbirds moved into the area, most Cooper's began laying. The peak of the songbird influx passed relatively quickly, and several pairs of Cooper's did not complete their clutches. At 1 nest the feeding of the ♀ by the ♂ increased greatly while the songbirds were present. Also, although laying dates within territories were generally consistent, there was a fair amount of variability between territories. This was attributed to differences in altitude and in habitat quality (N. Snyder and Wiley 1976).

In the Ithaca, N.Y., region, earliest record for laying of the 1st egg was Apr. 22. The majority of nests had their 1st egg on Apr. 24. Other dates for 1st-egg depositions in particular nests were Apr. 23 and 27 and May 1, 4, and 6. Later dates were 2d attempts, often after predation by raccoons.

Egg dates in Bent (1937) indicate when viable clutches were taken—that is, many were incubated to a variable extent: New Eng. and N.Y.—119 records Apr. 25–June 26 (60 in May 10–20); N.J. to Va.—48 records Apr. 7–May 23 (24 in Apr. 29–May 11); Ohio to Minn. plus Canada—52 records Apr. 26–June 21 (26 in May 8–21); Mo. to Colo.—7 records Apr. 23–May 30; Wash. to Calif.—58 records Mar. 31–June 13 (29 in Apr. 19–May 17); Fla. to Baja Calif.—21 records Feb. 22–June 16 (10 in Apr. 15–May 17). Two recent reports: in ne. Oreg., clutches completed May 12–31 (mean date May 22) (Henny et al. 1985), similar to se. Oreg. (in R. Reynolds and Wight 1978); in w.-cent. Ariz., earliest egg Mar. 28, and 50% of clutches complete by Apr. 25 (Millsap 1981).

Clutch size Usually 3–6, commonly 4–5 eggs. N. Am.: 3.5 ± 1.0 eggs in 72 clutches (Apfelbaum and Seelbach 1983); New Eng.: 112 clutches (of 4), 57 (5), and 17 (6) (F. Carpenter 1887); cent. N.Y.: 4 (of 3), 21 (4), 10 (5), and 1 (6) (Meng 1951); 30 clutches in nw. Ohio: 1 (1), 1 (2), 7 (3), 15 (4), and 6 (5) (H. Price 1941); 12 in Pa.: 8 (4), and 4 (5) (Street 1955); 40 in Wis.: 8 (3), 13 (4), and 19 (5) (R. Rosenfield); and in w.-cent. Ariz., mean of 46 clutches was 3.33 ± 0.62 (Millsap 1981). Bent (1937) noted that 6-egg clutches are rare; of 266 at W. Found. of Vert. Zool., Los Angeles, only 7 were of 6 eggs and none more (L. Kiff). A 7-egg clutch was found in Ariz. (Ellis and Depner 1979). In Ariz. and N.Mex., N. and H. Snyder (1973) suspected that clutch size is a function of habitat quality—that is, when prey is abundant, clutches are larger. It may also be a function of age—the occasional 2-egg clutch is presumably laid by a yearling.

One **egg** each from 21 clutches (Pa. 13, Ind. 1, Calif. 2, Tex. 1, Ohio 1, Ga. 2, and unknown 1) **size** length 48.17 ± 2.32 mm., breadth 38.01 ± 1.47 mm., and radii of curvature of ends 16.24 ± 0.96 and 12.50 ± 1.20; **shape** between elliptical and subelliptical, elongation 1.27 ± 0.059 mm., bicone −0.04, and asymmetry +0.124 (F. W. Preston). These align closely with Bent (1937)—62 eggs av. 49 × 38.5 mm. In cent. N.Y., 137 eggs: length 47–53, av. 49.1 mm., and breadth 36–42, av. 38.7 (Meng 1951).

In nw. Ohio, 121 eggs av. 47.8 × 37.6 (Price 1941). In Ariz. and N.Mex., 34 eggs: length 45.7–52.5 mm. (mean 48.9) and breadth 35.4–39.6 (mean 37.8) (Hubbard 1974a).

The shell is smooth. **Color** when fresh is pale cobalt; during incubation it fades gradually to a dirty white with bluish tinge. Some eggs are spotted with dried blood droplets, which can be rubbed off with a moistened finger. Bent (1937) stated that 25–50% of Cooper's eggs showed scattered spotting of "pale browns or buffs." A ♀ that lays spotted eggs does so year after year and can be recognized by her unique clutches. Some eggs become stained. A heavily spotted set (Am. Mus. Nat. Hist. #476) from Wis. are suspiciously like those of the Broad-winged Hawk. Bent mentioned a heavily marked set from Pa.

The av. **weight** of a fresh Cooper's egg is 43 gm. (range of 36–52), and the av. declines to 34 gm. just before hatching.

Activities during incubation   Incubation usually begins after the 3d egg is laid, and, since 1 or 2 eggs are usually yet to be laid, hatching is asynchronous. The ♀ sits quietly on the nest and, about once an hr., gets up to preen and to turn the eggs. Occasionally she leaves the nest to join the ♂ in his morning "singing," to receive quarry from him, or to defecate. She appears to like to watch the sun rise and set and so, at these times, usually sits facing it. She is very sensitive to motion, watching moving insects or birds with great interest.

Throughout incubation the ♂ comes to the nest 2–3 times daily; he sits on the eggs during the interval that the ♀ is away devouring the prey he has brought for her. When he arrives, he usually stands for a while, looking around nervously, then settles on the clutch and continues his nervous head motions. As soon as the ♀ touches the nest rim on her return from eating, he leaves instantly in the usual manner—diving headfirst out of the nest and flying at first close to the ground. Later in the day, while on his way to a hunting area, he occasionally alights within a m. or so of the nest and watches the ♀ for a min. or 2. In the evening he comes by once or twice, on inspection.

Incubation period   Generally, a clutch of 5 eggs may be laid in 10 days and hatch in a span of about 3 days. The incubation period was estimated in Oreg. as 30–32 days (R. Reynolds and Wight 1978). The same was given for Okla. by Schwabe (1940). In Ariz., it av. 32 days at 4 nests (Millsap 1981). In cent. N.Y., after 34 days the 1st 3 eggs became pipped; the next day slightly larger holes were present in the midsection, and on the 36th day they hatched and the 4th egg was pipped. On the 38th day the 4th egg hatched and the break in the 5th egg increased in size; the latter hatched on the 39th day. Shorter incubation periods are in the literature; for example, Burns (1915) and Bent (1937) stated 24 days—far too short. In an incubator at av. temperature of 38.5°C, Cooper's Hawk eggs hatched on the 36th day. The usual temperature of an adult Cooper's is close to 41.2°C.

Hatching   The future nestling moves its head inside the egg, causing the egg tooth to come forcefully into contact with the shell, thus cracking it. It is normally pipped for 2 days. Then the bird chirps even more inside the egg and pushes the shell apart with its neck, head, feet, and wings. A newly born nestling is wet and appears naked but is actually covered with whitish down that later dries. The ♀ is very attentive during hatching and will even assist the nestling in getting out of the shell. The shells are transported 50 m. or more by her and dropped. For the next 2 weeks the ♀ stays near the nest and often sits on its rim. In rainy weather and in brilliant sunshine she shelters the young with her spread wings and tail. She preens at the edge of the nest frequently.

Nest sanitation After the ♀ preens thoroughly, which ordinarily requires about 15 min., she rearranges sticks and bark flakes. The young move close to the nest edge and thus are out of her way. Sometimes she picks up a dried skeleton, bone, or pellet and flies off with it. The young back up to the very edge of the nest to defecate, and, since they are capable of expelling their liquid fecal matter outward, the nest is kept clean. The ground below, however, may be marked by this material, and its odor may attract such predators as raccoons.

Roosting The ♀ sleeps with her young for about 2 weeks, by which time they have a dense downy covering plus adequate temperature control for keeping warm. The following data are from flash photographs taken at night:

During the first 3 nights the young were not visible from above since they kept close to their mother's incubation patch. She slept with her head resting on the rim of the nest; the young huddled against her breast, and her extended neck and breast feathers covered them almost entirely.

As the young grew in size there was correspondingly less room for the ♀ and she was forced nearer the rim. During this 2d week the young slept in a semicircle around her head and breast. The heads of the young were touching each other, and the ♀'s head rested on the heads and necks of her brood. At the beginning of the 3d week there no longer was room for the ♀, so she roosted on a branch close by for 2 nights, then selected a perch within about 50 m. of the nest and used it for the remainder of the nesting season. Such a roost can be located by the abundant "whitewash" beneath it. Usually a deciduous tree is selected, even by ♀ ♀ nesting in conifers. The roosting bird stands vertically, head tucked between the upper back feathers and scapulars, tail straight down. One foot supports her; the other is folded against her body. During the night she alternates feet and appears to do this without awakening. Both parents and young out of nest roost in this manner.

After the young are about 2 weeks old the ♀ does not come to the nest very often except to feed her brood or occasionally add a stick.

Activities of the ♂ At beginning of nest construction the ♂ occasionally brings food for the ♀, but not until incubation starts does he supply all of her prey. After the morning duet the ♂ goes hunting and around 1000 hrs. has returned with food for her. Usually the head and viscera of the prey have already been eaten by the ♂ at the kill site. Around noon or soon after he goes on another hunting trip, and in early evening he goes on yet another.

The ♀ is ordinarily brought food 3 times daily during incubation. Usually she consumes her food on a stump or low branch within 50 m. of the nest, but occasionally she flies back to the edge of the nest to feed. The main feeding time for the ♂ is in late morning or early afternoon, and the food that he brings the ♀ at this time is usually the remains of his meal.

When the eggs are pipped the ♂ still is not hesitant about sitting on them, but he ceases "incubation" altogether once they have hatched. If a nestling becomes free of the eggshell while he is present, he will pick up part of it, carry it some distance, and drop it. Sometimes a shell is found under the nest, having been knocked out accidentally.

After the young hatch the ♂ increases his hunting trips in order to feed the rapidly growing brood; eventually he hunts all day. During the first 3 weeks the ♀ is very attentive, and so the ♂ delivers food to her and she takes it to the nest. Thereafter, the ♀ is often not in the vicinity when he calls, so he takes food to the young himself. If he sees a skeleton in the nest, he may take it away and drop it, but he is not seen to feed the young. Elsewhere, on a single occasion, both parents were seen together feeding the brood (Fitch et al. 1946a). A ♂ reared 2 young to flight age after his mate disappeared (N. and H. Snyder 1974b).

Usually the ♂ remains at the nest 3–4 sec. at most, but at 1 nest with 30-day-old young he came with prey and remained 3 min. He is not as wary as the ♀ when delivering food. Whereas she may shy away several times or not come near all day when there is a camouflaged camera or other suspicious object nearby, the ♂ is not disturbed by this and flies to the nest without apparent hesitation. The ♀, of course, is at the nest more often and is therefore much more likely to notice any change.

Most prey brought to the nest vicinity by the ♂ is deplumed and/or partially dismembered at the plucking stump (plucking post, or "butcher block"), which is sometimes instead a prostrate log or a horizontal tree branch. It is used for secondary plucking (most plucking occurs at the kill site), feeding, and food transfers and may be up to 9 m. above the ground. Usually 2 or 3 such sites are used at a nest area, typically well within 100 m. of the nest. As soon as the ♂ alights at 1 of these, he calls *kik*, plucks some fur or feathers, and calls *kik* again. This calling and plucking may be repeated 7 or 8 times before the ♀ answers *whaar* and flies to him for the food. He waits until she clutches the quarry, then both birds shriek for an instant and the ♂ leaves. The ♀ then flies to the nest with the prey in her talons. Just as she is landing on the nest she may transfer it momentarily to her beak; as soon as she has landed she clutches it with her talons.

Sometimes the ♂ arrives in the nest vicinity with food and the ♀ is absent—usually in the week before the young fly. He then utters a whining sort of note before each *kik* and, if the ♀ does not respond, eventually takes the food to the nest.

When the young are small the prey is well plucked, headless, and eviscerated; during the 4th and 5th weeks the ♂ brings quarry only ¾ plucked and whole.

During the 1st 2 or 3 days after the young have left the nest, the ♂ often arrives there with food. If he sees the young approaching he then leaves the prey in the nest and speedily departs. Otherwise, he usually takes the prey with him and tries to locate the young. On seeing the ♂ the young usually fly after him, and he will lead them to the nest, where he drops the food. As the young become more proficient on the wing, they will actually "attack" the ♂ while he is en route and force him to drop his prey.

Brood reduction Occasionally a nest is found with 3 young of different ages. In such a nest, probably 2 eggs of a 5-egg clutch did not hatch. Since incubation starts with the 3d egg, if 2 of the 1st 3 are infertile (or, more likely, have become addled), the remaining 3 eggs would hatch on 3 different days—36th, 38th, and 39th—resulting in quite different nestling sizes. The young from the 5th egg does not usually survive

342

more than a week if the 1st 3 eggs hatch. It has been suggested that, when a nestling is found dead in the nest or disappears, fratricide has occurred—but very young hawks, at least, have neither incentive nor strength to carry out a fatal attack. The youngest may weaken slowly because it cannot assert itself enough to get sufficient food and so eventually dies and is eaten, carried away, or accidentally pushed out by the others. Occasionally 1 disappears during a storm (Schwabe 1940). If 1 of the 1st 3 eggs fails to hatch, the young from the 5th egg has a good chance of surviving; if 2 of the 1st 3 fail, then it is almost certain to survive.

As just noted, very young nestlings do not have the physical capability of killing a nest mate, accidentally or purposely. By the time they are 3 weeks old, however, it could happen that a large ♀, attempting to seize prey in the nest, might inadvertently seize the head of a small ♂ and so kill him. This has happened under artificial conditions when the young were confined together out of the nest. It is probable that larger young do not attack their smaller siblings unless they are very hungry from shortage of prey.

In Ariz. and N. Mex., N. Snyder and Wiley (1976) reported possible cases of fratricide; they observed early stages of the process at several nests. It began with young pulling feathers out of the back of a sibling's head with their beaks. This led to open bleeding wounds that stimulated further attacks, since young Cooper's have a strong pecking or feeding response to the color red. They emphasized, however, that such behavior was never observed at a nest where adequate food was supplied.

In cent. N.Y., on visiting a nest in 1951, all 4 young were found dead. They were 2½-week-old ♂♂. At another nest at this time there were 3 ♀ and 1 ♂, 3½ weeks old. On inspection, the nest was found to contain 3 young plus legs of the 4th—the largest ♀. Fratricide might be suspected in this case but not the previous one. It had rained for almost a week, exceptionally hard the 2 days before these nests were visited. At a nearby game farm 600 young pheasants died of exposure, and the same fate probably befell the 4 ♂ Cooper's. Older downy young have considerable oil on their down, which aids in keeping them dry even in a heavy rain—but in a prolonged rain they are likely to die of exposure. A dead chick is evidently not considered a deceased member of the family; instead, it is prey; hence, partly eaten nestlings are found in nests.

Growth of young   When hatched and dry, a Cooper's is covered with white down that sometimes appears to have a faint tan tinge. The skin is pale pinkish, which shows through the down in places. The feet and tarsi are a pale flesh color and the talons are white, tinged pinkish dorsally. Very conspicuous are the large eyeballs, which appear pale bluish gray through the skin of the head. The eyes are open as soon as the hawk hatches; the irises are pale bluish gray with a faint brownish tinge. The cere is very pale pinkish tan and the upper mandible same; the lower mandible is pale gray-tan, becoming dark distally. The mouth lining is like that of the adult but much paler, with only a hint of pinkish and bluish gray.

During their 1st week the young do not grow as rapidly as later. When a week old, the av. erect sitting height is about 9 cm. The down is denser now and soft parts show more color. The beak is little changed, but the cere is pale greenish yellow, as are sides of the gape. The skin between the eyes and external ears and the back of the head has a bluish tinge, and the area immediately below, to the base of the neck, has a pale orange

343

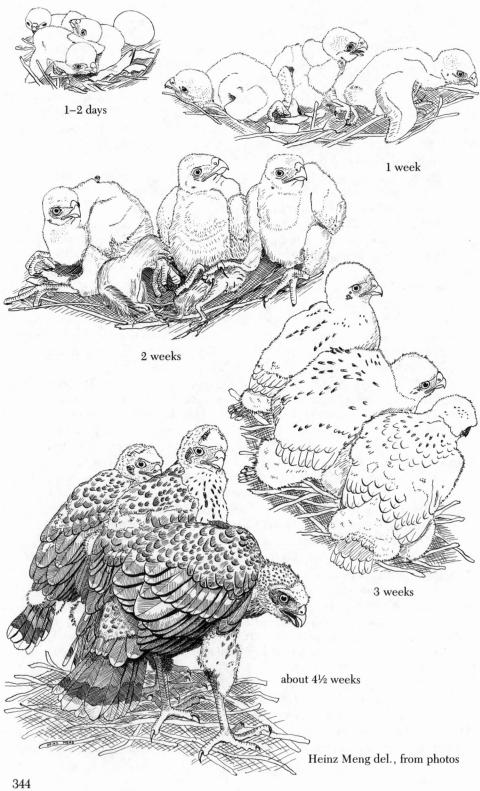

1–2 days

1 week

2 weeks

3 weeks

about 4½ weeks

Heinz Meng del., from photos

344

tint. This entire area is speckled with little tufts of white down. The eye has lightened somewhat, and a pale narrow brownish ring extends from and surrounds the pupil. The upper and lower ocular apteria are pale olive. Legs are pale orange-yellow, as are toes, although deeper yellow dorsally and distally; talons gray dorsally and white ventrally.

At 2 weeks the down is very deep and fluffy. Whereas it was white a week earlier, certain areas are now faintly buffy and grayish. The occipital region remains white and contrasts with the very pale yellowish buff of rest of head. The external ear is now almost completely hidden by this down. The cere is a deeper lemon yellow; feet and tarsi more vividly colored, and talons gray. The irises are a slightly paler bluish gray, and the brownish ring encircling the pupil has disappeared. The apteria around the eyes are a paler olive green. Pinfeathers with light bluish sheaths can be seen under the down.

At 3 weeks quite a number of feathers protrude through the dense down. Cere, feet, and tarsi are more vividly colored, talons almost black; irises have turned pale bluish gray; a brown patch, the protruding ends of auricular feathers, is visible close behind the eye. A tiny remnant of egg tooth may still be present.

During the 4th week most of the products of digestion evidently go into feather production, and so, by the end of this period, the young are feathered except for front of head, posterior part of auricular area, legs, and abdomen. Cere, tarsi, and toes have not altered in color, but irises have become preponderantly blue.

At 5 weeks the hawks are flying and have lost practically all nestling down. All soft parts are colored essentially as a week earlier. Feathers start to cover the legs and abdomen and, in the following week, the birds are feathered completely—although remiges and rectrices will not have attained full development until the young are almost 8 weeks old.

Weight of young At hatching av. about 28 gm., or 1 oz. During the 1st week, young of both sexes increase in wt. at about the same rate, but ♀♀ tend to av. about 7 gm. heavier. After this initial span of closely parallel growth, ♀♀ become much heavier and larger than ♂♂ and continue to get heavier until the 28th day, when their wt. begins to drop. This decline usually occurs 3–5 days before the young leave the nest; during the next 2 weeks, when they are getting practice at flying, it remains about the same; then another increase begins as the birds develop their muscles. The smaller ♂♂ develop more rapidly and so are ready to leave the nest 2–4 days before ♀♀. For a graph of wt.-increase of 4 young in Calif., see E. Sumner (1929b).

Developmental behavior The ♀ feeds the newly hatched, chirping youngsters with little pieces of meat held loosely in her beak; the young snatch and swallow them eagerly. As they swallow, their heads bob back and forth; this motion aids the food to pass into the crop. After stretching their necks for a few sec. they seem to be fatigued and rest their heads on the nest until they have regained enough strength to feed again. They are sensitive to food colored red and will snap at it. Indeed, N. and H. Snyder (1973a) noted a reluctance to strike at food that is not red, but such reluctance disappears as the young become older.

Behavior is about the same for the next several days; occasionally nestlings work on their downy covering in a manner suggestive of preening, but actual preening does not start until pinfeathers begin breaking through their sheaths. They back to the edge of the nest and defecate out over it, occasionally soiling the rim slightly; the nest bowl remains unsoiled.

At about 10 days the young are strong enough to stand feebly and to flap their wings. Now they begin to show fear of humans that climb to the nest. At 13 days they stretch their legs frequently, are curious about moving objects—insects, birds, falling leaves—and often "yawn."

From 16 days the young are aggressive if a person climbs noisly to the nest. They stand up, spread their wings, and open their mouths. Some feathers break from their sheaths on the 11th day, and from then on they attempt to preen, but not until about the 17th day do they do so thoroughly—that is, stand, preen, stretch, and exercise. At 18 days they stand well and are able to dismember prey themselves, but usually they still wait for the ♀ to tear it into little pieces. If there is a wind, the young may stand, face it, and flap vigorously.

It is not clear if or how a parent Cooper's can feed all nestlings with equal frequency, but Hamerstrom (1957) indicated that the young, when not quite fully feathered, appear to show considerably more expanse of white down when hungry; this may "lead" a parent to feed the hungriest and most conspicuous youngster 1st.

At age 21 days young ♀ ♀ often stand up and feed by themselves. If a young ♂ is hungry, he will move close to a feeding ♀ and, each time she tears loose a morsel, will snatch it away from her exactly as he obtains food from his mother. At this age the young can completely empty a full crop in 2½ hrs. If a person visits the nest; young ♂ ♂ are apt to strike at any hand that tries to pick them up; ♀ ♀ usually sit and observe the intruder with seeming great curiosity. If a ♀ is picked up, she may squeal a bit but seldom tries to grasp with her talons.

By 24 days the nestlings are feeding more by themselves, and if one of them tries to get the prey while another is feeding on it, the "owner" will scold vigorously and shield the food with extended wings—mantle over it, as a falconer would say. Not until this time do the young jump up and strike with their feet at sticks in the nest. From now on, much of the day is spent stretching, scratching, jumping, clutching objects in the nest, and flapping. Males are able to stand on 1 foot at 26 days and at 27 are very likely to jump from the nest and fly to a lower branch if molested. They are poor fliers and usually descend at about a 30° angle from the horizontal. The ♀ ♀ do this from age 29 days. Normal departure from the nest is on the 30th day for ♂ ♂ and 34th for ♀ ♀. In Oreg., young were in the nest 27–30 days (R. Reynolds and Wight 1978); in w.-cent. Ariz., all young av. 31 days in 6 nests (Millsap 1981).

After their initial departure, they become "branchers," and the young frequently return to the nest for food and rest. At first they roost on or beside the nest, but, as they gradually become more proficient fliers, they wander farther away. Food may be brought to the nest by the parents for as long as 10 days after the young leave for the 1st time. Schwabe (1940) mentioned 2 young that stayed in the nest for over 6 weeks, but they undoubtedly had returned there for food. Often a young bird will return to the nest when it is in direct sunlight; then it spreads its wings and tail and stretches its legs behind it. In the 1st few days after leaving the nest the young return to it in anticipation of food as soon as they hear the parents call. If the ♀ brings the food and the young are not too hungry, they gather about her and do not interfere as she dismembers the quarry, but should 1 of them be very hungry it will fly to the nest, seize the food, and mantle over it; by its aggressive actions it causes all others, including its mother, to leave. Then, having eaten its fill, it jumps to a branch and rests. The next hungriest may then come and feed. Even if a large ♀ and a small ♂ start fighting over food, the ♂, if he is the hungrier bird, wins. At this age, little aggressiveness by a youngster is needed to deter or intimidate all the others.

When the ♂ parent brings food, often the young fly and strike at it so vigorously that he is actually frightened by his onrushing progeny and leaves hastily. Soon the young move farther in the direction whence the ♂ usually brings quarry. They are often so eager for food that he is "forced" to leave the quarry on any stump or old platform of sticks that he can locate. But, if they are less hungry or do not see him, he brings the prey to the nest. According to McElroy (1974), when the young are in the brancher stage, a parent even may release live prey for them to catch.

Very soon after the young are flying, usually at about age 35 days, they begin to explore their surroundings. If there is water—especially running water—they fly down to investigate it. First they touch it with their beaks, then step into it, and often they take their 1st bath. As the young gradually become able to supply their own daily food requirements, they drift apart and lead a solitary life. In Oreg., dependency of young on parent(s) after attaining flight may last as long as 53 days (R. Reynolds and Wight 1978).

Food requirements   For a "typical" Cooper's Hawk nest with 4 young in N.Y., Meng (1959) reported that an av. of 266 prey items—mainly such medium-sized birds as Am. Robins and European Starlings—were brought to the nest during the 1st 6 weeks: 4 prey items/day in 1st week, 5 in 2d, 7 in 3d, 9 in 4th, 7 in 5th, and 6 in 6th. He thus figured that an av. of 66 prey items were required to raise a Cooper's Hawk to age 6 weeks; obviously this would vary depending on size and availability of prey. In Calif., Fitch et al (1946a) found that a young Cooper's requires 62.3 gm. of food/day or about 2,740 gm. during its 1st 6 weeks.

N. Snyder and Wiley (1976) reported the following feeding rates in Ariz. and N.Mex.: 0.267 prey/hr. and 0.564 prey/hr. at nests with 2 and 4 young respectively. They also altered the number of young in 2 nests to determine if feeding (hunting) rates varied with changing size of brood; since the number of feedings/day (4.67) remained the same, they concluded that pairs were operating at "maximum capacity" in procuring food for the young. They indicated that their results suggest that the young can survive for short periods under widely varying feeding rates/nestling.

A captive young between ages 6 and 10 weeks consumed an av. of 8 House Sparrows daily (Roddy 1888). A captive ♂, fed for 57 days in fall–winter, ate an av. of 63 gm./day; a ♀, fed for 20 days in spring–summer, ate an av. of 70 gm./day; these values represented 19.7% and 16% of the body wt. of these birds respectively (the Craigheads 1956).

Sex ratio   Nestlings in 20 nests in N.Y.: 36 ♀ and 35 ♂ (Meng); in Wis.: 137 (53.5%) ♂ and 119 (46.5%) ♀ (Rosenfield et al. 1985).

Breeding success   In cent. N.Y., 1948–1950, an av. of 4.2 eggs was laid in 36 nests. In w. Pa., 1947–1964, an av. of 3.2 young attained flight from 32 nests (Schriver, in Hickey 1969). In Mich. in 1942, 6 nests av. 4.3 eggs, 3.0 hatchlings, and 3.0 reared to flight; 7 nests in 1948 av. 4.0 eggs, 3.1 hatchlings, and 2.6 reared to flight (the Craigheads 1956). In the ne. U.S. and se. Canada, averages were: 4.18 eggs in 117 nests, 1880–1967; 3.53 young banded in 118 successful nests, 1929–1945; 3.08 banded at 26 successful nests, 1946–1948; and 2.67 banded at 54 successful nests, 1949–1967 (Henny and Wight 1972).

Recent studies: Oreg.—3.8 eggs, 2.8 hatchlings, and 2.1 young of age in 13, 13, and 24 nests respectively (R. Reynolds and Wight 1978); Utah—67 young flew from 23 nests (Hennessey 1978); Wis.—4.3 eggs, 4.1 hatchlings, and 3.5 bandable-aged (14+ days) young from 40, 26, and 57 nests respectively (Rosenfield and Anderson 1983); Md.—3.6 eggs and 2.0 flying young from 8 and 11 nests respectively (Janik and Mosher 1982); Ariz.—48 nests had 2.79 ± 1.37 eggs, with 41 successful nests that produced 2.23 ± 1.4 young to flight age (Millsap 1981).

Twenty-nine of 36 Cooper's nests (81%) in N.Y. produced young to flight age (Meng, in Henny and Wight 1972); the primary cause of nesting failure was predation by raccoons (Meng 1951). In w. Pa., 24 of 32 nests (75%) were successful; severe weather, raccoon predation, and unexplained losses reduced success (Schriver, in Hickey 1969). The Craigheads (1956) reported a greater loss of eggs (52%) compared with nestlings (18%) in Mich. In Oreg., 20 of 29 (69%) nests produced young to flight age, and greatest losses (to predation and unexplained factors) occurred in the nestling stage; this was reflected in a higher hatching success of 74% compared with 61.4% of young attaining flight (R. Reynolds and Wight 1978). In Ariz. and N.Mex., 18 of 79 (23%) nests failed during construction and incubation; 31 of 140 (22%) nests failed later—especially late in the preflight stage and when young 1st flew (N. Snyder and Wiley 1976). In Utah, 23 of 43 (53.5%) nests produced flying young; Great Horned Owl predation accounted for 22% of failures (Hennessey 1978), based on circumstantial evidence. In Wis., 13 of 23 (56.5%) nests failed during incubation and 4 of 10 during the nestling stage; 57 of 83 nests (68.6%) produced at least 1 young to bandable age (Rosenfield and Anderson 1983). In w. Md., 9 of 11 nests produced flying young (Janik and Mosher 1982). In w. Pa., 1947–1964, 24 of 32 nests were successful, av. 3.2 young reared to flight age—or, per occupied territory, av. 2.9 young, 1947–1957, but only 1.9, 1958–1964; Cooper's was one of the commonest nestling hawks in the late 1940s and is "now one of the rarest" (Schriver, in Hickey 1969).

In Oreg., mean clutch size (4.20 eggs) and young reared to flight age (2.64) thus were higher in older-aged ♀♀ than in yearlings (3.25 eggs, 1.73 young); the percentage of nesting attempts that produced at least 1 young to flight age was slightly higher in older birds (K. Moore and Henny 1984). In Ariz., on 54 territories 8 pairs did not lay; of the remainder, yearling ♀♀ were at 4 of 7 failed nests and at 7 successful ones (Millsap 1981).

Captives Cooper's has bred in captivity but is difficult to maintain.

These are data on a young bird in Calif. (Fitch et al. 1946a): When slightly over a month old (June 30), it was able to fly out of the yard and spent most of its time in nearby trees. A week later it was offered a small live snake but flew "in sudden fright" and could not be called down that day. The next day it took a lizard from the hand and killed and ate it. Three days later, when unusually hungry, it chased grasshoppers— apparently with no success. But it pursued a live deermouse dropped on the lawn, caught it, twice released its hold, and each time quickly recaptured it. It seemed unable to kill at first, but it eventually did and ate the mouse.

From various sights and sounds, the hawk learned to anticipate the release of live prey and became increasingly proficient at killing. In the latter half of July it pursued cottontails and various birds and apparently was occasionally successful; it wandered farther at times.

Thereafter, as the hawk became more independent it also became more hostile toward humans—but would still come for food. On Aug. 4 it was found ¼ mi. away in a quail trap with a dead and an injured quail. When approached, it attempted to escape and gave "adult" cackling notes (first heard July 18 when alarmed by a dog). The following day, it was again in a trap with a dead quail. The hawk was removed from the trap and killed.

Coues (1874b) wrote of visiting "Tennessee Bill," a frontiersman who had reportedly tamed 3 Cooper's Hawks. He whistled to his "pets," then shot a sparrow and fed it to the boldest of the 3. This, Coues stated, was the 1st time he ever saw a hawk at liberty come to a call and take food from the hand.

HEINZ K. MENG AND ROBERT N. ROSENFIELD

SURVIVAL   Based on rather small samples from ne. U.S. and se. Canada, Henny and Wight (1972) estimated mortality rates for the years 1925–1940 and 1941–1957. First period: shooting was a significant mortality factor; 1st-year rate was calculated at 82.5%, mean annual mortality rate for 2d–8th year at 44.0 ± 6.6%, and "overall annual mortality rate" at 71.6 ± 4.1%. The authors believed that these estimates were biased high. Second period: 77.8% (mean annual), 34.0 ± 4.0% (2d–8th years), and 60.5 ± 3.5% (overall annual), with slightly lower estimates based on "found dead" birds only. (The 2d period was in the DDT era.)

Judging from R. Reynolds and Wight (1978) in Oreg., Cooper's of breeding age probably suffer greatest losses during the nesting period.

From banding recoveries of 136 individuals deceased from man-caused and natural mortalities, Keran (1981) gave an av. survival of 16.3 mo.—below fully "adult" breeding age. There has been a marked decline in losses from shooting; for 1st-year birds, Henny and Wight estimated it at 28–47% in 1929–1940, 15–25% in 1941–1945, and 12–20% in 1946–1957.

Maximum recorded life span in the wild is 8 years (Henny and Wight 1972), although Meng (1951) suggested it might be much longer. ROBERT N. ROSENFIELD

HABITS   Cooper's is capable of extremely rapid flight over short (100 m.) distances, and its rounded wings and long tail permit skilled maneuverability. These adaptations facilitate the capture of quick and agile primary prey—birds of medium size.

Hunting range   The Craigheads (1956) reported a maximum area in nesting season of 5.3 sq. km. (2.05 sq. mi.) in Mich. and 2.0 sq. km. (0.79 sq. mi.) in Wyo. Also in Mich., the Hamerstroms (1951) noted that prey species most commonly taken were not the ones most common in the nesting area—the hawks left the forest reserve to hunt 0.8–1.2 km. (0.5–0.75 mi.) away on farmlands. In N.Y., Meng (1951) reported that adult ♂ ♂ usually hunted farther than 0.8 km. (0.5 mi.) from the nest and up to 3.2

km. (2.0 mi.) distant—but even farther if prey was scarce within the latter range. In Calif., Fitch (1958) found that adult ♂♂ foraged at least 1.2 km. (0.75 mi.) from the nest.

Hunting techniques   Cooper's Hawks, like our other accipiters, typically rely on concealment and surprise in order to capture prey. When hunting birds that are feeding on the ground, the hawk will skim along close to the ground, using bushes and trees to shield its approach. A sudden burst of speed is the usual type of pursuit when hunting from a perch (Meng 1951). These tactics are most often used at the forest edge (Meng, the Craigheads).

Cooper's is also known to hunt from higher flight, stooping falconlike at pigeons in the open (R. Mead 1963, R. Clark 1977). One caught a bat in midair (Leopold 1944), and near a Tex. cave free-tailed bats (*Tadarida*) were seized as the hawk flew through a stream of them on a fairly straight course (Sprunt, Jr. 1950). Cooper's will pursue prey into bushes, stalk or pursue it on the ground, and even attempt to flush it from cover (many authors; see Bent 1937). Prins (1946) noted it flying like the N. Harrier to approach grebes on a pond. It hunts over wet areas (R. Norris 1942, later authors) and open fields (Bacon 1981). It hunts Bobwhites by listening for their call notes (Stoddard, in Terres 1961).

Young Cooper's may practice hunting in association with their siblings during their early days of flying (Mailliard 1908, Meng 1951).

Attack, strike, and handling of prey   Marsh and Storer (1981) indicated that hunting success of Cooper's Hawks depends on a substantial power reserve over the minimum requirements for flight. They noted that this reserve allows for quick acceleration as well as for the hawk to carry prey equal to itself in body mass. Thus, as Cooper's gains wt., it must increase the power output available from the flight muscles in order to maintain its level of flight performance; they suggested that an increase in muscle mass could account for this. For further analysis, including comparison of Juv. and older birds, see especially Mueller et al. (1981c). In the breeding season, in Mo., ⅓ of 45 observed capture attempts were successful (Toland 1985a).

Goslow (1971) studied the attack and strike of an adult ♀ that was trained for falconry. In a "typical" strike, the hawk ceased flapping flight 12–15 ft. from the prey and, 5 ft. from contact, began swinging the legs forward with a moderate amount of extension. The feet attained velocities of 1,140 cm./sec. (25 mph.), 15% greater than that of the pelvis. Almost 100% of velocity of the feet was in a horizontal plane at time of impact. At the moment of contact the hawk set its wings in a braking position, held its toes extended, and maintained a body axis to a horizontal angle approaching 80°. Goslow also recorded pursuit of a Rock Dove in which strike posture at impact appeared to be that of the hawk on its back in the air. He noted that Cooper's showed a marked forward thrust of the pelvis and rapid extension of legs just before impact, thus using body speed to increase shocking power. Further, the feet usually were held chest-high, with much of the hawk's weight directly behind the extended toes. The hawk usually seized prey with both feet, but once with only one; other observers have also noted this.

Once quarry is caught, Cooper's—like our other accipiters—will respond to movement of the prey by strongly grasping it, then relaxing grip, and then clamping down again. It has been known to down its prey into water and hold it under until it ceased to move (Forbush 1927, M. Davis 1948, Gerig 1979). Typically, Cooper's holds onto the head of its prey and immediately begins to pluck it (or pull out fur); plucking can occur before the prey is dead (S. Jones 1979). Most prey is eaten in this sequence: head, viscera, meat (Meng 1951).

Miscellany As with other hawks, some individual Cooper's specialize, at least for a season, on a particular prey species. Examples: Bobwhite in Ga. (Stoddard, in Terres 1961), free-tailed bat in Tex. (Sprunt, Jr. 1950), and lizards in Calif. (Fitch et al. 1946a).

A Cooper's Hawk can be trapped and released repeatedly (Michener 1930), raising the question whether banding them causes them to become accustomed to man—hence easier to shoot (H. and H. Snyder 1974).

Many episodes revealing the **persistence** of this accipiter have been written, and it seems appropriate to cite 2 of them here. First, in Mass. (Foster 1959): The hawk watched a boxwood bush in which several House Sparrows had taken refuge. Then it flew to the top of the bush, balanced awkwardly there (the prey did not flush), then flew in tight circles in a *vertical* plane. Still no action. It alighted on the ground, then resumed circling. This 2d bout was too much, and the sparrows, in panic, bolted from cover. The hawk pounced—successfully. Presumably it was a hungry hawk, hence so persistent, and the bush was rather dense, or else the hawk would have gone right into it. This from Ohio (H. G. Smith 1963): A ♂ Cooper's came to a dooryard and perched. When it detected movement in a hemlock, it darted toward it, walked on the ground, and peered into the branches. Once the hunt lasted 45 min. before a capture. The hawk followed a sparrow from shrub to shrub, each time forcing it to flee by plunging into the branches.

"Enemies" Next to man, in part of its range the most important predator is probably the raccoon, which climbs to the nest at night and eats eggs or young hawks. A widespread major predator is the Great Horned Owl, which preys on the incubating ♀ and young—the latter even into the postnesting "brancher" stage. Crows are apparently a minor problem (see Reproduction, above).

Past numbers Around 1900 Cooper's was considered a common nesting raptor (various authors), but widespread decline occurred afterward—especially in e. U.S. In Mass., Bent (1937) found 3 times as many nests before 1920 as after that year. In Ohio, Trautman (1940) found only 3 pairs in 1933 compared with 18 in 1922 and 1924. In Pa., migration counts declined after 1937 (Spofford, in Hickey 1969, N. Snyder et al. 1973). Autumn migrants at White Marsh, Md., declined at an annual rate of 13% from 1951 to 1961 (Hackman and Henny 1971). Robbins (1975) reported similar declines from all fall migration indices and all but western Christmas counts. A general decline in ne. U.S. was recognized by the late 1960s (J. Anderson et al. 1968).

An extensive investigation of productivity in both ne. U.S. and se. Canada indicated a reduction (24.4%) in the number of banding-age Cooper's in successful nests for 1929–1945 to 1949–1967 with a 12.7% decrease already occurring by 1946–1948. Earlier in the century, substantially greater shooting pressure had probably affected population numbers (Henny and Wight 1972). The decline in production rates may have been underestimated as information on complete nest failures were not available and could not be included.

351

The numbers of Cooper's seen on Christmas counts declined 1952–early 1960s, when indices leveled off; in 1967–1971 numbers had decreased by 10% or more in 10 states and had increased in 7 others (W. Brown 1973), but Brown, and G. G. Daniels (1975), cautioned about biases (e.g., increased coverage, misidentification) in conclusions about population trends. A study (U.S. Dept. Interior 1976) incorporating Christmas counts, migration counts, and results of breeding bird surveys concluded that there were fewer Cooper's in the e. and cent. U.S. 1967–1974 than 1948–1966 but that there was some increase in the e. region, 1967–1974.

Environmental contaminants Biocides, especially DDT, have been associated with reduced productivity of Cooper's Hawks. These contaminants are long-lived and become concentrated in successive levels of longer food chains, as in raptors feeding on birds. After the aerial spraying of DDT, increased levels of DDT and DDE (a metabolite of the former) were detected in the plasma of Cooper's Hawks in Oreg. (Henny 1977b).

Correlations between thin eggshells and the presence of high levels of DDE in the eggs of Cooper's Hawks were reported by N. Snyder et al. (1973). A 7.0% decrease in eggshell thickness was found by D. Anderson and Hickey (1972). N. Snyder (1974) reported broken eggs in 11 of 16 clutches from Ariz. and N.Mex.; they had shells 16% thinner than eggs laid before 1947 (early DDT era). Populations reaching 15–17% shell thinning have serious reproductive difficulties (Hickey and Anderson 1968). Cooper's eggs had the greatest eggshell thinning (19.02%) of several raptors sampled in N.Y. (Lincer and Clark 1978).

N. Snyder et al. (1973) indicated that DDE contamination probably does not cause infertility or embryonic death but rather egg breakage and clutch desertion. It may also cause disturbed parental behavior—aberrant food transfer and desultory nest building in pairs with high levels of DDE. Stated otherwise, such behavior is drug-related (N. and H. Snyder 1974b). In Colo., a ♀ Cooper's apparently died of DDT poisoning; it had 62 ppm. DDT and DDE (combined) in its brain (Prouty et al. 1982).

Western populations have apparently remained relatively stable. Eastern Cooper's carried levels of DDE that were several times greater than in w. birds, probably because avian prey is a larger portion of the diet in the East. There is a significant correlation between percentage of birds in the diet and in levels of DDE in the eggs of Cooper's Hawks. Thus, the stability of w. populations was attributed to the consumption of less contaminated food (N. Snyder et al. 1973, N. and H. Snyder 1974b). Other contaminants—dieldrin, PCBs, heavy metals, and so on—have been detected in Cooper's Hawk eggs, but any stress they may put on populations is unknown.

Present numbers Regulations on use of pesticides and other potential contaminants plus legal protection for all raptors (under U.S.-Mexico treaty of Mar. 10, 1972) have apparently benefited Cooper's Hawk populations. Low levels of environmental contaminants and eggshell thicknesses that were at least 10% greater than the threshold at which breakage occurred in Cooper's Hawk eggs in Ariz. and N.Mex. were found for eggs in Wis. in 1980 (Rosenfield and Anderson 1983). Similar results have been reported from several other e. states (O. Pattee). Nests were few in Mich. in the late 1950s and 1960s, but recent reports suggest an increase (Postupalsky 1975). Further, the number of young banded per nest increased from an av. of 2.67 (1949–

1967) to 3.36 (1967–1976) in the ne. U.S. (Braun et al. 1977). Tate (1981) noted that numbers of Cooper's may be stable or increasing in the East and Southwest.

Numbers counted in fall at Bake Oven Knob, Lehigh Co., Pa., 1961–1981, show a striking increase in the terminal 6 years of this span; fall counts fluctuate, apparently with slight peaks at intervals of 3 or 4 years (Heintzelman 1982).

ROBERT N. ROSENFIELD

FOOD   Medium-sized wild birds, such as jays, thrushes, and flickers; some poultry and pheasants (latter, at least formerly, often at game farms); small mammals up to cottontail (*Sylvilagus*) size; a few reptiles, amphibians, and insects.

S. Jones (1979) calculated the following overall averages of prey groups from 9 studies: birds 70.4%, mammals 17.9%, lower vertebrates (reptiles, rarely amphibians) 8.9%, and insects 2.1%. Birds composed over 80% of the diet of Cooper's Hawks in the e. U.S. (S. Jones), but in Ariz.-N.Mex. only about 60% with remainder mammalian and reptilian (N. Snyder et al. 1973). R. Reynolds and Meslow (1984) contains a long list of prey from 2 areas in Oreg; mean prey size was significantly larger than that of the Sharpshin; in 1 area it was 74% birds and 25% mammals, in the other 47% birds and 53% mammals. In w.-cent. Ariz. in breeding season and winter, birds dominated numerically and by wt.—42 bird species, 6 mammals, 6 reptiles, and some invertebrates (scorpions and "other"); over ⅗ of prey taken by ♀♀ in breeding season were mammals, primarily cottontails and antelope ground squirrels (Millsap 1981).

Birds   McAtee (1935) reported the following from 261 Cooper's stomachs: poultry in 32, quail (4 species) in 16, Ring-necked Pheasant in 10, Ruffed and Spruce Grouse in 4, Gray Partridge in 1, sparrows and related groups in 84, and woodpeckers in 11. Blackbirds, thrushes, wood warblers, and vireos were taken infrequently.

Cooper's is a primary predator on the Bobwhite (Errington 1933, Stoddard 1931, Trautman 1940). In a Mich. area in winter, it took 3.4% of the local population in 1942 and 12.5% in 1948 (the Craigheads 1956).

A partial list of other avian prey: Eared Grebe (Sefton 1934), Merlin (McAtee 1935), Am. Kestrel (McAtee, Kirkpatrick 1980), Blue Grouse (Jewett et al. 1953), Greater Prairie Chicken (Bacon 1981), Least Bittern (McAtee 1935), Willet (G. Page and Whitacre 1975), Rock Dove (R. Mead 1963, R. Clark 1977), Screech Owl, (McAtee), Flamulated Owl (Borell 1937), and Am. Crow (G. Sutton 1929). Young ducks and teal occasionally (Coues 1874b, Swenk 1935). A Cooper's seized an Am. Coot, which had been shot, before it fell into water (R. Norris 1942). Nestling birds are also taken (the Hamerstroms 1951, Meng 1959, R. W. Nelson 1968), even a nest of Am. Goldfinches (Linduska 1943).

Mammals   Hares (*Lepus*, probably when young), cottontails, gray squirrel, red squirrel, cotton rat, several ground squirrel species (*Ammospermophilus*, *Spermophilus*), voles, deer mice, and shrews (S. Jones 1979). Chipmunks (*Tamias*, *Eutamias*) have been especially important, as noted by at least 8 authors. Bats, in 1 instance *Tadarida*, have been reported 3 times (Leopold 1944, Sprunt Jr. 1950, Toland 1985a).

Reptiles, amphibians, and fishes   Minor items; certain individuals or pairs of

353

Cooper's, however, specialize in particular prey items (S. Jones 1979). A pair in Calif. preyed predominantly on lizards (Fitch et al. 1946a). During a drought, 1 fed on minnows in dessicating pools (A. P. Smith 1915).

Insects Include grasshoppers, dragonflies, crickets, butterflies, and beetles.

Hawk size v. prey size R. Reynolds (1979) referred to Cooper's in Oreg. as "biomass maximizers" because they captured more animals of a large size (mean wt. 135 gm., or 4.8 oz.) than occurred proportionately in the environment. P. Kennedy (1980) found that both ♂ and ♀ preferred medium-sized prey, the ♀ selecting quarry from larger-sized categories. Storer (1966) found that Cooper's fed largely on prey weighing 15–166 gm. (0.5–5.8 oz.); he calculated mean prey wt. of 37.6 gm. for the ♂ and 50.7 gm. for the ♀. Other investigators have also reported that the larger ♀ captures larger prey more often than does the ♂. P. Kennedy and Johnson (1986) found no significant difference between the sexes in prey sizes delivered to 5 nests. Diet differences in the sexes have been studied in relation to the high degree of sexual size-dimorphism in this and the other N. Am. accipiters, but controversy exists over its significance and evolutionary consequences. ROBERT N. ROSENFIELD

Juv.   Def. Basic   R.T.T.

NORTHERN GOSHAWK

Accipiter gentilis

A large forest hawk having broad, rounded wings, fairly long tail (it is less rounded than Cooper's), and stout legs and feet.

The 3d functional primary from the outer is longest, the next outer slightly to 1½ cm. shorter, and the outermost 9–10 cm. shorter. The 5 outer primaries are emarginated on their outer web (as in Cooper's Hawk). The tarsus is feathered halfway down the front (only a third in Cooper's—a distinction in all ages). In much of N. Am. range the dark tail bands tend to have light margins in the Goshawk (tricolored tail), but not in Cooper's (bicolored tail), yet this distinction does not hold everywhere. Any accipiter in our area over 20 in. (50 cm.) long is a Goshawk. In proportion to its size, among our accipiters the Goshawk also has the stoutest tarsus, relatively shortest middle toe, and relatively smallest eye.

In our area (in e. Siberia the bird is **dimorphic**), this hawk is variably bluish gray dorsally, the cap usually blackish, and there is a white or whitish stripe above the eye; underparts are pale gray to whitish, barred (usually rather finely) very dark and with dark shaft streaks. The Juv. Plumage is more toward a blackish brown dorsally with light brownish feather borders; the venter is longitudinally streaked dark on pale buff to whitish; the tail has zigzag (not evenly transverse) barring.

The ♀ is larger than the ♂ with slight overlap of the sexes. The widespread race *atricapillus* in N. Am.: length 21–23 in. (53–58.5 cm., av. 56), ♀ 22½–26 (57.5–64, av. 61); wt. ♂ 25½–39 oz. (720–1,100 gm., av. 915), ♀ 32–39 (900–1,390, av. 1,130) (Mueller et al. 1979a). Wingspread 105 ♂ 101.8–111.7 cm., av. 107.1, and 181 ♀ 109.9–121.6, av. 116.8 (M. Wood 1938). The various figures align fairly well with those in McDowell (1941a). There is slight overlap with the smaller Cooper's Hawk.

355

Two subspecies in our area. There are at least 5 additional subspecies in Eurasia with collectively more variation in coloring and dimensions than those in N. Am.

DESCRIPTION *A. g. atricapillus*. Sexes nearly identical in definitive feathering. One Plumage/cycle with Basic II earliest definitive; molting is protracted, spring–fall; Basic I tends to be darker dorsally with heavy, partly transverse markings ventrally. Whether individuals with crown little or no darker than dorsum are more typical of Basic I is unknown.

▶ ♂ Def. Basic Plumage (entire feathering) early SUMMER to following early SUMMER. **Beak** blackish blue, cere yellow sometimes tinged greenish; **iris** typically rusty reddish to scarlet; **cap** very dark (blackish slate); forehead feathers usually edged white; superciliary stripe white, the feathers with blackish gray shaft streaks; auriculars blackish gray, sometimes mottled white; feathers on rear of head white basally (occipital spot). **Upperparts** medium to dark gray, often with bluish cast; **underparts** white to pale gray, the feathers with blackish gray to medium gray shaft streaks (usually absent from some lateral feathers) and dark barring that is very variable in width and quantity (heaviest on lower breast, belly, and tibiae); under tail coverts white, sometimes plain. **Tail** much like Cooper's Hawk (but see above), the barring sometimes almost obscured; more conspicuous ventrally are at least 4 visible transverse dark bars, narrower than the lighter intervening spaces, and the very tail-tip (bordering the terminal dark bar) white and often abraded or worn off. Legs and **feet** yellow, talons black. **Wing** upper surface as dorsum, the flight feathers patterned with very dark patches, wing lining whitish with more or less dark gray to blackish gray shaft streaks and barring.

▶ ♀ Def. Basic Plumage (entire feathering), worn a year, SUMMER to SUMMER. Eye usually scarlet, but orange in some (younger?) birds. Feathering as ♂ except, when specimens are viewed in series, ♀♀ av. slightly more toward brownish and paler dorsally and more coarsely marked ventrally—but sexes overlap completely in these characteristics.

Molting   The ♀ begins at about onset of incubation and has a pause beginning later when the nestlings are partly grown. The ♂ begins in the rearing period when the ♀ has begun assisting him in getting food for the nestlings. The ♀ resumes molting after the young are flying and learning to hunt on their own. Thus, the ♂'s delay is presumably a result of his being the sole provider for a considerable period (J. Platt 1973, McGowan 1975). The primaries are dropped from inner to outer (interrupted by pause in the ♀), the secondaries from 3 centers. In the tail, either the central or adjoining pair drop 1st (individuals vary), then the others (sequence varies). Little is known about body molting.

In a captive ♀ some feathers were retained in each of 6 consecutive molts. One or more pairs of secondaries were retained, but no primaries; the smallest alula feather in both wings was retained once; the tail was renewed completely twice, but 3 pairs of feathers were carried 2 years on 2 occasions and at next molting were 1st to be dropped. Duration of tail molting: 47–150 days, av. (of 6) "slightly over" 97 days (Stabler 1943). In Europe, wing molt extends up to 171 days (V. and E. Stresemann 1960). What is known of molting in Am. and European birds is essentially similar; see, for example, Schiemenz (1958).

AT HATCHING   Covered with a thin coat of short white down A, sometimes tinged grayish on head and dorsum. In about a week, down B begins to appear and is fully grown by age 16 days or older; it is long, dense, grayish dorsally and white ventrally. The nestling develops as in Cooper's Hawk, but slower—a day of Cooper's being equivalent to 1.27 days in the Goshawk. That is, in birds of same sex, if a Goshawk resembles a 14-day-old Cooper's, its age is approximately $14 \times 1.27 = 17\frac{3}{4}$ days (H. Meng). Soft-part coloring is slightly muted as compared with Cooper's of corresponding age. For Development of young, see Reproduction, below.

▶ ♂ ♀ Juv. Plumage (entire feathering) begins to show through the down by about age 17–18 days and is well developed in about 6½ (♂) or 7 (♀) weeks. Feather growth was "complete" (both sexes) in captivity in 58–60 days posthatching (Berry 1972). It is retained through WINTER and succeeded by Basic I beginning in early SUMMER (sometimes earlier) and extending into late FALL.

Banded Finnish Juv. birds (Haukioja 1967): wing length continues to increase slightly Aug.–Nov. (of hatching year); later it shows (from wear?) a small decrease in Mar.–Apr. (data for other months lacking).

Compared here with Cooper's Hawk: **Iris** pale grayish early in nestling stage, changing to pale yellowish by time flight attained and (McGowan 1975) yellow throughout 1st winter. **Head** as Cooper's but paler, the feathers with wider light margins; feathers of superciliary stripe usually white with blackish brown shaft streaks (the stripe obscure or lacking in some ♂ ♂). **Upperparts** as Cooper's but paler and with wider light feather margins. **Underparts** as Cooper's, the under tail coverts narrowly or even heavily streaked tan to blackish brown. **Tail** rather similar to Cooper's but crossed by 5 dark bands (7 on each outer feather), mostly edged pale smoky gray, the intervening light areas typically wider. Proximal 4 dark bands on central 6 feathers usually not aligned—the band-halves on a feather barely meet at the shaft. **Wing** as Cooper's, but wider light feather margins on dorsal coverts; a vestigial alulal claw is usually lost during preening.

▶ ♂ ♀ Basic I Plumage (entire feathering) acquired beginning in early SUMMER at age just over 1 year (occasionally earlier) and continuing into Oct. or early Nov. This molting usually begins later than subsequent Prebasics. The feathering is retained nearly a year. Iris variably orange, then varying toward reddish (especially in ♂ ♂). Although rather variable, feathering typically differs from definitive in that the venter tends to have heavier brownish shaft streaks and wider and browner transverse barring—see text and illus. in R. M. Bond and Stabler (1941). Some worn Juv. feathers may be retained, especially in dorsum and wing. There may be enough individual variation in this and succeeding Basics to eliminate any distinction sometimes, but a heavily barred bird, especially with orange (rather than scarlet) eyes, is presumably in Basic I. Occasional individuals of unknown age lack the "adult" head pattern, instead having its darker areas a grayed bluish (like the dorsum) with some paler streaking.

Color phases in the species   Beginning in nw. Siberia and increasingly e., in addition to "normal" birds, there are white or pale individuals; they compose about 50% of the birds in Anadyrland and Kamchatka (Vaurie 1965, Dementiev and Böhme 1970).

Variants   Perhaps, or perhaps birds distant from usual range, as listed by Taverner

(1940): ♂ Prince Edward I.—very similar to Vancouver I. birds; ♂ Vancouver I.—like lighter birds of e. N. Am.; ♀ Mackenzie Delta—heavily marked like nominate *gentilis* of Europe (= Basic I in N. Am.) mated to a ♂ *A. g. atricapillus;* unknown sex, Big Trees, Calif.—dark like birds of coastal is. of B.C.; unknown sex, Atlin, B.C. (mainland)—extremely pale like *A. g. albidus* of ne. Asia. Van Tyne (1943) reported a heavily marked ♀ from Labrador. It was presumably in Basic I, yet W. E. C. Todd (1963) listed it provisionally under *A. g. gentilis.* There is no certain evidence that European birds have occurred here naturally, but falconers have had them—hence a possibility of escapees.

A ♂ found dead in cent. Europe in Feb. was judged to be an aberrant local bird having characteristics of certain large tropical hawks (Voous and Wattel 1972, with illus.).

Measurements The Northern Goshawk is the largest and least sexually dimorphic in size of our accipiters (Storer 1966). Skin shrinkage confounds a direct comparison of live bird meas. with museum specimens, also feather wear to some extent (Henny et al. 1985). Live birds in Basic II Plumage and older have longer wings, shorter tails, and are heavier than those in Juv. Plumage (Mueller et al. 1976). This is true at least of ♀ ♀.

From widespread localities, dried "adult" specimens of 27 ♂ and 22 ♀, which meas. slightly smaller than live birds: BEAK from cere ♂ 20–26 mm., av. 21.9, and ♀ 21.5–26, av. 23.6; WING across chord ♂ 303–354, av. 325.2, and ♀ 321–368, av. 333.6; and TAIL ♂ 226.5–280, av. 245.7, and ♀ 250–301, av. 278.6 (Friedmann 1950).

WING chord of live birds in autumn in Wis. (mean and SD in paren.): Juv. 109 ♂ 301–334 mm. (319 ± 6.36) and 52 ♀ 330–361 (346 ± 6.93); Basic I 39 ♂ 314–335 mm. (324 ± 5.26) and 45 ♀ 337–367 (350 ± 6.34); Basic II and older 41 ♂ 309–336 mm. (323 ± 4.75) and 60 ♀ 339–365 (353 ± 6.22) (Mueller et al. 1976).

For "WING arc" of live birds, see Mueller and Berger (1968).

TAIL Juv. 106 ♂ 221–252 mm. (239 ± 6.11) and 53 ♀ 255–286 (272 ± 7.54); Basic I 39 ♂ 223–242 mm. (232 ± 5.28) and 45 ♀ 251–279 (267 ± 6.56); Basic II and older 41 ♂ 219–240 mm. (230 ± 5.37) and 60 ♀ 249–281 (266 ± 7.69) (Mueller et al. 1976).

Live birds in ne. Oreg.: "adults" BEAK from cere 16 ♂ 20.2–21.9 mm. (21.2 ± 0.55) and 26 ♀ 22.2–25.5 (24.1 ± 0.94); WING chord 22 ♂ 307–336 (321.1 ± 7.41) and 36 ♂ 340–370 (350.3 ± 7.85); and TAIL 21 ♂ 212–232 mm. (224.2 ± 5.34) and 37 ♀ 249–280 (262 ± 7.57) (Henny et al. 1985, which see for comparison with data from elsewhere).

Weight Live birds in Wis. in autumn (wt. of food in gullet estimated and subtracted from gross): Juv. 105 ♂ 664–988 gm. (808 ± 66.75) and 52 ♀ 878–1,253 (1,005 ± 79.03); Basic I 39 ♂ 756–1,029 gm. (900 ± 69.19) and 44 ♀ 845–1,345 (1,118 ± 103.75); Basic II and older 38 ♂ 735–1,099 gm. (925 ± 61.30) and 59 ♀ 1,005–1,364 (1,152 ± 77.50) (Mueller et al. 1976). Goshawks increase in wt. from fall into winter, with year-to-year and seasonal variation (Henny et al. 1985).

Live birds in ne. Oreg. in summer: "adults" 20 ♂ 655–838 gm. (741.7 ± 48.6) and 38 ♀ 860–1,085 (972.8 ± 63.0) (Henny et al. 1985). Oreg. summer wts. are lower than Wis. fall wts.

Winter wts of live birds in Alta. (averages): "adults" 6 ♂ 864 gm. and 12 ♀ 1,171; "immature" (Juv.) 21 ♂ 859 gm. and 15 ♀ 1,143. Lightest was an "immature" ♂ at 681 gm. and heaviest an "adult" ♀ at 1,304 gm. (Oeming 1958).

These wts. from Pa. are for Goshawks turned in for bounty in a 3-year period during which there was no pronounced incursion; extremes may indicate emaciated and gorged individuals: "mature" 62 ♂ 658–1,198 gm., av. 844, and 114 ♀ 730–1,562, av. 1,094; and "immature" 40 ♂ 631–1,107 gm., av. 795, and 40 ♀ 581–1,235, av. 972 (McDowell 1941a).

The wt. cycle in Juv. Finnish Goshawks for much of the year is as follows: from low in Aug. gradually to highest in Nov.–Dec.; moderately high (about as Oct.) in Mar.–May in the ♂ but in the ♀ highest in Mar. and declining greatly into May. This is based on banded birds (Haukioja 1967).

Hybrids   In the wild, a bird of the year much resembling *A. cooperi* was listed by Suchetet (1897), quoting at length a letter from M. Hardy of Brewer, Maine. His description did not include trenchant characters. W. L. Powers (1905) suggested other parentage.

Evidently in captivity, a ♂ *A. gentilis* × *Buteo buteo* "at 4 years of age was believed to be infertile" (Krings, in Gray 1958).

Since artificial insemination has been successful in the Goshawk and young have been reared (Berry 1972), attempts to produce captive hybrids are likely.

Abroad, a captive ♀ successfully reared 2 Sparrowhawk (*Accipiter nisus*) young (Mavrogordato, in Prestwich 1955), and a captive fostered the Common Buzzard (*Buteo buteo*) (Stohn 1974). In N. Am. in the wild, when nests were close, a ♀ fed a nestling Red-tailed Hawk (Gammon, in Shy 1982).

Geographical variation in the species   Ancestral stock presumably spread from Eurasia to N. Am. Presently the Goshawk has a vast breeding range across continental Eurasia and N. Am. and on some is. adjacent to both. Many Eurasian birds in definitive feathering are neutral colored dorsally and usually have wide, dark, transverse barring ventrally; in Juv. Plumage, the background color of the venter is very pale. The "adult" eye is orange to scarlet-orange in the Old World and scarlet ("deep red") in the New. According to Bahrmann (1974), there is less sexual size-dimorphism in N. Am. than in Europe. Eurasian variation is clinal—from smaller and darker s. to larger and paler n., with 2 morphs (1 whitish to white) from the Yana drainage e. There is a slight size increase going from w. (Europe) to e. (Kamchatka). There are limited annual migratory flights and periodic incursions. Outlying populations in the Mediterranean on Corsica and Sardinia and in the w. Pacific in Japan are darker and smaller than nearest mainland birds. The species also has close relatives; see Wattel's (1973) review of the genus.

In N. Am. the cap is darker (nearly black), the dorsum has a bluish cast, and dark markings on underparts are typically fine from Basic II Plumage onward. There is considerable size variation, and nw. continental birds av. somewhat paler. On the Queen Charlotte Is., B.C., and n. to some extent, they are darker overall; on Vancouver I., they are evidently variable in size and coloring. It is not yet demonstrated that southernmost continental breeders are our largest birds, in contradiction to a trend toward size increase going north.   RALPH S. PALMER

SUBSPECIES **In our area**   *atricapillus* (Wilson)—descr. and meas. given above; breeds in forests from Nfld. across N. Am. to nw. Alaska, se. at least to Pa., s. to nw.

Mexico, and w. to cent. Calif. Southerly birds (se. Ariz. and into Jalisco, Mexico) were named as another subspecies by van Rossem (1938) on minimal specimen material. These birds were included in *atricapillus* by Friedmann (1950), were not recognized in the 1957 AOU *Check-list,* and were included in L. Brown and Amadon (1968 **2**); Hubbard (1972) stressed WING length as a useful character, and they are not recognized here.

laingi (Taverner)—smaller, darker, rain forest birds of the Queen Charlotte Is., B.C. They apparently occur n. along the Pacific coast to the Gulf of Alaska and supposedly intergrade with mainland birds on Vancouver I. Almost no meas. have been published; see Friedmann (1950). They possibly occur rarely as incursion visitants away from their presumed range. If F. Beebe (1974) is correct that some Goshawks on Vancouver I. are very small, a redefinition of *laingi* might include more size variation and greater sexual size-dimorphism than so far reported.

Elsewhere How many Eurasian subspecies to recognize can be debated, but, going from w. to e., these names are in common usage: *gentilis* (Linnaeus)—moderately dark birds, n. and middle Europe (or with *gallinarum* (C. L. Brehm) split off for cent. Europe—see Eck [1982]); *arrigonii* Kleinschmidt—darker than the preceding, Corsica and Sardinia; *buteoides* (Menzbier)—pale birds, a small percentage in Siberia whitish, n. Sweden to at least the Urals; *albidus* (Menzbier)—the darker birds are paler than the preceding and about half are white (hence lighter than pale *buteoides*); *schvedowi* (Menzbier)—short winged, fairly dark, venter with much brownish barring, across e. Europe and Asia s. of the 2 preceding; *fujiyamae* Swann and Hartert— smaller and somewhat darker than the preceding, in Japan, where said to be resident on Hondo (Honshu), possibly elsewhere. For more details of each and for meas. of several, see Vaurie (1965). RALPH S. PALMER

FIELD IDENTIFICATION In N. Am. Our largest accipiter. Generally solitary except before the brood scatters. The main problem is to distinguish small Northern Goshawks from large Cooper's Hawks—see under the latter. In definitive feathering, underparts of the Goshawk are variably gray (not barred rusty) and the black cap is bordered laterally by a white or whitish superciliary stripe, usually conspicuous. Seldom is a Goshawk under 20 in. (50 cm.) long; Cooper's is smaller. In proportion to its larger size, the tail of the Goshawk appears shorter than Cooper's and is less rounded, appearing squarish when folded. The wings appear longer. In usual flap/sail flight, wingbeat is slower.

Goshawks in Juv. Plumage differ from Cooper's thus: the former has a light stripe over the eye (sometimes obscure in ♂ ♂): under tail coverts are streaked (seldom in Cooper's); and the underside of the spread tail shows a zigzag pattern of dark markings, or dark areas out of alignment (aligned in transverse barring in Cooper's).

The Goshawk tends to flap about 5–7 times, then glide on set wings. As with our other accipiters, it sometimes soars with tail at least partly spread.

In forest, the Goshawk usually comes into view swiftly and very suddenly, at fairly close quarters, and is quickly out of sight. It is remarkably adept for its size at avoiding obstacles and can fly through a dense stand of young birches or aspen with remarkable agility. It perches erect and is seldom seen except on the wing. A perched bird might possibly be confused with a gray Gyrfalcon, but the dark cap bordered with white is distinctive.

As stated under Cooper's and indicated above, the Goshawk is identified with most certainty by size and size-related characters; this requires experience and skill.

RALPH S. PALMER

VOICE   Often silent, but noisy in various seasons over territory and especially so at times during and after nesting. Both sexes seem to have an equally varied repertoire. As F. Beebe (1974) stated, some of the most intriguing calls heard in coniferous woods are made by this hawk. The ♂'s voice is higher pitched than his mate's. In general, the Goshawk's voice is like that of Cooper's. Perhaps surprisingly, in many respects it is even more like that of the diminutive Sharpshin, except much louder and fuller. The following is based on J. Schnell (1958), with added observations:

Both sexes may wail (or mew or scream, depending on one's definition) when circling over their domain on a warm winter's day. The call is a loud, clear, evenly spaced, gull-like *kree-ah kree-ah* and is at times long continued.

The morning duet commences at about the start of nest building. The ♂ awakes and gives a nasal *ki-ki-ki-ki* rather rapidly ("shrieking"); he may terminate with *gek* or some other sound and soon starts up again. This may last an hr. or longer. The ♀ joins in, calling similarly but at a lower pitch. This ceremony begins to wane during the incubation period: the ♂ "sings" longer but his mate does not join in. Later, when the preflight young are large, she may "sing" again in A.M., occasionally in P.M., but the ♂ seldom if ever calls. Both birds may cluck, chatter, or wail, but wailing seems to be primarily a ♀ call and generally precedes some action by her—such as taking wing to join her mate.

In alarm, both sexes call *ki-ki-ki-ki* (long series), the ♂ usually 2 notes higher than the ♀, but pitch varies. (The *ca-ca-ca-ca* of Cooper's is a higher *ki-ki-ki-ki* in the Goshawk.) When uttered very rapidly, as when attacking a predator at the nest (or an intruding Goshawk) and in mobbing, it becomes a chatter *gek-gek-gek*. The ♀ attacks with swiftness and persistence, her voice harsh, strident, and rasping. At highest intensity it has a piercing or screaming quality, and later, when the hawk has quit attacking and is perched, the notes become increasingly spaced out and finally cease as though the bird were out of breath. When cackling from a perch, she turns her head from side to side, causing the sound to seem to change direction. The ♂ attacks also, at times with less persistence and vigor.

The ♂'s more subdued and spaced-out calls evidently serve to keep contact with his mate or to announce his approach to her. When the pair is alone, her reply to this is typically a wailing, which, like cackling, is polyvalent. In intense form, it is used by both sexes during copulation.

The ♀ utters a distinctive "recognition scream" when the ♂ appears in the nest-area; it was used by the observer to determine the ♂'s presence. This call has a remote gull-like quality. Two variants: 1 food-transfer call, uttered "excitedly"; and 2 "dismissal call." An element of hostility is observable in the transfer procedure. The ♀ tolerates the ♂'s presence in the nest area and often waits expectantly for him to bring food. After it is delivered, however, she will not feed the nestlings until he has departed. This he does when she utters her dismissal call. The ♂ utters rather similar, more subdued, sounds, seldom recognizable as his voice unless both members of the pair are heard.

The ♂ has a special *guck* note not given by the ♀ (G. Sutton 1925). It is unmusical, like snapping the tongue away from the roof of the mouth, the beak open, head up and forward; when the sound is emitted, the head is brought abruptly downward. It is repeated at 5-sec. intervals and is audible at 300–400 ft. The ♂ utters this when he brings prey to the periphery of the nest area, and it indicates his presence and position to the ♀. A food transfer usually follows. The same is uttered when the pair meets at close range—a social or conversational function. A plaintive scream when delivering food to the nest area periphery is often uttered in its stead.

These data on nestlings are almost entirely from J. Schnell: At 9 days they make a "squealing whistle" that lasts about 1 sec. and is audible only at close range. At 11 days a rapid, high-pitched twitter like domestic chicks when caught and picked up; uttered when in pain, such as when stepped on by the ♀—"pain twitter." At 19 days a "contentment twitter," high pitched and staccato; uttered when well fed and the ♀ perched close by. By age 4 weeks, when alarmed, a rapid *kik-kik-kik-kik;* at this age, the ♂'s voice is 1½–2 notes higher than the ♀'s (H. Meng). At 31 days an aggressive *ke-ke-ke* call. A begging call usually given by the nestlings changes by age 41 days and sounds somewhat like the plaintive scream of the ♀ on sighting her mate. At 49 days the begging call resembles the recognition scream of the ♀. A twitter at start of flight.

Chick voices begin to differentiate into adult-type calls during nest life. The whistling food call evolves into wailing at about day 41. An early alarm call, a high-pitched twitter, is an antecedent of the chatter.

Young out of the nest also call *kree-ah* singly, irregularly but frequently. It can be mistaken for a buteo call. This is a contact call, used by young and adults at this stage and is audible at great distances.   RALPH S. PALMER

HABITAT   A forest hawk around the globe, from sea level to limits of trees. In N. Am., its hunting domain includes boreal areas with scattered patches of willow or alder, alpine country, farmland, prairie, and deserts, but it is generally near scattered trees or brushy areas—and preferably woodland. It seems to prefer habitat edges: changes in forest composition, as where conifers and brush meet, burned areas, or where a watercourse or bog interrupts a forest pattern. Presumably prey is more accessible there. It bathes as opportunity permits. It hunts very effectively within and below the forest canopy. Its haunts away from breeding range and during incursions are similarly varied.

Nesting sites in N. Am. are in almost any kind of forest and are not limited to conifers, as sometimes believed. Even so, habitat extends much farther s. in w. N. Am. where montane coniferous forest is more or less continuous to Mexico. Many nests are in patches of deciduous trees—white or yellow birches, beech, and various species of aspen. The approach is clear, especially before the leaves develop, and the nest is later concealed and shaded. In e. U.S., the birds nest in varied situations in s. areas that they have recently reoccupied.

In parts of Europe, the Goshawk has adjusted to human activity, living on mixed

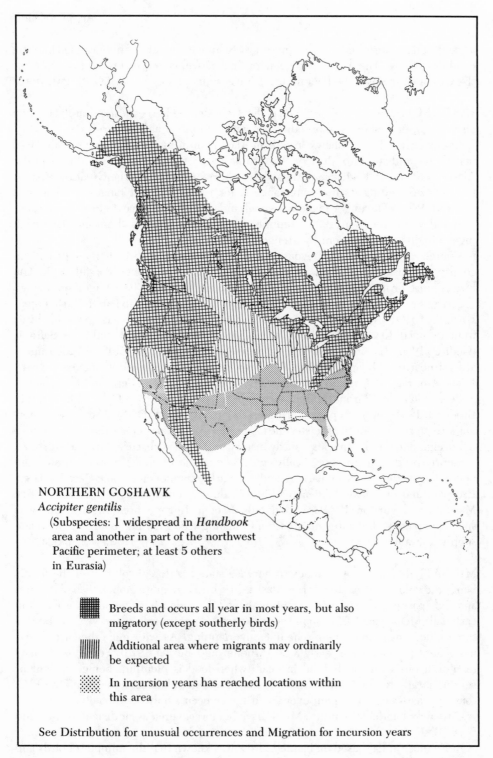

NORTHERN GOSHAWK
Accipiter gentilis
　(Subspecies: 1 widespread in *Handbook*
　area and another in part of the northwest
　Pacific perimeter; at least 5 others
　in Eurasia)

Breeds and occurs all year in most years, but also migratory (except southerly birds)

Additional area where migrants may ordinarily be expected

In incursion years has reached locations within this area

See Distribution for unusual occurrences and Migration for incursion years

363

agricultural and forest land, even quite close to human dwellings, finding good hunting conditions there. The domestic pigeon, or Rock Dove, is frequent prey. In e. N. Am., the Goshawk seems to be beginning a similar adjustment.   RALPH S. PALMER

DISTRIBUTION   (See map.) Since the Goshawk is a tree nester (rarely nesting elsewhere), upper limits of breeding are within forest or at least scrub.

In our area   The Goshawk **breeds** in Alaska and Canada, including certain large marine is., and sw. into Mexico. It is ordinarily present on the forested base of the Alaska Pen. and on Kodiak and Afognak Is. Approximately from the Great Lakes e., it has been expanding its breeding range s. (or recovering lost range) for at least 2 decades. When Passenger Pigeons were abundant in Pa., Goshawks bred there regularly and commonly (Bent 1937). Audubon may have seen this hawk associated with fall pigeon flights; see comment by Mengel (1965).

Winter   Present n. even beyond known breeding habitat—regularly in ptarmigan country in Alaska (E. W. Nelson 1887) and the Mackenzie Delta (Porsild 1943). The bird is more or less migratory as well as an incursion visitant (see Migration below).

Straggler   In Alaska to Semenof I. (Shumagins) and even w. to Dutch Harbor (near Unalaska I.) (O. Murie 1959). Recorded beyond on the Commander Is. (probably birds from ne. Asia). In Canada, n. to Horton R. in nw. Mackenzie Dist. and to se. Baffin I. (Godfrey 1966). In continental U.S., s. into states bordering the Gulf of Mexico and to at least near the Mexican border. Rarely to Bermuda (latest in 1982 incursion year).

The Am. race *atricapillus* is recorded from Ireland (5, Oct.–Feb.) and England (1).

Recorded as **fossil** from the Pleistocene of N. Am. at 2 sites in Calif. (references in Brodkorb 1964) and from **prehistoric sites** in Pa., Ill., and S.D. (3). There are numerous foreign records for the Pleistocene (19 or more) and from recent sites (26 or more).

Foreign data on the species   Early history in Britain is obscure, but the Groshawk evidently bred, at least sporadically, until late in the previous century, then again beginning in the 1930s or earlier, and regularly commencing some decades later. Escapees and/or released falconers' birds evidently contributed to this change. See Marquiss and Newton (1982) for full details. In cent. Europe, breeding distribution is spotty or patchy, but forested areas and ongoing tree planting assure an adequate supply of usable area.   RALPH S. PALMER

MIGRATION   In N. Am. unless otherwise stated. After dissolution of the family bond, the young scatter. In interior Alaska, Juv. birds are more mobile than older ones and ♂♂ (particularly Juv.) more mobile than ♀♀; evidently movement is greatest in early fall (McGowan 1975). Soon there is s. movement; birds of the year go 1st and some older ones later, their schedules overlapping. As with our other accipiters, movement peaks daily in early A.M. (Mueller and Berger 1973). Yet at least many territorial birds remain behind in years when food is plentiful, being resident or shifting locally to obtain prey. In some peripheral populations, as on is. off the B.C. coast, perhaps any movement over any distance occurs only occasionally.

Goshawks banded at Duluth, Minn. have been recovered as far distant as Alta. and B.C. (D. Evans).

In Fennoscandia, based on banded birds, it is known that the number of birds and distance traveled decreases going s., that the birds that travel later in the season go farther, and that this applies to all age classes, with fewer birds in their 2d calendar year or older going long distances. Birds are more nearly sedentary in cent. Europe, but there is still a dispersal of young and some fall movement. Judging from the geographic extent of irruptions in N. Am., the birds here often travel much greater distances.

Fall Movement begins in late Aug. or very early Sept.; the time to see peak numbers varies with year and place and may be any time from late Sept. to mid-Nov.; usually movement has terminated by sometime in Dec. There is little information from w. N. Am.

Spring The Goshawk is an early migrant. The birds are not easily seen, especially in poor weather, since they travel low and rapidly. Flight often begins by late Feb. and may continue into early May in coterminous U.S. An 11-year study was made in N.Y. at Derby Hill near se. L. Ontario; in years when few birds pass and most of those seen are "adults," a large portion has passed by Mar. 15 (G. Smith and Muir 1978).

Incursions Occur within N. Am. about once a decade, in response to a rapid decrease in snowshoe hares, but at 3–4 year intervals in n. Europe, where prey species are more diverse. In N. Am., evidently there are more prey species (more stable food supply) to the w. (F. Beebe 1974) and s. in the Goshawk's range, which may lessen regionally a tendency for it to irrupt. In 1916, large numbers of *A. g. atricapillus* invaded Calif. in Nov. (Grinnell 1917), a year before a massive e. flight. Some incursions consist almost entirely of "adult" Goshawks—evidently very few young have been reared because of food shortage.

In boreal N. Am. the snowshoe hare has a regular 10-year fluctuation, which is less regular s. At least to the n., peak Ruffed Grouse numbers tend to lag behind peak hare numbers. Also n., Goshawks (and usually Great Horned Owls) make s. incursions when hares suddenly become scarce (immediately after a peak); to the s., the Goshawk must increase its take of other prey than the almost nonexistent hares and so creates a predictable temporary scarcity of Ruffed Grouse.

According to Mueller and Berger (1967a), the hawks increase along with their preferred prey. Then a dense hawk population results in increased conflict between individuals. Such interaction increases further as prey numbers decline, requiring resident birds to expand their hunting areas. Many hawks then are unable to find suitable wintering areas within the breeding range. Since breeding Goshawks are presumably largely permanent residents, young birds without established territory probably are the first to be displaced. Mueller et al. (1977) carried this concept farther, suggesting that adults displace birds of the year, that ♀ ♀ displace ♂ ♂, and that adult ♂ ♂ cannot compete with the larger ♀ ♀ in a very harsh winter.

Because of inadequacies of reporting, it is difficult to compare incursions, which have been noted for over 120 years—see dates in Bent (1937), Palmer (1949), and in Mueller's papers. Definable incursions also occur at about the same time in the Great Horned Owl. In the Goshawk, they tend to last at least 2 years, the 2d a so-called echo effect. Incursion years include: winter of **1859**–1860 (Howe and Allen 1901); **1870**–1871 (Deane 1907); **1905**–1906–1907 (Deane, M. Hardy 1907); **1917**–1918 (Bent 1937, Palmer 1949, Bull 1964); **1926**–1927–1928, believed to have been the largest then known (Gross 1928, others); **1935**–1936 (Speirs 1939, Bryens 1941); **1954,** small (Mueller and Berger 1967a, but also note 1952 in table in Hofslund 1966); **1962**–1963 (Mueller and Berger 1967a); **1972**–1973, very large (Hofslund 1973, Mueller et al. 1977, G. Smith and Muir 1978), and 1972 was dramatic in Pa., followed there by declining numbers in 1974, 1976, and 1978 (Heintzelman 1981); **1982**–1983, very large and widely reported, Maritimes to n. Great Plains, s. to Gulf of Mexico and Ariz., w. into Calif., and includes the most recent Bermuda record.

Near Duluth, Minn., in 1972, the 1st birds were noted in the 1st week of Sept., the largest number was seen Oct. 14, and the flight declined after Oct. 18. There was a 7-day total (Oct. 11–17) of 3,908 Goshawks, and the entire flight, to end of Nov., yielded a count of 5,352. None of 382 birds trapped was wearing a band. Only about 15% were 1st year birds, most had empty crops, and a few were excessively thin (Hofslund 1973). For many further details, see especially Mueller et al. (1977). RALPH S. PALMER

BANDING STATUS   The total number banded to Aug. 1981 was 6,161, with 302 (4.9%) recoveries (Clapp et al. 1982). The 1985 figure from Duluth, Minn., was over 4,700 banded out of some 21,000 seen since 1972. Main places of banding have been in the Great Lakes region, to a lesser extent in Alta. and interior Alaska. Much more information is known from banded birds in Europe than in N. Am.

RALPH S. PALMER

REPRODUCTION   N. Am. data unless otherwise stated. Some **first breed** as yearlings, ♀♀ pairing with older mates (several authors). Bent (1937) stated, without details, that both sexes "rarely" breed in Juv. Plumage. In Europe, based on examination of testes, Hoglund (1964) concluded that yearling ♂♂ are typically incapable of breeding, but Glutz et al. (1971) reported 2 instances. In Oreg., 70 observed ♀♀ were in "mature" feathering, as were ♂♂ that were seen (R. Reynolds and Wight 1978). Also in Oreg., 2 (of 46) ♀ were Juv. and one of these laid 3 eggs and reared 2 chicks (Henny et al. 1985). In interior Alaska in 1971, a year of food abundance, 4 of 11 ♀♀ were "immature" (McGowan 1975). Thus, when there are numerous well-fed yearling Goshawks, some ♀♀ at least enter the breeding population.

Pair bond   Apparently lifelong. Displays on territory occur each year, whether mates were together continually during preceding months or not. In Europe, after loss of mate, a ♀ got a new one within 2 weeks (Holstein 1942).

Displays   HIGH-CIRCLING over the forest may be seen in almost any month by 1 bird or 2 (presumably a pair) advertising territorial ownership. The extended wings show the underwing pattern. Often the tail is no more than partly spread, but at times its white under coverts are alternately fluffed and spread laterally and retracted so that they are strikingly conspicuous—tail-flagging. In Feb.–Apr., both members make a fairly steep ascent, alternating brief spans of flapping with gliding or soaring; then they circle tightly on set wings or abruptly switch back and forth. Often the tail is spread during circling; at other times it is not, but the under coverts are flagged repeatedly. Sometimes a bird, presumably the ♂, dives toward the other, or he may dive toward her while she is perched. Tail-flagging is also done from a perch. The common call is a protracted wailing by both birds, the sexes distinguishable by lower voice of the ♀.

Two birds sometimes fly in a very deliberate manner, their wingbeats slow and deep, and wings (at least of ♂) held in high dihedral during the interspersed gliding. There are a few wingbeats to gain altitude, then a downward glide, and tail-flagging by at least the ♂. This is also performed singly (probably by either sex) or (F. Beebe 1974) with the ♀ close and leading. It may be a variant of the following.

The SKY-DANCE, variously described, is the most commonly seen display. Well above the forest a Goshawk makes a short downward glide, wings held close to the body, then with a few rapid wingbeats regains lost altitude, and again glides. The result is a series of shallow undulations, as in our other accipiters. After the upward portion of an undulation, the downward portion at times consists of a steep rapid dive, wings held close, into the forest. At other times the bird will flap-soar as it mounts several hundred m. overhead. Then it may circle, suddenly change course by doubling back, or undulate. Suddenly it climbs steeply, goes over the top of an undulation, and, with wings held close, makes a spectacular plunge. Zirrer (1947) stated that it is done silently, usually with a wavy gliding back and forth that brings the pair alternately close together and far apart. They are not always silent; both sexes may chatter, and a wailing is heard, probably from the ♀.

At least some aerial displays occur over a much larger area than the nesting territory. Displays also vary and combine in ways that, coupled with their presumably polyvalent functions, complicate any obvious pattern of which may relate to territorial ownership and which to pair formation or reformation. J. Schnell (1958) inferred that plucking prey has a "courtship" function. Continued mutual display surely indicates that a bond is formed.

Even on warm days in winter (in Calif.) the ♀ may bring green branches (see also Greenery, below) and deposit them on the nest without any attempt to work them into its structure (J. Schnell 1958). As with later building, this is a morning activity. This would seem to align with European authors that nesting territory is established and maintained by the ♀. At times in Wyo., territory was occupied by the pair up to 5 months before laying (the Craigheads 1956) as part of a large home range.

According to F. Beebe (1974), reproduction is dependent on a narrow range of resident prey species eaten by wintering adults. One or more of these must be sufficiently abundant to permit the ♀ to cease hunting altogether, or nesting does not occur. The ♂ usually captures all food from preincubation until well into the nestling period. In w. N. Am., an abundance of red squirrels or 1 or more grouse species makes possible the onset of reproduction.

Nesting density Norway, in 2 areas: 0–4 nests in 200 sq. km. over 13 years and 2–9 nests in 200 sq. km. over 7 years (Hoglund 1964). Interior Alaska: 1 pair/46–55 sq. km. for 1971–1973 (av. 8 active nests), then 1 pair/372 sq. km. in 1974; closest nests were 2.4 km. apart in 1971 and 3.1 km. in 1972 (McGowan 1975). Montane Colo.: 6 nests 1/13.3 sq. km. with the 2 closest 2.4 km. apart in 1974; also 6 nests in the area in 1975, but 4 active in 1974 abandoned with 2 having new ones a short distance away; the 2 closest were 0.8 km. apart (Shuster 1976). Oreg.: 1 pair/2,750 ha. in 1974 (4 nests), with mean distance apart 4.3 km. (R. Reynolds and Wight 1978).

Rust (1971) reported apparent clumping of nests in s. Bavaria at times. In n. Colo., a nest was seldom farther than 275 m. from standing water; Goshawk numbers were also highest near areas of high ground squirrel (*Spermophilus*) numbers—normally within 350 m. of them (Shuster 1980). Oreg.: quite obviously a pair may shift to a new site not far away, perhaps 3.5 km.; this can place pairs close together, "though none of these situations was found to persist for more than one breeding season" (R. Reynolds and Wight 1978). See R. Reynolds and Wight text figs. for distances between nests of our 3 coexisting accipiters in the same area and year.

Nest tree May be of any species as long as its structure provides a foundation. It may be forked, it may have several limbs on 1 side of the trunk (conifers), or it may have a tangle of small limbs and twigs (as in birches) on which to build. Rarely is a nest out on limbs away from the trunk. According to F. Beebe (1974), in mixed w. forest, trees that develop suitable crotches are selected, such as aspens among spruces, alders among firs, and so on. He stated, as have others, that sites are near standing water. Only on Vancouver I. did he find Goshawks nesting in continuous forest away from a lake or clearing. Various authors report that sites are on slopes.

Fifty-one of 62 nests were in deciduous trees and 18–75 ft. above ground (Bent 1937). Twenty sites in Colo.: preferably close to the trunk of large trees, at a major fork or branch at bottom of the living canopy, 12–15 m. up in aspen (*Populus*) and 8.5–12 m. in pines (Shuster 1980). When 3 trees died of beetle infestation they were no longer used (Shuster). According to J. Schnell (1958), conifers are preferred in the West when present, yet aspen is commonly used; reported heights are 15–45 ft. In interior Alaska, paper birch, less often aspen, the latter limited to ♀ ♀ that nest there as yearlings and return thereafter out of tenacity to such sites (McGowan 1975). In Wis., yellow birch (*Betula lutea*), with aspen 2d; tall pines and hemlocks are used as watchtowers (Zirrer 1947). In N.S., a marked preference for deciduous growth (Tufts 1962).

There are very few European records of nesting on the ground (Schweigman 1941). In Alaska it sometimes nests on rocky cliffs (Turner 1886). It probably sometimes nests in recesses in eroded stream banks. Olendorff (1980) listed 4 published references (none for N. Am.) of man-made nest bases provided for this species.

Reuse of sites The returning pair may use the same nest repeatedly, alternate between existing nests on the territory, or build a new nest. They tend to return to traditional areas, that is, places that have a special appeal; hence, one may find several old nests there. In interior Alaska, only 4 of 21 traditional locations contained only a single nest (McGowan 1975); most nest sites were active at least 2 consecutive years, some up to 5, and nontraditional sites were usually occupied by yearling ♀ ♀.

Nest building The ♀ fetches twigs or limbs from the ground or breaks them from trees—dead or alive. In Mass., the fresh fractures on many sticks showed that the hawk had broken them from living trees (Farley 1923). In Wis., the selection of a stick takes at times "wholly five minutes or even longer" (Zirrer 1947). If she drops a stick at the nest, she does not retrieve it but goes for another. All are carried in the beak. She builds in the morning for about 1 hr. Zirrer watched nest building for 7 consecutive seasons. The ♂, on guard nearby, did not fetch sticks or build. J. Schnell (1958) noted that the ♀ went out on a branch until suitable live twigs were encountered, then tore 1 off, leaning backward to do this and using her wings to regain balance; often she carried 2 or more at a time. The ♂ collected once in the ♀'s absence. The nest lining consists of dry bark or material of similar texture. **Greenery,** coniferous (frequently) or decid-

368

uous, is often added regularly from laying until the young depart (and in other seasons). New nests are not large, about 18–20 in. diam. and 10 in. high, but refurbished ones can be up to 36 in. diam. and 20 in. deep. Occasionally the Goshawk appropriates and refurbishes the old nest of a crow or a buteo (or a buteo uses a Goshawk nest). Goshawk nests are fairly easy to locate before the trees have leaved out.

Construction may continue for about a week, but observations are few. In Wis., Zirrer found the birds to be very persistent even after their structure was deliberately destroyed. The pair thrice attempted to nest again nearby. At 1 of the disturbed nests, 4 frozen eggs were found on the snow below and the ♀ was again sitting on the nest. The nest is defended vigorously against conspecific trespassers, various potential predators, and, in N. Am., against humans. (Striking is practically unknown in Europe, where the Goshawk has long been heavily persecuted by humans.)

Copulation During nest construction, the pair often interrupts to copulate, usually on a branch near the nest. The ♀ "solicits," facing away, her wings drooped and under tail coverts flared. The perched ♂ droops his wings, spreads his under tail coverts, begins calling, and then flies down to nearly ground level, gaining momentum to swoop upward and mount on her back. Much calling and slow wing-waving follow.

Plucking perch This may be a log, a stump, an old nest, or a limb but is preferably a bent-over tree or sapling—very reminiscent of the bow-perch of hawkers. The ♂ captures prey, decapitates it and eats the head, may pluck it slightly, and then carries it to a perch, where plucking is finished. Some prey, such as nestling birds, are not plucked but are delivered intact to the ♀. In Calif., 10 perches in 1 season at 1 nest were 100–425 ft., av. 225., distant from the nest (J. Schnell 1958).

Feeding the mate The ♂ delivers food in any daylight hr. beginning at least 14 days before egg laying, by which time the ♀ is wholly dependent on him (J. Schnell). It is brought 2–4 times daily, sometimes in response to the food call of the ♀ (Gromme 1935). The ♂ may, by his own calling, get the ♀ off the nest to join him. Thus, she may feed at his perch or carry the prey to the young, or it may be partly eaten and the remainder cached in the fork of a tree.

Caching Typically done when the young are too small to eat large amounts at a single feeding. After some hrs., or even 4–5 days, the prey is recovered and fed to the brood (J. Schnell). Occasionally, prey is transferred to the ♀ in an aerial food pass. Thus, the ♂ provides for his mate and, later, the brood. He seldom brings food to the nest and rarely tries to feed the young. If live prey passes the nest, the ♀ will sometimes drop off and capture it there or nearby; the ♂ may fetch it from a distance of up to 1½ mi. (Zirrer 1947). Zirrer mentioned a ♀ half-carrying, half-dragging a fully grown, freshly killed snowshoe hare across prostrate trees and other obstacles.

Laying interval Ordinarily 2 days.

Clutch size Usually 2–4 eggs, occasionally 1 and rarely 5; evidently, smaller clutches when food is scarce. Interior Alaska 1971–1973, 33 clutches of 1–4, av. 3.2 eggs (McGowan 1975); in Oreg., 5 clutches av. 3.2 (R. Reynolds and Wight 1978); 15 in Pa.: 6 sets (of 3) and 9 (2) (Street 1955); in N.S., 47 reportedly complete: 16 (of 2), 23 (3), and 8 (4) (Tufts 1962). For N. Am.: 2.7 ± 0.88 eggs (44 clutches) and 2.6 ± 0.81 young (50 broods) (Apfelbaum and Seelbach 1983).

One **egg** each from 20 clutches (Alaska 2, Sask. 2, Alta. 4, N.S. 1, Labrador 1, Pa. 9, and 1 not listed) **size** length 57.76 ± 2.05 mm., breadth 44.73 ± 1.67, radii of curvature of ends 18.51 ± 1.04 and 13.39 ± 1.23; **shape** slightly elongated elliptical, elongation 1.28 ± 0.052, bicone −0.080, and asymmetry +0.148 (F. W. Preston). Fifty eggs av. 59.2 × 45.1 mm. (Bent 1937). The shell is without gloss, slightly rough, **color** bluish white when fresh and without markings.

Egg dates Principal data are in Bent (1937) or the same as graphed by N. Snyder and Wiley (1976). The Goshawk is our earliest-nesting accipiter, laying about a month earlier than Cooper's Hawk, although southwesterly their timing is about the same. (The Sharp-shinned Hawk lays later than either.) Bent's dates for presumably viable eggs, with the long span probably including replacement clutches: 100 records Alaska to Labrador, Apr. 5–June 14 (50, Apr. 23–May 18), and 20 records in coterminous U.S., Apr. 1–June 3 (10, Apr. 17–30). In interior Alaska, most clutches are completed and incubation begun in the last week in April or the 1st half of May (McGowan 1975). Yearling ♀ ♀ lay later than older birds. In Oreg., earliest clutch completed Apr. 10 and latest June 2 (R. Reynolds and Wight 1978). In s. N.Mex., backdating from an estimated hatching date would indicate a clutch laid about a month earlier than in Wyo. (Shuster 1977).

Early in the season, mates roost some distance apart in the nesting territory. When laying begins, the ♀ is on or near the nest, the ♂ elsewhere (J. Schnell 1958); or, the ♂ is also in or near the nest tree, and the ♀ is on the nest, especially at night, even before laying (Zirrer 1947). Nights are cold in Apr. Probably, as in Cooper's, each ♀ has a fairly consistent schedule from year to year, some individuals starting their clutch early and others later. There is some difference, however, between early and tardy seasons.

Replacement clutches Repeated attempts by a pair in Wis. to renest are mentioned above. In Pa., 3 eggs were taken Apr. 2, and on Apr. 20 the bird was incubating a 2d clutch in an old Red-tailed Hawk nest in the vicinity; these were later destroyed, but on May 20 the Goshawk had laid a 3d clutch (of 2) in another old Redtail nest (R. B. Simpson 1909).

Incubation period Per egg, 32–34 days. They are typically warmed gradually for some time so that embryonic development begins late during the laying of the clutch. Variation in this pattern and up to at least 50 hrs. of pipping have contributed to (but do not entirely account for) stated periods of 21–42 days; 28 days has been widely quoted from Bent.

Hatching Requires less time than the laying span, and occurs when prey is plentiful. The eggshells are carried some distance, occasionally being found under the plucking perch, where the ♀ feeds. At hatching time in B.C. there is a flood of migratory passerines and waterfowl in the boreal forest. The principal prey species are then occupied with their own reproduction and the Goshawks have, if needed, alternative sources of food (F. Beebe 1974). A shift to ground squirrels often occurs somewhat before hatching.

Direct parental care By the ♀, the ♂ provisioning her and the brood except when, as noted earlier, she may make a chance kill in the nesting area. If so, she may feed on it away from the nest. By the time the young are a few days old, the ♂ is no longer allowed to linger and so leaves the nest immediately after a food transfer. That is, the ♀ repeatedly utters her dismissal call, not feeding her brood until her mate has departed (J. Schnell). If not expelled by the ♀, he would remain perched and not hunt; this was noted when the ♀ was absent. Later on, mere sight of the ♀ was enough to expel the ♂.

At first the ♀ holds a morsel in her beak, her head turned sideways, and the nestlings strike at the food. In about 13 days they also strike at food in her talons, but she may still endeavor to feed with her beak. She still divides the prey among them. At 3 weeks they are much less dependent; either parent may bring a plucked, decapitated prey to a nestling that is increasingly able to dismember it.

At first the young Goshawks utter their thin food calls while being fed. At 3 weeks, when they hear the ♀ calling at approach of the ♂ with food, they react to this by calling also. At about 23 days, in response to hostile action or voice of a sibling having food, a nestling may adopt an "appeasing" stance—it moves to the nest edge in a crouched-forward posture. A nestling with food may call, chase sibling(s) away, and strike with a foot. It "mantles" over the prey, "turning its back" on the others. Yet there is little conflict.

Siblicide? Although the young are ordinarily not aggressive toward one another, there is evidence from European studies that when food is scarce a larger nestling may kill and eat a smaller one. On the other hand, when the ♀ feeds her brood there is no aggression among them, and food is more evenly distributed; length of 75 feedings av. 11.5 min. (J. Schnell). The entire carcass, except a few hard parts, is usually fed to the brood; they seemed to "dislike" the intestines of most prey species (J. Schnell).

After the young have what food they want, the ♀ takes the remainder away and caches it for future use (J. Schnell). Then she goes nearby and fetches **greenery,** which thus continues to be delivered throughout the nestling stage but is not incorporated into the nest structure. Only once did a ♂ bring a twig. Also in Calif., J. B. and R. Dixon (1938) reported a nest covered with green pine sprigs and replenished as older sprigs turned brown. Another activity of the ♀, after having fed her brood, is to search for any dropped particles and to present them to the young or eat them herself. Then she begins "excavation" actions: pushing her head into the matrix of the nest, raising her head, and scattering the material about. This diminishes as the season advances (J. Schnell).

At some time, usually about 3½ weeks or longer into the nestling period, the ♀ does some hunting, going gradually farther away; in bad weather she stays close to the nest. Her return to hunting may correlate with a time when the brood may need more food than the ♂ can provide. This is also a time when the increasing size of the nestlings physically prevents her from brooding them. Presumably, she stays within, or at least very close, to the nesting territory until very late in the rearing period (but it could depend on prey availability), and she will attack any creature that comes near the nest that she regards as a menace. This includes humans, and such attacks can be dangerous. In Wis., Zirrer (1947) found that a ♀ attacked him regularly when he was not carrying a gun, but at sight of a weapon she remained hidden or disappeared. In Calif., as the season progressed, the ♀ left the nest area entirely (J. Schnell).

Development of young J. Schnell (1958) gave growth curves for each of 3 young in a brood; there was some interpolation, since he did not begin weighing right after hatching. Weight increase is gradual for over 2 weeks, then rapid for 20–25 days, and follows a steady upward trend thereafter to at least age 50 days. Schnell's paper should be read for changes in behavior and differences between members of the brood that hatched on different dates. (For another general summary, see McGowan 1975.) There is room for variance in the following material, since Schnell calculated a date when all eggs had presumably hatched. The **boldface numbers** are ages in days assigned in his paper.

9 Much brooded (this varies with weather); nestlings faced inward, in physical contact; their heads swayed, and when beaks of 2 nestlings came in contact, one thrust and poked vigorously at the other. When fed, they gave a squeaky whistle. They struck at the ♀'s beak, whether empty or not. When defecating, they oriented their aim over the nest rim. **11** More active, but coordination still poor; rudimentary "preening" motion noted; a rapid, high-pitched twitter uttered if in pain, as when accidentally stepped on. **13** First seen to strike at red meat held in the ♀'s talons; a nestling would maneuver to get near the nest edge and, in standing position, defecate over the rim. **15** Defecating, feeding, preening, and fly-shaking actions now more ritualized; in feeding, the nestlings continued to strike at red objects, in 3 instances at the eye of the ♀. **17** Much as before, but differences in behavior (as in preening) due to different chronological ages of the young very evident; older young showed an awareness of objects away from the nest. **19** Various new actions noted—pecking, peering, "contentment twitter" when well fed. **21** They related the ♀'s calls to arrival of food; thus, when she called on departing, they gave food-begging calls; a nestling regurgitated a pellet into the nest matrix; a nestling pecked vigorously at another. **23** Young attempted to dismember prey in absence of the ♀. **27** First flight motions. **29** Stretched out with a foot to grasp a twig, then released it; nestlings now able to stand. **31** Prey snatched from ♀; vigorous flight motions. **35** Could lift themselves above nest by wing action. **39** A nestling with food now turned away from others to retain it. **41** The young moved out—became "branchers"—and were as far as 50 ft. from the nest. They returned to the nest to be fed.

Late during nesting, if the ♂ encounters the ♀ at close range, he may utter a special, abrupt call; he faces her, his beak wide open, and while calling lowers his head forward and down. (See *guck* note under Voice, above.)

J. Schnell (1958) estimated the total wt. of prey delivered to 2 young in 49 days at 13 kg.

Breeding success In general, the number of young that attain flight is somewhat more than 1 less than the number of eggs/clutch. Averages: interior Alaska (33 clutches)—3.2 eggs and 2.0 young to flight age (McGowan 1975); and Oreg. (5 clutches)—3.2 eggs, 2.6 hatched, and 1.7 young reared (R. Reynolds and Wight 1978). In interior Alaska in a year of snowshoe hare abundance, the number of young Goshawks that attained flight reached 2.5/nest (McGowan).

Age at first flight Most indications are that the nestling period in undisturbed nests lasts about 37–41 days, ♂♂ flying several days earlier than ♀♀. Thus, in Colo., it lasted 34–37 days, and the faster development of ♂♂ (the smaller sex) accounted for much variation. (R. Reynolds and Wight 1978).

Brancher stage The young first leave while still bobtailed and incapable of climbing flight. They remain nearby, limb hopping, for a week or longer, during which time they return to the nest at night. At this stage their frequent calling appraises the parents of their whereabouts. Either parent may deliver food directly to a young bird, sometimes to the nest, where the young return to get it. In time, they fly on approach of a parent and there is an aerial food pass. Live prey is sometimes delivered. The young develop speed and aggressiveness; then they actively pursue adults bringing food, and this aggressiveness, often reinforced by hunger, is probably a major factor in dissolution of any family bonds.

In Wis., the young remained a few days near the nest tree, then were led a little farther from the nest daily by the parents. They were then about 50 days old, but it takes up to 6 weeks or longer before they leave the territory—unless unduly disturbed. The ♀ continued to attack anything and anybody coming near the young; sometimes the ♂ also attacked (Zirrer 1947). In Oreg., flying young were dependent on their parents for as long as 42 days (R. Reynolds and Wight 1978).

The parents gradually become less noisy and defensive. The young birds, after dissociation from their parents, roam the woods trying to catch and kill just about anything they see—but with poor success (F. Beebe (1974). In the Yukon in late summer, Rand (1948) saw young Goshawks approach a man, screaming at him, and following him through the forest, flying from tree to tree.

It is probable that the ♀, at least when food is available, often tends to remain on or near the nesting territory most of the year and that the ♂ may move away for some months beginning in autumn.

The Goshawk has bred in captivity (Cade et al. 1977).   RALPH S. PALMER

SURVIVAL   There are no useful N. Am. data. The several studies in Europe show a high mortality (to 80% in Sweden, where large numbers are shot) the 1st year, then half as high the 2d, and a gradual decline for several years to a leveling-off. For Finland/Sweden, E. and M. Haukioja (1970) recalculated the data thus: 63% (1st year), 33% (2d), 19% (3d), 17% (4th), and 11% (annual thereafter).

Maximum potential longevity of the Goshawk is probably about 20 years.

For accipiters, apparently the single most important mortality factor is starvation associated with difficulty or inexperience in gathering food or changes in local prey-species abundance and diversity (N. Snyder and Wiley 1976).   RALPH S. PALMER

HABITS   Goshawks roost solitarily, well within the forest canopy or, in the subarctic, perhaps occasionally on the ground. A series of sites are used; sometimes 1 is occupied for several consecutive nights. A perching bird lowers the right leg till the "heel" joint meets the perch; then, with toes clenched, the leg is raised and lowered, striking the perch several times, until the leg is abruptly contracted against the ventral feathers. In stretching, 1 side of the tail is spread and the corresponding leg extended stiffly backward; then the wing on that side is extended downward and back, partially covering the fanned tail. Then a return to normal perching stance. (From J. Schnell 1958.)

Outside the breeding season, a **hunting territory** is occupied by a bird or perhaps a pair, and it may shift during the winter. That is, an area may be hunted for a while, then the Goshawk moves on. In the process, an individual can have overlapping territories, and different individuals may hunt areas that overlap.

Hunting methods   The Goshawk tends to hunt lower in the forest canopy (as Cooper's Hawk), not in the upper canopy (as the Sharp-shinned Hawk). Most hunting is done **from a perch,** the hawk shifting at intervals; thus, the bird perches inconspicuously most of the time and spends relatively little time on the wing. Few pursuits are initiated **from flight,** and the chance of success then is probably much less than when the attack is initiated suddenly from a perch. This pattern has been verified from studies of radio-tagged birds in Sweden (Widén 1982, 1984); total activity increased with time after the last kill, the increase being in frequency rather than length of activity periods.

The attack is sudden, at tremendous speed, over short distances. Like our other accipiters, the Goshawk is reckless and will crash into thickets. A very persistent captor, it will walk or run on the ground to flush or seize prey. The shock of the strike is followed by a "killing reaction" (R. M. Bond 1942); the hawk reacts to any movement of the prey, grasping it strongly, relaxing the grip, then tightening again. Soon the hawk gets hold of the head of the prey and immediately plucks and eats it; this may be the ultimate cause of death. In N.H., Cram (1899) noted that Goshawks following the tracks of snowshoe hares walked and hopped where the brush was too thick to fly through it. For more on **terrestrial hunting,** see especially Forbush (1927), Bent (1937), and Bergstrom (1985).

In Alta. in winter, successful Goshawk traps baited with live pigeons were placed on high knolls or hills, prferably along wooded river valleys. The hills needed to be ringed with woods, since Goshawks prefer to attack with short, fast flight from the trees. Traps set in open fields were unsuccessful. (From Oeming 1958.) Other studies also indicate a preference for wooded edges.

Summer feeding   Since the av. body wt. of prey is related to predator size (Storer 1966, others), the ♀ has been said to take larger prey than the smaller ♂. From this it follows that smaller prey are preponderant in that portion of the breeding season during which the ♂ does the hunting. This concept has been questioned.

At Donner Lake, Calif., Goshawks capitalized on peak nesting populations of 2 birds—Am. Robin and Steller's Jay. The robin peak is slightly earlier; the Goshawks fed 1st on adults, then later had easy pickings of young birds to feed their own young. The ♀ was persistent; several times she was seen wading in shallow water searching for Mallard ducklings (she was aware of their presence). Another Goshawk was on the ground, trying to flush prey from around brush and logs. It seemed evident that the ♂ of this pair made repeated trips to nests of prey containing more than 1 nestling. Two young Steller's Jays were delivered within 21 min. and 2 robin nestlings within 36 min. (J. Schnell 1958).

In the Pacific NW the change to winter prey species does not begin until Sept. Migrants depart, ground squirrels commence hibernating, and the young of primary prey species are well grown. In most years, abundance of these young and their inexperience with danger ensures that young Goshawks get well trained and oriented to primary prey (F. Beebe 1974).

Winter feeding   At n. limits of range, the Goshawk probably competes with the Gyrfalcon for ptarmigan. Turner (1886, or in Bent 1937) described the Goshawk hunting them in Alaska. In Alaska/Yukon and n. B.C., large numbers of Willow Ptarmigan live on alpine uplands. In autumn and winter they move down to or even into forested country. The hawk can thus shift from its spring–summer diet, often largely the abundant arctic ground squirrel. Widespread primary winter prey includes other grouse, the snowshoe hare, and red squirrel. A captive "adult" ♂ Goshawk ate an av. of 124 gm. of food/day (14.1% of its av. wt.) in fall–winter (Fevold and Craighead 1958).

A major **incursion** of Goshawks in e. N. Am. (see Migration, above) can contribute to depressing the population of Ruffed Grouse. This large prey, if flushed away from dense cover, has no possible means of escape, since it is easily overtaken in flight. Long-term studies of Goshawk-Ruffed Grouse interrelationships on the 5-sq.-mi. Cloquet Forest in Minn. (where grouse are not hunted by man) have been discussed especially by Eng and Gullion (1962) and Gullion (1981a, 1981b, 1984). Losses have been estimated to exceed 270–315 birds annually in years when the hawks have been nesting residents. Drumming ♂ grouse are notably conspicuous in spring when other food is in short supply. Yet overall, diseases and hard winters can be more generally damaging, and grouse productivity has been such that Goshawk predation has not had a serious effect. In n. Europe, the Hazel Grouse (*Tetrastes* [=*Bonasa*] *bonasia*) is heavily preyed on. Yet perhaps the nearest the Goshawk has come to negatively affecting a species anywhere is on the Baltic is. of Gotland, where its prey species, the introduced Ring-necked Pheasant, is in marginal habitat.

There is evidence that individual Goshawks become **habituated** to 1 or 2 prey species. In N.S., a nest was located adjacent to 2 farms where many domestic chickens ran at large. The Goshawks fed their young smaller mammals and birds (3 Ruffed Grouse included), but they did not bother the chickens—nor had the farmers seen them (Tufts 1962). In an 8-year study of a pair in Wis., only twice were feathers and bones of Ruffed Grouse found; as long as hares, rabbits, and squirrels were plentiful, Goshawks did not chase many birds (Zirrer 1947). According to F. Beebe (1974), ♀ ♀ trained for hawking can be oriented to capture hares and rabbits, and once so conditioned they no longer exert themselves in pursuit of birds.

In York Co., Pa., in Oct. 1926 (incursion year) a man lost more than 40 chickens to Goshawks. Farmers told of chickens pursued into buildings and even carried away in the presence of human beings. A hunter saw 1 wait nearly ½ hr. at a rabbit burrow (G. Sutton 1927).

Cooperative hunting Zirrer (1947) described rather vividly how Goshawks "hunt together" in autumn for gray squirrels; they are noisy while doing it.

"Panic hunger" In Maine, several Goshawks were shot during the incursion winter of 1906–1907 after they either had struck or were in the act of striking dogs that were in pursuit of snowshoe hares (M. Hardy 1907). In Maine in Dec. 1980, the author saw a Goshawk fly from a conifer and strike a medium-sized dog walking nearby in a field; it was a young bird and was probably hungry.

Temperament Goshawks are easily livetrapped, and in hand some seem unconcerned, but others are shy and fearful (F. Beebe 1974).

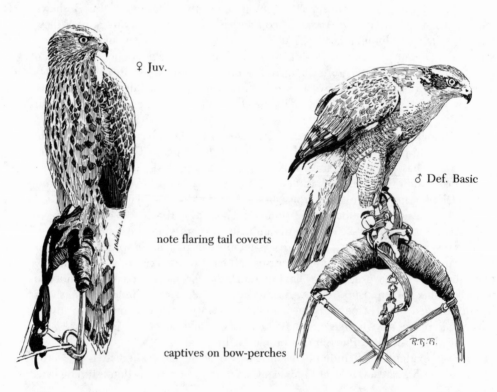

♀ Juv.

note flaring tail coverts

♂ Def. Basic

captives on bow-perches

Hawking Across Asia, from Turkey to Japan, this hawk is more prized than any falcon as a hunting bird. For much historical and other information and interesting illus.. mainly of Japanese hawking, see Jameson (1962). Even today, the bird is so valued in Japan that it is sold locally at good prices and is never exported. North America, on the other hand, lacks a background of traditional esteem, and the Goshawk is regarded as the worst of a bad lot (Beebe)—but its status has improved much of late.

Goshawks fall victim to frounce, a **disease** caused by the microorganism *Trichomonas gallinae*, which is endemic at a sublethal level in birds of the pigeon family. In an incursion year, Beebe thought it possible that pigeons indirectly caused more Goshawk deaths than human persecution, yet food habits studies generally do not reveal a predeliction for a diet of pigeons or doves.

There seems to be no evidence that pesticide levels have affected Goshawk numbers in N. Am.

In recent decades the Goshawk has been researched much more thoroughly in Europe than in N. Am.; the present account (with 109 references) is too brief to include so much material.   RALPH S. PALMER

FOOD   In N. Am. Mainly game birds, hares and rabbits, and squirrels (ground and tree) but also many other items depending on locality, season, and opportunity. Poultry principally during incursions. The usual caveat applies—some items are consumed and not seen at nests or in pellets, and some probably never in the latter.

The larger and more powerful ♀ can manage heavier prey than the ♂, as established in N. Am. and European studies. For a concise summary of 7 N. Am. sources on food, see Sherrod (1978). There is a useful list, emphasizing primary prey, in S. Jones (1979).

Excluding **carrion** (seldom reported), the largest **avian prey** species listed are Mallard and Black Duck; smallest are sparrow-sized birds and wood warblers. The only raptors are a Merlin and 3 Am. Kestrels. (Mainly in Europe, its food has included at least 4 falcons and 11 other diurnal raptors—principally the Kestrel [*F. tinnunculus*] and Sparrowhawk [*A. nisus*].) A spring–summer study in N.Y. and Pa. (Meng 1959) was notable for the extraordinary number of Am. Crows (*Corvus brachyrhynchos*) included; the number was also high at a Mich. nest (Pettingill 1976); and the Nw. Crow (*C. caurinus*) is a primary prey (F. Beebe 1974). Largest **mammals** are snowshoe hares (*Lepus*) and cottontails (*Sylvilagus*); very frequent are ground and tree squirrels and chipmunks (the last 2 also much favored by Cooper's Hawk); smallest are mice. Miscellaneous items include snakes, insects, and a few other invertebrates. Although the Goshawk is a generalist and an opportunist, it evidently tends to favor a few prey species at any time and place.

These are some findings; many of the older data are from Goshawks killed at poultry farms and game farms: McAtee (1935) reported on 243 stomachs: poultry in 116, game birds (chiefly Ruffed Grouse) in 40, other birds in 14, "rabbits" in 22, tree and ground squirrels 8, mice 5, other mammals (woodchuck, muskrat, kitten, weasel, shrew) 5, grasshaoppers and caterpillars 4. The 202 stomachs from Pa. examined by G. Sutton (1927) varied from the above: poultry 41, game birds (chiefly Ruffed Grouse) 79, small birds 27, cottontails 63, gray squirrels 10, small mammals 16, and snakes 2. Again Pa.,

377

for the period Nov. 1, 1936–Apr. 1, 1937, when Goshawk numbers were high, a total of 294 (156 contained food, 138 empty): Ruffed Grouse 40, flicker 2, crow 1, domestic fowl 45, domestic pigeon 1, unidentified birds 13 (total 102 birds); cottontail 23, deer mouse 1, chipmunk 1, red squirrel 4, gray squirrel 19, shrew 4, unidentified mammals 8 (total 60 mammals) (M. Wood 1938).

See earlier sections for data on food and its capture. Occasionally the Goshawk is very destructive to Bobwhite (Schorger 1929, Trautman 1940). During the incursion winter of 1906–1907 in Mass., largely Ruffed Grouse; 1st arrivals at Toronto, Ont., favored flickers (Deane 1907). Zirrer (1947) saw 1 capture a large fox snake, but it escaped. Introduction of Gray Partridge and Ring-necked Pheasant at Okanagan Landing, B.C., attracted an unusual number of Goshawks (J. Munro 1929b). Largely a ptarmigan feeder in parts of Alaska (several early authors). For w. data, in addition to F. Beebe's general statements for parts of B.C., there now are extensive summer data from Oreg. (R. Reynolds and Meslow 1984)—note the considerable number of snowshoe hares, chipmunks, and tree and ground squirrels.

Although the Goshawk has waded in shallow water to seek ducklings, apparently the only record of it fishing (Bertelson 1983) is from Sweden.   RALPH S. PALMER

LESSER BLACK HAWK

Buteogallus anthracinus

Black Hawk, Common Black Hawk, Mexican Black Hawk, Crab Hawk (in part of range). Rather stoutish hawk with short broad wings, longish legs, and short tail. Beak narrow (laterally compressed), loreal area largely unfeathered. Smaller than the similar-appearing Greater Black Hawk (*B. urbitinga*) of Mexico to Chile. **Color phases**(?)—see below.

Black with slaty bloom (soon lost in specimens), fading toward brownish; tail has wide (1⅓–3⅓ in.) white band midway across it. Feathers of rear of head white basally; some on dorsum marked with white or various browns (some more s. birds); upper and under tail coverts inconspicuously tipped white; tail squarish, black, narrowly tipped white, with white middle band and 1 to several much narrower white bars proximately and concealed under coverts. Primaries #6, #7, and #8 (counting from inner) or #3, #4, #5 (counting from outer) nearly equal in length, about 4 outermost slightly emarginated on inner web.

Juv. (**"normal"** feathering)—head to upper back with prominent heavy dark streaking on white or buffy (varies to head whitish with dark stripe through eye); remainder of upperparts very dark brownish, the feathers narrowly edged more or less reddish brown; feathers of underparts white to buffy with wide blackish center strip, forming heavy longitudinal streaking; tibial feathers and under tail coverts boldly barred blackish on white; tail dark ended, the remainder alternating very light (wider) and 5–7 very dark (somewhat narrower) exposed bars. **Rufescent** individuals have light areas cinnamon instead of white or buffy white (Wetmore 1965). **Pale variant** of small minority in part of range distant from our area—blackish is diluted (reduction of melanin) to brownish or yellowish, the head and anterior dorsum conspicuously light (Amadon 1961b, text and illus.).

Sexes similar so far as known, but ♀ larger and heavier; length (sexes combined) 17–

20½ in. (43–52 cm.), wingspread to 45 in. (114 cm.), approximate wt. 1⅛–2⅛ lb. (500–950 gm.).

As treated here, 1 subspecies in our area and 2 extralimital.

DESCRIPTION *B. a. anthracinus.* 1 Plumage/cycle with Basic I the earliest definitive.

▶ ♂ ♀ Def. Basic Plumage entire feathering ALL YEAR. **Beak** distally very dark, its base, the cere, and gape yellow to orange-yellow; **iris** dark brownish. **Feathering** as described above. Legs and **feet** as cere, talons black. All feathering is molted from late spring or summer into fall in our area. V. and E. Stresemann (1960) stated that the primaries are not molted in regular squence—possibly a misunderstanding of so-called stepwise molting.

AT HATCHING To age 1 week the nestling has short fluffy down, whitish (toward yellowish), with blackish brown patch through the eye and reddish brown dorsal areas on head, body, and upper surface of wings (J. Schnell). Earlier description: E. A. Mearns (1886).

Development of Juv. feathering At 2 weeks the down is not fluffy but is instead more woolly and whitish (toward grayish); dorsal areas are still reddish brown, and pinfeathers begin to show in the wings. At 3 weeks patch on side of head still discernible; many feathers have appeared on side of neck and anterior dorsum. At 4 weeks chick appears mostly dark (has many contour feathers) and feathering extends upward to a line above rear margin of eye; some feathers have appeared on thighs (crural tract). At 5 weeks cross-barring complete on thighs, neck fully feathered, and dorsal head feathering has advanced approximately to anterior margin of eye; standing young's tail does not touch the nest. At 6 weeks head fully feathered; standing young's tail touches the nest; flight feathers of wing and tail not fully grown. Data modified from J. Schnell (1979).

▶ ♂ ♀ Juv. Plumage entire feathering develops as described above, worn into the following SPRING or SUMMER, then molted gradually. **Beak** tipped black with base, cere, and gape yellow or greenish yellow; **iris** dark brownish. **Feathering** as described earlier. Underside of **tail** shows 5–7 dark bars 10–30 mm. wide. Legs and **feet** yellow, talons black.

Color phases See Juv. under diagnosis, above.

Measurements Wetmore (1965) measured birds from all parts of the range of this subspecies: 33 ♂ BEAK from cere 23.5–28.8 mm., av. (of 32) 26.2, WING across chord 354–378, av. 363; and 36 ♀ BEAK from cere 25.2–30.5 mm., av. 27.7, WING across chord 365–398, av. 377.

Mean for 20 ♂ and 20 ♀: BEAK from cere 26.6 and 27.0 and WING across chord 372.7 and 387.4 (N. Snyder and Wiley 1976).

Measurements and wt. of the sexes overlap.

Weight (With standard error of mean) in Panama: 6 ♂ 793 ± 95.8 gm. and 4 ♀ 1,199 ± 142 (Hartman 1961). A fall ♀ weighed approximately 700 gm. (Elwell et al. 1978), very early in Sept. an "adult" ♀ 866 gm. (White et al. 1983), and a ♂, unable to fly, in late Apr. 572 gm. (Wauer 1969).

Hybrids None reported.

Geographical variation In the species. Evidently omitting Cuban birds, A. Wetmore (1965) examined over 200 specimens; he concluded that there is so much individual variation in color and in extent and kind of lighter markings that the birds are best sorted primarily on size: 1 larger, from sw. U.S. through Mexico and Cent. Am. into S. Am., excluding 2 smaller ones of mangrove areas from s. Mexico (Chiapas) along the Pacific coast and on some is. into sw. Ecuador or beyond. The smaller birds had been treated by Monroe (1963) as a clinally varying (in color) separate species (composed of 3 subspecies)—a "suggestion" that Wetmore found "interesting" and in need of "careful consideration" in the future. Monroe was not adopted, for example, by L. Brown and Amadon (1968 2) or E. R. Blake (1977) but was followed by Amadon (1982b). Cuban birds have been treated as a separate species by some authors (e.g., Friedmann 1950, A. Wetmore 1965) but not by others. They differ from mainland birds in much the manner that smaller mainland ones differ from larger ones, and Amadon (1982b) left open the question of their taxonomic status. RALPH S. PALMER

SUBSPECIES Until there is reasonable agreement as to whether the birds included here compose a single species or more, the application of trinomials is unsatisfactory. Interested persons should consult and compare these authors, listed chronologically: Friedmann (1950), Amadon and Eckelberry (1955), Amadon (1961b), Monroe (1963), A. Wetmore (1965), L. Brown and Amadon (1968 2), E. R. Blake (1977), J. Bond (1979), and Stresemann and Amadon, in Mayr and Cottrell (1979). Quite arbitrarily, and for the time being, the principally mainland birds are treated here as in A. Wetmore (who examined the most material), with the geographically most isolated is. birds (of Cuba) added as not yet having evolved to separate species status.

In our area *anthracinus* (Deppe)—larger (mainly the WING); U.S. (principally Mexican border states) s. into S. Am. (except area listed below), also Cozumel I., Trinidad, and the Windward Is. Description and meas. given above.

Elsewhere *bangsi* (Swann)—smaller; more varied pattern and colors, especially underside of wing; pale birds (see Juv., above) included here. Mangrove areas adjoining the Pacific from s. Mexico (Chiapas) s. through Cent. Am. and beyond into S. Am. to extreme nw. Peru. Occurs on some is. For meas., see A. Wetmore (1965).

gundlachi (Cabanis)—somewhat smaller than *B. a. anthracinus*; rather brownish (not black) and with more white on underside of primaries. Juvenile crown nearly solid blackish, and very narrow, dark bars on the tail. Measurements: Friedmann (1950). Mangroves and coastal habitat of Cuba and adjacent cays and Isla de la Juventud [Isle of Pines]. RALPH S. PALMER

FIELD IDENTIFICATION **In our area** Medium-sized stocky black hawk with broad wings and rather short tail in which (in flight) the forward edge of the wide white band across its middle is nearly aligned with trailing edge of wing. Base of beak, cere, and gape vivid yellow or even toward orange—a useful field mark—and yellow legs. Soars with wings horizontal (no dihedral), with palish area at base of primaries faintly reminiscent of Black Vulture. Tends to perch in shade; more often seen soaring. Common call a series of far-carrying, more or less whistled, notes.

In flight, much broader winged and shorter tailed than the Zone-tailed Hawk, but when perched and tail pattern obscured appears nearly identical—that is, identification almost impossible until the bird takes wing. Sluggish in comparison to the Gray Hawk (which see).

The Juv. is very dark dorsally with some light spots or patches or feather edging; venter with very heavy, dark longitudinal streaking on whitish or buffy, and dark barring on flanks and under tail coverts. In flight—whitish area on underside of wings; tail with multiple alternating dark and light narrow bars.

Outside our area Often difficult or impossible to separate the lesser from the Greater Black Hawk (*B. urbitinga*). The latter has less color in beak, more white on rump (it shows), less white in wing lining, and, in addition to the white middle bar in the tail, a narrower bar may show nearer the body. Its voice is very different—often 4 notes, 2 quick, then 2 slower and drawn out.

Juvenal Lesser and Greater Black Hawks are very similar.   RALPH S. PALMER

VOICE Authors do not agree—queer whistling cry; weak, hoarse, squealing note; loudly whistled cry rendered with great power; high-pitched, eaglelike screams; harsh squawk resembling night heron; spinking like Bald Eagle; and so on. The usual call has a whistled quality and is far carrying. The following is condensed from J. Schnell (1979). The most common call, lasting 3–4 sec., is a series of 7 or 8 clear piercing notes, varying in pitch, increasing abruptly in intensity, then progressively decreasing. Far carrying. Uttered during displays, by adults alarmed by presence of humans or large birds of prey near nest, and often by the ♂ when (with or without prey) he approaches and leaves the nest. Duration and intensity varies.

During copulation, a monotonous series of 20–30 notes lasting about 10 sec.

A clear, high-pitched, rapid call (to 17 notes in 5 sec.), barely audible, from small chick; it later carries a considerable distance.   JAY H. SCHNELL

HABITAT **In our area** In breeding season, optimum environment includes permanent flowing water, trees for perching and nesting, a dependable vertebrate food supply, and relative isolation from human disturbance (H. Snyder, in Murphy 1978). Unaltered groves of mature trees in close association with water. Sometimes called an obligate riparian nester. A few nest near intermittent streams, impoundments, and elsewhere. (See also below.)

Elsewhere In all seasons, the upland birds occur in woodlands and scrub bordering streams and lagoons and are scarce in or absent from extensive forests; in lowlands occur especially in mangrove areas, thickets, and scrubby trees bordering beaches and mudflats, where crabs are a common—perhaps exclusive—prey in some areas.

RALPH S. PALMER

DISTRIBUTION (See map.) The species: sw. U.S. s. through Mexico and Cent. Am. (including some is.) and in S. Am. e. in coastal Venezuela (also Trinidad and some of the Windward Is.) to ne. Guyana; Cuba and Isla de la Juventud [Isle of Pines]; southward e. of the Andes in Colombia; and w. around the perimeter of Colombia and Ecuador to extreme n. Peru.

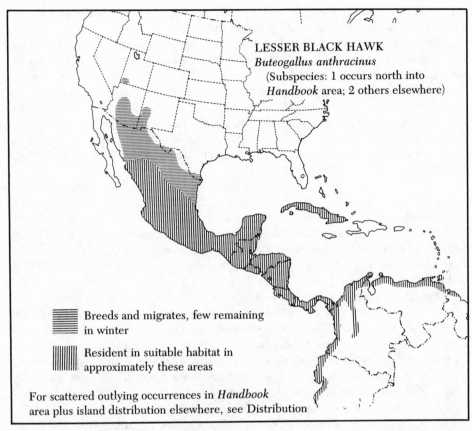

LESSER BLACK HAWK
Buteogallus anthracinus
(Subspecies: 1 occurs north into
Handbook area; 2 others elsewhere)

Breeds and migrates, few remaining
in winter

Resident in suitable habitat in
approximately these areas

For scattered outlying occurrences in *Handbook*
area plus island distribution elsewhere, see Distribution

In and near our area BAJA CALIF. One record in nw. part, May 7, 1967 (Short and Crossin 1967).

ARIZ. and N. MEX. Earlier published comments on the distribution of this hawk were made without knowledge of the entire breeding range. The relatively inaccessible character of Black Hawk habitat and irregular occupancy at some intermittent streams can also alter impressions of historic range. Such purported "new" areas as the Sierra Ancha Mts. are new only to the reporter. Similarly, there is little reason to suspect that this hawk did not occur (A. R. Phillips 1968) along the Gila R. before 1918; the negative is hard to prove. The Big Sandy R. is a classic example of an area that may be of marginal nesting use because of its variable flow. Its upper tributaries of Trout and Burro creeks, however, afford excellent nesting habitat and provide a reservoir of birds that nest occasionally along the Big Sandy during years of favorable waterflow and prey populations. This pattern is similar for other raptors and would be especially so for one that is dependent on a flowing stream, a factor that is quite variable in the arid Southwest. The pattern of Black Hawk occupancy as reflected in the literature's sparse records suggests that they are now more widespread than formerly. The quality of riparian habitats has generally declined since the turn of the century, and one would expect that the amount of its potential breeding habitat has diminished, thus reducing its density and possibly its breeding distribution.

Today, as no doubt formerly, Black Hawks can be found nesting in the Gila R. and Bill Williams R. watersheds of Ariz. and N.Mex., where perennial water exists between 2,000 and 6,000 ft. elevation. This includes the w.-cent., cent., and se. parts of Ariz. and the sw. and w.-cent. parts of N.Mex. Primary habitats are the tributaries of the following rivers: upper Bill Williams drainage, upper and middle reaches of the Gila, and upper and middle reaches of the Salt. Dispersed areas of good breeding habitat include the mt. drainages scattered in se. and w.-cent. Ariz. (R. L. Glinski). An adult ♀ was observed in Littlefield near the Utah–Nev. border, Aug.–Sept. 1980 (C. M. White, see also White et al. 1983).

UTAH Records for Springvale area, Washington Co. Seen near 2 nests in 1962 and sitting on one of them in 1963; the n. fork of the Virgin R. is here bordered with cottonwoods (Carter and Wauer 1965). Young bird seen July 9, 1964, and an adult June 27, 1965 (Wauer and Russell 1967). Male, unable to fly, captured Apr. 21, 1966 (Wauer 1969). The 1st record at Zion Natl. Park "since 1976" was a young bird seen Oct. 3, 1981 (1982 *Am. Birds* **36** 202). A young bird occurred again in Apr.–June 1985 (J. Gifford, C. M. White).

NEV. Davis Dam—reportedly seen Apr. 9, 1984 (1984 *Am. Birds* **38** 940).

TEX. The nesting population "collapsed" along the lower Rio Grande in early years of the 20th century—last recorded breeding in Cameron Co., 1937. In adjoining Tamaulipas (Mexico), Black Hawks were present in "apparently normal numbers" until about 1958. Southern Tex. nesters "probably were eliminated" by timber cutting, and the Tamaulipas birds "seem to have been done in" by DDT applied to cottonfields; the breeders in relatively unspoiled Jeff Davis Co. may have nested there for some time before their discovery in 1970. (From Oberholser and Kincaid 1974.)

Reportedly, the 1st record away from the Pecos region (N.Mex.–Tex.) and s. Tex. was of 2 birds in Lubbock Co., May–July 1982 (1982 *Am. Birds* **36** 869). Now seen regularly in Big Bend Natl. Park. For Tex. records up to the early 1970s, see text and map in Oberholser and Kincaid.

Winter—at least 2 records for the lower Rio Grande.

FLA. An "absolute minimum" of 4 Black Hawks were seen in s. parts of the state (principally in Dade Co.) in the period Aug. 12, 1972–June 29, 1976, and were thought (on geographical grounds) to have come from Cuba (Abramson 1976).

NOTES MINN. A ♀ collided with a truck at Bemidji, Sept. 18, 1976; how it reached there is speculative (Elwell et al. 1978). PUERTO RICO One shot in spring 1978, either a natural occurrence or perhaps an escapee (Perez-Rivera 1980). WINDWARD IS. The St. Vincent birds inhabit mountain forest (J. Bond 1956) and "do not differ" from *B. a. anthracinus* (L. Brown and Amadon 1968 **2**). Apparently very few birds and irregular occurrence elsewhere: St. Lucia, the Grenadines, Grenada.

This hawk has no known fossil or prehistoric record.   RALPH S. PALMER

MIGRATION The species is believed to be generally resident, but almost all birds at n. fringe of distribution withdraw seasonally. **Spring:** In Ariz. it has arrived as early as Mar. 11 and in the Davis Mts. in Tex. about Apr. 1 (in Schnell 1979). At Aravaipa

Canyon, Ariz., the birds returned from their wintering area Mar.–June (most sightings in May). Most were still in brown Juv. feathering, but some showed varying amounts of definitive coloration: some had blocks of "adult" flight feathers, others were almost fully "adult" but for a banded Juv. tail, a block of brown secondaries, and so on (J. Schnell). **Fall:** Most are probably gone from the U.S. by mid-Oct., but an occasional bird remains well into or through winter. Where migrants pass the winter is unknown (J. Schnell 1979)—"presumably" in Cent. Am. (Murphy 1978).

RALPH S. PALMER

BANDING STATUS   A few have been banded in Ariz. and fewer in N.Mex.

RALPH S. PALMER

REPRODUCTION   The following is from a study made in the Aravaipa Canyon, e. Ariz., as reported by J. Schnell (1979), with various additions.

Age when first breeds   Unknown.

Displays   Begin immediately on arrival in nesting areas—in 1 instance a ♂ displayed for a week before the arrival of a ♀. In HIGH-CIRCLING, the 2 birds soar, at times very high. In the SKY-DANCE, 1 (presumably the ♂) flies downward with legs dangling until very close to the other bird and repeats this several times. TUMBLING (Sky-dance component?) is common, a stalling maneuver close to the partner. In Brit. Honduras, G. Thomas (1908) observed a spectacular example. The ♂ circled high with dangling legs and then, with wings held close, plunged downward at tremendous speed, checking it at a dead tree, where it broke off a twig (symbolic, or actual nesting material?). It would appear that dangling yellow legs (and yellow cere?) are important in displays. There is considerable far-carrying vocalization during the several displays. In Ariz., maximum altitude of displaying birds was estimated at more than a mi.

Territories   Appear to be quite small compared with those of some of our other Falconiformes. They are permanent in terms of boundaries and dimensions and are used year after year by returning individuals. Boundaries are defended aggressively from neighboring individuals throughout the nesting season. The 1st spring arrivals are often observed in aerial combat. On Mar. 19, 1984, at 1800 hrs. (daylight fading), 3 individuals alternately circled and dived at each other with dangling legs. Often they came in contact and suddenly, on 1 occasion, at about 150–200 ft. altitude, 2 hawks began to descend rapidly in a corkscrew spiral; talons were locked together and neither bird was inclined to release its grasp. Just before striking the hillside, 1 hawk regained flight altitude and attempted horizontal flight, towing the other struggling individual, but spiraling resumed and the pair hit the ground. Five min. later, on approach of the observer, they separated, one still chasing the other. The demise of one of them might have resulted if they had been unmolested. Certainly territorial aggression is a mortality factor in this species (J. Schnell).

Nest site   Selection may begin as early as 5 days after arrival. Pair members (the ♂ most often?) visit old nests, which may be refurbished and used, and perch near them. Twelve pairs used cottonwoods exclusively for 3 seasons except for a nest in a sycamore 1 season. In Ariz. and N.Mex. they have also nested in alder, velvet ash, walnut, ponderosa pine, and Douglas fir. Reported nesting in cliffs in Ariz. (F. Fowler 1903)

385

has not been verified by other observers. Pines are used commonly in parts of Cent. Am. Average nest height in Ariz. was 55 ft. (max. 82), and nest trees av. 80 ft. from running water. Nests have been found at various elevations from a low of 1,420 ft. to a high of 6,000 ft.

In Sonora, Mexico, this hawk apparently nests before summer rains (Short 1974).

Nest The ♂ collects and delivers most of the building material—twigs of ¼ in. av. diam.—from ledges or hillsides within about 200 ft. of the nest or breaks them from nearby trees. The ♀ does all construction. A newly constructed nest had a diam. of about 15 in., height about 8 in., and rather shallow bowl (Bendire 1892). East of Ft. Verde, Ariz., a nest in a cottonwood had evidently been the birthplace of many generations—the accumulation measured 4 ft. high and 2 ft. in diam.; it was lined with cottonwood leaves to a depth of several in. (E. A. Mearns 1886). For photograph of Mexican nests, see Rowley (1984).

Greenery As the nest nears completion, a greater number of leafy twigs is delivered. One nest was composed entirely of leafless twigs, but 10 days later leafed-out cottonwood twigs had been added. This is in part because leaves do not emerge early in the season, but evidence also indicates that the ♂ selects leafless ones initially and leafy ones later. During incubation a ♂ persisted in delivering leafless sticks (after the cottonwoods had leaved out) and the ♀ brought only leafy twigs. The ♀ was never seen to bring leafless twigs, and she was primarily responsible for fetching leafy ones, which are compressed into a nest lining. Until the young depart, the parents continue to deliver leaved twigs, which raises the floor of the nest above the past year's decaying material and its invertebrate inhabitants.

The ♀ roosts at night progressively closer to the nest during construction and may stand on it for long periods before egg laying.

Copulation Occurs 50–300 ft. from the nest, on a branch or prominent rock, and increases to about 4 times a day as time of laying nears. The ♂ may swoop down, alighting directly on the ♀, or may sometimes perch beside her and then mount, flapping his extended wings to maintain balance. At this time 1 bird (♀?) utters the distinctive copulation call.

Eggs are probably laid at intervals of 2–3 days. In the present study, 7 clutches had 2 eggs. In the same area, B. Millsap found a 3-egg clutch and suspected that the original ♀ had been killed (carcass found) and was succeeded immediately by another that laid the 3d egg. According to Bent (1937), **clutch size** is 1–3 eggs—in 13 clutches, 3 (of 3), 6 (2), and 4 (1). In Ariz., an av. of 1.67 eggs in 12 clutches (J. Schnell, in Mader 1982). "According to several good authorities," clutch sizes are 2 and 3, but in Brit. Honduras 27 clutches consisted of 26 (of 1) and 1 (2) (G. Thomas 1908). This hawk eats mainly lower (cold-blooded) vertebrates, and clutch size may be enhanced by rodent eating (I. Newton 1979). Apparently, clutch size also varies geographically.

One **egg** each from 20 clutches (Ariz. 3, Tex. 5, Mexico 11, Brit. Honduras 2) **size** length 56.54 ± 2.69 mm., breadth 44.90 ± 1.59, radii of curvature of ends 19.16 ± 1.30 and 15.49 ± 1.33; **shape** between elliptical and subelliptical but somewhat variable, elongation 1.25 ± 0.046, bicone −0.023, and asymmetry +0.104 (F. W. Preston). Texture is finely granulated, without sheen; **color** whitish, blotched or marked in

386

variable extent with lavenders and light to dark browns; some have few and faint markings, occasionally none.

Incubation period Approximately 37 days (Millsap 1981) and 39 ± 1 (Schnell 1979). The ♀ always covers the eggs at night. At 1 nest the ♂ incubated 54% of daylight hrs. (at midterm); the ♀, however, controlled the ♂'s total because she yielded her position on the eggs only occasionally; the ♂, in contrast, always relinquished his position whenever the ♀ came to the nest (J. Schnell).

Replacement clutches In Brit. Honduras, according to G. Thomas (1908), if a nest is robbed, work begins at once on another nest; he claimed to have taken 3 clutches in a season from the same bird.

Hatching dates Seventy-five percent of the Aravaipa clutches hatched May 18–30, the latest (a single egg) July 28, 1977. In 1 nest 2 eggs hatched 44 hrs. apart.

Nestling phase When pipping begins, the ♀ prevents the ♂ from incubating; henceforth she attends the young, and his role is to provide her and the young with food, which she parcels out to them until they can manage this themselves. Early in the nestling phase she is rarely absent from the nest; if she is away, the ♂ often attempts to feed the young. If prey is too large to be consumed at once, the ♀ caches it—once a fish was cached 75 ft. away beside a tussock of grass. As the young grow the ♀ spends less and less time at the nest. Once, 3 weeks posthatching, she returned with a fish, which she presumably caught. When the young are 5 weeks old, the ♀ no longer returns to the nest at night.

At 22 days a nestling swallowed a 5-in. lizard intact; the nestling could not yet walk in a standing position. At 29 days it stood for 9 min., attempted to dismember a fish, and for the 1st time was seen to flap its wings. At 36 days it stood for more than 1 hr., and at 43 days it stood for 3 hr., 43 min.

Age at first flight Varies 43–50 days; an av. of 1 nestling attained flight in 58 instances (Schnell, in Mader 1982). When first out of the nest the young are secretive, moving about very little, and the parents seek them out when delivering food. Older ones, better able to fly, return to the nest at intervals and also fly to their parents to receive food. They become independent 1½–2 months after attaining flight.

Jay H. Schnell

SURVIVAL No information.

HABITS Data from Ariz. **Hunting methods** This hawk hunts primarily from a stationary perch, often near the ground—from branches to a height of 50+ ft., on boulders, on gravel beds along streams, and so on. High perches are often used initially to discern if prey is present; the hawk then shifts to a lower perch before striking. Fish and other swimmers are taken as they pass either close to the perched hawk or sufficiently near the water's surface to be grasped. Rarely is a capture made at a depth greater than the length of the hawk's legs (J. Schnell 1979). Diving directly from a perch was the most frequently observed method of catching frogs and snakes that were swimming or resting on mats of algae (B. Millsap). Other observed successful prey captures in water were made when the hawk stalked and then made a forward thrust at small fish (J. Schnell 1979). A wading Black Hawk was observed waving the tips of its primaries in water, apparently to herd and concentrate prey in shallows (B. Millsap).

On 2 occasions an Aravaipa ♂ was observed actively coursing through a territory, apparently attempting to capture prey opportunistically. In 1 instance the hunter flew rapidly from perch to perch at midcanopy level, covering a circular distance of about 500 ft.; on another occasion he flew from rock to rock upriver, then returned along the same route, covering a total distance of perhaps ¼ mi. (J. Schnell 1979).

Capture of flying prey was observed on 1 occasion at Aravaipa; during a lean season (frogs and fish were scarce), a young Hooded Oriole was captured about 4 ft. above ground while attempting to escape (J. Schnell).

Captured prey Plucked, or fins of fish removed, before delivery to nestlings. If young are unable to consume it entirely, the ♀ usually caches it nearby.

Interrelationships As observed, usually some form of aggression toward other avian raptors. Near its nest, this hawk has been observed to attack Golden Eagles, Red-tailed Hawks, Peregrines, vultures, and ravens (J. Schnell). Great Horned Owls are probably a threat to nestlings (Webster 1976 *Am. Birds* **30** 975–978).

Bathing A ♀ bathed at approximately noon on Mar. 20, in 2–3 in. of water, within sight of the nest and incubating ♂. She stayed only about a min., then continued hunting (J. Schnell).

Mortality factors On the Arivaipa study area 2 dead Black Hawks were found near nests (causes of death unknown), and another, when moisture was high, was electrocuted on a power pole (J. Schnell). (See also Territories, above.) In the U.S. some losses probably occur from shooting (N. Snyder, in J. Schnell 1979), but this is seldom seen (see White et al. 1983). These hawks were reportedly killed (Zimmerman 1965) on the Gila R. to reduce the number of predators in release areas for exotic gamebirds.

Numbers and preservation In the early 1980s it was estimated (R. Glinski, N. Snyder) that there were about 200 pairs of Black Hawks in the U.S. The continued health of these birds depends on the preservation of relatively isolated natural riparian habitat that contains permenent flowing water (supporting aquatic and semiaquatic vertebrates) and gallery-forest tree species for nesting. A short-term management procedure to enhance their productivity would be the erection of low crossdams near nest sites. These should not stop natural flow but should form impoundments large enough to concentrate frog and fish populations, important components of this hawk's diet. Long-term management objectives must include continued regeneration of gallery-forest seedlings by periodic suppression or elimination of livestock grazing.

JAY H. SCHNELL

FOOD Of the species. Invertebrates (crabs, insects, etc.), fishes, amphibians, reptiles, birds (mainly small), and mammals (mainly small). Retrieved cached prey, also carrion.

The literature contains a long list of prey items; the Black Hawk is by no means a specialist. It takes the most vulnerable and available invertebrates and vertebrates that coexist in its living space. Poisonous animals appear to be a notable exception. Further, frogs are not recorded s. of the U.S. border—perhaps their capture or transportation must be observed, since they are digested very rapidly. Main foods of a pair nesting in a wide valley were reptiles and birds (67%), whereas fish and frogs were main foods (74%) of a pair nesting in a narrow canyon. Furthermore, annual differences in prey numbers are reflected in diets; when frogs were scarce (1976) on the Aravaipa study area, they represented only 20%, and when high (1967) constituted 42% (J. Schnell 1979). A cursory summary of items reported in the literature follows. **Invertebrates** In parts of range outside U.S., crabs are reported by about a dozen authors. Centipedes (Mexico), various insects and allies (U.S., elsewhere), and crayfish (U.S.). **Fishes** About 11 species (U.S. mostly, Mexico). **Amphibians** At least 3 frog species, also toad (U.S.). **Reptiles** About 10 species of lizard (mainly U. S.), 6 snakes, mud turtle (mostly U.S., but also Mexico). **Mammals** About 10 species (mainly U.S.), cottontail to mouse size; unidentified bats.

Carrion The retrieval of cached food items is evidence that Black Hawks occasionally eat dead and dried flesh in times of food scarcity, but this is unusual. Abramson (1976) reported a young bird feeding on a dead duck in Fla. Carter and Wauer (1965) noted a Black Hawk eating a dead mammal on a highway in Utah. L. Brown and Amadon (1968 2) stated that stranded dead fish are often eaten. At Aravaipa this was never seen. The Fla. bird, being young, could have lacked hunting skills; both it and the Utah bird may have experienced a food shortage while they were outside "normal" environment (J. Schnell 1979).   JAY H. SCHNELL

BAY-WINGED HAWK

Parabuteo unicinctus

Harris's Hawk (n. birds); Dusky Hawk (the species—Friedmann [1950]).

Medium-sized tricolored hawk. Beak fairly long; eye to cere naked except for a few bristles; primaries #6 and #7 (counting from inner) longest and nearly equal in length, the outer 3 progressively much shorter, and outer 4 with inner webs emarginated (incised) and outer web of at least 5 outer ones narrow; feathering rather soft, the feathers on outer side of flanks large but not much elongated; legs and feet stout; tail slightly rounded. Sexes similar, but ♀ larger. Generally speaking, the birds are browner to the s. (S. and Cent. Am. northward) and darker, nearer black, to the n. (darkest ones concentrated but not restricted to nw. Mexico and nearby). "Brown," "black," and intermediate individuals occur in some n. areas.

Basic feathering—largely various darker browns to sooty blackish, depending on individual; at least lesser upper wing coverts, wing lining, and flanks rusty to rich reddish brown (although sometimes reduced or obscure); vent to tail and upper tail coverts white; tail black with proximal quarter and terminal inch white, the areas sharply delineated. Juv.—variegated; head–neck mostly streaked dark and palish; dark brownish dorsal feathering with some rusty edging; most upper wing coverts usually with considerable palish rusty; underwing varies with individual, mostly palish to mostly rusty or darker; underparts nearly white with heavy, dark, longitudinal streaks or spots (in dark individuals they coalesce into nearly solid dark venter); flanks rusty with dark barring; upper tail coverts and vent area whitish with tawny tinge and sometimes black streaks ventrally; tail pale and more or less crossed by many fine dusky bars, the tip white.

Tex. data: wt. ♂ 20½–26½ oz., av. 24 (580–750 gm., av. 680), and ♀ 30¼–39½, av. 34¾ (856–1,118, av. 983). Note no overlap (and there is essentially none in chord of

WING). The sexes combined: length about 18–23 in. (46–58 cm.), wingspread to 46 in. (117 cm.).

Three subspecies, 2 marginally in our area.

DESCRIPTION *P. u. harrisi.* One Plumage/cycle with Basic I earliest definitive; scant information on molting; the following supplements the above diagnosis.

▶ ♂ ♀ Def. Basic Plumage (entire feathering) worn about a year. **Beak** variably bluish with dark tip; cere, lores, and eyelids yellow; **iris** a medium brownish; most of **head–body** a dark neutral color tinged brownish ("chocolate"), with concealed white on lower rear of head; flanks reddish brown (unbarred); vent to tail and upper tail coverts white; **tail**—see diagnosis; legs and **feet** yellow, talons black. In the **wing** the median and lesser upper coverts mostly cinnamon-rufous or variant, wing lining same, and flight feathers very dark.

Molting E. and V. Stresemann (1960) stated that some individuals of this species renew their primaries from inner to outer (descendant, regular) and others irregularly. This could be a difference between Prebasic I (regular) and later Prebasics. There is at least 1 molt center in the primaries and additional ones in the secondaries. In El Salvador, "adult" ♂ ♂ (Aug. 16, Sept. 8) were "just finishing the annual molt" and were otherwise in "full breeding condition." An "adult" ♀ in Calif. (Jan. 1) was in an "identical stage" of molting. A known-age (banded) yearling ♀ with young in Aug. was beginning to molt from Juv. to Basic I (Mader 1977b).

AT HATCHING Tex.: upperparts "uniform light tawny," lores and underparts white with tawny tinge on foreneck (Sennett 1887). Ariz.: a light brown down at first; in 9–13 days a gray down emerges (Mader 1975a); see Mader for graph of wt. increases of 2 nestling ♀ ♀.

▶ ♂ ♀ Juv. Plumage (entire feathering) fully developed at about age 40–45 days and evidently retained about a year (and may be found in any month, since birds nest year-round). **Head–neck** whitish or buffy brownish streaked dark, the dark nearly solid on crown, superciliary line brownish, concealed white on rear of head; **upperparts** a sooty brownish, some feathers margined rusty; underparts near-white or toward buffy with bold, dark, elongated spots and streaks, the vent to tail and upper tail coverts white tinged tawny (the ventral feathers sometimes with dark shaft streaks); flanks variable, often with alternating bars of palish tawny and much darker narrow ones; legs and **feet** yellow, talons black; **tail** feathers preponderantly whitish tinged brownish basally, this increasing and with many narrow sooty bars until distally almost entirely dark, then a white tip. **Wing** as in earlier diagnosis.

NOTE Northwesterly birds in N. Am. might be regarded as a dark phase; in Basic, upper wing coverts and flanks often with greatly reduced brown (many individuals appear largely blackish); Juv. birds "chocolate" rather than normal (light venter streaked dark). Perhaps most birds are dark in Baja Calif., adjacent mainland Mexico, and n. into Calif. and Ariz., but dark birds also occur widely among "normal" ones elsewhere in Mexico.

Sex differences These criteria were used in Tex. for distinguishing sexes of live birds (the Hamerstroms 1978): 1 trapped birds may be immobilized temporarily in holding tubes having an inside diam. of 106 mm. for ♂♂ and 128 mm. for ♀♀, the degree of reliability not entirely established (may slightly overlap); **2** ♂♂ take standard Fish and Wildl. Service bands size 7a, and ♀♀, which have stouter legs, size 7b; only 11 individuals (4 ♂ and 7 ♀) of 614 birds banded took the "wrong" size; **3** meas. and **4** wts. differ and are diagnostic of sex.

Measurements Live birds in Tex. in winter, sexed by the above criteria (the Hamerstroms 1978): definitive feathering WING across chord 221 ♂ 303–342 mm., av. 324, and 176 ♀ 340–383, av. 360.9; Juv. 37 ♂ 299–330 mm., av. 311.7, and 38 ♀ 327–367, av. 348.3. The same birds WING flattened: definitive ♂ 313–350 mm., av. 333.2, and ♀ 351–397, av. 373.6; Juv. ♂ 307–340 mm., av. 320.7, and ♀ 335–380, av. 360.3. There was extremely little overlap when WING was meas. across chord and none when it was flattened; it is unusual among raptors for the definitive wing to be longer than the Juv. In this species, "immatures closely correspond in size to adults" (van Rossem 1942).

Livetrapped birds in Ariz. had no overlap of the sexes in WING (Mader 1975a).

Weight of live birds in Tex. in winter: definitive feathering 220 ♂ 550–829 gm., av. 689.7, and 177 ♀ 825–1,173, av. 997.7; Juv. 37 ♂ 536–755 gm., av. 636.8, and 39 ♀ 789–1,137, av. 935.1. Weights of 19 winter birds from Tamaulipas did not differ greatly.

Livetrapped birds in Ariz.: 37 ♂ 634–877 gm., mean 725, and 14 ♀ 918–1,203, mean 1,047 (Mader 1975a).

The ♂ av. about 300 gm. (over 10 oz.) less than the ♀ in all age classes. There is almost no overlap between the sexes in Tex. Mader (1975a) found none in Ariz., nor did the Hamerstroms in a small sample from Sonora.

Hybrids None reported; young have been fostered by the Red-tailed Hawk.

Geographical variation Darkest overall and av. largest in Baja Calif. and an adjoining strip of the Pacific side of Mexico from within Nayarit n. into extreme sw. U.S.; lighter, especially venter, and smaller from s. Ariz. to Tex. s. through Cent. Am. and the nw. perimeter of S. Am.; smallest, with white showing in venter, from ne. Colombia down through much of S. Am. and mostly w. of the Andes.

Affinities Amadon (1982b) speculated that this hawk may be close to *Buteogallus*.

RALPH S. PALMER

SUBSPECIES Their distribution as currently defined seems unusual. Because of lack of regional information on both size and coloring, the following is tentative.

In our area *harrisi* (Audubon)—size intermediate; descr. and meas. of Tex. birds given above. Occurs from s. Tex. locally through much of Mexico except nw. (areas of intergradation unknown), much of Cent. Am., and S. Am. more or less peripherally from Venezuela (including Margarita I.) counterclockwise to parts of Colombia, Ecuador, and n. Peru.

superior van Rossem—largest birds; exclusively(?) dark (darkest have upper coverts of wing and the flanks often with little brown; i.e., many appear almost entirely blackish); Juv. almost entirely "chocolate" rather than with venter whitish marked dark as in normal phase. Sw. Calif. and s. Ariz. southward to include Baja Calif. and adjacent mainland Mexico down into Nayarit, here extended on size of birds (J. D.

Webster 1973) to Zacatecas City. Although darkest individuals of the species presumably are in the n. of the area just given, equally dark birds in both Basic and Juv. occur at other "Mexican points" (Dickey and van Rossem 1938); they noted that there is a "decided tendency" for some individual variation "to become localized."

WING across chord 5 ♂ 335–355 mm., av. 342.5, and 6 ♀ 360–390, av. 375 (van Rossem 1942); 4 ♂ 324.4–357.1 mm., av. 337.8, and 9 ♀ 351–388, av. 370.4 (Friedmann 1950)—perhaps some of the same birds included on both series.

Elsewhere *unicinctus* Temminck—av. smallest; "normal" coloring. See Blake (1977) for details of descr., meas., and map. Large portions of S. Am. except the nw. perimeter (see above), the Amazon basin (evidently), and from s. Argentina southward, and so on. RALPH S. PALMER

FIELD IDENTIFICATION **In our area** and nearby. Readily recognized. At long distance, perched, might possibly be confused with the Black Vulture, but not on the wing. Size approximately of a large buteo, but very different configuration. In coursing flight it is graceful and harrierlike, but, except for white rumps, the differences are great. Some authors claim that its flight appears sluggish at times.

Basic feathering—very dark bird with large areas of brownish red on both surfaces of wings and the flanks more or less evident. The rather scarce dark phase of the Ferruginous Hawk lacks the banded tail with much white basally.

Juv.—individuals vary from having underparts streaked light to overall dark, the tail always encircled with white basally. Lighter ones might be confused with some Ferruginous Hawks, which have decidedly light-colored heads. Both have tan or rusty flanks. Young Red-tailed Hawks, seen from below, are more stocky, with body and underwing at least partly white.

At rest the Bay-winged perches erect on a pole, saguaro cactus, or other high point. When alert, its body is close to horizontal, and it is rather trim and long tailed. If one is seen, there are often up to several more close by, since it commonly occurs in groups. Sometimes it is noisy (rasping or croaking voice). In the warmer part of the day it may soar to a great height. RALPH S. PALMER

VOICE In s. Ariz. (Mader 1975a): **1** alarm *iirr* lasting about 3 sec., when an intruder entered the nesting area; **2** cackle call, quick succession of 4–5 chirps at 1-sec. intervals for 5–10 sec., somewhat like the cackle of Cooper's Hawk, seldom uttered; **3** chirp *eerrp* lasting 1–3 sec., usually by "adult" anticipating prey exchange or food delivery; and **4** begging by young and 1st-year birds, a plaintive scream *eechip* lasting about 2 sec.

The following is from other sources without attempt to correlate with the above: Tex. (Oberholser and Kincaid 1974): **1** usually a loud harsh *karrr*, seldom heard; and **2** a rather weak *eee-eee-eee-eee* when disturbed. Costa Rica (Slud 1980): **1** "typical cry" of "adult," an angry sounding, lengthened, heavy, harsh note that rapidly lost intensity; **2** hoarse scream of a sort associated with *Buteo;* **3** from "subadults," unclearly screamed *oo-eek* calls; and **4** rhythmical sets of usually 5–6, sometimes 10, simple peeping notes, "uttered with monotonous regularity" by any of several "adults and subadults" spaced well apart. Sometimes shrill, other times lisping. Stronger peeps singly and "out of context" were *Buteo*-like in quality and power. Venezuela (Friedmann and Smith 1950): harsh wheezy *uerr* not unlike note of Turkey Vulture but considerably louder and of much longer duration.   RALPH S. PALMER

HABITAT   The species—open and semiopen dry terrain with more or less shrub, scattered trees, or cacti; in Cent. and S. Am., dry grassland to agricultural and ranch lands, also such wetlands as mangrove swamps. In some parts of our area there is some shifting, evidently related to drought, rainfall, and changes in prey availability; one might expect less of this in wet areas.

In sw. U.S., current habitat varies from occasionally used riparian areas with cotton-wood and other native trees to scrub or cactus desert. In Ariz., it is most commonly associated with saguaro-paloverde desert scrub; formerly, drowned trees of the lower Colorado R. from Yuma to Topock and vicinity, mesquite near Tucson, and saguaro and paloverde in foothills. In Tex., for the most part, and N.Mex., mesquite (desert) brushlands (Griffin 1976).

In adjacent n. Mexico, habitats much as in U.S.—open flat or rolling desert-brushland.   WILLIAM J. MADER

DISTRIBUTION   (See map for our area.) Breeding distribution tends to be spotty, with large vacant areas, and with occasional birds fairly remote from limits of usual occurrence. The species is present all year, apparently with some seasonal movement and other shifting. The map is tentative and changes are to be expected.

Distributional changes   Nesting distribution in the U.S. has shrunk greatly in this century. Once the Bay-winged Hawk was a common breeder along the lower Colorado R. To control flooding, several dams were built in the 1930s and 1940s. Agricultural

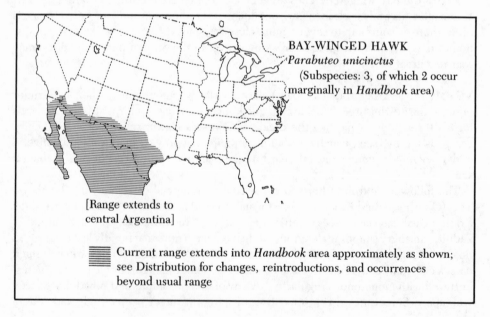

BAY-WINGED HAWK
Parabuteo unicinctus
(Subspecies: 3, of which 2 occur marginally in *Handbook* area)

[Range extends to
central Argentina]

Current range extends into *Handbook* area approximately as shown; see Distribution for changes, reintroductions, and occurrences beyond usual range

activities increased, and salt cedar (*Tamarix pentandra*) spread widely, competing with the cottonwood community. Dredging may have had a negative effect. By the 1950s, formerly inaccessible areas could be reached by motor-powered recreational watercraft. At Havasu Natl. Wildl. Refuge, where the birds nested in drowned mesquite, they were vulnerable to disturbance and destruction. Thus habitat alteration and increased recreational and other activities eliminated them (but note restocking, mentioned below). Habitat has also been severely altered where the birds bred along the Gila, Santa Cruz, and San Pedro rivers. Urban sprawl has reduced or eliminated suitable habitat near Tucson and Cave Creek, and the Bay-winged is similarly threatened near Rio Verde, Apache Junction, and Florence. See Whaley (1986) for further details.

Evidently, similar reductions have occurred in N.Mex. and Tex. In the latter, such rapid habitat alteration as loss of mesquite areas is a severe threat in places (Oberholser and Kincaid 1974), yet Griffin (1976) thought that this hawk had extended its range in w. Tex.

Isolated occurrence An area near Meade, Kans., is virtually an oasis in dry terrain. This hawk occurred there in winter of 1962–1963, bred in the latter yr, and, on Jan. 7, 1963, one was found dead many mi. away near Hunter, Lincoln Co. (Parmelee and Stephens 1964).

By 1981 there were groups on the Ariz.-N.Mex. border, distant from other known birds in either state, in dry washes with dead mesquite and a few old cottonwoods (W. R. Spofford). It is, of course, possible that these originated from released birds.

Other occurrence beyond usual range On geographical grounds, perhaps the following were natural occurrences: n. and e. Tex., La., Okla., Kans. (in Dec., in addition to the above sightings), s. Nev., s. Utah, and sw. Calif. On the other hand, since this hawk is easy to maintain and is a favorite of falconers, more distant occurrences presumably were escapees, as in Iowa, Ohio, N.Y., and Fla. (several).

Reintroduced Beginning in the late 1970s along the lower Colorado R. (Calif.-Ariz. boundary), whence extirpated by 1969 if not earlier. This has included release of flying birds and the placing of preflight young in Red-tailed Hawk nests for rearing, for a total of several score.

Extralimital Distribution in lower Cent. and in S. Am. was mapped by E. R. Blake (1977).

Recorded as **fossil** from the Pleistocene of Nuevo León, Mexico, also in Peru.

WILLIAM J. MADER

MIGRATION   In Ariz., this hawk has a long breeding season, "which affords no time for migration" (Whaley 1986).

Bay-winged Hawks occasionally wander in winter; families often remain together. Twice Whaley saw winter groups of 7 and 8 hawks ("adults" plus color-marked young), and Wilder (1916) noted groups of 10–20 along the Colorado R. in Dec. In Tex., the birds are more nomadic, with shifts in breeding distribution related to changes in rainfall pattern and prey abundance (Griffin 1976).

In s. Ariz., 21 banded individuals (13 banded as young) were last sighted or retrapped 44–1,319 days after their 1st capture at distances av. 1.3 km. (0.8 mi.) away; an "immature" was recorded 70 km. (43.5 mi.) n. of its initial sighting (Mader 1978). There is thus no strong tendency for Juv. birds to disperse. Based on 13 records, Juv. birds traveled less than 5 mi. (♂ during 3 years) to 30 mi. (♀ in 6 months), an av. of 15 mi. from their natal area. Exceptionally, a ♂ banded as a nestling May 20, 1977, was trapped on its own nesting territory 35 mi. s. on Jan. 12, 1985. (From Whaley 1986.) In 9 instances where nesting occurred twice a year in 1977, color-marked birds of earlier nestings were in the immediate vicinity of—even on the nests containing eggs or nestlings of—subsequent attempts (Whaley).

NOTES   Reports by Chambers (see Bent 1937) of migrant flocks in s. Calif. evidently pertain to misidentified darker and redder Swainson's Hawks; see A. R. Phillips et al. (1964).

Farther s., this hawk is an "abundant winter visitant" to Colima, Mexico; noted as early as Sept. 16 one year; the species was common until mid-Apr. (Schaldach 1963). No similar data for anywhere else have been located.   WILLIAM J. MADER

BANDING STATUS   To Aug. 1981, a total of 1,883 had been banded in the U.S. and there were 39 recoveries (Clapp et al. 1982). In Tex., the Hamerstroms (1977) reported having banded 652 and retrapped 13; this work has continued. In Ariz., Whaley banded 212 nestlings in 1977; he and others have banded additional birds of various ages. Main use of banding data has been by Mader (1978) and Whaley (1986).

WILLIAM J. MADER

REPRODUCTION   Mostly Ariz. data, principally from Mader (1975a) and Whaley (1985); also some from Tex., and very little from elsewhere.

The majority **first breed** after attaining Basic feathering, but Juv. birds of both sexes (although mostly ♀♀) are also known to breed. In s. Ariz., a ♀ hatched in 1973 laid eggs in Aug. 1974, approximately 7.2 km. from where she had hatched; this was a trio-bond, and her 2 mates were "adult" ♂♂ (Mader 1975b). Ten "sub-adult" (= Juv.) ♀♀ raised 7 young; 7 of the ♀♀ had "adult" mates and 3 had Juv. mates only (Whaley 1986).

Breeding season   In Ariz., nests with eggs have been found as early as Jan. Laying typically reaches a peak in Mar.; hence, hatching is often in Apr., and young attain flight in May–June. The season is prolonged largely because many pairs and trios either attempt to raise or raise 2 (or, occasionally, 3) broods. Saguaro-paloverde habitat provides comparatively abundant and varied food resources (includes animals with long breeding seasons) governed principally by rainfall; where trio-bonds exist, the food supplied by the "extra" ♂ may increase the chances of a successful 1st nesting and of the ♀ laying again (Mader 1978). Thus the breeding season is long in Ariz. and Tex. (where laying peak is later); this is presumably so elsewhere in the large range of the species. In Sonora, Mexico, eggs are laid even in Dec., which suggests continuous breeding in the s. Sonora Desert.

Displays   HIGH-CIRCLING: On Feb. 18, 1977, Whaley saw 8 "adults" together, flying at about 150–180 m. altitude—soaring, tail chasing, and stooping, with much vocalizing. There were long vertical stoops, often involving all 8 hawks, then tail chasing and eventual return to former altitude to begin again. SKY-DANCE: The ♂, wings partly folded, stoops from a height. Once 2 ♂ made identical dives in the presence of a ♀ with nestlings. Sometimes the ♀ joined in; on several occasions, all 3 stooped together in a group or in single file. Although this dance in hawks typically has a territorial function, it may also have others. In the Bay-winged, often the ♂ swings upward from the bottom of the dive, alights on the back of the perched ♀, and then copulates for about 13–24 sec. In trios, and evidently from at least very early in the reproductive cycle, both ♂♂ deliver food to the ♀.

Copulation   Seen Jan. 28–July 26 in Whaley's study, duration 15–40 sec., av. 24, and not necessarily preceded by display. On 1 occasion a ♀ copulated with both ♂♂ of the trio 7 times in 2 hrs. Similar polyandrous behavior had been reported earlier by Mader (1975a).

Sexual nexus   Cooperative polyandry is not the exclusive mating system, since there also are breeding pairs; the ratio of twosomes to threesomes is unknown, but threesomes are much more frequent in Ariz. than in Tex. Commonly, 2 ♂ are bonded to a single ♀; both provide her with food, copulate, participate in nest construction, participate to some extent in covering the eggs, and supply food for the young during nest life and subsequent lengthy dependency. Whaley (1979) occasionally saw 4 "adults" at a nest, but whether the 4th was yet an additional "helper" or merely a visitor is uncertain. For example, birds from neighboring home ranges may join in soaring over a nest when its owners are disturbed—up to 7 in 1 instance.

Nesting density   The greatest reported concentration (Whaley 1986) was 2.5 sq. km. per active nest in saguaro-paloverde in s. Ariz.; Mader found 5 sq. km. in similar habitat there. The birds undoubtedly are more scattered where prey is scarce. A typical home range (territory) contains several old nests, generally within 0.5 km. of one another, but sometimes up to twice that far apart. In a 2-year period in Ariz., 15 of 17 home ranges were reoccupied (Mader). Whaley's study: 123 territories were occupied in 1976, and 84% were reoccupied and used the next year, with "adults" also present at 9 additional ones. Of 19 nesting "adults" in an area, 6 marked birds were present the following year, and, since not all individuals were checked, the return rate was probably higher. Seven nests active in 1976 were used the following year by Great Horned Owls, and another was used by a pair of Red-tailed Hawks. This seemed to have little effect; Bay-winged Hawks built a new nest 160 m. from the Redtails.

Nest site   Arizona nests are mostly in saguaro cacti (preferred, with substantial arms) and paloverde; in N. Mex. and Tex. in mesquite, hackberry, and spanish dagger. Arizona sites also include pine, palms, cottonwood, mesquite, ironwood, and towers supporting electrical transmission lines. Saguaro nests av. just under 6 m. from the ground and paloverde av. 4.4–6.3 m. Whaley recorded heights up to 21.3 m. on a transmission tower and 14.3 in a pine. Nineteen nests in Tex.: hackberry 7, mesquite 6, spanish dagger 5, and desert sumac 1, with av. height 3.4 m. (Griffin 1976). In S. Am., reportedly a cliff nest in Colombia (Lehmann V 1957).

Nest building   Some groups begin construction about 5 weeks before laying. A ♀ fetched sticks from the ground and broke others from trees; these were transported in the beak, once in the feet. She gathered nesting materials within 90 m. of the nest, but a ♂ delivered from distances up to 530 m. The structures they build are usually bulky, but this depends on adequacy of support at the site. For dimensions of 19 Tex. nests,

397

see Griffin (1976). They often build on mistletoe. a good support that provides partial concealment from below. Finer twigs or, where available, grass is used for lining. Such **greenery** as leafed-out twigs, and pieces of prickly-pear cactus, and assorted debris is added continually while eggs or nestlings are in the nest. At times the ♀ "rearranges" the lining, using her beak.

Building a nest or refurbishing 1 or more existing nests occurs in Ariz., Jan.–Aug. Some pairs or trios build or add material to as many as 4 nests, some to only 1. There were 8 nests in 1 territory, 1 repaired and ready for eggs on Feb. 10 (copulation observed Jan. 28). Supernumerary nests may be used for feeding platforms. In 4 observed cases the hawks used a particular nest 1 year, nested elsewhere the 2d year, and returned to their former nest the 3d year. In 3 renestings after loss of 1st clutches, the birds built and successfully used new nests 400–960 m. from their previous sites (Mader).

Laying season Nests have been found with eggs as early as Jan. and with nestlings as late as Dec. (but no eggs laid in Oct.–Dec.); that is, reproduction is year-round (Mader, Whaley). Various prey species of this hawk also have extended breeding seasons. To the s. in Sonora, Mexico, eggs are laid even in Nov., which suggests continuous breeding in s. parts of the Sonora Desert.

Clutches/season In Whaley's study, double or triple clutching occurred 61 times at 50 of the nests studied; 39 of these followed a successful initial breeding cycle, and 22 followed failure. When the 1st was successful, the av. lapsed time to the next completed clutch was 106 days. In 8 territories, a short interval (mean: 75 days) indicated a repeat clutch before the initial brood had attained flight (2 eggs were laid in a nest alongside a nestling aged 23–25 days). For 6 2d attempts in Tex., the interval between 1st brood flying and completion of 2d clutch was 7–59 days, av. 28 (Brannon 1980). In Ariz., whenever the initial clutch was laid early, there were 3 clutches/breeding season (Whaley 1986).

Laying interval Not reported.

Clutch size One to five eggs, with 3–4 common. In Ariz.: 4 clutches (of 1 egg), 29 (2), 73 (3), 51 (4), and 5 (5) (Whaley). Mean clutch size was 3.04 in 1976 (67 clutches) and 3.22 in 1977 (95 clutches). Mean figures for different studies: 2.85 for 20 clutches in Tex. (Griffin 1976), 2.96 for 50 in Ariz. (Mader 1975a), and 3.16 for 162 in Ariz. (Whaley 1986). Some ♀ ♀ are exceptional layers: 2 each laid 16 eggs in a 2-year period; another laid 4 clutches of 4 in 2 years (and all but 1 clutch in the same nest) (Whaley).

One **egg** each from 20 clutches (Tex. 17, Mexico 3) **size** length 53.29 ± 3.02 mm., breadth 41.81 ± 0.96, and radii of curvature of ends 17.59 ± 0.88 and 13.20 ± 1.24; **shape** usually short subelliptical, elongation 1.28 ± 0.041, bicone −0.060, and asymmetry +0.134 (F. W. Preston). Fifty-two av. 53.7 × 42.1 mm. (Bent 1937). The shell is smooth but without gloss, **color** very pale bluish (fades to white), plain or with a few small dots or spots of pale brownish or lavender.

Incubation Evidently may begin with laying of the 1st or any later egg. At a nest intensively studied, the 3 "adults" visited it regularly and to near the time the brood could fly. During incubation, visits av. 19.1/day—the ♀ 6.4, ♂ #1 6.4, and ♂ #2 6.2. All 3 birds were at the nest simultaneously 12 times. Although both ♂ ♂ sat on the eggs, incubation was mostly by the ♀; see details in Mader (1979). The ♂ ♂ had 3 roles:

to supplement the ♀'s incubating duties, to supply the ♀ with food, and to chase predators. Incubating individuals regularly relieved one another, with fewer change-overs in cool weather, and the ♀ dominated the ♂ ♂ at the nest. She did not hunt. All 3 birds commonly exchanged food with one another, and occasionally the remains of prey were carried from the nest and left nearby.

Incubation period Thirty-three to thirty-six days, av. 35 (Mader 1975a); 34 days in captivity (Nice 1970).

Hatching dates For 284 clutches in Ariz., extended over 8 months (mode: Apr.) (Whaley).

Nestling period At the well-studied nest mentioned above, the ♀ brooded, shaded, and fed the young, and all "adults" continued to visit regularly. Twenty-five percent of the visits were to deliver prey and 10% to deliver sticks. The ♀ av. 10.5 visits/day, ♂ #1 3.6, and ♂ #2 3.9. The ♀ got all her food from the ♂ ♂. Male #1 was known to have caught at least 11 prey items, ♂ #2 brought 27, and no doubt others were taken. A ♂ was seen to feed nestlings both in the absence of the ♀ and in her presence, and once both fed at the same time. Prey remains may be carried away (such material decomposes rapidly in the desert heat). No aggression among siblings has been observed, and "immatures" (in Juv. feathering) occasionally visit nests in active use.

On May 12, 1977, Whaley observed 2 young, only 2–3 weeks out of the nest, incubating 3 eggs of their parents' 2d clutch. In Tex., Brannon (1980) observed prey deliveries 3 times by Juv. birds to nests where their parents were again breeding.

Not only the owners of the nest intensively studied but also other Bay-winged Hawks from nearby joined in defense against other hawk species, owls, and coyotes. Occasionally the 2 ♂ cooperated in an attack. There was no evidence of serious conflict between this hawk and the Great Horned Owl or the Red-tailed Hawk.

Age at first flight In Ariz., dates are spread over 7 months (mode: May), with Oct. 28 the latest noted (Whaley). A very late date for Tex. is Nov. 8 (in Brannon 1980). The young become "branchers" (perch near the nest) at about age 40 days, then gradually improve their flight capability. Usually they stay in the close vicinity for at least 2–3 months.

Breeding success The evidence suggests that success rate (for nests rearing at least 1 young to age 4 weeks or older) is higher in Ariz. and N.Mex. than in Tex. In Ariz., 68% for 50 nests (Mader 1975a) and 72% for 319 nests (Whaley 1986); it was about 44% for 18 nests in Tex. (Griffin 1976). Similarly, the number of young produced per nesting attempt (begun with at least 1 egg) was lower in Tex. (0.83) than in Ariz. (1.60–1.62), based on the same sources.

Apparently nests maintained by trios are more successful than those maintained by pairs—78% v. 59% in 50 nests (Mader), and 97% v. 71% in another sample (Whaley). The number of young per successful nest was greater for trios (2.5 v. 2.19), and the number of young produced per nesting "adult" was lower in trios at 0.65 vs. 0.73 for pairs. Thus, it is questionable whether trios produce more young to flight age. Trios possibly contribute more young at the stage where the latter are flying but dependent than do pairs. See discussion of polyandry in Mader (1979).

Some trios can be extraordinarily successful; 1, in a 3-year period, bred 6 times and produced 14 young to flight age (Mader 1977b). Also, at one point, a ♂ gave prey to a crippled 4-month-old bird from the previous brood of the year at a time when there was a 2d brood of nestlings (Mader 1975a, 1978). In Tex., on the other hand, a trio maintained territory, built 2 nests, and failed to lay (Griffin 1976).

Dependency   Some family groups are present into winter, the young uttering a food-begging call (as when nestlings) to at least 8 months after they are on the wing.

Sex ratio   For 212 nestlings of banding age in Ariz., ratio was 1.2 ♂:1.0 ♀ (Whaley 1985) and 1.1 ♂:1 ♀ in 107 broods (Mader 1975a). Allowing for possible biases in livetrapping, data suggest that, at least in some areas in Ariz., "adult" ♂♂ outnumber ♀♀. Thirty-one of 42 trapped birds were ♂. In winter trapping in Texas, the Hamerstroms (1978) found a ratio of 1.2 ♂:1 ♀ in 397 trapped "adults." Polyandry seems to be less frequent there (Griffin 1976).

Trio-bond duration   At least sometimes, the 3 birds remain together for several years. Additionally, the Bay-winged Hawk is our only N. Am. buteonine known to breed more than once a year; indeed, even 3 clutches are laid by a ♀ member of a trio. The reproductive pattern thus much resembles that of the insular Galapagos Hawk.

For many further details of reproduction, see Mader (1979) and Whaley (1986) and papers they cited.   WILLIAM J. MADER

SURVIVAL   In Ariz., an "adult" trio remained together for at least 3 years.

Also in Ariz. (Whaley 1986), high egg loss results from infertile eggs (in 2 successive years a pair incubated 4-egg clutches that did not hatch), destruction of nests, and so on, and 47 young disappeared or died (cause of 27 deaths undetermined). Some flying birds get electrocuted, some are caught in coyote traps, and a few drown in livestock watering tanks (the only water source in the dry May–June period). Two flying young were injured by cholla cactus joints.

As of Aug. 1981, the oldest banded birds recovered was aged 10 years (Clapp et al. 1982).   WILLIAM J. MADER

HABITS   In U.S. This hawk gives the impression of being rather sluggish and unwary, keeping just ahead by moving from perch to perch if approached. Yet it is a surprisingly swift and agile hunter, dashing around obstacles close to the ground in pursuit of rodents, rabbits, birds, and lizards. Oddly, perhaps, there is little mention of it still-hunting from a perch, nor is it known to stoop from overhead.

Bay-winged Hawks can often be seen in **groups.** Sixty-four of these contained an av. of 2.7 individuals (Mader 1975a). **Cooperative hunting** is well developed. Of 67 observed attempts to capture prey near a trio nest, 2 "adults" participated in 17 hunts and all 3 in 12. Such cooperation, plus later exchanges of prey, may ensure an adequate food supply not only for dependent young but also for "adults"; it does not seem to increase prey captures, yet it likely provides more food for each bird than if each hunted singly. In a cooperative hunt, if 1 hawk misses the prey and the 2d is successful, the former also may feed when there is enough for more than 1 individual. With 1 trio, over ⅓ prey observed brought to the nest or nearby during incubation was partially consumed by all 3 "adults"; it also occurred in 12.8% of instances during the nestling phase.

Sometimes a hawk may actually alight on another perched individual, without apparent hostility; perhaps the later arrival wanted a particular perch.

Falconry This hawk is popular because it is easily maintained (has a good disposition), is aggressive and quicker than most buteonines, and takes a wide variety of quarry. Typically, it is flown from the fist or trained to follow the falconer by going from perch to perch until quarry is flushed. Casts (pairs) are occasionally flown together, this approximating cooperative hunting by wild birds (McElroy 1977).

Factors affecting populations In the U.S. (and Mexico undoubtedly), the biggest threat is destruction of habitat. This is indeed the case in Ariz., where its preferred environment is considered scenic and is often chosen for real estate or other development. There is similar loss of habitat in Tex. and N. Mex. As for hydrocarbons, although a 5-egg clutch was contaminated (Mader 1977a), there was no indication of eggshell thinning and no evidence of biocides affecting the population. Shooting and electrocutions along powerlines have contributed to mortality (Whaley 1979), but whether significantly is questionable. WILLIAM J. MADER

FOOD Data from our area, supplemented by information from elsewhere (as indicated). Small mammals, many birds, some lizards, and occasionally insects.

Mammals Ground squirrels (*Spermophilus*), wood rats (*Neotoma*), Kangaroo rats (*Dipodomys*), cottontails (*Sylvilagus*), and jack rabbits (*Lepus*) reported consistently. Occasionally pocket gophers (*Thomomys*) and pocket mice (*Perognathus*).

In Chile, Jaksic et al. (1980) and Schlatter et al. (1980) reported that it consumes large numbers of a diurnal rodent (*Octodon degus*) that weighs about 3 times as much as a large vole.

Birds From wren to pheasant and small heron size (night herons frequently); many of flicker to quail size. It has taken other raptors: Am. Kestrel, Cooper's Hawk, Screech and Elf Owls (Whaley 1986).

It attacked and killed poultry in Dec. in Ohio (Earl 1918); it is considered an inveterate poultry thief in Costa Rica (Nutting 1882), where one was seen feeding on a dead fowl in 1969 (Slud 1980). It raids chicken roosts and dovecotes in Chile (A. W. Johnson 1965).

Reptiles Principally common lizard species in these genera: *Sceloporus, Callisaurus, Cnemidophorus*, and *Phrynosoma*—see Mader (1975a, 1978, 1979) and Whaley (1986). In general, these do not comprise much biomass (volume). It seems odd that snakes are not reported.

Amphibians In Chile, frogs (A. W. Johnson 1965).

Fishes In Baja Calif., an emaciated bird "made desperate by starvation" was shot while attempting to catch goldfish in a tank (Brewster 1902).

Insects Large species in some numbers; see Sherrod's (1978) summary of sources.

Offal Listed by A. K. Fisher (1893). If in the hot season, this needs confirmation; during much winter hawk-trapping in Tex., the Hamerstroms have observed it no more than 3 times. WILLIAM J. MADER

GRAY HAWK

Asturina plagiata

Northernmost birds were long called Mexican Goshawk. The species as treated here has been included in *Buteo nitidus* by many authors.

Similar in shape and slightly smaller than the Red-shouldered Hawk; a bird of patchy woodlands and tropical lowlands. Middle toe more than half as long as the rather stout tarsus, which has more than upper third feathered in front. Fairly short wing, the 4 outer primaries emarginated on inner web and the 3 longest (#6, #7, and #8 counting from inner) nearly equal in length. Tail squarish when folded. The characters illus. in Friedmann (1950); for photograph of undersurface of bird in flight, see Zimmermann (1976a).

Basic Plumage—upperparts gray or blue-gray, plain or nearly so (northerly), varying to barred dark and light; some white on rump; underparts and axillars white barred more or less finely with medium or darker gray, the under tail coverts white. Tail appears mostly very dark with a broad, white, subterminal band but also has 1 or 2 inconspicuous, narrow, sometimes incomplete, white bands. Wing above as back, the primaries dusky ended and secondaries white tipped, wing lining white with variable amount of darkish barring—a pattern that extends out onto the flight feathers.

Juv.—very dark above, the feathers bordered brown; underparts off-white to buff with nearly black markings (much more heavily marked than young Broad-winged Hawk); tail has variable number (to 9) blackish bars alternating with buffy brown—more barring than in later life.

The ♀ av. larger, darker dorsally, with heavier ventral barring. Sexes combined: length 16¼–18 in. (41–46 cm.), wingspread 32–39½ in. (81–98 cm.), wt. 13–23 oz. (360–650 gm.).

As treated here, the Gray Hawk has 2 subspecies, the range of the northernmost extending into our area.

DESCRIPTION   A. *P. plagiata* of our area and most of Mexico. One Plumage/cycle with Basic I earliest definitive.

▶ ♂ Def. Basic Plumage (entire feathering) ALL YEAR, with fairly protracted molting beginning early in breeding season. **Beak** blackish blue, cere and gape yellow to orange-yellow, **iris** dark brownish. **Upperparts** slaty bluish, somewhat paler on head (which has considerable concealed white), and in some with paler barring in "shoulder" region; upper tail coverts white ended. **Underparts** white, finely barred transversely (including axillars and flanks) with dark gray; under tail coverts white. **Tail** as described earlier. **Wing** as described earlier, with rather sparse darkish barring on undersurface.

▶ ♀ Def. Basic Plumage av. darker dorsally and more coarsely barred ventrally than ♂.

Molting   From Basic to Basic, begins early in the breeding season and is fairly prolonged; feathers are commonly found near nests. Bent (1937) saw one molting its tail in June, the other completing wing molting in Feb. (which may be exceptional). (Molting is said to differ from *Buteo* species, which led V. and E. Stresemann (1960) to restore the genus *Asturina*.)

AT HATCHING   No information. At age about 1 week, not white but light gray (Stensrude 1965). A ♂ nestling, clad in white down and tinged pale gray on lower back, already weighed 363 gm. and showed much Juv. feathering when described by Amadon and Phillips (1939). The beak was black, skin of lores and eyelids cobalt blue, iris grayish brown, legs and feet yellow.

▶ Juv. Plumage (entire feathering) acquired during nest life and worn for ABOUT A YEAR. **Beak** nearly black, cere and gape yellow, **iris** gray-brown to medium brownish. On **upperparts** the feathers are margined blackish brown and terminally notched cinnamon. **Underparts** toward pinkish buff, paler and boldly streaked blackish anteriorly, grading to much broader markings of same on sides and belly—heavy and conspicuous; under tail coverts plain, light. Leg feathers barred or vermiculated, legs and **feet** yellow, talons black. **Tail** (longer than in Basic) notably paler above than upper side of wing, with 6 or 7 transverse blackish bars (progressively narrower proximally), the intervening bars off-white (toward brown). **Wing:** upper surface as back except cinnamon also internally in the feathers; undersurface of secondaries have faint darker barring, also some on primaries, and both are tipped off-white; wing lining more or less buffy.

♀ Juv. similar to ♂, "but the brown averaging lighter, and more approaching umber" (Friedmann 1950).

Measurements   Mexican birds: 12 ♂ BEAK from cere 20.9–22 mm., av. 21.6, WING across chord 232.5–252, av. 244.6, and TAIL 146–163, av. 155.9; and 6 ♀ BEAK from cere 24–25.5 mm., av. 24.9, WING across chord 254–259, av. 256.7, and TAIL 161–167, av. 164.3 (Friedmann 1950). Note no overlap in size of sexes except for 2 mm. in tail. Oddly, the mean figures for larger series, for WING (♂ 262.1, ♀ 283.9) in N. Snyder and Wiley (1976) exceed the corresponding upper extremes of range in Friedmann.

Another series from Mexico: 28 ♂ BEAK from cere 20–24.5 mm., av. 21.5, WING across chord 232.5–272, av. 252.8, and TAIL 146–187, av. 165.9; and 17 ♀ BEAK from cere 22.5–25 mm., av. 24.1, WING across chord 254–289, av. 273.2, and TAIL 161–195, av. 178.9 (E. R. Blake 1977).

Weight A nesting pair in Ariz.: ♂ 434 and ♀ 636 gm. (Amadon and Phillips 1939). Also for n. birds: ♂ 364 and 404, ♀ 572 and 655 (L. Brown and Amadon 1968 2). From specimen labels: mean wt. 5 ♂ 415.7 gm. and 4 ♀ 636.6 (N. Snyder and Wiley 1976).

Hybrids None reported.

Geographical variation Gray Hawks have been treated by some authors as composed of 2 species—*plagiatus* (U.S. states bordering Mexico down to nw. Costa Rica) and *nitidus* (sw. Costa Rica to well down in S. Am.). Others have united them (as *nitidus*), for example, L. Brown and Amadon (1968 2). They are separate in Millsap (1986). Whether a tropical moist forest "barrier" of at least 10,000–12,000 years' duration s. in Cent. Am. resulted in separation long enough for entities above and below it to evolve to the level of separate species is a matter than cannot be decided to everyone's satisfaction.

According to Millsap, n. of the barrier, birds in definitive feathering: 1 have significantly longer wings and tails, 2 lack prominent dorsal barring, and 3 have a complete next-to-distal white bar within the tail, with a 3d (more proximal) often present. Juv. birds: 1 crown dark, 2 light bars on dorsal webs of outer primaries ("wing panels") white, 3 an av. of at least 2 more dark tail bars than s. birds, 4 small dark streaks and spots on breast and abdomen, and 5 barred thighs.

From sw. Costa Rica s., in definitive feathering: 1 wings and tails are significantly shorter, and 2 there is prominent barring on crown and dorsum. Juvs.: 1 crown primarily light with a few dark streaks, 2 "wing panels" orange or buffy, 3 av. 2 fewer tail bars, 4 dark ventral markings coalesce into large spots or patches, and 5 thighs are immaculate or streaked.

Within each area there is clinal variation in WING length and at least 1 fairly abrupt change. In the n. entity, WING decreases in length going s. and in the s. entity it increases going s. As far as is known, only the most n. birds of the n. entity tend to vacate their range seasonally (response to decreased prey availability in cold weather), but there is apparently considerable wandering. RALPH S. PALMER

SUBSPECIES **In our area** *plagiata* Schlegel—see Description, above; see also Millsap (1986). From s. in Ariz., N.Mex., and Tex. s. to the Isthmus of Tehuantepec, but absent from Baja Calif. and, apparently, the cent. Mexican highlands. According to Millsap, who plotted isophenes for WING flattened, going up the w. side of Mexico into the U.S. there is considerable increase in s. Sonora; going up the e. side, clinal variation is gradual over the entire distance. Northwesterly birds (*maxima* van Rossem), although recognized by Millsap, are included here (also see E. P. Edwards and Lea 1955).

Elsewhere *micra* W. deW. Miller and Griscom—somewhat smaller; not well differentiated and perhaps not separable; Isthmus of Tehuantepec to nw. Costa Rica.

(Treating the birds beyond to the s. separately as *A. nitida*, they comprise 2 subspecies: *nitida* (Latham)—sw. Costa Rica through S. Am. to intergrade s. with *pallida*

404

Todd—w. of the Mato Grosso Plateau in Brazil and through the Chaco in Paraguay, Bolivia, and nw. Argentina. Names and distribution as in Millsap [1980].)

RALPH S. PALMER

FIELD IDENTIFICATION **In our area** primarily. Definitive feathering—perched bird at a distance appears dark with conspicuous white bar in black tail. Somewhat larger than Broad-winged Hawk, approaching size of Red-shouldered Hawk. Fine, dark, ventral barring on white shows only at close range. Not easily confused with any hawk occurring in its U.S. range.

In flight, very fast flapping, then a glide. Appears evenly gray dorsally and also underwing, without noticeable difference between wing lining and underside of flight feathers. Conspicuous white band in tail, and 2 proximal bands visible at some distance. Ordinary call rather musical and whistled, less harsh than voice of Roadside Hawk.

Juv. (differs markedly from "adult")—in n. Mexico "can be the bane of a field observer's life, as they invariably resemble something else!" (Schaldach 1963). In general, suggests Juv. Broadwing or Roadside, but underparts more heavily marked dark and dorsum appears nearly black.

RALPH S. PALMER

VOICE Data primarily from our area. Noisy, especially about its nest. Call at onset of breeding season variably rendered *Cree-ee-ee*, also *Kree-ee-ah*, and *pee-yeer*. Flutelike, reminiscent of Long-billed Curlew (Bendire 1892).

Each of the 3 following calls is uttered variably, also differently by each sex (but details unavailable). **1** *Cree-ee-ee* given in series of 6–8, the "Peacock call" of Stensrude (1965); signals maintenance of pair or territory (R. Glinski). **2** *Pee-yeer* and variants, usually given singly, but at times precedes series of *Cree* calls; given when birds are upset (Glinski). **3** *Yee-ee-ee* uttered comparatively softly, usually in series of 2–5; often precedes a *Pee-yeer* call and usually indicates stressful mood, as in territorial encounter (Glinski). These statements are more or less at variance with Slud (1964) and Stensrude (1965).

RALPH S. PALMER

HABITAT **In our area** Ariz.—formerly common along wooded watercourses and in areas of mesquite, but much of this now destroyed by human occupation. At present, patches of thornscrub along rivers (R. Glinski). Nests in groves, especially in cottonwoods, and hunts in areas of mesquite and scrub. For further information, see Porter and White (in Chancellor 1977). Also found breeding in "unexpected" places (A. R. Phillips et al. 1964); for example, at high elevations in the Huachuca and Chiricahua mts. N.Mex.—as Ariz. Southern Tex.—formerly nested in cottonwoods and willows along the lower Rio Grande (Oberholser and Kincaid 1974).

To the south Hot open country with patches of well-watered woods (mostly deciduous). Colima and Jalisco, Mexico—Schaldach (1963) found it abundant, almost ubiquitos, in thorn forest. Cent. Am.—tropical lowlands.

RALPH S. PALMER

DISTRIBUTION (See map.) In historic times has nested in the U.S. in at least the s. ⅓ of Ariz., s. N.Mex., and s. Tex. Recent information is as follows:

405

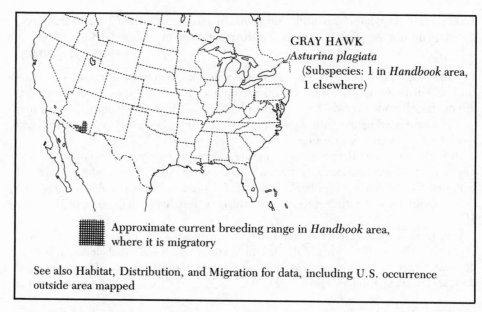

GRAY HAWK
Asturina plagiata
(Subspecies: 1 in *Handbook* area,
1 elsewhere)

Approximate current breeding range in *Handbook* area,
where it is migratory

See also Habitat, Distribution, and Migration for data, including U.S. occurrence
outside area mapped

ARIZ.   Watersheds of the Santa Cruz and San Pedro rivers at 2,000–4,000 ft.
elevation; population in the state estimated at about 45 pairs. Recent scrub invasion
since early 1900s along the San Pedro has afforded increased habitat, and about ⅓ of
state's Gray Hawks now nest there (R. Glinski).

In the previous century the Gray Hawk was locally plentiful. The Ariz. portion of the
Santa Cruz ceased to be a permanent stream about 1948, and the species may have
been absent from the state for a decade beginning about that time. There were records
for 1958 and (breeding) 1959, and in 1963 pairs appeared in various places. Glinski
(Porter and White, in Chancellor 1977) estimated a total of 39 nesting territories in se.
Ariz. since 1973, some in marginal habitat and unproductive. He knew of 7 additional
sites occupied since 1963 and later abandoned. In 1974 he located 25 nests where pairs
of adults had clutches. In 1975 that part of the population in the Santa Cruz drainage
was studied intensively: 23 occupied territories were active, and 16 of them produced a
total of 34 young to flight age.

N. MEX.   Probably now nests (2–4 pairs in marginal habitat?) in the sw. (Porter and
White, in Chancellor 1977). There are 2 old nesting records for Ft. Bayard, Grant Co.,
1876, which evidently are authentic (Zimmerman 1976a). An adult and flying young
were seen on the Gila R. near Cliff, July 24, 1953 (J. S. Ligon 1961). There were
sightings in Apr. 1961 and May and Aug. 1973, also others (not precisely recorded) in
the 1960s. A feather was found near Mangas Springs in Oct. 1974 (Zimmermann).

TEX.   Formerly bred—3 nesting records in Webb Co., Feb. 2 and May 8, 1892,
and Feb. 3, 1913; may have nested formerly from mouth of the Rio Grande upriver to
Eagle Pass (Oberholser and Kincaid 1974).

Now rare and local in the Rio Grande delta—sightings in the past 25 years principally at 2 localities in Hidalgo Co. but has also wandered to Corpus Christi, Oct. 27,
1945, to Refugio Co., Mar. 14, 1968, and to Brewster Co. Apr. 4, 1967, and late Mar.

and Apr. 3, 1970. A Juv. found dead in the Davis Mts., Jeff Davis Co., Aug. 28, 1969. See Oberholser and Kincaid (1974)—text, map, and occurrences into 1970. Sighted in Big Bend Natl. Park, June 24, 1980 (1980 *Am. Birds* **34** 909).

NOTES E. C. Jacot suggested that the range of this hawk in the U.S. probably depends on availability of lizards as food—a viewpoint agreeable to Amadon and Phillips (1939) and Zimmerman (1976a). Some reappraisal may be needed, especially since this bird occurs even in winter, when such food must be unavailable.

Old records for Ill. in 1871 and Iowa in 1895 were "considered unsatisfactory" by Bent (1937).

Recorded as **fossil** from the Pleistocene of N.Mex. (P. Brodkorb).

RALPH S. PALMER

MIGRATION The species has been labeled nonmigratory, except for withdrawal for the colder season from northernmost part of range, but note the following:

ARIZ. Banding returns for 6 birds indicate that Gray Hawks from this state migrate to n. Mexico near Culiacan, Sinaloa. Departure from Ariz. usually occurs in Sept.– Oct., but a pair was still present at a nest site on Dec. 19. Spring arrival usually is in mid- to late Mar. (R. Glinski). Long ago, when Gray Hawks were plentiful, Bendire (1892) stated that they arrived in early Mar. or, in tardy seasons, at the beginning of Apr.

N.MEX. No specific data, but probably comparable to Ariz.

TEX. Migratory. Also formerly wintered (specimen Brownsville, Dec. 5, 1885) and occasionally does so now (Oberholser and Kincaid (1974). Records "liberally sprinkled" in 1 area, winter of 1982–1983 (1983 *Am. Birds* **37** 317).

MEXICO (Sonora) There are "no northerly winter records"; earliest Mar. 29 and latest Oct. 26 (van Rossem 1945). RALPH S. PALMER

BANDING STATUS A few have been banded in Ariz. (almost none elsewhere in U.S.), and recoveries of 6 are mentioned above. RALPH S. PALMER

REPRODUCTION U.S. data unless otherwise indicated.

Displays Known ones are as follows: HIGH-CIRCLING: Pairs circle, flap-sailing gracefully over treetops and openings, the ♀ closely followed by the ♂, according to Bendire (1892), uttering a flutelike and "very peculiar piping note." SKY-DANCE: In Tamaulipas, Mexico, on Mar. 3: the smaller bird, swooping gracefully upward, turned a backward flip, plunged deeply, and again shot upward, letting momentum carry it into a position in front of the other bird before flipping backward or sideways again (G. Sutton 1953). TUMBLING (exaggerated Sky-dance?): In Ariz., 2 climbed to an esti- mated 1,000–1,500 ft. and then both dived rapidly, their paths crossing, then 1 bird climbed up again "with closed wings and plummeted straight downward at tremen- dous speed" (Stensrude 1965). This was repeated several times.

Nest site In a grove much more often than in a solitary tree, and often the tallest tree, frequently a cottonwood (*Populus*). Other nest trees include sycamore, oak, ash, mesquite, hackberry, even (in Oaxaca, Mexico) pines. The nest is built within the crown, as high up as adequate support can be found (Bendire 1892, later authors).

Often in the general vicinity there are stands of mesquite (*Prosopis*)—hunting areas. The nest is built both of green leafy and dead leafless twigs and is lined with leafy twigs (R. Glinski). Usually it is well hidden.

Territory Gray Hawks will nest within 100 m. of Cooper's Hawks, Zone-tailed Hawks, Red-tailed Hawks, and Lesser Black Hawks, also within 1,000 m. of other Gray Hawks. Under such crowded conditions, there is usually much aerial display and vocalizing by both sexes (R. Glinski). Turkey Vultures, however, passed overhead without conflict (Stensrude 1965).

Copulation Can occur at any time of day, usually in Apr., and lasts up to 10 sec. (R. Glinski). It was seen in early A.M. and was repeated several times by the same pair, the ♀ on a horizontal dead limb (Stensrude).

Breeding season Begins progressively earlier with decreasing latitude down through Cent. Am. (G. Sutton 1953), apparently before summer rains (L. Short 1974).

Egg dates Southeastern Ariz.—earliest are mainly in 2d and 3d weeks of May (Hubbard 1974a). Ariz. and N.Mex.—48 records (presumably of viable eggs) Mar. 16–July 2, with 24 of them Apr. 19–May 31 (Bent 1937). Sonora, Mexico—18 clutches "represent dates between 5 May and 19 June" (L. Short 1974).

Clutch size Usually 2–3 eggs, ¼ of the (U.S.) sets, according to Bendire (1892), containing the higher number.

One egg each from 20 clutches (Mexico 11, Ariz. 8, N.Mex. 1) size length 50.67 ± 2.10 mm., breadth 40.41 ± 1.31, radii of curvature of ends 16.76 ± 0.85 and 12.50 ± 1.38; shape nearly elliptical, elongation 1.25 ± 0.069, bicone −0.090, and asymmetry +0.132 (F. W. Preston).

Fifty eggs length 47.3–50 mm., av. 50.8, and breadth 38.2–43.5, av. 41 (Bent 1937). Twenty-five from Ariz.: length 47.8–56.7 mm., mean 52.1, and breadth 39.2–44.4, mean 41.0 (Hubbard 1974a). Hubbard also gave the following for 21 eggs from s. Tamaulipas, Mexico, which are smaller: length 45.6–51.2 mm., mean 49.1, and breadth 35.4–42.5, mean 39.3.

Egg color commonly white or (when fresh) pale bluish, often plain, but Bendire (1892) mentioned a set "marbled with a few buffy brown spots," hardly visible, and Kiff (in Hubbard 1974a) stated that, at least in Sonora, Mexico, the frequency of spotted eggs "is greater than is generally believed." Often they become stained.

Fresh **egg wt.** 43 gm. (Glinski, in I. Newton 1979).

Zimmerman (1976) cast doubt on Hubbard's (1974a) contention that 2 clutches taken in N.Mex. in 1876 and mentioned by Bendire were misidentified Cooper's Hawk eggs.

Incubation By the ♀, although the ♂ will stand over the eggs in her absence; **period** 32 days (Glinski, in I. Newton 1979).

Nestling period Poling (in Bendire 1892) stated that a ♀ flew a distance to catch cottontails for her brood. She was shot, and evidently the ♂ of this pair raised the young to flight age. After departing, the young returned at least once for the night, remained about for several days, then disappeared. Parent birds deliver live lizards to nests containing young (Glinski, in Sherrod 1983). The nestling period is 42 days (Glinski, in I. Newton 1979); then the young frequently return to sit on or lie in the nest but are not dependent on it (Glinski).

In the Santa Cruz R. drainage of Ariz., in 1973 the av. number of young reared to

408

flight age in 13 nests was 2.4, and in 1974 it was 1.1 (lower because of climatic factors). In 1975 (see Distribution, above), from 16 of 23 occupied territories, 34 young were raised (Glinski, cited by Porter and White in Chancellor 1977). RALPH S. PALMER

SURVIVAL   No data.

HABITS   **Hunting methods**   The Gray Hawk is graceful and quick moving—some rapid wingbeats followed by sailing or a glide. It often circles and soars rather low, and its broad square-ended wings endow it with "amazing skill in avoiding obstacles as it darts among trees in pursuit of avian prey" (Stensrude 1965).

During perch- (or still-) hunting, prey may be spotted on the ground or on a tree trunk. If the quarry escapes on the 1st pass, the hawk may alight on the ground and pursue it or land on a low perch. This is especially effective for capturing lizards. Another method, perhaps more suitable for obtaining rodents and small birds, is to circle low over clearings in wooded areas.

In Ariz., Stensrude (1965) observed that a pair was less active on windy and cloudy days, possibly because such weather inhibits the activity of its favorite prey—a spiny lizard (*Sceloporus clarkii*) that is an arboreal inhabitant of mesquite forests (Stensrude 1965).

In ne. Mexico young Gray Hawks, especially, are mobbed by Brown Jays (G. Sutton 1953).

This hawk apparently has had no problems from pesticides (Oberholser and Kincaid 1974). Destruction of habitat is by far the major hazard to it. The U.S. nesting population in the mid-1980s is about 50 pairs.   RALPH S. PALMER

FOOD   Principally lizards and small birds, but also a variety of other quarry (mostly vertebrate); some insects. Sherrod (1978) summarized several published sources plus unpublished Ariz. data from R. Glinski. See that source for quantitative data. The following is an indication of size and variety of prey:

ARIZ.   Lizards, birds, rodents, small lagomorphs, beetles, and large grasshoppers (Bendire 1882, 1892); snakes (Bent 1937); ground squirrels, remains of fish (Brewster 1883); very young doves (apparently from nest), and remains of a quail (Swarth 1905); large lizard (*Sceloporus magister*) (Amadon and Phillips 1939); and Clark's spiny lizard (*Sceloporus clarkii*) frequently.

Mice (*Peromyscus*), wood rats (*Neotoma*), and rabbits (*Sylvilagus*); adult and young Gambel's Quail, White-winged and Mourning Doves, and kingbirds (*Tyrannus*); lizards (*Holbrookia, Sceloporus, Urosaurus*, many *Cnemidophorus*); and snakes (*Masticophis, Thamnophis*) (Glinski). Adult Brown Towhees and unidentified fledglings carried to nest (Stensrude 1965).

MEXICO   Lizards, small snakes, "field mice," birds, young domestic fowl, young Chachalaca, rats, and insects (G. N. Lawrence 1874, 1875). Small heron or bittern (Neff 1947).

NOTE   For comparison, these are some data of interest on the more southerly *A. nitida*. In some areas, stated to feed largely on lizards or fish. El Salvador—shot while trying to carry a white hen from a dooryard (Dickey and van Rossem 1938). Panama—

was eating a worm lizard (*Amphisbaena*) (S. West 1975). Suriname—dashed into a tree and captured a honeycreeper (*Cyanerpes*); an "immature" seen with a lizard (*Tupinambis*) it was barely able to carry; stomachs contained lizards (*Amieva*) and 1 a small mammal (Haverschmidt 1962); stomach contents of 7: small mammals in 2, small birds in 3, bird egg in 1, lizards in 4, snakes in 3, and insects in 4 (Voous 1969). In ne. Venezuela— ♀ in Feb. contained bits of an iguana; "imm." ♀ in Apr. had eaten a lizard (Friedmann and Smith 1950).   Ralph S. Palmer

ROADSIDE HAWK

Asturina magnirostris

Insect Hawk. Formerly placed in *Buteo*. Proportions and size (length 14–16 in., or 35–40 cm.) but not pattern nearest to the Broad-winged Hawk. Abbreviated description here applies to *A. m. griseocauda*, presumably the subspecies that has occurred in our area.

▶ ♂ ♀ Basic feathering—**iris** orange-red or reddish (beginning at age unknown); **upperparts** predominantly dark grayish brown; **underparts:** breast as dorsum but somewhat lighter; sides, abdomen, and flanks palish buff or whitish, variably barred some variant of cinnamon; **tail** tipped white and remainder of its undersurface palish gray or brownish crossed with 4 exposed blackish brown bars (2 more are concealed), which are usually much narrower than the intervening light ones; undersurface of **wing** shows some rufous in the primaries and secondaries, and the lining is predominantly buffy.

▶ ♂ ♀ Juv. Plumage—**iris** yellow (when it becomes reddish is not reported); **upperparts** muted dark, more brownish than Basic, with some lighter mottling; basal color of **underparts** whitish, the breast with muted brownish longitudinal streaks, the abdomen with warmer brownish broken transverse barring; **tail** ventrally may show up to 6 dark bars (distal one wide, others narrower), the intervening light ones a light grayish brown.

For photographs of the ventral surface of specimens in Basic and Juv., see N. Johnson and Peeters (1963).

The ♀ is larger, but sexes overlap considerably in meas.; wt. (sexes combined) about 7¼–12¼ oz. (200–350 gm.).

Geographical variation   Some in size and much in pattern and coloring in the species, from n. Mexico into Argentina and including some nearby is. Iris color varies (yellow in birds from part of the species' range). L. Brown and Amadon (1968 **2**) listed 12 subspecies; E. R. Blake (1977) listed 14 in addition to the 1 occurring in our area. For detailed description of n. birds, see especially Friedmann (1950).

RALPH S. PALMER

FIELD IDENTIFICATION   In and near our area. Compare with the Broad-winged Hawk (the Roadside Hawk has been called Tropical Broadwing) in both Basic and Juv., especially tail barring and underparts. Both species occur in similar habitat—lowlands, forest edges.

In Basic Plumage the Roadside Hawk is quite reddish ventrally; usually the dark bands in the tail (except the most distal one) are much narrower than the light ones; in flight, undersurface of wings may show some reddish brown in flight feathers and buff in lining. Not a high-soaring hawk. It flaps briefly, then glides briefly, as when crossing clearings, appearing indolent or sluggish, and often perches in shade where there is a fairly unobstructed view. Frequent along roadsides. It is tame, even curious to a degree, taking wing on close approach and sometimes flying toward the observer. Common call is a reedy drawn-out *eeyaaaa* uttered while perched or on taking wing and in flight. Voice resembles Red-tailed Hawk (Rowley 1984). Useful illus.: 1982

Birding **14** (6): cover (monochrome); perched pair, also downies, and so on (monochrome) (Rowley 1984); and L. Brown and Amadon 1968 **2** pl. 95 (color).

In Juv. feathering can be confused with Juv. Gray Hawk, a species that occurs in much the same habitat. The Roadside Hawk is more heavily marked ventrally and has more tail bars; see under Gray Hawk for more details.   RALPH S. PALMER

DISTRIBUTION   **In our area** recorded from Tex. Specimen ♂ Cameron Co., Apr. 2, 1901, identified as *B. m. griseocauda* (Trautman 1964). Sightings: "adult" at Bentsen-Rio Grande Valley State Park, Oct. 23, 1982, photographed Dec. 5 (see earlier ref. to illus.), and remained at least until mid-Feb. 1983 (1983 *Am. Birds* **37** 153, 317); an apparent "immature" at Santa Ana Natl. Wildl. Refuge, Oct. 3, 1983, and remained through Nov. (and also photographed) (1983 *Am. Birds* **37** 153, 200).

Elsewhere   In L. Brown and Amadon (1968 **2** map 56) the ranges of 12 subspecies are indicated; a later map, for Cent. and S. Am. (E. R. Blake 1977) has distribution of subspecies added in text.

OTHER TOPICS   Not far distant from our area, in e. Mexico, the Roadside and the Gray are the 2 common hawks. The nest of the former varies from bulky to compact, clutch size is 2 eggs, and incubation period is apparently unrecorded. Seven nests in Oaxaca, Mexico, were compact and concealed in upper crowns of deciduous trees, 25–35 ft. up; they contained 2 eggs (Apr.–May) or 2 downies (May); eggs varied from nearly plain to heavily marked and 10 (5 clutches) av. 45.10 × 37.08 mm. (Rowley 1984). Usually this hawk still-hunts by watching from a tree or pole, and when prey is sighted it goes down in a long glide. It may hunt occasionally from low flight. Information from scattered parts of this hawk's range indicates that it feeds on invertebrates (various insects, scorpions), cold-blooded vertebrates (arboreal lizards commonly, some snakes), and warm-blooded vertebrates (young birds taken from nests, some small mammals). For an interesting description of this hawk following brush and grass fires in Guatemala to feed on dead and dying insects, small reptiles, and other victims, see Dickey and van Rossem (1938).   RALPH S. PALMER

dorsal

Florida
subspecies

RED-SHOULDERED HAWK

Asturina lineata

The Redshoulder fits better morphometrically in *Asturina* than in *Buteo;* it is placed in the former here, based on Millsap (1986).

Approximately crow-sized; larger than the Broad-winged Hawk and smaller than the Red-tailed Hawk but with roughly similar proportions. Four outer primaries emarginate—inner web abruptly incised (as in the Redtail); less than half of the tarsus is feathered (half in the Redtail). Sexes similar, except ♀ larger, with some size overlap.

Basic feathering—upperparts dark, but somewhat blotchy, the lesser upper wing coverts rusty reddish; underparts with transverse rusty to rufescent barring; in se. U.S. overall coloring appears diluted or bleached, and w. of the Sierra Mts. the rufescent barring is vivid and coalesces. The tail has several wide and very dark bars, the intervening narrow stripes and tip white.

Juv.—dorsum dark, dullish, paler to se.; white of underparts varies from streaked in ne. to more spotted, irregularly marked, or even somewhat barred elsewhere. The Juv. tail has more dark bars than Basic.

There is geographical and some sexual variation in number of tail bars in both Basic and Juv. Plumages.

The usual dimensions given are for ne. birds, which are largest: length ♂ 17–23 in. (43–58 cm.), ♀ 19–24 in. (48–61 cm.); wingspread (J. B. May 1935) ♂ 32½–44 in. (90–112 cm.) and ♀ 39–50 in. (99–127 cm.). Southerly and w. birds are perhaps 10–15% smaller.

Approximate wt. of ne. birds ♂ 16½–21 oz. (475–600 gm.) and ♀ 22–27 oz. (625–775 gm.); s. and w. birds weigh less.

Five subspecies, all in our area.

DESCRIPTION   *A. l. lineata* of e. N. Am. One Plumage/cycle with fairly prolonged molting beginning early in the breeding cycle. Basic I is earliest definitive.

▶ ♂ ♀ Def. Basic Plumage (entire feathering). **Beak** black, cere yellow to orange-yellow; **iris** dark brownish; **head** mos streaky (feathers dark with light edges), chin mostly whitish, occipital area has white feathers tipped dark (to blackish). **Upperparts** mostly dark browns, but some light portions of feathers may show. **Underparts** white to buffy brownish, heavily barred rich rusty, the barring thinning out on lower abdomen and posteriorly; legs and **feet** vivid yellow, talons black. **Tail** dorsally has the very tip white, and there are narrow, white stripes separating at least several very dark, wide bars. Flight feathers of **wing** dark dorsally (primaries largely blackish), with clear-cut contrasting pale buffy to whitish barring; wing lining has broken pattern, rusty (mostly) and lighter.

Molting   Entire feathering begins "sometimes" in Apr. and "in some cases" is not completed until Oct., according to Bent (1937), who noted that molting birds are scarce in collections. (The same had been stated earlier by Forbush 1927.)

AT HATCHING   beak black, cere light; down-A 10–15 mm. long, very soon fluffs out and is light buffy brown, darkest in scapular area and upper surface of wings; talons gray (D. and N. Wetherbee 1961). Down-B is thick, woolly, densest on venter, where it is white, and whitish gray dorsally (Bent 1937).

▶ ♂ ♀ Juv. Plumage (entire feathering) well developed by flight age and retained through 1st WINTER into late SPRING or thereabouts, then gradually succeeded by Basic I.

Much of **head** (it has a concealed white occipital spot, as in later life) and **upperparts** various dark and muted browns, the feathers with varying amount of tawny edging; **underparts** whitish to buffy, the feathers usually with more or less elongated or oval spots, largest on breast and sides, and spaced rather sparingly; abdomen to tail whitish with few or no markings; flank feathers longitudinally streaked; legs and **feet** palish yellow, or with a hint of greenish, talons black; **tail** has very tip white, then there are wide darkish drab bars (distal is widest) and the intervening narrow ones are pale (toward a brownish or grayish). **Wing** flight feathers patterned much as in Basic, but the light barring has more of a cinnamon or tawny cast.

There is no useful information on molting out of Juv. (Prebasic I), but it may presumably begin and end somewhat earlier than the corresponding molting of breeders.

Color phases   None; a few completely white (albinistic) individuals are known.

Measurements   Birds from all parts of range of this subspecies: 26 ♂ BEAK from cere 19.1–23.7 mm., av. 21.6, and WING across chord 309–346, av. 320.8; and 22 ♀ from N.Y. to Va. and w. to Ark. BEAK from cere 20.6–25 mm., av. 23.1, and WING across chord 315–353, av. 339 (Friedmann 1950). Note that there is great overlap of the sexes, although av. quite different.

414

N. Snyder and Wiley (1976) gave means for WING of 20 of each sex as ♂ 323.6 mm. and ♀ 342.9.

Weight Mean for 25 ♂ 550 gm. and for 24 ♀ 701 (N. Snyder and Wiley).

Hybrids None.

Geographical variation Not great in size. A series of 26 ♂ Apr.–Aug. demonstrates that WING across chord increases clinally n. and w. from Fla. (Frances James 1970). Birds approaching the ne. ones in size, and the richest in coloring (especially ventrally), are w. of the Sierras. Ventral markings in Juv. feathering are streaky in the ne. but vary toward barring elsewhere. There is geographical variation in tail barring; see details in next section.

Clutch size varies geographically—an increase from s. to n. and from e. to w.— smallest in Fla. (av. 2.36) and largest in Great Lakes region (av. 3.45); most of this was based on clutches taken before 1930 (Henny 1972). Based on extant evidence (Bent, F. W. Preston), there is some variation in egg size: smallest in Texas, larger and about equal in Fla. and w. of the Sierras, and largest in the ne.

Affinities No useful information.

RALPH S. PALMER

SUBSPECIES All 5 occur **in our area,** although 2 extend (or did in the past) s. into Mexico. Evidently only the 1st and part of the last have significant seasonal movement. Some of the data here, mainly on number of tail bars, is based on N. Johnson and Peeters (1963).

lineata (Gmelin)—descr. and meas. given above; largest; much of underparts evenly barred rusty; at least several (often 3 in ♂ and 4 in ♀) dark bands exposed dorsally in tail. The Juv. has streaks and tear-shaped spots sparingly on venter, and the tail commonly has 6–7 dark bands showing. Large ne. breeding range, extending w. into Nebr. and Tenn. Largely migratory.

alleni Ridgway—smaller and paler than preceding (appears bleached or faded), yet some rusty usually remains on smaller upper coverts of wing; usually 3 dark bands (occasionally 4 in ♀) show dorsally in tail. The Juv. typically has the ventral feather markings somewhat transverse, rather heavy, and within the feather; tail usually with 5–6 exposed dark bands. Southeastern U.S. down to include upper mainland Fla. and w. to e. Okla. and e. Tex. Not migratory. Thirty ♂ BEAK from cere 18–25.5 mm., av. 21, and WING across chord 284–330, av. 300.9; and 14 ♀ BEAK from cere 20–23.5 mm., av. 22.7, and WING across chord 281–340, av. 316.2 (Friedmann 1950).

extima Bangs—on av., even smaller than the preceding and slightly paler overall, although the tail bands (3–4?) are dark. The few Juvs. examined have ventral pattern "essentially intermediate" between the 2 previously listed subspecies, even though geographically separated from the 1st by the 2d (Johnson and Peeters). Visible tail bars 5–5½. Florida from L. Okeechobee s. to include the Fla. Keys and the Dry Tortugas. Five ♂ BEAK from cere 18.8–21.1 mm., av. 20, and WING across chord 278–291, av. 282.2; and 2 ♀ BEAK from cere 21–22 mm., and WING across chord 299–305 (Friedmann 1950).

texana Bishop—individual size-variation about as nominate *lineata*, but av. smaller (especially ♂); rich rufous cast overall; breast feathers have conspicuous dark shaft lines; tail dorsally shows 3–4 dark bars. The Juv. is barred ventrally, thus being more

415

like the se. birds than the nominate race (Johnson and Peeters); tail shows 5–6 bars. Southeastern Tex. and, at least formerly, to Valley of Mexico. Six ♂ BEAK from cere 20.1–22 mm., av. 21, and WING across chord 302–313, av. 309; and 3 ♀ BEAK from cere 22–23 mm., av. 22.6, and WING across chord 329.6–337, av. 334.2 (Friedmann 1950).

elegans Cassin—somewhat smaller (av. considerably smaller) than nominate *lineata*. The dorsum is dark, the rufescent or rusty on the venter is merged into nearly solid color anteriorly, then becomes progressively more open-spaced barring to none past the vent; evidently only 2–3 dark bars show dorsally in tail. The Juv. is heavily marked below with very dark triangular and diamond-shaped dark markings, the flanks evenly barred transversely; the tail dorsally shows 3½–4 dark bands—fewer than Juv. of any other subspecies. Five ♂ BEAK from cere 20.3–21.3 mm., av. 20.7, and WING across chord 288–305, av. 299.2; and 4 ♀ BEAK from cere 20–22 mm., av. 20.9, and WING across chord 298–312, av. 302 (Friedmann 1950). West of the Sierras, from n. Oreg. s. and continuing (formerly?) into nw. Baja Calif. Apparently a few of the more n. ones are migratory.   RALPH S. PALMER

FIELD IDENTIFICATION   The buteo-like outline is evident; the Redshoulder is more buoyant and trim and has relatively longer tail than the larger Red-tailed Hawk. The tail is comparatively short in the compact-appearing Broad-winged Hawk. A circling Redshoulder continuously alternates a few quick flaps (like an accipiter) with rather short glides; the Redtail flaps once or twice, then glides or sails for a much longer time. In transmitted light, the Redshoulder's tail is black crossed by several narrow white bars—a diagnostic feature. (In the Broadwing the white is about as wide as the dark.) A Redshoulder in flight overhead shows white barring in basal half of the primaries, forming a translucent patch or "window"—the only "necessary" field mark (Forbush 1927); it is crescent shaped and not always evident. Reddish breast and wing lining generally show well, but the reddish "shoulders" on upper surface of wing, which are also diagnostic, may be difficult to see unless the bird is near eye-level.

A perched Redshoulder almost invariably has at least a reddish cast and usually shows mixed white and very dark in the folded wing.

The above features typically hold throughout the Redshoulder's range, allowing for the "washed out" coloring s. (but contrasting tail pattern holds up well) and for the rich coloring w. of the Sierras (Red-bellied Hawk).

Young (Juv.) Redshoulders have fluffy whitish underparts, more or less streaked or spotted dark. Thus there is dark anteriorly on the venter, an area that is plain in "normal" phase young Redtails (but there is coloring laterally and on the abdomen). In flight the "window" often shows in the Juv. wing. The tail, compared with older birds, usually has 1 or 2 additional bars. Young Redshoulders are trimmer than young Broadwings and have, in proportion to their size, decidedly longer tails.

This woodland hawk seems unwary at times, but much less so than the Broadwing. If you hear its downward-slurred call, dribbling off to nothing, but do not see the bird, perhaps you are hearing the Blue Jay's convincing imitation.

Doubtfully, the Redshoulder can be confused with the Rough-legged Hawk or with the Ferruginous, White-tailed, and Bay-winged Hawks.   RALPH S. PALMER

416

VOICE Most common call may be written *Kee-aah*, accent on 1st syllable, and 2d extended and with falling inflection—as though the bird were tired. Repeated rapidly 2–4 times or, occasionally, in fairly long series. In early July in Fla. a perched bird called continuously for ½ hr., then departed (Funderberg 1967). There are variants, but general pattern as in buteos. Bent (1937), who had much field experience with the Redshoulder, stated that he also had heard a plaintive *ke-we-e-e-e*, much like the Broadwing but in lower key, shorter, with accent on 2d syllable. There is a single or repeated *kip*, which the ♂ utters when fetching prey and nearing the nest, and the ♀ responds similarly. A scolding *cac, cac, cac* reported by O. W. Knight (1908) was suspected by Bent to have been Cooper's Hawk. Yet an aggressive pair, when a person climbed to the nest, may have uttered sounds of this sort—attacking and calling "fiercely" and "shrilly" (E. B. Williamson 1913).

A melee of displaying Redshoulders in spring: long, drawn-out, 3-syllabled yell *kee-ann-errrr* 15–25 times, then shortened and in faster tempo to *kee-yerr*, and finally *kendrick* 6–8 times (W. R. Spofford).

In Fla. in Feb. a ♀ gave "short cries before, during and for some time after copulating." Two days later she gave the same cries in series of 3–5 every 15–20 sec. during most of the 30 min. she and mate perched in a tree. It seemed as though she were inviting him to copulate (Kilham 1981).

Keeo-keeo in winter in Pa. (B. H. Warren 1890).

Nestlings have a chirping call (Portnoy and Dodge 1979).   RALPH S. PALMER

HABITAT **In breeding season** generally described as preferring mature lowland forest with open water and with clearings nearby. The older literature would seem to indicate that, before the drastic decline in numbers, this woodland hawk may have occupied more varied habitat. Since it is recorded as having nested in at least 43 species of trees, evidently the general aspect of the forest is more important than the particular site. Conversion from forest to farmland has favored the Redtail over the Redshoulder. The following summarizes some of the habitat studies:

SW. QUE. Nests preferably in large beeches and sugar maple, with height of nest positively correlated with height of tree; nesting habitat has been analyzed and is predictable (M. Morris and Lemon 1983).

MASS. and NEW ENG. Old-growth hardwoods; also white pine forest (Bent 1937). In cent. Mass., e. and ne. slopes, in mature deciduous forest (Portnoy and Dodge 1979). It is fully capable of maneuvering within and below the forest canopy and thus can nest in shaded places.

MD. In the Patuxent R. drainage, a combination of fairly extensive deciduous floodplain forest with adjacent clearings and along waterways. Sweet gum, river birch, pin oak, red maple, tulip tree, beech, and hornbeam were dominant; well-developed understory; consistently near water; nests were spaced at fairly regular intervals (R. Stewart 1949). In a later study there, the most commonly used nest trees were beech and sweet gum rather than river birch; numbers of breeding pairs remained unchanged where habitat had not been altered, and nests were roughly equal distances apart (Henny et al. 1973). Cent. Appalachians in w. Md.: old growth timber with mature understory, near water (Titus and Mosher 1981).

417

Iowa Variable general habitat—floodplain forest, upland forest, and marsh; the many small marshes and wet meadows form a great amount of edge; if floodplain forest was lost, upland forest compensated for it (Bednarz and Dinsmore 1981).

SE. MO. In Mingo Swamp; bottomland hardwoods; bald cypress, water tupelo, and pumpkin ash were dominant on wetter sites, and 4 oak species where slightly drier; nests were a mean distance of 572 m. from water, and all were near roads (Kimmel and Fredrickson 1981).

FLA. Many nest on hammocks of an acre or less (Bent 1937).

E. TEX. Primarily heavily timbered river bottoms—many enormous trees: pecans, hickories, cottonwoods, live oaks, pin oaks, hackberries (Bent 1937). Harris Co., Tex.: tall pines.

The drier SW: riparian woodlands, but cutting of trees and drying of streams has reduced available habitat.

CALIF. Wooded river bottoms; a "great fondness" for eucalyptus groves, making nests at times in masses of bark that have sloughed off and collected in some large crotch of the main branches (C. S. Sharp 1906). Now nests in residential areas, as Ojai, Ventura Co., some distance from water; suspected of nesting in areas previously unoccupied in s. Calif. and Nev., since water development projects may have increased their attractiveness (Wilbur 1973).

Prebreeders are apparently in the same habitat as breeders.

The Redshoulder and the Barred Owl share much the same habitat and are, in some measure, antagonists.

In other seasons Occurs more widely. In winter, mostly such lowland areas near standing or running water as river valleys, swamps, marshes, the Everglades, and perhaps canyon bottoms. No data for Mexico where this species is very scarce—now perhaps present only in winter. RALPH S. PALMER

DISTRIBUTION (See map.) **Breeding** The area mapped is an approximation. Breeds in much of the East, also w. of the Sierras; in a large area from the prairies w. and s. it has been reported as a rare breeder, as only a straggler, or as unrecorded. Eastern birds have declined drastically; this accelerated beginning in the 1950s or earlier. South of the Mexican border a drastic decline apparently began at least 50–60 years ago, and there is inadequate information for defining either past or present (if any) breeding range. Going clockwise from the sw. U.S., the following pertains mainly to edges of breeding range (breeding, stragglers) n. of Mexico:

N. MEX. A few sightings. ARIZ. Bones, accumulated in the 15th–17th centuries, from the Hopi Reservation at Awatovi; a few sightings; a 1970 nesting in sw. corner of the state (Glinski 1982). CALIF. Considerable breeding range; numbers have not declined in recent decades; may have expanded recently in s. Calif. and in NEV. because of environmental changes caused by water impoundments (Wilbur 1973). OREG. Eggs were taken in Harney Co. Apr. 17 and May 6, 1878, and an additional undated report of occurrence published in 1880. The recent increase in occurrences up through w. Oreg. would seem to reflect an increase in birds probably beginning in the 1960s. There were 46 field observations 1971–1983 (Henny and Cornely 1985), but no recent confirmed nesting. Has occurred in winter. WASH. Seen; no breeding

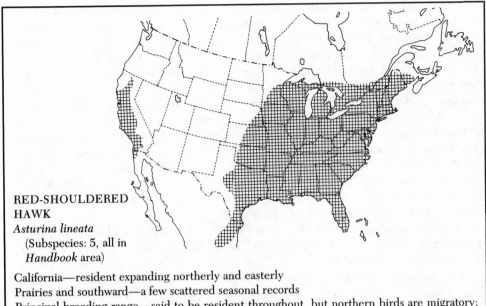

**RED-SHOULDERED
HAWK**
Asturina lineata
  (Subspecies: 5, all in
  Handbook area)

California—resident expanding northerly and easterly
Prairies and southward—a few scattered seasonal records
Principal breeding range—said to be resident throughout, but northern birds are migratory;
most numerous in winter (within range of resident birds) in eastern Texas, also from Missouri
and Indiana southward, and from North Carolina through Florida. May breed far down in
eastern Texas, but nearly extinct beyond (range extended to the Valley of Mexico)
For details and occurrence beyond usual range, see also Subspecies, Distribution, and
Migration

record. BRIT. COLUMBIA Various old sightings and an alleged capture—but no
specimen known (Bent 1937); a sighting in late 1940s. PRAIRIE PROVINCES Sightings;
that 2 pairs nested at Eastend, Sask., in 1909 and 1910 was mentioned by Bent, but
Godfrey (1966) showed no Canadian breeding range w. of s.-cent. Ont. ONT. and
QUE. Breeds in the s.; a short-distance straggler farther n. MARITIMES Very few
breed in s. New Bruns.; even its occurrence was hypothetical in N.S. (Tufts 1962), but
it has been sighted recently. SE. U.S. The Redshoulder nests plentifully on the s.
Fla. mainland and occurs on the Fla. Keys, where burgeoning human activity certainly
restricts available breeding area. Long ago, Bent (1937) traveled extensively over
many of the keys, and, although he saw a few birds, he never saw a nest. DRY
TORTUGAS Has nested (regularly?).

   Winter The Calif. birds are resident. Eastward from the prairies, the number of
Redshoulders that are absent seasonally varies from nearly 100% at upper limits of
breeding, diminishing progressively down to 0% about at the latitude of Va.; that is; to
the s. they are resident; details in Henny (1972). It seems likely that the influx of e.
winterers, especially birds of the year, is greatest from S.C. into upper Fla. and w. to
the Mississippi Delta.

   Extralimital MEXICO So great has been the decline in numbers that a person can
spend a lifetime without seeing this species. In winter it now rarely reaches Tamaulipas and Coahuila (A. R. Phillips), although in winter of 1983–1984 a valid sighting

419

in state of Mexico (Richard Wilson). In extreme n. Baja Calif., Huey (1941) had seen a single pair in 17 years of experience. In their Mexican list, Friedmann et al. (1950) listed 2 subspecies (of 4 reportedly having occurred) as breeding in Mexico—*elegans* in Baja Calif. and Sonora, and *texanus* from ne. Mexico s. to the Valley of Mexico. BERMUDA   Specimen and sighting (Bradlee et al. 1931). (Note Atlantic records, below.) SCOTLAND   Invernesshire, Feb. 26, 1863, reportedly a specimen "has been recorded (Yarrell 1 113)" (Witherby 1939); "identification open to question" (Friedmann 1950); not included in the 1950 British national list; included in recent Am. lists, evidently in error. ASSISTED PASSAGE   In the Atlantic—reportedly 2 "immatures." The 1st boarded "almost exactly midway" between New York City and Southampton, England, Oct. 20, 1961; it fed on Leach's Petrels and was last seen aboard Oct. 22 "near the Isles of Scilly." The other boarded Sept. 5, 1964, fed on Leach's Petrels, and departed before the ship was "three quarters of the way" to Fastnet Light off nw. Ireland. These sightings were by Durand (1972).

Recorded as **fossil** from the Pleistocene of Calif., Va., and Fla. (2 sites); and from **prehistoric sites** in Ariz., Calif. (2), S.D., Iowa, Ill., Ohio (2), Pa., and Ga. (from Brodkorb 1964, with additions).

A hawk, possibly this species, from the Pleistocene of Little Exuma, Bahamas (Olson and Hillgartner 1982).   RALPH S. PALMER

MIGRATION   The following pertains mainly to ne. N. Am., where the birds are migratory. There is no published information on any age or sex differences in dates or peaks, but such would be expected. This hawk is an excellent example of a species that avoids crossing water by tacking into the wind to stay over land—that is, goes around the Great Lakes. Spring migration comes in a rush, early, when Red-tailed and Rough-legged Hawks are beginning to move, and thereafter numbers are almost negligible; fall movement is more protracted, yet peak numbers are more concentrated than with some of our other hawks. These phenomena may indicate that breeders, especially, may not travel far. Here are a few dates:

Fall   MASS. mid-Sept. through Oct. (Bent 1937). N.Y. at Tuckahoe, Oct. 29, 1944, a total of 122 seen, all but 2 "adults" (Bull 1964). ILL. (Chicago): an "immense flight" preponderantly of this species in Oct. 1854 (Kennicott, cited in Bent 1937), at a time when this bird was abundant. OHIO (Buckeye L.): Oct. 20–Nov. 15; a few remain in warmer winters (Trautman 1940). MD. and D.C. Sept. 10–20 to Nov. 20–30, peak Sept. 20–Nov. 15; maximum count 115 on Nov. 12, 1952 (R. Stewart and Robbins 1958).

Spring   MD. and D.C. Feb. 15–25 to Apr. 10–20, peak Mar. 1–Apr. 5; maximum of 36 on Mar. 26, 1954 (R. Stewart and Robbins 1958). OHIO (Buckeye L.): Feb. 15–Mar. 20; migration chiefly in early Mar., and by Mar. 10 almost all pairs on nesting territories (Trautman 1940). N.Y. (Derby Hill, near Rochester): Mar. 5–May 10, but almost all pass early, Mar. 10–30 (Haugh and Cade 1966). MASS. (Lexington): In span of over 20 years arrived Mar. 3–30, av. Mar. 16, but Bent found them working on their nests in Bristol Co. as early as Mar. 5 (Bent 1937). (The latter could have been birds that had wintered over.) QUE. (sw.): Arrive late Mar. and soon begin nesting activities (M. Morris 1981).

420

For other spring arrival and fall departure dates, see Bent (1937).

NOTE   In Calif., Bloom (1983) stated that the birds are territorial all year and that no migrants are ever seen. Earlier, Binford (1979) had indicated that there was some migration near San Francisco at Point Diablo; it begins Sept. 1, peaks last ⅓ of the month, and ends Nov. 10, but only 99 birds were seen 1972–1977.

RALPH S. PALMER

BANDING STATUS   To Aug. 1981 a total of 6,111 had been banded and there were 442 recoveries (7.2%) (Clapp et al. 1982). Main places of banding: Md., Ohio, Fla., Calif., Wis., Mich., Pa., and N.J.   RALPH S. PALMER

REPRODUCTION   Data on various subspecies, but mostly on e. birds, are listed here; included is older information from the time when the Redshoulder was much more plentiful in the East.

First breeds   Age usually at least 2 years, with exceptions. In Ohio in 1928 a Juv. ♀ (collected) was at a nest with 3 eggs; the ♂ was "adult" (Trautman 1940). On nests under observation in s. Calif., 3 had yearling ♀ ♀, and 2 of these produced flying young (J. Wiley 1975a). In Md., there was a Juv. ♀ plus "adult" ♂ nesting pair that produced 2 young (Henny et al. 1973, Apanius 1977). Again Ohio, in 1974–1975 pairs at 5 of 58 nests had ♀ ♀ in Juv. feathering, and none produced young—no eggs (3 pairs) and infertile eggs (2 pairs)—but in 1973 both birds of a pair were Juv., and there were nestlings (Apanius 1977).

Sexual mexus   "We believe" they mate for life with continuity, since a lost mate is succeeded "promptly" by a new one sharing the territory (Bent). In N.Y., a ♀ was shot May 12 during incubation; the ♂ flew about, calling, for a week and on May 19 had a new mate; she was on the nest the next day (A. Perkins 1922). At C. Sable, Fla., there was evidently a **trio bond** of ♀ plus 2 ♂ attending a nest with 4 nestlings (J. Ogden 1974a). In Calif., a ♀ was seen copulating with 2 ♂; details in McCrary and Bloom (1984).

Displays   HIGH-CIRCLING   The birds are noisy and conspicuous, circling over territories with tails fanned, near and then away from each other; one may also gain altitude and swoop or dive toward the other. This was well described by J. B. Dixon (1928). It is done annually "even by mated pairs" (Bent 1937). In Fla., circling begins in early Dec. among resident birds (Nicholson 1930); migrants far n. begin immediately or soon after arrival on territory.

SKY-DANCE   The ♂, presumably, mounts upward, usually calling while in circular flight, loudest at the zenith. In 1 instance, on appearance of a ♀, the ♂ went into steep dives, each time checking his flight and "sweeping a wide spiral" before again shooting upward (Shelley, in Bent). Early in the 1926 nesting season at Berlin, Mass., there were at least 6 pairs in an area of a few mi. Aerial displays were frequent. Nesting pairs at 1 site were affected by activities at another, and on several occasions displays over a nesting place attracted others—soon an aggregation of over 10 birds, circling, diving, and yelling. A Redshoulder would get up 600 ft. or more, then plunge vertically, "wrists" out and wing tips held in, dropping a couple of hundred ft. A real melee of birds and yelling. After about 20 min., pairs began drifting away. The observer (W. R.

421

Spofford), hidden, could imitate the yelling; immediately, crows and Redshoulders would come over, and the din was astonishing.

Copulation   Occurs repeatedly and over considerable time. A Sky-dance ended in a rapid dive by the ♂ to the perched ♀; he alighted on her back, briefly copulated, then dismounted and hopped about 1 ft. away on the branch, and they stood apart facing each other for about 10 min. Then he took flight and went so high that he disappeared.

Territory   For the Patuxent R. drainage in Md., R. E. Stewart (1949) mapped locations of nests and centers of territories in which nests were not found; the regularity of their spacing was evident. On the upper river (where the floodplain was widest) nests were closest—mean distance apart 0.67 mi.—and were farthest—mean 1.34 mi.—on the w. branch (floodplain narrowest). Along the Kissimmee R. in Fla. there were 65 nests in an area measuring 10 × 5 mi. (Bent 1937), a density of 0.8 sq. mi. per pair, very close to Stewart's findings. The latter author thought that these figures indicated approximately the minimum optimum breeding density in optimum environment. In s. Calif., distances between adjacent nests ranged 0.37–1.27 km. (av. 0.66) in creek bottoms (Wiley 1975a).

McCrary (1982) worked with a few radio-tagged birds in Calif. The maximum "breeding home range" of ♂ ♂ (mean: 61.8 ha.) was larger than and encompassed that of their mates (mean: 36.8 ha.); there was a small percentage of overlap between adjacent pairs (mean: 8.4%). The birds were essentially sedentary, and he found that they used less space when not breeding than during reproduction.

An abundance of food can result in high nesting density. This may explain Hahn's (1927) report that, along the Nueces R. in Tex., they sometimes nest "real close." He took clutches from 4 nests in a grove of trees less than ½ mi. sq. and stated that there was also a 5th nest.

Territorial conflicts between Redshoulders are seldom reported in detail. An exception is Kilham (1981), who saw 2 birds whirling downward (cartwheeling) with talons locked. This was in Fla. in Feb.; both were presumably ♂, and 1 had invaded the other's territory.

Long occupancy of territories   Both J. B. Dixon (1928) in Calif. and Bent (1937) in New Eng. emphasized the long period of usage of suitable territories. Bent described an unbroken record of 26 years, another in which a nest was found in 31 of 43 years, and other incomplete records for spans of 45, 47, and 51 years. The greatest hazard was tree-cutting. Once, after Redshoulders vacated an area, Red-tailed Hawks moved in.

Some raptor interactions   Bent considered the Redshoulder and Barred Owl to be mutually tolerant, frequenting similar haunts, eating much the same food, and hunting on different schedules. He stated that they often use the same nest in alternate years and that the owl and then the hawk occasionally use the same nest successively in the same season. Other observers have noted conflict between this hawk and owls. In 1 instance in Fla., for example, J. Ogden (1974a) considered the outcome to be a standoff with neither pair able to nest. A Calif. nest contained 3 Redshoulder eggs and 1 of the Long-eared Owl (C. S. Sharp 1906).

In Calif., a nesting Redshoulder pursued a Great Horned Owl while the hawk's mate robbed an owlet from the nest and dismembered and ate it in a nearby tree (Huey

1913). A pair of Redshoulders nested above a pair of these owls in a sycamore, and both nestings were successful, but 2 other Redshoulder nests were robbed of young by this owl (J. Wiley 1975c). Owl predation in Mass. included loss of an entire brood of Redshoulders when about 28 days old (Portnoy and Dodge 1979). There are several reports of Great Horned Owls occupying formerly active Redshoulder nests. In Calif., when the owl's hoot was imitated, the hawk flew toward the source (L. Miller 1952).

It was Bent's experience that Redshoulder and Redtail never nest "near together." Yet he cited W. Ralph (in Bendire 1892) on the Redshoulder nesting near both Redtail and Great Horned Owl in 1 instance and of the Redshoulder nesting very near Sharp-shinned and Cooper's Hawks and the Long-eared Owl. That Redshoulder and Redtail have mutually exclusive territories is established, although they may slightly overlap if they hunt on different schedules (areas less hunted are less defended). Near Skanea-teles, N.Y., on Apr. 19, 1959, a Redshoulder was incubating in a 3- or 4-acre woodlot. Her mate chased a Redtail (it was calling with sharp "barks") to a perch some 200 yds. from the nest. An auto flushed the Redtail, which flew toward the Redshoulder nest and was again attacked by the ♂ Redshoulder some 80 yds. from the nest. The ♂ dived repeatedly at the interloper; suddenly the ♀ stood up on the nest and, flying fast and "determined," came directly at the facing Redtail, which sprung up just as the ♂ Redshoulder came down from above and behind and the ♀ struck from in front. The ♂'s attack prevented the Redtail's escape, and it was hit on the breast by the ♀, making a distinct sound on contact. All the while there was much yelling by both Red-shoulders. The Redtail departed (W. R. Spofford).

In known cases where Redshoulder territories were occupied by Redtails, the environment had been altered, as by tree removal.

Nesting site Typically, a large tree in a stand of mature trees is chosen. The site is on solid ground, about 30–50 m. from water, and there is usually a well-developed understory. From Bent (1937)—177 nests in hardwoods in Mass.: chestnut 49, red oak 26, white pine (usually scattered among hardwoods) 26, white oak 19, swamp white oak 15, scarlet oak 13, maple 8, and ash 1; and 41 in white pine region: pine 31, beech and red oak 4 each, maple and chestnut 1 each. Forty-five nests in N.Y.: beech 26, maple 12, ash 3, basswood, 2, oak 1, and hemlock 1. In parts of Calif. eucalyptus is favored. Fla. (Kissimmee R.), 65 nests: cabbage palmetto (nests in dead stalks just below the living fronds) 35, live oak 15, gum 10, bays 3, maple 1, and myrtle 1. Carter (1960) reported a ground nest on the Kissimmee Prairie; it had 2 eggs on Mar. 17, 1959.

Nest Generally somewhat above halfway up the tree, below the canopy crown (the Redtail builds much higher and larger). Nest height: 274 widespread records 47 ± 18.3 ft., range 18–110 (Apfelbaum and Seelbach 1983). It is usually in a main fork, such as where the trunk divides, and is securely built. It may remain for several years, even if not refurbished. If in a pine, it sets on part of a whorl and against the trunk. Nests out on lateral foundations of any sort are rare. There seem to be no data on roles of the sexes in construction. Much of the material, such as sticks, is evidently obtained nearby. Some, obviously, is gathered from standing trees—loose bark, leaves, Span-ish moss, fresh twigs, and so on—generally a considerable mixture. The cavity is lined with finer material of the same sort. Outside diam. to 2 ft. (60 cm.), height 12 in. or more (30 cm.), with cavity about 8 in. (20 cm.) diam. and 2–3 in. (5–7.5 cm.) deep.

Bent (1937) gives a few more details, while Oberholser (1896) measured 10 nests in Ohio. The nest seems tidy, not scraggly and loosely built as is that of the Broad-winged Hawk. Because a nest may receive attention over a long span, Bent thought construction required 4–5 weeks, but a nest can be built in a few days at most.

A nest may be refurbished and reused another year or more. Unlike some raptor nests, it does not become bulky, since only some lining is added (J. B. Dixon 1928). Bent stated that Redshoulders prefer to build a new nest each year. He also stated that, after a lapse of 2–3 years, they repossess an old one (**alternative nest**) and that whether a nest is robbed of its eggs makes little difference. Two nests may be built in the same grove or even in adjoining trees, even in the same season. Redshoulders may alternate between adjoining nests in the same season. Bent mentioned a pair (or possibly an unmated bird) that built a nest and did not use it. One year a "good" nest was built, then the materials were reused in an inferior one; the bird was flushed from the latter but never laid in it. Supernumerary nests may be used for plucking and/or feeding platforms. Occasionally an old Cooper's Hawk nest or an occupied or vacated gray squirrel drey is used as a foundation.

Greenery and other "decoration"　If a previous nest is to be reused, ownership is indicated by deposit on it of 1 or more symbolic objects—generally sprigs of greenery. The resident birds in Fla. may do such "marking" up to 2 months before laying (Savery, in Bent); for months before laying, a Fla. bird repeatedly placed fresh green branchlets on a nest (J. Ogden 1967). Among migrants far to the n. the sign is the same: a nest with a sprig of green is occupied (or reoccupied).

Bent stated that he did not find fresh deciduous leaves in nests until after hatching, but deciduous twigs must grow their leaves before they are used. Singley (1887a) and others have reported greenery added during incubation and later. The recorded list of what are apparently "decorations" (equivalent of greenery) is interesting. Wood (in Bent) stated that the majority of nests in Mich. are decorated after the eggs are advanced in incubation and that in 1 instance there was a complete green lining. He listed not only leaves but even various plants in their entirety—nightshade, violets in flower. Rathbun wrote Bent of finding blades of cornstalks and dried tent caterpillar webs. He thought that green hemlock sprigs, often found in nests, were gleaned from the ground after being blown off trees—material used in windy weather and sometimes lacking in calm seasons. In Mass., an adult carried greenery in its beak and carefully arranged it on the nest before departure; this behavior appeared to increase as nestlings grew (Portnoy and Dodge 1979). In N.Y., Burtch (1905) found nearly all nests decorated with old tent caterpillar nests. He also found ears of corn, corncobs, corn husks, tissue paper, nests of N. Oriole, Wood Pewee, and Red-eyed Vireo, and straw, mullen leaves, twine, and conifer twigs.

Clutch size　Varies geographically (Henny 1972), as previously mentioned. Two eggs are more common than 3 in Fla.; elsewhere, 3 most often and 4 quite often. Smallest clutches are from Fla.; largest are from the Great Lakes region, while New Eng. and Calif. are runners-up. New Eng.: 104 sets (of 2), 393 (3), 84 (4), and 9 (5) (F. Carpenter 1887). N. Am.: 2.5 ± 1.0 (101 nests), and in the Midwest 3.2 ± 2.4, which aligns with Henny's data (Apfelbaum and Seelbach 1983). Tex.: 3 eggs, sometimes 2, never 4, in over 75 clutches examined (Singley 1887a). A few 1-egg clutches are reported. At the other limit, Bendire (1892) listed 2 clutches of 5, and Henny (1972) listed 5 (of 5) and 1 (6). Analysis of 322 clutches taken in s. Calif. 1880–1961 (mostly pre-1928) showed a mean of 3.08 ± 0.65 eggs/clutch; the figure was significantly lower for 29 clutches in 1973 (J. Wiley 1975a), but the latter may be a more reliable sample.

Laying interval   Usually 2 or 3 days; incubation usually begins before the clutch is completed (Bent 1937).

These data are for nominate *lineata*: 1 egg each from 22 clutches (Pa. 14, Ohio 3, N.Y., Mich. and Ind. 1 each, and 2 without locality) **size** length 54.01 ± 1.50 mm., breadth 43.32 ± 1.00, radii of curvature of ends 18.20 ± 0.75 and 14.60 ± 1.01, **shape** short elliptical, elongation 1.25 ± 0.04, bicone −0.052, and assymetry 0.104 (F. W. Preston). Fifty eggs length 51–59 mm., av. 54.7, and breadth 40–47, av. 43.9 (Bent). Also see F. W. Preston (1968) for meas. of 72 eggs in 22 clutches.

Omitting full details, some geographical size-variation is indicated by these series: *alleni* 53.71 ± 1.85 × 43.64 ± 1.32, *texana* 52.68 ± 2.31 × 42.99 ± 1.38, and *elegans* 53.54 ± 2.89 × 42.30 ± 1.72 (F. W. Preston).

The shell is smooth, without gloss. Bent stated that Redshoulder eggs are "perhaps the handsomest" of all "*Buteo*" eggs, showing an "almost endless variety of types and colors of markings." The ground **color** is white or very pale bluish (which fades). It is overlaid with blotches and markings of various browns and lavenders; some are finely spotted; unmarked eggs are rare. A fresh egg weighs about 57–60 gm.

Some clutches can be mistaken for some Broad-winged Hawk clutches; a set closely resembled those of the Swallow-tailed Kite (Singley 1887a).

Egg dates   For Canada and the U.S., Bent listed 979 records (for presumably viable eggs) as follows: s. Canada, Apr. 16–May 25 (peak Apr. 24–May 7); New Eng. and N.Y., Mar. 5–May 31 (peak Apr. 18–29); N.J. to Va., Mar. 19–June 28 (peak Apr. 10–25); Ohio to N.D. and Colo., Mar. 13–June 2 (peak Apr. 13–May 1); Wash. to Calif., Feb. 12–June 19 (peak Mar. 23–Apr. 13); and S.C. to Fla. and Tex., Jan. 20–June 3 (peak Mar. 2–Apr. 14). Street (1955) gave av. date of completion of 62 1st clutches in the Pocono Mts., Pa., as Apr. 21.

Replacement clutches   Certainly some are included in the above spans of egg dates. If the 1st clutch is taken, another will be laid, usually in another nest some 3–4 weeks later; occasionally there is a 3d attempt (Bent).

Incubation   May be largely by the ♀, but J. B. Dixon (1928) stated that mates "seem to share equally" in this function. According to Bent, the ♂ comes in low, calling, and swings up to the nest rim; the ♀ rises and flies away, and the ♂ settles down. The changeover is done so swiftly and smoothly that it is difficult to determine whether the departing bird is the one that just arrived. The ♂ delivers food to the ♀ on the nest or to a perch nearby, where she joins him. Aerial transfers have not been reported. A ♂ roosted on the limb of a nest tree while his mate incubated (Bent).

Temperament   Varies; some sitters depart when a person is a long way off, others on closer approach, some not until the tree is rapped on or climbed, and occasionally a bird is so aggressive that it will strike a climber. In Skaneateles, N.Y., in 1958, a nest was some 35 ft. up in a beech. The Redshoulder left only when W. R. Spofford started climbing. Suddenly he was hit on the head; the bird made off with his old felt hat and was soon again perched, watching closely as he examined the 3 nestlings. Three weeks later he climbed again, this time losing a new hat. He found the old one nearby in a hayfield but never found the new one!

Incubation period   (Per egg) 33 days; an incorrect shorter period commonly given was based on F. Carpenter (1882). In Ky., eggs that did not hatch were incubated for 8 weeks (Covert 1949). In Calif., infertile eggs are "not at all uncommon"—it is rare for all of a clutch of 4 to be fertile (J. B. Dixon 1928).

Hatching   Spread over some days.

Rearing   In Mass., Portnoy and Dodge (1979), using time-lapse photography, found that the number of daily feedings was high, about 10 at first, then declined by half around 20 days posthatching, occurring thereafter at an intermediate level. The decline came at 16–21 days, when the chicks began to feed themselves. They were capable of self-feeding by day 18. Brooding by the ♂ was the "dominant behavior" during the 1st week of nest life. Nestling activity increased steadily, and, from day 19 on, attentiveness by the parents rarely exceeded 10 min./day and consisted almost entirely of feeding. Chipmunks were a major prey, delivered decapitated to the nest.

Breeding success   In Calif., 29 nests produced an av. number of young to flight age of 1.34 ± 1.14; subtracting 10 nests that yielded no flying young, the successful nests give a figure of 2.05/nest. In an area where the young were not taken by people, the overall figure was 1.82, comparable to Mich. (the Craigheads 1956), lower than in Md. (Henny 1972), and enough that year to sustain the population. Eggshells were thinner than in pre-1947, but no eggs were broken. (From J. Wiley 1975a.) In 17 active nests in w. Md., mean clutch size was 3.1 and 9 nests produced young to flight age; counting all nests, this gives 1.8 young "per attempt" (Janik and Mosher 1982). This compares with 1.7 young/attempt and 2.3 young/successful nest as derived from 6 earlier papers. Success is very poor on keys in Fla. Bay, where food is scarce (J. Ogden 1974a).

Age at first flight   Median for 25 Redshoulder broods in Calif. was 45 days (J. Wiley 1975a, 1975c); some stay considerably longer if not disturbed. As "branchers," they continue to return to the nest to feed and to roost at night for some time thereafter (Wiley).

Duration of family bond   In Calif., where the birds are sedentary, 2 broods began to hunt about 2 weeks after attaining flight; their parents, however, continued to supply them with food for 8–10 weeks (N. Snyder and Wiley 1976). These authors graphed feeding rates (gm./hr./bird) for the 2 broods, and intake was fairly stable throughout the period. See their paper for full details.   RALPH S. PALMER

SURVIVAL   From birds banded as nestlings, 1946–1965, Henny (1972) calculated the 1st-year mortality rate as 0.587, and for the 2d and later years as 0.297. Human-caused mortality has been high; see, for example, Keran (1981).

Clapp et al. (1982) reported a Redshoulder recovered at 19 years, and 11 months. Earlier, Schmid (1963) gave a list of 7 birds recovered at ages 6+ and 18 years; also another individual, banded as an "adult," recaptured approximately 440 yds. from place of original capture and having a "minimum possible age" of 20 years.
   RALPH S. PALMER

HABITS   The Redshoulder is a woodland dweller, **hunting** there beneath the forest canopy and on more open nearby terrain that is preferably moist or near water. **Perch-**

and-wait: It perches quietly, often not high up, watching for prey, which is attacked with suddenness. This is apparently how it obtains many chipmunks, shrews, some small birds, and at times even insects. **From flight:** Out in the open it does not circle and stoop but flies low, rather like a harrier, surprising its prey at close range. Many such prey are slow moving and easily taken, as amphibians, snakes, and small turtles. The Redshoulder's hearing is "extremely keen," and it may hunt as much by it as by sight (J. B. Dixon 1928). Not only does it get quarry on and near the surface of the water but it is also fond of bathing. In general, its hunting flight requires its close attention but not much speed, and its progress seems rather leisurely.

A lone individual in Kans. in winter had an elliptical territory of some 180 acres that overlapped broadly with that of a pair of Broad-winged Hawks and a Red-tailed Hawk; the birds were "somewhat intolerant" of each other (Fitch 1958).

From Md., Kilham (1964) reported the "usual indifference" of crows to the Redshoulder—even to the extent of the hawk alighting among them. In Apr., crows assembled to mob a Barred Owl, and 2 Redshoulders were screaming from the periphery of the group; neither crows nor hawks paid any evident attention to each other, and both followed closely when the owl moved on. Similar activity was seen in Oct.

In N.H. in spring, Redshoulders and crows associated in mobbing a Great Horned Owl, which they followed on each occasion that it flew. Kilham thought that the crows initiated the mobbing. In Fla., mobbing was apparently stimulated by piles of turkey feathers on the ground; both crows and Redshoulders mobbed them (Kilham 1982b). Also in Fla., crows scavenged fish heads left by a river otter. Once a hawk landed among crows and made off with a catfish head. Another time the hawk landed almost on top of an otter that had been feeding; there was no fish head, and the hawk departed. A crow tried to hold 2 fish heads at the same time; the hawk swooped, the crow dropped both, and the hawk made off with 1 of them. When crows tried to retrieve a catfish head cached in a grassy area, the hawk took possession in the face of crow hostility and departed. A crow perched in a tree delivered blows with its bill to a piece of sod held in its feet. A Redshoulder swooped at it, perhaps mistakenly regarding the sod as prey in possession of a crow (Kilham 1982a).

In early Jan. in Bay Co., Fla., an "adult" Redtail was flushed from a patch of rushes. Immediately an "immature" Redshoulder that had been perched nearby attacked it from above. Both flew out over water, and the Redshoulder struck the lower bird several times on the rump with its talons. Then the attacker flew a short distance to the beach, picked up an oyster shell, again took station above the flying Redtail, and dropped the shell, which hit the back of the other bird. The Redtail departed, and the Redshoulder returned to its perch (Stedman 1983).

In Apr. in N.Y., Burtch (1927) found a still-warm, dead Redshoulder and flushed a Redtail nearby; on returning an hr. later, the Redtail was feeding on it. On the other hand, the Redshoulder is known to have fed on Am. Kestrel, Screech Owl, and at least 1 crow. On Nov. 1 in Pa., a migrant Redshoulder harassed a migrant Golden Eagle, which turned over, seized the hawk, and plunged downward into the woods (Broun 1947). Redshoulders have had accidents, such as being overpowered by a large snake, getting caught in a mink trap, and becoming entangled in Spanish moss.

The Redshoulder is able to transport, or sometimes drag, surprisingly heavy prey, as Edscorn (1974) reported from Fla. (where the hawks are relatively small). One flew

427

toward the observer, carrying a Tricolored Heron considerably larger than itself, then fed on it on the ground. An "immature" Redshoulder with a full-grown gray squirrel got away from the observers "by dragging and actually lifting it in very short, laborious flights." An "adult" flew strongly, carrying a small opossum. Some of these prey may have been as heavy or heavier than the hawk that carried them.

Numbers The former plenitude of Redshoulders in ne. N. Am. seems almost unbelievable today. In se. Mass., Bent (1937) and 2 field companions, over a period of 50 years, examined perhaps 250 nests. Near Berlin, Mass., in the mid-1920s, in patchy woodlots the ratio was 10–12 pairs of Redshoulders to 1 of Redtail, with only a single Broadwing nest found (W. R. Spofford).

Migrant Redshoulders are seldom concentrated, at least today. Fall counts for 1934–1975 at Hawk Mt., Pa. (Nagy, in Chancellor 1977), show a decline beginning in the mid-1950s, but for the entire span they average out to some increase. In cent. Ill., Christmas counts 1903–1955 showed "no consistent declining trend" (Graber and Golden 1960); probably few birds are resident there. An analysis of Christmas counts in general for the years 1959–1969 showed a steady decrease in wintering birds in all states except Calif., where no significant change occurred, and W. Va., where there was some increase (W. H. Brown 1971). In Ont., a "crash" in numbers began about 1964–1967 (C. A. Campbell 1975). It was concluded that the Redshoulder population (Calif. excluded) "has declined in recent years as a result of reduced reproductive success," but the annual rate cannot be estimated due to lack of information (Henny 1972). Based on studies in an area of good breeding habitat in Md., it is doubtful that the low pesticide levels in eggs has had a detrimental effect on reproduction (Henny et al. 1973).

RALPH S. PALMER

FOOD Of the species. Mainly reptiles, amphibians, small mammals and birds, and some insects. Occasionally carrion.

Over 3 dozen papers contain important data on foods. A starting point for anyone interested would be the 9 sources summarized by Sherrod (1978). Information consists of identification of contents of digestive tracts (earlier studies), items found at nests, and what the birds are seen killing, transporting, and eating. Studies of contents of digestive tracts are probably biased, since some aquatic vertebrates may be digested entirely and rapidly. In summary, this hawk tends to specialize on cold-blooded vertebrates and, in some places seasonally, on small mammals. The following may be regarded as commentary on papers read, since listing all reported items and quantities would serve little purpose.

These are observations of birds with prey or found at nests. In Ohio, on at least 50 occasions individuals were seen carrying or eating food—in more than 40 instances cold-blooded vertebrates (toads, frogs, snakes), on 10 occasions mice or shrews (Trautman 1940). In Mich., food delivered to a nest containing 1 nestling included: 15 mammals, 13 birds, 8 snakes, and 1 frog (positively identified were *Blarina brevicauda*, Ruffed Grouse, Eurasian Starling, and smooth green snake); the next year (3 young in same nest): 1 mammal, 3 snakes, 4 frogs, an unidentified mammal, and later a N. Flicker (Pettingill 1976). In Iowa, in a drought season (1977) 92% mammals, but in the next breeding season 85% amphibians and arthropods (Bednarz and Dinsmore

428

1985). In Calif., prey delivered to a nest included insects 14, small reptiles and amphibians 13, mammals and a small bird 6; and at a Fla. nest, insects and small amphibians 37, reptiles and large amphibians 28, mammals 3, and birds 2 (N. Snyder and Wiley 1976). In the Okefenokee Swamp, Ga., they are partial to frogs (Hebard 1941).

Prey captured, possibly found injured, or some perhaps carrion, include items too large to transport. Examples: Philippine Mallard (Ripley 1951), Blue-winged Teal (E. G. Holt and Sutton 1926), possibly a Wood Duck (Rapp 1941b), a young Wild Turkey (Hebard 1941), and see Edscorn's data under Habits, above. In Maine, a Redshoulder killed 2 radio-tagged ♀ Black Ducks (Ringelman and Longcore 1983). From digestive tracts: opossum, skunk, rabbits, muskrat, and waterfowl—perhaps young individuals, or carrion. A 4-ft. rat snake was too much to manage (G. Williams 1951).

Much prey consists of snakes of moderate size, amphibians up to bullfrog size, mammals mostly from shrew to chipmunk size, small lizards and young turtles, birds to grackle size and evidently not in numbers, a few small fishes, a few crayfishes, insects in considerable numbers usually of cricket and large grasshopper size, and a miscellany including centipedes, earthworms, and snails.

Although domestic chicken remains have been found in digestive tracts (McAtee 1935), chickens are often not taken when readily available; see examples in Bent (1937). Dead ones were formerly used to bait traps for predatory birds at game farms.

There are regional and seasonal differences. Eastern chipmunks are a mainstay in the breeding season at some localities. Shrews, perhaps surprisingly, are reported in greater numbers than are voles. Lizards can be important, but snakes are generally more so. A few fishes (McAtee 1935, Ernst 1945). Crayfishes are reported in Fla. and Calif. In Mass., Kennard (1894) invariably found feathers and bones of birds.

RALPH S. PALMER

List of literature cited in this volume is combined with that of vol. 5 and precedes the index in vol. 5.

INDEX

431

433